Coordination of Internet Agents

Springer

Berlin
Heidelberg
New York
Barcelona
Hong Kong
London
Milan
Paris
Singapore
Tokyo

Andrea Omicini • Franco Zambonelli •
Matthias Klusch • Robert Tolksdorf (Eds.)

Coordination of Internet Agents

Models, Technologies, and Applications

With 89 Figures and 16 Tables

Springer

Editors

Andrea Omicini
Università di Bologna
Dipartimento di Elettronica,
Informatica e Sistemistica
Viale Risorgimento 2
40136 Bologna, Italy
E-mail: aomicini@deis.unibo.it

Matthias Klusch
DFKI GmbH
German Research Center for AI
Multi-Agent Systems Group
Stuhlsatzenhausweg 3
66123 Saarbrücken, Germany
E-mail: klusch@dfki.de

Franco Zambonelli
Dipartimento di Scienze dell'Ingegneria
Università di Modena e Reggio Emilia
Via Vignolese 905
41100 Modena, Italy
E-mail: franco.zambonelli@unimo.it

Robert Tolksdorf
Technische Universität Berlin
Fachbereich Informatik, FLP/KIT
Sekr. FR 6-10
Franklinstr. 28/29
10587 Berlin, Germany
E-mail: tolk@cs.tu-berlin.de

Library of Congress Cataloging-in-Publication data applied for

Die Deutsche Bibliothek – CIP-Einheitsaufnahme

Coordination of Internet agents: models, technologies, and
applications; with 16 tables/Andrea Omicini... (ed.). – Berlin;
Heidelberg; New York; Barcelona; Hong Kong; London; Milan; Paris;
Singapore; Tokyo: Springer, 2001
  ISBN 3-540-41613-7

ACM Subject Classification (1998): I.2.11, C.2, D.1.3, D.2-D.4, H.3-H.4, H.5.3

ISBN 3-540-41613-7 Springer-Verlag Berlin Heidelberg New York

Springer-Verlag Berlin Heidelberg New York
is a member of BertelsmannSpringer Science+Business Media GmbH

http//www.springer.de

© Springer-Verlag Berlin Heidelberg 2001
Printed in Germany

The use of general descriptive names, trademarks, etc. in this publication does not imply, even in the absence of a specific statement, that such names are exempt from the relevant protective laws and regulations and therefore free for general use.

Typesetting: Camera-ready by the authors
Cover Design: d&p, design & production, Heidelberg
Printed on acid-free paper   SPIN 10796140 – 06/3142SR – 5 4 3 2 1 0

Foreword:
Coordination and the Internet

The Internet changes everything. Not only does the Internet change the applications that people use and the systems with which they interact, it also changes the way we model, design, and build those applications and systems. Moreover, the Internet changes the theories with which we understand computation.

All of these changes in theory and practice are manifested in the coordination, broadly understood, of software components. All of these changes are necessary because the Internet promotes – indeed, all but requires – the autonomy of the software components. Coordination is essential if for no other reason than to control this autonomy.

It is instructive to consider at least three main forms of autonomy corresponding to the three main roles that people play in networked computing environments. Design autonomy, also termed heterogeneity, reflects the independence of designers and vendors to build their software components as they please. This is realized in the schemas and representational assumptions of the designs and implementations of the various components. Configuration autonomy reflects the independence of system administrators to set up individual hosts and networks as they see fit. This is realized in dynamically linkable libraries and directories, sometimes through arbitrary choices among incompatible libraries and services. Execution autonomy reflects the independence of end users – both consumers and enterprises – to act as they prefer. This is realized in software tools such as browsers and personal assistants.

The forms of coordination that arise correspond directly to the forms of autonomy that occur in open environments. Design autonomy forces coordination about schemas and ontologies. When the components are created by different designers, without such coordination, they would not be able to understand each other enough to interoperate coherently. Configuration autonomy forces coordination for resource discovery so that components can be linked up with other components that can supply the services they require. Without such coordination, system administrators would not be able to set up large distributed systems. Execution autonomy forces coordination at run time, e.g., through interaction protocols. Without such coordination, users would not be able to interact coherently and would fail to carry out even the simplest business transactions with each other.

Prior to the expansion of the Internet into our daily personal and business activities, all forms of coordination were exercised solely by humans. Moreover, they were exercised before a given distributed system was instantiated and applied. The components of a running distributed system had no autonomy. Designers chose a fixed, usually proprietary, schema and ensured that the various components worked together. System administrators were forced to adopt closed solutions, typically provided by some major vendor. Users were forced to act strictly as required by whatever application program had been configured to run on their computers. For anything nontrivial, users, especially enterprises, were forced to follow a preset sequence of actions that had been deemed acceptable.

Because the traditional approaches required human effort, they simply would not scale to Internet-sized systems. Further, for the same reason, they would not be able to accommodate its dynamic nature where components and users can arbitrarily come and go. The obvious solution has been to delay the coordination as much as possible. Thus the scope of design coordination narrows to include only the most basic meta information, so that design decisions about schemas and ontologies can be deferred to configuration. Likewise, the scope of configuration coordination narrows so that a separate phase of configuration prior to execution becomes vanishingly small. With minimal human-supplied information, configuration protocols arrange for automatic resource discovery and binding, leading to efficient, low-cost configurations. Conversely, the scope of execution coordination grows to include many of the tasks of the other two forms of coordination. Discovery protocols apply at run time to autoconfigure a system; moreover, they acquire richer structures to accommodate discovery based on increasingly subtle semantic properties that were heretofore the domain of design coordination.

Coordination is a good thing, but contrary to Mae West's famous dictum, too much of a good thing is not necessarily wonderful. Coordination can be expensive to achieve because it requires additional computation and communication beyond the basic application itself. By definition, coordination reduces the autonomy of the participating components. Moreover, whenever applied, it reduces the set of allowed computations, thereby increasing the overhead on computational resources. In other words, coordination is like friction – we need some, but the less we have of it the better.

To achieve coordination in this minimalist fashion presupposes subtle models of interaction that enable us to specify the required coordination with great finesse. Such models would need to be integrated with programming models and software architectures. The models would need to be operationalized in infrastructure that accommodates any special properties of the underlying information resources. For the above reasons, coordination would be most naturally realized through an application of agents.

The changes that the Internet brings about not only affect wide-area public networks, but virtually all forms of networked computing. This is because what was essential for the Internet at large is highly desirable even for smaller networked computing environments such as within enterprises. Indeed, the additional knowledge available to designers and components alike in such environments facilitates the development of richer forms of coordination, which lead to greater efficiency and effectiveness of the resulting distributed systems.

For this reason, I believe that the scope of coordination includes all of modern computing. To live up to our own expectations, however, we will need to develop increasingly rich models for coordinating components and increasingly sophisticated platforms for realizing and operationalizing those models.

That great progress is being made along the above lines is evidenced by the excellent volume you are now reading. I applaud the editors, Andrea Omicini, Franco Zambonelli, Matthias Klusch, and Robert Tolksdorf, for the quality of the works that they have assembled and organized for our reading pleasure. Enjoy!

Munindar P. Singh
North Carolina State University
Raleigh, North Carolina

Preface:
Coordination of Internet Agents

The Internet is broadly accepted as *the* technology of today, agents are expected to be *the* paradigm of tomorrow. This book relates the two topics by discussing *models* for the *coordination* of *Internet agents*, their *technologies* and *applications*.

The field of coordination models and languages is a very lively one from both the research and the application sides. It can look back on a history of more than fifteen years [267] which was very profitable, indeed. A huge amount of excellent work been performed; interesting results are ready and available; many good papers on the models and language for the coordination of processes, objects, activities, agents [530, 531, 529, 165, 263, 174] and other entities have been written and published.

Although so many results have already been obtained, many are still to be achieved. This book is meant to address some of these remaining gaps.

Firstly, it is not easy for anybody from Computer Science, Software Engineering, or AI, to get a comprehensive view of the whole coordination field from the literature. Although a few surveys are available [482, 163, 167], they focus on some partial view, some limited criteria, or some particular classification scheme.

Secondly, many researchers in the field had the feeling that coordination models should be as inter-disciplinary as the very general notion of coordination, and that their application should have a significant impact on a wide range of complex systems [393]. However, few people are actually using coordination models and languages consciously and explicitly outside the research area itself, and that no systematic exploitation of its results had been attempted yet.

This book aims at providing a snapshot of the area at the time when the key transition from theoretical results to industrial applications is apparently taking place. It should help both practitioners to take advantage of all the research work done till now, and researchers to cross the boundaries and set new paths to follow. Two major audiences are distinguishable:

− To the researcher, the practitioner, the developer and the engineer working on Internet- or agent-based systems, the contents of this book help to provide an understanding of how the notion of coordination model relates to the respective fields of interest and how the conceptual results and the

technologies emerging from the coordination area can be usefully exploited. Usually, one is already modelling or building systems whose components interact and coordinate in some way – thus, there already exist implicit coordination models, coordination technologies, and coordination applications. This book argues in favor of an *explicit* consideration of coordination.
– For the experienced researcher or practitioner in the area of coordination models and languages, the book gives a comprehensive view of a rich and inter-disciplinary area. A wide range of coordination-related issues is covered in depth, as well as some hopefully inspiring views of the role of coordination models and technologies in future systems.

This volume brings together contributions by well recognised authors in the field of coordination models and languages, as well as in some of the most closely related research fields. They have written original essays *ex novo* according to both their perspective and the context of this book, without limitations in length or content.

Consequently, most of the material contained in this book cannot be found anywhere else in the literature – and the authors have done a great job in combining known results and ideas with new views and perspectives. As a result, this book could be read as a whole, from the first page to the last. Alternatively, the reader may just as easily choose to read each chapter independently, or use the book as a reference for specific topics of interest.

Two choices guided the selection of chapters for this book. On the one hand, agent-based systems on the Internet represent one of the most important trends in both research and industry in recent years. On the other hand, by emphasising the role of interaction, both agents – as interactive and social entities – and the Internet – as an infrastructure to support distributed and open interaction – implicitly put coordination at their core from both a conceptual and a pragmatic viewpoint.

Coordination

What is *coordination*, after all? Several different definitions have been given, and several you will find throughout this book. The notion of coordination that this book mostly relies on was inspired by the works of Malone [393], Gelernter [269] and Wegner [623, 624], among many others. The most accepted view understands coordination as managing the interaction and dependencies between the entities of a system – whether they are agents, processes, molecules, individuals, or whatever. The notions of interaction used in this book cover a broad range – from subjective inter-dependencies (like intra-organisation relationships) to physical interactions (like communication acts). The term "coordination" affects a wide spectrum of research areas where it is commonly used: Programming Languages, Parallel and Distributed Systems,

Artificial Intelligence, Distributed Artificial Intelligence and Multi-Agent Systems, Internet Technologies, and Software Engineering.

This book tries to put all the coordination-related issues in perspective, and provides a conceptual kernel around which a huge amount of seemingly heterogeneous material can be structured and organised. A coordination model (as defined by [269, 163, 482, 168] among the others) is first of all a conceptual framework to model the space of interaction. According to [163], coordination models allow systems to be represented as multi-component assemblies, by defining which are the entities whose mutual interaction is ruled by the model, by providing the abstractions enabling the interaction between the entities, and by expressing the system's governing rules.

Coordination of Agents on the Internet

The Internet is today much more than a mere distributed information repository, or a world-wide collection of network services. Instead, the Internet itself constitutes a global, distributed, open, heterogeneous, decentralised, and unpredictable computing environment. On the Internet, applications are made up of a multiplicity of different components, which are likely to be heterogeneous in their design, source, technology, architecture and ownership. Interaction is a key issue in Internet-based systems, where components interact with each other at the application level, as well as with the infrastructure at several levels – from network devices to operating systems to language executors. Correspondingly, coordination plays a central role in Internet applications, where not only coordination models, but also *coordination technologies* [167] can test their effectiveness.

In particular, the Internet makes clear that coordinating an open system is not the same thing as coordinating a closed one, that a coordination model that fits a homogeneous system does not necessarily fit a heterogeneous system as well, and that a coordination technology supporting static components does not trivially adapt to mobile entities. Issues like security, mobility, or scalability have obviously to be taken into account when designing Internet-based systems, in particular when choosing the models and the technologies – and this also applies to coordination systems.

As a result, this book tries to provide the reader with a comprehensive view of how coordination models and technologies are affected by the emergence of such relevant Internet-related issues, and how they can be exploited to deal with such issues.

Thus, the issues arising from coordination models and technologies are inescapable, in particular when the environment of choice for a system is at such a level of complexity as the Internet. The coordination viewpoint may then successfully be adopted to supply a unified view of this wide and heterogeneous range of topics, from security to software architecture, from mobility to emergent behavior.

This book does not introduce a new definition of the term "agent": there are several already, coming from the Multi-Agent System field [643, 248], each one emphasising different aspects of what being an agent means. This book focuses on understanding those aspects of agenthood that relate to coordination in general, and what role and impact coordination models and languages could have in multi-agent systems.

A widely accepted notion understands agents as autonomous software or hardware entities which are *situated* in some environment where they live and interact. Such an environment typically features some characteristics of its own – like heterogeneity, dynamics, or unpredictability. Since agents are supposed to be *reactive*, that is, responsive to the dynamics of their surrounding world, these features affect the way in which agents are conceived, designed, and built.

It is also frequent to find that agents are defined as *social entities*, which interact with other entities of the same sort in order to achieve their goals. The ways in which this interaction is conceived, organised and performed, which models are adopted, which languages are used, and which technologies are exploited, are again a matter of coordination.

So, how agents manage to live in their environment and how they interact with other agents are, in essence, coordination problems. The final feature that almost everybody recognises in agents is their *pro-activeness*: agents are not objects which can be invoked, but act on their own initiative. Then, once we start thinking of agents as individuals, and multi-agent systems as societies, issues like mobility, identity, social rules in multi-agent systems clearly reveal themselves as coordination-related topics.

Agent-based approaches [644] are currently showing how the agent abstraction can be exploited to address issues like distribution, heterogeneity, decentralisation of control, unpredictability, and the need for intelligence [643]. Agents' reactivity helps in dealing with dynamic and unpredictable environments, their pro-activeness in pursuing goals makes it possible to abstract from control issues and to easily deal with decentralisation of control, and so on. The Internet is today the most complex environment in which systems have to be built, and the level of abstraction provided by the metaphors of agent and agent society is likely to be the most suitable for tackling the complexity of Internet-based applications. As a result, the need for modelling and building systems on the Internet is pushing scientists and engineers more and more towards the adoption of the multi-agent paradigm.

Here is where coordination models for multi-agent systems meet coordination technologies for Internet-based applications.

Agent societies could be organised around coordination media supplied as coordination services by an Internet-based infrastructure [471]. The access of intelligent agents to heterogeneous information in a distributed and decentralised environment like the Internet might easily be enabled and ruled by a suitable coordination infrastructure providing authentication, authorisation, knowledge indexing and mediation, and so on [197].

In the end, many of the advanced systems of today are likely to exploit Internet agents – and dealing with Internet agents is mostly dealing with coordination models and technologies of many different sorts.

Structure of the book

In this book, the authors of the chapters write about models, technologies, and applications for the coordination of Internet agents. So, this book starts with a bird's-eye view on coordination models (Part I), maps models onto technologies for Internet-based (Part II) and multi-agent (Part III) systems, and explores the emerging related issues from both a conceptual and a technological viewpoint (Part IV). Then, it deals with the application issues (Part V) and ends by supplying some visions on the future (Part VI).

Part I, edited by Andrea Omicini, is intended to provide the reader with the comprehensive view that is required to enter the field of coordination models. There, two surveys allow two different viewpoints to be adopted: roughly speaking, the Computer Science (Chapter 1) and the Software Engineering viewpoints (Chapter 2).

Chapter 1, by Nadia Busi, Paolo Ciancarini, Roberto Gorrieri, and Gianluigi Zavattaro, takes the reader on a "guided tour", which first supplies a basic ontology for coordination models and languages, then exploits a clean formal framework to represent a wide range of different coordination models, which are defined, explored and classified.

Chapter 2, by George Papadopoulos, provides a comprehensive survey on coordination models and technologies specifically focussing on Internet agents. In spite of the number of models and systems surveyed, the author shows the reader a clear path from basic coordination infrastructures up to high-level agent coordination models.

Part II, edited by Andrea Omicini, deals with the basic issues of coordination systems as technological infrastructures which enable complex systems to be built by putting components together, making them interact, and ruling their interaction so as to achieve global application goals. There, the relationship between the notions of *coordination services* and *middleware* are clarified in different contexts: run-time systems (Chapter 3), tuple-based models (Chapter 4), standards and technologies for distributed systems (Chapter 5), and scripting languages (Chapter 6).

Chapter 3, by Antony Rowstron, surveys the systems providing run-time support for coordination services, by supplying both a historical perspective and a bridge between the conceptual issues and the implementation problems.

Chapter 4, by Davide Rossi, Giacomo Cabri, and Enrico Denti, provides the reader with a comprehensive survey on tuple-based coordination systems, a taxonomy as well as a set of criteria for the classification of the models of this class.

Chapter 5, by Paolo Bellavista and Thomas Magedanz, takes an apparently more traditional approach to the middleware topic. However, after a report on the state of the art, it shows how models and infrastructures for mobile agent support could be effectively integrated with interoperability standards, like CORBA, to provide multi-component systems with the basic enabling technologies for interaction and coordination.

Chapter 6, by Jean-Guy Schneider, Markus Lumpe, and Oscar Nierstrasz, defines the notion of coordination in the field of scripting languages, which singles out the main features of these languages in terms of the mechanisms and abstractions they supply, in particular in the context of agent coordination.

The contributions of part III edited by Matthias Klusch are centered around the topic of high-level enabling coordination techniques. As the Internet is an open system where heterogeneous agents can appear and disappear dynamically, and the number of such agents increases steadily there is a particular need to cope with (a) the connection problem means to locate agents that provide relevant data and services, (b) the issue of conversations on top of any inter-agent communication, and (c) transparent location and migration of mobile agents.

Chapter 7, by Robert Scott Cost, Yannis Labrou, and Tim Finin, proposes a formalism based on colored petri nets for modeling and verifying conversation policies. It also presents some examples of using this formalism to specify conversations among agents.

Chapter 8, by Matthias Klusch and Katia Sycara, gives a compact guide to the basic concepts of capability-based matchmaking and brokering for coordination of agent societies in the Internet by respective types of middle-agents. It provides examples of both coordination techniques as they are available in several multiagent systems which have been developed by different research labs and universities so far.

Chapter 9, by Gul Agha, Nadeem Jamali and Carlos Varela, presents techniques for higher-level actors (agent) naming and coordination models and infrastructures which enable agents in the Internet to transparently migrate in a coordinated manner with appropriate runtime support. This is demonstrated by an example of coordinating travel agents.

Part IV, edited by Franco Zambonelli, focuses on a specific set of issues that are emerging as being of primary importance in the development and management of coordinated Internet applications, i.e., mobility (Chapter 10), security (Chapter 11), and scalability (Chapter 12). All three chapters are representative of the convergence – induced by agent-based Internet computing – of the issues faced by different research communities, such as Software Engineering, Distributed Systems, Coordination Models and Languages.

Chapter 10, by Gruia-Catalin Roman, Amy Murphy, and Gian Pietro Picco, addresses the issues of mobility and coordination in a very general way. The authors introduce a working definition of coordination and explore the problems related to coordination and mobility in a way that makes it possible to transcend the distinctions between mobility of software and devices.

Chapter 11, by Ciaran Bryce and Marco Cremonini, analyses the issues arising in the definition of a secure coordination architecture for open and distributed agent systems. The authors show the variety of models, technologies, and architectural solutions for security that can be adopted in the context of coordinated Internet applications.

Chapter 12, by Ronaldo Menezes, Robert Tolksdorf, and Alan Wood, discusses the scalability issues that arise in Linda-like coordination systems for the Internet. By analysing several models and systems, the authors show that Linda-like coordination on the Internet can be adopted without undermining the main advantages of the Linda model.

Part V, edited by Robert Tolksdorf, studies issues of the application of coordination technologies. It shows that coordination, while being mostly invisible in application, is pervasive to all aspects of applications, be it their development (chapter 13), the coordination patterns embedded in applications (chapter 14), the coordination of actors in workflows (chapter 15), or the embedding of coordination technology within some other basic technology like constraint solving (chapter 16).

Chapter 13, by Franco Zambonelli, Nicholas R. Jennings, Andrea Omicini, and Michael Wooldridge deals with the development of complex Internet based applications. The authors propose to apply a coordination model within a methodology for the development of agent-based applications.

Chapter 14, by Dwight Deugo, Michael Weiss, and Elizabeth Kendall presents a set of reusable patterns for agent coordination. The five patterns for agent coordination are described with respect to the most important forces of mobility and communication, standardisation, coupling, problem partitioning and failures which drive the design of agent-oriented applications.

Chapter 15, by Monica Divitini, Chihab Hanachi, and Christophe Sibertin-Blanc is devoted to how actors involved in business processes coordinate. A framework for the support of inter-organisational workflows is proposed and used to study two existing approaches.

Chapter 16, by Eric Monfroy and Farhad Arbab, gives an example of applying coordination models by embedding them in yet another technology. It advocates the use of coordination models for cooperation of distributed constraint solvers and demonstrates two possible approaches for doing so.

Part VI, edited by Franco Zambonelli, concludes the book with two chapters that present a forward look at the next generation of agent systems, showing how coordination models and technologies can effectively rely on models and concepts inspired by those already driving our real-world organisations. The two chapters show that, even if it may still take a long time before autonomous organisations of agents populate the Internet, the research is already suggesting the feasibility of the approach.

Chapter 17, by Jonathan Bredin, David Kotz, Daniela Rus, Rajiv T. Maheswaran, Çagri Imer and Tamer Başar, focuses on market-based models and architectures for mobile-agent systems. The results presented in the chapter encourage the development of a future generation of agent systems in which coordination activities can occur according to market-based models.

Chapter 18, by Rune Gustavsson and Martin Fredriksson, puts the emphasis on a next generation of agent-based Internet applications, e.g., distributed health-care and smart homes. By focussing on the engineering of such systems, the authors show how concepts inspired from our real-world societies and organisations will play a primary role in their design.

An extensive bibliography collecting all references from the chapters conclude the book.

Acknowledgements

This book is a collaborative effort. The editors would like to thank foremost the contributing authors of the chapters and the foreword for their outstanding work. It was a pleasure to cooperate with them. Last but not least, we are particularly indebted to Alfred Hofmann and Ulrike Stricker from Springer publisher for their kind and supportive assistance during the whole book project.

Enjoy reading this book!

Andrea Omicini, Franco Zambonelli, Matthias Klusch, Robert Tolksdorf
Bologna – Modena – Saarbrücken – Berlin
Fall 2000

Table of Contents

Part III. High-Level Enabling Coordination Technologies

Part VI. Visions

List of Figures

List of Tables

Part I

Coordination Models and Languages:
State of the Art

Coordination Models and Languages: State of the Art

Introduction

The notion of *coordination model* is the conceptual foundation for the two notions of coordination language and system. A *coordination language* represents a linguistic reification of a coordination model, whereas a *coordination system* provides for the model's implementation in terms of either a programming environment, an architectural framework, or an infrastructure.

We may define a coordination model as a formal framework for expressing the interaction among components in a multi-component system [163]. Or, we may say as well that a coordination model is a conceptual framework for shaping the space of component interaction. These two different definitions are apparently very similar, and can be easily reconciled – but in fact, they come from two different perspectives on what the essence of coordination models and languages is: two viewpoints that we may term the Computer Science and the Software Engineering ones, respectively.

According to the former acceptation, a coordination model supplies notation and rules for the formal characterisation of coordinated systems. Several formal frameworks have been defined for this purpose [166, 658, 470], partially borrowed from other research fields (like Concurrency [418]), partially defined *ex novo* in the Coordination field. There, an ontology is either implicitly or explicitly adopted, emphasising relevant properties of a coordinated system while abstracting away from non-relevant ones. Symbols and rules are defined to enable all the relevant interactions occurring in a coordinated system to be formally expressed. In these models, focus is definitely on the formal properties of the space of component interactions. Thus, the main purpose of these approaches is typically to provide computer scientists with the theoretical tools required to model, analyse, and validate properties of the interaction space.

Instead, the latter notion of coordination model emphasises its role as a source of the abstractions and mechanisms required by software designers and developers to effectively manage the space of inter-component interactions [168]. After recognising that interaction is an independent dimension in the engineering of complex multi-component systems – like Internet-based multi-agent systems – then a coordination model is primarily meant to provide engineers with the conceptual tools for the engineering of the interaction space. For instance, coordination media can be exploited as core abstractions around which the interaction can be organised and ruled – as in the case of agent societies in multi-agent systems [471]. In this context, the emphasis is more on the expressive power of the abstractions provided by a coordination model, and on their effectiveness in helping engineers to manage the intricacies of interaction in non-trivial multi-component systems, rather than on the formal properties of the model itself.

Linda [267], which started a long history of scientific consideration of coordination models and languages, was for a long time a model without a formal semantics. So, since its very beginning, the conceptual relationship between the two definitions (and the corresponding acceptations as well) has not been easy and straightforward. This has apparently had no consequences on the success of Linda and its extensions, which are today becoming a sort of mainstream [249, 648]. However, some recent works revealed that the absence of a formal characterisation has led to inconsistent implementations and systems – surprisingly, not due to the unclear definition of the *eval* primitive (a well-known and underestimated problem, such that many Linda-based systems simply do not implement *eval*), but to the apparently simple *out* primitive [105].

As a result, making the two acceptations coexist and work together is nowadays a fundamental issue of the research on coordination. This is far more true when we take as understood that coordination models and languages will play a key-role in the modelling and engineering of complex systems of tomorrow, especially when agent societies in open and unpredictable environments like the Internet are concerned.

This part of the book has a twofold goal. First, to provide readers with an entry point to the issue of coordination models and languages in general, and of Internet agent coordination in particular. Then, to give readers the chance to adopt either of the two perspectives on the notion of coordination model as well as on the related concepts – with each the two chapters of this part supplying one of them.

The contributions

Chapter 1, by Nadia Busi, Paolo Ciancarini, Roberto Gorrieri, and Gianluigi Zavattaro, provides the reader with an original entry point to coordination models as formal frameworks. First, the authors define the basic ontology for coordination models, then they bring the reader along a "guided tour" which covers a broad range of different models, starting from the basic Linda (called here the *shared dataspace* model) and exploring three different lines for its extension. In particular, every extension is first explained both in its goals and in its realisation, then few formal rules are introduced which map the ideas presented into a very simple formal framework – as if the Linda model and its extensions were built step by step under the reader's eyes.

Chapter 2, by George Papadopoulos, is an effort to put altogether and in some meaningful perspective all the vast amount of material which might be placed in any sense under the wide umbrella of "coordination of Internet agents", by defining a novel three-layer taxonomy. At the lower level, we find the basic enabling technologies for building agent coordination frameworks and infrastructures – e.g., Agent Communication Languages. The middle level deals with the frameworks providing agent coordination as Internet-based services – e.g., tuple-based coordination systems. At the upper level, the logical, high-level aspects pertaining the organisation of the collective behaviour of agent societies on the Internet are taken into account and categorised.

1. Coordination Models: A Guided Tour

Nadia Busi, Paolo Ciancarini, Roberto Gorrieri, and Gianluigi Zavattaro

Dipartimento di Scienze dell'Informazione, Università di Bologna
Mura Anteo Zamboni 7, I-40127 Bologna, Italy
mailto:{busi,cianca,gorrieri,zavattar}@cs.unibo.it

Summary.
In this paper we survey and discuss a number of coordination models
for agents. We define a framework general enough to be able to capture
the main ideas underlying the major coordination models for agents. The
framework is based on three key concepts: the *coordinables*, the *coordination medium*, and the *coordination rules*. We start modeling a simple
dataspace-based model. Then we structure our discussion along three directions: more advanced coordination primitives exploitable by the coordinables, reshaping the coordination medium, and programming the coordination rules.

1.1 Introduction and Motivation

Coordination languages are a class of programming notations which offer a
solution to the problem of specifying and managing the interactions among
computing agents. In fact, they generally offer language mechanisms for composing, configuring, and controlling software architectures made of independent, even distributed, active components.

Gelernter and Carriero introduced a programming-specific meaning of the
term *Coordination* presenting the following equation [269]:

$$\text{Programming} = \text{Computation} + \text{Coordination}$$

They formulated this equation arguing that there should be a clear separation
between the specification of the components of the computation and the
specification of their interactions or dependencies. On the one hand, this
separation facilitates the reuse of components; on the other hand, the same
patterns of interaction usually occur in many different problems – so it might
be possible to reuse the coordination specification as well.

A number of interesting models have been proposed and used to design,
study, and compare coordination languages. Examples include "tuple spaces"
as in Linda [267], various forms of "multiset rewriting" or "chemical reactions" as in Gamma [50], and models with explicit support for coordinators
as in Manifold [39]. Some of these models have been informally defined, as in
the case of Linda. A major aim of this chapter is to offer a coherent framework
for describing and comparing coordination models for agents.

The relationship between a coordination language and its underlying coordination model is a complex one. Ideally, according to Gelernter, a coordination language *"is the linguistic embodiment"* of a coordination model.

Currently, it is more and more clear that a coordination model is similar to an ontology for agent-based software design. The inventor of a coordination model is usually interested in defining a concept of computing agent, that can be mobile, autonomous, or even "intelligent", but in any case has to interact with some environment including some other agents.

Coordination languages are sometimes confused with Linda, especially because it was the first language that got such a classification. Actually coordination languages include notations which have nothing to do with Linda, thus it is difficult to precisely define what a coordination language is. However, the pragmatics of coordination languages shows that:

- A coordination language like Linda has been shown to be sufficiently general to be used for building parallel applications [137], for designing distributed computing platforms [648, 619], and for programming agent-based systems [172, 167].
- In general, coordination languages are not fully-fledged, general purpose programming languages; rather, they are often defined as language extensions or scripting languages and they are exclusively concerned with coordination issues. In fact, a significant number of coordination models and languages are "minimalist", meaning that they are based on a small set of notions, however powerful enough to deal with the complexities of coordination. An obvious example is Linda,which offers only four coordination primitives. Other less obvious examples include Gamma [50], which has only a fixpoint-based coordination construct (called the Gamma operator), and the Interaction Abstract Machines [27], an object-based model for pattern-based, associative coordination of either inter-agent or intra-agent entities.
- Coordination languages are especially relevant in the context of open systems like the Internet and related services, where the coordinated entities and their overall software architectures are not predefined; here they have much in common with object-based approaches. In order to operate in an open system, computing entities must be encapsulated (that is, their implementation details should be hidden from other entities) and they should persist beyond a single transaction. Moreover, in a heterogeneous system, in which the computing entities are written in different languages, the data must be stored in a common format. In the past such considerations have led to the development of object-based modelling techniques; the design of coordination languages is leading to the development of agent-oriented modelling techniques.

The designer of a coordination language has to address a number of issues:

1. *What is being coordinated?*
   The coordinated entities are usually actively computing entities – we usually call them *agents* or *processes*. The agents, or processes, may have been programmed in a variety of different languages. For instance, in the

original Linda system it was not difficult to coordinate together both C and FORTRAN processes. However, Linda coordination primitives were included in the source code of processes. An interesting issue from the viewpoint of agent-oriented programming is that the coordination of the agents should not require any re-programming of the agents themselves; the inter-agent coordination mechanisms should possibly act as wrappers around the existing, independent agents.

2. *What are the media for coordination?*

Conventional languages for distributed programming, like for instance ADA, usually adopt a naive approach to communication, assuming the existence of channels or ports and introducing some low-level primitives, like send and receive, to transmit messages over channels. Instead, in many coordination languages, as in Linda, coordination is accomplished via a shared dataspace. In such models, communication is *generative*: agents communicate by "generating" data in the shared space. Data are then available to any agent that has access to the space – this contrasts with the message-passing paradigm where communication is usually a private act between the participating agents, which have to share some channel. Messages in the dataspace can be manipulated, either by the dataspace itself, which in such a case plays a role of active channel, or by third-party agents. The dataspace itself can have a complex structure, for instance in the form of multiple nested dataspaces. Moreover, in the most recent coordination models the dataspace is complemented by event-based mechanisms.

3. *What are the protocols and rules used for coordination?*

By *coordination rules* we intend the laws which rule the relationship between the coordinables and the coordination media. These laws may be expressed in an operational way, for instance introducing some language primitives and their operational semantics, or in a more abstract, declarative way. The Linda proposal identifies a set of coordination primitives which may be used to access a shared dataspace – the primitives are normally implemented as library routines which are called from some host language such as C or FORTRAN. In contrast to Linda, many of the recent proposals have been for rule-based languages; one consequence of this shift to a more declarative view of coordination is an increased reasoning power. In either case the coordination rules supply a level of abstraction which hides much of the complexity of coordination from the programmer.

According to the three issues above, we consider key concepts for the definition of a coordination model the adopted *coordinables*, the considered *coordination medium*, and the corresponding *coordination rules*.

The main contribution of this chapter relies, on the one hand, on the proposal of a formal framework for the representation of the three concepts described above and, on the other hand, on the instantiation of this framework to a variety of coordination models and languages for agents proposed in the literature. The starting point is the basic coordination dataspace-based model of Linda; this model is then extended in three different directions in order to capture the main aspects of many other models. The three directions are briefly described as (i) more advanced coordination primitives exploitable by the coordinables, (ii) reshaping the coordination medium, and (iii) programming the coordination rules. The chapter has the following structure: Section 1.2 introduce the formal framework and adopts it for the description of the basic Linda coordination model; Sections 1.3, 1.4, and 1.5 respectively describe the three directions of extension; finally, some conclusive remarks are reported in Section 1.6.

1.2 The Starting Point: The Dataspace Model for Coordinating Agents

In this section we start by providing a representation of the *coordinables*, that is of the agents. As our focus is essentially on the description of the coordination capabilities, we will abstract away from the many details of real agents and focus only on the basic features that are relevant from the coordination point of view, i.e., the basic actions that are used for the interaction with the environment where the agent is.

Our starting point is the shared dataspace model, which is at the base of Linda. Agents interact directly with the dataspace (the *coordination medium*) to insert or extract tuples/messages. Asynchronous associative inter-agent communication is realized indirectly: a message (which is a tuple, i.e., an ordered sequence of data) produced by a sender is collected in the dataspace; then a receiver can receive the message by reading or removing it from the dataspace. The access to the messages is associative in the sense that the receiver specifies via a template the kind of tuples in which it is interested, and one tuple matching the template, if available, is selected to be read or consumed from the dataspace.

When a message is emitted by an agent, it has an independent existence in the dataspace until it is explicitly withdrawn by a receiver; in fact, after its insertion in the dataspace, a message becomes equally accessible to all agents and it is bound to none. These are the basic features of the so-called Linda generative communication.

In our presentation we abstract away from the templates and the matching rules between tuples and templates; we consider three basic operations (*out*, *in*, *rd*) managing messages and one (*eval*) for agent generation. The output operation $out(a)$ denotes the insertion of a new instance of message a in the dataspace. The input operation $in(a)$ denotes the consumption of an instance of message a from the dataspace; if a is not available the operation is blocked. The read operation $rd(a)$ is similar to $in(a)$, but a is not removed from the dataspace. The spawn operation $eval(A)$ adds the agent denoted by A to the multiset of currently active agents.

By borrowing typical techniques from the tradition of process calculi for concurrency (e.g., Milner's CCS [418]), an agent is described as a term of an algebra where the basic actions are of the four kinds listed above. To be general, we consider a generic set of messages, called $Data$, ranged over by a, b, ... The set $Agent$ of agents, ranged over by A, A', ..., is the set of closed terms generated by the following grammar:

$$A \quad ::= \quad \mathbf{0} \mid \mu.A \mid \sum_{i \in I} A_i \mid K$$

$$\mu \quad ::= \quad out(a) \mid in(a) \mid rd(a) \mid eval(A)$$

where μ denotes an instance of one of the possible coordination primitives, and K stands for a generic element of a set $Name$ of agent names; we assume that all agent name occurrences are equipped with a corresponding (guarded) defining equation of the form $K = A$. Agent names are used to support recursive definitions as, for example, in the term $Ren_{ab} = in(a).out(b).Ren_{ab}$, which represents an agent able to repeatedly rename messages of the kind a in messages of the kind b.

Agent $\mathbf{0}$ is an agent that can do nothing. Agent $\mu.A$ is an agent that can do the action μ and then behaves like A. Agent $\sum_{i \in I} A_i$ is an agent that can behave like any of the A_i's in the summation (alternative composition).

A system configuration is composed by a multiset of active agents and by a multiset of available messages. Formally, a system configuration is a pair $(Ag, DS) \in \mathcal{M}(Agent) \times \mathcal{M}(Data)$ (where $\mathcal{M}(Set)$ is used to denote the set of the multisets of elements taken from Set). A multiset is usually represented by the classic set notation (using the brackets { } which we omit in the case of singletons), but where multiplicity of occurrences is relevant. Multiset union is denoted by $\oplus$ (we will use also $\bigoplus_i M_i$ to denote the multiset union of an indexed sequence of multisets). With abuse of notation we sometimes use $\oplus$ also for set union, and the actual meaning is made clear by the context.

A system configuration evolves according to the execution of coordination operations. We formally describe this presenting a transition system defined in a variation of the CHAM style [71]; we define a set of rewriting rules on system configurations representing the *coordination rules*. These rules for the basic dataspace model are listed in Table 1.1 where we use characters in bold to emphasize the elements directly involved in the considered transitions.

The rules are very intuitive. The execution of the output operation has the effect of adding the emitted datum to the dataspace. On the contrary, the input operation removes the datum, if it is present, otherwise the rule does not apply (blocking operation). Similarly for the read operation, where however the datum is not removed. The execution of $eval(A')$ enables a new instance of agent A' to be added to the multiset of agents. The choice among the many A_i's is resolved by taking one that can do a move. Finally, an agent name K can do what its defining agent A can do.

$$(\mathbf{out(a)}.\mathbf{A} \oplus Ag, DS) \longrightarrow (\mathbf{A} \oplus Ag, DS \oplus \mathbf{a})$$

$$(\mathbf{in(a)}.\mathbf{A} \oplus Ag, DS \oplus \mathbf{a}) \longrightarrow (\mathbf{A} \oplus Ag, DS)$$

$$(\mathbf{rd(a)}.\mathbf{A} \oplus Ag, DS \oplus \mathbf{a}) \longrightarrow (\mathbf{A} \oplus Ag, DS \oplus \mathbf{a})$$

$$(\mathbf{eval(A')}.\mathbf{A} \oplus Ag, DS) \longrightarrow (\mathbf{A'} \oplus \mathbf{A} \oplus Ag, DS)$$

$$\frac{(\mathbf{A_j}, \mathbf{DS}) \longrightarrow (\mathbf{A'}, \mathbf{DS'})}{(\sum_{i \in I} \mathbf{A_i} \oplus Ag, \mathbf{DS}) \longrightarrow (\mathbf{A'} \oplus Ag, \mathbf{DS'})} \quad \text{if } j \in I$$

$$\frac{(\mathbf{A}, \mathbf{DS}) \longrightarrow (\mathbf{A'}, \mathbf{DS'})}{(\mathbf{K} \oplus Ag, \mathbf{DS}) \longrightarrow (\mathbf{A'} \oplus Ag, \mathbf{DS'})} \quad \text{if } K = A$$

Table 1.1. The shared dataspace coordination model.

1.2.1 Remarks

The first observation is that we have not modeled templates and matching rules between tuples and templates, as we have abstracted away from the actual structure of the data. However, this is not a real problem and can be easily accommodated if we extend the modeling with features like value passing in process algebras. For a description of the typical Linda matching rules, see [166] (where also different semantics for the basic calculus above are reported, using Petri nets and value passing CCS).

The second observation is that the read operation $rd(a)$ is semantically redundant as it can be equivalently modelled by an input $in(a)$ immediately followed by an output $out(a)$ of the same datum a. This result is not general; for instance, it does not hold when enlarging the basic calculus with additional operators (e.g., the test operators as in Section 1.3.2), nor when considering semantics that may describe simultaneous executions because in such a case one datum is enough to enable simultaneous read operations but not simultaneous input operations.

The third observation is about the existence of alternative semantics for the output operation. According to [107], we can imagine at least three different semantics: *instantaneous*, *ordered* and *unordered*. According to the instantaneous semantics, the configuration $(out(a).A \oplus Ag, DS)$ is actually the same configuration as $(A \oplus Ag, DS \oplus a)$, i.e. the datum a is already in the dataspace. This very abstract semantics is adopted in some process calculi, e.g., the asynchronous π-calculus [310]. The ordered semantics is precisely the semantics outlined in Table 1.1: in one single step, the datum is emitted by the agent and reaches the shared dataspace. The name ordered reflects the fact that the order of emission of data is coherent with the order they reach the dataspace. On the contrary, in the unordered approach, the emission and the insertion of the datum into the dataspace represent two separate steps; hence, an emitted datum can reach the dataspace with an unpredictable delay and the order of emission may be not respected by the order of arrival to the dataspace. Formally, this semantics can be described by the following a first rule which substitute the first of Table 1.1:

$$(\mathbf{out}(\mathbf{a}).\mathbf{A} \oplus Ag, DS) \longrightarrow (\langle\langle \mathbf{a} \rangle\rangle \oplus \mathbf{A} \oplus Ag, DS)$$

where $\langle\langle a \rangle\rangle$ denotes the datum that has been sent but not yet received; the presence of this new term requires the addition of a second rule:

$$(\langle\langle \mathbf{a} \rangle\rangle \oplus Ag, DS) \longrightarrow (Ag, DS \oplus \mathbf{a})$$

Process calculi are usually equipped with observational equivalences; their aim is to define equivalence relations which equate processes that can be considered observationally indistinguishable (see, e.g., bisimulation and weak bisimulation in [418]). Despite of the fact that the three semantics above are very different at the implementation level, it can be proved that they are actually indistinguishable if we consider weak bisimulation. This result does not hold as soon as the test-for-absence operators, discussed in the next section, are introduced.

The last remark is concerned about the expressiveness of the basic calculus above; it is possible to prove that it is not even Turing complete. This result is proved in [108], where it is shown how to map agents to finite Place/Transition nets, a formalism in which termination is a decidable property.

1.3 Extending the Coordination Primitives

In this section we consider three classes of extra coordination primitives that could be added besides the standard output, input, and read operations.

The first class consists of transaction operations which have the ability to act atomically on a group of data instead of a single data item (e.g., multiset input operations); the second class comprises operations which requires a global vision of the data actually available in the dataspace, in other words, requires a snapshot of the state of the dataspace (e.g., test for absence); the third class consists of operations which comprise both the two abilities above (e.g., the complete consumption of all the data of a certain kind).

1.3.1 Transaction Operations

One of the main limitations of the basic shared dataspace model is that the considered coordination primitives act atomically on one datum only. A typical problem which arises in this scenario is the realization of transaction operations involving more than one datum. A standard solution to this problem is the adoption of specific transaction protocols which ensure that the execution of the transactions preserves some minimal consistency properties.

This approach for the realization of transactions, for example, has been adopted in JavaSpaces [249] where, any time a new transaction is started, a customized *transaction manager* is elected responsible for the preservations of the so called ACID properties:

1. **Atomicity:** This is the typical all-or-nothing condition: all the operations grouped under a transaction occur or none of them do.
2. **Consistency:** The completion of a transaction must leave the system in a consistent state; this is a semantic condition related to what the dataspace is actually representing.
3. **Isolation:** Ongoing transactions should not affect each other; more precisely, participants in a transaction should only see intermediate states resulting from the operations of their own transaction, not the intermediary states of other transactions.
4. **Durability:** The results of a transaction should be as persistent as the entity on which the transaction commits: they should be maintained until other explicit variations are performed.

An alternative approach is to extend the set of the available coordination primitives by, e.g., adding operations which atomically produce and/or consume multisets of data. For example, in T Spaces [648] the *multiwrite* primitive permits to atomically introduce inside the dataspace all the data contained in an array.

As an example of a transaction primitive we model a $rew(m_1, m_2)$ operation which atomically consumes the multiset of data m_1 and then produces the multiset of data m_2. We do not consider any ability to read multisets of data: indeed, this can be simulated by atomically consuming and producing the data to be tested for presence.

Formally, the syntax is extended by introducing a new prefix:

$$\mu ::= \ldots \mid rew(m_1, m_2)$$

and the semantics by adding the axiom:

$$(\mathbf{rew(m_1, m_2).A} \oplus Ag, DS \oplus \mathbf{m_1}) \longrightarrow (\mathbf{A} \oplus Ag, DS \oplus \mathbf{m_2})$$

The considered $rew(m_1, m_2)$ primitive has been inspired us by a class of coordination languages advocating the so-called chemical reaction metaphor (see, e.g., Gamma [50], CHAM [71], and LO [28]). According to these languages, the items in the dataspace are seen as molecules that freely move in a chemical solution. The molecules react when they come in contact provided that they satisfy certain constraints.

Gamma is one example of coordination language inspired by the chemical metaphor which has been proposed as a means for the high level description of parallel programs with minimum explicit control. The conditional rewriting rules are defined by a pair (R, A), where R is a *reaction condition* (which is a boolean function on multisets of data) and A is a *rewriting action* (which is a function from multisets to multisets of data). When a group of molecules satisfies the reaction condition, then it can be rewritten in the way stated by the corresponding rewriting action.

For instance, a Gamma program which computes the maximum element of a non-empty multiset of integers can be defined as:

$$(R_{max}, A_{max}) \text{ with } R_{max}(\{x, y\}) = true \text{ and } A_{max}(\{x, y\}) = max(x, y)$$

where $max(x, y)$ returns the maximum between x and y. The above program repeatedly compares pairs of numbers, and each time eliminates the smaller one; the computation terminates when only one number remains in the dataspace (this number is the maximal one).

The Gamma notation can be mapped into our coordination model extended with the $rew(m_1, m_2)$ primitive; given a Gamma program (R, A) it is enough to define an agent $[\![(R, A)]\!]$ which is able to repeatedly perform rewriting operations (defined accordingly to the function A) on those multisets of data which satisfy the reaction condition R:

$$[\![(R, A)]\!] = \sum_{m_i \ s.t. \ R(m_i) = true} rew(m_i, A(m_i)).[\![(R, A)]\!]$$

An interesting observation is related to the atomicity of the rewriting operation $rew(m_1, m_2)$: it is not important that the emission of the multiset of data m_2 is executed atomically with the consumption of m_1. This is a consequence of the fact that the two programs below can be proved to be weak bisimilar:

$$rew(m_1, m_2).A \text{ and } rew(m_1, \emptyset).out(a_1). \ldots .out(a_n).A \text{ with } m_2 = \{a_1, \ldots, a_n\}$$

Intuitively, this result holds because it is not possible to observe the delays in the production of data. On the other hand, as we will discuss in the following, test-for-absence operators permit to observes such delays; thus, in the presence of these operators, the above equivalence does not hold any more.

It is interesting to observe that on the contrary the atomicity on the execution of the consumption of the data is important. This problem has been discussed in [658] where the expressiveness of an operation $min(m)$, which is the same of $rew(m, \emptyset)$, is investigated. Indeed, it is proved that it is not possible to provide a general encoding of the $min(m)$ operator using the standard Linda primitives; this allows us to conclude that the min operations strictly increases the expressiveness of the Linda coordination model.

1.3.2 Global Operations

Here we consider primitives which require, in order to be executed, a global vision of the actual state of the shared repository. Coordination primitives of this class are, e.g., tests-for-absence or operation which count the actual number of instances of a certain kind of datum. Even in this case, T Spaces provides interesting primitives: the *count* operation returns the actual number of data inside the repository which satisfy a certain condition.

A test-for-absence of data verifies that no data of a certain kind are actually available; we can model this operation in our calculus simply by considering a new operation $tfa(a)$, a blocking primitive which can be executed only if no data a are actually available. Formally, we extend the syntax by introducing a new prefix:

$$\mu ::= \ldots \mid tfa(a)$$

and the semantics by adding the axiom:

$$(\textbf{tfa(a)}.\textbf{A} \oplus Ag, \textbf{DS}) \longrightarrow (\textbf{A} \oplus Ag, \textbf{DS}) \qquad \text{if } a \notin DS$$

The necessity of a global vision of the actual state of the dataspace is reflected by the side condition which considers the global multiset DS.

Some versions of the Linda coordination language comprises also other two operations which are non-blocking versions of the *in* and *rd* operations, called *inp* and *rdp* respectively. They are non-blocking as, in the case no data of the required kind is actually available, they can terminate by failing. More precisely, these operations are predicates which may return *true* or *false*. In the case the required datum is available they behave like *in* and *rd* respectively and return *true*. On the other hand, if the datum is not available, they terminate by returning false.

In [106] the *inp* and *rdp* operators have been formalized by using terms with two possible continuations, the first chosen in the case the operation succeeds, the second chosen otherwise. In our setting we can model the same operator by exploiting the $tfa(a)$ primitive:

$$inp(a)?A\_B = in(a).A + tfa(a).B$$
$$rdp(a)?A\_B = rd(a).A + tfa(a).B$$

In [108] the expressiveness of this operation is investigated and it is proved that the simple non-Turing powerful calculus introduced in Table 1.1 becomes Turing complete when the *inp* operation is added. Even more interesting is the fact that the Turing-completeness result holds only under the instantaneous and ordered interpretations of the output operation, while it does not hold under the unordered one. Intuitively, the discrimination between the different interpretations of the output operation follows from the fact that a test-for-absence permits to observe the delay between the execution of an output operation and the effective introduction of the emitted datum inside the shared repository.

Other results which does not hold any more under the presence of test-for-absence is the fact that a read operation is the same as an input followed by the output of the same operation, and the observation regarding the fact that atomicity is not needed in the execution of the output part of the $rew(m_1, m_2)$ primitive.

A possible extension of the test-for-absence primitive is to associate to it the execution of output operations. For example, an interesting operation representing a sort of negative test&set operation is analyzed in [657, 107]; there, it is proved that this kind of operation strictly increases the expressive power of the standard Linda coordination model.

Another interesting remark is that in the presence of primitives which require a global vision, monotonicity is lost. By monotonicity, we mean the fact that the addition of other data inside the shared repository does not alter the previously available computations. Formally, monotonicity holds if the following condition is satisfied for any multiset of data DS'':

$$\text{if } (Ag, DS) \longrightarrow (Ag', DS') \text{ then } (Ag, DS \oplus DS'') \longrightarrow (Ag', DS' \oplus DS'')$$

Apart from a theoretical relevance, monotonicity is a property which is particularly useful in the implementation of the coordination operations, in particular in the case the shared data are distributed across a net and not centralized in a unique storage device. Indeed, if monotonicity is satisfied, the execution of a coordination operation can be safely executed simply by considering the subset of data directly involved in the operation, without having to check the entire distributed state of the repository.

1.3.3 Global Transaction Operations

We now consider primitives which combine the two abilities described in this section, thus obtaining transaction operations which are able to perform tests on the global state of the shared repository. Typical operations of this class are global read or input primitives which atomically read or consumes all the data satisfying a certain condition.

In [526] Rowstron and Wood have proposed a *collect* primitive which removes all the data satisfying a specified pattern. Collect (and its non-destructive counterpart *copy_collect*) is proposed as a solution to the *multiple-rd* problem. of Linda. By multiple-rd, we mean the fact that two distinct read operations may return the same object. Multiple-rd becomes a problem when we need to read all the data satisfying a certain pattern inside a transaction; indeed, in the basic Linda model it is not possible to observe the difference between, on the one hand, the reading of two distinct instances of the same datum and, on the other hand, the double reading of the same instance.

We can extend our formal model with the *collect* primitive simply by extending the syntax with a new prefix:

$$\mu \quad ::= \quad \ldots \mid collect(a)$$

and the operational semantics with the new rule:

$$(\mathbf{collect(a).A} \oplus \mathbf{Ag, DS}) \longrightarrow (\mathbf{A} \oplus Ag, \{\mathbf{b} \in \mathbf{DS} \mid \mathbf{b} \neq \mathbf{a}\})$$

1.4 Reshaping the Coordination Media

In the previous section we have analyzed and formalized many proposals of extensions of the coordination primitives for the Linda shared dataspace model. Here, we consider extensions devoted to the reshaping of the coordination media, moving from the idea of a single shared dataspace to a collection of either named independent spaces or structured nested spaces.

Several advantages are advocated in order to justify the introduction of multiple spaces. First of all, it provides modularity in the sense that one can restrict the visibility to only data present in a particular dataspace. Moreover, it allows a network-aware style of programming, e.g., simply by allocating spaces to a particular node of the net. Finally, there are proposal for promoting dataspaces to first class citizens of the coordination languages, thus permitting, e.g., to consume, duplicate, and move entire spaces.

In our formal framework we model two different approaches for the introduction of multiple spaces. On the one hand, we consider multiple spaces, each one identified by a unique name as happens for example in Klaim [453]. On the other hand, we consider a hierarchy of anonymous nested spaces as happens for example in Bauhaus Linda [138]. In the first case names are used in order to specify the space target of a particular coordination primitive; in the second case the specific structure of the dataspace is used instead. More precisely, each process is associated to a dataspace and indicates the target space by specifying its relative location (e.g., the "parent" space, that is the preceding space in the hierarchy).

1.4.1 Multiple Flat Dataspaces

Let $Space$ be a denumerable set of space names, ranged over by $r, s, \ldots$. A system configuration is now a subset of $Conf = Space \times \mathcal{M}(Agent) \times \mathcal{M}(Data)$ with typical element denoted by $s.(Ag, DS)$; this term represents a shared space identified by s, which contains the data in DS, and such that the processes actually associated to it are exactly those in Ag. In the following we use C, D, ..., to range over system configurations. In order to ensure unique names we will consider only configurations C in which all the space names are distinct, i.e., $s.(Ag, DS) \in C$ and $s.(Ag', DS') \in C$ imply $Ag = Ag'$ and $DS = DS'$.

The syntax of the basic formalism is extended with the new versions of the coordination primitives having the associated space name. The idea is that coordination primitives with a specified space name are executed in the indicated space, while those without name are executed on the local dataspace of the agent.

$$\mu ::= \ldots \mid out(a)@s \mid in(a)@s \mid rd(a)@s \mid eval(A)@s \mid new(s)$$

A further $new(s)$ primitive is considered which permits the dynamic creation of a new space. The name s is formal, and the actual name is chosen at run-time in such a way that the uniqueness of space names is preserved.

The operational semantics for the new configurations is defined by the new transition system, with typical transition $C \longrightarrow C'$, defined in Table 1.2 where we do not report the rules for the operations which act on the local dataspace (i.e., without explicit indication of the target space) as they are trivial adaptations of the rules in Table 1.1.

$$r.(\textbf{out(a)@s.A} \oplus Ag, DS) \oplus s.(Ag', DS') \oplus C \longrightarrow$$
$$r.(\textbf{A} \oplus Ag, DS) \oplus s.(Ag', DS' \oplus \textbf{a}) \oplus C$$

$$r.(\textbf{in(a)@s.A} \oplus Ag, DS) \oplus s.(Ag', DS' \oplus \textbf{a}) \oplus C \longrightarrow$$
$$r.(\textbf{A} \oplus Ag, DS) \oplus s.(Ag', DS') \oplus C$$

$$r.(\textbf{rd(a)@s.A} \oplus Ag, DS) \oplus s.(Ag', DS' \oplus \textbf{a}) \oplus C \longrightarrow$$
$$r.(\textbf{A} \oplus Ag, DS) \oplus s.(Ag', DS' \oplus \textbf{a}) \oplus C$$

$$r.(\textbf{eval(A')@s.A} \oplus Ag, DS) \oplus s.(Ag', DS') \oplus C \longrightarrow$$
$$r.(\textbf{A} \oplus Ag, DS) \oplus s.(Ag' \oplus \textbf{A}', DS') \oplus C$$

$$r.(\textbf{new(s).A} \oplus Ag, DS) \oplus C \longrightarrow$$
$$r.(\textbf{A\{u/s\}} \oplus Ag, DS) \oplus u.(\emptyset, \emptyset) \oplus C \qquad u \text{ is a fresh space name}$$

$$\frac{r.(\mu.\textbf{A} \oplus Ag, \textbf{DS}) \oplus C \longrightarrow r.(\textbf{Ag}', \textbf{DS}') \oplus C}{r.(\mu @ \textbf{r.A} \oplus Ag, \textbf{DS}) \oplus C \longrightarrow r.(\textbf{Ag}', \textbf{DS}') \oplus C}$$

$$\frac{r.(\textbf{A}_\textbf{j}, \textbf{DS}) \oplus \textbf{C} \longrightarrow r.(\textbf{A}', \textbf{DS}') \oplus \textbf{C}'}{r.(\sum_{i \in I} \textbf{A}_\textbf{i} \oplus Ag, \textbf{DS}) \oplus \textbf{C} \longrightarrow r.(\textbf{A}' \oplus Ag, \textbf{DS}') \oplus \textbf{C}'} \quad \text{if } j \in I$$

$$\frac{r.(\textbf{A}, \textbf{DS}) \oplus \textbf{C} \longrightarrow r.(\textbf{A}', \textbf{DS}') \oplus \textbf{C}'}{r.(\textbf{K} \oplus Ag, \textbf{DS}) \oplus \textbf{C} \longrightarrow r.(\textbf{A}' \oplus Ag, \textbf{DS}') \oplus \textbf{C}'} \quad \text{if } K = A$$

Table 1.2. The multiple flat dataspace coordination model.

In this scenario in which processes have a specific location, we could some form of mobility of processes by introducing a primitive $moveto(s)$ which moves the agent to the remote space s. This kind of primitive can be simply implemented exploiting the $eval(A)@s$ primitive which permits to move the code in A to the remote space s:

$$[\![moveto(s).A]\!] \quad = \quad eval(A)@s.\textbf{0}$$

As already explained the addition of multiple spaces is useful because it permits some form of modularity, a network-aware style of programming, or some form of mobility. Nevertheless, formally speaking, we have that the real novelty is not in the fact that we have spaces with names that we can use in the standard coordination primitives, but in the fact that the structure of the spaces can be dynamically modified by the $new(s)$ primitive. Indeed, in the absence of this operation it is possible to map the new framework with multiple spaces to the previous calculus with a single dataspace. The idea is to associate to each single datum the name of the space where it actually resides. More formally, we consider data taken from $Data \times Space$ and translate, e.g., $in(a)@s.A$ into $in(\langle a, s \rangle).[\![A]\!]$. The complete definition of the mapping is defined in Table 1.3.

$$[\![\bigoplus_i s_i.(Ag_i, DS_i)]\!] = (\bigoplus_i [\![Ag_i]\!]_{s_i}, \bigoplus_i (DS_i \times \{s_i\}))$$

$$[\![out(a).A]\!]_s = out(\langle a, s \rangle).[\![A]\!]_s$$

$$[\![in(a).A]\!]_s = in(\langle a, s \rangle).[\![A]\!]_s$$

$$[\![rd(a).A]\!]_s = rd(\langle a, s \rangle).[\![A]\!]_s$$

$$[\![eval(A).A']\!]_s = eval([\![A]\!]_s).[\![A']\!]_s$$

$$[\![out(a)@r.A]\!]_s = out(\langle a, r \rangle).[\![A]\!]_s$$

$$[\![in(a)@r.A]\!]_s = in(\langle a, r \rangle).[\![A]\!]_s$$

$$[\![rd(a)@r.A]\!]_s = rd(\langle a, r \rangle).[\![A]\!]_s$$

$$[\![eval(A)@r.A']\!]_s = eval([\![A]\!]_r).[\![A']\!]_s$$

$$[\![\textstyle\sum_{i \in I} A_i]\!]_s = \textstyle\sum_{i \in I} [\![A_i]\!]_s$$

$$[\![K]\!]_s = K_s \quad \text{with } K = A \text{ and } K_s = [\![A]\!]_s$$

Table 1.3. Encoding multiple flat dataspaces in a single dataspace.

This approach for providing the Linda model with multiple spaces has been adopted in Klaim [453]. Klaim considers both logical and physical names for the spaces and uses two scoping disciplines in order to bind logical to physical names: one static (used in the *out* primitive) and one dynamic (used in the *eval* primitive). Due to the presence of this dynamic scoping the encoding reported in Table 1.3 cannot be extended to Klaim.

1.4.2 Multiple Nested Spaces

An alternative approach consists of adopting a hierarchy of spaces structured according to the typical parent/child relationship. This structure permits to avoid the use of space names as identifiers of the space target of a particular coordination primitive.

Many Linda-like languages exploiting a hierarchical structure of nested dataspaces have been proposed, see, e.g., Bauhaus Linda [138], Melinda [317], and Polis [164]. Even if it is not proposed as a coordination language (but a calculus for mobility) another interesting example of language with nested spaces is Ambient [126]. Mobility is achieved by allowing a dynamic reconfiguration of the structure of the spaces by, e.g., permitting to move a space inside another one.

All the above proposals mainly differ in the kind of primitives which permit the inter-space communication or the dynamic modification of the structure of the spaces. As an example of possible inter-space communication mechanism we consider a proposal of [164] to extend the Linda generative communication mechanism to nested dataspaces. The idea is that two brother spaces communicates by introducing and retrieving messages in the parent space. This can be simply achieved by adding the possibility to indicate the parent space as target of the standard Linda primitives. Moreover, we do not consider here mechanisms for the treatment of spaces as first-order objects, that is, they cannot be removed, copied, or moved; they can only be dynamically created. The syntax of the new calculus is obtained by adding the following prefixes:

$$\mu ::= \dots \mid\ out(a)\uparrow\ \mid\ in(a)\uparrow\ \mid\ rd(a)\uparrow\ \mid\ eval(A)\uparrow\ \mid\ new(A)$$

The new set of system configuration $Conf$ is inductively defined as:

$$Conf ::= \mathcal{M}(Agent) \times \mathcal{M}(Data) \times \mathcal{M}(Conf)$$

We omit the third element of the configurations when it is empty, that is (Ag, DS) is a space without subspaces. As an example, we consider the term $(Ag, DS, \{(Ag', DS'), (Ag'', DS'')\})$ as the representation of a configuration with the root space containing the data in DS, the agents in Ag, and two subspaces represented by (Ag', DS') and (Ag'', DS'').

The operational semantics (denoted also in this case with $\longrightarrow$) is defined in Table 1.4; also here we do not report the rules for the operations acting on the local dataspace as they are trivial adaptations of the rules in Table 1.1.

Observe that the coordination primitives considered here may act only inside the local or in the parent space. Nevertheless, communication between spaces which are not in a direct parent/child relation may happen via the least common ancestor, provided that each intermediary space contains processes able to move the messages along the considered path, thus moving the messages up and down in the hierarchy from the source to the target space.

As a last remark, we have that an encoding similar to the one of Table 1.3 can be defined also here to map the hierarchically nested dataspace model to the single dataspace model. Thus, the observations in the previous subsection can be reported also here.

$$(Ag, DS, (\mathbf{out(a)} \uparrow .\mathbf{A} \oplus Ag', DS', S') \oplus S) \longrightarrow$$
$$(Ag, DS \oplus \mathbf{a}, (\mathbf{A} \oplus Ag', DS', S') \oplus S)$$

$$(Ag, DS \oplus \mathbf{a}, (\mathbf{in(a)} \uparrow .\mathbf{A} \oplus Ag', DS', S') \oplus S) \longrightarrow$$
$$(Ag, DS, (\mathbf{A} \oplus Ag', DS', S') \oplus S)$$

$$(Ag, DS \oplus \mathbf{a}, (\mathbf{rd(a)} \uparrow .\mathbf{A} \oplus Ag', DS', S') \oplus S) \longrightarrow$$
$$(Ag, DS \oplus \mathbf{a}, (\mathbf{A} \oplus Ag', DS', S') \oplus S)$$

$$(Ag, DS, (\mathbf{eval(A)} \uparrow .\mathbf{A'} \oplus Ag', DS', S') \oplus S) \longrightarrow$$
$$(\mathbf{A} \oplus Ag, DS, (\mathbf{A'} \oplus Ag', DS', S') \oplus S)$$

$$(\mathbf{new(A)}.\mathbf{B} \oplus Ag, DS, S) \longrightarrow$$
$$(\mathbf{B} \oplus Ag, DS, (\mathbf{A}, \emptyset, \emptyset) \oplus S)$$

$$\frac{\mathbf{C} \longrightarrow \mathbf{C'}}{(Ag, DS, \mathbf{C} \oplus S) \longrightarrow (Ag, DS, \mathbf{C'} \oplus S)}$$

Table 1.4. The multiple nested dataspace coordination model.

1.5 Programming the Coordination Rules

Here, we consider recent extensions which permit a dynamic modification of the coordination rules thus obtaining a programmable coordination medium.

Examples of coordination languages of this class are TuCSoN [472], Law-Governed Linda [424], and MARS [114]. In all the cases, the introduction of the programmability of the medium is justified as the attempt to enable some form of control of the access to the shared repository. For example, a repository may be programmed in such a way that the no read or input operation are enabled to unknown agents.

We need to revisit our formalism in order to model the dynamical modification of the coordination rules. First of all, some mechanism is required to identify the rules to change. One possible approach is to define a one-to-one mapping between rules and coordination primitives. More precisely, we define Op as the set of all the possible prefixes μ (e.g., $in(a)$ and $out(a)$) and we use the elements in Op as the identifiers for the rules. Let $\mathcal{R} = Op \times \mathcal{M}(Data) \times \mathcal{M}(Agent) \times \mathcal{M}(Data)$ be the set of possible rules (ranged over by R). We will denote elements of $\mathcal{R}$ by $\mu : DS \triangleright [Ag', DS']$ where μ is the identifier of the rule, DS is the part of dataspace which is consumed, Ag' is the set of new spawned agents, and DS' is the part of dataspace created.

As an example, we have that the original single shared dataspace model reported in Table 1.1 can be described by the following rules:

$out(a) : \emptyset \triangleright [\emptyset, a]$
$in(a) : a \triangleright [\emptyset, \emptyset]$
$rd(a) : a \triangleright [\emptyset, a]$
$eval(A) : \emptyset \triangleright [A, \emptyset]$

As the rules may change during the computation, we need to introduce also the set of rules inside the description of the configuration. Formally, a system configuration is a triple (Ag, DS, R) in $\mathcal{M}(Agent) \times \mathcal{M}(Data) \times \mathcal{P}(\mathcal{R})$ where $\mathcal{P}(\mathcal{R})$ denotes the set of all possible sets of rules. We assume that for each operation μ there exists one and only one rule with this identifier.

This kind of system configuration may evolve according to the considered coordination rules. Formally, we need the following rule:

$$\frac{(\mu : \mathbf{DS} \triangleright [\mathbf{Ag'}, \mathbf{DS'}]) \in R}{(\mu.\mathbf{A} \oplus Ag_c, \mathbf{DS} \oplus DS_c, R) \longrightarrow (\mathbf{A} \oplus \mathbf{Ag'} \oplus Ag_c, \mathbf{DS'} \oplus DS_c, R)}$$

In this new scenario it is easy to model a primitive $newRule$ responsible for the modification of the set of the actually active rules. First of all we extend the syntax adding the new prefix:

$$\mu ::= \ldots \mid newRule(\mu : DS \triangleright [Ag', DS'])$$

and then add the new rule:

$(\mathbf{newRule}(\mu : \mathbf{DS} \triangleright [\mathbf{Ag'}, \mathbf{DS'}]).\mathbf{A} \oplus Ag_c, DS_c, (\mu : \mathbf{DS_o} \triangleright [\mathbf{Ag'_o}, \mathbf{DS'_o}]) \oplus R)$
$\longrightarrow (\mathbf{A} \oplus Ag_c, DS_c, (\mu : \mathbf{DS} \triangleright [\mathbf{Ag'}, \mathbf{DS'}]) \oplus R)$

1.5.1 Event Notification in the Shared Dataspace Model

Recently, we have assisted to the definition of coordination languages based on the shared dataspace model which consider also mechanisms inspired by the event reaction metaphor. In particular, JavaSpaces and T Spaces allows for the creation, during the computation, of listeners which are able to observe the occurrence of some particular events inside the data repository. The reaction to the event consists of the activation of a process.

In JavaSpaces the observable events are of a specific kind: "introduction inside the data repository of a new object satisfying a certain pattern". The primitive which permits to create a new listener is called $notify$. This new primitive has been formally modeled and analyzed in [111] (see [109] for a complete modeling of JavaSpaces).

Even if the concepts of programmable medium and event-notification metaphor have been defined in different contexts with different aims, it is interesting to see that we can model the $notify$ primitive of [111] in our framework adopting the same approach described above for the modeling of programmable media. We can simply add the following new prefix:

$$\mu ::= \ldots \mid notify(a, A)$$

where a is the kind of object which the created listener is interested in, and A is the agent that will be eventually activated as reaction.

The presence of a listener observing the introduction of data of kind a can be realized by modifying the semantics of $out(a)$ in such a way that its execution will activate also all the associated reactions. Formally, we have:

$$(\mathbf{notify}(\mathbf{a}, \mathbf{A}').\mathbf{A} \oplus Ag_c, DS_c, (out(a) : DS \rhd [Ag', DS']) \oplus R) \longrightarrow$$
$$(\mathbf{A} \oplus Ag_c, DS_c, (out(a) : DS \rhd [\mathbf{A}' \oplus Ag', DS']) \oplus R)$$

In [111] the expressiveness of this $notify$ primitive is investigated in the setting of a Linda-based process calculus. Several interesting results are proved there. First of all it is shown that $notify$ strictly increases the expressiveness of a simple Linda-like coordination language with output, input, and read operations only; indeed, there exists no general encoding of $notify$ in terms of these three standard primitives. On the other hand, in the presence of the inp operation it is possible to simulate the $notify$ by activating a special protocol each time an output operation is executed: first the presence of interested listeners is tested, then an activation message is sent to each listener, and finally an acknowledgement from the listeners is required. Another interesting result is that even if $notify$ strictly increases the expressiveness of the basic shared dataspace model, it is still strictly less expressive than the complete Linda model comprising also the inp operation. This because it is not possible to provide a general encoding of inp in terms of output, input, read, and notify operations only.

In [110] it is shown that the notify primitive makes the unordered semantics, recalled in Section 1.2, as expressive as the ordered one. The result is achieved by providing an encoding of the calculus interpreted with the ordered semantics on top of the calculus with the unordered one.

1.6 Conclusions

Coordination languages offer a bridge between concurrency theory and software engineering, as they single out those concurrency principles and primitives that have been more widely accepted by the software engineering community, for their simple understanding, easiness of use and for their support to software reuse and heterogeneity. Indeed, these are the main features explaining the great success of this class of languages.

Even if we expect the readership for this chapter is mainly composed of software engineers, we have presented a panorama of models for coordinating agents in a style that reminds classic concurrency theory. Indeed, we have used notations and techniques similar to those used for process calculi such as CCS. In fact, the theory of coordination can be seen as a new branch of concurrency theory: while in classic process algebras (such as CCS, CSP and related calculi) communication takes place by message passing, by synchronous handshake (point-to-point as in CCS or broadcast as in CSP), in coordination languages on the contrary the emphasis is on the shared communication medium (reminiscent of shared memory systems and related architectures, e.g., blackboard) that implements the Linda-like generative communication mechanism (hence, communication is asynchronous, anonymous and by pattern-matching).

The foundations for this class of languages is still poor, if compared with classic process algebras. For instance, a basic open problem is the definition of suitable behavioral semantic equivalences for the many Linda-like languages discussed here (some initial work is in [106]). Nonetheless, the problem raised by this class of languages are very challenging as, contrary to many process calculi, coordination languages are widely used in practice and so a good foundational theory for them can really be of practical help, e.g., in devising tools for reasoning about coordination architectures or multiagent systems.

Acknowledgements

This paper has been partially supported by Italian Ministry of University – MURST 40% – Progetti SALADIN and TOSCA, and by a grant by Microsoft Research Europe.

2. Models and Technologies for the Coordination of Internet Agents: A Survey

George A. Papadopoulos

Department of Computer Science, University of Cyprus
75 Kallipoleos Street, P. O. Box 20537, CY-1678, Nicosia, Cyprus
mailto:george@cs.ucy.ac.cy

Summary.

Agent technology has evolved rapidly over the past few years along a number of dimensions giving rise to numerous "flavours" of agents such as intelligent agents, mobile agents, etc. One of the most attractive and natural fields for the development of agent technology is the Internet with its vast quantity of available information and offered services. In fact, the term "Internet agent" is effectively an umbrella for most of the other types of agents, since Internet agents should enjoy intelligence, mobility, adaptability, etc. All these different types of agents must be able to somehow interact with each other for the purpose of exchanging information, collaborating or managing heterogeneous environments. This survey presents some of the most common models and technologies that offer coordination mechanisms for Internet agents. It argues for the need of using coordination, then it presents some basic infrastructure technologies before examining in more detail particular coordination models for Internet agents, themselves classified into some general categories.

2.1 Introduction

Agent technology has evolved rapidly over the past few years along a number of dimensions giving rise to numerous "flavours" of agents such as *intelligent agents, mobile agents*, etc. One of the most attractive and natural fields for the development of agent technology is the Internet with its vast quantity of available information and offered services. In fact, the term *"Internet agent"* is effectively an umbrella for most of the other types of agents, since Internet agents should enjoy intelligence, mobility, adaptability, etc. All these different types of agents must be able to somehow interact with each other for the purpose of exchanging information, collaborating or managing heterogeneous environments. This survey presents some of the most common models and technologies that offer coordination mechanisms for Internet agents. It argues for the need of using coordination, then it presents some basic infrastructure technologies before examining in more detail particular coordination models for Internet agents, themselves classified into some general categories.

The rest of this chapter is organised as follows. In the rest of this introductory section we give some preliminary information regarding the relationship between Internet agents on the one hand and the notion of coordination on the other. In the process, we identify three main basic areas where the notion of coordination is involved, namely: basic (coordination and communication) infrastructure, coordination platforms (i.e. models and languages that offer coordination functionality as a first class citizen) and "logical" coordination at the level of agent behaviour. The next three sections present in more detail some representative approaches in introducing coordination behaviour into these three levels. The chapter ends with some conclusions and references.

2.1.1 Internet Agents

The issue of what is precisely a (software) agent is a rather hot topic of discussion and has attracted much controversy. Traditionally, the notion of agents has its roots in areas such as Distributed Artificial Intelligence, Distributed Computing and Human Computer Interaction, as entities that enjoy such properties as proactivity, reactivity, autonomous behaviour or adaptability. Thus, it is often taken as a default that an agent is, in general, intelligent and a non-intelligent agent is, in a way, a contradiction in terms. However, many people have questioned this approach (see for instance the discussion in [491] where it is claimed that an agent can be autonomous without being also intelligent and, in fact, intelligence is not always necessarily a useful property); another related discussion can be found in [243]. The rapid growth of the Internet has further complicated this issue, where now in addition to being intelligent an Internet agent is also expected to be mobile.

Thus, in this chapter we will refrain from adhering to a particular definition or assume that an Internet agent has some specific properties. In fact, for the purposes of this work we do not have to do that since all definitions of what an agent (Internet or otherwise) is, agree that an agent should be able to: (i) *communicate* with other agents, and (ii) *cooperate* with other agents. In particular, an agent should be able to engage in, possibly, complex communications with other agents in order to exchange information or ask their help in pursuing a goal. The latter leads naturally to the notion of a number of agents cooperating with each other towards the accomplishment of some common objective. The need to communicate and cooperate leads to the need for coordinating the activities pursued by agents in order to both simplify the process of building multi-agent systems but also provide the ability to reuse descriptions of coordination mechanisms and patterns.

2.1.2 Internet, WWW and Coordination

Recently, there has been an increase in the development of applications that need to cooperate, coordinate and share their information with other applications, either with or without user intervention. This is particularly true for Web-based applications that operate in an open system environment and where data and resources are distributed. This leads to the need for developing techniques that allow negotiation and cooperation. In particular, it has been suggested that basic services for collaboration that include the coordination of activities and the exchange of information should be provided by the Web infrastructure and related enabling technologies. More to the point, some approaches refer to the development of infrastructures for sharing artifacts, the use of shared languages for exchanging information, and the creation of shared working spaces for providing collaboration [629]. This leads to the notion of having coordination architectures for the purpose of building collaborative applications.

2.1.3 Coordination and Internet Agents

Coordination has been defined as the process of managing dependencies between activities. In a seminal paper, Crowston and Malone [393] characterise coordination as an emerging research area with an interdisciplinary focus, playing a key issue in many diverse disciplines such as economics and operational research, organisation theory and biology. In the field of Computer Science coordination is often defined as the process of separating computation from communication concerns and a number of coordination models and languages have been developed [482].

From the discussion so far it has become clear that the need for coordinating activities is inherent in both the case of building (multi-) agent systems and in the case of developing Web-based environments, independently from each other. Therefore in the case of Internet agents which combine the notion of multi-agent collaboration with that of using a Web-based environment, the development of suitable coordination technologies is of paramount importance.

In the rest of this chapter we present some representative approaches in developing such coordination frameworks. However, before we embark on this era, we would like to put the rest of the work into some perspective and we argue that one way to classify these approaches is to group them into three categories as follows:

- *Basic coordination infrastructure.* The most primitive form of coordination is that of communication. In this first, "lower", level of coordination formalisms we present the elementary enabling technologies for building coordination frameworks. We can identify two such groups of enabling technologies: various families of Agent Communication Languages (ACLs) such as KQML and its variants, and support computing technologies that act as compositional platforms for multi-agent systems executing in a distributed environment.
- *Coordination frameworks.* In this second, "middleware", level we examine some representative frameworks that offer mechanisms for modelling coordination activities and expressing them as first class citizens. At this

level we have the traditional approach to developing coordination models and languages, with emphasis on issues particularly pertaining to Internet agents.

- *Logical coordination.* In this third, "upper", or user-level we present some approaches which deal with the coordination functionality of the agents themselves such as contracting, planning or negotiation. Such coordination agents include cooperation domain agents, interface agents, and collaborative agents.

Thus, we approach the issue of coordination in Internet agents from a more general perspective examining not only the mainstream coordination notions (the second level) but also the issues of information exchange (the first level) and managing interdependencies between agents (the third level). In the next three sections we elaborate further on these three dimensions of coordination.

2.2 Basic Coordination Infrastructure

2.2.1 Agent Communication Languages

Aside from how one perceives the notion of an agent, one has to accept the fact that an agent should be able to communicate with other agents and cooperate with them. Typically, agent-based applications comprise many agents (possibly of different type and functionality). In order to enhance such a multi-agent framework with communication and cooperation capabilities we need an *Agent Communication Language* (ACL) which will be used for the purpose of exchanging information, intentions or goals. An ACL is also used to allow agents to ask for support from other agents in order to achieve collectively some goal, monitor agent execution, report the status of some computation, organize task allocation, etc. In other words, an ACL offers the ability to formulate basic coordination patterns.

There are basically two main categories of ACLs [461]: Traditional third generation multiple-purpose languages that are used, among other things, for agent communication. Such languages are C and Java, AI languages such as Lisp, Prolog and Smalltalk, and OOP languages. We will not elaborate further on this category. The second category involves the development of language formalisms specifically designed for the purpose of offering inter-agent communication and cooperation. Below, we review some of these approaches.

KQML. The Knowledge Query and Manipulation Language (KQML) is probably one of the most widely accepted and used ACLs [239]. It has been developed as part of the DARPA Knowledge Sharing Effort project and is considered an evolving standard. KQML is based on the notion of modelling illocutionary acts, such as requesting or commanding an agent to perform certain things. These requests are called *performatives* and can be classified into nine categories, some of which are directly related to the notion of coordination. More to the point, there are performatives that offer basic communication capabilities; for instance, the *networking* performative offers the primitives `register`, `unregister`, `forward`, `broadcast`, `pipe`, and `break` with self-explanatory functionality. However, there is also the *facilitation* performatives with the primitives `broker-one`, `broker-all`, `recommend-one`, `recommend-all`, `recruit-one`, and `recruit-all` which offer more sophisticated coordination patterns. The facilitation performatives are used by a special class of agents, called *facilitators* or *mediators*, which are used effectively as coordinator agents for the rest, and whose purpose is to manage various communication actions such as maintaining a registry of service names, forwarding messages to named services, routing messages based on content, providing "matchmaking" between information providers and clients, providing mediation and translation services, etc.

KQML can be viewed as comprising three layers of abstraction:

- The bottom layer, referred to as *content layer*, specifies the actual content of the message. This can be represented in any programming language, as long as it is ASCII-representable.
- The middle layer, referred to as *message layer*, consists of the primitives that comprise the nine classes of performatives, and forms the core of the language. This layer specifies the protocol for delivering the message, whose contents are specified by the previous layer.
- The upper layer, referred to as *communication layer*, is used to encode communication parameters such as the identities of senders and receivers.

The actual format of a KQML message is shown below:

```
(register
            :sender        agentA
            :receiver      agentB
            :reply-with    message
            :language      common_language
            :ontology      common_ontology
            :content       "something_to_do"
)
```

The first keyword identifies the particular performative that is being used (in this case it is the `register` one), followed by the a number of parameters. These include the parameter `ontology` which identifies the ontology (i.e. the specification scheme for describing concepts and their relationships in a domain of discourse) to interpret the information in the content field of this message.

As a particular example, the agent `customer` could ask for all the different types of 4x4 cars from an agent `seller`, as follows:

```
(ask-all
            :sender       customer
            :receiver     seller
            :content      "cars(4by4(Type,Price))"
            :reply-with   4by4-request
            :language     Prolog
            :ontology     CARS
)
```

The agent seller receiving this message would interpret the request using the ontology CARS and bearing in mind that the request was formulated in the language Prolog. In due time, it will reply using the identification 4by4-request so that the agent customer would know for which of its (potentially many) requests this message constitutes a reply. Such a reply message could be the following:

```
(tell
          :sender       seller
          :receiver     customer
          :content      "[4by4(honda,15000), ...]"
          :in-reply-to  4by4-request
          :language     Prolog
          :ontology     CARS
)
```

A coordinator agent, monitoring continuously the changes in the 4x4 cars market and informing the agent customer, could be defined as follows:

```
(monitor
            :sender       customer's_agent
            :receiver     seller
            :to           customer
            :content      "cars(4by4(Type,Price))"
            :reply-with   4by4-request-for-customer
            :language     Prolog
            :ontology     CARS
)
```

In the above example, the intermediary agent customer's_agent has used the performative monitor (which is an abbreviation for a combination of some other primitives) to keep itself informed of all future changes to the 4x4 cars and inform the agent customer.

Although KQML has been criticized for a number of shortcomings, such as the lack of precise formal semantics, it is interesting to highlight the three layer abstraction that separates the communication aspect of the language from the way the actual information is being computed and presented. This separation of concerns is one of the most important features of coordination languages and thus KQML can be seen as a truly, if elementary, coordination language.

Agent Oriented Programming. AOP is a more elementary, compared to KQML, framework for agent programming, and can be considered a specialisation of OOP where agents are viewed as objects with *mental* states (such as beliefs, desires and intentions) and a notion of time. AOP is effectively a family of evolving formalisms. A program written using the first member of this family, Agent-0 [552], executes at each time step the loop comprising two steps: during the fist step incoming messages are gathered and the mental state of the agent is updated appropriately, and during the second step *commitments* (i.e. guarantees that the agent will carry out an action at a certain time) are executed using *capabilities* (actions the agent is able to perform). Basic communication in Agent-0 is achieved by means of the primitives (INFORM t a fact), (REQUEST t a action), (UNREQUEST t a action) and (REFRAIN action) where t specifies the time the message is to take place, a is the agent that receives the message, and action is any action statement. An INFORM action sends the fact to agent a, a REQUEST notifies agent a that the requester would like the action to be realized. An UNREQUEST is the inverse of a REQUEST. A REFRAIN message asks that an action not be committed to by the receiving agent.

PLACA [588] extends Agent-0 with *intentions* (a commitment to achieve a state of the world) and ability to plan composite actions. New syntactic structures added to PLACA include the following: (INTEND x) intending to make sentence x true by adding it to the list of intentions, (ADOPT x) adopting the intention / plan x to the intention / plan list, (DROP x) dropping the intention / plan x, and the set (CAN-DO x), (CAN-ACHIEVE x), (PLAN-DO x), (PLAN-ACHIEVE x), (PLAN-NOT-DO x) which are truth statements used in mental conditions. For the purposes of this chapter, we can view the primitives of Agent-0 as offering basic coordination at the level of communication whereas those of PLACA as offering basic logical coordination.

Agent-K [199] is an attempt to standardize the message passing functionality of Agent-0 by combining the syntax of Agent-0 with the format of KQML. In the process, the communication primitives of Agent-0 have been replaced by a single generic message action kqml(time,message) where message is of the form [performative,keyword(action)].

A simple communication pattern in Agent-K between two agents agent1 and agent2 would be modelled as follows:

```
commit([clock(Now),b([Now,alive(agent2)])],
    kqml(Now,['ask-all',sender(agent1),
        receiver(agent2),content(...),language(...)]))

commit([clock(Now),b([Now,alive(agent1)]),
    kqml(Now,[reply,sender(agent2),
        receiver(agent1),content(...),language(...)]))
```

where b(...) represents a belief and a predicate clock provides the current time.

Market Internet Format. We include in our survey the MIF [227] formalism, as an example of how KQML can influence the design of more specialized ACLs which are designed and oriented towards specific applications. In the

case of MIF this application is e-commerce which has attracted a wide interest
and has shown to be a natural application domain for both agent technology
and coordination models. In MIF agents share a common language which is a
formalized subset of commerce communication. MIF agents leave within the
MarketSpace, a medium reflecting a market place where consumer goods and
services can be offered and bought. Interaction between agents is modelled in
MIF, a Lisp-like frame language, which has both a textual and graphical representation. Typical MIF expressions of interest for e-commerce transactions
are the following one:

```
(def car "trade-object"
     color (instance "red"))
... )

(instance "contract"
   date(interval 1/1/2000 1/1/2001)
   buyer(instance "person"
         (name "John Brown")
         (address ...) ...)
   goods(instance "car"
     color(instance "red") ...)
```

MIF expressions are exchanged using messages written in the Market Interaction Language (MIL) which have the following format:

```
(offer
           :from          url
           :to            url
           :in-reply-to   message_id
           :language      "MIF 1.0"
           :content       <MIF expression>
)
```

The basic communication primitives that can be used to formulate complex
coordination patterns can be grouped into two categories: non committing
messages (ask (for an expression-of-interest), tell (an eoi) and negotiate
(an eoi)) and committing ones that are understood to make legally binding
agreements (offer (an offer), accept (an offer), and decline (an offer)).
The involvement of specific agents in such communication scripts can be
parametrised, thus rendering frequently used scenarios (such as auction protocols) reusable.

April. The Agent PRocess Interaction Language [404] is a process oriented
symbolic language influenced by the actor paradigm. April is oriented primarily towards offering a basic language for modelling agent interactions rather
than a high-level set of agent related features such as planners, knowledge
representation systems, etc. In that respect April is used mainly for managing the processes representing agents and their actions as the former interact
with each other in a distributed system. The following example shows how a
broker agent can be modelled in April:

```
agent_record ::= (handle?agent,symbol[]?relnames);
subscription_record ::= (handle?agent,symbol?relname);
broker(){
    agent_record[]?has_rels := [];
    subscription_record[]?sub_for := [];
    repeat {
        (advertise,symbol[]?rels) -> { ... }
        | (subscribe,symbol?rel) -> { \ldots }
        | (remove_subscription,symbol?rel) -> { \ldots }
        | ...
    until quit ::= sender == creator()
}
```

The code starts with the declaration and initialisation of the data structures
that will hold the data on those agents that have advertised or subscribed to
the broker. The process then enters a loop to handle the requests for its services, such as advertising something, registering or removing a subscription,
etc. (the particular actions taken for each request are not shown above for
reasons of brevity). This process executes until its creator has sent it a quit
message. Recently [560] April has been used as a component-based platform
for implementing KQML in a distributed environment.

2.2.2 Compositional Platforms

In this subsection we briefly describe some approaches that lend support in
the development of Internet agents-based systems. We refer to both general
purpose technologies that are used in distributed computing but also to those
that have been designed primarily to assist in the development of agent-based
systems.

Java-Based Agent Toolkits. The rapid developments in object-oriented
programming and wide area networking has led to the integration of these
technologies and the formation of distributed object-based computing platforms. These platforms allow the development of systems as a synthesis of
pre-existing components. Furthermore, they provide a natural medium for
constructing agent layers. This has led to the development of agent toolkits that are typically Java-based. One such toolkit is JavaSpaces [249] and
its associated infrastructure Jini [619]. JavaSpaces allows dynamic sharing,
communication and coordination of Java Objects. It is a loosely coupled cooperative marketplace model, based on the metaphor of Linda like models (see
next section), whereby producers store objects in a shared working space
and consumers lookup and retrieve objects from this shared medium. The
shared medium is effectively a networked repository of Java Objects where
the latter exist in the form of *entries* (serialized objects with both data and
behaviours) and their lookup is done via *templates* allowing type and value
matching. JavaSpaces is 100% pure Java-based and provides a simple solution
to lightweight distributed applications. Furthermore, it decouples requestors

from providers, thus relieving responsibilities and complexity and reducing the difficulty of building distributed applications and maintaining them. The model supports five simple but very powerful primitives:

- write, puts a copy of an entry into the space.
- read & readIfExists, (blocking and non-blocking versions) return a matching entry from the space.
- take & takeIfExists, (blocking and non-blocking versions) remove the matching entry from the space.
- notify, sends an event when the matching entry is written to the space.
- snapshot, returns another entry object that contains the snapshot of the original one.

As a basis technology, JavaSpaces uses Jini, a protocol allowing "plug and play" functionality for new entities connected to the network. Such an entity can be a device or a software service, which when connected to the network announces its presence. Clients can then use lookup facilities to locate and invoke the services offered by such entities. Thus, a Jini environment is made up of three main parts: the services offered, the clients that will invoke the services, and a service locator that implements the lookup capability.

There are a number of other similar toolkits which for reasons of brevity we will not describe in this chapter. These include Concordia by Mitsubishi [183], IBM's Aglets [12], Odyssey by General Magic [466], and Voyager by ObjectSpace [615]. The interested reader can consult the relevant references for further details.

Law Governed Interaction. One of the most important problems that must be faced in open distributed systems, such as Internet (multi-) agent ones, is that of security. A framework based on specifying and enforcing "laws" which must be obeyed by all entities involved in an application and which provide, among others, safe communication is described in [425]. The model has a wide applicability, but is particularly attractive to the case of Internet agent-based systems. In Law Governed interaction protocols, there exist a set of *controllers*, one controller per entity involved in an application, which intercept all communication between this entity and the rest in the apparatus. Each controller executes a copy of the law which defines in precise ways how the communication between the entities must be realized. The controllers monitor all message exchanges and allow the completion of only those which do not violate the law. As an example, the following is part of a law which establishes a secure bidding policy between agents involved in an e-commerce transaction:

```
R1. sent(C1,out([requester(C2),service(S)]),ts :-
    C1==C2, do(forward).
R2. sent(C1,in([requester(C2),service(S)]),ts :-
    C1==C2, do(forward).
R3. sent(C1,in([offerFor(C,S),fee(f),provider(P),
    provider(P),contact(Addr)]),ts) :-
```

```
C1==C2, do(forward).
```

In the above example we assume that the agents communicate via a common medium, referred to as `ts`; furthermore, a message can be sent to `ts` by means of an `out` primitive and retrieved from there by means of an `in` primitive. Assuming further that a controller monitoring an agent `C1` executes the above law, then the first rule of the law says that `C1` can request a service provided it is for himself, the second one allows the withdrawal of the request, and the third rule allows `C1` to retrieve an offered service if it has been posted to `ts` (by some other agent) for `C1`'s sake.

IMPS. The Internet-based Multi Agent Problem Solving (IMPS, [198]) is a compositional platform for developing Internet multi-agent systems. It features the use of *Problem Solving Models* (PSMs) which may be used in ontology construction and knowledge acquisition. A knowledge library is available to all agents containing information about PSMs in terms of their competencies and domain knowledge requirements, and about types and locations of domain knowledge sources and how to extract different kinds of information from them. This library can be distributed over the Internet and is designed to be modular and extensible by means of 'plug-and-play' new classes written in Java. More to the point, knowledge sharing in IMPS is realized by means of using emerging standards such as KIF, KQML and Java, thus ensuring interoperability.

IMPS is built on top of JAT (Java Agent Template), an agent-level architecture featuring the use of two specialist server agents; these are the Knowledge Extraction Agent (KexA) and the Ontology Construction Agent (OCA) which are used for providing on-demand knowledge to Inference Agents (IAs). IAs specialize in performing particular process or inference steps; thus, IMPS enhances *cooperation* between agents collaborating towards the achievement of a common goal, reduces *redundancy* and increases *reusability* of agent cooperation patterns. The use of KQML allows the dynamic configuration of agents and further enhances the coordination capabilities of this framework. IMPS can be viewed as an enabling technology for modelling logical coordination (see Section 2.4 below).

ADK. The AgentBean Development Kit (ADK, [291]) is a component-based framework for developing mobile multi-agent systems with some emphasis on network and system management issues. In ADK an agent is understood to be composed of components belonging to one of the following three sets:

- *Navigational* components. They are responsible for managing the itinerary of an agent which may be static of dynamically modifiable at run time.
- *Performer* components. They are responsible for carrying out the management tasks that should be executed at the host of the currently visited place. Tasks performed by agents comprise one or more components.
- *Reporter* components. They are responsible for delivering agents' results to designated destinations. Delivery can be a simple point-to-point exchange

of messages of more complicated – for instance, collecting a number of messages (possibly from different sender agents) and forwarding all of them to some recipient agent.

For the purposes of this chapter, the above separation of concerns between the three categories of components enhances the coordination capability of the system. For instance, the reporter components can be seen as encapsulating the coordination activities of some ensemble of agents, thus separating them from other concerns, but also rendering useful coordination interaction patterns reusable. The interaction between components is done in an *event/action*-based fashion: events generated by one component may trigger actions to be performed by another.

JGram. JGram [572] is another multi-agent development platform using the component-based approach. Agents' services are specified in the JGram Description Language and automatically converted into Java source templates. These services may then be invoked synchronously or asynchronously in a manner transparent to the services' implementation. Compositionality of tasks is realized by means of the notion of *pipelining*: an agent may dynamically delegate tasks to other agents and chain together their results. Thus, the complexity of handling a task is distributed across a number of agents, each being aware of only part of it. This notion of pipelining can be seen as an extension of the Unix pipes where the agents involved in a pipeline can be distributed across the network. Furthermore, it is possible to form hierarchies of pipelines with transparent propagation of results.

Communication between the agents involved in pipelines is realized by means of JGram *slates*, consisting of a header specifying addressing information and delivery instructions and a body containing a set of typed entities. Slates are passed over from one agent to another for the purpose of accessing and if necessary modifying the entries in it. The system adheres to elementary coordination principles by taking the responsibility itself for performing parameter checking, thread management, authentication, agent name service and error handling. Thus, the user can concentrate only on creating and using agent services. In particular, the JGram Description Language provides high-level concepts for agent behaviour in the form of (offered) *services* and *requests* (for services). A user expresses an interaction scenario among a number of involved agents using these two notions and the underlying system handles the low level communication details.

RETSINA. The REusable Task Structure-based Intelligent Network Agents (RETSINA, [272]) system plays particular emphasis to the process of formulating planning actions between a number of agents involved in the pursuing of a common goal. The RETSINA system architecture is composed of four autonomous units as follows:

– *Communicator*. It is responsible for exchanging requests between agents in KQML format.

- *Planner*. It transforms goals into plans that solve these goals.
- *Scheduler*. It schedules for execution the tasks representing the plans.
- *Monitor*. It monitors the execution of the plans.

The above separation effectively provides elementary coordination capabilities to the system. Furthermore, the system employs a *planning* and *refinement* algorithm which decomposes a complex plan into a *Hierarchical Task Network* (HTN) of more elementary plans. Every partial plan in the HTN is handled by the planner (and the rest of the units as listed above) of some agent, irrespective of how other agents deal with the rest of the plans. Thus, at any moment in time each agent is aware and interested only in his own local partial plan with the positive consequence that agents may dynamically join and leave the system. This mechanism provides further potential for developing parametric and reusable coordination patterns between cooperating agents.

Domain Specific Languages. The advantages of using Domain Specific Languages (DSLs) for modelling collaboration scenarios between Internet agents is discussed in [252]. DSLs provide a common communication language between all types of agents (human or other) involved in Internet applications. In DSLs a clear separation is enforced between syntax and semantics, so that each agent in a collaboration is capable of applying a behavioural semantics appropriate to its role (e.g., buyer, seller, etc.). Thus, DSLs support the development of multi-agent applications from heterogeneous agents, an issue of importance to coordination frameworks.

Language semantics in DSLs are separated into two levels: the abstract semantics refer to the objects in the domain itself whereas the operational semantics refers to how the messages received by objects will be processed by the machine. What differentiates DSLs from ordinary languages in that respect, is that the "machine" is a specialized computational entity according to what precisely is the domain in question. So, this entity could be a machine specialized in playing bridge or a whole corporation with workflow infrastructure, databases and Internet communication mechanisms, according to the application framework.

[252] uses SGML/XML as a metagrammar for defining DSLs. The following piece of code defines the grammar of part of the scenario that models a game of bridge:

```
<!ELEMENT bridge (player+,deal,bidding,dummy,play)>
<!ELEMENT player #EMPTY>
<!ATTIST player  position (north|south|east|west) #REQ
                 name cdata #REQ>
<!ELEMENT deal (card+)>
<!ELEMENT card #EMPTY>
<!ATTIST card    suit (spades|hearts|diamonds|clubs) #REQ
                 face cdata #REQ>
 ...  ...  ...
```

Part of an actual scenario (for dealing only), based on the above grammar is shown below:

```
<bridge>
<player position='north', name='george'> ...
<deal><card suit='spades', face='king'>, ... </deal>
... ... ...
</bridge>
```

In a distributed realisation of this game, each agent will receive and interpret a bridge string as the one shown above. This string may be parsed as a data structure by a computational agent or be presented to a human agent in some visual and interactive form. The instance of a bridge game, as specified by the code enclosed in the `<bridge>`...`</bridge>` tags, will be played according to the rules for bidding, passing and using trump cards (not shown above) as they have been defined in the grammar above.

2.3 Coordination Frameworks

In this section we describe a number of approaches where coordination between Internet agents is supported as a "first class citizen". Contrary to the previous section where the emphasis was on systems whose principles have the *potential* of developing coordination frameworks, here we concentrate on genuine coordination models and languages that have specific features for Internet agents. Many of these models have evolved from earlier, more conventional versions, that deal with non (Internet) agent-based distributed computing [482]. Most of the models in this section adopt the notion of a Linda-like shared dataspace; however, some follow a more control-driven approach [482] and a few are based on other notions such as using graphical notations.

2.3.1 Shared Dataspace Models

TuCSoN. TuCSoN [196, 197] addresses in particular two important problems that must be faced in open Internet agents-based systems: those of security and authentication. The model is an extension of the Linda framework and it uses the same set of primitives for dealing with tuples. As in other variations of the vanilla model, TuCSoN introduces multiple tuple spaces, referred to as *tuple centres*. Thus, an ordinary Linda tuple operation op(tuple) is now parametric to the particular tuple centre tc which is being accessed and takes the form tc?op(tuple). Furthermore, the tuple centres are associated with their own policies for being accessed by agents; an agent attempting to access some tuple centre will undergo an authentication screening according to the particular policies of the tuple centre that it tries to access. Thus, the tuple centres become *programmable media* that define locally the way agents will interact with them. TuCSoN views the Internet world as a hierarchical collection of different tuple centres. For instance, one tuple centre can be the main gateway of some Web site (e.g. the gateway for some organisation), comprising a number of subordinate tuple centres (e.g. local departments within the organisation). This allows the optimisation of enforcing security policies in the sense that the programmable "logic" of a tuple centre for some tree hierarchy regarding how it is being accessed by external agents, may refrain from authenticating an agent that tries to access a sub-domain of the tree if that agent has already received security clearance from the top domain.

The consequences of the tuple space acting as a programmable medium means that there exist now two different levels of perception: that of the agents accessing it and that of the medium itself handling the queries. Thus, every logical operation at the level of the agent must be mapped onto one or more corresponding system actions at the level of the medium and vice versa. This introduces the notion of *reactions* and the primitive reaction(Operation, Body) where every logical Operation is mapped onto one or more system operations (Body). As an example, consider the problem of coordinating the well-known dining philosophers to access their forks:

```
reaction(out(forks(F1,F2)),
  (in_r(forks(F1,F2)), out_r(fork(F1)), out_r(fork(F2))))

reaction(in(forks(F1,F2)),(pre,out_r(required(F1,F2))))
reaction(in(forks(F1,F2)),(post,out_r(required(F1,F2))))
reaction(out_r(required(F1,F2),
  (in_r(fork(F1),in_r(fork(F2)),out_r(forks(F1,F2)))))

reaction(out_r(fork(F)),(rd_r(required(F1,F)),
  in_r(fork(F1)),in_r(fork(F)),out_r(forks(F1,F))))

reaction(out_r(fork(F)),(rd_r(required(F,F2)),
  in_r(fork(F)),in_r(fork(F2)),out_r(forks(F,F2))))
```

In the above modelling of the problem in TuCSoN, two points of reference are being involved. The agent philosopher perceives the fork resources as pairs and asks for them in that fashion, namely forks(F1,F2). The programmable medium however must map the agent's perception of pairs-of-forks to single forks and furthermore, ensure that these are accessed atomically and in a way that is fair to all philosophers. This is achieved by means of a number of reaction rules. The first one changes a release of the left and the right fork as a pair to two single releases. The next two rules refer to the case of an agent requesting a pair of forks in which case a request is posted to the medium (first rule of this group) and is retracted when the forks have been allocated to the agent (second rule of this group.). These requests are handled by the last three rules; the first rule of this group allocates immediately the two forks if they are both available whereas the last two rules handle the case when only one of the two forks can be immediately given to the requesting agent.

KLAIM. The Kernel Language for Agent Interaction and Mobility (KLAIM, [453]) is another Linda variant for coordinating Internet agents with similar characteristics to TuCSoN. A KLAIM program is a *net*, comprising a set of *nodes*. Each node has a name and is associated with a process component and a tuple space component. The name of a node is effectively an Internet site and allows access to the network. Processes access tuple sites via symbolic *locality* references; in other words, they need not know explicit network references. Thus the net can be seen as a distributed infrastructure for coordinating processes in accessing and sharing resources.

In particular, each node in a net is of the form e {P | T} where e is an allocation environment that maps symbolic locality references to actual tuple spaces, P is a set of running processes, and T is a tuple space. Consider the following piece of KLAIM code:

```
def Client = out(Q)@l ; nil
def Q = in('foo',!X)@self ; out('foo',X+1)@self ; nil
def Server = in(!P)@self ; eval(P)@self ; nil
```

In the above example, the first line of code defines a process Client that outs a process Q to the environment l. The actual definition of Q is given in the second line and involves the increment of the value of some variable X. The third line of code defines a process Server which retrieves a process P from its own tuple space and executes it. The idea in this example is that Client sends an increment process Q to some other process Server which will then execute Q and send the new increment value back to Client. Assuming that Client and Server run on the nodes s1 and s2 respectively, this will work provided that l is mapped to s2 and the self references of Client and Server map themselves to s1 and s2 respectively. Furthermore, we assume that before the execution of these processes commences, an initial tuple <'foo',1> exists in the tuple spaces involved in the scenario. These are achieved by the following piece of code:

```
node s1 :: e1 {Client | out('foo',1)} ||
node s2 :: e2 {Client | out('foo',1)}
```

When Client sends Q for execution to Server's tuple space, it will appear there as the process:

```
Q' = in('foo',!X)@s1 ; out('foo',X+1)@s1 ; nil
```

Thus, Server will execute Q' in its own tuple space s2 but post the result to the tuple space s1, i.e. will effectively send the result back to Client.

KLAIM has a capability-based type system to express and enforce access control policies and thus provide security. These types provide information regarding the intention of some process with respect to producing or using tuples, creating new nodes or activating processes. Permissions have a hierarchical structure in the sense that if a process is allowed to perform an operation of a certain generality or "strength", then by default it is also allowed to perform all other operations that are less general or weaker. For instance, if it is allowed to read a real value then it is also allowed to read an integer value, and if it is allowed to remove a tuple (in) then it is also allowed to simply read it rd). As an example, the following KLAIM code specifies access control rights for the processes Client and Server:

```
def Server = out(<1:void,Top>)@self ; nil
def Client = read(!u:<[self > e], ac>@1-S;
             eval(P)@u ; nil
```

According to the above definitions, Server adds a tuple containing the locality 1 to its own tuple space; no access restrictions are specified on 1. The process Client first accesses the tuple space 1-S to read an address u before sending process P to execute at u. However, this will only be possible to achieve if P is of type ac, because the second rule states that only processes of this type are allowed to be sent from the site of Client to the site u.

LIME. Linda in a Mobile Environment (LIME, [493]) is yet another extension of the Linda model for coordinating Internet agents. However, contrary to the previous two models that develop fully-fledged languages, LIME offers only a minimalist set of constructs. The philosophical difference between models like the previous two and those such as LIME is that in the former case the user has direct and explicit control on how to deal with coordination matters specific to Internet agents (such as mobility or security) while in the latter case the user only implicitly expresses the intended actions to be performed and it is the system that is primarily responsible for dealing with such issues.

The fundamental abstraction provided by LIME is that of a *transiently shared tuple space*. In particular, each agent is associated with its own personal tuple space, referred to as *interface tuple space* (ITS). An agent may have one or more ITSs identified by a separate name. The union of the ITSs with the same name that belong to all the agents that are co-located at some host form the transiently shared tuple space for that host with respect to the currently residing there agents. When a new agent moves to some location, the LIME system recomputes the transiently shared tuple space for that location taking into consideration the ITSs of that agent. This process is called *engagement*. When an agent leaves the host, LIME again recomputes the transiently shared tuple space for that host by removing those tuples that belong only to the ITSs of the departing agent. This reverse process is called *disengagement*.

Thus, if two agents A and B reside on the same host and A performs the operation out(t) to its own ITS (we assume for simplicity here that only one ITS per agent is involved in our scenario), then because the two agents are co-located and the two ITSs form a common transiently shared tuple space, B can perform the operation in(t) and retrieve the tuple t (which can be seen by B through his own ITS). Care must be taken when, after performing the operation out(t),A migrates to some other host. In this case, the transiently shared tuple space between the ITSs of A and B does not exist any more and the tuple t would go along with A and would not be any more accessible to B for retrieval. In order to allow access to t even after the departure of A, the latter must out it to the ITS of B, rather than to its own ITS by means of executing the primitive out[B](t). In this case, t becomes part of B's ITS and will remain there even after the departure of the agent (A) which created it, although the two agents are not co-located on the same host any more.

Berlinda. Berlinda [596] is a meta- coordination Linda-based platform developed in Java. The system offers a highly abstract model of coordination that can be used as the basis for developing more concrete coordination frameworks for Internet agents. As in all Linda models, there exists a common communication medium in the form of *multisets*, which comprises a collection of *elements*. Elements carry *signatures* with meta information and provide a *matching function* for their access by agents according to the semantics of the particular coordination framework that is being employed. All these entities are implemented as Java classes that form a hierarchical structure and provide appropriate operations that realize the functionality of the coordination framework.

The Berlinda platform has been used for developing coordination frameworks for Linda and KQML. As an example, the following piece of code creates a set of agents in a Linda coordination framework that traverse a file system and remove unnecessary files, i.e. those files that can be generated from some other file:

```
public class SweepAgent extends LindaAgent {
public static void main (String argv[]) {
    // create tuple space
    TupleSpace ts = new TupleSpace();
    // create agents
    for (int i=1; i<=walker; i++) ts.eval(new Walker());
    for (int i=1; i<=sweeper; i++)ts.eval(new Sweeper());
    // allocate work to agents
    ts.out(new Tuple("Sweeped", new Integer(0)));
    ts.out(new Tuple("Walker",start_directory_path));
    ... ... ...
    }
    ... ... ...
}
```

The Walker agents traverse a directory, spawning themselves to traverse in parallel any subdirectories. The results of their search are passed on to the Sweeper agents that remove the selected files.

PageSpace. The PageSpace platform [173] is effectively a meta-architecture or reference architecture for developing Internet agents-based applications.

Applications are composed of a set of distributed agents and are conceived as comprising three layers: a *client* layer, a *server* layer and an *application* layer, that coordinate modules belonging to client agents, server agents or intranet applications respectively. These applications may be distributed transparently across a network and used in serving several users who independently access a shared Linda-like environment via their WWW browsers. Independently progressing applications may interact with each other in order to cooperate towards the achievement of a common goal. Furthermore, the configuration of users, applications and hosts may change dynamically without disrupting the offered services.

Depending on their functionality, PageSpace distinguishes several kinds of agents, such as *user interface* agents, *application* agents (that manage the running of some application), *gateway* agents (that provide access to the outside world), *kernel* agents (that perform management and control tasks), etc. PageSpace is effectively the product of combining related research at the University of Bologna and the Technical University of Berlin and it thus uses a number of more specialized software architectures and associated coordination models and languages that have been developed by the two groups such as MUDWeb, Shade/Java, or MJada [516]. As an example of Internet agent coordination in PageSpace, we show extracts of a Shade/Java program that coordinates the process of bidding in an e-commerce scenario involving three groups of agents: an auctioneer agent that sells items to participant agents while some observer agents passively watch the process. Shade/Jada is a combination of Java with the Linda-based coordination language Shade. A Shade program is a collection of classes and each object in a Shade application is a class instance. Objects communicate by means of Linda-like communication primitives. Thus, Shade/Java is a syntactic extension of Java with the coordination features of Shade [516]. Regarding the example in question, the code is part of the auctioneer agent functionality:

```
class auctioneer extends ShadeObject {
  in ("begin");
  out ("bid","bid1"), ("next_item","next1"),
      ("cartoon","car1"), ("display","dis1"),
      ("BasePrice",5000), ("next_init","init_2"),
      ("item#",1);
  #
  in ("BasePrice",?i:base_bid);
  out (("display",?s:display), ("item#",?i:num);
  send [bid,  ("begin_auction","auctioneer",base_bid,0),
             ("item#",num)],
  send [display, ("begin_auction","auctioneer",base_bid, 0)];
  out ("auction_active"), ("first_timer"),
      ("current_bid",base_bid), ("TimeStamp",0);
  #
  ... ... ...
```

The above piece of code shows two of a number of methods that the auctioneer agent comprises (the code for each method is separated by '#'). The auctioneer starts the auction when it receives the tuple begin in which case the first method above is activated. This method broadcasts a number of initialisation tuples that activate the agents to be engaged in the scenario. Furthermore, when the first item goes on sale, it is displayed by the agent dis1 of class display. The second method commences the coordination of the bidding process. An auction starts from a base price which is sent to all participating agents (the tag item# on some item denotes that that item is to be sold). Further methods receive bids, validate them and modify appropriately offered prices for sellable items.

MARS-X. MARS-X [118] is a programmable coordination architecture for Internet agents based on a combination of XML and a Linda-like communication mechanism. The XML component enhances interoperability by separating the treatment of data from its representation. The Linda-like communication mechanism offers the required coordination mechanisms for modelling cooperation between agents. MARS-X is a four layer architecture: at the lowest layer lays the actual information being manipulated and in the next level the XML dataspace; the third layer comprises the Linda-like interface (based on Sun's JavaSpaces) and at the upper (application) level lie the executing agents. There exists a local per node in the network XML dataspace, and when a mobile agent arrives at a node it is provided with a reference to this dataspace. Groups of nodes can create shared federated dataspaces. Access to a dataspace is realized by means of the operations read, take and write which correspond directly to Linda's rd, in and out. There are also the aggregate variants readAll and takeAll which retrieve all matching tuples. The following piece of codes illustrates the modelling of agents in MARS-X:

```
<?XML version="1"?>
<course>
  ...
  <lesson>
    <lessonname>Introduction</lessonname>
    <lessonnumber>1</lessonnumber>
    <abstract></abstract>
    ...
</course>

class_lesson extends AbstractEntry {
  static private URL DTDfile = new URL(http://);
  public String lessonname;
  public Integer lessonnumber;
  public String abstract;
  ... }

lesson tmplesson = newlesson();  // template lesson
tmplesson.abstract="networks"  // partially def field
for (i=0; i<number_of_federation_sites; i++)
```

```
{go(site[i];              // current site in the federation
 if(lesson=S.read(tmplesson,)  // if a lesson with
   go(home);  // the right keyword is found go home
}
```

In the above example, the first part of the code describes in XML the structure of a lesson, as part of some course. The second part defines as extended Java classes the MARS-X tuple corresponding to a lesson. Finally, the last part makes use of the Linda like primitives to define the behaviour of an agent which roams a federated site (i.e. a collection of local XML dataspaces) in order to find and retrieve the lesson with the keyword "networks".

2.3.2 Other Coordination Models for Internet Agents

We present below some other coordination models, particularly suited to Internet agents, which however are not based (at least directly) on the Linda model. Here we find a variety of flavours: those that use a point-to-point communication mechanism and can be characterized as being control-oriented [482], or others which are based on extension of existing programming paradigms such as logic programming or visual programming.

STL++. The Simple Thread Language ++ (STL, [540]), an evolution from earlier coordination languages, is a control-driven coordination formalism for Internet agents which is based on the Encapsulation Coordination Model (ECM). Unlike the members of the previous category of coordination models in this section which are variants of Linda (and therefore they are relying on a notionally shared dataspace), ECM and its associated language ECL++ are relying on point-to-point communication. In particular, there exist five building blocks:

- *Processes*, as a representation of active entities.
- *Blops*, as an abstraction and modularisation mechanism for a group of processes and ports.
- *Ports*, as the interface between processes/blops and the outside world.
- *Events*, as a mechanism for synchronising the execution of processes and blops.
- *Connections*, as a means of connecting ports.

A coordination ensemble in STL++ is a collection of agents, themselves grouped in blops, with well defined port-based input-output interfaces which communicate via their respective ports by means of port-to-port connections, and synchronize their activities by means of events. The language is object-oriented and has been realized as an extension of C++. As an example, the following is an extract from an STL++ program coordinating the activities in a restaurant:

```
void Waiter :: start() {
  Agent :: start();
  int income;
  table_port = new BB_Port<int>(this,nV("MealBB"),INF);
  int i, j;
  for (i=0; i!=nbrOfClients; i++) {
    j=(i+1)% nbrOfClients;
    createAgent(Client,&i,&j);   // Create the clients
  }
  // Restaurant closes - take the money
  income=table_port->get("money");
  while (income) {
    total_income+=income;
    income=table_port->get("money");
  }
  stopMe();
}
```

The above code refers to a `Waiter` agent which manages the diner area in a restaurant. It is responsible for organising a place for each newly arriving customer. It initializes the scenario by creating an initial number of customers. Finally, it collects the money for providing dinner and closes the restaurant. `Waiter` creates a port `table_port` with the name `MealBB` which will be used to collect money. Then it creates a number of clients, and finally it receives the money through `table_port` and sums up the income. The setting up of a connection between an appropriate port of the agents of type `Client` and `table_port` so that the money can be received, is not shown above and is part of the code for `Client`.

Mobile Streams. Mobile Streams [505] is a middleware platform for the development of distributed multi-agent systems. What is of particular importance to the issue of coordination, is that Mobile Streams is especially suitable for applications that require dynamic (re-) configuration. Furthermore, the system is event-driven in the sense that its components (namely mobile agents) synchronize their cooperation by means of sending and receiving events. The combination of these two features (event-driven dynamic reconfigurability) is typical of a particular class of control-driven coordination formalisms [482] and Mobile Streams can be seen as being a mobile version of them.

A Mobile Stream (MStream) is a globally unique name for a communication end-point in a distributed system that can be moved from machine to machine, during the course of a computation and preserving the order of messages. A MStream is part of a hierarchical tree structured logical organisation whose root is a *Session*, namely a distributed application. A *Session* comprises a set of *Sites*, at each one of which a number of agents execute and communicate via one or more MStreams. Each agent comprises a number of *Event Handlers* which handle events. This apparatus separates the logical design of a distributed application from the physical placement of components.

A distributed application is constructed by first specifying the communication end-points as MStreams and attaching agents to them. The latter create event handlers, one (and only one) for a different event associated with an agent. When an event occurs, the appropriate handler in each agent is concurrently and independently invoked with appropriate arguments. When a MStream moves from one site to another, it (logically) moves the code of all the agents attached to it to the new site along with their state. The code can have initialisation and finalisation parts that execute once the agent first arrives at a site or when it is about to be killed. As an example, consider the following piece of code:

```
stream_create foo
stream_create bar
stream_move foo 1
stream_move bar 2

# external input
stream_open bar
stream_append foo "Hello World"

register_agent foo () {
    stream_open bar
    on_stream_append {
            stream_append bar $argv
    }
}

register_agent bar () {
    on_stream_append {
            puts $argv
            stream_relocate 1
    }
    on_stream_relocation {
            set my_loc [stream_location]
            puts "I am at $my_loc"
    }
}
```

The above script initially defines two streams, foo and bar, and locates them at different sites (1 and 2). We further assume that a string is sent to foo from an external source. The MStream foo receives the string message and sends it to the MStream bar, which outputs the message via its handler. Finally, bar moves to the site of foo and prints an appropriate message to announce its new location.

GroupLog. The agent coordination language GroupLog [52] is based on an extended Horn Clauses formalism. Elementary agents in GroupLog are modelled as (possibly perpetual) processes which receive messages and react to them by invoking appropriate methods. A clause can have AND-conjunctions with sequential or parallel operational semantics. Sets of clauses defining the overall behaviour of agents are grouped into modules. In that respect, GroupLog is very similar to object-oriented concurrent logic programming languages such as POOL. What is particularly relevant to the notion of co-ordination however is the notion of *group*, which effectively structures the communication space of agents and allows the modelling of various cooperation patterns between them. Agents can dynamically join and leave groups and can be members of multiple groups at the same time. Group communication can be either broadcast or point-to-point. The following code defines such a group:

```
group meet_schedule {
    context().
    interface(begin).
    meet_schedule(Id) : begin :-
        members(meet_schedule(Id),[H,I]),
        rd(meet_schedule(Id),meet(MeetId)),
        H << begin(I,MeetId) || I << begin(H,MeetId)
                | meet_schedule(Id).
    meet_schedule(Id) : new | meet_schedule(Id).
}
```

The group meet_schedule defines a broadcast communication mechanism between a number of agents [H,I] belonging to the same group MeetId. Using the communication operation <<, and the predefined primitives members (returns the agents belonging to the same group Id and rd (returns the subset from a set of agents belonging to the same group), meet_schedule sets up communication paths between all members of this group so that they can exchange messages in a broadcast fashion. An agent joining the group meet_schedule will automatically become part of this communication apparatus. Furthermore, the communication strategy of this group may change dynamically without the agents belonging to it realising any difference.

Little-JIL. We end this section with a brief description of Little-JIL [334], a visual language for agent coordination. Little-JIL has been designed to address in particular the problem of knowledge discovery in databases, an issue of particular interest to Web environments, especially with regard to aspects of traffic analysis, fraud detection, etc. Activities of processes in Little-JIL are represented as *steps*, decomposed into *substeps*. Substeps belonging to a step can be invoked either proactively or reactively. Steps may have *guards* to be executed upon entering or exiting a step, as well as handlers to deal with exceptions. They can also include *resource* specification. One special resource associated with each step is an *agent* which is responsible for initiating and carrying out the work of the step.

Coordination of agents is achieved by means of an *agent management system* (AMS). An AMS is based on the metaphor of to-do lists for activities to be performed by agents, human or automated. Assignment of tasks to be executed by some agent(s) are placed on the to-do lists of those agents. Agents monitor to-do lists (they may be associated with more than one list if they are involved in performing several disjoint processes), in order to receive tasks to perform. Any changes in the to-do list cause notification to be sent to the interested agents which then execute the corresponding tasks. Task execution causes changes to the system state and these changes are recorded by the AMS. Thus, the AMS provides language-independent facilities that allow coordination to take place in a way that separates the concerns about why and when coordination should occur (handled by AMS) from how it will be achieved (handled by the agents).

2.4 Logical Coordination

The previous two sections have dealt with a rather "technical" aspect of coordination, as it applies to the field of Internet agents. In particular, we first examined some enabling technologies that provide the necessary infrastructure for building coordination frameworks. We then presented some approaches in developing models and languages for Internet agents where coordination is treated as a first class citizen. However, the concept of coordination exists also at a higher, more logical, level where we are interested in organising the cooperation behaviour between the members of a multi-agent ensemble. In this case, *middle agents* are used with the sole purpose of acting as coordinators managing the activities of other agents. Such coordination can be done centrally or in a distributed fashion. Depending on precisely what sort of coordination these agents realize, they can belong to a number of different categories, some of which are the following [243]:

- *Facilitators* or *Mediators*, which satisfy requests on behalf of other agents, usually by offering certain services to these agents.
- *Brokers*, which also satisfy requests received by other agents but often by using services provided by third parties rather than themselves.
- *Matchmakers* (*Yellow Pages*), which offer look-up services.
- *Blackboards*, which are repository agents that receive and hold requests for other agents to process.
- *Local area coordinators*, which are agents responsible for assisting the other agents in some well defined area to initiate and conduct inter-agent communication and interaction.
- *Cooperation domain servers*, which provide agents in some domain with facilities to subscribe, exchange messages and access shared information.

Logical coordination techniques have been classified by [462] into four main categories:

- *Organisational Structuring*, which provides a framework for activity and interaction through the definition of roles, communication paths and authority relationships; here classic *master-slave* or *blackboard* coordination techniques are being employed.

- *Contracting*, which involves the use of manager agents who break a problem into subproblems and assign each one of them to some contract agent to deal with them. This apparatus is often referred to as *contract-net protocol*.
- *Multi-Agent Planning*, where the agents build a plan that defines all current and future interactions among them in such a way that avoids inconsistent or conflicting actions. There are two ways to execute the plan: in *centralized* planning, a coordinating agent is responsible for setting up and executing the plan, whereas in *distributed* planning each agent is aware of the plans of the other agents and acts appropriately.
- *Negotiation*, involves a particular form of coordination where a number of agents interact with each other in order to reach a mutually accepted agreement on some matter. Negotiation techniques can be *game theory*-based, *plan*-based, or *human inspired*.

In the rest of this section we will present some approaches in realising logical coordination at the level of modelling the behaviour of agents. The models in this section try to address such questions as how agents communicate and coordinate themselves in achieving a common goal, how are problems stemming from dynamical evolutions of agents or incomplete knowledge handled during the coordinated behaviour, or how patterns of interaction and interoperation that characterize coordinated behaviour are modelled. A major consequence of addressing these issues is the ability to *reuse* descriptions of generally useful coordination mechanisms.

COOL. The COOrdination Language [54] is part of an effort to develop a more general Agent Building Shell that will provide reusable languages and services for agent construction that will relieve developers from the burden of developing from scratch essential interoperation, communication and cooperation services. The COOL architecture comprises three layers, with a basic KQML-like communication mechanism at the lower level, an agent and conversation management at the middle level for defining and executing agents and coordination structures, and an upper level that supports in context acquisition and debugging of coordination knowledge. We will not elaborate on the lowest level which is covered adequately by the material in Section 2.2. Regarding the way the agent and conversation management models the behaviour of agents, we note that every agent is associated with a name and an interpreter which then selects and manages its conversations. The interpreter applies continuation rules to determine which conversation to work on next. The interpreter may also invoke more specialized agents for knowledge acquisition and/or debugging services. Such a scenario is shown below:

```
(def-agent 'customer
  :continuation-control 'agent-control-ka
  :continuation-rules '(cont-1 cont-2 cont-3 cont-4))
(def-agent 'logistics
  :continuation-control 'agent-control-ka
  :continuation-rules '(cont-1 cont-2 cont-3 cont-4))
```

```
(def-agent 'plant
  :continuation-control 'agent-control-ka
  :continuation-rules '(cont-1 cont-2 cont-3 cont-4))
```

In the code above three agents are defined, part of a supply chain application. The execution and control of these agents is managed by a conversation manager like the one below:

```
(def-conversation-manager 'm1
  :agent-control 'execute-agent
  :agents '(customer logistics plant ...))
```

This manager decides which agent to run next, manages message passing, etc. Agents interact with each other by means of carrying out *conversations*; such a conversation for the agent customer is defined below:

```
(def-conversation-class 'customer-conversation
  :name 'customer-conversation
  :content-language 'list
  :speech-act-language 'kqml
  :initial-state 'start
  :final-states '(rejected failed satisfied)
  :control 'interactive-choice-control-ka
  :rules '( (start cc1) (proposed cc-13 cc-2)
            (working cc-5 cc-4 cc-3)
             (counterp cc-9 cc-8 cc-7 cc-6)
              (asked cc-10) (accepted cc-12 cc-11)))
```

The above code associates with some agent the conversation rules that govern its interaction with other agents. What particular activities are performed during the execution of such a rule is illustrated by the following code:

```
(def-conversation-rule 'crn-1
  :current-state 'start
  :received '(propose   :sender customer
                        :content(customer-order :item ?l))
  :next-state 'order-received
  :transmit '(tell      :sender ?agent
                        :receiver customer
                        :content '(working on it)
                        :conversation ?convn)
  :do '(put-conv-var ?conv '?order
                        (cadr(member :content ?message)))
  :incomplete nil)
```

This code defines the behaviour of the agent logistics in our scenario of supply chain management. When logistics is at the start state, it receives a proposal for an order and informs the sender (customer) that it is working on it before going to the next state order-received. The language also allows the formulation of two other coordination dimensions, cooperative information distribution and cooperative conflict management, but for reasons of brevity we do not discuss them here.

Agent Groups. The model described in [60] introduces the notion of Agent Groups, comprising agents working together on a common task. Agent groups may be arbitrarily structured and highly dynamic. Communication and synchronisation between the agents of a group is event-driven; the model assumes the existence of a mechanism for sending and receiving events. The group model used involves the following types of agents:

- A *Group Initiator*, which creates the agent group, an activity that involves assigning agents to groups, defining group coordinators, administrators and receivers of results.
- *Group Members*, which is the collection of agents forming a group, according to a common task pursued.
- A *Group Coordinator*, which models dependencies within an agent group but also between the group and the outside world. Dependencies are implemented as condition-action pairs, where the condition is defined by means of event types received and the action can be internal to the group or external, in the latter case involving entities existing outside the group.
- A *Group Administrator*, which manages the group as a whole and decides on issues such as the life span of the group or orphan detection.
- A *Results Receiver*, which is an agent collecting the results of the agents forming a group.

The above logical organisation of a multi-agent system has been applied by the authors to their system Mole [59] while allows migration of agents and supports a distributed event service.

Dynamic Agents. Dynamic Agents [150] is a similar model to the one presented above, based on the dynamic modification of the behaviour of agents. In an ordinary (mobile) agent its behaviour is fixed at the time of agent creation, and in order for this behaviour to change this agent must effectively be replaced by another agent with the newly required behaviour. A dynamic agent, however, is not designed to have a fixed set of predefined functions, but instead to carry application specific actions, which can be loaded and modified on the fly. In that respect, dynamic agents can adjust their capabilities to accommodate changes in the environment and requirements, and play different roles across multiple applications.

Dynamic agents are created by an *agent factory* running on each local site. Each such agent is identified by a symbolic name and an Internet address (including a socket number) which are unique within the boundaries of some *agent space*, itself defined in terms of the agents residing within. The agent space is managed by an *agent coordinator* which maintains the agent name registry of this space. The coordinator is the first agent to be created within an agent space. When it is created, it publishes its socket address to a designated location and in that respect it makes it known to all other dynamic agents. A dynamic agent that is being created, first registers its (unique) name and address with the coordinator. In that respect, any other agent who wishes to send a message to the agent in question and does not know its address, consults the coordinator. The coordinator keeps also an address list for any services offered in its space (e.g. program utilities) and any agent wishing to use some service can again consult the coordinator. The address list of agents is kept up to date, so any agent termination, for instance, results in the name and address of the agent being removed from the list. The coordinator also broadcasts an appropriate message to all the agents in the agent space so that they become aware of the termination of that agent. Hierarchical groups of agent spaces with associated coordinators can also be formed.

Finally, the proposed system offers other types of coordination services in terms of more specialized dynamic agents. In particular, there exist *resource brokers* that provide global resource management services, *request brokers* that provide look up services for service requests, and *event brokers* that manage event-based synchronisation between agents.

Role Models. In [350], it is argued that a way to express coordination and collaboration relationships between agents is by means of roles. A role model identifies and describes an archetypal or recurring structure of interacting entities in terms of roles. The latter define a position and a set of responsibilities within role models. External interfaces are used to make a role's services and activities accessible. In addition to responsibilities and external interfaces, an agent role comprises a number of other parameters such as collaborators (roles it interacts with), and *coordination and negotiation* information related to communication protocols, conflict resolutions, permissible actions, etc. The author presents a UML-based formal notation (which can be also presented in terms of Patterns) for describing agent roles and shows how executable code can be generated using Aspect Oriented Programming techniques. She further argues that the model can be used at the systems analysis and design phase of developing a multi-agent system.

TRUCE. The TRUCE [325] coordination language can be seen as a concrete realisation of some of the above mentioned notions such as roles, groups and dynamic agents. TRUCE is a *scripting* language where scripts define a protocol specification for coordination. Such a script is given to all agents that are members of some collaboration group and they interpret it in a concurrent fashion. An agent receiving a script does not execute it in its entirety, but chooses to execute only that part which is relevant to its activities, as the latter are defined from the *role* that has been assigned to it.

Every instruction in a script has two components: an *action* to be executed and a set of *collaborators* that participate in carrying out this action. Every such collaborator has a specific role, e.g. initiate the action, receive the result of the action, etc. Depending on the state of the system, an agent may execute different parts of the script and play different roles, thus exhibiting behaviour similar to that of dynamic agents (see above). The following fragment of code shows the modelling of some coordination scenario:

```
protocol selling-protocol {
  when { $selling=true {
        sellers.if {myturn=true} {
              set $"current-seller"=_me;
        }
        retract {selling-protocol};
        facilitator.set {$selling} false;
        auction {facilitator, $"current-seller"
              {buyers, sellers} };
        recover {selling-protocol};
        facilitator.proceed {$"current-seller"};
    }
}
```

This code is part of a more elaborate scenario on auctions. Roughly speaking, the protocol is triggered by a global property $selling which is set by some seller agent. Only sellers test the value of their local parameter myturn. They then set current-seller to _me which causes the temporal suspension of the protocol until the selling has taken place (not shown above) in which case the protocol is re-activated. The roles facilitator, buyers and sellers are bound to agent names according to other parts of the rest of the script.

E-Commerce Mediators. The survey paper by [295] discusses a rather important type of Internet agents which act as coordinators, the Electronic Commerce *mediators*. The authors define a set of characteristics that these mediators should possess, namely *need identification* that assists the consumer to define precisely his needs, *product brokering* that helps to determine what must be bought, *merchant brokering* that helps to determine where to buy from, *negotiation* that determines the terms of conducting a business transaction, *purchase* and *delivery* of the bought product, and post *analysis* of quality of service. A number of tools and products are then analysed against these parameters, namely Personal Logic, Firefly, Bargain Finder, Jango, Kasbah, Auction Bot and Tete-a-Tete. According to the authors' survey, only the last model addresses all the requirements they have defined.

2.5 Conclusions

In this survey chapter we have presented an overview of the various types of models and technologies that enable the use of coordination principles in the development of Internet (multi-) agent systems. As in another survey of similar nature [482] we have advocated a rather liberal approach in what constitutes a coordination framework. In particular, for the case of Internet agents we have identified three broad categories of associated coordination models and languages. The first category comprises those approaches which can be viewed as providing the basic coordination infrastructure. The models in this category do not deal with coordination mechanisms *per se*, but instead they provide the means necessary to build fully-fledged coordination frameworks. We can identify two subcategories here; the first one deals with the most fundamental issue of coordination, namely that of communication. Therefore this subcategory comprises the Agent Communication Languages, where prominent members are KQML and its derivatives. The second subcategory comprises those approaches which provide useful infrastructure to other important aspects of developing Internet (multi-) agent systems such as security or basic mechanisms for building compositional environments.

The second main category presents some fully-fledged coordination models and languages where coordination principles are treated as first class citizens. Historically, many of these models have evolved from more traditional (non-agent-based) versions that have been developed as proposals to advance the Software Engineering techniques for building Parallel and Distributed Information Systems. Here we can also identify two subcategories. The first deals with those approaches that have been inspired from the Linda model of coordination and the use of a Shared Dataspace. Many researchers agree that the concept of having a common forum of communication and cooperation among a number of processes (or agents) is particularly appealing to the case of Internet-based Information Systems. The second subcategory comprises the rest of the proposals, which use some alternative approach.

The final main category is concerned with those approaches which deal with coordination at a higher, logical or algorithmic, level. In this category we review some models whose main aim is to program coordination techniques into the behaviour of the agents that comprise an application. This leads to the creation of specialized types of Internet agents that deal with one or another aspect of inter-agent coordination (contracting, negotiation, etc.), and languages able to express coordination patterns of agent behaviour at a higher level.

Needless to say, the above three-level organisation of the presented approaches in this chapter is hardly the only one that has been suggested. There is a number of other survey papers that the interested reader may want to consult. [462] present a survey on the basic infrastructure technologies for developing agent-based systems with emphasis on the Agent Communication Languages. [117] present a similar in scope survey where the taxonomy used is based on the criterion as to whether a model is independent or not in time and/or space. [278] presents another survey where the main aspect of coordination which is of concern in this work is that of the different cooperation patterns employed by the various systems examined. The author focuses his analysis on the issue of application frameworks suited to each model with particular emphasis to e-commerce ones. A similar survey, with even more emphasis on e-commerce issues, is reported in [351]. However, all these surveys deal with only one aspect of coordination, as this notion is conceived in this chapter. Effectively, [462] deals with the first level of our taxonomy, [117] is focused on the second one, and [278] and [351] examine models belonging to the third level.

It should be clear from the various trends that have been presented in this chapter, that the notion of coordination is inherent and important in building Internet multi-agent systems. We believe we will see in the future more models and languages that will advance this framework in all three dimensions as we have used them to classify the different approaches. At the lower level, we will see more advanced techniques for dealing with issues of basic inter-agent communication (i.e. more powerful and expressive KQML or otherwise based ACLs), security, etc. The middle level will continue to populate with know-how from mainstream coordination technologies and further associated coordination languages will be proposed. The upper level will also evolve, driven by the needs for coordination patterns from important Internet-based applications such as e-commerce or Cooperative Information Systems.

Finally, one should note that one of the aims of this chapter is to become a roadmap for the more focused and specialized chapters that follow and which shed even more light in the usefulness and importance of using coordination principles in developing Internet-based multi-agent systems.

Acknowledgements

This work has been partially supported by the INCO-DC KIT (Keep-in-Touch) program 962144 "Developing Software Engineering Environments for Distributed Information Systems" financed by the Commission of the European Union.

Part II

Basic Enabling Technologies

Basic Enabling Technologies

Introduction

Suitable infrastructures are what is going to make agents an everyday technology for Internet-based systems – like railways for trains in the transportation system, or satellites for cellular phones in the communication system. In simple terms, an infrastructure is meant to factorise the most effective and efficient solutions to the most common problems, so as to minimise the efforts of engineers when building complex systems. So, singling out the common sources of complexity for agent-based applications in the Internet environment, finding which mechanisms and abstractions best solve the most frequent problems, and encapsulating them into easily deployable Internet-based services, is the process that determines what should be featured by an infrastructure for Internet-based multi-agent systems.

As far as agent coordination is concerned, the relevant issues obviously come from agent interaction – both agent-to-agent and agent-to-environment interactions. A coordination infrastructure should then enable agents to live on an Internet node and there coexist with other agents, to possibly move from one node to another, to find resources and access them, to communicate and coordinate with other agents.

At the most basic level, an infrastructure for the coordination of Internet agents should provide agents with both their "life support" – possibly including support for mobility – and the simplest interaction capabilities – like accessing resources on a host, or exchanging messages with other agents. Roughly speaking, this represents the "level zero" of coordination, since it simply deals with *enabling* agent interaction and communication.

However, in its non-trivial acceptation, the term "coordination" essentially means governing (agent) interaction, rather than simply enabling it [623]. So, the "level one" of a coordination infrastructure for Internet agents should provide engineers with the tools for effectively *ruling* agent interaction so as to achieve global system goals. Coordination tools, like tuple spaces or scripting languages, should then be provided as services, possibly based on run-time systems.

So, this part of the book is mainly meant to provide the reader with the fundamental notions on coordination infrastructures, while making the relationship between the two notions of *coordination services* and *middleware* as clear as possible. In particular, such a relationship is explored by surveying, analysing and classifying models, languages, and systems from many different contexts, like run-time systems, tuple-based models, standards and technologies for distributed systems, and scripting languages.

The contributions

Chapter 3, by Antony Rowstron, first presents the notion of run-time system for coordination, and advocates the role of tuple-based models in this context. Then, it surveys the systems supplying run-time support for tuple-based coordination services, by providing the reader with an intriguing perspective on the historical evolution of the notion and goals of tuple-based run-times, from the first Linda systems to the most advanced implementations of today. During this process, the author also clarifies the implications of implementing a coordination model as a run-time system, thus bridging the conceptual issues with the implementation problems.

Chapter 4, by Davide Rossi, Giacomo Cabri, and Enrico Denti, is an outlook on tuple-based coordination, covering many of the models, languages, and systems of this class. The authors provide the reader with a novel viewpoint on the matter, by devising out an effective taxonomy for the plethora of successors and extensions of the Linda model. A novel set of criteria is introduced and used throughout this chapter to classify and compare all the many instances of this class of coordination models.

Chapter 5, by Paolo Bellavista and Thomas Magedanz, is the "middleware chapter". It supplies a comprehensive report on the state-of-the art infrastructures for distributed agent systems by discussing in depth both the CORBA standard for agent interoperability and the technologies for mobile agent support. Then, the authors present their perspective on the matter, and show how models and infrastructures for mobile agent support can be effectively integrated with interoperability standards, like CORBA, to provide multi-agent systems with the basic enabling technologies for interaction and coordination.

Chapter 6, by Jean-Guy Schneider, Markus Lumpe, and Oscar Nierstratz, brings a new perspective in the Coordination field, by starting from component-based system development, and defining the role of scripting languages in this context. Besides singling out the main features of these languages in terms of the mechanisms and abstractions they supply, the authors discuss their impact in the context of agent coordination, where scripting languages can be exploited not only to manage the interaction between distributed agents, but also to script the agents themselves.

3. Run-Time Systems for Coordination

Antony Rowstron

Microsoft Research, 1 Guildhall Street, Cambridge, CB2 3HN, UK
mailto:antr@microsoft.com

Summary.

This chapter presents an overview of the past, current and possible future run-time systems for coordination. The main coordination language considered in the chapter is Linda. This is because Linda has clearly been the most successful coordination language that has made the transition from academic curiosity to wide-spread commercial use.

The review focuses on the last fifteen years of implementations, from the early closed compile-time analysis versions for parallel computing, which are now mature, through LAN based systems that provided support for parallel and distributed applications. Finally, the review ends with a summary of the work on large-scale implementations supporting coordination over the Internet, in particular PageSpace and WCL. Throughout the review many of the issues that have concerned implementors are raised and discusssed.

The chapter concludes by drawing on the authors experience of developing run-time systems by attempting to envisage where run-times might go next, briefly describing a "tuple mega-server".

3.1 Introduction

This chapter talks about run-time systems for coordination, and in particular about tuple-based run-time systems. In many ways the title seems odd, perhaps "Middleware for the coordination of agent systems" might have been better. However many of the run-times described here were developed long before the terms agent and middleware were widely in use, and it seems only fitting to use a title that lacks "buzzwords".

Any coordination language requires a run-time system of some description. The run-time system provides the functionality offered by a coordination language. The run-time system deals with the problems of heterogeneous environments, so masks the heterogeneity of the computers being used, and manages the communication over the networks connecting these computers. For example, when information is passed between two computers it takes care of converting multi-byte numbers when one computer uses big-endian and another uses little-endian.

In the next section, we will briefly look at coordination languages and systems in general. However, most of the rest of the chapter is then dedicated to tuple-based run-time systems. Over the last two decades there have been many coordination languages proposed, but few have been as long-lasting and as successful as Linda [267]. If you look for successful coordination languages developed in an academic environment there are very few, if any, which have had as much impact. Indeed, implementations embodying the basic ideas of Linda have become ubiquitous, choose any set of devices capable of computation connected by a network and you will probably find somewhere a Linda implementation for them. Linda-like systems have been implemented to support supercomputers, networks of workstations on a local area network (LAN), to large-scale interaction over the Internet. If anything the popularity of Linda-like systems today is greater than at anytime before, with the adoption of the technology in Sun's JavaSpaces [249] and IBM's T Spaces [648]. Linda coordination languages are described in detail in Chapter 4 and the access primitives provided by Linda-like coordination languages are not covered in this chapter, only the run-time systems.

The challenge to writers of run-time systems is to create efficient run-times systems. In general, the higher-level the coordination language the harder it is to create efficient run-time systems. Tuple-based run-time systems are also interesting because the tuple model is simple and provides tremendous opportunities for different implementation strategies. As will be seen in this chapter, this has been exploited in many different and varied ways. Over the last 15 years there have probably been more than 100 different implementations of tuple-based run-time systems created – few other coordination languages can claim such a rich set of run-time systems! It is impossible to cover all of these implementations, and only a few can be seen as innovative. Therefore, in order to help describe the innovations and approaches to creating run-time systems, the run-times are classified as either implementations designed for Local Area Networks (LANs) and parallel computers, or those implementations designed for Wide Area Networks (WANs). In Section 3.3 the difference between these classifications is discussed, and then a review of the implementation issues and techniques used for both types of implementations is given.

Following the review of these two types of tuple-based run-time systems, Section 3.8 presents an overview of where we feel the future of tuple-based run-time systems lie: the tuple mega-server. A tuple mega-server is a run-time system running on a cluster (or cluster of clusters) of computers, where the computers are located at a single geographical site, providing ubiquitous access to tuple-spaces from anywhere on the Internet.

3.2 Coordination Systems in General

If two agents, programs, or applications executing on different computers or processors wish to interact with each other then there needs to be some way of allowing them to communicate. The software that facilitates this communication is called often referred to as *middleware* (see Chapter 5). The middleware resides between the application and the network, and presents an abstract way of allowing interaction, hiding details such as the physical properties of the network.

Most middleware platforms provide an Application Program Interface (API) to the application. The API is a library of functions that provide the functionality (or services) offered by the middleware for use in an application. Different middleware platforms provide different services to allow interaction between the entities wishing to communicate. Examples of different types of services are message passing, remote procedure call, distributed shared memory, distributed shared objects, event based, shared space and so on. All these represent different ways of allowing information to be exchanged, and all require a run-time system to perform marshalling and management facilities. It is often the case that one middleware is built using services provided by another lower-level middleware.

The two most widely used interaction mechanisms are message passing and remote procedure call (RPC). Message passing middleware provides mechanisms to send and receive messages. This includes services to help pack information into messages, and services to manage the queues of incoming messages. In addition, most message passing middleware provide different types of message transmission, such as synchronous, asynchronous, reliable, unreliable, ordering of messages, broadcasting of messages and so on. Examples of such systems are PVM [573] and MPI [245], and these can be considered as well supported and mature systems. Such middleware is predominantly used for parallel processing applications, and these systems offer the advantage of providing standard APIs. The advantage of standard APIs means that the same source code can be compiled on many different platforms. Message passing is very low-level. A good programmer can generate very efficient distributed programs using message passing (in the same way a good programmer can produce better machine code than a compiler), however it is not particularly easy.

The second approach to facilitating interaction is the remote procedure call (RPC) [448, 74]. The middleware attempts to make the interaction appear similar to a local procedure call in the host programming language, except the procedure is actually invoked on another computer across a network. The middleware provides all the marshalling services required to pass the parameters across the network and to pass the result of the invoked procedure back to the initiating computer. RPC has become very popular, and is used in DCOM [414], CORBA [463] and Java RMI [416] for example. Most RPC programs are of a client-server form, where a program acts as a server providing services, and clients contact the server and request to use a service. The general principles of RPC mean that is a synchronous mechanism, where a thread of execution invoking a RPC blocks until a reply is received from the invoked remote procedure. It should be noted that in some systems asynchronous RPC mechanisms have been incorporated. Also, one of the aims of RPC is to make the invocation appear as though it is local, however, it is difficult to obtain the same semantics when making a RPC. For example, many languages provide call-by-reference semantics for local method invocation, and then provide call-by-value for the RPC invocations. In addition, care has to be taken to ensure that the programmer understands that an RPC is not as cheap as a local procedure call.

Whilst message passing and RPC have enjoyed being the predominant approaches to interaction up to now, there are many approaches vying to become the next middleware of choice. The run-time systems supporting these richer coordination models are usually built utilising either message passing or the RPC middleware they provide significantly more functionality. Examples of these alternative coordination models include event based systems, distributed shared memory [238], distributed shared objects, streaming, and shared spaces, eg. Linda-like. It is unlikely in the future that one particular approach will become the ubiquitous one because different approaches suit different applications; for example, a video streaming application is unlikely to stream video through a tuple-space, but it may pass control information through a tuple space! The recent resurgence in interest in Linda-like systems means that these may well be the next technology to become widely accepted as the middleware of preference for agent based systems and general coordination over the Internet.

What is clear is that with each generation of middleware the complexity of the middleware increases. The more general and abstract the coordination supported, the m ore freedom the middleware programmer has.

3.3 Taxonomy of Tuple-based Run-time Systems

All tuple-based implementations require a run-time system that from this point in this chapter will be referred to as the *kernel*. In some implementations this is a set of library routines which are linked in at compile time, in other implementations it is a library and a single separate process, and in some other implementations it is a library and a set of distributed processes. If the kernel is distributed then the different processes will be referred to as *kernel processes*. Different implementations and implementors refer to these kernel processes by different names, for example *tuple-space manager, TS-manager* and *TSM* have all been used. In this chapter the term *kernel process* will be used regardless of what the authors originally christened their processes.

Kernels for tuple-based languages, as in Linda, can be subdivided into implementations for parallel computers, for Local Area Networks (LANs) and for Wide Area Networks (WANs). A further distinction can be made between *homogenous* and *heterogeneous* implementations. Homogenous implementations are normally associated with parallel computer implementations and LAN implementations, when all the workstations might need to be from the same family, or the processors are connected by a bus with particular properties. As we move towards WAN implementations, environments that are more heterogeneous are supported, different hardware, operating systems, networks and so on.

The major distinction between implementations is whether they are open or closed. A *closed implementation* is considered an implementation that requires information about all processes that are to communicate via tuple-spaces to be available when the kernel starts. The implication of using a closed implementation is that processes cannot leave and join at will. Most closed implementations require either the object code or source code for all processes to be available at link or compile time. Such closed implementations have the advantage of being able to use compile-time analysis for performance optimisation, and therefore, normally consist of two sections; a pre-compiler (or compiler) and a kernel. The compilers perform some form of compile time analysis to enable better control and management of tuples. Most early implementations of Linda were closed implementations and were produced by researchers at Yale University [129, 76, 379, 659].

An *open implementation* is defined as an implementation where the agents communicating through tuple-spaces need no information about the agents with which they share tuples and vice-versa. In addition, the kernel requires no prior knowledge about agents when it starts. This means that agents can leave and join at will, because no information about agents is required when the *kernel* starts. The communicating agents can be written independently, and even in different programming languages. Open implementations consist of a kernel and sometimes a pre-compiler or compiler. The role of the pre-compiler is normally to provide a more natural syntax for the Linda primitives embedded in the host language. Because not all the agents are available to the pre-compiler less analysis of tuples and tuple usage can be performed. Some of the first open implementations were [215, 521, 555, 496, 24, 234, 51, 595].

The distinction between open and closed implementations is quite dramatic, with the nomenclature changing. In closed implementations, the things interacting are called processes, and in the open implementations, the things interacting are called agents. Closed implementations are used for parallel processing; open implementations are used for more general computing, from Internet agents to computer-supported cooperative working applications. In closed implementations a single global tuple space is shared by all the processes[1], in open implementations multiple tuple spaces are required. Closed implementations have a single application running at any one time. Open implementations support many independent applications running concurrently, and allow interaction between these applications if required. This distinction also defines different requirements for the run-time systems; in closed implementations, performance is of paramount important, whereas in open implementations the emphasis has traditionally been on supporting heterogeneity, security, reliability and availability. However, the need for per-

---

[1] It should be noted that some closed implementations have been extended to support multiple tuple spaces.

formance may soon become a major driving force in the future development of open implementations.

The next major distinction is the approach taken to managing tuples. Broadly, all implementations can be considered as either centralised or distributed. A centralised implementation has a single process that manages all the tuples in the systems, and in a distributed implementation, there are multiple processes managing the tuples. Distributed implementations normally provide concurrent access to the tuple-space or spaces.

Table 3.1 shows how the tuple distribution policies (centralised and distributed) have been applied to open and closed run-time systems have be used in different environments. The environment is classified as one of parallel computers, LANs or WANs. To summarise, open implementations are

	Centralised		Distributed	
	Open	Closed	Open	Closed
Parallel Computer	No	Yes	No	Yes
LAN	Yes	Yes	Yes	Yes
WAN	Yes	No	Yes	No

Table 3.1. Taxonomy of tuple-based run-times.

used on LANs and WANs, and closed implementations are used on parallel computers and LANS. Both open and closed implementations can use distributed or centralised tuple management, although for high performance distributed tuple storage is better.

Most of the recent work on tuple-based run-time systems has been on the development of open implementations. The performance achievable by open implementations is currently below that of closed implementations which use compile time analysis because of the performance increases that compile time analysis can provide. Closed implementations have the ability to alter the kernel's fundamental characteristics based on knowledge of how a program uses tuples. This should lead to a reduction in the number of messages being sent between the user processes and the kernel, and as the communication costs are significant, there should be an improvement in performance. The best closed implementation using compile-time analysis is the SCA C-Linda, a commercial system based on the implementations produced at Yale University.

However, the drawback with closed implementations is that they are restrictive. Closed implementations were designed for parallel programming, whilst open implementations are designed for distributed computing. With parallel programming, it is easier to control the whole system, a group of programmers create the application and they are able to design the coordination patterns of the application. There is little use of spatial and temporal separation, because all the processes are available at compile time. In contrast distributed computing (or agent computing) uses more of the general features of Linda, such as the ability to support processes which are spatially and temporally separated [51, 353, 132]. Applications need to be able to join and leave the kernel at will. Open implementations leverage the concept of persistence of tuple-spaces. One agent can place information in a tuple-space and then another agent can use that information at any time in the future. Indeed, it has even been proposed that tuple-based systems can provide file systems by using persistent tuple-spaces to store the contents of files [268].

3.4 LAN and Parallel Computing Implementations: The First and Second Generation

In this section of this chapter, we review the first and second generation of Linda implementations. These implementations are characterised as by-and-large implementing variants of Linda, and represent the work between about 1987 and 1995.

3.4.1 Closed Implementation Techniques

The development of closed implementations played a vital role in the acceptance of Linda. The ability to take a program using three simple tuple-space access primitives and, through compile time analysis, to transform this program into one that achieves the same performance as a message passing program is phenomenal. It made this simple paradigm acceptable and usable. Indeed, still to this day highly optimised closed implementations of Linda are available for the parallel processing community.

Carriero [129] implemented the first Linda system for both shared memory parallel computers (Encore Multimax and Sequent Balance) and a distributed memory parallel computer (S/Net). The Encore Multimax and Sequent Balance were closed implementations and relied on the use of compile-time analysis. The compile-time analyse involved the examination of the tuples and templates to enable efficient data structures to be constructed for storing the tuples. The analysis specifically examined field types and values present within the templates and tuples. Once this information is known the fields that need to be matched at run-time can be calculated, and redundant fields can be removed. The shared memory implementation placed the data structure in which the tuples are stored in the shared memory. The S/Net distributed memory implementation did not use any compile time analysis and simply replicated a simple data structure for storing tuples within each processor module of the computer, and used broadcasts to all nodes to ensure that the data structures were kept synchronised.

The same compile time analysis techniques used in the Encore Multimax and Sequent Balance implementations are used by Bjornson et al. [76, 75] and

Zenith [659]. However, both these implementations examined how the kernel could be implemented for distributed memory parallel machines where the replication of all tuples on all the nodes is unacceptable. In these implementations, the kernel is distributed over several processors within the parallel machine and the tuples stored on one of the many kernel processes. The tuples are distributed across the kernel processes using a hashing function. For a given tuple, the hashing function identifies a unique kernel process for that tuple. For a given template, the hashing function identifies the kernel process on which a matching tuple would reside. The kernel architecture used within these implementations provides the basic architecture that has been widely used in most kernels since then.

The next major advancement of compile time analysis was again introduced by Carriero [133, 132, 134]. Instead of just analysing the tuples and templates to generate efficient data structures, and detect which fields need to be matched at run-time, the compiler actually performed "partial evaluation" of the Linda primitives. The basic approach is to recognise how tuples are being used and then implement a suitable approach to deal with the coordination patterns. For example, if there are a number of processes performing `in("semaphore")` followed by `out("semaphore")` the compile-time analysis recognises this as a coordination pattern (a semaphore). Once recognised the kernel at run-time can create a counter to act as that particular tuple. Whenever an `in("semaphore")` is performed the kernel simply decrements the global counter if it is greater than zero otherwise the primitive blocks. Whenever an `out("semaphore")` is performed the kernel increments the counter. The compile time analysis recognises a particular coordination pattern (in this case a tuple being used as a semaphore) and instructs the kernel to use a more efficient mechanism to control that tuple. The kernel is also able to ensure that the mechanism is placed in a kernel process close to the user processes using the semaphore. The compile time analysis is also capable of recognising when tuples are being used as global counters, and instead of removing the tuple, updating it and then replacing it, the operation is implemented as a counter stored within the kernel. The analysis also improves the placement of tuples, for example with the ability to detect that tuples can only be consumed by a particular user process implies that the tuples can be sent directly to that user process. Also, if a tuple, once produced, is only non-destructively read then it can be broadcast to all user processes that could potentially access it.

Work outside Yale University on closed implementations has been limited. This has mainly concentrated on the development of "hierarchical" kernels [200, 176, 177, 403]. The underlying idea is that by grouping processes which "share" tuples a more efficient implementation can be made.

Matos et al. [403] have created an implementation based on the use of multiple tuple-spaces called Linda-Polylith. The multiple tuple-space model adopted is a hierarchical one and the compile time analysis analyses the program and produces a tree, where the nodes represent a tuple-space and the leaves represent user processes. If a process is to access a tuple-space then the process must be a descendent of the node that is the tuple-space. The root node is the global tuple-space; so all processes can access it.

Clayton et al. [177, 200] described their kernel as a hierarchical kernel. They use compile time analysis to group tuples in a similar manner as Carriero [129] to allow distribution across a number of kernel processes. They also use compile time analysis to create a static placement mechanism for spawned processes [200, 176]. This relies on a machine description; compile time information about when processes are spawned; and heuristic rules to decide statically (at compile time) where the processes should be placed.

3.5 Open Implementation Techniques

Within a LAN setting, the basic role of a kernel in an open implementation is to manage tuples stored within tuple-spaces. The run-time is divided into the kernel and an API library that is linked into the agent that wishes to access the shared tuple-spaces. The kernel "receives" messages containing instructions it from the agent, processes these messages, and returns, if appropriate, a tuple or reply message.

There is normally a clear separation between the kernel and the API library, however, some implementations have less of a separation than others. For example, the York Kernel II [519] has the concept of local and remote tuple-spaces, where local tuple-spaces are managed within the library and the remote tuple-spaces are managed by the kernel.

All kernels have a number of basic characteristics that are:

- *Tuple distribution*, which is how the tuples are going to be distributed *across* a number of kernel processes,
- *tuple format*, which is the format of the tuples,
- *tuple storage*, which is how the tuples are stored within a single kernel process, and
- *eval implementation*, which is how the `eval` primitive is implemented.

The characteristics are not disjointed and making decisions about using one approach for one characteristic can often limit the choices for another characteristic.

Tuple format and tuple storage are important because this impacts heavily on the performance of the kernel. In general, there is a trade off between data structure complexity for the data structure used to store the tuples within a process and the cost of comparing tuples and templates. For a given template, the more tuples that need to be checked the higher the tuple access cost, but the more complex the data structure the higher the cost of inserting and removing tuples from within it. The format of the tuples is also important, a simple and precise format will reduce the cost of checking tuples against templates. Another consideration is if the run-time system supports multiple host languages or a single host language. If multiple host languages are supported then a "language independent" way of encoding the tuples and templates is required.

The tuple distribution mechanisms and the implementation of `eval` are considered in more detail in the next two sections.

3.5.1 Tuple Distribution

How are sets of tuples distributed across the kernel (as opposed to within kernel processes)? There are four approaches used within the first and second generation kernels to controlling the distribution of tuples across a kernel [16, 128]. These four approaches are:

Centralised. This is where the kernel is a single process. All tuple-space operations are sent to this single process, and all the tuples are stored in it.

The advantages of such an approach is that the kernel is simple and all the tuples are kept together which means it is easy to take a "snapshot" of the current state of the tuple-space. This property has made the centralised approach popular in many implementations supporting fault tolerant tuple-spaces, such as PLinda [338, 337] and Paradise [541].

The disadvantage of having a centralised kernel is that the single kernel process becomes a bottleneck. As more processes try to perform tuple-space operations concurrently, the kernel simply cannot service them fast enough. If either a small number of user processes are to be used, or the number of tuple-space accesses that a set of user processes are to perform is low then a centralised approach provides acceptable performance. This type of approach is used in Parlin [555], TsLib [556], PLinda [338, 337], Paradise [541] and Glenda [546].

Uniform Distribution. This is where the kernel is distributed (there is more than one kernel process) and the tuples are distributed evenly over the kernel processes. This is often achieved by every user process having two sets of kernel process identifiers called an *in-set* and an *out-set*. Whenever a tuple is placed into a tuple-space the tuple is broadcast to all the kernel processes in the *out-set*. Whenever a tuple is required from a tuple-space, the request is sent to all the kernel processes in the *in-set*. If the tuple is retrieved using an `in` primitive then all the kernel processes in the *in-set* have to synchronise to update the tuple-spaces to ensure that two user processes cannot retrieve the same tuple. If there are t tuple-space servers the cardinality of the *out-set* can vary from one to t (and the cardinality of *in-set* will vary from t to one). All the *out-sets* present within the user process must include a member from each of the *in-sets* in all of the user processes and vice-versa. Carriero's S/Net implementation [129] uses this approach with an *in-set* being a local kernel process (one that resides on the same processor as the user process) and the *out-set* being all kernel processes. This is because the S/Net provided

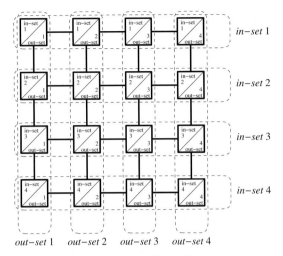

out−set 1   out−set 2   out−set 3   out−set 4

Fig. 3.1. Intermediate uniform distribution using 16 kernel processes.

a cheap broadcast function. If this kind of approach is required then it is more common to adopt an approach known as *intermediate uniform distribution*.

Intermediate Uniform Distribution. This is a particular case of uniform distribution. If there are t nodes then the cardinality of both the *in-set* and the *out-set* are $\sqrt{t}$. This is shown in Figure 3.1.

This variant of uniform distribution has been proved the most optimal uniform distribution [16] in terms of the number of nodes involved in an **in** primitive and an **out** primitive. This particular approach is adopted in the Linda machine [16, 361, 362], where the bus that joins the different Linda nodes provides the arbitration necessary to ensure that the tuple-spaces remain consistent when several **in** primitives are performed by different processes concurrently. A number of other implementations have used the same approach, X-Linda [228] (for transputer meshes) and the Bag-machine implementation [592] (network of workstations). In these cases the communication costs of synchronising the duplicated tuples is too great [228] to make the method efficient without specialist hardware support (as in the Linda machine). Whenever a tuple is retrieved by a user process from a kernel process, the kernel processes that are members of the *in-set* used by the user process have to determine which can provide a suitable tuple. If many kernel processes can provide a suitable tuple then one has to be chosen. Once the kernel process has been chosen it then has to inform the kernel processes that are in the same *out-set* that the tuple is being removed. Without the support of special buses such an approach requires a large amount of communication to control all the arbitration that is needed [228]. Tolksdorf [595] has created a kernel that can dynamically change over time allowing the number of kernel processes to be both increased and decreased, where the distribution strategy is based on intermediate uniform distribution.

This leads to the final general type of tuple distribution; *distributed hashing*.

Distributed Hashing. Distributed hashing is another distribution mechanism for use in distributed kernels, and the kernel process which stores a particular tuple is chosen by using the properties of the tuple or template being used. In order to do this a hashing function is used which when applied to a tuple or template provides the kernel process on which either the tuple should reside, in the case of a tuple, or where a matching tuple would reside in the case of a template. Hashing is discussed in detail by Bjornson [75], and is used as the basis for most open implementations, including several previous implementations at the University of York [215, 521]. The aim is to develop a hashing function that has two properties. Firstly, this should provide a unique mapping between every tuple and a template that matches it to a single kernel process and secondly it should provide a good distribution of the tuples over the kernel processes. This has the advantage that the kernel process given by the hashing algorithm will contain a matching tuple, if there is one in the tuple-space, which removes the problems of searching multiple kernel processes. However, pragmatically this has only been achieved effectively in closed implementations. For open implementations no general purpose hashing algorithms have been created because of the limited amount of information potentially provided within a template and the lack of compile-time analysis of all tuples and templates used within a system. Therefore, in open systems, hashing functions are chosen that enable every *tuple* to be hashed to a unique kernel process and a template hashed to a set of kernel processes. In the best case, the cardinality of this set will be one because the information the hashing algorithm uses for a tuple is present in the template. The request for the tuple is then either broadcast to all the kernel processes produced by the hashing algorithm for a particular template, or to a particular kernel process. If there is a broadcast to more than one kernel process then some form of arbitration has to be performed by the user process (transparent to the Linda programmer) as there may be more than one tuple returned. If the request is sent to a single kernel process and that kernel process cannot find the tuple it will then broadcast the message or pass it to another kernel process. The original kernel process then deals with the arbitration. An interesting point is that the kernel created by Bjornson [75] provides dynamic analysis of tuple accesses. Therefore, if a particular process is consuming tuples of a particular kind, then the hashing functions in the user processes are dynamically altered (by messages from the kernel) to send the tuples to the kernel process that is local to the user process consuming the tuples. This technique is called *bucket switching*.

The choice of the distribution approach used depends largely on the requirements of the system. Most current LAN implementations use the distributed hashing approach, because it is more efficient and it does not require the synchronisation of kernel processes in *out-sets* whenever a tuple is destructively retrieved.

3.5.2 The `eval` Primitive

The issue of how to create new agents has always been a difficult one for Linda implementations. The original Linda contained a primitive called `eval`. This primitive creates an *active* tuple, which is a tuple with one (or more) of the fields is a function to be evaluated concurrently with the agent producing the tuple. Whenever the evaluation of a particular field is completed, the value produced is placed within the active tuple. Once all the fields have been evaluated, the active tuple becomes a passive tuple. The need for active tuples appears unclear in the early implementations as they cannot be matched or manipulated by any user process.

Implementation strategies vary from not providing any sort of `eval` primitive, through mapping the `eval` primitive onto the basic spawning characteristics of the system being used (for example, Glenda [546], PLinda [338], eLinda [628] and York Kernel I (PVM version) [521]) to providing a mechanism that literally places an "active tuple" within the tuple-space that can be manipulated by other processes, for example MTS-Linda [454] (although not fully implemented).

The creation of a tuple in the tuple-space when all the functions have been evaluated appears desirable. It provides a simple and effective mechanism to allow other processes to detect when a set of processes have terminated. Allowing active tuples to be retrieved raises many questions. How are active tuples matched, and in particular how is a field that is a process matched. How does a process know if it is getting a process or a value? What happens to the matched process and what does it mean to perform a `rd` primitive matching an active tuple? Nielsen et al. [454] discusses these issues, proposing that matched processes are bound to variables, and the addition of a `touch` primitive which forces the functions to be evaluated before the tuple can be retrieved.

There has been some research into how the `eval` primitive can be implemented to provide a passive tuple upon completion, without supporting the manipulation by user processes as active tuples [316, 513]. Both approaches are similar and require compile time analysis which makes them useful for closed implementations, but not for open implementations. Both approaches use the concept of "eval servers" which receive instructions to execute particular functions. When a user agent performs an `eval` primitive the description of the function or functions to be executed are sent to the `eval` servers. When each function has been evaluated, the `eval` server updates a shared structure (which is a special tuple), inserting the resulting value. When all the functions are evaluated and the values inserted the tuple becomes a passive tuple. All the communication is achieved using tuple-spaces (including the passing of arguments to the functions). In both approaches care has to be taken to ensure that "spurious" deadlocks do not occur if there are fewer `eval` servers than spawned processes, because the `eval` servers can only sequentially evaluate a single function. Spurious deadlocks can be produced if there is a synchronisation between two agents that are considered to be executing concurrently but are in fact not.

In the ISETL-Linda implementation [215, 214] a similar approach is used. The ISETL engines use threads and can therefore evaluate more than one function concurrently which ensures that spurious deadlocks, due to functions not executing concurrently, cannot occur.

An alternative adopted by Clayton et al. [176] in a transputer implementation of Linda involves the development of a static heuristic approach to the placement of processes. The approach is only suitable for a closed implementation and is restrictive, assuming certain types of characteristics about the use of Linda programs, and is not suitable for use in open implementations.

3.6 Adding Explicit Information to Linda Programs

One of the drawbacks of open LAN implementations is that they, in general, provide poor performance when compared to closed LAN implementations. This has led to people adding explicit information to Linda programs to improve the performance of the kernel.

The explicit information can take many forms including special primitives and "hints" (or *pragmas*). The special primitives are treated in a more efficient manner than the equivalent using Linda primitives. Eilean [128] uses programmer hints which are used to aid in the distribution of tuples. The hints take the form of library calls indicating how certain tuples are used within a program, typing the tuples as being one of the following classes: producer-consumer, result, write-many, read-most and general read/write. Once classified the kernel treats each type of tuple differently, allowing more efficient placement and retrieval of tuples. A more specific approach has been suggested by Wilson [635] where configuration files are created to allow the kernel to be configured and then the programs explicitly state where individual tuples should be placed. Such an approach may lead to increased performance but degrades Linda into little more than a system providing asynchronous buffered communication channels between processes, similar to many message passing systems such as PVM [573].

In the description of the implementation of MTS-Linda [454] it is suggested that tuple-spaces should be explicitly tagged to indicate their use. Therefore, a tuple-space could be tagged as a persistent tuple-space, a tuple-space to be replicated, a tuple-space that compile time analysis should be performed on, a local tuple-space, etc. The kernel then treats the tuple-space appropriately.

A programming tool called the Linda Program Builder [14] is an interactive tool which supports the design and development of Linda programs. The user is able to design programs by choosing code templates that generate the code for different coordination patterns and constructs. Because the Linda Program Builder is aware of which code templates were used to generate a sequence of Linda primitives, it knows more information about how the tuples are being used. This extra information has been used in conjunction with the Yale C-Linda compiler [132] to enable the compiler to further optimise the programs. Therefore, although a standard Linda program is produced by the Linda Program Builder it is able to add compiler hints. Unfortunately many of the optimisations used within the Linda Program Builder are suitable for closed implementations rather than for open implementations. All communicating processes are developed using the Linda Program Builder, and consistency in the use of particular tuples can be checked and enforced. All the compiled processes know how a particular tuple or tuples are stored or how a coordination construct is implemented.

3.7 From LAN to WAN: The Third Generation

Since 1995 a new generation of implementations have been created with the aim of supporting Linda in WAN environments. These implementations tend not to be interested in performance, but rather in demonstrating the expressiveness of the coordination language being implemented. These implementations are characterised as providing different access primitives Linda (or adding many new primitives), and subsequently provide far richer access mechanisms to tuple-spaces, for example supporting a streaming of tuples from tuple-spaces to clients.

One of the issues this that is not covered in this chapter is the introduction and development of fault-tolerance within the run-time systems. This is something that is vital to the development of run-time systems for WAN environments, and this is being covered in Chapter 12.

Jada [162] was the first Java run-time implementation, and integration of tuple-space access primitives into the Java programming language. Whilst interesting from this perspective the underlying run-time system introduces little new. TuCSoN [472] is another interesting coordination language that extends the basic tuple-space model to make the tuple-spaces reactive (programmable tuple-spaces). Tuple-spaces can be made to react to events happening, such as the inserting of tuples, and this requires support in the run-time system. The TuCSoN run-time extends LuCe [205]. It makes programmable tuple-spaces (called tuple centres) available as Internet services. That is, there is a TuCSoN port where each "local coordination space" (made up of all the tuple centres on the host) is made available to local and remote TuCSoN agents.

Probably the two most well known new generation tuple-based coordination languages are JavaSpaces [249] and T Spaces [648], but from an run-time perspective they are not inspiring. Details of the implementation strategy adopted in the reference JavaSpaces implementation have not been given. T Spaces presents the view that the tuple-spaces would be ubiquitously available from all networked devices, but the implementation is a centralised Java based system, aimed at demonstrating the functionality of T Spaces.

However, there have been two serious attempts at creating large-scale implementations: PageSpace [173] and WCL [524]. Both of these could not be considered as complete proposals but as demonstration systems proving particular aspects of how a run-time for a WAN Linda may be developed. Interestingly both take very different perspectives, and these are now considered in detail.

3.7.1 PageSpace

PageSpace [173] is the first implementation to really explore the large-scale use of Linda. What is interesting is that the system does not expose the tuple-spaces to the agents running over the Internet. The "PageSpace" is run on a LAN, and is composed of a number of agents:

Beta Agent: A representation of a user, interacts with other agents in the PageSpace using tuple-spaces. The agent is persistent and agents outside the PageSpace, for example running in a Web browser, connect to this Beta Agent (using HTTP).

Delta Agent: Provide services to other agents, but have no interface to allow agents outside the PageSpace to communicate with it.

Gamma and Epsilon Agents: Provide administrative functions within the PageSpace.

Zeta Agent: Acts as a gateway between the PageSpace and external environments, for example a CORBA gateway or a NNTP news.

The external agents (for example those running in Web browsers) connect with the Beta Agent, so the state stored within the PageSpace is never explicitly removed from the PageSpace. State manipulation within the system can only be performed by Beta Agents, and therefore, the tuple-space access primitives are not exposed to the external agents, they simply receive information to display and provide commands back. The Beta Agents convert these into tuple manipulations.

Should the external agent fail the Beta Agents are not affected, and can complete any state manipulations they were performing. This ensures the tuple-spaces stay in an application consistent state. The Beta Agents are written in such a way that they can have external agents reconnect.

This is an interesting approach, and the use of tuple-spaces to coordinate within large servers is interesting. However, the creation of a Beta Agent for every user means that the ability of the PageSpace to scale may be limited.

3.7.2 WCL (and Bonita)

WCL [524] is a tuple-space based coordination language that attempts to provide a very broad set of access primitives, including the asynchronous versions of in and rd as first introduced in Bonita [525]. The aim from the beginning is to create a system where the tuple-spaces are exposed to agents geographically distributed over the Internet. In other words, the agents remove and insert tuples into the shared tuple-spaces.

The run-time system for WCL is equally as radical. The first run-time system produced for WCL was based on an extension of York Kernel II [519], and adopted a similar approach to that used in PageSpace, except the tuple-spaces were directly exposed to the agents [522]. However, the centralised architecture appeared not to be ideal for scalable run-times.

The second attempt at developing a run-time system [523] attempted to create a run-time system that was geographically distributed. The run-time is composed of multiple servers, where each server stores entire tuple-spaces (each server can store many tuple-spaces). The run-time also contains a control layer which monitors how the tuple-spaces are being used, and instructions the tuple-space servers to migrate tuple-spaces as necessary. The control layer attempts to balance the location of a tuple-space depending on the geographical location of the agents that are using the tuple-space. So for example, if two agents using a tuple-space are located in Germany, and the tuple-space is currently being stored in the UK, the control layer would decide a location to move the tuple-space to in Germany.

The control layer used a simplistic approach to analysing the information to decide where to place tuple-spaces, and a better oracle is a subject for future research. The run-time makes a clear distinction between control and the accessing of tuple-spaces. This means that the control layer works independently of the tuple-space servers, and therefore, if the control layer becomes saturated the performance of the tuple-space servers is not degraded.

More recently the WCL run-time systems has been extended again providing *mobile coordination* [520], which addresses the issue of providing a fault tolerance mechanism at the coordination language level, which was not within the original WCL run-time.

However, WCL remains a research vehicle, and as such leave many questions unanswered.

3.7.3 Mobility

The use of mobility in coordination is being considered in Chapter 10. In this section, we briefly look at a number of run-time systems that use mobility, but in different ways.

PLinda 2.0. Plinda 2.0 [337] was a run-time system developed to support coarse grained long lived parallel computation. Fault tolerance was very important in the development of the system and as such, it introduced transactions into Linda, and a mechanism to allow agents to checkpoint their state to tuple-spaces was provided. This mechanism allowed an agent to be resumed if it should fail. The same mechanism allowed the movement of agents from one machine to another machine. However, the agents themselves could not request to be moved. The movement of the agents was controlled by the system, which moved them should machines fail, or if the (human) user requested their movement.

In order to support this a particular programming style had to be adopted (the agents were written in C). The run-time system was centralised, but is interesting because it is probably the first implementation to support the (strong) migration of agents.

KLAIM. KLAIM [453] is another implementation that provides strong mobility. However, KLAIM aims to support a distributed implementation. The kernel is composed of multiple servers, where each server can be considered as representing a (geographical) location. Each location contains a single named tuple-space. Tuple-spaces can be accessed by agents using the traditional Linda primitives and the Linda `eval` primitive is supported for creating new agents at particular locations.

Unlike most platforms for experimenting with mobile agents, KLAIM supports *strong* migration of agents. Strong migration means that an agent can request at a particular point in its execution to migrate. However, this is achieved through using a special Pascal-like language for writing the agents. This language is translated into Java, is such a way to give the impression that strong migration is being supported.

The agents can choose to access the tuple-space stored at a particular location by either moving to the location or by remotely accessing the tuple-space.

From a run-time perspective, the run-time can be seen as providing a standard implementation, and the agent migration can be seen as a separate operation, independent of the tuple storage mechanisms.

LIME. LIME [493] is interested in the development of Linda implementations that support mobile users rather than mobile agents. In LIME, tuple-spaces are created transiently based on currently visible agents. Each agent has a number of tuples associated with it, and the shared tuple-space at any point is composed of the tuples from all the visible agents.

Obviously a run-time system to support such a system is complex, however, little details of how the run-time system works have been published.

3.7.4 From LAN to WAN: Conclusions

In the move from LAN to WAN the development of run-time systems appears to have become less important. When looking at the LAN implementations, many papers were published on the run-time systems and how performance was improved within them. However, in a WAN setting the engineering of the run-time systems used for many implementations remains a mystery. This is probably partly attributable to the difficulty of creating large-scale implementations, the increasing interest in proving formal aspects of languages rather than demonstrating that efficient systems can be built.

Although the access primitives used in each of the implementations differ, what is clear is that, in general, the underlying properties of the run-time system vary little, with a few exceptions such as PageSpace and WCL, and in general make little effort to address the issues of scalability. What can be said is that in general, the underlying run-time stores and manipulates tuples. A clear conclusion is that it is quite feasible to produce a single run-time system that provides general tuple-space access functionality, which then allows the creation of domain specific tuple-based coordination languages.

So, from a run-time perspective, the next important evolution that will enable the use of tuple-based coordination for large-scale Internet computing is the development of generic large-scale tuple servers, coupled with domain specific API's providing domain specific tuple-space access primitives.

3.8 The Future: The Tuple Mega-Server?

When talking about services offered over the Internet it is increasingly common to talk of "mega-servers". A mega-server is a geographically localised cluster (or collection) of computers that between them provide a service to be used over the Internet. Although the computers are referred to as a cluster, it is often a cluster of clusters depending on the topology of the network connecting them. The computers are connected by low-latency, high bandwidth networks. Examples of currently existing mega-servers include the Microsoft Hotmail service and the Microsoft Passport service.

There are several points to note about mega-servers. One is that they are often currently created in an ad-hoc fashion, usually utilizing low level sockets for communication between the components running on the different machines in the cluster. Another interesting point this is that these mega-servers usually provide persistent stores for relatively small units of information and ways of reading, writing and updating this information. The final interesting point is that these systems do not always present information that a human would use directly (in other words they do not all serve human viewable documents). For example, Microsoft operate a web server called "MS Passport" that provides an authentication service for all the web sites operated by Microsoft. Hence, once the user has been authenticated by the Passport Web server, all other Microsoft sites can be accessed without having to enter a user name and password.

Given these characteristics it is clear that a tuple-space mega-server could be created that could provide these types of services to agents distributed across the Internet. The mega-server would probably accept tuple-space instructions and tuples encoded using XML, and then return tuples encoded in XML.

The internal architecture of the mega-server would be organised into multiple tiers, with at least a front end managing the incoming and outgoing tuples, and then a second tier manage the storage of the tuples. The mega-server will have to achieve a high throughput of I/O operations per second. In order to achieve an acceptable level of throughput, it is likely that the mega-server will have to be highly optimised. Static optimisations and dynamic optimisation will be required. An example of a static optimisation is the one presented in Rowstron [520]. This optimisation allows tuples to remain partially visible once they have been destructively removed from a tuple-space. This has the advantage of reducing the number of tuple-space accesses that need to block, which in turn reduces the load within the run-time system and therefore increases the potential throughput obtainable. Dynamic optimisations have been used in some implementations, for example Bjornson [75] showed that dynamic optimisation of tuple storage was possible, with his bucket switching techniques.

It is highly likely that in a mega-server the dynamic analysis of access patterns of the agents will be very important. This is motivated by the observation that there will be many different *instances* of the *same type* of agent accessing the mega-server. This means that coordination patterns will be similar for all instances of the same type of agent. This can be demonstrated by considering an instant messenger type application. It is possible to consider the instant messages being stored in a tuple-space, and having a more persistent type of instant messaging system. All the clients will use the tuple-space is the same way, perhaps reading the last n entries in the tuple-space and then adding entries. If this can be observed then the storage of the tuple-space can be optimised for this type of access pattern.

We are currently working on the development of such analysers, and one such optimisation is the spotting of tuples that are being used as locks/semaphores on the tuple-space. Simply, a tuple is considered as a lock/semaphore on a tuple-space if an agent is required to remove the tuple before inserting any other tuples into the tuple-space.

Figure 3.2 shows an example output from a current prototype lock analyser looking for tuples that are acting as a write lock on the tuple-space. The output shown is a post-execution summary from the analyser. The analyser examines a trace of tuple-space accesses (either statically or dynamically). The analyser determines the template (or templates) being used to access a lock tuple (if there are more than one it shows them too) – and provides. It provides a type classification of the of lock tuple seen indicating either as a full lock (lock), which means that for all the tuple-space accesses seen the tuple has remained as a lock, or as a partial lock, whether it was a lock for only part of the accesses seen. It provides the time (relative to when the

```
Template: ([ ],[Int])
Type: lock
Create time: 10 ms
Last access time: 21580 ms
Average release time: 237 ms (std: 226.3 ms)
   Agent A: 40 out of 161, Average hold: 25 ms (std: 40.7 ms)
   Agent B: 40 out of 161, Average hold: 11 ms (std: 18.0 ms)
   Agent C: 81 out of 161, Average hold: 56 ms (std: 74.9 ms)

Template: ([Counter,  ],[String, Int]) and ([ , ],[String, Int}])
Type: lock
Create time: 10 ms
Last access time: 21400 ms
Average release time: 65 ms (std: 60.7 ms)
   Agent D 52 out of 215, Average hold: 211 ms (std: 192.7 ms)
   Agent E 42 out of 215, Average hold: 153 ms (std: 121.9 ms)
   Agent F 81 out of 215, Average hold: 52 ms  (std: 87.0 ms)
   Agent G 40 out of 215, Average hold: 176 ms (std: 102.8 ms)
```

Fig. 3.2. Tuple usage analyser output.

system started) the tuple acting as the lock was created, and the time when the tuple acting as the lock tuple was last accessed[2]. It then provides the average release time and its standard deviation, and then a break down for each agent that uses the lock tuple. For each agent it indicates how many operations have been performed using that lock tuple (out of the total number of operations performed on the tuple), and the average time (with its standard deviation) that the agent has held the lock.

Figure 3.2 shows the results for two different locks being used in a system. The second lock is being accessed with two different templates, and it can be quite clearly seen that the locks are being used in different ways. The times that the locks are held and release vary between the two locks. Although the work is in its initial stages we intend to use the information generated by the analyser to optimise the storage (and location) of the tuples (obviously lock tuples have a tendency to act as bottlenecks), and information about how long locks are likely to held for may be used to order the tuple-space accesses from the agents. Using this information will make the mega-server adaptive, which should provide far better performance that if this analysis was not being used. Future work will look at extending this work, recognising different coordination patterns and how to combine dynamic analysis with stored histories for other agents of the same type.

---

[2] It should be noted that the field values of the lock tuple may vary over time.

3.9 Conclusions

In general, the first ten years of Linda were dominated by the drive to create highly efficient Linda implementations. The next five years we have seen the assessment of tuple-based coordination languages for use in large-scale environments. What can be said is that run-times systems developed in the last five years have largely ignored performance and the need to create large-scale implementations, in favour of allowing the evaluation of more expressive coordination languages to address the needs of complex multi-component systems.

The original challenge to Linda implementers was to demonstrate that Linda was viable as an alternative to the traditional pure message-passing paradigms that existed. The challenge now is to create *efficient* large-scale implementations, that provide general purpose access to tuple-spaces, and to demonstrate these are efficient and effective for the coordination of large-scale multi-component systems distributed over the Internet. These implementations will build on the work on implementations outlined in this chapter and will also need to use other run-time system developments not outlined in this chapter (such as tuple-space garbage collection [408] and fault-tolerance). It is only when we address this challenge will we have truly demonstrated the true flexibility of the tuple-space model.

This is possible and this chapter started by describing the impact that Linda has had since it was first described 15 years ago, and it is certain that Linda is not simply a passing fad. This chapter is concluded with the statement that the author hopes in another 15 years time to be writing about the impact over the last 30 years of tuple-based coordination languages, and the impact that Gelernter has had on computing.

4. Tuple-based Technologies for Coordination

Davide Rossi[1], Giacomo Cabri[2], and Enrico Denti[3]

[1] Dipartimento di Scienze dell'Informazione, Università di Bologna
Mura Anteo Zamboni 7, I-40127 Bologna, Italy.
mailto:rossi@cs.unibo.it
[2] Dipartimento di Scienze dell'Ingegneria, Università di Modena e Reggio Emilia
Via Campi 213b,I-41100 Modena, Italy
mailto:giacomo.cabri@unimo.it
[3] LIA, Dipartimento di Elettronica, Informatica e Sistemistica
Università di Bologna, Viale Risorgimento 2, I-40136 Bologna, Italy
mailto:edenti@deis.unibo.it

Summary.

By *tuple-based technologies* we refer to any coordination system that uses associative access to shared dataspaces for communication / synchronization purposes.

The idea of using a shared dataspace to coordinate concurrent activities first appeared in the Linda coordination language, which defined a coordination model based on the so-called *tuple space*, as well as a set of primitives, that extend a host computational language, to access it. The basic Linda model has been extended in various ways by different languages / architectures in order to deal with the different requirements of different application areas, from high speed parallel computations (the context in which Linda was designed) to Internet-based multi-agent architectures.

This chapter surveys various tuple-based coordination systems and models, introducing a taxonomy (based on the enhancements with respect to the original Linda model) as well as a set of criteria to classify the considered projects. Our aim is not just to supply an updated reference to existing tuple-based coordination systems, but also to provide the reader with some helpful guidelines to compare coordination models and systems.

Given the book focus, we will restrict our survey to the technologies that are explicitly targeted to open distributed systems, trying, at the same time, to offer a perspective that is as wide as possible.

4.1 The Origins

The use of a shared dataspace for agents communication was first investigated in the Artificial Intelligence field with *blackboards* [225], which are information spaces where messages can be put and retrieved from.

However, the first coordination model (and language) actually adopting a dataspace with associative access for coordination purposes was Linda [269]. Linda introduces an abstraction for concurrent agent programming, and consists of a small set of coordination operations (the *coordination primitives*) combined with the *tuple space*, a shared dataspace containing *tuples*, that is, ordered collections of elements. The coordination primitives are orthogonal to any particular programming language: in fact, they are part of the coordination language, which can be added to any other computation language.

Research showed that, using Linda, a large class of parallel and distributed problems can be efficiently expressed, thus alleviating many of the pitfalls of building networked systems [135]. This demonstrated that tuple-based systems are not only simple and elegant, but also expressive.

Linda primitives provide means for agents to manipulate the shared tuple space, thereby introducing *coordination operations*. A tuple can be emitted to the tuple space by an agent performing the out primitive. As an example, out("amount", 10, a) emits a tuple with three fields: the string amount, the integer 10 and the contents of the program variable a.

Two primitives are provided to associatively retrieve data from the tuple space: in and rd. A *matching rule* governs tuple selection from the tuple space in an associative way: input operations take a *template* as their argument, and the returned tuple is one *matching* the template. In order to match, the template and the tuple must be of the same length, the field types must be the same, and the values of constant fields have to be identical. For instance, the operation in("amount", 10, ?b) looks for a tuple containing the string amount as its first field, followed by the integer 10, followed by a value of the same type as the program variable b: the notation ?b indicates that the retrieved value is to be bound to the variable b after retrieval. The difference between in and rd is that the former removes the matching tuple, while rd leaves it in the tuple space. Both operations are *blocking*, that is, they return only when a matching tuple is found. If multiple tuples match a given template, Linda does not specify how the tuple selection mechanism is expected to work. As a consequence, if a tuple is to wake up a suspended operation, no guarantee is given on which suspended operation is actually selected.

Other Linda operations include inp, rdp – the predicative, non-blocking versions of in and rd, which return true if a matching tuple has been found and false otherwise – and eval. eval creates an *active tuple*, i.e., a tuple where one or more fields do not have a definite value, but must be computed by function calls. When such a tuple is emitted, a new process is created for each function call to be computed. Eventually, when all these processes have performed their computation, the active tuple is replaced by a regular (passive) tuple, whose function calls are replaced by the corresponding computed values. This feature provides for the dynamic creation of processes in a Linda system. It has been demonstrated [135] that Linda is capable to express all the major styles of coordination in parallel programs.

Altogether, Linda operations define a *coordination language* [269]: the combination of a coordination language and a sequential programming language generates a new language, suitable for concurrent systems. This combination, which is called *embedding*, can be implemented in various ways – by changing the sequential programming language syntax and runtime, by preprocessing source code, by supplying proper libraries, or as an extension to the operating system services (see Chapter 3).

Though defined in the framework of concurrent (and typically closed) systems, Linda-like coordination is attractive for programming open distributed applications, too, because of its features, which are summarized below:

- **Uncoupling**. The use of a tuple space as the coordination medium uncouples the coordinating components both in space and time: an agent can perform an out independently of the existence of the retrieving agent, and can terminate its execution before such a tuple is actually retrieved. Moreover, since agents do not have to be in the same place to interact, the tuple space helps to abstract from locality issues.
- **Associative addressing**. The template used to retrieve a tuple specifies *what kind* of tuple is requested, rather than *which* tuple. This way of accessing information is more abstract than retrieving a specific message.
- **Asynchrony and concurrency**. These notions are intrinsic to the tuple space abstraction.
- **Separation of concerns**. Coordination languages focus on the issue of coordination only: they are not influenced by characteristics of the host programming language, which leads to a clearer coordination model.

4.2 Towards Open Distributed Systems: A Taxonomy for Linda-derived Systems

Linda originated in the parallel programming research field using run-times environments based on closed systems (see Chapter 3). Modern software applications, however, are open with respect to different points of view – in particular, topology, platform and evolution [209]. In fact, they could run on a single host or over a network of workstations, on heterogeneous as well as on homogeneous systems, and are subject to extensions and incremental refinement due to evolving requirements.

In this context, Linda's ability to dynamically glue software entities together is an attractive feature: actually, it was soon recognised that the original model could be very useful in open distributed systems, too. Despite its success, however, the original Linda model suffers from some limitations: there is only one (unnamed) tuple space, there is no support for transactions, there is no way to solve the so-called "multiple read problem" (see Sect. 4.3.1), nor is there a way to identify and to authenticate agents.

For these reasons, many projects have extended the original Linda model under different aspects. Several systems, for instance, are able to deal with multiple tuple spaces, both user-created or handled transparently to the user. The multiple read problem suggested the definition of "bulk primitives", and partial failures have been faced by means of some kind of transactional model.

In the remainder of this chapter, we introduce a broad taxonomy of Linda-derived models, which assumes the extensions to the original Linda model as the main classification criteria. Three major categories can be devised:

- **Extensions of the set of the coordination primitives.** The set of the Linda primitives is extended, introducing new primitives to address specific problems or to enrich the expressiveness of the coordination language. Examples are: WCL, KLAIM, Jada, T Spaces, JavaSpaces (see Sect. 4.3).
- **Programmability of the semantics of the language.** The semantics of the primitives can be customized or their use can be subject to control rules. Examples are: Law-Governed Linda, MARS, LuCe, TuCSoN (see Sect. 4.4).
- **Modification of the model.** The primitives are changed or the associative access to the shared dataspace is changed (or both). Examples are: Bauhaus Linda, Laura, LIME (see Sect. 4.5).

In the following of this chapter we try to survey the wide set of tuple-based systems with respect to some relevant criteria (features), in order to help to compare the systems against each other based on the features they support.

The identification of an extensive set of criteria, wide enough to include most aspects, but small enough to include only the relevant ones is not a trivial task. On the basis of our experience in designing, developing and using tuple–based coordination systems, we selected the following set:

- Extensibility
- Data Space Structure
- Platform-related Issues
- Technological Extensions
- Other features (mobility, security, development tools)

For each system, we try to overview its main features with respect to the applicable criteria. Of course, not all the criteria are meaningful in all contexts: in these cases, we restrict our analysis to the meaningful ones. The details of the criteria are shown in the following sections.

4.2.1 Extensibility

The flexibility of a tuple–based system strongly depends on its extensibility. A system can be extensible in several different ways: extensible (or customizable) can be the set of coordination primitives, the operations performed by the primitives or the matching mechanism. Rather obviously, a very extensible and flexible system often implies some inefficiencies, since it is harder to find optimization paths when everything is subject to changes. Linda efficiency, in fact, is mostly due to its non-extensible, closed-system-targeted nature. In most systems, extensibility is achieved in one of the following forms:

- **Extensible set of primitives.** New coordination primitives can be added to the system.
- **Extensible primitive semantics.** The behaviour of the primitives can be changed.
- **Configurable matching.** The matching mechanism and its policies can be customized. Examples of configurable matching are:
  - matchings that are programmable on a per-item basis;
  - matchings based on the host language facilities (for example, Prolog's unification).

4.2.2 Data Space Structure

The original Linda model is based on a shared space of tuples, which are as typed sequences of fields. This basic approach has been widely extended in several ways: by replacing tuples with more complex data structures (sometimes to accommodate the peculiarities of the host language), by enabling the use of multiple spaces (along with mechanisms to reference and create new spaces), by nesting spaces; often the distributed nature of the tuple space has been changed to a more usual client/server architecture. Some of the most relevant features concerning the data space structure are:

- **Single or multiple spaces.** Does the model support multiple tuple spaces?
- **Space naming and creation issues.** How is (are) the space(s) created and referred to?
- **Distributed or centralised.** Is the space centralised on a single execution environment, or is it distributed over a network?
- **Flat or hierarchical structure.** Are multiple spaces just a flat collection of items, or are there hierarchical relationship among them?
- **Content (tuples, objects, other complex data types).** What kind of data are exchanged via the data space?

4.2.3 Platform-related Issues

Adapting a coordination language to a given platform often leads to a certain degree of "contamination". While the coordination model can, in fact, be very generic, its actual implementation has often to deal with the platform it is targeted to. Sometimes this is due to limitations of the platform, sometimes it is because an in-depth knowledge of the platform can allow some optimizations. Here are some platform-related issues:

- **Host language.** Is the coordination language available only with a given host language (C, Java, Prolog, ...)?
- **Portability.** Is the system portable among different architectures?
- **Architecture.** Does the architecture of the platform influence the coordination language?

- **Run-time system.** What kind of run-time support does the coordination system need?

4.2.4 Technological Additions

Basically, technological additions consist of the integration of existing technologies into coordination systems. Different technological additions are included in several systems presented in this chapter: some are inherited from database systems, others are inspired by new trends in distributed systems (like mobility). Features referred to technological additions include:

- **Transaction support.** Does the system supply some kind of transaction support? If so, at what level, with which granularity?
- **Mobility support.** How is mobility addressed at the coordination language level? Can mobile agents/processes use the coordination system transparently? Is there a notion of locality expressed by the coordination model?
- **Security support.** Is the system "secure" in some sense? If so, what kind(s) of security does it provide for? Indeed, security concerns several aspects: agent identification/authentication, message encryption, access policies, protection models, overall system safety, etc. So, can agents/processes be authenticated (with respect to each other or with respect to the run-time system)? Are the communication streams encrypted somehow? Are there access rights, and if so, at what level? Is there an overall security model, enabling the use of the system for critical applications?
- **Availability of development and analysis tools.** Is the system provided with some kind of development tools? If so, how are these tools related to the model's metaphors? What kind of support are these tools aimed to supply?

4.3 Systems Extending Primitives

This section describes the systems that extend the set of Linda primitives by adding new primitives or by changing the existing ones. Usually, such an extension is related to the specific context where the given system is used.

4.3.1 WCL

WCL [524] is a coordination language designed to support agent coordination over the Internet. WCL is based on multiple Linda-like tuple spaces and supplies synchronous, asynchronous, bulk and streaming access to each tuple space. Associative access to tuple spaces uses the same matching mechanism as Linda. The number of primitives, 19, though not extensible by the programmer, is larger than in many coordination languages, mostly because WCL:

- extends the Linda model with new coordination constructs useful in open systems;
- enables the programmer to explicitly choose between synchronous and asynchronous tuple space access, a lower-level approach with respect to Linda which is useful when fine tuning applications for high-latency networks, like the Internet.

Some primitive of WCL are inherited from Bonita [525], notably the bulk primitive `collect` that returns, in a single operation, a copy of every tuple in the space that matches a given template. `collect` solves the multiple read problem [526], that is the impossibility to read each tuple matching a given template exactly once, without reading the same tuple twice.

WCL makes a clear distinction between the agents and the run-time system. All the primitives invoked by an agent are passed to the run-time system that is distributed among all the hosts that are part of the system. The implementation language of the run time system, too, is independent from the agents' implementation language – in fact, bindings for agents written both in C++ and Java are supplied.

The actual distribution of tuples and tuple spaces depends only on the run-time system, and is transparent to the agents. The semantic of the primitives is guaranteed to be kept consistent independently of the actual implementation of the tuple store as a centralised or (partially) distributed entity. The current run-time system (evolved from the original one based on C^2AS) uses centralized tuple repositories which can be moved to different hosts to automatically optimize the agents' access to the tuple space. Some efficiency results for this approach are discussed in [524].

WCL also allows an agent to move part of its code to the host where the tuple space is actually located, which is useful to overcome high network latency. Moreover, this feature can be used to lower the overall computational effort required in the tuple space host, when the computational effort required by the moved code is small.

WCL does not provide support for transactions or log-based checkpointing, though the latter is on the works. However, the chance of moving the coordination code from agents to the tuple space host makes it possible to avoid transactions, moving the chunk of code that should be enclosed in a transaction to the remote host. In this way, it can be ensured that the code will not fail because of a network trouble between the agent and the tuple space. Finally, WCL support for mobile code also enables agents to move a *will* to the tuple space host. In this context, a will is a chunk of code whose task is to maintain consistency in the tuple space if the agent dies during a coordination operation.

4.3.2 KLAIM

KLAIM (*K*ernel *L*anguage for *A*gent *I*nteraction and *M*obility) [453] is a language that supports a programming paradigm where processes can be moved from one computing environment to another. This language derives from Linda, which is extended to suit distributed and location-aware environments. In KLAIM processes are *network-aware* in the sense that the network is not seen as a whole flat environment, but is composed of *locations*, considered at both logical and physical level, where processes can move and execute.

The KLAIM model consists of a Linda core with multiple tuple spaces and a set of operators borrowed from CCS [418]. The main concepts used to model network environments are:

- **Processes.** Processes represents the active entities of the system, and are located at a given location.
- **Nodes.** In KLAIM, locations are called nodes. Each node is a triple (s, P, ρ), where s is a site – i.e., a physical location –, P represents processes, and ρ is the allocation environment.
- **Nets.** KLAIM nets are sets of nodes. A net represents a logical network where processes can move and execute.

Since KLAIM relies on a strong concept of *locality*, both tuples and operations are located at specific sites of a net. So, all Linda operations can be invoked by specifying a given location where the operation is actually performed. For instance, the invocation of an operation such as out(t)@l means that tuple t has to be written at the location l.

Besides mobility, the key issues addressed by KLAIM are *privacy* and *integrity* of data, enforced by enabling a strict check on the actions that agents perform on tuple spaces, based on their access rights.

KLAVA. KLAVA is an implementation of the KLAIM model in Java. The Java language has been chosen to achieve portability over heterogeneous and widespread networks like the Internet.

KLAVA introduces two new Java packages: Linda and Klaim. The Linda package implements Linda primitives: to this end, it defines the classes Tuples and TupleSpace. The former supplies methods to create and handle tuples, while the latter supplies mechanisms to create and access tuple spaces – namely the methods to implement the in, out and read operations.

The Klaim package contains the implementation of KLAIM's concepts, by means of Net, Node and K-Process classes. Net is the core class, which acts as a server in charge of managing nodes and sites. The Node class encapsulates a tuple space and a set of processes, and supplies KLAIM's primitives, i.e. the distributed versions of the Linda operations. The instances of the K-Process class represent KLAIMprocesses: an execute() method works similarly to the run() method of the Java Thread class. In the current implementation, the localities are represented as strings, while sites correspond to Internet addresses.

4.3.3 Jada

Jada [169] is a coordination language for Java that can be used to coordinate parallel/distributed components. This model extends Linda's basic concepts by implementing new primitives, replacing tuple spaces with object spaces (i.e. specialized object containers) and enabling the creation of multiple spaces.

Jada's basic coordination entity is the *Space*. Concurrent threads can access a space by using a small yet effective set of Linda-inspired primitives that are made available as methods of the Space class. Besides the usual in, read and out operations, Jada provides users with some "bulk" primitives: readAll, inAll, getAll and getAny. The first two return all the objects that match a given template, while getAll returns all the objects that match *a set* of templates, and getAny returns *any* object that matches a set of templates.

All the input primitives can be associated to a timeout, interpreted as the time within which the primitive has to be performed. Unlike other systems, input primitives are never blocking: they return an object that is an instance of the Result class. This object provides users with methods to check whether the operation has been successfully performed, whether it has been cancelled (either by the user or because the timeout is over), and to gather its result. Gathering the result is a blocking operation: if the result is not yet available, the calling thread blocks until either the operation is successfully performed, or it is cancelled. Output primitives can specify an associated time-to-live: when this time is over, the object emitted in the object space can be reclaimed by the garbage collector.

The matching policy used by Jada is very simple and easily extensible. Templates (formals) are represented by instances of the Class class, the Java meta-class. A template representing an Integer class, for instance, matches any Integer object. Actual to actual matching is delegated to the standard Java equals method in the general case, and to the ad hoc matches method when objects implement the JadaObject interface. This mechanism is used in particular to customize the matching rule in the Tuple class, which is an ordered object container used to mimic Linda tuples. This class defines its matching policy by implementing the matches method so that two Tuple objects a and b match iff a and b have the same number of fields, and each field in a matches the corresponding field in b using the standard Jada matching mechanism. The same mechanism can be applied to any user-supplied class.

Jada provides users with a client/server-based technology that enables distributed components to access an object space uniformly. Two versions of the server/client pairs are provided: one based on a simple stub/skeleton mechanism that uses socket connections, and another based on Java RMI. Currently only the latter is supported: the former was implemented for historical reasons (the first version of Jada appeared before RMI). Moreover, since an object space is a Java object, an application can create several object spaces and even several server objects spaces. The same paradigm can then be used to achieve data driven coordination in both parallel and distributed applications – though the access to a remote object space can obviously fail because of network troubles.

Security in Jada is addressed at two levels: by enforcing access control policies on a per-space basis, and by supporting data encryption when accessing a remote space. While the second mechanism applies to remote spaces only, the first can also be used when concurrent threads access a local, shared object space. One of the advantages of this approach is that a space-based access control enables uniform security policies to be used for both the concurrent and the distributed case, which is particularly useful for mobile agents. Though agents running on the same place (i.e., on the same Java Virtual Machine) can use a local space for coordination purpose (i.e., a space running on the same JVM as well), accessed without remote protocols, the security policy should be consistent between local and remote access.

Moreover, Jada intrinsically supports mobile code: by using the `eval` primitive, *evaluable* objects are moved to the server space JVM and (like in WCL, see Sect. 4.3.1), executed as new threads.

In the last few years Jada has been used for several research projects and to implement quite different systems, from parallel computing to Internet card games, from distributed collaborative applications to mobile agents systems. In particular, it has been used to provide coordination support for applications based on PageSpace [173], a reference architecture for distributed applications running on the World Wide Web.

4.3.4 T Spaces

T Spaces [648] is a product from IBM Research Division proposed as a coordination-based middleware for a broad range of software architectures, from small embedded systems to large-scale distributed systems. T Spaces exploits monolithic Java-based tuple space servers, accessed from remote Java-based clients through a client library that interfaces with the server by means of a proprietary protocol designed on top of a TCP/IP stack. Tuples, that are stored in flat spaces, are sequences of (potentially named) fields: a field can be any serializable Java object. Tuples themselves are instances of classes that extend the abstract `SuperTuple` class.

Multiple tuple spaces can be created by running multiple instances of the server application. Clients address a tuple space by specifying the host/port pair of the corresponding server, and can perform the usual Linda-like operations on the remote space (though operation names have been subject to aesthetic changes). Bulk primitives, such as multiple in and read, are available, too. A novel blocking *rendez-vous* operation, `rhonda`, is also introduced, which takes a tuple and a template as its arguments, and succeeds when another client performs another `rhonda` operation with a matching tuple/template pair. Moreover, the T Space API makes it possible for the programmer to

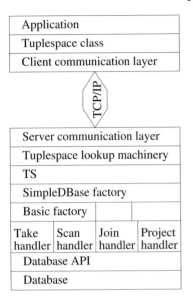

Fig. 4.1. T Spaces design overview.

define new primitives, whose code can then be downloaded to the server: the
structure of a T Space system is shown in Fig.4.1.

In T Spaces, a tuple and a template match iff the tuple type is a subclass
of the template type, the tuple and the template have the same number of
fields, each tuple field is an instance of the type of the corresponding template
field, and, for each non-formal field of the template, the field value matches
the value of the corresponding tuple field. Optionally, tuple fields can be
named, which enables matching to be performed on just a subset of the tuple
fields.

Associative access to the tuple space can also be performed by *queries*,
a mechanism that extends the basic notion of matching by exploiting the
database backend used by T Spaces. Queries enable matching operations to
be combined by means of **and** and **or** operators: in particular, the combination
of queries with bulk primitives makes it possible to perform SQL's **Select**-
like operations.

T Spaces also provides for both intra-operation and inter-operation consistency. The first is ensured by a checkpoint/recovery mechanism based on
an operation log file, while the latter is achieved by means of a transaction
system, like those available in relational databases.

Security support includes authentication (based on simple username/pass-
word pairs) and access control lists on a per-tuple space basis: each operation
defined on a tuple space is associated to a list of access attributes that must
be satisfied by any client trying to execute that operation. In addition to
the standard *read, write, owner* and *admin* permissions, T Spaces also allow

specific permissions to be associated to a single command, which may be a need when defining new operators.

Other salient features of T Spaces include:

- **Database indexing.** The data manager indexes all the tagged data to improve retrieval efficiency.
- **Event notification.** Agents can register to be notified when new tuples are inserted into the space or when tuples are removed from it.
- **XQL queries.** XML fields can be used in tuples, and are handled in a special way: once in the tuple space, they are decomposed in the corresponding DOM tree. A subset of the XQL query language can then be used to perform queries on such XML data.
- **Customizable database engine.** Different database engines can be used to handle the tuples in the tuple space. The system ships with three data manager units: two are memory-based, while the third is a wrapper interface towards IBM DB2 systems.
- **Direct thread access.** When the server and the client are both running on the same Java Virtual Machine, it is possible to avoid the communication through the TCP/IP stack and use the shared memory instead. Though this is not as efficient as using direct method calls, yet it can help improving the performance in a local execution environment.

In the actual usage, T Spaces design reflects its designers' background in database systems. While this may be of help for programmers coming from the database field, it may make the system unfamiliar to people with a tuple-based coordination background. This "database-oriented" approach also led T Spaces designers to view tuple spaces mostly as a data repositories, putting great care in data management and retrieval. While that makes it possible to search for large amounts of data using complex queries, it can cause low performance when dealing with just few tenth of tuples, which is quite a frequent situation when using a tuple space as a coordination medium. Even if integrating this model with object-oriented systems leads somehow to an extension of the basic matching policy, the choice of supporting complex queries and indexing techniques seems a different approach rather than an extension.

A known limitation of the T Spaces system is that the data exchanged between the server and the clients is not encrypted, with obvious (in)security implications. Moreover, the client/server communication protocol is proprietary and, unlike RMI, cannot be used across a firewall. This problem, however, can be overcome by using an RMI-based communication layer in place of the internal one.

Thanks to its client/server structure, which fits well in the architecture of many multi-agent systems, and to its flexibility, T Spaces can be a good choice for many Java-based systems, especially when performance and strong security are not a major requirement; however, integrating its security system may sometimes require some effort since it is not integrated with the standard Java security model.

4.3.5 JavaSpaces

JavaSpaces is a technology developed by SUN Microsystems in the framework of distributed network services [249], aimed at providing distributed repositories of information, similar to Linda tuple spaces. The goal is to ease the design and the implementation of distributed applications, while providing users, at the server side, with a uniform interface to different kinds of information services.

JavaSpaces are Java tuple spaces, whose tuples are Java objects: more precisely, tuples are instances of classes implementing the `Entry` interface. Therefore, the JavaSpaces world consists of distributed tuple spaces, which can be accessed by anyone that adheres to the above interface. The access to the tuple spaces is defined in terms of Java methods, which are declared in the `JavaSpace` interface (see Table 4.1). Tuples are stored in their *serialized form*: in particular, each field of the tuple object is serialized separately. Consequently, the pattern-matching mechanism relies on the serialized form of the tuples: two tuples match if their serialized forms match. The Java keyword `null` is used with a twofold meaning in tuples and in tuple templates: in the former case, it actually stands for "no object", while in the latter it has a wildcard (any value) meaning. Since Java classes belong to the same hierarchy, rooted by `Object`, tuples that are instances of different classes can match, too, if the common fields match. In this case, the matching rule follows the standard Java assignment rule: a tuple template which is an instance of class `A` matches a tuple which is either an instance of class `A`, or an instance of a class `B` which is a subclass of `A`.

The `JavaSpace` interface (Table 4.1) defines the basic Linda operations, though some names have been changed (`out` becomes `write`, `in` becomes `take`). The main enhancements introduced by JavaSpaces with respect to the basic Linda model are:

- **Rich typing.** The adoption of (possibly user-defined) classes for both tuples and tuple fields makes it possible to exploit Java's strict typing to enhance the matching mechanism, taking into account the field types besides the field values.
- **Methods associated with Entries.** Since entries – and fields – are objects, it is possible to define methods in the corresponding classes: the represented information is therefore enriched so as to include its behaviour.
- **Matching of subtypes.** The adoption of an object-oriented language, enabling classes to be used as tuple types and tuple field types, enhances the pattern matching mechanism by introducing the chance of considering the subtype relationship induced by inheritance in the matching policy, too.

```
public interface JavaSpace {

Lease write(Entry e, Transaction txn, long lease)
    throws RemoteException, TransactionException;

public final long NO_WAIT = 0; // don't wait at all

Entry read(Entry tmpl, Transaction txn, long timeout)
    throws TransactionException, UnusableEntryException,
        RemoteException, InterruptedException;

Entry take(Entry tmpl, Transaction txn, long timeout)
    throws TransactionException, UnusableEntryException,
        RemoteException, InterruptedException;

EventRegistration notify(Entry tmpl, Transaction txn,
    RemoteEventListener listener, long lease,
    MarshalledObject handback)
        throws RemoteException, TransactionException;
    ...
}
```

Table 4.1. The main methods of the JavaSpace Interface.

- **Lease.** Each tuple in the space is associated to a *lease time*, which can be considered as the tuple lifetime: when it is over, the tuple is removed from the space.
- **Transactions.** Transactions are often required in practical systems to ensure the correctness of the performed operations. JavaSpaces transactions can rely on external transaction services (provided that they implement the Transaction Service API), for example the one supplied by the Jini technology [619].

Another relevant JavaSpaces feature is the capability of *notifying* the writing of a given tuple to an external object that registered its interest on this event. To do so, an object willing to be notified when a given kind of tuple is written in the space must first register as a *listener*, specifying the proper tuple template. In the Java event model, a *listener* is an object that can be registered for a given event: when such an event occurs, a specified method of the listener object is called. So, in JavaSpaces, each tuple written in the space is pattern-matched against the specified template: if they match, all the registered listeners are notified. Then, each notified listener knows that a possibly interesting tuple has been written in the space, and can consequently act as appropriate.

4.4 Systems Adding Programmability

The last kind of enhancement is towards programmability. These systems give the capability of modifying the standard behaviour of the tuple space by programming it, without changing the set of primitives.

4.4.1 Law-Governed Linda

The Law-Governed Linda (LGL, [424]) technology exploits the power of the Linda model for the coordination in open and distributed systems, but recognizes the limitations of this model in terms of insecurity and inefficiency. LGL is an instance of the more general concept of *law-governed architecture* [423], which defines interactions governed by a global law specified in the architecture. Originally created for systems modelled around the notion of *process*, LGL has been easily adapted to agent-based systems. The LGL architecture includes the five basic components of the general law-governed architecture:

- **Communication medium.** The communication medium is the means used by the system actors to communicate and interact. In LGL, it is a Linda tuple space.
- **Sequential processes.** Processes (also referred to as *agents*) are the system actors, which interact via the communication medium.
- **Control states.** Control states are the new concept introduced by LGL to maintain information about processes and their action history during time. To this end, each process is associated to one control state. Control states can be exploited to keep the history of the accesses to the communication medium.
- **Global law.** The global law is defined by the architecture, and is therefore unique throughout the system. Composed of several *rules*, it is aimed at governing the interactions that take place in the communication medium.
- **Law enforcement mechanism.** The global law is enforced by means of *controllers*: each process is associated to a controller, which acts as a mediator between the process and the communication medium.

In LGL, the communication medium is accessed by processes exactly as a Linda tuple space, by means of the `read`, `in`, and `out` operations. Unlike Linda, however, each LGL process accessing the tuple space generates an *event*, which is caught by the associated controller. The controller calculates the *ruling* of the law associated the event, taking into consideration the process control state, and carries out the ruling.

    The law can be exploited to control the execution of the Linda-like operations, without formally adding any new operation. This calls for a language to express the rules of the law, and for an execution model defining how events are to be handled. The LGL language for expressing the rules is based on some primitive operations, which can be put together to compose the rules of the law. The execution model establishes that all rules are triggered whenever an event occurs. For this purpose, LGL defines two main kinds of events that may occur in the basic Linda operations:

- **Invocation events.** These events occur when a process invokes an operation (`out`, `in`, `read`) on the tuple space. These events express only the attempt to perform an operation, not the actual execution of the operation itself, which will take place only if the law allows it.
- **Selection events.** These events occur when a matching tuple is found in the tuple space. As above, the occurrence of such an event does not mean that the matching tuple is actually returned to the invoking process: this action has to be allowed by the law.

When an event occurs, LGL searches the law for a rule that describes the occurred event. If it finds one, it executes all the primitive operations in the rule, which are supposed to express how to carry out the invoked process operation. The primitive operations that can be included in the ruling of the law are:

- `complete`. The effect of this operation is to actually carry on the operation requested in an invocation event. If the invoked operation was an `out`, the supplied tuple is actually written in the space, while if it was a `rd` or an `in`, the pattern matching mechanism is triggered. A parameter for the `complete` can be specified, in which case it takes the place of the parameter of the invoked operation.
- `return`. This primitive allows the matching tuple to be returned to the invoking process. As in the previous case, a parameter may be added to `return`, in which case it is returned to the invoking process instead of the matching tuple.
- `out(T)`. This primitive operation writes tuple T in the space, without activating any further rule.
- `remove`. This primitive operation removes a process from the system.

In the context of agents, LGL explicitly addresses the problem of making peer-to-peer coordination within a group of agents obey to a set of specified rules.

The LGL model is particularly useful and effective to control interactions and enforce security in an open system. Although LGL does not supply security mechanism such as access control lists, several kinds of security policies can be implemented by exploiting the programmability of the law rules [425].

4.4.2 MARS

MARS (*M*obile *A*gent *R*eactive *S*paces) is a coordination architecture developed at the University of Modena and Reggio Emilia [116], implementing *programmable reactive tuple spaces* for Java-based mobile agent applications. Of course, it can be fruitfully exploited by static agents, too. MARS is a

```
public interface MARS extends JavaSpace {
// inherited from JavaSpace

  ...
// Lease write(Entry e, Transaction txn, long lease)
//    throws RemoteException, TransactionException;
// Entry read(Entry tmpl, Transaction txn, long timeout)
//    throws TransactionException, UnusableEntryException,
//           RemoteException, InterruptedException;
// Entry take(Entry tmpl, Transaction txn, long timeout)
//    throws TransactionException, UnusableEntryException,
//           RemoteException, InterruptedException;
// defined by MARS
Vector readAll(Entry tmpl, Transaction txn, long timeout);
//    throws TransactionException, UnusableEntryException,
//           RemoteException, InterruptedException;
Vector takeAll(Entry tmpl, Transaction txn, long timeout);
//    throws TransactionException, UnusableEntryException,
//           RemoteException, InterruptedException;
}
```

Table 4.2. The MARS Interface.

service for mobile agents that roam the network in a *network-aware* fashion (i.e., the network is modelled as a set of sites).

The MARS model assumes the existence of one (unnamed) tuple space locally to each execution environment, which is independent of the other sites' spaces. This tuple space represents the only means that agents can use to interact both with the local execution environment and with other agents. The MARS tuple space is only loosely coupled to the agent server and can be associated with different systems and implementations. Incoming (or newly-created) agents are provided with a reference to the local tuple space as soon as they appear on a node, and can use it to coordinate with other entities.

Agents access the MARS tuple space by means of the MARS interface, which is derived by the JavaSpace interface (see Table 4.2). Also, MARS tuples are Java objects, and are managed exactly as in JavaSpaces. With respect to JavaSpaces, MARS adds two operations (readAll and takeAll) which make it possible to retrieve *all* the matching tuples from the space. While the latter may be seen as a language shortcut, the first helps to face the so-called "multiple read problem" (see Section 4.3.1), that is, Linda's inability of reading each matching tuple exactly once.

The key feature of MARS, however, relies in the notion of *programmable reactive tuple space*, which makes it possible to embody computational abilities within the tuple space itself (*programmable* property), assuming specific behaviours in response to access events (*reactive* property). So, a MARS tuple space is no longer a mere tuple repository with a built-in and stateless pattern-matching mechanism, but an active component with its own state, which can be programmed so as to react to tuple access operations by performing specific (re)actions. Reactions can access the tuple space, change its content, and influence the semantics of the access operations. Rather than adding new primitives, MARS allows the *effects* of the operations to be changed by programming proper reactions. For example, a reaction may change the pattern matching mechanism so as to let agents specify a range of values, rather than a fixed value, in the template of an input operation [117].

Programmable tuple spaces enable the specification of inter-agent coordination rules in terms of reactions, thus achieving a clear separation between algorithmic and coordination issues: agents are in charge of embodying the algorithms to solve the problems, while reactions represent the application-specific (or site-specific) coordination rules.

The MARS reaction model complies with the standard tuple space model: reactions are coded as *meta-level tuples* (*meta-tuples* for short) stored in a local *meta-level tuple space*. Each meta-tuple represents a kind of access event – in terms of involved operation, tuple(s) and agent identity – and specifies the reaction to be triggered when a matching access event occurs. The reaction itself is a method of a Java object. Whenever an access occurs, the system searches the meta-level tuple space for a matching meta-tuple. If such a meta-tuple is found, the corresponding reaction object is retrieved and its reaction method is executed, providing it with useful pieces of information, like a reference to the tuple space. In order to avoid endless recursion, reactions are not allowed to trigger other reactions in a chain: this is why a reaction access to the local tuple space is called *passive*, opposite to the *reactive* access performed by agents. Meta-tuples can be stored and retrieved at run time, leading to dynamic insertion and removal of reactions, both by the local administrator and by agents.

Since the MARS model is specifically designed for mobile agent systems, tuple space *locality* – that is, the choice of supplying one independent tuple space for each site – is a fundamental property. This property helps to overcome the resource binding problems due to the change of the execution environment (see [253]), and leads to the implementation of the *context-dependent interaction* concept.

From the security viewpoint, MARS implements basic access control list mechanisms, which make it possible to define the allowed operations on tuples on the basis of agent identities. MARS allows also a more sophisticated and flexible security schema that relies on the definition of *roles*, which can be dealt with in a more general way, overcoming the limitations related to the identification based on the single agent identity. Peculiar security policies can also be implemented by means of reactions: in particular, the administrator of a site can define a local policy and implement it as a reaction, relying both on the visibility of the entire tuple space and on its own state to store general information.

To achieve portability across different platforms, MARS has been written in 100% pure Java. In addition, MARS tuple spaces are loosely coupled with the mobile agent system of the single nodes [115].

In the forthcoming future MARS is expected to provide support for the XML format inside tuples [118], so as to improve the integration with the Internet environment: this should enable MARS to play the role of a coordination interface to the rich world of XML documents.

4.4.3 LuCe

LuCe (from Logic Tuple Centres) is a coordination model, system and technology for the construction of multi-agent systems involving autonomous, pro-active, possibly heterogeneous agents [205]. The key contribution of the model consists in the introduction of the concept of *tuple centre* as an enhanced tuple space, which can work as a *programmable coordination medium* [203]. In LuCe, tuples are used not only to represent the application data, but also to describe tuple centres' behaviour: these further tuples are called *specification tuples*.

The ability to define the tuple centres' behaviour makes it possible to uncouple the actual representation of knowledge in a tuple centre from the agents' perception of such knowledge, enabling interaction protocols to be defined at the most natural level, according to simple data-oriented criteria. Moreover, LuCe promotes a clear separation between *individual tasks* and *social tasks*: individual tasks can be designed around the previously-defined interaction protocols, while the accomplishment of social tasks is charged mainly upon the suitably-programmed coordination media.

LuCe is both a theoretical model and an actual *coordination technology*, made available by the LuCe *system* [207]. Developed in Java over a lightweight Prolog engine, the LuCe system integrates Prolog and Java within the Internet platform, effectively supporting the construction of portable Prolog and Java agents. In addition, it is fully *coordination transparent* – that is, tuple centres can be freely distributed over a LAN or an intranet, yet agents can access them by name, with no need to know anything about their physical location [206].

The key difference between a tuple space and a tuple centre is that a tuple space supports only the coordination policies that can be directly mapped onto its fixed behaviour, while a tuple centre can be programmed so as to bridge between the different representations of information shared by agents, to provide new coordination mechanisms, to support the full monitoring of agent interaction, and, above all, to embed the laws for agent coordination [204]. In particular, LuCe tuple centres are logic-based: so, they exploit Prolog both as the inter-agent *communication* language – that is, to *enable* inter-agent communication – and as the *coordination* language – that is, to *rule* communication (see [470] for a formal description of the LuCe communication and coordination languages).

Tuple space access and modification	
out_r(T)	succeeds and inserts tuple T into the tuple centre
rd_r(TT)	succeeds, if a tuple T unifying with template TT is found in the tuple centre, by unifying T with TT; fails otherwise
in_r(TT)	succeeds, if a tuple T unifying with template TT is found in the tuple centre, by unifying T with TT and removing T from the tuple centre; fails otherwise
no_r(TT)	succeeds, if no tuple unifying with template TT is found in the tuple centre; fails otherwise
Communication event information	
current_tuple(T)	succeeds, if T unifies with the tuple involved by the current communication event
current_agent(A)	succeeds, if A unifies with the identifier of the agent that triggered the current communication event
current_op(Op)	succeeds, if Op unifies with the descriptor of the operation that produced the current communication event
current_tc(N)	succeeds, if N unifies with the identifier of the tuple centre performing the computation
pre	succeeds in the *pre* phase of any operation
post	succeeds in the *post* phase of any operation
success	succeeds in the *pre* phase of any operation, and in the *post* phase of any successful operation
failure	succeeds in the *post* phase of any failed operation

Table 4.3. Main ReSpecT predicates for reactions.

Agents perceive a LuCe tuple centre as a (logic) tuple space, which can be accessed through the typical Linda-like operations (out, in, rd, inp, rdp). Each tuple centre is uniquely identified by a ground Prolog term and, conversely, any ground term can be used to denote a tuple centre. What makes a (logic) tuple centre different from a (logic) tuple space is the notion of *behaviour specification*, which defines how a tuple centre reacts to an incoming/outgoing communication event. The behaviour of a LuCe tuple centre is defined through the ReSpecT specification language [204], a logic-based language where *reactions* in response to communication events are defined by means of first-order logic tuples, called *specification tuples*. A ReSpecT reaction consists of as a sequence of *reaction goals*, which can access properties of the triggering event, perform simple tests on terms, and operate on the space of tuples through the out_r, in_r, rd_r, and no_r predicates (see Table 4.3 for details). Unlike the MARS approach, in LuCe these may trigger further reactions in a chain: this property is fundamental for the Turing-equivalence of the ReSpecT reaction model.

Reaction goals are executed sequentially: a reaction as a whole either succeeds or fails depending on whether all its reaction goals succeed or not, and is executed with a transactional semantics. So, a failed reaction has no effect on the tuple centre state. Since all the reactions triggered by a communication event are executed before serving any other event, agents perceive the result of serving the communication event and executing all the associated reactions altogether as a single transition of the tuple centre state (see [204] for more details on the ReSpecT language and its computational model).

As a result, the effect of a communication primitive is no longer limited to adding, reading, or removing a single logic tuple, as in the case of logic tuple spaces: instead, it can be made as complex as needed in order to uncouple the agent view of the space of tuples from its actual state, and to relate them so as to embed coordination laws into a new observable behaviour of a tuple centre. Since ReSpecT is Turing-equivalent [204], any computable coordination law can be in principle encapsulated into the coordination medium.

A logic tuple centre is then conceptually structured in two parts: the *tuple space*, containing ordinary communication tuples, and the *specification space*, containing specification tuples. By representing at any time the current state of agent interaction, the state of the space of (ordinary) tuples provides for the *communication* viewpoint. Instead, the space of the specification tuples provides for the *coordination* viewpoint, since the behaviour specification of a tuple centre governs inter-agent communication, and specification tuples actually define agent coordination rules. So, in principle, (intelligent) agents can reason on the system behaviour by taking both the communication and the coordination theories into account, possibly refining / changing the coordination laws if appropriate.

The tuple centre notion impacts over the whole LuCe development system [207]: in particular, specialised tools provide agents with the proper tuple centre *views*. Since a tuple centre is characterised by three sets – the set T of its tuples, the set W of its pending queries waiting to be served, and the set S of its reaction specifications [470] –, three ad-hoc agents, the T, W and S *Inspectors*, provide agents with the ability to edit and control tuple centres from the data, the pending query and the specification viewpoints. By making tuples observable, the T Inspector enables developers to monitor communication from a *data-oriented* viewpoint, while the W Inspector, supporting communication events' observability, provides for the *control-oriented* viewpoint. Finally, by making tuple centre's specification tuples accessible and modifiable, the S Inspector provides for the *coordination* viewpoint.

The possibility of specifying tuple centres' behaviour has a strong impact on the way applications are designed: in particular, agents can be provided with a view of the domain representation that is specific to their own task, independently of representation of knowledge as tuples in the tuple centre. In turn, this one should be chosen according to what is most natural in the application domain, independently from agent protocols' needs. The bridge between agents' own domain representation and tuple centre's representation of shared knowledge is then meant to be provided by suitably-programmed tuple centres.

This approach leads to a neat separation between individual tasks, involving the single agents, and social tasks, involving the multi-agent system as a whole [206]. In particular, agents are to be designed around their individual tasks, tailoring their interaction protocol to the agents' desired perception of the interaction space: interaction protocols are then naturally modelled in terms of reading, writing, and consuming tuples in tuple centres. Tuple centres behaviour is instead aimed to harness collective behaviours towards the accomplishment of social tasks, governing agent autonomy: coordination rules are designed so as to accomplish such social tasks, bridging amongst the different agents' perceptions and ontologies.

Finally, the clean separation between computation and coordination [624] carried out by agents and coordination media (respectively) promotes design incrementality since the earliest design phases: so, for instance, adding a new agent with a new task to a LuCe-coordinated system typically does not imply a system re-design, but simply the modification of the existing coordination rules or the definition of new ones, in terms of tuple centre's behaviour specification.

LuCe has been successfully exploited to build several test applications: from the classical Dining Philosopher problem [203, 205], in two versions, to more complex and realistic application scenarios such as a distributed version of classical games like TicTacToe and Reversi [206, 207], with different agent types to be coordinated (Java agents providing for the graphical interface, Prolog agents taking care of game supervision, etc).

4.4.4 TuCSoN

Inspired to the LuCe model, from which it borrows both the tuple centre concept and the ReSpecT specification language, TuCSoN [472] exploits tuple centres to define an interaction space spread over a collection of Internet nodes. Each tuple centre is associated to a node, and is denoted by a locally unique identifier: so, each node provides agents with its own version of the TuCSoN name space (i.e., the set of the admissible tuple centre names), by virtually implementing each tuple centre as an Internet service.

A TuCSoN tuple centre can be denoted either by means of its full *absolute name*, or by means of its relative *local name*: the first one is unique all over the Internet, while the latter is unique only within a single node name space. The tc@node syntax uniquely identifies the specific tuple centre tc hosted by node, while the relative name tc refers to the local tuple centre of the node where the mobile agent currently is. So, while LuCe is always *network-transparent*, TuCSoN allows agents to perform tuple centre operations both in a *network-aware* and in a *network-transparent* fashion: the first form is typically used by an agent wishing to interact with a node locally, while the latter allows an agent to remotely look for its next hosting environment.

The above duality enforces the separation between network-related issues, such as agent migration across nodes, and purely computational issues, such as interaction with the local resources. In particular, since each node implements its own version of the TuCSoN name space, the network-transparent form allows mobile agents to adopt the same interaction protocol across all nodes, independently of the specific hosting environment, charging the handling of heterogeneity onto the different tuple centres' behaviour specifications.

4.5 Systems Modifying the Model

The systems described in this section enhance Linda by modifying its model. In this case, too, the modifications reflect the requirements of the context where the system operates.

4.5.1 Bauhaus Linda

Bauhaus Linda [138], or just Bauhaus, generalizes Linda in order to support multiple first-class tuple spaces and to handle both data and processes using the same primitives. The goal is achieved by a generalization that leads to a simpler model than the original Linda, which is generalized in the following ways:

- Linda's distinction between tuples and tuple spaces is eliminated: the only coordination structure is, in fact, the *multiset*. Output primitives add a multiset to a destination multiset, input primitives read (and possibly remove) a multiset from a target multiset.
- Linda's distinction between tuples and templates in eliminated: Linda's type- and position-sensitive associative matching rule is replaced by simple set-inclusion.
- Linda's distinction between data and processes is eliminated: while passive data and active processes remain distinct species, the coordination language itself makes no distinction between active and passive entities. In Bauhaus, then, out is used to put both data and processes inside a multiset; in the same way, rd and in retrieve both data and processes from a multiset (in returns the process itself, rd returns a "freezed" copy of the process).

Bauhaus is thus simpler that Linda, in that both tuples and tuple spaces are replaced by multisets, templates are eliminated, distinction between processes and data is eliminated, and the primitives are reduced from four to three. On the other hand, Bauhaus is more powerful than Linda: the use of multisets as the only coordination entity naturally accommodates a hierarchy of multiple spaces. Moreover, since the coordination primitives operate on multisets, Bauhaus' (multiple) spaces are first class objects – i.e., coordination operations can be applied to whole spaces.

For these reasons, Bauhaus is elegant, simple, and powerful. However, distributed implementations of Bauhaus have to support the capability of dealing with copies of processes and processes that move around the network. These features are not usually supported by classic operating systems, and can lead to complex scenarios requiring support for performance, security, and heterogeneous systems altogether.

4.5.2 Laura

Laura [595] is a coordination model based on Linda, where the tuple space is enhanced to a *service space*. A service space is a collection of special tuples called *forms*. A form can be a description of a *service offer*, of a *service request*, or of a *service result*.

Interaction consists of either posting a service request to the service space, so as to find a matching offer form, or trying to get the results of a service, by finding a matching result form. Since the service provider and the service consumer remain unknown to each other, interaction is completely uncoupled.

A service is described through an *interface*, which specifies a set of operation signatures. A signature describes an operation in terms of its name, arguments and result type: interfaces are then used to identify the required service.

To ask for a given service, users just insert the proper service request form into the service space. This action triggers the search of a service offer form whose interface matches the interface of the request form. By doing so, Laura emphasizes *what service* is requested, not *which agent* is requested to perform it. Service identification is then a crucial point.

For this purpose, interfaces are described using a *service type language*. The semantics of interface definitions is formally given by means of a suitably-defined type system (see [594]), which includes rules for subtyping: these are the key for service identification. In fact, given the interface descriptions, a service offer form matches a service request form if the type of the offered interface is a subtype of the requested one. Subtyping is defined so that a type A is a subtype of B if any value of type A can be used instead of a value of type B, where "values" are services. This makes it possible to supply a service of type A whenever a service of type B is requested. Laura type system deviates from other approaches to the management of types in open systems under three viewpoints. First, it abolishes global names for service interfaces and relies on interface matching only. Second, it does not consider the names of structured types. Finally, it adopts just syntactic equivalence for checking the names of interface operations.

A service is the result of interaction between a *service provider* and a *service user*, which are coordinated by two operations, **serve** and **result**. An agent willing to offer a service to other agents adds a service offer form to the service space by executing the **serve** operation, whose arguments are the offered service type and a list of binding rules: the latter specify the bindings between the program variables and the above arguments. When `serve` is executed, a service offer form is built from the specified arguments. Then, the service space is scanned for a service request form whose service type matches the service offer form according to the above type rules. Arguments are then copied to the service offer form and bound to the program variables. If no matching request forms can be found, `serve` blocks.

After performing the requested service, the service provider delivers a result form to the service space by means of the `result` operation. Such a result form consists of the service interface and, depending on the operation, of a list of result values according to the binding list. It is the agent's responsibility to properly store the service results in those variables. The `result` operation is performed immediately, and the form is inserted into the service space. So, an agent offering services typically operates in a loop consisting of the sequence `serve` / *perform the service* / `result`.

On the client side, an agent willing to use a service should execute Laura's third operation, `service`, whose arguments are the requested service type, the requested operation along with its arguments, and a binding list. When executing `service`, two forms are involved: a *service put* form and a *service get* form. The first represents the requested service: it is constructed from the service interface and from the specified arguments, and then inserted into the service space. If another agent performs a `serve` operation and its service offer form matches this agent's put form, arguments are copied as described above and the service provider starts processing the requested operation. The service get form is used, instead, to retrieve the service results. First, this form is constructed from the service interface and the binding list. Then, a matching result form is sought in the service space: when available, the results are copied and bound to the program variables.

Laura has been used to provide coordination support for applications based on PageSpace [173], a reference architecture to support distributed applications on the World Wide Web.

4.5.3 LIME

LIME means "*LI*nda in a *M*obile *E*nvironment": as expected, the main issue focused by this technology is *mobility* [493], addressed from both the logical (*mobile agents*) and the physical (*mobile computing*) viewpoints uniformly. In the following of the section we will focus on the former one.

Linda's static, global and persistent tuple spaces show several limitations when inserted in a context of mobile entities: LIME tries to adapt the advantages of the Linda model – in terms of uncoupled interactions – to the dynamicity of a mobile world, by focusing on the description of the model of the tuple spaces, disregarding the actual implementation, which can rely on different programming languages and platforms. Unlike MARS, mobility has a strong influence in the definition of the LIME tuple space model.

LIME relies on the concept of *transiently shared tuple space.* Each mobile entity – whether it is an agent or a physical device – is associated to an *Interface Tuple Space* (ITS), which can be seen as a personal tuple space where tuples can be stored and retrieved from. When mobile entities meet in the same physical place, their ITSs are automatically merged, thus enabling Linda-like coordination among mobile entities via temporarily shared tuple spaces. The merged tuple spaces become a single tuple space from the viewpoint of agents, which, therefore, do not have to worry about the actual location of tuples. When a new agent arrives, its ITS is merged with the current one, and the content is dynamically recomputed. The sequence of actions involved in sharing and merging tuple spaces is called *engagement,* while the opposite sequence (enact when an agent leaves the site) is called *disengagement.*

Agents can be associated to multiple ITSs, each identified by name. This makes it possible to rule the ITS sharing on the basis of the names that are common to other agents. Agents can also define *private* ITS that are not shared with other agents, to be exploited to store private information. LIME also defines a system tuple space for each agent at the environment level, called the *LimeSystem* ITS.

LIME implements the three fundamental Linda operations: `read`, `in` and `out`. The main difference between LIME and the basic Linda model is the capability of defining *personal* tuple spaces that can be shared and joined with other tuple spaces transparently to the agents, enabling temporarily shared tuple spaces. In this way, the semantics of the tuple space operations is not altered, but the tuple space content changes according to the agent's current location. The uncoupled form of interaction proposed by Linda is preserved, but the absence of a global and static tuple space better fits a highly dynamic scenario.

Another interesting feature of LIME is its event reaction capability: to this end, LIME introduces the reactive statement $T.\texttt{reactsTo}(s,p)$, where s is a code fragment to be executed when a tuple matching the template p is found in the tuple space T. There are several system events that are monitored and can be coded as tuples in the *LimeSystem* ITS by the run-time support, such as the agent arrival / departure, changes in connectivity, changes in the system, etc. Along with the `reactsTo` statement, the above monitoring capability enables tuple spaces to react to system events. In this way, LIME provides its tuple spaces with a form of programmability: a mobile entity can program the behaviour of its own ITS, so as to provide more flexible control on the accesses to it.

The concept that a tuple space may be both *personal* and *shared* can be exploited to support *agent communities.* Specific tuple spaces can be used as points where agents with a given goal can meet and interact: so, agents can access information belonging to the whole community without having to know all the community members. At the same time, private information can be protected by the definition of private tuple space, which can be accessed only by the owner agent.

4.6 Conclusions

In this chapter we surveyed several tuple-based coordination models and systems, introducing a framework to classify them on the basis of the extensions to the original Linda model. In our intention, the criteria used to define the taxonomy should ease the comparisons between the different approaches, as well as define a reference framework useful for design purposes.

Of course, other models and systems do exist, which may well be of interest in specific environments and application areas: in this chapter we restricted to those that are related to the book focus.

Acknowledgements

The authors would like to thank Robert Tolksdorf for his clear explanation of Linda (on which the one presented here is based) and Andrea Omicini for his feedback and suggestions.

This work has been partially supported by Italian Ministry of University - MURST 40% - Progetto SALADIN, by a grant by Microsoft Research Europe, by the Italian National Research Council (CNR) in the framework of the project "Global Applications in the Internet Area: models and programming environments", and again by the Italian MURST in the framework of the Project MOSAICO "Design Methodologies and Tools of High Performance Systems for Distributed Applications".

5. Middleware Technologies: CORBA and Mobile Agents

Paolo Bellavista[1] and Thomas Magedanz[2]

[1] LIA, Dipartimento di Elettronica, Informatica e Sistemistica
Università di Bologna, Viale Risorgimento 2, I-40136 Bologna, Italy
mailto:pbellavista@deis.unibo.it
[2] IKV++ GmbH, Bernburger Strasse 24-25, D-10963 Berlin, Germany
mailto:magedanz@ikv.de

Summary.
The design, implementation and provision of services in the Internet scenario are forcing both the traditional area of client/server distributed systems and the emerging sector of agent technology towards the definition of
a common distributed middleware, i.e., a set of basic facilities that can be
ubiquitously accessed by any distributed component as an integrated part
of the enhanced communication infrastructure. This middleware should
not only be the basis where designers start for the realization and deployment of their services, but also be flexible enough to permit the easy and
rapid extension of the common infrastructure to accommodate evolving
system/service requirements and expectations of final users.

Among the technologies for middleware implementation, the chapter
describes the state-of-the-art of two approaches: the Common Object Request Broker Architecture (CORBA) technology and the Mobile Agent
(MA) one, which are different from several points of view (interoperability
and location transparency vs. mobility and location awareness). However,
in contrast to using them separately, the chapter claims that an integration
of both middleware technologies represents the most promising solution to
achieve the maximum flexibility in the implementation of an open service
infrastructure. In this context CORBA-based MA platforms demarcate
an important evolution step into the direction of mobile and interoperable object systems, on which Internet services could be realized through
dynamically distributed and reusable object-based components.

5.1 Middleware Technologies for Open and Global Distributed Systems

In the last years, the widespread diffusion of Internet technologies has
changed the way of thinking about service provision. The availability of a
global communication infrastructure and its ubiquitous accessibility suggest
to implement services as the result of interworking resources and service components that are geographically distributed and intrinsically heterogeneous
due to the openness of the Internet scenario. Whereas the standardization
of communication protocols has made possible to consider the Internet as
a global distributed system, its extensive usage for the implementation and
provision of distributed services demands the additional availability of basic common facilities, provided at the infrastructure level, to simplify the

interworking and coordination between distributed components [79]. For instance, any Internet service implemented in terms of cooperating components needs a naming infrastructure to simplify the dynamic identification and location of required entities, even based on a partial knowledge of searched resources (e.g., by knowing their functionality but not their interface). Naming is probably the most evident example of a general-interest facility for distributed systems: single applications that implement their proper *ad hoc* naming service not only force their designers to a considerable implementation effort but, most important of all, lead to competing and incompatible solutions that are in contrast with the reuse and interoperability principles emerging in the Internet environment.

At the same time, the diffusion of agent technologies has further stimulated the re-thinking of software implementation in terms of coordinated groups of autonomous components. While first research activities obviously aimed at the definition of models, design principles and methodologies for agents, as the focus has moved to the implementation of agent systems and agent-based complex applications, one of the main objectives is becoming the identification and provision of a common infrastructure of basic services. This infrastructure should provide application designers with a wide set of "horizontal" general-purpose facilities, possibly designed according to a layered architecture, to simplify the rapid prototyping of agent-based distributed services and to support their deployment and execution at run-time [62].

In short, the Internet is forcing both the traditional area of Client/Server (C/S) distributed systems and the emerging sector of agent technology towards the definition of a common set of basic facilities that can be ubiquitously accessed by any distributed component as an integrated part of the communication infrastructure. These facilities should not only be the basis where designers leave from when realizing and deploying their applications, but also should be flexible enough to permit to easily extend the infrastructure in order to accommodate evolving system/service requirements and expectations of final users. This kind of infrastructure is the current vision of what is traditionally known as *middleware*.

While there is a general agreement on the necessity of providing middleware solutions for Internet services, researchers hardly agree when they have to define exactly what middleware is, which facilities and services are part of it, and which ones have to be considered either at a lower layer (as components of the network infrastructure) or at a higher one (as application-specific components). In fact, the concept of middleware tends to depend on the subjective perspective of those trying to define it. It is even dependent on when the question is asked, since the middleware of yesterday (e.g., Domain Name Service, Public Key Infrastructure and Event Services) may become the fundamental network infrastructure of tomorrow. Final users and programmers usually see everything below the Application Programming Interfaces (API) as middleware. Networking gurus see anything above IP as middleware. Researchers and practitioners who work between these two extremes consider it as somewhere between TCP and the API, with some even further classifying middleware into application-specific upper middleware, generic middleware, and resource-specific lower middleware [17, 450].

To briefly present a historical evolution of the middleware definition, some of its earliest conceptualizations originated with the distributed operating research of the late 1970s and early 1980s and were further advanced by the I-WAY project [246]. The I-WAY linked high-performance computers nation-wide over high-performance networks such that the resulting environment functioned as a single high-performance system. As a consequence of that experiment, the involved researchers re-emphasized the fact that effective high-performance distributed computing required distributed common resources and facilities, including libraries and utilities for resource discovery, scheduling and monitoring, process creation, communication and data transport. In May 1997, the members of the Next Generation Internet (NGI) consortium extended the traditional definition of middleware by stressing requirements such as reusability and expandability [450]. Their definition includes persistent services, such as those found within traditional operating systems, distributed operating environments (e.g., the Java framework), network infrastructure services (e.g., the Domain Name Service), and transient capabilities (e.g., run-time support and libraries).

The chapter has neither the presumption nor the objective of presenting a conclusive and totally accepted definition of middleware. Its aim is, instead, to give some details about widely diffused and recently emerging middleware technologies and to describe which coordination models are at the basis of the presented distributed infrastructures. So, to fully understand the following, it is sufficient to adopt a popular definition of middleware as "the intersection of the stuff that network engineers do not want to do with the stuff that application developers do not want to do" [324]. By accepting this informal definition, the largest part of both research and industrial work in distributed systems in the last years can be classified as middleware, from the area of distributed operating systems [256] to the one of distributed objects [186, 544], from the area of distributed multi-agent societies [637, 331] to the one of tuple-based distributed coordination [44].

Among the middleware supports for distributed objects, the Object Management Group (OMG) Common Object Request Broker Architecture (CORBA) is certainly the most widespread, complex and mature infrastructure, also because the major competing support, Microsoft Distributed Common Object Model (DCOM), has started later and with different aims in terms of openness and generality [186, 544, 159]. Since 1989, the OMG consortium, which includes the quasi-totality of companies (except for Microsoft) has been defining CORBA. CORBA is a middleware that permits a very rich variety of coordination modalities between its components. The architecture is based on the concept of a common software bus allowing for distributed object interoperability and providing a wide set of bus-related services to interacting objects. The main aim is to release application developers from all the duties that stem from the possible heterogeneity and distribution of C/S components: CORBA client objects have no visibility of the location of the CORBA server objects they collaborate with, and their interaction is completely independent of both their implementation language and the platform where they are running. The most notable consideration in this context is that CORBA, apart from the variety of available policies for communication and coordination between components, has been designed from the beginning as a complex and layered architecture of facilities and services to support the implementation of distributed C/S applications.

A significant novelty in the distributed systems of the last years is the introduction of the Mobile Agent (MA) programming paradigm that is contributing with new energies and different perspectives to the definition and implementation of a distributed middleware of common facilities and services. The crucial point of the MA technology is to give to location-aware computing entities the possibility of migrating (with their code and the reached execution state) from one network host to another one while in execution [253]. The property of mobility makes the MA programming paradigm significantly more flexible than the traditional C/S one, by permitting to exploit locality in agent access to distributed resources and to perform distributed operations in a completely asynchronous way with respect to the commanding users and the originating hosts [253, 518, 45]. Several heterogeneous MA platforms have recently emerged [12, 18, 284, 563], and coming from a completely different direction with respect to CORBA, they are also trying to identify a middleware of basic services to provide to mobile agents, in order to simplify and stimulate the implementation of industry-scale MA-based applications for the Internet.

Both CORBA and mobile agents propose middleware approaches to support the implementation of Internet services, but the properties of their solutions are very different due to the fact that CORBA mainly focuses on interoperability and location transparency while mobile agents concentrate on mobility and location awareness. As previously cited, they are not even representative of any possible middleware approach. For instance, Jini has recently emerged as a very interesting technology for the coordination of Java-based distributed components, with a solution that is certainly more lightweight and perhaps less general than the CORBA one [44]. However, in this chapter we have decided to present and compare CORBA and MA technologies because they have achieved the same goal of providing a distributed middleware for Internet services, even if their approaches originate from very different directions and perspectives, being the CORBA middleware a basic element of its initial design, the MA one a necessity emerged during the realization of first MA platforms and MA-based services. Most important of all, we claim that CORBA and MA should not be considered alternative one to the other: on the contrary, several properties exhibited by the two technologies are complementary and motivate their integration to provide application designers with a very flexible middleware infrastructure that is able to cover different levels of abstraction.

The remainder of the chapter is structured as follows. Sections 5.2 and 5.3 are devoted to a brief description of the middleware frameworks and the coordination possibilities offered by, respectively, CORBA and MA. Section 5.4 tries to demonstrate the suitability of the integration of CORBA distributed objects with mobile agents due to the partial complementation of the two approaches. Section 5.5 exemplifies the claim of the previous section by presenting the architecture of two MA systems integrated with CORBA (Grasshopper and SOMA) and their application to the domains, respectively, of enhanced Intelligent Networks (IN) services and of management of distributed Video on Demand (VoD) applications. Concluding remarks and emerging directions in current and future work follow.

5.2 Common Object Request Broker Architecture (CORBA)

The OMG CORBA technology has gained wide acceptance in the late 1990s and has become the standard *de-facto* for the integration and support of possibly heterogeneous distributed objects in large-scale industrial applications. Born with the main aim to facilitate interoperability between C/S distributed components (including the integration with legacy systems and services), CORBA has been designed from scratch as a very articulated and layered architecture of services, at different levels of abstraction, that should cover all aspects and duties of designing and implementing distributed applications, from basic communication between objects to the provision of more complex and dynamic modalities of coordination, from general-purpose low-level services that can help in the implementation of any kind of distributed application to higher-level common and domain-specific facilities.

The independence of both the implementation language and the execution platform is guaranteed in CORBA by the specification of a standard language to define object interfaces, the Interface Definition Language (IDL). CORBA server objects that publish their IDL interfaces can be invoked by any CORBA client object that has an a-priori knowledge of server interfaces, by exploiting static mechanisms of interaction based on pre-compiled proxies both on the client side (stubs) and on the server one (skeletons). It is also possible to have more flexible and sophisticated modalities of coordination between CORBA objects, based on the availability of dynamic invocation mechanisms that permit to defer the knowledge of the IDL interfaces of the involved objects. A CORBA client can dynamically build an invocation request from scratch by exploiting the Dynamic Invocation Interface (DII). A

CORBA server can analogously be unaware at compile-time of its skeleton by exploiting the Dynamic Skeleton Interface (DSI) functionality. Any possible combination of static/dynamic clients invoking static/dynamic servers is supported. In any case, object interactions in CORBA are mediated by runtime services for object activation on the server side (Basic/Portable Object Adapter - BOA/POA) and for dynamic retrieval of information on currently available CORBA interfaces (Interface Repository - IntR) and CORBA object implementations (Implementation Repository - ImpR).

All the above mechanisms are components of the CORBA core, i.e., the software bus that realizes the transparency of allocation and implementation between CORBA objects and that is called Object Request Broker (ORB). They are mandatory in any vendor implementation of the CORBA specifications. Upon the ORB core, the OMG specifies the possibility to implement a layered architecture of additional modules to help in the design and deployment of distributed applications. These facilities are organized into a structured architecture called Object Management Architecture (OMA) and classified as CORBA services, horizontal/vertical facilities and application objects.

In the following, we try to give some insights about the OMG architecture model and about the mechanisms available in the ORB for object communication and coordination. The objective is to illustrate the variety of interactions that are possible between CORBA objects, in order to acquire the elements required to compare it with the corresponding modalities available in common MA platforms and presented in Section 5.3.

5.2.1 Object Management Architecture

The OMA has been defined by OMG in 1991 with the goal of providing a high level specification of the functionality needed for an object-oriented C/S distributed processing, that is: how distributed objects should be defined and created, what communication mechanisms are required and how methods should be invoked on remote objects.

The architecture includes an Object Model and a Reference Model. The Object Model shows how objects must be described in the context of a heterogeneous distributed environment, while the Reference Model describes the possible interactions between distributed objects.

In the Object Model, an object is an encapsulated entity, characterized by a specific identity. Any object is supposed to provide external objects with services, which are accessible only through well-defined interfaces without requiring the knowledge of the object specific implementation.

The Reference Model identifies and characterizes the components, interfaces and protocols that compose the OMA. It includes the ORB (also referred to as CORBA object bus), which represents the core of the OMA architecture by providing the support to object location transparency, server object

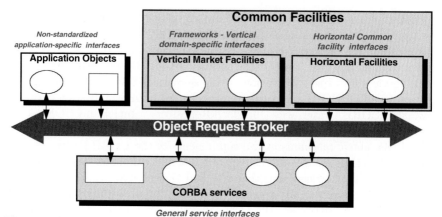

Fig. 5.1. OMG Object Management Architecture Defining DifferentInterface Categories.

activation and inter-object communication, and four categories of object interfaces (as depicted in Figure 5.2.1):

- *Object Services,OMGServ* are a collection of domain-independent low-level services that extend the ORB functionality with basic functions that are likely to be used in any program based on distributed objects (such as lifecycle management, naming, persistence, transactions, ...). These components provide the generic environment where single objects can perform their tasks. Adopted OMG Object Services are collectively called *CORBA Services*;
- *(Horizontal) Common Facilities,OMGFacil* are interfaces for horizontal facilities that are oriented to final users and applicable to most application domains (such as user interfaces, information management, system management, task management, ...). They may be based on object services;
- *(Vertical) Domain Interfaces,OMGFacil* are application interfaces tailored to specific domains and areas (such as electronic commerce, telecommunications, tele-medicine, ...), which may be based on object services, common facilities and application interfaces;
- *Application Interfaces* are non-standardized application-specific interfaces, which also allow to wrap existing interfaces into the CORBA framework (such as legacy switch control and management interfaces). Since the OMG is interested in the specification of middleware components and not of final applications, these interfaces are not subject to standardization.

A peculiarity of the OMA architecture is that the same object can alternatively play the client and the server roles in different times.

A second part of the Reference Model introduces the notion of domain-specific *Object Frameworks*. An Object Framework component is a collection of cooperating objects that provide an integrated solution within an application or technology domain and which is intended for customization by either service developers or final users. They are vertical slices down the OMG "interface stack". This means that Object Frameworks are collections of cooperating objects categorized into Application, Domain, Facility, and Service Objects. Each object in a framework supports (through interface inheritance) or makes use of (via client requests) some combination of Application, CORBA Facilities, and CORBA Services interfaces.

Through a series of Requests for (specification) Proposals (RFPs), the OMG is populating the OMA with detailed specifications for each component and interface category in the Reference Model. Adopted specifications include the Common Object Request Broker Architecture (CORBA), CORBA Services, and CORBA Facilities. The following section focuses on the specifications and functionality of the CORBA components that represent the core of any implementation of the OMA.

5.2.2 Common Object Request Broker Architecture

CORBA defines the programming interfaces to the OMA ORB. The ORB is the basic mechanism by which objects transparently make requests to (and receive responses from) each other, either on the same host or across a network. A CORBA client object need not to be aware of the mechanisms used to either communicate with or activate a server object, how it is implemented, and where it is located. So, the ORB forms the foundation for building applications constructed from distributed objects and for interoperability between applications in both homogeneous and heterogeneous environments.

The CORBA specification [186] provides the description of the interfaces and services that an OMA-compliant ORB must implement to be aligned with the OMG standards. In addition, it defines a software infrastructure to facilitate the development of reusable and portable applications in distributed environments. 5.2.2 shows its architecture consisting of various structural components, each responsible for a specialized functionality: the ORB, the IDL Stubs and Skeletons, the Dynamic Invocation Interface (DII), the Dynamic Skeleton Interface (DSI), the Interface Repository (IntR), the Implementation Repository (ImpR), and the Object Adapter (OA).

The ORB is responsible for establishing the communication relationships between client and server objects in the distributed environment. It is in charge of identifying the server object that must satisfy the client request, activating it if necessary, passing the input parameters and the operation type, and returning the result and the output parameters. The ORB implements a mechanism similar to remote procedure calls applied to objects. The CORBA specification requires that the ORB mediates the communications between distributed objects since the client must be aware neither of the server location nor of the server programming language. Clients need only to care about object interfaces.

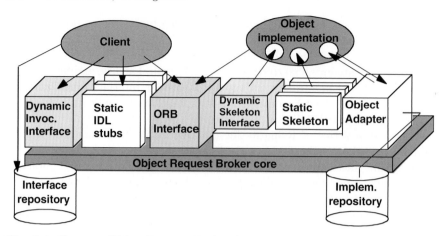

Fig. 5.2. Common Object Request Broker Architecture.

Before invoking an operation on a target object, the client must obtain its object reference, for example by interacting with the naming service that will return the needed object reference as output parameter. The ORB creates a new object reference once the target object has been activated, but the object itself is responsible for the distribution of its reference via the registration with the naming service or by other distribution mechanism, if it wants to be reachable. An object reference can be stored and used later since the ORB guarantees that the associated target object will be available to satisfy client requests as long as it is active. The object reference can be exchanged between interacting objects in a string format, but its usage requires to preventively re-convert the string into an object. In summary, the ORB offers to client objects the following services:

- *Object localization.* The client does not need to know if the target object is active either within a process running on a remote machine or in a process within the same machine or even within the same process of the client.
- *Object implementation.* The client must not be aware of the programming language used to implement the target object, of the operating system or the hardware platform on which the server program is executed.
- *Object execution state.* The client does not need to know if the target object is already active within the corresponding server process and ready for accepting the incoming request. The ORB is responsible for transparently activating the target object before forwarding the client request.
- *Object communication mechanism.* The client can ignore the communication mechanism used by the ORB to send the incoming request to the target object and to return the response to the client.

Interface Definition Language. The OMG IDL provides a standardized way to define the interfaces to CORBA objects. The IDL definition is the contract between the implementer of an object and the client. IDL is a strongly-typed declarative language that is independent of the programming language chosen to implement either the server object or the client one. IDL-to-anyLanguage mappings enable objects to be implemented and to send requests in the developer programming language of choice, in a style that is natural to that language.

A client can determine the services offered by an object on the basis of its IDL interface. In fact, an interface describes the attributes and the operations that a server object makes available to any possible client. The IDL permits to define modules, interfaces, attributes, operations and data types. A module is a namespace where interface names must be unique. An interface defines a set of object attributes and operations. Attributes are object values, which can be directly accessed for reading and writing or only for reading, by using the standard *get* and *set* operations. Operations are methods whose signature is described in terms of operation name, parameter modes (*in, inout, out*), names and types, result type and exceptions. Finally, data types describe the types of values (either basic or constructed) used for parameters, attributes, exceptions and return values.

One of the key characteristics of IDL is the abstraction of object implementation details, being focused only on the interfaces and on the public attributes of an object, which are the only relevant for object interaction scenarios. The concept is that, in a distributed environment, clients should never be interested in implementation issues but only on offered services.

Static Invocation Interface. Once the IDL definition of the object interface is available, it is used to generate automatically the proxies needed to link CORBA clients to the implementation of CORBA server objects. The IDL specification must be mapped onto a target implementation language using the IDL pre-compiler. Once applied, this pre-compiler will generate the necessary stub and skeleton files, required for the communication between client and server.

The *skeleton* files contain the server-side code that implements the communication between the ORB and the server object. Anytime the skeleton receives a service invocation from the ORB, it forwards the request to the object implementing the corresponding operation. To realize a server object, the programmer must only write the code implementing its interface operations, i.e., the methods present in its skeleton. The *stub* files contain the client-side code that implements the communication between the client object and the ORB. When the client invokes an operation on a remote object, the stub resulting from the pre-compilation of the server IDL in the client programming language is responsible for forwarding the service invocations to the ORB.

Stubs and skeletons interact with the ORB for the marshalling and unmarshalling of the operation parameters in order to map them from the local programming language (e.g., Java, C++) format to a common format, i.e., the General Inter-ORB Protocol - GIOP. When either stubs or skeletons mediate the interactions between the objects and the ORB, this is referred to as Static Invocation Interface. The term static indicates that stubs and skeletons are respectively part of the client application and of the server object implementation and therefore the server object IDL interface must be known at compile-time to both the client and the server.

Dynamic Invocation and Dynamic Skeleton Interfaces. In addition to the Static Invocation Interface based on stubs and skeletons, CORBA provides other two mechanisms: the Dynamic Invocation Interface (DII) and the Dynamic Skeleton Interface (DSI), allowing modalities of C/S coordination that are more flexible and changeable at run-time. In particular, the DII mechanism makes a client object independent of the knowledge of the target object stub at compile-time. This means that it is not necessary to have an a-priori knowledge of the server object the client will interact with. Analogously, the DSI mechanism allows the server object to be unaware of its object skeletons at compile-time, i.e., it does not force a server object to know its own IDL interface and, therefore, the specific object it is implementing. In short, DII and DSI make possible to provide new services by defining at execution-time the operations that have to be invoked and the parameters to be returned.

The DII and DSI mechanisms exploit a set of ORB interfaces that are independent of the IDL interfaces of the implemented objects. To support these features CORBA has introduced standard APIs that enable run-time binding mechanisms.

Repositories and Object Adapters. The knowledge of the IDL interfaces implemented by target objects can not only be fixed in stubs and skeletons, but can also be stored in a middleware database component that is called *Interface Repository* (IntR). Whenever a distributed application uses the DSI mechanism, the knowledge of object IDL interfaces is embedded in the application code. Therefore, if the IDL interfaces referenced by the application change during the application lifetime, the application needs to be recompiled. The IntR is the response of the CORBA middleware to avoid this rigidity. The IntR is a CORBA object that manages an online database containing the description of the interfaces defined via the IDL. The stored information is used by the ORB to check the method signature correctness, to provide meta-data information to CORBA clients and to dynamically get the description of the interfaces implemented by any registered CORBA object.

The *Object Adapter* (OA) is the glue between the implementations of CORBA objects and the software bus. The OA provides object implementations with a set of services, such as object instantiation, server class registration in the *Implementation Repository* (ImpR), object reference generation, forwarding of incoming service invocations to interface stubs/skeletons, and dispatching of incoming requests to target objects. Similarly to the IntR, the ImpR is a runtime database containing object references, types and classes of the instantiated objects of all registered server processes. The ORB exploits this information to locate active objects and to request the activation of new objects within a server.

Since an OA defines how an object must be activated, different OAs could be implemented to support different object activation policies, possibly required by different applications. For instance, the server-per-method activation policy specifies that a new server process is activated for each method invocation (the ORB does not need to know if the object is already active). The persistent-server policy, instead, imposes that the server process is not activated automatically by the OA at the first client invocation, but it has to be started manually by invoking an explicit operation of connection to the ORB.

5.2.3 Integration with Internet Technologies

The emergency of widely diffused Internet services and the increasing relevance of a full integration with the Web are probably the major driving force behind the evolution of CORBA specifications. With the publication of the first CORBA 1.0, a number of commercial ORB implementations appeared, thus emphasizing the problem of ORB interoperability when objects reside on different ORBs and need to communicate, as it is in an open and global distributed system such as the Internet. This problem has been overcome by the CORBA 2.0 specification that faced the interoperability issues by defining an interoperable format for object references (Interoperable Object Reference) and the mandatory Internet Inter-ORB Protocol (IIOP) that specifies how GIOP messages have to be transported over a TCP/IP network. Even if GIOP messages can also be mapped into other connection-oriented transport protocols, an ORB must always support IIOP to be CORBA 2.0 compatible. In addition, Environment Specific Inter-ORB Protocols (ESIOPs) have been defined for handling interoperability also with distributed platforms that are not compliant with CORBA (e.g., the Open Software Foundation Distributed Computing Environment - OSF DCE [475].

The primary goal of the current CORBA 3.0 specification is to simplify the use of the CORBA technology for the development of Internet-oriented distributed object applications, by providing a CORBA version with full integration with the Internet. To increase the acceptance of CORBA also by other technology providers, a rich support for legacy environments was included:

- *CORBA Java to IDL Mapping.* The mapping allows Java application developers to build distributed application purely in Java and then to generate the CORBA IDL from compiled Java class files. This permits an easy integration with CORBA without writing IDL interfaces and allows other CORBA-compliant services to access Java applications over IIOP;
- *CORBA Firewall.* Many Internet applications and legacy systems are behind a firewall for security reasons. The specification defines a set of in-

terfaces for passing IIOP requests and replies through a firewall. It encompasses configuration mechanism for allowing the firewall to perform filtering and proxying on both the client side and the server one. This enables a controlled and secure use of CORBA-based applications from the Internet;

- *CORBA Interoperable Naming Service.* Until recently, pure CORBA clients could access CORBA object interfaces only via CORBA object references. There was no other mechanism to reach a server object, even if the client knows the server location. This naming service defines an Internet-like format for object references based on URLs, that can be used to reach defined services at a remote location.

Finally, it is important to notice that the most diffused Web browsers (e.g., Netscape Communicator 4.x and Microsoft Internet Explorer 5.x) currently support full integration with CORBA by permitting to encapsulate Java-based CORBA clients in standard Web documents.

5.3 Mobile Agents

The appearance of the Mobile Agent (MA) concept can be derived mainly by a new technology called TeleScript developed by General Magic in 1994 [630]. It was the period when scripting languages, such as the Tool Command Language (TCL) and its derivative SafeTCL [83] gained much attention, since they enabled rapid prototyping and the generation of portable code. The concept of smart messaging [359], based on the encapsulation of SafeTCL scripts within emails [83], made new mail-enabled applications possible. In the same years, the concept of mobile computing, intended as the possibility of moving users and terminals in the Internet with no need to suspend service provision, has gained increasing importance and has further stimulated the research on mobile code technologies [153]. Last but not least, it was the beginning of the Java age, and Java is the basis for the largest part of current MA systems.

Nowadays there has been a lot of development and general excitement in the area of the MA technology, much of which has evolved from the platform independence of the Java language with its object serialization and network communications support. We can summarize that, based on this coincidence of the appearance of various agent concepts, agents become a fashion technology for the research and development communities. However, this also created confusion, since there was a lack of common definitions and standards, resulting in various concepts, languages, architectures, technologies and terminology. This situation is now going to change thanks to the work accomplished for the definition of the first standard proposals in the MA area (see Subsection 5.4.1 for details about the current status of MA standard specifications).

Mobile agents, also referred to as transportable agents or itinerant agents, are based on the principle of code mobility. In the C/S paradigm the server is defined as a computational entity that provides some services: the client requests the execution of these services by interacting with the server; after the service is executed, the result is delivered back to the client. Therefore, the server provides the knowledge of how to handle the request as well as the necessary resources. Mobile code enhances the traditional C/S paradigm by performing changes along two orthogonal axes:

- Where is the know-how of the service located?
- Who provides the computational resources?

Three main programming paradigms based on the possibility of dynamic code migration have been identified [253]: *Remote Evaluation* (REV), *Code on Demand* (CoD), and *Mobile Agents*. These paradigms differ in how the know-how, the processor and the resources are distributed among the components S_A and S_B of a distributed system (see Table 5.3). The know-how represents the code necessary to accomplish the computation. The resources (i.e., the file system where application-specific data are stored) are located at the machine that will execute the specific computation.

In the REV paradigm [565], a component A sends instructions specifying how to perform a service to a component B. For instance, the instructions can be expressed in the Java bytecode. B then executes the request on its local resources. Java Servlets are an example of REV [282]. In the CoD paradigm, the same interactions take place as in REV. The difference is that component A has resources located in its execution environment but lacks the knowledge of how to access and process these resources. It gets this information from component B. As soon as A has the necessary know-how, it can start executing. Java applets fall under this paradigm.

The MA paradigm is an extension of the REV one [253]. Whereas the latter primarily focuses on the transfer of code, the MA paradigm involves the mobility of an entire computational entity, along with its code and the reached execution state. In other words, if component A is a mobile agent, it has the know-how capabilities and a processor, but it lacks the resources where to perform its operations. The computation associated with the interaction takes place on component B that has a processor and the required resources. For instance, a client owns the code to perform a service, but does not own the resources necessary to provide the service. Therefore, the client delegates the know-how to the server where the know-how will gain access to the required resources and the service will be provided. An entity encompassing the know-how is a mobile agent. It has the ability to migrate autonomously to a different computing node where the required resources are available. Furthermore, it is capable of resuming its execution seamlessly, because it preserves its execution state.

This means that a mobile agent is not bound to the network host where it begins execution. The ability to travel permits a mobile agent to move to

Paradigm	Before		After	
	S_A	S_B	S_A	S_B
Client/Server	A	Know-how Resource B	A	Know-how Resource B
Remote Evaluation	Know-how A	Resource B	A	Know-how Resource B
Code on Demand	Resource A	Know-how B	Resource Know-how A	B
Mobile Agent	Know-how A	Resource	—	Know-how Resource A

Table 5.1. Classification of Programming Paradigms based on Code Mobility [253].

a destination agent system that contains the resources with which the agent wants to interact. Moreover, the agent may be interested in exploiting the services offered by the destination agent system. When an agent travels, its state and code are transported with it. The agent state can be either its execution state or agent attribute values that determine what to do when execution is resumed at the destination agent system. The agent attribute values can include the agent system state associated with the agent (e.g., time to live).

The MA paradigm is important for network-centric systems because it represents an alternate, or at least complementary, solution to traditional C/S models of interaction [153]. MA solutions may contribute to a reduction of the overall communication traffic in network. For example, mobile code has the ability to engage with a server locally for searching large databases; the proximity to the server ensures high communication bandwidth.

The adoption of the MA technology is encouraged by many researchers in the distributed system area, by citing the following deriving benefits [154]:

- *Asynchronous/autonomous task execution* - After the injection of an agent into the network environment, both the commanding user and the originating network host have no control duties on the launched agent and can perform other tasks.
- *Reduction of network traffic and client processing power* - Massive data exchanges are handled locally at the nodes hosting the data, and client computers could concentrate on performing only limited local tasks.
- *Increased robustness* - The reduction of dependence between interworking components allows MA-based applications to overcome temporary unavailability of both the network and the needed C/S resources. Once the agent arrived at a target system, the originating host may crash or the network may become unavailable without any drawbacks on the task processing.

- *Automation of distributed task processing* - Agents can exhibit an autonomous behaviour and can have built-in itineraries which determine which tasks they have to perform and where, without the need of any user interaction.
- *Decentralized control and management* - Dynamic agent migration and their possible cloning significantly simplify the automated distribution of formerly centralized programs for the control and management of network resources and distributed applications.
- *Flexibility* - Software can be distributed at run-time and only when needed (on-demand software distribution). Service software can be encapsulated within mobile agents, instantly downloaded to both client and server nodes, and installed by transporting mobile agents even when possibly complex installation operations have to be performed on target hosts.

This means that mobile agents provide flexibility in dynamically (re-)distributing intelligence inside a distributed network environment, in particular to reduce network load and to optimize service performance. The MA benefits listed above permit to overcome various problems and inefficiencies of traditional C/S architectures. The possible drawback of the MA technology is represented by the security risks introduced, since from some points of view a computer virus is some kind of mobile agent, too. Furthermore, an agent may be attacked, modified or deleted by a hostile agent platform on a malicious network host. Another typically stated and obvious concern related to mobile agents is the question if agent migration is always of advantage if compared with message passing. For example, it is probably better to interact by message passing in case the agent code is bigger than the expected data volume to be exchanged.

In summary, it has to be stated that agent technologies have a lot of appealing advantages compared to traditional technologies for solving specific requirements that are emerging in the provision of distributed services in the Internet environment. But the agent support imply the introduction of middleware components in the target environment in order to enable mobility, local agent execution and advanced facilities for inter-agent communication and coordination. In addition, to be effectively usable in the short term, mobile agents require mechanisms and tools to interact with existing services and legacy systems designed according to the traditional C/S programming paradigm.

5.3.1 Mobile Agent Platforms

The boom of research activities related to MA platforms started in the mid nineties, motivated by the several advantages promised by this new technology and presented in the previous section. Many research labs and manufacturers were involved in the development of various platforms, built on top of different operating systems, and based on different programming languages and technologies. Even new languages have been realized, exclusively designed for the support of mobile agents (e.g., TeleScript).

However, what is more relevant for the middleware perspective we are trying to present in this chapter, is that common trends in MA platforms have started to emerge evidently within the last few years. Interpreter-based programming languages, particularly Java, are forming the basis for most of today's agent platforms, mainly due to their easy portability over heterogeneous platforms. In addition, Java is frequently chosen for the available support, directly at the language level, of fine-grained security policies and transport facilities via object serialization [282]. Moreover, even if coming from different experiences and domain-specific design constraints, the implementers of MA platforms are achieving a general agreement on the architecture of middleware services that are necessary for supporting mobile agents in open and global environments and for leveraging the diffusion of MA-based services in the Internet. Finally, several approaches have recently explored the possibility of integrating mobile agents and RPC-based middleware like CORBA, possibly stimulated by the research work accomplished for the definition of agent interoperability standards [660].

MA platforms typically realize a distributed processing environment, consisting of several middleware components, and usually referred to as *Distributed Agent Environment* (DAE). In the following of the section, we will look closer to the structure of state-of-the-art MA platforms and to their middleware capabilities [98], while Section 5.4 will be completely devoted to a detailed presentation of why and how to integrate the CORBA and MA middleware technologies.

Good examples for existing state-of-the-art MA systems are Aglets Workbench from IBM Japan [12], Concordia from Mitsubishi [183], Odyssey from General Magic [466], Voyager from ObjectSpace [615], Ajanta from the University of Minnesota [18], TACOMA from Universities of Cornell and Tromso [582], Grasshopper from IKV++ GmbH [284], and SOMA from University of Bologna [563]. An extensive description and comparison of MA platforms is out of the scope of this chapter and can be found in [487].

Structure of Mobile Agent Platforms. DAEs usually support a hierarchy of locality abstractions (regions, places and agent systems) to model network physical resources, and two different types of agents (mobile and stationary). The same terms are standardized by the OMG MASIF standard that will be presented in Subsection 5.4.1. Figure 5.3.1 depicts an abstract view of these entities.

The actual runtime environment for agents is called *agent system*: on each network host, at least one agent system has to run to support the execution of agents. Agent systems are structured by means of places, i.e., isolated execution contexts that are able to offer specific additional services. For example, there may exist a communication place offering sophisticated communication

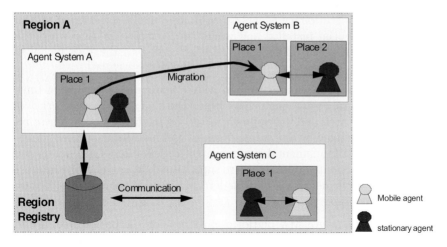

Fig. 5.3. Structure of a Distributed Agent Environment (DAE).

features, or there may be a trading place where agents offer/buy information and service access. Agent systems can be grouped into domains, called regions, that usually model a physical local area network: each region has an associated (region) registry that maintains information about all registered agent systems, places and agents.

The region concept facilitates the management of the distributed components (agent systems, places and agents) in the DAE. Agent systems, as well as their places, can be associated with a specific region by registering them within the accompanying region registry. All agents that are currently hosted by those agent systems will also be automatically registered by the region registry. If an agent moves to another location, the corresponding registry information is automatically updated. A region can be used also to comprehend in a unique logical entity all agent systems belonging to a specific company or organization.

The region registry maintains information about all components that are associated to a specific region. When a new component is created, it is automatically registered within the corresponding region registry. While agent systems and their places are associated to a single region for their entire life time, mobile agents are able to move between different agent systems of possibly different regions. The current location of mobile agents is updated in the corresponding region registry after each migration. By contacting the region registry, other entities (e.g., agents or human users) are able to locate agents, places, and agent systems residing in a region. Besides, a region registry facilitates the connection establishment between agent systems or agents.

Two types of agents are distinguished: mobile agents are able to move from one physical network location (agent system A in Figure 5.3.1) to another one (agent system B); stationary agents, instead, are bound to the agent system where they have been installed and where they remain for their whole life time to provide a place persistent service according to the C/S model of interaction.

Common Capabilities emerging in MA Platforms. In course of time, several fundamental requirements have been identified due to the experiences made during research and development activities in the MA area. These requirements are fulfilled by any state-of-the-art MA platform, and their identification is the first fundamental step towards the definition of a common and interoperable distributed middleware to support mobile agents in the Internet scenario. The implementation of a modern MA system requires middleware components to support:

- *Agent Execution* - An MA platform must provide the basic capability to put incoming mobile agents into execution, taking into account possible agent-specific requirements regarding the runtime environment (e.g., binding to specified local resources). The platform has to retrieve the agent code that may be either delivered with the migration request or downloaded separately from an external code base;
- *Transport* - A special mobility support must be provided by the platform, not only to facilitate the network transport of agent code and execution state, but also to permit MA system administrators to command remote execution and migration. Note that both agent execution and transport cannot be sufficiently handled without a strict interworking with the security support mentioned in the following;
- *Unique Identification* - Mobile agents as well as agent systems have to be uniquely identifiable in the scope of the entire Internet environment. Thus, special support is required for the generation of unique agent and agent system identifiers;
- *Communication* - Agents should be able to communicate with each other as well as with platform services. Several mechanisms are possible, such as messages, method invocation, object sharing and tuple-spaces, with different levels of expressive power and of temporal/spatial coupling between coordinating entities. Communication through messages may be done point-to-point, by multicasting, or by broadcasting. In addition, several MA communication modules include support for semantic analysis;
- *Security* - Basic issues are authentication (i.e., the determination of the identity of an agent or an agent system), and access control of resources/services depending on the authenticated identity of the requesting entity. To guarantee privacy and integrity, crucial information such as code and state of a migrating agent should exploit public-key cryptographic encryption before transfer over an untrusted network;
- *Management* - It is necessary for agent administrators to be able to monitor and control their agents, also remotely. Control functions include temporary interruption of the execution of an agent task, agent premature

termination, and modification of its task list. The monitoring of an agent is associated with its localization in the scope of the whole distributed environment. Regarding an agent system, all hosted agents as well as the occupied system resources have to be monitored and controlled, possibly to notice and avoid denial-of-service attacks.

Figure 5.3.1 shows the structure of a core agent system that includes several services in order to fulfil the basic functional requirements identified above. Note that some of the services provide remote interfaces in order to be accessible by external actors, such as other agent systems, agents, or human users.

Apart from the basic capabilities shown in the Figure, additional ones have been taken into consideration in some of the most recent and evolved MA platforms [284, 563]. The most relevant one in the context of this chapter is certainly the interoperability module, offered to permit the integration of heterogeneous agents and agent systems with already existing services and legacy components. This interoperability is obtained via compliance with emerging standards in the MA area, all based upon the CORBA middleware, and is the object of the whole Section 5.4. Other capabilities have started to be accepted as fundamental and tend to be integrated in MA platforms. For instance, a persistency service can permit to temporarily suspend executing agents and to store them on a persistent medium. Persistency allows agents not to waste system resources while they are waiting for external events such as the reconnection of one user or terminal where they have to yield back the results of their operations. In addition, a module for the support of mobile computing is provided in some MA systems to accommodate the nomadicity of users, terminals and service components, which can move with no need to suspend offered/accessed services; it is the MA distributed middleware that maintains traceability of the mobile entities and re-organizes accordingly the service provision [63]. These additional features usually benefit from the modular organization of MA platforms and should be handled as add-ons that can be "plugged" into a core MA system to dynamically extend its basic functionality.

5.4 Middleware Technologies: the Integration of MA and CORBA

The two previous sections should have put into evidence the several differences between MA and CORBA as enabling technologies to implement distributed middleware for Internet service provision. The most evident one is that CORBA tends to suggest a model where objects are allocated once and for all at a fixed location before their registration at the CORBA ORB, while mobile agents can dynamically and autonomously migrate during execution depending on time-dependent system conditions. It is possible in CORBA to

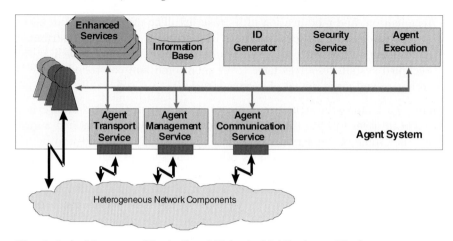

Fig. 5.4. Architecture of Basic Capabilities in Mobile Agent Platforms.

mimic a certain kind of object mobility by replicating different instances of the same object at different locations and by tailoring the object adapter to forward different client requests for the same object to the different locations hosting one of its replicas. This replication (with the consequent issues of maintaining consistency in case of writable replicas) can be motivated by objectives of fault-tolerance, scalability and load balancing. However, the single instance of the CORBA object is thought to be at a fixed location for its whole lifetime, possibly activated/deactivated automatically by the CORBA object adapter.

Another relevant point of difference is the fact that mobile agents are entities aware of their current locations and of the locations of needed resources (e.g., other agents, execution places, service components), since this awareness is basic to permit dynamic decisions about agent migration. On the contrary, CORBA tends to hide the physical location of a server object when answering to a client invocation. Obviously, the ORB has visibility of the allocation of registered objects, but this information is typically not visible to client objects and application designers. This is coherent with the principles that inspired the CORBA specification and design, that is to simplify as much as possible the programmer duties while implementing services in distributed systems, by giving the impression of the availability of a local concentrated computing environment. In addition, due to its origins in the traditional area of distributed computing, CORBA suggests a C/S model of interaction between its objects while mobile agents, also because of the influence of the multi-agent research community, typically adopt a peer-to-peer model of interaction. However, the distinction is not so rigid either in CORBA, since CORBA objects can play the role of both clients and servers during their lifetime.

All above differences between CORBA and MA technologies stem from their different vision of the role and objectives that a distributed middleware must have in the support of application design, implementation and deployment. CORBA has been thought mainly to simplify the duties of distributed service implementers, by providing a transparent middleware that is in charge of solving the largest part of the issues related to the integration of distributed and heterogeneous components. From a certain point of view, the CORBA middleware tends to take some decisions in place of programmers, by leaving them the specification of even articulated and complex policies (e.g., for object activation, security, replication and persistency). On the contrary, the MA-based distributed supports have generally grown from the bottom, by first providing the mobility capacity to objects, and then trying to organize common capabilities into a layered architecture. This architecture aims at simplifying the work of application designers by supporting most common functionality, in order to avoid useless duplications of design work and implementation code. In MA-based infrastructures, application programmers usually have complete visibility of the operational environment where agents execute, and have the opportunity whether to exploit or not the provided mechanisms and services.

Finally, the last relevant distinction between CORBA- and MA-based middleware infrastructures is that, at the moment, CORBA has reached a widely accepted standardization and has a very large installed base of compliant resources, systems and service components. On the contrary, mainly due to the novelty of the MA technology, the research on mobile agents has produced a great variety of different and non-interoperable MA platforms, where the common facilities provided at the middleware layer are strictly dependent of the specific platform used.

All these considerations suggest that the two presented middleware solutions have not to be considered alternative the one to the other, but they can integrate and complement very well. In fact, a flexible middleware for the realization of Internet services can significantly benefit from the expressive power of agent mobility at run-time together with the possibility of transparent remote agent coordination, from the availability of different degrees of visibility of resources in the global system together with the capacity of simply integrating legacy service components via standard interfaces. System- and application-specific considerations typically guide the selection of the most suitable characteristics to exploit; for this reason, we claim that a general-purpose middleware solution for the Internet scenario should give service designers the possibility to dynamically choose the proper solution among a wide variety of available ones.

To show the opportunity of the integration of CORBA and MA, the following of the section reports two notable examples. On the one hand, in the area of the extension of MA platforms to achieve interoperability, we present the two most relevant research activities that have led to the specification of the MASIF [401] and FIPA [240] standards. It is not a case that both the proposals, even if coming from different research communities and different scientific backgrounds, adopt CORBA as the standard bridge to overcome heterogeneity. On the other hand, in the area of the extension of the CORBA distributed middleware, we shortly describe the work undergoing in the OMG towards the definition of a CORBA migration service [187]. We will show, in particular, how the migration service calls for a set of basic middleware facilities that are very similar to the ones identified and implemented in the most diffused MA platforms.

5.4.1 MA Integration with CORBA-based Standards

The international standardization of agents started relatively late in 1997. Two main forums have to be considered in the context of agent standardization today, namely the OMG, which has initially investigated MA system interoperability aspects and is currently looking at the integration of distributed object and agent technologies, including both intelligent and mobile agents, and the Foundation for Intelligent Physical Agents (FIPA) [240], which mainly focuses on intelligent (co-operative) agents. In the following, we look in more detail at the OMG and FIPA agent standards and to describe how they exploit the underlying CORBA distributed middleware to permit the interworking of heterogeneous Internet agents.

OMG Mobile Agent Systems Interoperability Facility. Interoperability among different MA systems is, in our opinion, a key issue for widening the diffusion of MA-based commercial Internet services. At the same time the goal of interoperability requires the identification of the aspects in the MA technology subject to standardization.

Recognizing the emergence of different MA systems, which are based on different approaches regarding implementation languages, protocols, platform architectures and functionality, the OMG aimed for a standard to ensure the interoperability between heterogeneous MA platforms and the (re-)usability of (legacy) CORBA services by means of agent-based components. Therefore OMG ORB and Object Services (ORBOS) Group issued a Request for Proposal for an MA facility in November 1995 that resulted in a corresponding Mobile Agent System Interoperability Facility (MASIF) specification adopted in 1997 [401]. MASIF is built within the CORBA framework and shows the interest in integration between CORBA distributed objects and mobile agents.

The idea behind the MASIF standard is to achieve a certain degree of interoperability between MA platforms of different manufacturers without enforcing radical platform modifications. MASIF is not intended to build the basis for any new MA system. Instead, the provided specifications shall be used as an "add-on" module to plug-in to already existing systems. The standard includes CORBA IDL specifications supporting agent transport and management, including localization capabilities. It has to be stated that the

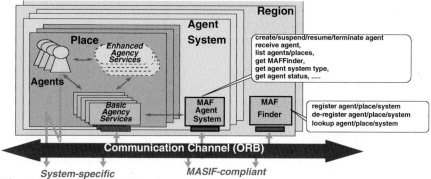

Fig. 5.5. OMG MASIF Interfaces.

target of agent transport between different agent systems is not fully enabled through the given specifications. This transport capability would only become possible through mutual agreements on a common agent exchange format of MA system vendors.

As shown in Figure 5.4.1, MASIF has adopted the concepts of places and regions that are used by various existing agent platforms (see Grasshopper and SOMA in Section 5.5). A place groups the functionality within an agent system, encapsulating certain capabilities and restrictions for visiting agents. A region facilitates the platform management by specifying sets of agent systems that belong to a single authority and possibly are mapped to a physical network locality (e.g., a Local Area Network).

MASIF does not suggest standardization of local agent operations such as agent interpretation, serialization, execution and deserialization, because these actions are application specific, and there is no reason to limit MA system implementations. Instead, MASIF only proposes standardization for agent and agent system names, for agent system types and for location syntax. It specifies two interfaces: the MAFAgentSystem interface provides operations for the management and transfer of agents, whereas the MAFFinder interface supports the localization of agents and MA systems in the scope of an administered locality. A MAFAgentSystem object should interact internally with MA system-specific services, and provides the associated CORBA interface to external users.

Any external system can control agents of a MASIF-compliant MA system via the MAFAgentSystem interface: MASIF defines methods for suspending/resuming/terminating agents and for moving agents from one MA platform to another one. The interoperation is significant only when the two interworking systems present a compatibility base, that is the same implementation language, or compatible externalization mechanisms. Agent tracking functions permit the tracing of agents registered with MAFFinder, introduced to provide an MA name service, because the CORBA Naming Service is not suitable for entities that are intrinsically and frequently mobile. Agent communication is outside the scope of MASIF (while it is the focus of other MA standardization proposals, such as FIPA, described in the following): SOMA agents communicate via proprietary mechanisms, but they may also decide to use the CORBA middleware for object communication.

As part of any MASIF-compliant agent system, the MAFAgentSystem object interacts internally with platform-specific services while it provides the associated CORBA interface to external users. In this way, it is possible to communicate with an agent system either in a MASIF-compliant way (using the MAFAgentSystem interface and the CORBA ORB) or in a platform-specific way (using platform-specific interfaces that may provide additional functionality, not handled by MASIF).

Apart from the agent-specific CORBA interfaces MAFAgentSystem and MAFFinder, the MASIF standard explains in detail how existing CORBA services, e.g., the Naming, Life Cycle, Externalization, and Security Service, can be used by agent-based components to enhance the provided functionality. For instance, interoperability also means opening MA systems to new security threats coming from the interaction with external components. The MASIF standard recognizes the need for security and for its management: all MASIF implementations are required to introduce security mechanisms, policies and tools, built upon the CORBA Security Services in order to overcome the possible heterogeneity in the security solutions adopted by the interworking components.

Note that the current MASIF specification only represents the first approach for an MA standard. It is believed that the work of the OMG Agent Platform Special Interest Group will result in further specifications. For more details on MASIF, see [401].

Foundation for Intelligent Physical Agents. FIPA is a non-profit association whose purpose is to promote agent technology through the development of specifications that maximize interoperability across agent-based applications, services and equipment [240]. FIPA specifies the interfaces of the different components in the environment with which an agent can interact, i.e., humans, other agents, non-agent software and the physical world. Being mainly composed by researchers with background in the intelligent agent area, FIPA puts main emphasis on the standardization of agent communication, and a dedicated Agent Communication Language (ACL) is proposed for all communication between FIPA agents.

FIPA specifications are developed in a yearly manner. In October 1997, FIPA released its first set of specifications (FIPA'97, Version 1.0) [240]. The three main specifications (parts 1-3) focus on agent management (in particular, defining a FIPA agent platform), define an agent communication language, and deal with agent/software interaction.

The Agent Management System specification provides the normative framework within which FIPA Agents exist and operate. It establishes the logical reference model for the creation, registration, location, communica-

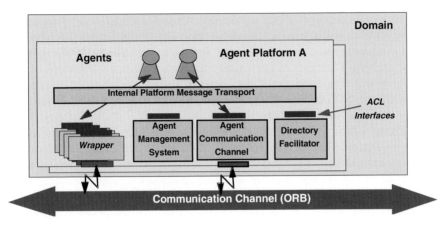

Fig. 5.6. FIPA Agent Management Reference Model.

tion, migration and retirement of agents and thus is very much related to capabilities of a FIPA agent platform. Figure 5.4.1 depicts the agent management reference model. FIPA proposes the concept of an Agent Platform (AP) offering three basic services. These services are namely the Agent Management System (AMS), the Directory Facilitator (DF) and the Agent Communication Channel (ACC). Agents may offer their services to other agents and make their services searchable in a yellow pages manner by the DF. Registration on a DF is optionally while registering on the AMS is mandatory on any agent platform. Finally, the ACC is enabling agent communication between agents on a platform and between possibly heterogeneous platforms, by offering a message forwarding service. Reachability between platforms is gained by making the forward service available over the CORBA ORB whose integration is considered mandatory for any FIPA-compliant MA platform. Agent messages are transferred via CORBA IIOP.

The AMS is the core of any agent platform. It is responsible for registering agents on their home agent platform. Registering on an AMS is done by calling the AMS message method with a request to register encoded in the FIPA ACL. Other functionality offered by the AMS is deregistering of agents, modification of the agent description and modifying the agents life cycle state. The DF offers services similar to those of the AMS, but with an additional search functionality. Thus, the DF acts as a yellow pages directory where agents may register to offer their services in a dynamic manner to other agents. The registration is done in the same way as with the AMS. Agents can deregister with the DF by calling the deregister service.

If the AMS and DF services provide functionality that are similar to the MASIF MAFAgentSystem and MAFFinder, a peculiar characteristic of the FIPA standardization proposal is the concept of agent communication by means of a special ACL. Agents have predictable behaviour by common semantics defined in common interpretation of a common language. This is achieved by the concept of communication acts. The registering of an agent with an AMS is realized as a communication act of the action registration. In this communication act the roles of the agent and the AMS are clearly defined and the reactions of each party are determined by the state of the agent platform. For instance, if the agent is already registered, it is clearly defined that it can not be registered again, and an answer message denoting exactly this must be sent to the agent.

FIPA proposes the implementation of a communication channel (ACC) per agent system that is responsible for forwarding the ACL messages between agents. As platform local communication is free to the implementor of an MA system, it is clear that the simplest solution for local communication between agents is realized by the platform native communication protocol. Inter-platform communication, that means communication between agents on different and possibly heterogeneous platforms, is mandatory to be realized by offering the forward service over CORBA IIOP.

Integration of OMG MASIF and FIPA Concepts. As can be observed from the above presentations, the OMG MASIF architecture puts more emphasis on the physical migration/operation support for mobile agents and on their physical object view, while FIPA has more emphasis on the logical and service view. This difference reflects the different focal points and constitutions of the two organizations. It is interesting to note that, notwithstanding their different perspectives and research background, both have decided to specify their middleware proposals on top of the CORBA standard.

Both MASIF mobile agent and FIPA intelligent agent approaches aim at adaptive and flexible interoperability and coordination among dynamic autonomous systems. Some correspondences between concepts in the MASIF and FIPA frameworks are particularly significant because they come from different research communities, and can play an important role in the future evolutions and in the convergence of the agent standardization efforts. In this context, it is worth to observe that:

– a mobile agent in the MASIF framework specifies a kind of message which migrates between software systems and has the similar functionality as an intelligent agent communication message in FIPA framework. The current MASIF middleware does not support MA communications, but a flexible and rich communication capability should be integrated in any MA platform for the provision of Internet services. With such communication capability, a mobile agent will also have the features of an intelligent agent in FIPA;
– a place in the MASIF framework provides the operation environment for the mobile agents, with its capabilities (local services) and restrictions. Examples of such capabilities and restrictions can be database services, network resource management functions, security monitoring and management. All these capabilities are supported by special intelligent agents within the FIPA agent platform;

- The MASIF agent system is the group of places that provides the platform for mobile agent migrations and operations. Therefore a MASIF-compliant agent system corresponds to a FIPA agent platform. More specifically, the DF and AMS in FIPA framework corresponds, respectively, to the `MAFFinder` and `MAFAgentSystem` functions in MASIF, while the other MASIF agent system component/services (offered to mobile agents via places) become specific intelligent agent services within a FIPA agent platform (e.g., wrapper, resource broker, and other intelligent agents for specific applications).

It is obvious that both intelligent agent and mobile agent religions have their strength and weakness in the versatile application fields for the agent technology. Therefore it is very likely that both paradigms will converge in the near future. A more detailed discussion of these aspects can be found in [660]. Nevertheless we have briefly tried to show in this section that both intelligent and mobile agents have a lot of commonalties in regard to the capabilities required to the distributed middleware for their support in an open and global scenario. These similarities suggest the realization of a common and flexible CORBA-based middleware for the provision of Internet services designed according to the agent programming paradigm.

5.4.2 Mobile CORBA Objects - Towards a CORBA Migration Service

As a further sign of the importance of code mobility in the provision of modern distributed middleware for Internet services, the OMG ORBOS Task Force has recently started to work on the possibility to integrate object mobility into a CORBA environment, by extending the OMA with a dedicated CORBA service for migration [187]. The objective is to design a flexible and unified CORBA environment, supporting both remote interactions and object migration, by considering already existing CORBA services as a basis, determining missing functionality, and specifying a minimal set of new functionality in order to fill the gap.

The proposed service model is composed by the Life Cycle and Externalization services and uses the Naming Service for identification and resolving matters [188]. The Life Cycle specification provides conventions for creating, deleting, copying, and moving objects, while the Externalization service is used for the serialization/deserialization (marshalling/unmarshalling) procedure of objects needed for the transfer operation.

A mobile CORBA object - in short, mobile object - is a set of traditional CORBA objects, forming a unit of computational community. Such a mobile object provides multiple CORBA interface implementations. An instance of it has the ability to migrate from one physical network location to another one, without loosing its internal state. By definition, a mobile object is transformed into a package, which includes the object code and possibly a

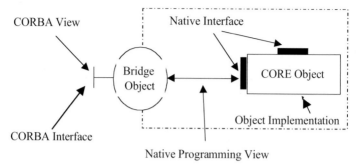

Fig. 5.7. The Structure of a Mobile Object According to the OMG Migration Service RFP.

serialized version of its state. The state consists of the contents of the instance variables, so-called data state, and the execution state. Nevertheless, since the execution state is rather physical, this state should be manually coded into the data state which will make the implementation of the migration easier. The mobile object package can then be delivered to another location or be preserved within a database for persistency purposes. By transforming back this package, a new mobile object is created and reinstated with the preserved state. The creation and reinstatement of a mobile object can be either done from templates (classes) or by cloning an existing instance. In the connection with mobility, it should be noted that migrating an object means to freeze its execution at one location and to continue it at a different location. It is not a copy, since only one instance is running at a time.

The basic structure of a mobile object is relatively simple. There are two kinds of object types, a core (containing the state) object type, also referred to as object implementation, and a bridge (stateless) object type, which represents a CORBA object, i.e., it is visible through an IDL interface. Figure 5.4.2 shows the proposed structure for a mobile object. A core object type contains the state of a mobile object and a set of local interfaces, and its implementation must be completely local. This object has no identity and is not registered with the ORB. The realization of the provided service is contained within this object that supports local interfaces (API) and can be composed by native implementation objects.

The OMG ORBOS claims that mobile objects need a run-time environment that supports their entire life cycle, including their creation, termination, and migration. Besides, users must be able to monitor and control their objects. The basic procedures of the distributed middleware for mobile objects that have started to be identified by the ORBOS are exactly the same ones we have presented in Subsection 5.3.1 as basic capabilities emerging in MA platforms. In particular, the migration of mobile objects can be split into the following procedures:

– Externalizing (marshalling) the object execution and data state;

- Packing the externalized state and the code into a stream and transfer it to the receiving side;
- Creating and reinstating the serialized state by internalizing (unmarshalling) the stream into a new object instance at the receiving side;
- Finally, removing the instance at the sending side.

The new instance at the receiving side is not identical with the one at the sending side. After the removal of the instance at the sending side, in fact, the CORBA objects associated with the new mobile object instance at the receiving side have to register themselves to the ORB and thus, will receive new Inter-Orb References (IORs) associated to them. In the specification of the GIOP, an approach for handling this IOR modification is given: an ORB must provide so-called agents which are responsible for handling client incoming requests. Such an agent has the following possibilities to handle client requests if the IOR specified by the client is not associated with an active object (e.g., object has moved to another destination), with different degrees of migration transparency for the final CORBA client:

- It knows the new IOR of the object and forwards the request to the new address. The result of the request is sent from the object back to the agent which forwards it back to the client. This is achieved transparently to the client which means that the client is not aware of the forwarding procedure and of the new server side location;
- It knows the new location of the object, but is not able to forward the request to the object. Instead, the agent delivers the new IOR to the client which is then able to establish a new connection to the object at the new location;
- It is not aware of the new IOR and returns an exception to the client, indicating that the object is not any more reachable. In this case, the client may retrieve the current IOR of the object by contacting either the Naming Service or a trader. For this purpose, it is necessary that the object must have its entries modified in either the Naming Service or the trader, respectively.

5.5 CORBA/MA Integrated Supports: Grasshopper and SOMA

Our claim about the suitability of the integration of CORBA and MA technologies is exemplified by two emerging MA platforms that have been developed in the last years with different features and objectives.

Grasshopper is a commercial MA platform realized jointly by TUB OKS, GMD FOKUS and IKV++ GmbH [284]. Grasshopper is a development platform and run-time support, built on top of a DAE that integrates mobile agents with the traditional C/S paradigm by exploiting CORBA as a standard bridge for interoperability. Grasshopper is based on the Java 2 programming environment and its newest version is compliant with the MASIF and FIPA specifications.

Secure and Open Mobile Agents (SOMA) is an MA platform, resulting from a research project at the University of Bologna [563]. SOMA has not been realized for commercial purposes, but mainly to explore and propose innovative solutions to still open issues in the MA technology (e.g., the protection of the state of mobile agents against malicious executing environments [189], and the integration of differentiated naming services for mobile computing in the Internet scenario [63]). SOMA is implemented in the Java 2 programming framework, is designed according to the architecture principles of the Telecommunications Information Networking Architecture, and specifically focuses on the provision of a wide set of facilities for security and interoperability.

Thanks to the deep integration of both Grasshopper and SOMA with CORBA, the two platforms are extensively used in application domains that are characterized by a high degree of resource heterogeneity and the frequent presence of legacy systems and services. In the following, we will briefly describe the distributed middleware architecture implemented by the Grasshopper and SOMA platforms and we will present how the integration of MA and CORBA is strategic for the implementation of Grasshopper-based enhanced Intelligent Networks (IN) services and of SOMA-based Quality of Service (QoS) management of multimedia flows.

5.5.1 Grasshopper and the Telecommunication Domain

Grasshopper realizes a DAE composed by regions, places, agent systems (called agencies) and different types of agents, as described in Section 5.3. A Grasshopper agency consists of two parts: the core agency and one or more places. Core agencies represent the minimal functionality required by an agency in order to support the execution of agents. The following basic capabilities are provided by a Grasshopper core agency (see Figure 5.5.1):

- *Communication and Transport Service.* This service is responsible for all remote interactions that take place between the distributed components of Grasshopper, such as location-transparent inter-agent communication, agent transport, and the localization of agents by means of the region registry. All interactions can be performed via IIOP, Java Remote Method Invocation (RMI) [282], or plain socket connections. Optionally, RMI and plain socket connections can be protected by means of the Secure Socket Layer (SSL) [589] that is nowadays a widely diffused Internet security protocol. The communication service supports synchronous and asynchronous communication, multicast communication, as well as dynamic method invocation. As an alternative to the communication service, Grasshopper can use its OMG MASIF-compliant CORBA interfaces for remote interactions. For this purpose, each agency provides the interface `MAFAgentSystem`, and the region registries provide the interface `MAFFinder`;

- *Registration Service.* Each agency is able to know about all agents and places currently hosted, both for external management purposes and for delivering information about registered entities to hosted agents. Furthermore, the registration service of each agency is connected to the region registry which maintains information of agents, agencies and places in the scope of a whole region;
- *Security Service.* It supports mechanisms for external and internal security. External security protects remote interactions between the distributed components of the Grasshopper middleware, i.e., between agencies and region registries. For this purpose, SSL and X.509 certificates are used [232]. By using SSL, confidentiality, data integrity, and mutual authentication of both communication partners can be achieved. Internal security protects agency resources from unauthorized access by agents. Besides, it is used to protect agents from each other. This is achieved by authenticating and authorizing the user on whose behalf an agent is executed. Due to the authentication/authorization results, access control policies are activated. The internal security capabilities are mainly based on Java 2 security mechanisms;
- *Persistency Service.* It enables the storage of agents and places (the internal information maintained inside these components) on a persistent medium. This way, it is possible to recover agents or places when needed, e.g., when an agency is restarted after a system crash;
- *Management Service.* It allows the monitoring and control of agents and places of an agency by Grasshopper system administrators. It is possible, among others, to create, remove, suspend and resume agents, services, and places; in addition, the management middleware component permits to get information about specific agents and services, to list all agents residing in a specific place, and to list all places of an agency.

Apart from these core services, any Grasshopper agency implements two modules for compliance with MASIF (the `MAFAgentSystem` component is present in any agency, while there is only one `MAFFinder` for any region) and FIPA, both based on an underlying CORBA ORB. A peculiarity of the Grasshopper MA platform with respect to other CORBA-integrated MA systems, such as SOMA (presented in Subsection 5.5.2), is that Grasshopper realizes some forms of location transparency for its mobile agents. It is as if the Grasshopper focus on interoperability and its tight integration with CORBA have superimposed the location transparency of the CORBA standard on the location awareness typical of the MA programming paradigm. The result is that not only that Grasshopper agents do not care about the location of a desired communication peer, but also that there is no difference between remote method invocations and local method invocations within the agent

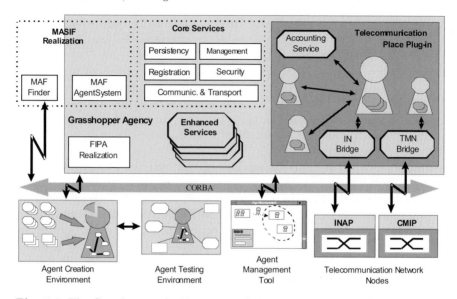

Fig. 5.8. The Grasshopper Architecture and the Telecommunication Place "Plug-in".

code. The last feature is achieved by means of proxy objects that are directly accessed by a client agent. The proxy object forwards the call via the ORB to the remote target object. In this way, these proxy objects are equivalent to the client stubs used by CORBA implementations.

This kind of location transparency certainly simplifies the programming work in the implementation of MA-based services, but it may significantly limit the visibility of designers when realizing applications that must have a high degree of knowledge about the hosting environment, such as in the domains of performance monitoring and distributed management [62]. For this reason, other MA platforms pursue integration with CORBA without exploiting its ORB for agent operations in "homogeneous" environments, i.e., within their proprietary agent systems, even if, however, they usually provide location transparency for peer communications [563].

Grasshopper is a very complete MA programming environment also for the rich variety of support tools offered to MA application designers (see Figure 5.5.1). An agent creation environment enables the "plug and play" composition of mobile agents out of reusable functional building blocks. An agent testing environment allows for the simulation of the whole distributed environment by means of a single agency, so that the entire execution of an agent can be simulated locally, without endangering the real resources. Finally, a graphical agent management tool enables the monitoring and control of agents and agencies in the scope of one or more regions.

Special emphasis lies on the opportunity to easily enhance the platform capabilities in order to fulfil individual needs, depending on concrete application scenarios. To achieve this goal, a Grasshopper core agency comprises only those capabilities that are inevitably necessary for the support of mobile agents. Additional, application-dependent functionality is realized by modular and reusable building blocks. Examples of such building blocks are adapter services for the access to telecommunication hardware for IN service provision, based on either proprietary protocols/technologies or compliance with CORBA.

In fact, one emerging application area of the MA technology is the telecommunications sector. The following section tries to outline how the current IN architecture can be enhanced significantly and flexibly by means of mobile agents, in particular if they are integrated with interoperability standards. For information about the basics of INs, please refer to [391].

MA-based IN Service Provision. The current IN architecture is C/S-based. The Service Switching Points (SSPs) act as clients, requesting the execution of service logic from the Service Control Points (SCPs), acting as servers. This architecture provides several important advantages, e.g., the opportunity to create or modify network capabilities without any changes at the switches. However, due to the rising number of service users and the increasing number of provided IN services, the centralized SCPs are likely to become the bottleneck of the whole system. Even now the SCP capacity is temporarily overdrawn. Besides, the deployment and subscription of services by the Service Management System (SMS) is not efficient and open enough to handle the demands of the emerging open service market. Finally, due to the centralized architecture, an SCP server failure would cause immense costs for service providers.

Because of these limitations, the adoption of standard distributed object technology, such as CORBA, has been considered in the IN world in the last 1990s. Also taking this into account, some research projects have proposed the introduction of the MA technology, when integrated with the CORBA middleware, into the IN environment in order to achieve ultimate flexibility [392]. This means that enhanced IN services can be implemented by either CORBA objects and/or by mobile agents on top of CORBA.

Focusing specifically on the last issue, the realization of IN services in terms of mobile agents can extend the traditional IN model in several ways. Services can be provided time-dependently, i.e., installed for a limited time duration. Distributed provision of services and service components can enable load balancing in the network. Finally, the service management can be facilitated by dynamically installing, maintaining and extending ad-hoc management agents only on those network nodes where they are currently needed.

Figure 5.5.1 depicts the proposed approach. The main idea is to introduce services on demand and ultimately distribute service logic and data from the centralized SCP to switches and final user devices by means of mobile agents. To support agent technology, the different network nodes should

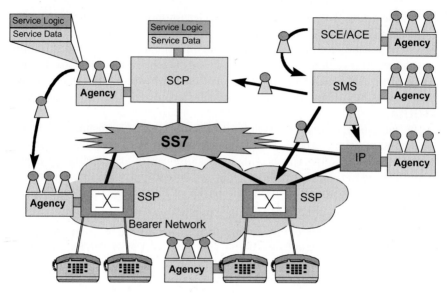

Fig. 5.9. MA-based IN Architecture.

contain Grasshopper agencies. In this way, agents representing IN service logic and data can be sent dynamically to those network locations where the functionality is currently required. An agent-enhanced Service Creation Environment (SCE) allows to develop appropriate IN service logic and data, including the envisaged itinerary of the agent. The outlined integrated approach, combining both agent and C/S technology, allows to enhance the current IN architecture instead of completely removing it [392]. Note that the agent transport shown in Figure 5.5.1 is not performed via the IN standard signalling system no.7 (SS7), but instead via a CORBA-based data network that interconnects the agencies.

The Grasshopper agents implemented for IN service provision consist of two parts. The first part (core component) is devoted to the agent nature of being an autonomous mobile entity: it includes all functionality required for agent lifecycle management and mobility support, and these functions are realized by strongly interworking with Grasshopper agency services.

The second part (application component) is related to the provision of the specific IN service, e.g., the control and management of telecommunications switches. Therefore, the agent application part contains appropriate IN logic and data, and makes use of either external interfaces (e.g., INAP interface at the switch and SCP) or adapted interfaces already offered within the agency (e.g., a CORBA object mapping INAP operations into CORBA object invocations, as depicted in Figure 5.5.1). In the first case traditional IN logic may be used, whereas in the second case advanced logic based on object-oriented programming may be used. Note that the availability of the second choice also permits the fast prototyping and deployment of functionality for service subscription, customization, and service logic maintenance (including appropriate GUIs).

Three kinds of actors are involved in the Grasshopper solution: a Web-accessible agent provider, a customer representing a company or organization, and various final users. Each actor requires access to an agency. Additional agencies are connected to the different network elements, i.e. SCP and switches. Figure 5.5.1 presents the scenario, which is initiated by the customer accessing the provider via the Internet and requesting an IN service agent (0). The provider sends the requested agent to the customer (1) who is now able to pre-configure it (2). The pre-configuration comprises the selection of desired final users and the specification of their various access restrictions. Afterwards, the service agent is sent to the final users (3) where it is supplied with individual service logic configurations (4). Before the agent executes its designed task, it automatically migrates back to the provider (5) to allow security checks, e.g., the determination of code modifications (6). Only if the security checks have been successful, the agent moves to a specific network node. Three possibilities are taken into account: agents representing global services (e.g., free phone) migrate to the agency connected to the centralized SCP (7a); agents realizing called party services (e.g., call forwarding) move to the agency at the called party switch (7b); agents representing calling party services (e.g., abbreviated dialing) move to the agency at the calling party switch (7c). After reaching their destination agency, the agents connect themselves to specific IN service adapters that can either be realized by enhanced agency services or in turn by special (stationary) agents. Finally, the service execution starts (8a-8c).

5.5.2 SOMA and the Management Domain

SOMA is an MA-based programming framework designed to support the easy definition, deployment and tailoring of general-purpose network-centric services. In the following, however, apart from briefly presenting the architecture of the SOMA DAE, we will concentrate specifically on its application to the management of distributed and heterogeneous network resources, systems and services. In this domain, SOMA has already achieved interesting results [61, 62], also due to its full integration with the standard CORBA technology.

The main idea in applying SOMA agents to the management domain is that mobile agents can fulfil administration needs by moving and executing on different nodes. Automation of control is obtained through the possibility of delegating management actions to agents, that act autonomously and in a completely asynchronous fashion with respect to the administrator, thus relieving her duty; for instance, one agent can automatically take care of software upgrading on dynamically selected nodes of a managed network. Mobile agents permit to adapt to system modifications by tuning the behaviour of

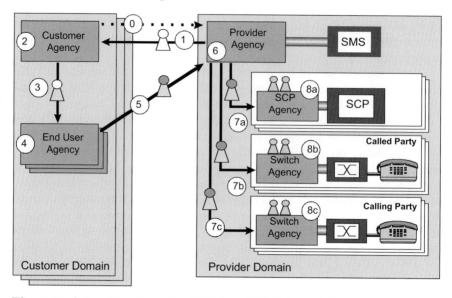

Fig. 5.10. A Provision Scenario of MA-based IN Enhanced Services.

network resources and services at run-time; for instance, any administrator can modify and propagate security policies at any time, with no need to shut-down the whole system, by dynamically instantiating new mobile agents to propagate the new policies in the administered domains.

Also SOMA realizes a DAE consisting of regions (called domains), places and different types of agents, as described in Section 5.3. The SOMA DAE offers a distributed middleware with a rich set of interacting and coordinated facilities for the design and development of complex network-centric applications. In addition, the openness property of the SOMA infrastructure [64] permits to extend the programming framework by dynamically adding new services, even built on the already provided functionality.

SOMA DAE facilities are split in two levels, the lower one that groups the basic and primary mechanisms, the upper one that comprehends more evolved tools and services, as depicted in Figure 5.5.2. The SOMA Upper Layer Facilities (ULF) represent advanced operations and support directly the development of applications and services (see [64] for details):

– *Agent Interoperability Facility (AIF)* - The AIF offers interfaces to simplify the calls from SOMA components (included either in the DPE layer or in the service one) to external CORBA components or services. In addition, it supports the registration of SOMA-based services as CORBA servers and, finally, it provides interoperability with different MA systems by implementing the MASIF standard interface;

– *Agent Security Facility (ASF)* - The ASF provides all the mechanisms for authentication, authorization, integrity and privacy. SOMA integrates a

security framework based on standard security providers and certificate infrastructures [318, 226]. The current ASF implementation is based on agents but can also interoperate with CORBA Security Services [188];
- *Agent QoS Facility (AQoSF)* - The AQoSF provides both QoS monitoring and adaptation functionality. It is in charge of observing resource properties, from disk free space to effectively available network bandwidth, from CPU usage to allocated space in heap memory for any thread, thanks to the integration with the Java Virtual Machine Profiler Interface (JVMPI) [343] and with platform-dependent monitoring modules via the Java Native Interface (JNI) [280]. Any authorized mobile service can access the monitored properties, and, depending on this information, can decide a strategy suitable for adapting to the current environment conditions, without suspending service provision (see also Subsection 5.5.2 about the dynamic adaptation of multimedia streams).

The AIF, ASF and AQoSF can make use of the lower facilities in their implementation; for instance, the QoS facility exploits the underlying coordination facility to command collaborative operations to try to restore the requested quality after the degradation of a network link. The SOMA Lower Layer Facilities (LLF) include:

- *Agent Coordination Facility (ACF)* - The ACF provides mechanisms and tools to simplify coordination and communication between entities. Agents in the same place interact by means of shared objects, such as blackboards and reactive tuple spaces [114]. Any place hosts a Local Resource Manager module that regulates agent access to the node resources. This module controls the authorization of agents and enforces the place security policy. Whenever one agent needs to share one resource with another agent that resides in a remote place, it is forced to migrate to that place. Outside the scope of the place, agents can perform coordinated tasks by exchanging messages delivered to agents even in case of migration;
- *Agent Migration Facility (AMF)* - The AMF gives service designers the possibility to simply reallocate network resources and service components at run-time. Entities capable of reallocation are represented by agents, that can move in the network either via MA native migration methods or via standard interfaces such as MASIF over CORBA IIOP;
- *Agent Naming Facility (ANF)* - A basic identification mechanism permits to dynamically assign tags to any entity in the system. Globally unique identifiers are the basis for the realization of the multiple naming systems provided by the ANF that puts together a set of different naming systems, possibly characterized by different policies. For example, it realizes a Domain Name Service and a Directory Service functionality. The ANF dynamically maintains and permits to access the information about the current state of any (possibly mobile) entity in the SOMA distributed middleware.

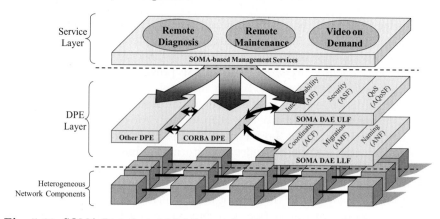

Fig. 5.11. SOMA Distributed Middleware for Management Applications.

The above facilities are available in different flavours, depending on system and service needs. For instance, the ANF, currently permits the coexistence of the SOMA proprietary naming service deriving from DNS with the CORBA Naming Service. Other LDAP-compliant naming and directory services are under integration to let users and designers choose among multiple name spaces [313]. System- and application-specific considerations typically guide the selection of the available facilities to use; for this reason, a flexible management environment has to give service designers the possibility to choose the proper solution among a wide variety of available ones.

SOMA-based Resource and Service Management. SOMA provides a wide range of management tools, from the monitoring of the state of the distributed system to the possibility to control and coordinate replicated resources, from the dynamic installation and configuration of new network resources to the optimization of access to replicated information by considering both current traffic level and query locality. The full integration with CORBA and the implementation of the MASIF interface gives to SOMA management agents the capacity of interworking in different contexts (see Figure 5.5.2):

- any SOMA service can perform management operations on legacy systems via third-party CORBA gateways to either the IETF Simple Network Management Protocol (SNMP) [299] or the ISO Common Management Information Protocol (CMIP) [622];
- any SOMA service may call external CORBA objects, included either in CORBA Services/Facilities or in other systems management frameworks that offer a CORBA interface (SOMA agents as CORBA clients);
- any SOMA service may register its interface to an ORB and offer the implemented services to any recognized external CORBA client (SOMA agents as CORBA servers);

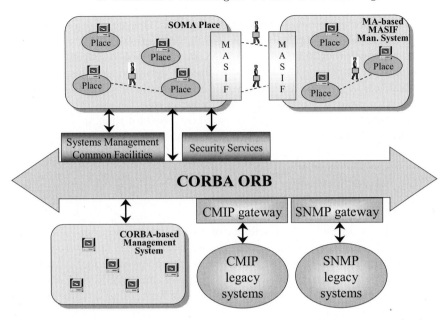

Fig. 5.12. Different Contexts of Interoperability for SOMA Management Agents.

- any external entity, whether MA-based or not, may ask SOMA agents for agent management and tracing services defined by the MASIF standard;
- mobile agents can be moved between different type-compatible MA-based management environments compliant with MASIF.

SOMA has demonstrated its suitability in the implementation of several monitoring and controlling tools [61]. In addition, a main goal of SOMA is also to manage complex Internet services, even obtained by tailoring and composing existing ones, and to dynamically introduce new services in the existing infrastructure with no need to suspend operations.

In the area of the management of multimedia streaming over best-effort standard networks such as the Internet, we have implemented a Video on Demand (VoD) SOMA-based service [62]. It is based on a set of lower-level services, implemented in terms of mobile agents dynamically distributed over the paths between the source and the targets of the video stream. SOMA VoD permits users to require a QoS level for any multimedia stream, and allows to manage and adjust the requested quality during service provision, to respond to dynamic modifications of network resource availability. The VoD service is realized by coordinating two different types of SOMA management agents: the QoS Negotiators (QoSNs) that define and grant a specific level of quality for the service, and the Admission Controllers (ACs) that manage the resources to be engaged by local intermediate nodes (see Figure 5.5.2).

ACs are present on every node of the network; this assumption is not severe because they are implemented by mobile agents that can move and be installed whenever they are needed. Each AC manages local resources and keeps track of their current commitment to already accepted streams. The flow specifications of streams are recorded in a local table of <receiving-host, bandwidth, delay, loss> tuples. Any tuple represents the statistics of VoD traffic between the local and the receiving host: the first time, it contains values calculated upon a short sample of communication; then, it is updated by monitoring real traffic of current VoD sessions. ACs are in charge of answering to reservation requests from QoSNs.

The VoD service requires the coordination of a set of QoSN agents located at the source, at the target and at some intermediate nodes. QoSNs maintain session state: they record user preferences and flow specifications for a video stream. QoSNs evaluate the feasibility of meeting these requirements against the local AC database and exploit the SOMA coordination facility to perform the negotiation phase for the definition of the achievable QoS. After the negotiation phase, during multimedia streaming, any QoSN is in charge of receiving packets from the previous QoSN and of forwarding them to the next QoSN.

Let us first consider the case of a video stream addressed to one target only. The path between the source and the target is automatically determined at run-time, by tracing the route via one dummy packet sent from source to target. QoSNs move to the chosen hosts on the path and interrogate the AC database: if available resources are not enough for the desired QoS, QoSNs can coordinate and reduce their requests by scaling the stream (at the moment, by dropping frames in Motion JPEG streams or by reducing resolution in MPEG-2 ones [273]). Only if these diminished reservation requests cannot be satisfied, the VoD service is denied. After a successful negotiation phase, the (possibly scaled) multimedia stream starts to flow. During the video distribution, a link can fail or its quality can deteriorate, thus making impossible to a particular QoSN to maintain the negotiated quality. In that case, the interested QoSN can enhance the throughput of its link via stream striping on non-corouted paths [603]. In this case, it sends back a message to temporarily stop the stream, and forwards a message to suspend updates in AC tables on the path. Then, it sends its clones to handle new non-corouted paths and starts the negotiation phase with the clones. When negotiation completes, the QoSN sends back a message that restarts the stream: apart from a delay in receiving the stream, the VoD target goes on transparently.

In the case of multicast distribution of the same video stream (for N targets), the generated network traffic can be limited by exploiting location awareness of agents. While in traditional VoD systems the source generates N packet streams, one for each target, SOMA QoSNs can ascertain whether there are several targets within the same domain locality, and can split packets only when it is necessary, in general only at the last hop.

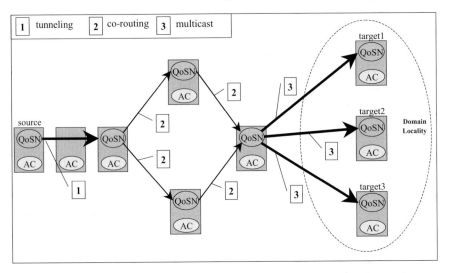

Fig. 5.13. Tunnelling, Co-routing and Multicast in the SOMA-based VoD Service.

5.6 Concluding Remarks

Based on the findings of sections two and three, namely that each of the presented middleware technologies has some drawbacks or limitations for its exclusive use to realize a very flexible platform for the realization of Internet services, this chapter has presented an emerging approach for the integration of MA and CORBA technologies in order to take advantage of both when needed. This means that service components could be dynamically deployed in a distributed service provisioning environment and moved during runtime to more appropriate network hosts if required (e.g., for system recovery, upgrading, extending and load balancing). Nevertheless, remote inter-object coordination and communication between distributed service components is maintained as a fundamental paradigm of the proposed service middleware for open and global systems.

We have described how it is possible to extend MA systems via the CORBA C/S middleware technology that is today the most accepted and diffused standard for interoperability between heterogeneous distributed objects. This approach currently enables a pragmatic short-term way to enhance CORBA-based distributed processing environments with object mobility through the provision of an add-on middleware layer, i.e., the distributed agent environment. In addition, we have illustrated how two state-of-the-art MA platforms (Grasshopper and SOMA) exploit this integrated and flexible middleware respectively for the provision of enhanced IN services and for the management of Internet multimedia streams with QoS requirements.

The resulting integrated technology suggest to imagine and provide new and flexible service creation environments, which require an evolution of the current ones in order to reflect the capability of object mobility. Mobility could be made visible at a high level of applications design for developing specific applications that can benefit from the explicit notion of locality, or (more in line with the overall CORBA principles) can be exploited at a lower level of application engineering, where object mobility is employed by the middleware support in response to specific run-time requirements, such as potential interconnectivity of ORBs, performance, replication, and so on.

Much research work is still to be done, as some mobility aspects have not reached yet a widely accepted and standardized solution. All of them have to be analysed and considered in the future in order to provide a consistent model which is inline with the latest developments within the CORBA community. For instance, still an open point is the dynamic detection of object relationships, which is required when the middleware is requested to freeze (i.e., to serialize on a transportable format) the state of a mobile object. The CORBA Relationship Service may be a starting point, but does not provide a complete solution at the state-of-the-art of its specification [188]. Finally, also as a proof of the heat of the subject and of the interest raised in the OMG itself, interested readers are referred to the recent activities of the OMG Agent Special Interest Group, which has issued a Request for Information on "Agent Technology in OMA" addressing the need for object mobility [187]. It is likely that a corresponding Request for Proposal for the standardization of a CORBA Migration Service will be issued at the time of publication of this book.

6. Agent Coordination via Scripting Languages

Jean-Guy Schneider, Markus Lumpe, and Oscar Nierstrasz

Institute of Computer Science and Applied Mathematics (IAM),
University of Berne, Neubrückstrasse 10, CH-3012 Bern, Switzerland

Summary.

In recent years, so-called *scripting languages* have become increasingly popular as they provide means to build quickly flexible applications from a set of prefabricated components. These languages typically support a single, specific architectural style of composing components (e.g. the *pipes and filters* architectural style), and they are designed to address a specific application domain. Although scripting languages and coordination languages have evolved from different roots and have been developed to solve different problems, we argue that both address similar *separations of concerns*. Scripting languages achieve a separation of *components* from the *scripts* that configure and compose them, whilst coordination languages separate *computational entities* from the *coordination* code that manages dependencies between them. In this chapter we will define coordination in the context of a conceptual framework for component-based software development. Furthermore, we will discuss main properties and abstractions of scripting languages and will compare selected scripting languages with respect to the identified core concepts. Finally, using a small set of sample applications, we will illustrate the power and the limitations of these concepts in order to define agent coordination.

6.1 Introduction

It is widely accepted today that closed and proprietary software systems cannot keep up with the pace of changing user requirements. In order to overcome the problems of these systems, modern applications are being built as collections of distributed software agents. Since these agents run in a distributed environment and concurrently access resources, they not only need to exchange information, but they must coordinate their actions to achieve the required functionality. Unfortunately, the corresponding coordination code is often intermixed with computational code, which reduces the flexibility and adaptability, hence the reusability of distributed agents.

Talking about agents, it is often not clear what kind of entities we should consider as being agents. In this chapter, we will not worry to much about giving a precise notion of software agents, but simply adapt a definition given in [419]. From our point of view, an agent should be considered as a software program that can act autonomously on behalf of a human or another software or hardware system. Agents represent well-defined services, but are not required to be either mobile or intelligent [456].

There are several approaches to separate the coordination part of agents from the computational part. Common to all these approaches is the goal to make a *clear separation between computational entities and their relationships*.

Software architectures, for example, focus on describing software systems at a level beyond simple algorithms and data structures, including global organization and control structure. They express the structure of applications in terms of processing elements, data elements, and explicit connecting elements (also known as connectors). Furthermore, architectural styles abstract over a set of related software architectures and define a set of rules how the elements can be combined [490, 547].

A similar approach is taken in the field of component-based programming, where applications are expressed as compositions of plug-compatible software components [455]. Of particular interest is the fact that coordination aspects can be encapsulated into reusable coordination components [590]. This approach not only enhances the explicit separation of coordination and computational code, but also allows application developers to reuse coordination aspects in different settings.

A third approach in this direction is the concept of aspect-oriented programming (AOP). AOP aims at separating properties of software systems which can be cleanly encapsulated in a generalized procedure (i.e., components) from properties for which the implementation cannot be cleanly encapsulated (i.e., aspects) [352]. Aspects and components generally cross-cut each other in a system's implementation.

Naturally, it is not enough to separate different concerns of systems into deployable entities, but one needs a way to build applications as assemblies of such entities (i.e., to express applications as compositions of composable elements).

In recent years, *scripting languages* have become increasingly popular for quickly building small, flexible applications from a set of existing components. These languages typically support a single, specific architectural style of composing components (e.g., the *pipe and filter* architectural style supported by the Bourne Shell [86]), and they are designed with a specific application domain in mind (system administration, graphical user interfaces etc.). Furthermore, scripting languages are extensible as new abstractions can be integrated into scripting environments. Finally, it is often possible to embed scripts into existing components, offering a flexible way for adaptation and extension. Hence, scripting languages seem to be ideal tools for building open, distributed systems in general and for both implementing and coordinating software agents in particular.

In this chapter, it is not our goal to focus on basic coordination models and abstractions of scripting languages alone. We would like to view coordination from a different perspective, set the relation to other approaches which aim at separating independent concerns into deployable entities, in particular to component-based software development, and discuss the influence of scripting on building applications as assemblies of these entities. Furthermore, we would like to stress the fact that scripting languages do not only allow us to coordinate distributed agents, but also to implement the agents themselves as scripts.

The remaining parts of this chapter are organized as follows: in section 6.2, we clarify important terms used throughout this chapter and define coordination in the context of a conceptual framework for component-based software development. In section 6.3, we discuss the main properties and abstractions of scripting languages, compare selected scripting languages, and illustrate some important concepts of each of these languages. In section 6.4, we show how the concepts discussed previously are applied in practice by illustrating a small set of sample applications and discuss limitations of existing scripting languages. Finally, we conclude this chapter in section 6.5 with a summary of the main observations and a discussion about related and future work.

6.2 A Conceptual Framework for Software Composition

It is generally accepted that modern software systems are increasingly required to be open, flexible conglomerations of distributed software agents rather than monolithic heaps of code. This places a strain on old-fashioned software technology and methods that are based on the maxim

$$\text{Applications} = \text{Algorithms} + \text{Data}.$$

This maxim has some relevance for well-defined and delimited problems only and is often applied in imperative programming languages that focus on top-down decomposition.

Coordination approaches, on the other hand, view systems as (i) computational entities that encapsulate well-defined functionality and interact with each other in order to achieve a common goal and (ii) coordination entities that manage the corresponding interactions [269]. These approaches can be best described by the maxim

$$\text{Applications} = \text{Computation} + \text{Coordination}.$$

Coordination can be seen as the management of dependencies between computational entities, or as the "glue" between distributed software agents [482].

Recent work in the area of coordination has focused on the development of particular coordination languages that realize a particular model of coordination (the interested reader may find corresponding overviews in chapters 2 and 4 as well as in [482]). Coordination problems, however, cannot always be solved by solely using a particular model. Furthermore, data-driven coordination approaches such as Linda [136] do not enforce a clear separation of concerns as a mixture of coordination and computation code within an agent is still possible. Finally, coordination languages generally do not allow the definition of reusable coordination abstractions at a higher level than the basic mechanisms and paradigms supported by the underlying model. In order to tackle the problems related to the development of open distributed systems, we need an approach which not only enforces a clear separation between computational and compositional entities, but also overcomes other problems with existing coordination models and languages (e.g., the interleaving of coordination and computation code in Linda-based systems).

In the last decade, component-based software technology has emerged as an approach to cope with the advances in computer hardware technology and rapidly changing systems requirements [581]. Component-based systems aim at achieving flexibility by clearly separating the stable parts of the system (i.e., the components) from the specification of their composition (i.e., scripts). Hence, a component-based engineering style can be best described by the maxim

$$\text{Applications} = \text{Components} + \text{Scripts}.$$

Components are black-box entities that encapsulate services behind well-defined interfaces whereas scripts define how the components are composed. More precisely, scripts specify connections between the services of components. In contrast to data-driven coordination models, which only make the distinction between computation and coordination *functionality*, component-based software technology aims at encapsulating coordination functionality into independent units of deployment (i.e., components) [590].

It is important to note that scripts may not only be used for composition, but also for implementing components (i.e., a composition of components is again a component). Hence, if we use the term *scriptability*, we either mean components offering an interface for scripting (scriptable components) or the possibility to implement components or agents as scripts.

The importance of component-based engineering in the context of open systems development is probably best underlined by the following quote:

> What I think is quite important, but often underrated, is the dichotomy that scripting forces on application design. It encourages the development of reusable components (i.e., "bricks") in system programming languages and the assembly of these components with scripts (i.e., "mortar"). *Brent Welch*

Our experience in developing component-based systems has shown that components and scripts are only half of the truth if we want to build flexible and extensible distributed systems. It is necessary that we also think in terms of *frameworks, architectures*, and *glue* [537]. In this section, we will define and clarify the relevant terms and propose a conceptual framework where these five techniques are combined.

A *software component* is a static abstraction with plugs and can be seen as a kind of black-box entity that hides its implementation details [455]. It is a static entity in the sense that it must be instantiated in order to be used. A software component has plugs which are not only used to *provide* services, but also to *require* them. It is important to note that components are never used in isolation, but according to a software architecture that determines how components are plugged together. Therefore, a software component has to be considered as a composable element of a component framework [387].

A *component framework* is a collection of software components and architectural styles that determine the interfaces that components may have, the connectors that may be used to plug components together, and the rules governing component composition. In contrast to an object-oriented framework where an application is generally built by subclassing framework classes that respond to specific application requirements (also known as *hot spots* [501]), a component framework primarily focuses on object and class (i.e., component) composition (also known as *black-box* reuse).

The main idea behind component-based software development is that an application developer only has to write a small amount of *wiring code* in order to establish connections between components. This wiring, or *scripting*, can take take various forms, depending on the nature and granularity of the components, the nature and problem domain of the underlying framework, and the composition model. Composition may occur at compile-time, link-time, or run-time, and may be very rigid and static (like the syntactic expansion that occurs when C++ templates are composed [446]), or very flexible and dynamic (like that supported by Tcl or other scripting languages [480]).

In an ideal world, there are components available for any task an application has to perform and these components can be simply plugged together. However, it is sometimes necessary to reuse a component in an environment different than the one it has been designed for and that this environment does not match the assumptions the component makes about the structure of the system to be part of. In such a situation, *glue* code is needed to overcome the mismatched assumptions and to adapt components in order to be composable.

The question arises how and where coordination concerns fit into this conceptual framework. The purpose of a coordination model is to separate computational entities from their interactions and, therefore, needs to provide abstractions for controlling synchronization, communication, creation, and termination of concurrent and distributed computational activities. The main idea behind coordination in component-based software development is to encapsulate the first two concerns of a coordination model (i.e., synchronization and communication) into separate components (also known as *coordination components* [590]) and to handle the other two concerns (i.e., creation and termination of activities) in scripts. This approach enhances the flexibility to exchange individual synchronization and communication concerns (e.g., different network protocols) as "ordinary" components are simply plugged together using appropriately selected coordination components (refer also to the Bourne Shell example given below). Therefore, *coordination can be considered as scripting of concurrent and distributed components* [537].

At present, however, there does not exist a programming language or system that supports general-purpose software composition based on the conceptual framework presented in this section. Although scripting languages and 4GLs (such as Visual Basic [415]) go a long way in the direction of open systems development, they mainly focus on special application domains and offer only rudimentary support for the integration of components not built within the system. The reason for this situation is not only the lack of well-defined (or standardized) component interfaces, but also the ad-hoc way the semantics of the underlying language models are defined.

In order to illustrate how the conceptual framework illustrated above is applied in practice, consider the Bourne Shell script given below which prints the names of all users who were recently working on a UNIX machine. The Bourne Shell defines a simple component framework where UNIX commands (usually called *filters*), files, and character streams are the components and the pipe operator '|' as well as the other stream redirectors (such as '<', '>' etc.) are the corresponding connectors. The standard input stream and the command line arguments of a filter can be considered as required services whereas the standard output and error streams as provided services, respectively.

```
last | awk '{ print $1 }' | sort -u | rsh server expand | awk '{ print $1 }'
```

Analysing this Bourne Shell script, it is easy to identify components and connectors, the underlying architecture, as well as other interesting properties:

- the script consists of five components (the filters `last`, `awk`, `sort`, `expand`, and `awk`), each fulfilling a well-defined task,
- a data source (i.e., a system file read by the filter `last`) and a data sink (the standard output stream of the second `awk` filter),
- successive components are connected by a pipe (indicated by the '|' symbol) and interact using characters streams,
- the filter `rsh` is used to communicate with the filter `expand`, which runs on a remote server,[1]
- the components have to be instantiated, and the functionality of each component can be specialized at instantiation by passing different (command line) arguments (e.g., the filter `sort` is used with the argument `-u`).

The components and the character streams of the script form a pipeline, where each component only depends on the output of its predecessor. Since many Bourne Shell scripts fulfill similar restrictions, they are often associated with a *pipe and filter* architectural style [547]. However, scripts are not restricted to this style, and it is possible to define more complex unidirectional data-flow architectures [58] by connecting the standard error stream of a filter to the standard input stream of another filter using the connector

---

[1] The information about the full names of users is only available on a dedicated server (indicated by *server* in the script above).

'|&'. The composition of filters using the pipe connector again leads to a filter (i.e., a UNIX process which reads from the standard input stream and writes to the standard output and error streams).

In the script given above, the filter rsh, which is used to communicate with the filter expand running on a remote host, deserves a special attention. From the perspective of the conceptual framework, rsh acts both as a generic *glue component* and a *coordination abstraction*, as we will explain in the following.

Since the information about the full names of users is only available on a dedicated server, the filter expand cannot be run locally, but must run on the corresponding remote server. However, the pipe connector of the Bourne Shell only allows connections between filters running on the same host. In order to overcome the resulting architectural mismatch [262], we need a way to (i) start the process expand on the remote server and (ii) connect with its input and output streams. This is exactly what the filter rsh does: it starts a process on the remote server and forces this process to use rsh's input and output streams as standard I/O medium. This has the effect that the remote process expand created by rsh reads the output of the filter sort and produces the input for awk, hence ensuring the correct communication between the two hosts and the three processes involved. Note that rsh is a *generic* glue abstraction as it can be used to instantiate and communicate with any UNIX process running on a different host.

On the other hand, rsh can also be considered as a *coordination abstraction*. Due to the inherently concurrent nature of UNIX processes, the character streams act as coordinators (synchronizers, buffers) between the filters, as UNIX commands generally do not specify any particular synchronization model; they simply read from/write onto their I/O streams. In addition to local synchronization, rsh has to open an network connection, synchronize the communication between the remote process, itself, and the local I/O streams, and close the network connection upon termination of the processes. Hence, rsh takes care of all coordination-related concerns we have previously given in this section. Due to the fact that rsh encapsulates all this functionality as a single unit of deployment, it must be considered as a coordination abstraction or as a coordination component.

The reader should note that the filters of the example given above could also be plugged together using a system programming language like C. However, C only offers low-level (library) abstractions for connecting the standard output stream of a command to the standard input stream of another command or for invoking a process on a remote server. Hence, it is not easily possible to make the architecture of the application explicit, especially as C does not offer such a convenient syntax for expressing connections of UNIX commands as the Bourne Shell.

6.3 Scripting Languages at a Glance

6.3.1 What is Scripting?

Unfortunately, this question does not have a generally accepted answer. Consider the following two definitions:

> "A scription language is a language that is primarily interpreted, and on a UNIX system, it can be invoked directly from a text file using #!."
> *Anonymous Usenet User*

and

> "A scripting language introduces and binds a set of software components that collaborate to solve a particular problem [457]."

These two definitions mark the lower and upper bound of possible applications of scripting languages. However, they fall short of giving us an intuition when and how we should use a scripting language to solve a given problem. Furthermore, these definitions are rather vague and lack a precise characterization in terms of provided features or supported application domains.

Many researchers have been working on a characterization of scripting languages. We will summarize the most prominent contributions in this field and elaborate our own definition.

John Ousterhout argues that scripting languages are designed for "gluing" applications [480]. They provide a higher level of programming than assembly or system programming languages, much weaker typing than system programming languages, and an interpreted development environment. Scripting assumes the existence of powerful components and provides the means to connect them together. However, scripting languages sacrifice execution efficiency to improve speed of development. Please note that in this context, Ousterhout uses the term glue in a much broader sense than we have defined it in the previous section.

Guido van Rossum, the inventor of Python [610], defines the main characteristics of scripting languages as follows: scripting languages should (i) provide text processing primitives, (ii) offer some form of automatic memory management, (iii) not require a mandatory separate compilation phase, (iv) favour high-level expressiveness over execution speed, and (v) interface well with the rest of the system.

Brent Welch puts emphasis on two aspects: *embeddability* and *extensibility*. In his view, scripting languages should (i) be interpreted, not compiled, (ii) be dynamically typed, (iii) offer abstractions for introspection, (iv) be embeddable and extensible, and (v) have a simple syntax.

Embeddability and extensibility are two important properties of scripting languages, which tells them apart from other programming languages. Extensibility is needed in order to incorporate new abstractions (components or connectors) into the language, encouraging the integration of legacy code.

Embedding a script into an existing component or application (e.g., Visual Basic [415] as scripting facility for Microsoft Word or Excel) offers a flexible way for adapting and extending this component, enable to configure applications to user defined needs, or simplify repeated complex editing as in case of Microsoft Word.

Finally, Clemens Szyperski claims that scripting is quite similar to application building, but unlike mainstream (component) programming, scripts usually do not introduce new components [581]. Scripts are used to simply plug existing components together: scripts can be seen as introducing behaviour but no new state. Therefore, *scripting* aims at late and high-level gluing.

Summarizing the definitions given above, we argue that scripting languages can be characterized as follows:

- The purpose of a scripting language is the development of applications by plugging existing components together (i.e., the primary focus is on *composition*).
- Scripting languages generally favour *high-level programming* over execution speed.
- Scripting languages are *extensible* and *scalable*: they are designed for extending the language model with new abstractions (e.g., new components or connectors) and for interoperating with components written in other languages.
- Scripting languages are *embeddable*: it is possible to embed them into existing components or applications (e.g., Microsoft Word), offering a flexible way for *adaptation, configuration,* and *extension*.
- Scripting languages are in general *interpreted* and offer *automatic memory management*.
- Scripting languages are *dynamically* and *weakly typed* and offer support for runtime *introspection*.

Using these properties, we define scripting and scripting languages as follows:

> "Scripting is a high-level binding technology for component-based application development. Scripting itself is done using a high-level programming language (i.e., a scripting language) that allows us to create, customize, and assemble components into a predefined software architecture [536]."

6.3.2 Characterization of Scripting Languages

We have now identified the most distinguished properties of scripting languages. However, not all scripting languages aim to address the same application domain (e.g., Perl [621] is primarily used for text manipulation, whereas AppleScript [29] is used to configure and control "Part Editors" in the *Open Scripting Architecture* (OSA) of OpenDoc). In order to appropriately characterize scripting languages, we also have to classify them by the features they provide.

Like system programming languages (such as C or Java), scripting languages are generally not categorized according to their syntax or their semantic domain, but according to the language constructs (or *features*) they offer (or do not offer). For example, depending on the provided features, a scripting language is better suited for text-processing (e.g., Perl) than for building graphical user interfaces. For Tcl [479], on the other hand, the opposite holds.

We have carried out a detailed analysis of existing scripting languages. In the following, we will identify the most important features that modern scripting languages support. We will, however, distinguish between *essential features* and *characterizing features*. Essential features are those that must be supported by any scripting language while characterizing features classify scripting languages in terms of the language design space.

We have identified two concepts which are essential for scripting languages: (i) *encapsulation and wiring* and (ii) *external interoperability*.

Encapsulation and wiring. In order to build an application as a composition of components, a scripting language must support some notion of components and connectors. More precisely, a scripting language must offer mechanisms for encapsulation and wiring.

Besides the notion of components, a scripting language must offer a set of mechanisms which allow one to connect provided and required services of corresponding components. Such mechanisms can be as "low-level" as a function call or as higher-level as the pipe-operator in the Bourne Shell language.

An important aspect of encapsulation and wiring is whether a language is *compositionally complete* (i.e., it is possible to encapsulate a composition of components as a composite component). For example, a Bourne Shell script can be used as a component of another shell script.

External interoperability. In order to use components not written in the language itself, it is necessary that a scripting language provides features to interoperate with components written in other languages. We denote these features as external interoperability.

Interoperability features are important if a component is implemented as a composition of other components, but does not completely fulfill all actual requirements (e.g., it does not have the required run-time performance). In this kind of situation, it must be possible to reimplement this component with more favourable run-time behaviour and integrate this new component into the scripting environment using interoperability features.

Characterizing features are summarized in the following list. The reader should note that these features are not only important for scripting languages, but for programming languages in general.

Embeddability. Scripting languages may be directly embedded into an application or component (e.g., JavaScript [242] or Visual Basic [415]) while others offer an interface to embed them into other programming languages (e.g., Python offers an interface for C/C++).

Extensibility. Scripting languages often provide an approach to extend themselves with additional abstractions (new components and connectors). As an example, the core of Tcl [479] does not offer the concept of classes and objects, but the stooops extension (which is fully written in Tcl) introduces abstractions for object-oriented programming [244].

Objects. A comparison of popular scripting languages reveals that they either directly support the notion of objects (e.g., Python or JavaScript) or there are extensions which introduce objects (e.g., stooops).

Exceptions. For programming in the large and for testing applications, it is useful if a language has features to explicitly cope with errors and exceptions.

Execution model. A criterion to distinguish scripting languages is whether they are *event driven* or *data driven*. In the case of an event driven language, it is important to know what kind of call-back mechanisms it supports (e.g., the concept of event listeners in Java) and how closures [545] can be specified.

Concurrency. Some scripting languages are inherently concurrent (e.g., Bourne Shell or Piccola [4]), while others provide abstractions for concurrency (e.g., threads, monitors). In both cases, the kind of built-in *coordination abstractions* are of interest.

Introspection. Scripting languages generally offer features for run-time introspection or even reflection, although these features often only have a limited functionality. From our point of view, both dynamic creation and execution of code (often referred to as an *eval*-feature) and the concept of *call-by-name* are part of this dimension. Whereas languages like Tcl only offer low-level introspection mechanisms, Python goes a step further and offers a meta-level protocol.

Typing. According to Ousterhout [480], scripting languages tend to be weakly typed. However, an analysis of popular languages reveals differences in the type system: some languages are untyped (e.g., Bourne Shell) or dynamically typed (e.g., Perl) whereas others have a mixture of static and dynamic typing (e.g., Visual Basic). This analysis also revealed different strategies for resolving type mismatches (e.g., implicit type conversions vs. exceptions).

Scoping rules. The scope of a name (variable, function etc.) is the range of program instructions for which the name is known. The scoping rules of a language defines the strategy how name-value bindings are established. Most scripting languages tend to be *dynamically scoped* (e.g., Python), although there are languages which also offer *static scoping* (e.g., Visual Basic).

Built-in data abstractions. Besides low-level data abstractions such as integers and strings, many scripting languages offer built-in *higher-level data abstractions*. Examples of such abstractions are key-based data abstractions (e.g., dictionaries), ordered data abstractions (e.g., lists), or data abstractions without a particular order or access strategy (e.g., sets). In addition, many languages offer specialized operations on high-level data abstractions (such as iterations), and Perl even has a special syntax for these operations.

Persistence. Only few scripting languages (e.g., AppleScript) offer general-purpose support for making complex configurations or properties of applications and components persistent.

6.3.3 Selected Systems and Languages

In the following, we will briefly illustrate important concepts and features found in selected scripting languages.

Bourne Shell is an interpreted scripting language for the UNIX operating system and offers a simple component model based on commands and character streams. Commands can be connected by using higher-level connectors (e.g., the pipe operator '|'), which makes the architecture of a Bourne Shell script explicit in the source code. The language is compositionally complete (i.e., a composition of commands is again a command) and supports a declarative style of programming.

Tcl is a dynamically compiled, string-based scripting language and is available on all popular platforms. The basic abstraction in Tcl is a command (comparable to a procedure in an imperative programming language), and since every programming construct is achieved with commands (and not special syntax), commands are the unifying concept of the language. The concept of commands allows a user to extend the language using the same syntactical framework as is used for all built-in commands.

Perl can be considered as a uniform selected merge of sed, awk, csh, and C. It offers higher-level data abstractions such as lists, arrays, and hashes and syntactic sugar for processing instances of these higher-level data abstractions. Perl introduces the notion of contexts for evaluating expressions, offers support for operator overloading based on contexts, and has both lexical and dynamic scoping rules.

Python is an object-oriented scripting languages that supports both scripting and programming in the large. Objects are the unifying concept (i.e., "everything is an object") and, therefore, all abstractions are first-class values. Python offers a meta-level protocol which can be used for extending and adapting existing abstractions as well as for operator overloading. Finally, the language model supports keyword-based parameter passing.

Language	Domain and/or Paradigm	Extensible	Embeddable	Reflection support
Bourne Shell	administration, commands	any	no	no
Tcl	GUI, commands	C, Java	yes	yes
Perl	text-processing, object-oriented	C/C++	yes	yes
Python	object-oriented	C/C++	yes	yes
AppleScript	object-oriented, events	any	yes	no
JavaScript	object-based, events	Java	yes	yes
Visual Basic	object-based, events	C/C++	yes	no
Haskell	functional	COM	no	no
Manifold	coordination, process-based	C, (Java)	yes	no
Piccola	process-based, object-based	Java	no	yes

Table 6.1. Functional properties of selected scripting languages.

AppleScript is a dynamically typed, event- and object-oriented scripting language which only runs on the MacOS platform. In fact, AppleScript is not a scripting language on its own, but it should be considered as a front-end to a framework based on scriptable applications (also known as component parts). The concepts of AppleScript are heavily based on similar concepts defined in the Open Scripting Architecture (OSA) for OpenDoc [233]. The main purpose of AppleScript is to automate, integrate, and customize scriptable applications. The language is compositionally complete, but in contrast to many other scripting languages, it does not offer an equivalent to an "eval" feature (i.e., it is not directly possible to create and execute scripts at runtime).

AppleScript comes with an application called *Script Editor* which can be used to create and modify scripts. Although this editor has access to the dictionary of scriptable applications (i.e., the set of messages a scriptable applications supports), to our knowledge AppleScript scripts cannot introspect these dictionaries (refer also to Table 6.1).

JavaScript is a (general-purpose) object-based scripting language embedded into a web browser [242]. The main predefined components in JavaScript are windows, forms, images, input areas, and menus. In general, JavaScript is used to control the browser and web documents. JavaScript scripts are attached to events and executed when the corresponding event occurs. JavaScript enables the interaction of the user with a web-document by providing means to read and write content of document

Language	Platform portability	Implementation technique	Module concept	Application area
Bourne Shell	UNIX	Interpreter	(yes)	adm. tasks
Tcl	major	Bytecode	yes	GUI
Perl	major	Bytecode	yes	Text
Python	major	Bytecode	yes	adm. tasks
AppleScript	MacOS	Interpreter	no	configuration customization
JavaScript	Netscape	Interpreter	(yes)	WWW
Visual Basic	Windows	Bytecode	yes	GUI/COM
Haskell	major	Bytecode	yes	COM
Manifold	UNIX	Compiled/PVM	yes	coordination
Piccola	major	Virtual machine	(yes)	composition coordination

Table 6.2. Non-functional properties of selected scripting languages

elements. However, JavaScript does not provide any graphic facilities, network operations other than URL loading, or multithreading.

Visual Basic is a visual programming environment for object- and component-based application development, focusing on wiring components. In particular, in Visual Basic one defines the wiring-code (e.g., event handling) while objects and components are usually developed in a language like C, C++, or Java. Visual Basic programs can be compiled to native code. However, components and the runtime system are packaged into separate run-time libraries (DLL's). Visual Basic provides a static typing scheme for variables and a dynamic typing scheme for components. Furthermore, Visual Basic supports keyword-based parameters (enabled by the IDispatch interface of COM-components). At present, Visual Basic is only available on Windows operating systems.

Haskell is a pure functional programming language that provides a COM binding [492]. Haskell is not really a scripting language, but due to its features like a polymorphic type system, higher order functions, lazy evaluation, or convenient syntax it is an attractive language for scripting components. The COM integration into Haskell is strongly typed. Haskell is an interpreted language and the Haskell system provides garbage-collection. Haskell provides an unconventional and new way for scripting.

Manifold is a coordination language for managing complex, dynamically changing interconnections among sets of independent, concurrent, and cooperating processes [38]. It should be considered as a scripting language for concurrent and distributed components. It is particularly suitable for specifying and implementing reusable, higher-level coordination abstractions and protocols as well as for dynamically evolving architectures.

Piccola is a simple untyped language and has been designed to be a general purpose "composition language" [4, 5]. Piccola is primarily used to express how components are composed, i.e., it is used to define the connectors, coordination and glue abstractions needed for an actual composition. Piccola uses the unifying concept of *forms* (immutable, extensible records), which represent almost everything in Piccola, including *namespaces, interfaces, parameters, scripts,* and *objects.* This unification results in an extremely simple but expressive language. Since Piccola is based on a formal process semantics [386, 536], it is a prime candidate for coordination and configuration of internet-based agents.

The reader should note that other scripting languages (e.g., DCL [25], Icon [289], Lua [319], Obliq [124], Rapide [383], or Rexx [193] also support some of the features that we have illustrated in this section, but a detailed discussion is beyond the scope of this work.

6.4 Scripting in Practice

In the previous section, we have discussed the main properties of scripting languages and compared selected scripting languages using these properties. In this section, we show how scripting languages are used in distributed applications where coordination concerns are of importance. More precisely, we illustrate CyberChair [609], an on-line submission and reviewing system for scientific conferences, a case study carried out in the context of the FAMOOS project,[2] where CORBA [464] is used as a medium to connect heterogeneous components [300], and the implementation of a Wiki server in Piccola [4].

Common to first two sample applications is that Python [610] is used as the underlying scripting language. These examples illustrate the application of a data-driven (i.e., CyberChair) and a control-driven coordination model (i.e., scripting of CORBA components) in Python, respectively. The Wiki server shows how user-defined operators are used to make the architecture of an application explicit.

In this section, we will only focus on selected aspects related to scripting and coordination; a detailed description of the three sample applications is beyond the scope of this work. We forward the interested reader to the corresponding references for details.

6.4.1 CyberChair: A Conference Management System

Most scientific communities have established policies and mechanisms aiming at minimizing the organizational efforts of conference management, while

---

[2] FAMOOS was an industrial ESPRIT Project (No 21975) in the IT Programme of the Fourth ESPRIT Framework Programme on reengineering object-oriented legacy systems towards component-based frameworks.

keeping a high quality of accepted papers and a fair selection process. Generally, authors interested in presenting their work at a conference submit their papers to the program chair. Under the guidance of the program chair, a program committee (i) reviews all submitted papers and (ii) selects the papers to be accepted. Finally, the authors are notified about the evaluation process, and authors of accepted papers and are invited to submit a camera-ready copy. The whole process of submission, reviewing, selection, and notification requires many activities, and the corresponding workload can be substantially reduced by the aid of an appropriate software system.

An example of such a software system is CyberChair, which was first developed in 1996 at the University of Twente in order to offer automatic conference management support for ECOOP, the annual European Conference on Object-Oriented Programming. In the past years, CyberChair has evolved and matured, covers most administrative tasks of the submission and review process, and has been successfully adapted for about ten different conferences.

The activities supported by CyberChair roughly correspond to the activities of a series of related case studies used to evaluate various coordination models and languages in real world problems (refer to [517, 543] for details). A detailed description of all activities has therefore been omitted here.

The overall structure of CyberChair conforms to a client-server architecture organized around a central data repository, where all the data of the submission process is stored. In order to enhance the access to the data repository and to reduce conflicting accesses as much as possible, the information for each paper submission, the status of each paper (accepted, rejected, withdrawn etc.), the distribution of papers to reviewers, and each review report are stored in separate files on the server system.

For each of the management task supported by CyberChair, there exist an agent which implements the corresponding functionality. Most of these agents are simple CGI-programs (in particular those agents which directly communicate with users) while other agents run as batch processes and periodically update HTML pages used to access specific services.

To transparently access the data repository and to encapsulate the concrete structure from client agents, CyberChair offers a set of basic Python routines which are used to create, modify, and access the data repository (i.e., the access functionality is encapsulated into a single Python module).

The agent for submitting abstracts, for example, is a CGI-program and can be actived using a simple web-browser (the corresponding URL is available form the main web-page of the conference). This agent creates an HTML form for submitting information about the authors, their affiliations, the title, and the abstract of a paper. The information submitted using this form is checked by another agent, which (i) stores the necessary information in the data repository and (ii) notifies via email both the contact author of the paper and the program chair about the submission. This email message also contains an identification and an URL which are needed to submit the electronic version of the paper in a later stage. The identification for each submission is again stored in the data repository.

In order to fulfill the security policy imposed by the conference management, access to restricted services (e.g., services only available to members of the program committee or the program chair) is given by password-enabled agents or password-protected web-pages. Note that these web-pages are periodically updated by the system in order to reflect changes in the data repository (e.g., all review reports of a paper are made available to those reviewers who review the same paper).

From a coordination point of view, there are three main concerns which must be considered by a conference management system like CyberChair: (i) concurrency concerns (i.e., ensure correct transaction protocols), (ii) security concerns (i.e., granting and revoking access rights to agents and/or data elements), and (iii) dependency concerns (i.e., tasks depend on the termination of other tasks). In the following, we will discuss each of these concerns in further detail.

Concurrency concerns. Generally, web-servers allow several CGI-programs to run concurrently. Hence, it might be possible that more than one active agent wants to update data stored in the same file (e.g., all identification keys for the authors are stored in a single file). At the level of accessing the files representing the persistent data repository, a two-phase locking protocol (based on POSIX file locks) prevents concurrent modification of files and ensures correct transaction protocols. Other access protocols (such as immutable data entries) are ensured by checking the presence or absence of the corresponding files.

Security concerns. As mentioned above, the access to several services is restricted to a particular set of users only. In order to achieve a fine-grained security policy, password-enabled web-pages are created which contain the access points (i.e., hypertext links) to dedicated services (agents or other web-pages). The access points given in the password-enabled web-pages use an identification mechanism to prevent users from "guessing" the access points to other restricted services. The system periodically updates the contents of the access pages in order to allow for an up-to-date view of the data repository (e.g., additional hypertext links are created when new review reports have been submitted). Finally, the access of particularly critical services is logged by a security agent.

Dependency concerns. It is obvious that some management tasks depend on the termination of other tasks. The coordination of these dependencies can be easily achieved by (i) defining deadlines for the critical tasks, (ii) preventing access to the corresponding services once the deadline has exceeded, and (iii) only granting access to the dependent tasks from this moment on (e.g., access to all abstracts is only granted when the submission phase has been completed, electronic versions of papers can only be downloaded when all papers have been submitted). In CyberChair, this concept is implemented using simple boolean flags in the corresponding Python scripts.

6.4.2 Scripting CORBA Components

The second sample application we will discuss was conducted in the context of an industrial ESPRIT project our research group participated in. The goal of this project (called FAMOOS) was to support the evolution of first generation object-oriented software, built with current analysis and design methods and programming languages, to frameworks – standard application architectures and component libraries which support the construction of numerous system variants in specific domains. Methods and tools were developed to analyse and detect design problems with respect to flexibility in object-oriented legacy systems and to transform these systems efficiently into frameworks based on flexible architectures.

Each of the FAMOOS project partners was interested in different aspects of reengineering and developed their own tools to conduct experiments in their field of interest. These tools were implemented in a heterogeneous environment using various programming languages (C/C++, Smalltalk, Java, and Python). Hence, there was a need to find a way to easily combine these tools in order to perform experiments where several tools were involved.

As a first step towards an integration of these tools, a common data exchange model was defined which represented object-oriented source code in a language-independent format [202]. Using such a language-independent exchange format allowed developers to implement their tools with a much broader functionality (i.e., metric tools could handle source code written in any object-oriented language). Furthermore, the character-based CDIF format the exchange model was based upon reduced the need for data marshalling between different operating system platforms and enhanced the interoperability between the tools.

All tools were either written in a language where a CORBA binding was defined or had an API in such a language. Hence, it was a natural decision to convert all tools into CORBA components, i.e., to define a wrapper for each tool with a CORBA compatible interface. These wrappers were defined using standard wrapping technology and, therefore, details of the wrapping process have been omitted here (refer to [300] for details).

However, wrapping the tools as CORBA components was not enough as languages like C++ or Java do not offer abstractions to wire CORBA components in a flexible and extensible way. Hence, there was the need for an environment fulfilling this requirement.

Fnorb is an experimental CORBA ORB [157] which allows users to implement and compose CORBA components using Python. Of particular interest in the context of the FAMOOS project was the second property as it made Fnorb an ideal tool for experimenting which CORBA architectures, for scripting CORBA components, and for building test harnesses for CORBA development projects.

In order to enhance the transparent scripting of CORBA components, it was necessary to encapsulate CORBA-related protocols as much as possible. An approach to achieve this goal was to represent CORBA components in the scripting environment using proxy objects [258]. Hence, an application programmer was freed from directly referring to the components themselves, but could instead refer to local representatives (i.e., the proxy objects), being responsible for (i) instantiating the (possibly remote) CORBA components and (ii) coordinating the communication between the components and their clients. Proxy objects either forward requests to the actual components or, in case of "intelligent" proxies [300, 441], handle request themselves.

It is important to note that an implementation of component proxies in Python substantially benefits from the dynamic typing and the underlying metalevel protocol, in particular the way attribute accesses in objects are performed (refer to [536, 610] for details). As a consequence, it was possible to implement a single generic proxy class (and not a new class for each component). This proxy class heavily uses the *dynamic invocation interface* (DII) of CORBA for a correct handling of requests.

Using a middleware environment such as CORBA for interconnecting heterogeneous components has the advantage that several "lower-level" coordination aspects (such as intercomponent communication and synchronization, data marshaling etc.) are directly handled by the involved ORBs. At a higher level, the usage of generic component proxies enables a complete abstraction from the underlying middleware and application programmers are freed from CORBA-related protocols. If further coordination concerns have to be taken care of, it is possible to define specialized component proxies and implement these concerns in the corresponding proxies. As a result, all coordination concerns can be encapsulated into independent units of deployment and computational entities are freed from coordination code.

The efforts to (i) wrap tools as CORBA components and (ii) integrate them into a scripting environment resulted in the desired framework for conducting various reengineering experiments. The approach taken also reflects the elements of the conceptual framework given in section 6.2, in particular the usage of generic glue abstractions for interoperation with components not being part of a scripting environment.

6.4.3 Observations

Although the two sample applications do not cover all aspects of open systems development, they, nevertheless, indicate some benefits and limitations of scripting languages for coordinating distributed software agents.

The two sample applications we have given in this section show that Python is a suitable scripting language for both a control- and data-driven coordination models. It has enough expressiveness to plug existing components together, to implement the missing functionality where needed, and to encapsulate (low-level) coordination concerns into independent units of deployment.

Due to dynamic scoping rules and the lack of static typing, many scripting languages (including Python) ease the implementation of generic glue abstractions. In particular the lack of static typing makes it easier to interoperate with components written in other languages and, therefore, encourages the use of legacy components.

Application development using scripting languages naturally leads to the maxim of viewing applications as combinations of components and scripts and, therefore, a scripting approach encourages the development of reusable components highly focused on the solution of particular problems, and the assembly of these components by means of scripts.

However, scripting languages also have their limitations. Consider the fact that the overall architecture of both sample applications given above is not made explicit in the underlying source code. It is important to note this that observation can be made in many applications where scripting languages are used to wire components together.

Furthermore, scripting languages typically support a single, specific architectural style, which makes them ideal tools for solving problems where this style is appropriate. However, as soon as a different style is required, most scripting languages fall short of giving the required flexibility to adapt to the new style (refer also to the discussion about the Perl Wiki given in the next section).

Only a limited number of scripting languages offers built-in support for concurrency; most languages only provide concurrency by libraries. Therefore, it is not possible to express concurrency issues directly in the source code. Finally, scripting languages are suitable to build small applications, but only offer limited support (if at all) for programming in the large. Interested readers may find further details concerning scalability issues in chapter 12 of this book.

6.4.4 A Piccola Wiki

In the previous section we have illustrated why scripting languages alone do not allow for flexible composition, adaptation, and configuration of existing components and to explicitly represent higher-level design elements (such as software architectures or coordination concerns) in applications. What we would need is something we call a *composition language* that (i) supports application configuration through a structured, but nevertheless flexible wiring technology and (ii) enforces a clear separation between computational elements and their relationships. In the following, we will briefly illustrate why Piccola can be considered as a step into this direction.

A Wiki Wiki Web Server (Wiki for short) is a simple hypertext system that lets users both navigate and modify pages through the World-Wide-Web, and was originally implemented by Ward Cunningham as a set of Perl scripts (available at c2.com). Wiki pages are plain ASCII text augmented with a few simple formatting conventions for defining internal links, bulleted lists, emphasized text etc. and are dynamically translated to HTML by the Wiki server. Generally, a Wiki is used as a medium to collaborate on documents and information webs.

Although the original Perl implementation is perfectly robust and widely used for many Wiki installations around the world, the style of programming that Perl encourages poses some problems for extensibility. In the available Perl implementation, it is not easy to understand the flow of control as the procedural paradigm of Perl is mixed with the stream-based processing of the web pages. Execution is sensitive to the sequence in which the declarations are evaluated. In particular, the architecture of the scripts are not evident, which makes it hard to adapt them to new functionality.

The Piccola Wiki implementation illustrates how the architecture of a scripted application can be made explicit by means of a data-flow architectural style (refer to [4] for details). More precisely, it shows that (i) a clear separation between components and their connections is enforced and (ii) glue abstractions adapt components that are not part of the underlying component framework. In particular, the Piccola Wiki implementation

- illustrates the implementation of an object-oriented (white-box) framework incorporating *streams, transformers*, and *files* that corresponds to a pull-flow stream-based architectural style [58]. Note that Java streams are integrated into this framework by means of gateway agents.
- substantially benefits from the fact that (i) the language offers user-defined operators which allow us to use a syntax that highlights the architectural style of the component framework and (ii) users can create new transformer and stream components without subclassing framework classes (i.e., the component framework supports *black-box extension*).
- integrates components of a push-flow architectural style (i.e., components which *push* data downstream instead of *pulling* it from upstream). Glue components are used to adapt push-flow components so they can work within a pull-flow architecture.
- defines a top-level script that implements the Wiki by composing components that conform to the architectural style mentioned above.

Maintaining a system such as the Piccola Wiki is much easier than the original Perl implementation and substantially benefits from an explicit architecture. Changing requirements, for example, may be addressed by reconfiguring individual components (i.e., replacing their required services), reconfiguring interconnections between components (i.e., adapting the scripts), incorporating additional external components (i.e., using glue abstractions), and deriving new components from old ones (i.e., support for black-box extension).

6.5 Summary, Conclusions

Although scripting languages and coordination languages have evolved from different roots and have been developed to solve different problems, we argue that there is a strong affinity between them. In particular, scripting and coordination address similar *separation of concerns*. Scripting languages (ideally) achieve a separation of *components* from the *scripts* that configure and compose them, and coordination languages separate *computational entities* from the *coordination* code that manages dependencies between them.

This affinity, we believe, will become only more important in the coming years as pervasive computing is becoming a reality, and agents representing hardware devices, internet services, and human clients will have to spontaneously interact and coordinate with other agents as a matter of routine. Building such flexible and dynamically evolving agent systems, on the other hand, will not be a trivial task, and we believe that scripting languages offer the only paradigm that has any hope of meeting the challenge.

If we examine the state of the art of today's scripting languages, however, we see that, although they offer many useful concepts and mechanisms for high-level programming, they are still a long way from fulfilling the coordination needs of tomorrow's agent systems. In particular, we see the need for improvement in the following areas:

- *Abstraction:* most scripting languages offer relatively weak abstraction mechanisms. To implement high-level abstractions, one is often forced to resort to techniques like generating code on-the-fly. As a consequence, higher-level coordination abstractions are cumbersome to implement in most scripting languages, if they are not already built into the language.
- *Software architecture:* the compositional (or "architectural") style supported by any given scripting language is usually fixed in advance. A truly general purpose scripting language would support the definition of new kinds of composition mechanisms for different application domains.
- *Concurrency:* concurrency, if supported at all, is provided by libraries, and is not explicitly supported by the language (both the Bourne Shell and Manifold are notable exceptions).
- *Coordination styles:* the fact that many different coordination models and languages have recently been proposed suggests that there does not exist a single approach suitable for all coordination problems. Similar to architectural styles, a catalogue of coordination styles that exhibit properties more suitable for some problems than others could be expressed in terms of components, connectors, and composition rules.

- *Reasoning:* scripting languages, as a rule, have no formal semantics, making it hard to reason about scripts. Since the behaviour that is coordinated by scripts is provided by components typically written in a separate programming language, a formal semantics for the scripting language is not enough to reason about overall behaviour, but it is certainly a prerequisite for making any progress.

In the Software Composition Group, we are attempting to address several of these problems with Piccola, a small language with a formal process calculus semantics, that is intended to be used as a general-purpose "composition language" for different application domains. In particular, we are currently working on formalizing and implementing various coordination styles based on the idea of a component algebra [3].

Acknowledgements

We thank all members of the Software Composition Group for their support of this work, and Richard van de Stadt for helpful comments on CyberChair. This research was supported by the Swiss National Science Foundation under Project No. 20-53711.98, "A framework approach to composing heterogeneous applications."

Part III

High-Level Enabling Coordination Technologies

High-Level Enabling Coordination Technologies

Introduction

Coordination is the process of managing dependencies between activities of one or multiple actors performed to achieve a goal and to avoid conflicts. It involves, amongst others, task decomposition, resource allocation, synchronization, group decision making, communication, and often the preparation and adoption of common objectives. A variety of approaches for coordination models and strategies including multiagent planning and decentralized negotiation protocols for different multiagent environments exist.

Coordination models have been extensively studied not only in the context of distributed systems but mobile agents and open multiagent systems deployed in the Internet. The *coordination medium* of a model supports interaction among coordinable, the agents in a multiagent system. The coordination model of the Linda language, for example, consists of a shared structure providing multisets of elements which can be constructed and manipulated by operations of an appropriate coordination language. In a more broader perspective sharing of elements is not necessary for coordination media like the interface repositories in the CORBA OMG architecture. An *interaction space* of a coordination model is constituted by the rules which govern the interaction among the agents on and the behavior of the coordination media. Such spaces can be accessed, for example, transparently in the Internet, for example, via object references, or explicitly via respective URLs. The interaction rules are typically defined in terms of both a given low-level communication and high-level coordination language. *A coordination language* defines the syntax and semantics of a set of admissible coordination primitives; the semantics of the primitives are typically expressed in terms of effects on the considered interaction space of the agents. Prominent examples of coordination models are Linda-like, client-server, meeting oriented, and blackboard based. In terms of coordination models agents in the Internet may interact with each other at given interaction spaces and use a coordination language to manipulate their coordination media such as channels, monitors, connectors, meeting places and blackboards.

However, in contrast to the rather syntax-based data communication, for example, in Linda-like coordination models there is an obvious need for some higher-level coordination in terms of a semantically meaningful communication between agents to let them accomplish their tasks and goals. In communicating information among different agents it is essential to preserve the desired semantics of utterances transmitted via messages. Both the intention of the message as well as its data content has to be understood correctly by the agents. Regarding the first issue agents may use a common *agent communication language* (ACL) for message exchange based on speech acts such as KQML and FIPA ACL. However, each ACL focuses on the interaction among agents only, leaving open the semantics of the content of the messages. In this respect, any ACL can be considered as a coordination language. On top of that, any *conversation* among agents is a pattern of message exchange that two or more agents agree to follow in communicating with one another. Thus, a conversation can be seen as a simple coordination protocol for agents itself using an ACL as its coordination language.

How can separate computational activities of heterogeneous agents be coordinated in collaborative or competitive settings in the Internet? We may roughly distinguish between the following two approaches:

1. *Direct communication*, in which agents handle their own coordination in asynchronous ensembles, or
2. *Assisted coordination*, in which agents rely on so-called middle-agents to achieve coordination in the context of service and data mediation within agent societies.

An individual agent in a multiagent system may perform its actions devoted to, for example, utilitarian coalition forming, team building, and distribution of tasks and responsibilities in the system exclusively via bi- and multi-lateral communication with relevant agents. There is an obvious trade-off between the amount of communication and quality of coordination in terms of completeness and efficiency. It depends on both the given application domain and environment as well as the type of interaction the agents in a society jointly agreed upon to accomplish their goals if and to what extent assisted coordination by middle-agents like yellow-page server, recommender, broker, and arbitrator agents is necessary.

In both cases, direct communication or assisted coordination, the agents may follow fixed or emerging policies, social obligations, and styles of conversations to coordinate their activities, for example, in negotiation settings at interaction spaces such as free market places in the e-commerce domain. However, interaction rules in assisted coordination typically turn out to be more rigid than in non-assisted coordination. This is particularly due to the introduction of trusted intermediaries as central control units to assist in the coordination among agents in a society.

In summary, high-level enabling techniques for coordinating agent societies include (1) agent naming and registration for localizing and identifying available agents in the system, (2) agreed use of agent communication languages for meaningful message exchange enabling task-oriented conversations among agents, and (3) mediation techniques and protocols to cope with the connection problem in open agent societies in the Internet.

Regarding assistance of coordination the only decisive issue is that of how to perform mediation amongst agents. In particular, mediation protocols such as for service matchmaking or recommendation determine which agents are involved in what kind of conversations at any instant in time. Thus, any mediation protocol is a high-level coordination protocol on top of the rather simple ones related to the respective conversations. Latter, in turn, rely on the high-level coordination mechanism of agent naming and a commonly agreed ACL as the coordination language. In non-assisted coordination settings mediation such as capability-based agent matchmaking has to be appropriately distributed among the agents. This still appears to be an unscarted territory, though first steps have been made in this direction. The following chapters provide overviews of the high-level enabling mechanisms for coordination of agent societies mentioned above, and report on ongoing significant research and development in the respective areas.

The contributions

In chapter 7, Robert Scott Cost, Yannis Labrou, and Tim Finin argue the usefulness of conversations and protocols for agent coordination on top of agent communication languages such as KQML and FIPA ACL. The authors are suggesting the utilization of colored petri nets for the purpose of a formal specification of conversations among interacting agents. One main motivation behind this proposal is that it enables to clearly specify and verify the semantics of such conversations. In particular the implied ability to validate properties of the conversations that are important in the context of coordinating agent societies such as liveliness, fairness, and reachability is essential for the design of vivid multiagent systems in many application domains.

Middle-agents perform assisted coordination by means of helping agents locate others that provide requested data and services in the Internet and Web. In chapter 8, Matthias Klusch and Katia Sycara introduce several different classes of basic services any middle-agent needs to appropriately instantiate to be able to perform a meaningful, effective, and reliable mediation between agents. Accoridng to these mediation service classes the authors propose a skill-based classification of middle-agents and have a closer look at the functionality of some special kinds of middle-agents, namely mediator, broker and matchmaker agents. A comprehensive description of prominent examples for multiagent systems and platforms which are coordinated by middle-agents and related work round this survey off.

Flexible and efficient naming, migration and coordination schemes are critical components of concurrent and distributed systems. In chapter 9, Gul Agha, Nadeem Jamali and Carlos Varela describe high-level actor naming in terms of a naming scheme with location and migration transparency called Universal Actor Names. On top of that, the authors present so-called ActorSpaces as an abstraction for decoupled publish-and-subscribe pattern-based communication. Latter enables the unanticipated connection of users, agents and services in the open, dynamic nature of today's networks. In addition, an actor-based architecture, the so-called World Wide Computer, is introduced as a basis for implementing the above concepts of high-level naming and multiagent coordination by means of synchronized migration of co-located sets of tightly constrained actors encapsulated in a so-called cyber organism (cyborg). Cyborgs is presented as a model for resource-bounded agent systems, an abstraction which provides a unit for group migration and resource consumption. The authors use a travel agent example to motivate the requirements and proposed solutions for naming, migration and coordination.

7. Coordinating Agents using Agent Communication Languages Conversations

R. Scott Cost, Yannis Labrou, and Tim Finin

Department of Computer Science and Electrical Engineering
University of Maryland Baltimore County
Baltimore, Maryland 21250
{cost,jklabrou,finin}@csee.umbc.edu

7.1 Introduction

Internet agents are expected to accomplish their tasks despite heterogeneity; agents of different designs and of varying skills and domain knowledge need to interact successfully through knowledge and information exchange and effective coordination. We identify two distinct and separate problems that Internet agents are faced in an open and dynamic environment: knowledge sharing and coordination.

The knowledge sharing problem between heterogeneous agents has a long thread of work behind it. For a large category of agent systems, the main mechanism for knowledge sharing is the Agent Communication Language (ACL). An ACL relies on a three-layer conceptual breakdown of the knowledge sharing problem. The concepts originated in the work of the Knowledge Sharing Effort (KSE) [447] and have found their way into Knowledge Query Manipulation Languages (KQML) [323] [368], the first ACL, and in FIPA ACL, the ACL proposed by the Foundation for Intelligent Physical Agents (FIPA), a standardization organization in the area of agents. A simple formulation of the *knowledge sharing* problem between heterogeneous intelligent agents is: "expressions in a given agent's native language should be understood by some other agent that uses a different implementation language and domain assumptions".

The three-layered approach distinguishes between propositions and *propositional attitudes*. The first and the second layers are concerned with sharing the meaning of propositions and the third layer is concerned with sharing the meaning of propositional attitudes. So, the first layer is that of (syntactic) translation between languages in the same family (or between families) of languages [1]. The second layer is concerned with guaranteeing that the semantic content of tokens is preserved across applications; in other words, the same concept, object, or entity has a uniform meaning across agents even if different "names" are used to refer to it. Every agent incorporates some view of the domain (and the domain knowledge) to which it applies. The technical

---

[1] The Object Management Group (OMG) standardization effort is an example of work in this direction, within the family of object-oriented languages.

term for this body of "background" knowledge is *ontology*. More formally, an ontology is a particular conceptualization of a set of objects, concepts and other entities about which knowledge is expressed and of the relationships that hold among them. An ontology consists of terms, their definitions, and axioms relating them [290]; terms are normally organized in a taxonomy. The final layer addresses the communication between agents. This is not merely about transporting bits and bytes between agents; agents should be able to communicate complex "attitudes" about their information and knowledge content. Agents need to ask other agents, to inform them, to request their services for a task, to find other agents who can assist them, to monitor values and objects, and so on. Such functionality, in an open environment, can not be provided by a simple Remote Procedure Call (RPC) mechanism. Agents issue requests by specifying not a procedure but a desired state in a declarative language, *i.e.*, in some ACL.

Assuming effective translations between their respective representation languages, with shared ontologies, an ACL allows them to share their knowledge content. But knowledge sharing alone does not guarantee effective problem solving any more than superb language skills guarantee effective performance for a human agent. Accomplishing tasks requires coordination.

Coordination is the process by which agents reason about their local actions and the (anticipated) actions of others in order to ensure that all agents in a community act in a coherent manner towards a goal or a set of goals. The actions of multiple agents need to be coordinated because of dependencies between agents' actions, there is a need to meet global constraints, and no one agent has sufficient competence, resources or information to achieve such system goals. Examples of coordination include supplying timely information to other agents or ensuring that the actions of agents are synchronized. In an environment of heterogeneous agents coordination is a difficult task because agent must reconcile conflicting or incomplete views of the environment they are acting upon or interacting with.

An ACL offers agents building blocks for coordination. To the extend that coordination is communicative, as is often the case in heterogeneous agent communities, agents can use the propositional attitudes supplied by ACLs in order to sustain the complex interactions with other agents that are necessary for coordination. The ACL alone, though, does not help agents to decide when to "talk" and what exactly to "say" when they do so. Ideally, agents would possess such a rich understanding of themselves, their environment and other agents, that, like human agents, they could decide what to "say" and for what purpose. There is a sizable amount of work in this direction, the problem is extremely difficult in an open and dynamic environment. The direction we explore in this chapter in differs in that it is not concerned with the internal structure of agents. ACL research has been exploring *conversation protocols* as mechanisms for structuring agent interactions. Such protocols serve as pre-arranged protocols for coordinating specific task-related agent interactions.

We are concerned with a suitable formalism for expressing such coordination protocols. Our goal is a formalism that guarantees certain useful properties for such protocols.

We next outline the organization of this chapter. In Section 7.2 we very briefly outline the basic concepts of ACLs and conversation protocols for ACL-speaking agents. In Section 7.3 we discuss conversation protocols, their use for coordination between agents and related work by other researchers. We continue by presenting our formalism for specifying conversation protocols, which is based on Colored Petri Nets CPNs), in Section 7.4, complete with examples of conversation protocols specified in our formalism. In Section 7.5 we discuss the merits of CPN-based descriptions of conversation protocols for agent coordination and in Section 7.6 we present relevant work on CPNs.

7.2 From Agent Communication Languages to Conversation Protocols

An Agent Communication Language provides agents with a means to exchange information and knowledge. ACLs, such as KQML or FIPA ACL, are languages of propositional attitudes. Propositional attitudes are three-part relationships between: (1) an agent, (2) a content-bearing proposition (*e.g.*, "it is raining"), and (3) a finite set of propositional attitudes an agent might have with respect to the proposition (*e.g.*, believing, asserting, fearing, wondering, hoping, *etc.*). For example, $< a, fear, raining(t_{now}) >$ is a propositional attitude.

ACLs are intended to be above the layer of mechanisms such as RPC or RMI because: (1) they handle propositions, rules and actions instead of simple objects (with no semantics associated with them), and (2) the ACL message describes a desired state in a declarative language, rather than a procedure or method. But ACLs by no mean cover the entire spectrum of what agents may want to exchange. More complex *objects* can and should be exchanged between agents, such as shared plans and goals, or even shared experiences and long-term strategies.

At the technical level, when using an ACL, agents transport messages over the network using some lower-level protocol (SMTP, TCP/IP, IIOP, HTTP, etc.). The ACL itself defines the types of messages (and their meaning) that agents may exchange. Agents though, do not just engage in single message exchanges but they have *conversations*, *i.e.* task-oriented, shared sequences of messages that they observe, in order to accomplish specific tasks, such as a negotiation or an auction. At the same time, some higher-level conceptualization of the agent's strategies and behaviors drives the agent's communicative (and non-communicative) behavior.

Traditionally, we understand the message types of ACLs as *speech acts*, which in turn are usually accounted for in terms of beliefs, desires, intentions and similar modalities. This kind of intentional-level description can either be just a useful way to view a system or it can have a concrete computational aspect. The latter case describes a large range of BDI^2 agents which have some (implicit or explicit) representation of the corresponding modalities. This representation is built on top of a substrate that describes the conceptual model of knowledge, goals and commitments of an agent, commonly known as a BDI theory. Despite the criticism that BDI theories and BDI agents have faced, such as the number and choice of modalities and the fact that multi-modal BDI logics have neither complete axiomatizations nor they are efficiently computable, they offer an appealing framework to account for agent communications, because agents, when communicating, they communicate their BDI states and/or attempt to alter their interlocutors BDI states.

While an ACL is good for message-passing among agents, on its own it does not offer much in terms of agent coordination. But when an agent sends a message, it has expectations about how the recipient will respond to the message. Those expectations are not encoded in the message itself; a higher-level structure must be used to encode them. The need for such conversation policies is increasingly recognized by both the KQML [369] and the FIPA communities [241, 212].

A conversation is a pattern of message exchange that two (or more) agents agree to follow in communicating with one another. In effect, a conversation is a pre-arranged coordination protocol, A conversation lends context to the sending and receipt of messages, facilitating interpretation that is more meaningful.

Although, conversations have become part of many infrastructures for ACL-speaking agents, relatively little work has been devoted to the problem of conversation specification and implementation. For conversations to be used for agent coordination, the following three issues require attention:

1. Conversation specification: How can conversations best be described so that they are accessible both to people and to machines?
2. Conversation sharing: How can an agent use a specification standard to describe the conversations in which it is willing to engage, and to learn what conversations are supported by other agents?
3. Conversation aggregation: How can sets of conversations be used as agent 'APIs' to describe classes of capabilities that define a particular service?

Although we have worked on items (2) and (3) (see [192]), our primary focus, in arguing the usefulness of conversations for agent coordination, is on their specification with emphasis on the ability to validate properties that are important in the context of coordination, such as liveliness and reachability.

---

^{2} BDI stands for *Belief*, *Desire* (or Goal) and *Intention*.

7.3 Coordination using Conversation Protocols

Well-defined, sharable conversation protocols, with testable, desirable properties, can be used to coordinate agents that attempt to accomplish specific tasks. Typically, a conversation protocol is associated with a specific task, such as *registration*, or a particular type of a *negotiation*. Agents adhering to the same conversation protocol, can coordinate their communicative actions as they attempt to accomplish the task suggested by the conversation protocol. Such a coordination is akin to a scripted interaction, with specific properties, rather than coordinated action resulting from a deep understanding of the domain and the task at hand. Nevertheless, it can be effective for tasks that can be adequately described in the form of possible sequences of communicative interactions.

A specification of a conversation that could be shared among agents must contain several kinds of information about the conversation and about the agents that will use it. First, the sequence of messages must be specified. Traditionally, deterministic finite-state automata (DFAs) have been used for this purpose; DFAs can express a variety of behaviors while remaining conceptually simple. For more sophisticated interactions, however, it is desirable to use a formalism with more support for concurrency and verification. Next, the set of roles that agents engaging in a conversation may play must be enumerated, and the constraints and dependencies between individual messages need to be captured. Many conversations will be dialogues, and will specify just two roles; however conversations with more than two roles are equally important, representing the coordination of communication among several agents in pursuit of a single common goal. For some conversations, the set of participants may change during the course of the interaction.

These capabilities will allow the easy specification of individual conversations. To develop systems of conversations though, developers must have the ability to extend existing conversations through specialization and composition. Specialization is the ability to create new versions of a conversation that are more detailed than the original version; it is akin to the idea of subclassing in an object-oriented language. Composition is the ability to combine two conversations into a new, compound conversation. Development of these two capabilities will entail the creation of syntax for expressing a new conversation in terms of existing conversations, and for linking the appropriate pieces of the component conversations.

The set of conversations in which an agent will participate defines an interface to that agent. Thus, standardized sets of conversations can serve as abstract agent interfaces (AAIs), in much the same way that standardized sets of function calls or method invocations serve as APIs in the traditional approach to system-building. That is, an interface to a particular class of service can be specified by identifying a collection of one or more conversations in which the provider of such a service agrees to participate. Any agent that wishes to provide this class of service need only implement the appropriate set of conversations.

Implementing and expressing conversations for software agents is not a new idea. As early as 1986, Winograd and Flores [636] used state transition diagrams to describe conversations. The COOL system [55] has perhaps the most detailed current FSM-based model to describe agent conversations. Each arc in a COOL state transition diagram represents a message transmission, a message receipt, or both. One consequence of this policy is that two different agents must use different automata to engage in the same conversation. COOL also uses an :intent slot to allow the recipient to decide which conversation structure to use in understanding the message. This is a simple way to express the semantics of the conversation, though it is not sufficient for sophisticated reasoning about, and sharing of conversations.

Other conversation models have been developed, using various approaches. Extended FSM models, which, like COOL, focus more on expressivity than adherence to a model, include Kuwabara et al. [365], who add inheritance to conversations, Wagner et al. [617], and Elio and Haddadi [218], who defines a multi-level state machine, or Abstract Task Model (ATM). A few others have chosen to stay within the bounds of a DFA, such as Chauhan [148], who uses COOL as the basis for her multi-agent development system [3], Nodine and Unruh [459], and Pitt and Mamdani [498], who uses DFAs to specify protocols for BDI agents. Also using automata, Martin et al. [398] employs Push-Down Transducers (PDT). Lin et al. [381] and Cost et al. [191] demonstrate the use of CPNs, and Moore [437] applies state charts. Parunak [485] introduces Dooley Graphs. Bradshaw [91] introduces the notion of a conversation suite as a collection of commonly-used conversations known by many agents. Labrou [367] uses definite clause grammars to specify conversations.

While each of these works makes contributions to our general understanding of conversations, more work needs to be done to facilitate the sharing and use of conversation policies by agents.

In the next section of this chapter we describe a formalism based on Colored Petri Nets, which can be used to specify conversation protocols.

7.4 Modeling Conversation Protocols with Colored Petri Nets

7.4.1 Colored Petri Nets

Petri Nets (PN), or Place Transition Nets, are a well known formalism for modeling concurrency. A PN is a directed, connected, bipartite graph in which each node is either a *place* or a *transition*. *Tokens* occupy places. When there

---

[3] More recent work with this project, JAFMAS, explores conversion of policies to standard Petri Nets for analysis [255].

is at least one token in every place connected to a transition, we say that the transition is *enabled*. Any enabled transition may *fire*, removing one token from every input place, and depositing one token in each output place. Petri nets have been used extensively in the analysis of networks and concurrent systems. For a more complete introduction, see [7].

CPNs differ from PNs in one significant respect; tokens are not simply blank markers, but have data associated with them. A token's *color* is a schema, or type specification. Places are then sets of tuples, called *multi-sets*. *Arcs* specify the schema they carry, and can also specify basic boolean conditions. Specifically, arcs exiting and entering a place may have an associated function which determines what multi-set elements are to be removed or deposited. Simple boolean expressions, called *guards*, are associated with the transitions, and enforce some constraints on tuple elements. This notation is demonstrated in examples below. CPNs are formally equivalent to traditional PNs; however, the richer notation makes it possible to model interactions in CPNs where it would be impractical to do so with PNs.

CPNs have great value for conversational modeling, in that they are a relatively simple formal model with a graphical representation and support for concurrency, which is necessary for many non-trivial interactions. Additionally, CPNs are well researched and understood, and have been applied to many real-world applications. As such, many tools and techniques exist for the design and analysis of CPN-based systems.

7.4.2 Conversation Protocols using Colored Petri Nets

As mentioned earlier, conversations are often specified by simple or modified DFAs. For the purposes of example, we will consider conversation definition in JDFA, a loose Extended Finite State Machine (EFSM) for modeling conversations, introduced in [192], [486]. The base model is a DFA, but the tokens of the system are messages and message templates, rather than simply characters from an alphabet. Messages match template messages (with arbitrary match complexity, including recursive matching on message content) to determine arc selection. A local read/write store is available to the machine.

CPNs make it possible to formalize much of the extra-model extensions of DFAs. To make this concrete, we take the example of a standard JDFA representation of a KQML Register conversation[4] and reformulate it as a CPN. The graphic depiction of this JDFA specification can be seen in Figure 7.1.

There are a number of ways to formulate any conversation, depending on the requirements of use. This conversation has only one final, or accepting, state, but in some situations, it may be desirable to have multiple accepting states, and have the final state of the conversation denote the *result* of the interaction.

---

[4] A *register* conversation is one the most basic KQML conversations, used for an agent to register its name and availability with an agent service. FIPA ACL uses a similar concept.

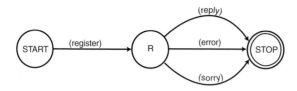

Fig. 7.1. Diagrammatic DFA representation of the simplified KQML Register conversation

In demonstrating the application of CPNs here, we will first develop an informal model based on the simplified Register conversation (in KQML) presented, and then describe a complete and working CPN-ML model of the full Register conversation.

Some aspects of the model which are implicit under the DFA model must be made explicit under CPNs. The DFA allows a system to be in one state at a time, and shows the progression from one state to the next. Hence, the point to which an input is applied is clear, and that aspect is omitted from the diagrammatic representation. Since a CPN can always accept input at any location, we must make that explicit in the model.

We will use an abbreviated message which contains the following components, listed with their associated variable names: performative(p), sender(s), receiver(r), reply-with(id), in-reply-to(re), and content(c)[5].

We denote the two receiving states as places of the names **Register** and **Done** (Figure 7.2). These place serve as a receipt locations for messages, after processing by the transitions **T1** and **T2**, respectively. As no message is ever received into the initial state, we do not include a corresponding place. Instead, we use a a source place, called **In**. This is implicit in the DFA representation. It must serve as input to every transition, and could represent the input pool for the entire collection of conversations, or just this one. Note that the source has links to every place, but there is no path corresponding to the flow of state transitions, as in the DFA-based model.

The match conditions on the various arcs of the DFA are implemented by transitions preceding each existing place. Note that this one-to-one correspondence is not necessary. Transitions may conditionally place tokens in different places, and several transitions may concurrently deposit tokens in the same place.

Various constants constrain the actions of the net, such as performative (Figure 7.3). These can be represented as color sets in CPN, rather than hard-coded constraints. Other constraints are implemented as guards;

---

[5] These variable names correspond to attributes of a typical ACL message. Syntactically, a ACL message is a balanced parenthesis list that begins with the *performative* (or message type, or propositional attitude) followed by attribute-value pairs for the sender of the message, the intended receiver and so on

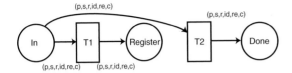

Fig. 7.2. Preliminary CPN model of a simplified KQML register conversation.

boolean conditions associated with the transitions. Intermediate places **S**, **R** and **I** assure that sender, receiver and ID fields in the response are in the correct correspondence to the initial messages. **I** not only ensures that the message sequence is observed, as prescribed by the message IDs, but that only one response is accepted, since the ID marker is removed following the receipt of one correct reply. Not all conversations follow a simple, linear thread, however. We might, for example, want to send a message and allow an arbitrary number of asynchronous replies to the same ID before responding (as is the case in a typical Subscribe conversation), or allow a response to any one of a set of message IDs. In these cases, we allow IDs to collect in a place, and remove them only when replies to them will no longer be accepted. Places interposed between transitions to implement global constraints, such as alternating sender and receiver, may retain their markings; that is implied by the double arrow, a shorthand notation for two identical arcs in opposite directions.

We add a place after the final message transaction to denote some arbitrary action not implemented by the conversation protocol (that is, not by an arc-association action). This may be some event internal to the interpreter, or a signal to the executing agent itself. A procedural attachment at this location would not violate the conversational semantics as long as it did not in turn influence the course of the conversation.

This CPN is generally equivalent to the JDFA depicted in Figure 7.1. In addition to modeling what is present in the JDFA, it also models mechanisms implicit in the machinery, such as message ordering. Also, the JDFA incorporates much which is beyond the underlying formal DFA model, and thus cannot be subjected to verification. The CPN captures all of the same mechanisms within the formal model.

7.4.3 A Conversation protocol for a simple Negotiation between Agents

In this section we present a simple negotiation protocol proposed in [151]. The CPN diagram in Figure 7.4 describes the pair-wise negotiation process in a simple MAS, which consists of two functional agents bargaining for goods. The messages used are based on the FIPA ACL negotiation performative set.

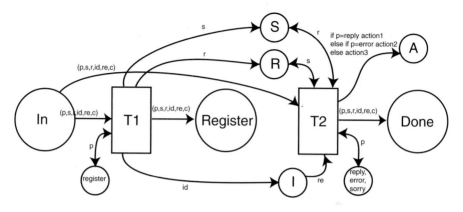

Fig. 7.3. Informal CPN model of a simplified KQML register conversation.

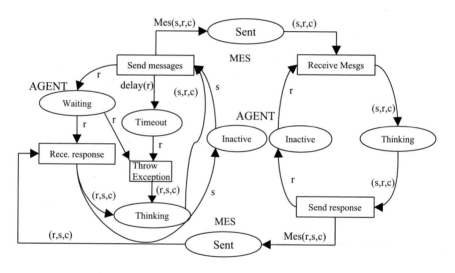

Fig. 7.4. Pair-wise negotiation process for a MAS constituted of two functional agents.

The diagram depicts three places places: **Inactive**, **Waiting**, and **Thinking**, which reflect the states of the agents during a negotiation process[6]; we will use the terms state and place interchangeably. Both agents in this simple MAS have similar architecture, differing primarily in the number of places/states. This difference arises from the roles they play in the negotia-

---

[6] It is not always the case with such a model that specific nodes correspond to states of the system or particular agents. More often the state of the system is described by the combined state of all places.

tion process. The agent that begins the negotiation, called the *buyer* agent, which is shown on the left side of the diagram, has the responsibility of handling message failures. For this, it has an extra 'wait' state (**Waiting**), and timing machinery not present in the other agent, *seller*. For simplicity, some constraints have been omitted from this diagram; for example, constraints on message types, as depicted in the previous examples.

In this system, both agents are initially waiting in the **Inactive** places. The buyer initiates the negotiation process by sending a call for proposals ('CFP') to some seller, and its state changes from **Inactive** to **Waiting**. The buyer is waiting for a response ('proposal', 'accept-proposal', 'reject-proposal' or 'terminate'). On receipt, its state changes from **Inactive** to **Thinking**, at which point it must determine how it should reply. Once it replies, completing the cycle, it returns to the **Inactive** state. We have inserted a rudimentary timeout mechanism which uses a delay function to name messages which have likely failed in the **Timeout** place. This enables the exception action (**Throw Exception**) to stop the buyer from waiting, and forward information about this exception to the agent in the **Thinking** state. Timing can be handled in a number of ways in implementation, including delays (as above), the introduction of timer-based interrupt messages, or the use of timestamps. CPN-ML supports the modeling of time-dependent interactions through the later approach.

Note that this protocol models concurrent pairwise interactions between a buyer and any number of sellers.

7.5 Advantages for Coordination when using CPN-described Conversations

There are a number of benefits to be derived from modeling agent coordination with a formal system, and with CPNs in particular. Formal models have a more clearly defined semantics, and are more amenable to standardization, exchange and reuse. They also facilitate analysis, both empirical and analytic.

The ability to verify the properties of a specification is one of the important benefits of applying formal methods. These benefits can be derived in two ways:

– Verification of the conversation policies or protocols directly, and
– Verification of agents or Multi Agent Systems (MAS) that are based on such protocols.

We will first consider the range of properties amenable to analysis, and then discuss their value in the two contexts described. The focus will be on the methods provided by Design/CPN and associated tools.

In addition to 'proof by execution', CPNs can be checked for a variety of properties. This is done by way of an Occurrence Graph (OG) [208]. Each node in an OG consists of a possible marking for the net. If another marking (B) can be reached by the firing of a transition, the graph contains a directed arc from the node representing the initial marking to B. All nodes in an OG are therefore derived from some initial marking of the net.

The properties subject to verification are:

1. Reachability Properties: This relates to whether or not the marking denoted by node B is reachable by some sequence of transition firings from node A.
2. Boundedness Properties: The upper or lower bound on the contents of place X in the net, over all possible markings. This can be the cardinality of the multiset at node X, or the greatest or least multiset itself.
3. Home Properties: The marking or set of markings which are reachable from all other markings in the OG define a homespace. One can verify that a marking or set of markings constitutes a homespace, or determine whether or not a home marking exits, and what the minimal such marking is.
4. Liveness Properties: A marking from which no further markings can be derived is 'dead'. Liveness, then, relates to the possible progressions from a given node in the OG. One can verify that a marking is dead, or list dead markings in the OG.
5. Fairness Properties: Relates to the degree to which certain transition instances (TI) will be allowed with respect to other TIs.

Many of these properties have different values depending on whether we are regarding a conversation protocol or a Multi Agent System, and also on the complexity of the net. Conversation protocols describe/operate on a message stream, which in most cases is finite; they are themselves static. One can imagine analyzing a conversation protocol in the context of (1) a single message stream, or (2) in the presence of a generator for all or many representative streams. In that sense, we may be interested in boundedness or home properties, and possibly reachability or fairness, but not liveness. On the other hand, liveness and fairness will often be more important in the analysis of a system as a whole.

It is possible to verify properties even for very large and complex nets. The version of Design/CPN used in this research supports the computation and analysis of OGs of 20,000 - 200,000 nodes and 50,000 to 2,000,000 arcs.

7.6 Related Work

CPNs are not new, and they have been used extensively for a broad range of applications (see [336] for a survey of current uses). Since their target domain is distributed systems, and the line between that domain and MASs is vague at best, there is much work on which to build. We will review here a few of the more directly related research endeavors.

Holvoet and Verbaeten have published extensively on the subject of agents and PNs. In their 1995 paper, "Agents and Petri Nets" [306], they introduced the idea of enhancing AOP by using high-level nets to model agents, and extended this thought in [307] to a variant called 'Generic Nets'. In 1997, Holvoet and Kielmann introduced PNSOL (Petri Net Semantics for Objective Linda) [308, 309], used to model agents which live in and communicate through the Objective Linda [353] tuple space.

Yoo, Merlat and Briot [652] describe a contract-net based system for electronic commerce that uses a modular design. Among the components are BRICS (Block-like Representation for Interacting Components) [237]), which are derived from CPNs.

Fallah-Seghrouchni and Mazouzi have demonstrated the use of CPNs in specifying conversation policies in some detail, using FIPA ACL as a framework [230, 229, 231]. This work suggests an approach for hierarchical construction of conversations.

Moldt and Wienberg have developed an approach called AOCPN (Agent Oriented Colored Petri Nets) [634, 428]. This system employed an object-oriented language, syntactically similar to C++, which maps onto CPN, extended by 'test arcs' [158, 370]. They show how this approach can be used to model societies of agents as described by Shoham [552]. Their model extends down to the level of individual agent theorem provers, facilitating the logical specification of agent behavior.

Other work of note includes Billington et al. [73], Purvis and Cranefield [503], Lin et al. [381] (above), and Merz and Lamersdorf [412].

7.7 Conclusions

An Agent Communication Language is a powerful framework for interacting agents in an open and dynamic environment. Although an ACL provides a framework for knowledge sharing between agents, it is, by itself, inadequate for coordination between agents. Conversations, i.e., well-specified sequences of message exchanges geared towards particular tasks, use ACL messages as building blocks for scripted, task-oriented interactions between agents. Such well-specified conversations, with testable properties, can be used to coordinate the behavior among communicating agents that attempt to accomplish the tasks specified by conversations.

While FSMs have proven their value for describing conversation policies, we feel that inherent limitations necessitate the use of a model supporting concurrency for the more complex interactions. CPNs provide many of the benefits of FSMs, while allowing greater expression and concurrency. We presented a CPN-based formalism for modeling conversation policies and we presented examples of using this formalism to specify conversations. This formalism provides for the testing of properties that are valuable for agent coordination.

8. Brokering and Matchmaking for Coordination of Agent Societies: A Survey

Matthias Klusch[1] and Katia Sycara[2]

[1] German Research Center for Artifical Intelligence, Multiagent Systems Group, D-66123 Saarbrücken, Germany.
[2] Carnegie Mellon University, Robotics Institute, Pittsburgh, USA.
E-Mail: klusch@dfki.de, katia@cs.cmu.edu

8.1 Introduction

A vast majority of enterprises continue to operate in the physical world, doing business as usual, but increasingly adopt the Internet in every aspect of their business operations. Internet-based coordination and collaboration between supply chain partners is expected to create new value and increase the productivity and efficiency of both digital and physical product companies. To date, the Internet has already created a complete electronic economy which is rapidly growing and comprising, in particular, an open and globally accessible networked environment; interconnected electronic markets, online consumers, producers, and electronic intermediaries; and legal and policy frameworks.

Intermediaries in the Internet economy provide market-maker services, domain expertise, trust, visibility, assurance, and certification that enable buyers to choose sellers and products. They also provide the search, retrieval, and aggregation services that lower online transaction costs for businesses. Like intermediaries in the physical economy, intelligent middle-agents can be considered as electronic intermediaries in the digital economy[57]. These agents provide means of meaningfully coordinating activities among agent providers and requesters of services (information, goods, or expertise) in the Internet [201]. Their main task is to locate and connect the ultimate service providers with the ultimate requesters in open environments, that is to appropriately cope with the connection problem.

Various distributed and centralized settings exist to solve this problem. In general, we roughly distinguish three agent categories, service providers (P-agents), service requester (R-agents), and middle-agents. The basic process of capability-based mediation by middle-agents has the following form: (1) P-agents advertise their capabilities to middle-agents, (2) middle-agents store these advertisements, (3) a R-agent asks some middle-agent to locate and connect to P-agents with desired capabilities which may include complete transaction intermediation and other value-added services, and (4) the respective middle-agent processes this request against its knowledge on capabilities of registered P-agents and returns the result. The result may be either a subset of the stored advertisements with names of respective providers to contact, or the result of the complete transaction for the most suitable service.

While this process at first glance seems very simple, it is complicated by the fact that the Internet considered as an open social, information, and business environment is in a continual change. The driving force which precipitate or demand change may arise anywhere at any time. Dynamic changes concern, for example, location and heterogeneity of available resources and content as well as different user communities and societies of agents each of which is pursuing its goals that may conflict with the goals of others. In addition the number of different agents and multiagent systems that are being developed by different groups and organizations significantly excarbates the connection problem. Thus, the essential capabilities of any kind of middle-agents are to facilitate the interoperability of appropriate services, agents and systems, building trust, confidence and security in a flexible manner, and to comply to regulatory and legal frameworks when available. This depends on the specific requirements implied by given specific application, information, and system environment. Given the fact that different types of middle agents provide different performance trade-offs what types of middle-agents are appropriate depends on the application. The overall challenge of a middle-agent based solution is to fit in with the considered situation most effectively, efficiently and reliably.

The structure of the remainder of this chapter is as follows. Section 8.2 provides a general skill-based characterization of middle-agents. In particular, we will give a compact guide to the basic concepts of matchmaking and brokering for coordination of agent societies in the Internet by respective types of middle-agents. Section 8.3 gives examples of both coordination techniques as they are available in several multiagent systems which have been developed by different research labs and universities so far. Finally, section 8.4 concludes this chapter by briefly summarizing the main results.

8.2 Coordination of Agent Societies via Middle-Agents

8.2.1 Middle-Agents

The notions of middle-agents, matchmakers, brokers, facilitators, and mediators are used freely in the literature on the subject without necessarily being clearly defined. In the following we address this terminological issue. In general, middle-agents are agents that help others to locate and connect to agent providers of services [201]. Furthermore, any middle-agent can be characterized by its core skills of

1. providing basic mediation services to the considered agent society,
2. coordinating these services according to given protocols, conventions, and policies, and

3. ensuring reliable service mediation in terms of leveled quality of services as well as trust management within and across multiagent systems borders.

Provision of mediation services. In open information and trading environments in the Internet a middle-agent has to provide basic mediation services for the

1. processing of agent capability and service descriptions
2. semantic interoperation between agents and systems,
3. management of data and knowledge, and
4. distributed query processing and transactions.

We will briefly discuss each of these service types in the following and propose a respective service-oriented classification of middle-agents in section 8.2.2.

1. *Processing of agent capability and service descriptions.* Basic requirement to understand and automatically process requests for and descriptions of services and capabilities of agents is the agreed use of a (set of) common agent capability description language such as LARKS [579, 577], CDL [144], or XML-based service description frameworks, like RDF(S)[507] or eCo system's server and common business library (CBL) of generic XML document models for e-commerce [277]. In general, the middle-agent has to in real time parse, validate, understand and respectively process capability and service descriptions it receives. This is in order to efficiently determine which of the advertised services and capabilities of currently registered P-agents are most appropriate for a given request of an R-agent. The choice of a suitable matching mechanism certainly depends on the structure and semantics of the descriptions to be matched as well as on the desired kind and quality of the outcome of the matching process; it may rely, for example, on simple keyword and value matching, use of data structure and type inferences, and/or the use of rather complex reasoning mechanisms such as concept subsumption and finite constraint matching. Semantically meaningful matching requires the matching service to be strongly interrelated particularly with the class of services enabling semantic interoperation between agents. We describe selected approaches for specifying and matching capability and service descriptions with given requests in more detail in section 8.2.3.

2. *Semantic interoperation.* One main obstacle of a meaningful interoperation and mediation of services is the syntactic and semantic heterogeneity of data and knowledge the middle-agent does access and receive from multiple heterogeneous agents, information systems and sources. The functional capability of a middle-agent to resolve such structural and

semantic heterogeneities refers to the knowledge-based process of semantic brokering [550].

a) *Knowledge-based reconciliation of heterogeneities.* Most methods to resolve semantic heterogeneities rely on using partial or global ontological knowledge which may be shared among the agents. This requires a middle-agent to provide some kind of ontology services for statically or dynamically creating, loading, managing, and appropriately using given domain-specific or common-sense ontologies as well as inter-ontology relations when it processes requests and data from different agents. For example, the agreed use of some common metadata catalogue and XML-based frameworks like Dublin Core and RDF(S)[507], respectively, a standardized ontology exchange language (OEL) such as XOL[649] or OIL[468] could be used by different agents in a multiagent system to represent and exchange individual ontological knowledge of given domains.

The transformation into a unified knowledge representation supports the middle-agent to (a) understand the semantics of requests and advertised capability or service descriptions it receives from heterogeneous agents and (b) to reconcile discovered semantic heterogeneities. The type of application and mediation of the middle-agent requested determines which kind of ontology and reconciliation service is most appropriate. A comprehensive survey of methods and techniques for knowledge-based resolution of different types of heterogeneities can be found, for example, in [357].

b) *Integration of information.* A middle-agent may create and maintain an integrated partially global view on available information for internal processing and restricted inspection by other agents and users on demand. Such an information model can, for example, take the static form of a federated schema in a multidatabase system [548] or a dynamically updated and categorized collection of capability and service descriptions annotated with relevant ontological information. The latter can be stored, maintained and queried like in XML-based data warehouses.

3. *Management of data and knowledge.* Basic internal services of the middle-agent include the efficient storage and management of data and knowledge about itself and other agents. Such data are, for example, sets of capability advertisements of registered P-agents, past and current requests of known R-agents, ontological knowledge shared among agents and other auxiliary data for internal processing. The corresponding databases, repositories and knowledge base of a middle-agent may be inspected by other agents and users for different purposes such as, for example, the specification of appropriate requests in the domain or monitoring activities according to given valid access restrictions and security policies.

4. *Distributed query processing and transactions.* In some cases the middle-agent has to put forward queries to multiple relevant external databases or other sources to gather information on behalf of its requesters. This requires the middle-agent to perform distributed query planning and execution of transactions in collaboration with respective systems and agents.

Coordination of mediation services. The coordination of mediation by a middle-agent requires in particular its ability to meaningfully communicate with agents, systems, and users which are involved in the overall mediation process according to given protocols, conventions, and policies. As a basic additional means agent naming and registration is needed to enable the middle-agent to locate and identify its providers and requesters within and across multiple agent societies.

Agent registration and naming. Location of relevant agents by the middle-agent presumes that its clients are registered and can be named at any instant; this implies utilization of basic services of agent registration and naming for example agent name servers within the network domain covered by the middle-agent. Regarding scalability the middle-agent may also have to be able to dynamically cross register agent capabilities from one agent society to another so as to maintain maximum accessibility of involved societies to each other's capabilities. R-agents within one agent society may benefit from services and data provided by P-agents in another one without being aware of the fact that each of them belong to a different multiagent system. This can be achieved by the middle-agent which is initially contacted by the R-agents by exploiting its semantic interoperation services and appropriate collaboration with relevant middle-agents of and interoperators between heterogeneous agent societies [272].

Inter-agent interactions. Any coordinated interaction between the middle-agent, registered R-/P-agents and other middle-agents basically relies on the agreed use of one or more standardized agent communication languages (ACL) like FIPA ACL or KQML, given conversation protocols, and policies [366]. In communicating information among different agents it is essential to preserve the desired semantics of utterances transmitted via messages of an ACL. Both the intention of the message as well as its data content has to be understood correctly by the middle-agent and its clients to perform and support required service mediation, respectively.

Accessing sources of data and information. In case the middle-agent has to access database systems, knowledge bases or other sources of information by itself it can do so either via standardized APIs or transparent remote access methods such as JDBC/ODBC, OKBC[469], Java RMI, and CORBA, respectively. In a different approach the middle-agent may retrieve the required data in collaboration with so-called wrapper agents which are encapsulating the relevant systems and sources. The middle-agent forwards appropriate subqueries to the wrappers each of which transforming the received request to a query in the proprietary query language of the particular system and returns the result of its execution in the desired format to the middle-agent. The middle-agent then has to merge all of these partial results for further processing. Such a scenario is in compliance with the paradigm of a mediator for intelligent information systems introduced by Wiederhold in 1992 [633].

Interfacing with users. In addition to the requirement of a middle-agent to appropriately communicate with its clients and relevant systems, it may also provide interface services to human users to let them, for example, browse available information they are interested in such as parts of a local domain or shared global ontology, sets of actual service descriptions, or registered service providers. These interface services have to be restricted according to given security policies and requirements.

Mediation protocols and policies. Any activities related to service mediation within an agent society can be organized and coordinated according to given protocols, conventions, and policies of interaction between agents. The middle-agent by definition plays a central role of initializing and coordinating the interaction among agents in collaborative or competitive settings. Most common forms of mediation protocols include matchmaking, brokering, and arbitration in negotiations between P- and R-agents, for example, at virtual marketplaces or auctions. The general protocols for brokering and matchmaking are described in section 8.2.3 below.

Reliability of mediation. Each client requires the contacted middle-agent to be reliable in terms of trust and quality of service. That means that the middle-agent should perform its designated mediation services at any given instant in a trustworthy manner and in compliance with given security and quality policies of individual agents or the considered agent society as a whole. This particularly requires the middle-agent to cope with different kind of policies in a coherent and consistent manner.

Quality of service. A middle-agent has to assure that the data it stores, processes and provides to the agents in the society comply with desired data quality requirements, standards, and policies. In this context data policy is the overall intention and direction of an agent with respect to issues concerning the quality of data products and services it will receive either from the middle-agent or the respective P-agents. The specification, management and evaluation of quality of mediated data and services may follow corresponding methods, standards and metrics used for data warehouse quality management [326] and software implementation quality such as the ISO 9126 standard.

Regarding the usage of mediated services and data, common quality requirements are that they are accessible and useful to the agents in terms of, for example, secure availability, interpretability and timeliness in order to detect changes and reasons for them. Other quality factors include correctness, completeness, consistency, and redundancy of data as well as functionality, efficiency, maintainability and portability of the implementation of mediated services. Latter factors particularly also concern the quality of the mediation services of the middle-agent itself. For example, the provided mediation should be accurate, fault-tolerant to potential service failures, adaptive, time and resource efficient, and stable. It also requires the middle-agent to guarantee against loss of data or revenue as a result of its mediation which in turn, may increase the level of trust in its mediation services.

Trust management. Besides the client-sided demand to the middle-agent of providing quality of services there is also the essential requirement of a middle-agent to behave in a trustworthy manner to its clients in terms of guaranteeing desired data privacy, anonymity, and verification of claimed agent capabilities [640, 402]. In this sense, a middle-agent acts as a trusted intermediary among the agents of the considered agent society according to given trust policies of individual agents and the whole society.

Both internal data and knowledge of, and the computational processes of mediation executed by the middle-agent should be robust against external manipulation or attacks of malicious agents, systems, or users. On the other hand, clients of a middle-agent should have no incentive to misuse any information which has been revealed by the middle-agent during mediation. In this respect most common trust actions are authorization and verification of credentials of all parties which are involved in the mediation.

These actions have to take different trust relationships into account which may exist among the R-agents, middle-agents, and the P-agents within one or more connected agent societies. Can a contacted middle-agent, for example, be trusted by R- or P-agents to not resell (parts of) private profile information, copyrighted data, and so forth, to other middle-agents or P-agents it collaborates with potentially across multiagent systems borders? R-agents also might want to verify certain facts about relevant P-agents before contracting them either by itself or the middle-agent as a trusted intermediary.

In summary, there is an obvious need for all agents involved in the mediation process to use an appropriate trust model to analyse and assess the risks of and methods to prevent and counteract attacks against their data and knowledge. Models, methods and techniques supporting the establishment and management of mutual trust between a middle-agent and its clients in an open environment include

— the use of expressive trust establishment certificates useful for, e.g., binding agent identity to public key infrastructures such as IETF's SPKI [301, 564], and other standard security mechanisms and protocols, the use of mechanisms to bind agent names to their human deployers, so that the human would bear responsibility in case his/her agent misbehaves.

- the formal specification of agent trust policies, and
- the respective update, propagation, and transitive merge of trust matrices to calculate an overall trust relationship that accounts for the trust values in each and every individual trust relationship which is relevant to the considered mediation process [395]. An option is the application of distributed history-based reputation mechanisms to agent societies [653].

8.2.2 Types of Middle-Agents: Mediators, Brokers, and Matchmakers

Decker et al. [201] investigated different roles of middle-agents in the solution space of the connection problem from the standpoint of privacy considerations. The authors particularly examined knowledge about R-agent preferences, and P-agent capabilities; in this view specific requests and replies or actions in service of a request are interpreted as instances of preferences of R-agents and capabilities of P-agents, respectively. Both preference and capability information can initially be kept private at the R-agent, be revealed to some middle-agent, or be known by the P-agent. This leads to a categorization of some middle-agent roles as shown in the following table.

Preferences initially known by	Capabilities initially known by		
	P-agent only	P-agent + middle-agent	P-agent + middle-agent + R-agent
R-agent only	(Broadcaster)	"Front-agent"	Yellow-Pages, Matchmaker
R-agent + middle-agent	Anonymizer	Broker	Recommender
R-agent + middle-agent + P-agent	Blackboard	Introducer	Arbitrator

Table 1: Middle-agent roles categorized by initial privacy concerns [201].

For example, a broker agent understands but protects the initial privacy of capability and preference information of both the R-agent and P-agent; neither the R-agent nor the P-agent ever knows directly about the other in a transaction which is intermediated by the broker agent. In contrast, any R-agent can query capability information of registered P-agents at a matchmaker or yellow-page server such that this information is revealed initially to both requesters and providers. However, this categorization of middle-agent roles does not reflect the possibility of learning of preferences and capabilities over time.

In addition to this perspective on middle-agents restricted to initial privacy concerns we propose a more general skill-based, means service-oriented, classification of middle-agents. This classification is implied by the extent a middle-agent is providing mediation services as they are described in section 8.2.1. Figure 8.1 summarizes these service classes for middle-agents in general and for some common types of middle-agents in particular, namely mediators, brokers, and matchmakers. Latter is illustrated by means of object-oriented inheritance and instantiation of service classes for each of the agents. The corresponding classification matrix based on the differences in services is given in figure 8.2.

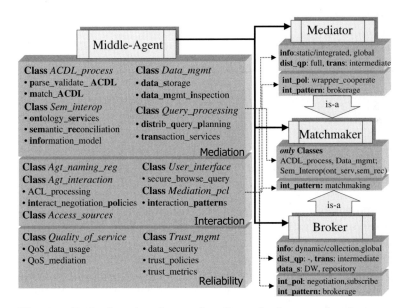

Fig. 8.1. Derived service classes of mediator, broker, matchmaker agents

In the following we briefly discuss mediator, broker and matchmaker agents in general, then focus on particular enabling techniques of brokering and matchmaking, and finally survey some of the prominent examples.

Mediator. A mediator agent in its original definition by Wiederhold (1992) [633] is dynamically and actively interfacing users (R-agents) to relevant data and knowledge resources. In this context, the term 'mediation' includes the processing needed to make the interface work, the knowledge structures that drive the transformation needed to transform the data to information, and any intermediate storage that is needed. In general, a mediator focuses on the provision of services devoted to semantic information brokering. That encompasses services to (1) dynamically determine information services and products; (2) arbitrate between consumer and provider agents by means of resolving different world-views (information impedance), and (3) dynamically

Mediation Services	Matchmaker	Broker	Mediator
Class *ACDL_process*			
• parse_validate_ **ACDL**	X	X	X
• match_**ACDL**	X	X	X
Class *Sem_interop*			
• ontology_**services**	X	X	X
• semantic_**reconciliation**	X	X	X
• information_model		dynamic collection	static/integrated global
Class *Data_mgmt*			
• data_storage/**mgmt/inspect**	X	data warehouse repository	federated db/repository
Class *Query_processing*			
• distrib_**query_planning**			X
• transaction_services		intermediate	intermediate
Class *Agt_interaction*	register/matching only	negotiation,	wrapper,
• interact_negotiation_**policies**	no negotiation	subscribe, coop.	(mediator) coop.
Class *Mediation_pcl*			
• interaction_**patterns**	matchmaking	brokerage	brokerage
Class *Access_sources*		X	X

Fig. 8.2. Service-oriented classification of mediator, broker, matchmaker

create or compose information products by correlating or assembling components and services from various providers.

As mentioned above, the most common scenario of a mediator in an intelligent information system is that it acts as a central unit collaborating with a set of wrapper agents (P-agents) each of which is providing access to and data of some available information source in a common data model. A mediator is creating and managing a partial global information model on the environment and other agents through knowledge based integration of received information from different sources, and offering domain and application specific value-added services. It takes requests from user agents (R-agents) and answers them either using its global information model or forwarding appropriate requests to the relevant wrapper agents based on respective distributed query planning and processing. In this sense information is gathered following a pull mechanism initiated by the mediator on demand.

In contrast to broker agents mediators do not simply collect information from different providers similar to data warehouses but integrate them into a global information model by resolving inconsistencies and conflicts. This model is typically hidden in the definition of the mediator, and is either statically or dynamically generated. In addition, a broker agent usually is considered not to be able to do any distributed query planning and processing. Examples of mediator-based information systems are Infomaster [271], TSIMMIS [259], Observer [549], MIX [56, 426], and SIMS/Ariadne [40].

Broker. A broker agent may actively interface R-agents to P-agents by inter-mediating requested service transactions. All communication between paired R- and P-agents has to go through the broker. It typically contacts (a set of) the most relevant P-agent, negotiates for, executes and controls appropriate transactions, and returns the result of the services to the R-agent.

This is in contrast to the functionality of a matchmaker agent but is sub-sumed by that of a mediator. But unlike mediators, broker agents typically do not provide a global, semantically integrated, consistent information model to their clients but store collected information maybe together with associated ontological annotations in some standardized data (structure) format in one (or multiple) appropriate repositories like in a data warehouse. In addition, a broker typically does not have a comparably extensive set of value-adding mediation services like a mediator; in this respect a broker may rely on differ-ent types of task-oriented agents it is able to collaborate and negotiate with. Broker may subscribe to certain P-agents if needed. Unlike a mediator agent, the interaction of brokers with other agents is neither restricted to wrappers or mediators nor committed to a fixed number of agents. This ability is par-ticularly useful since brokers are usually acting in dynamic environments in which resources and agents may continually enter and leave the agent society. In such environments it turns out to be inappropriate to maintain a static pre-integrated global model which is valid for a rather closed society of agents and systems.

However, it is noteworthy that the semantics of the terms matchmaker and broker as well as mediator and broker are often used interchangeably in the literature; brokers are also often called facilitators. Examples of bro-ker agents and broker-based systems include XML-based GMD Broker [315], OntoBroker [474], SHADE, and COINS [364].

Matchmaker. A matchmaker agent just pairs R-agents with P-agents by means of matching given requests of R-agents with appropriate advertised services of registered P-agents. In contrast to the functionality of both the broker and mediator it simply returns a ranked list of relevant P-agents to the requesting agent. As a consequence the R-agent has to contact and nego-tiate with the relevant P-agents itself for getting the services it desires. This direct interaction between R-agent and selected P-agents is performed inde-pendently from the matchmaker. It avoids, for example, data transmission bottlenecks or single point of failure at the matchmaker but increases direct communication overhead between matched R-/P-agents.

One could consider matchmaking as subsumed by brokering but it also extends it in the sense of giving the R-agent the full choice of selecting a (set of) P-agents a-posteriori out of the result of service matching. In settings with brokers instead, any R-agent choice a-priori by specifying respective constraints in its request for service to the broker. Examples of matchmaker-based multiagent systems and platforms include IMPACT [42], InfoSleuth

[458], and RETSINA/LARKS [579, 577] each of which is described in section 8.3.

8.2.3 Coordination Techniques for Middle-Agents: Brokering and Matchmaking

The coordination of mediation activities within and across agent societies can be performed by a middle-agent, for example, via brokering or matchmaking. Both types of mediation imply different requirements and protocols for interaction among agents which are involved in it. According to the skill-based classification of middle-agents as described in section 8.2.1 any method and technique for capability and service matching can be utilized for implementing both the brokering and matchmaking. In addition, ontology services are typically used to perform meaningful automated reasoning on capability and service descriptions specified in a given ACDL.

In the following we briefly summarize the high-level interaction patterns for both the matchmaking and the brokering protocol. Additionally we adopt the approach by Wong and Sycara [639] to give a formal specification of the respective protocols by means of state-transition relation based input/output (IO) automata [388]. An IO automaton performs an action in a given state such that it may transition to a new state according to a given transition relation. This relation is described in a precondition-action-effect style to specify the changes that occur as a result of an action in the form of a simple pseudo-code that is applied to a pre-state to yield another state. Each agent is modelled as a process which, in turn, is specified as an IO automaton.

Matchmaking. When a service-providing agent registers itself with the middle-agent together with a description of its capabilities specified in an agreed ACDL, it is stored as an advertisement and added to the middle-agent's database. Thus, when an agent inputs a request for services, the middle-agent searches its database of advertisements for a service-providing agent that can fill such a request. Requests are filled when the provider's advertisement is sufficiently similar to the description of the requested service (service matching). As mentioned above the requesting agent has to directly interact with the relevant provider to obtain the service and data it desires (service gathering). Figure 8.3 gives an overview of the interaction pattern of this two-parted matchmaking process.

According to this interaction pattern an IO automaton for a matchmaker agent can be specified as follows.

Definition 1: *(Matchmaker automaton)*

Variables $provID, reqID, req, pref, capDescr, servParam, transID, match$ are drawn respectively from the set of P- and R-agent ids, requests, preferences, capability descriptions, service parameters, transaction ids, and an ordered list of service-request matches. The set of states and the signature of automaton A is

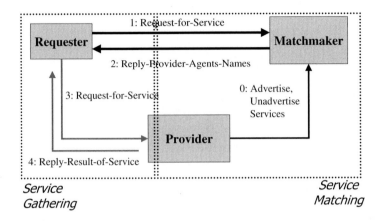

Fig. 8.3. Interaction pattern of capability and service matchmaking between agents

denoted by $states(A)$ and $signature(A)$, respectively. The set of actions $acts(A)$ includes $receive(msg)$, $send(msg)$, and $match(db, (req, pref, reqID), k)$ denoting functions for receiving and sending messages of type 'advertise-capability', 'request-for-service', 'result', and returning a decreasingly ordered list of k tuples $((provID, capDescr), req, reqID)$ denoting the k best matching P-agents $provID$ (with respective capability description $capDescr$), respectively.

The set of transitions $trans(A) \subseteq states(A) \times acts(signature(A)) \times states(A)$. A middle-agent performs actions triggered by its input which transition A into a valid state and produce some output. Input and output are defined in terms of message types the middle-agent can receive and send, respectively.

Signature:
        input: (advertise-capability $(provID, capDescr, servParam)$)
                (request-for-service $(reqID, req, pref, k)$)
        output(msg), $msg \in \{success, fail\}$
                (result $(match)$), $match = [((provId, capDescr), req, reqID)]$

States:
- $capDB$: database of capability descriptions.
- $ackQ$: queue of acknowledgements containing tuples $(provID, success/fail)$ each of which is indicating the result of an advertisement.
- $delQ$: queue of delegations containing tuples $(reqID, (req, pref, input))$ each of which is representing a request which has not yet been processed by the middle-agent.
- $matchQ$: queue of matching pairs of R-/P-agents containing tuples $((provID, reqID), (req, pref))$ with $provId$ indicating the P-agent that best matches the request req of R-agent $reqID$.

Transitions:

    receive((advertise-capability $(provID, capDescr, servParam)))$

        Precondition: -

        Effect: $capDB :=$ add$(capDB, (provID, capDescr, servParam))$;

        if add$(capDB, (provID, capDescr, servParam))$ succeeds

        then $ackQ :=$ append$(ackQ, (provID,$success$))$ else

        $ackQ :=$append$(ackQ,(provID,$fail$))$

    send$(msg, provID)$

        Precondition: head$(ackQ) = (provID, msg)$,

        Effect: $ackQ :=$tail$(ackQ)$.

    receive(request-for-service $(reqID, req, pref))$

        Precondition: -

        Effect: $delQ :=$ append$(delQ, (reqID, req, pref))$.

    match$(capDB, (req, pref, reqID), k)$

        Precondition: head$(delQ) = (reqID, req, pref)$.

        Effect: $delQ :=$ tail$(delQ)$;

        $matchQ :=$ append$(matchQ,$

                $(reqID,$ match$(capDB, (req, pref, reqID), k)))$.

    send((result $(match))$, $reqID)$

        Precondition: head$(matchQ) = (reqID, match)$

        Effect: $matchQ :=$ tail$(matchQ)$;

□

Brokering. Based on the functional capability of broker agents informally described in section 8.2.2 the interaction pattern of brokering is shown in figure 8.4 below.

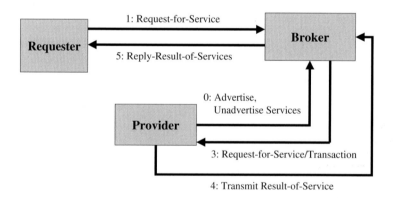

Fig. 8.4. Interaction pattern of capability and service brokering between agents

According to this basic interaction pattern an IO automaton for a broker agent can be defined as follows. Due to space constraints we omitted to include the option of the broker to individually negotiate services execution with the relevant P-agents on behalf of its clients.

Definition 2: *(Broker automaton)*

See definition 1 for definition of states, variables, actions, message types. In addition, variables *input*, *ResultOfService*, z are drawn from the set of inputs needed for service executions, results they generate, and integer, respectively. The message type 'brokerage-RFS' and 'perform-SE' indicate that the middle-agent has to broker the request for service, and that each of the contacted P-agents has to perform requested service execution (transaction) given the id, and preferences of the requesting R-agent, respectively. It is assumed that the additional input needed for intermediation of transactions (such as payment information) is known to the broker agent. The states are meant to be in addition to the states already described in definition 1.

Signature:
> input: (advertise-capability ($provID, capDescr, servParam$))
> > (brokerage-RFS ($reqID, req, pref, input, k$))
> > (result ($ResultOfService, transID$))
>
> output: (msg), $msg \in \{success, fail\}$
> > (perform-SE (($req, pref, input$), $reqID, transID$))
> > (result ($ResultOfService, req$))

States:
- *AsyncResWait*: set of tuples (reqID, transID) indicating that the middle-agent is still waiting for the result of the transaction transID to be sent to the respective requester reqID.
- *resQ*: queue of service execution (transaction) results containing tuples ($reqID$, $ResultOfService$, $transID$) each of which includes the result of the transaction $transID$ ready to be transmitted to the respective R-agent $reqID$. set of tuples ($req, transID$) each of which denotes the mapping of a request to its transaction id.

Transitions:
> receive(((advertise-capability ($provID, capDescr, servParam$)))
> > Precondition: -
> > Effect: $capDB$:= add($capDB, (provID, capDescr, servParam)$);
> > if add($capDB, (provID, capDescr, servParam)$) succeeds
> > then $ackQ$:= append($ackQ, (provID$,success))
> > else $ackQ$:= append($ackQ,(provID$,fail))
>
> send($msg, provID$)
> > Precondition: head($ackQ$) = ($provID, msg$)
> > Effect: $ackQ$:= tail($ackQ$).
>
> receive(brokerage-RFS ($reqID, req, pref, k$))
> > Precondition: -
> > Effect: $delQ$:= append($delQ, (reqID, req, pref)$), z:=k;
>
> match($capDB, (req, pref, reqID), k$)
> > Precondition: head($delQ$) = ($reqID, req, pref$).
> > Effect: $delQ$:= tail($delQ$);

$$matchQ := \text{append}(matchQ,$$
$$(reqID, \text{match}(capDB, (req, pref, reqID), k))).$$

send(perform-SE $((req, pref, input), reqID, transID), provID)$
   Precondition: head($matchQ$) =
   $(reqID, [((provID, capDescr), req, reqID)])$; $z_i 0$
   Effect: $matchQ := \text{tail}(matchQ)$; $z-$;
   $AsyncResWait := AsyncResWait \cup \{(reqID, transID, req)\}$;
receive((result $(ResultOfService, transID)), provID)$
   Precondition: -
   Effect: $resQ := \text{append}(resQ,$
            $(reqID, ResultOfService, transID))$;
   $AsyncResWait := AsyncResWait \setminus \{(reqID, transID, req)\}$;
   $TR := TR \cup \{(transID, req)\}$
send((result $(ResultOfService, req), reqID)$
   Precondition: head($resQ$) = $(reqID, ResultOfService, transID)$;
   $(transID, req) \in TR$
   Effect: $AsyncResWait := AsyncResWait \setminus \{(reqID, transID)\}$;
   $TR := TR \setminus \{(transID, req)\}$;
   $resQ := \text{tail}(resQ)$.

□

8.3 Examples of Coordination via Service Matchmaking and Brokering

In the following we describe prominent examples of implemented multiagent systems and platforms which are coordinated by middle-agents via the mediation protocols for service matchmaking and brokering. These examples are IMPACT, RETSINA/LARKS, and InfoSleuth, respectively. Other related work is surveyed in section 8.3.4.

It is noteworthy that mediation across multiagent systems boundaries has still not received much attention though it is a crucial issue in open environments like the Internet. First steps in this direction include the RETSINA interoperator [272] between heterogeneous agent societies and multi-agent systems.

8.3.1 InfoSleuth

InfoSleuth [458] has been developed by MCC Inc. in Austin, Texas, USA. It is an agent-based system that can be configured to perform different information management activities in distributed applications such as in an evironmental data exchange network and competitive intelligence system. InfoSleuth offers a set of various agents with different roles as follows.

User agents act on behalf of users and interface them to the rest of the agent system, resource agents wrap and activate databases and other information sources; "broker agents" perform syntactic and semantic matchmaking;

ontology agents collectively maintain a knowledge base of the different ontologies used for specifying requests and return ontological information on demand; multi-resource agents process complex queries that span multiple heterogeneous resources, specified in terms of some domain ontology. Further agent roles concern task planning and execution, monitoring of data streams and system operations, and other specialized functions.

Any P-agent in a given InfoSleuth system announces itself to one or multiple matchmaker agents (called "broker agents") by advertising to it, using the terms and attributes described in a common shared ontology (called "infosleuth ontology") attributes and constraints on the values of those attributes. This special ontology is shared by all agents to use for specifying advertisements and requests. It contains concepts useful to define (a) what kind of content is accessible by an agent, (b) what services an agent can do for whom, (c) what are the interfaces to those services, (d) how well can an agent perform those services at the moment, and (e) other properties of an agent such as location, used communication protocols, etc.

Agent capabilities are represented in InfoSleuth at following four levels:

1. the agent conversations that are used to communicate about the service,
2. the interface to the service,
3. the information a service operates over, and
4. the semantics of what the service does.

Figure 8.5 shows an example of the specification of a pair of matching query and capability description in InfoSleuth adopted from [141].

In this example a resource agent named 'tx-env-resource' is able to provide environmental contamination information related to contaminated sites in Texas. In this respect it advertises generic capabilities such as the ability to be monitored, to be queried and subscribed to. Latter capability consists of a set of related ontology fragments according to the levels of capability representations mentioned above: the conversation ontology fragment specifies that the agent accepts conversations of the form used by subscriptions, using the language KQML. The sql ontology fragment specifies that queries have to be specified in the relational database query language SQL. The environment ontology fragment specifies classes and slots which contain data in the agent. Finally, the service ontology fragment specifies that the advertised service is accessed locally within the agent as well as other properties.

R-agents formulate request for services like the one shown in the example above in terms of the infosleuth ontology. The matchmaker then matches the request to P-agents whose advertisements correspond to the constraints specified in the request, and returns a recommendation containing those P-agents to the R-agent. Resource agents whose databases do not maintain data in terms of the common ontology access special mapping agents to perform appropriate ontology mapping actions.

Given a query over a single domain-specific ontology, a query agent coordinates the processing of the request by (a) collaborating with one or multiple

Advertisement

capability env-subscription

  ontology conversation
  class conversation
    slot conversation-type **in** {subscribe}
    slot language **in** {kqml}
  ontology sql
  ontology services
  class data-response
    slot language **in** {tuple-format}
    slot delivery **in** {http,inline}
  class subscription
    slot computation **in** {direct}
  ontology environment
  class site
    slot contaminant
    slot remedial-response
    slot city
    slot state **in** {Texas}

Query

capability subscribe-to-capability

  ontology conversation
  class conversation
    slot conversation-type **in** {subscribe}
    slot language **in** {kqml}
  ontology sql
  ontology services
  class data-response
    slot language **in** {tuple-format}
    slot delivery **in** {inline}
  class subscription
    slot computation **in** {direct}
  ontology environment
  class site
    slot contaminant
    slot city **in** {Austin}
    slot state **in** {Texas}

Fig. 8.5. Example of query and capability descriptions in InfoSleuth

matchmakers to identify relevant resource agents, (b) decomposing the query into a collection of subqueries each addressed to these agents, and (c) fusing the subquery results into an integrated answer to the original global query. Issues of subquery translation and execution being encapsulated with the respective resource agent. The resource agents may continually enter and leave the system, such that the query agent does not create and maintain a global integrated information model of the agent society. In summary, in InfoSleuth the query agent and the "broker" agent acts as a broker and a matchmaker, respectively.

Unfortunately, the exact and complete process of query decomposition for general queries (not just data base queries) or the process of matching in the InfoSleuth system has not yet been revealed in the literature. However, what is known from the literature is that service matching occurs at different levels: Syntactic, semantic, and pragmatic matching. In InfoSleuth, syntactic matching refers to the process of matching requests on the basis of the syntax of incoming messages which wrap the query; semantic matching refers to the process of matching the internal data structures of and constraints used in request and capability descriptions; pragmatic matching includes considerations such as the performance of the machine the agent is running on and security requirements.

8.3.2 IMPACT

The IMPACT (Interactive Maryland Platform for Agents Collaborating Together) platform [42, 322] has been developed at the University of Maryland, College Park, USA. It supports multiagent interactions and agent interoperability in an application independent manner. For this purpose IMPACT provides following set of connected servers:

1. *Yellow-pages server* performs basic matchmaking among R- and P-agents based on two weighted hierarchies it maintains - a verb and a noun hierarchy of synonyms - and retrieval algorithms to compute similarities between given service specifications,
2. *registration server* for agent registration and maintaining an agent service index used by the yellow-pages server,
3. *type server* maintains a hierarchical ontology of standard data types and concepts, as well as
4. a *thesaurus* and a *human interface* allowing a human to access all the above servers in an IMPACT system.

The IMPACT software provides the infrastructure upon which different IMPACT agents may interact; multiple copies of it may be replicated across the network and get synchronized when needed.

Any service provided by an IMPACT agent is specified in a special markup service description language. A service specification consists of (a) a service name in terms of a verb-noun(noun) expression such as rent:car(Japanese), (b) typed input and output variables, and (c) attributes of services such as usage cost, average response time to requests for that particular service, etc. Services may be either mandatory or discretionary. Agents may request services in one of the following forms.

- *k-nearest neighbor request*: Find the k-nearest service names (pairs of verb and noun term) such that there exists an agent who provides that service and identify this agent
- *d-range search*: Find all service names within a specified distance d.

Searching of appropriate services in IMPACT essentially relies on the exploitation of given weighted verb hierarchy and noun hierarchy each of which are special cases of the general concept of a term hierarchy. Similarity between verbs and nouns in the verb and noun hierarchy, respectively, is computed via a given distance function on paths of weighted edges in the hierarchies. A composite distance function then combines both distance functions to calculate the combined similarity value for two word pairs (verb,noun) of service names. The authors suggest to take addition as composite distance function. If a word cannot be found in the respective hierarchy a synonym will be searched in the thesaurus instead.

Figure 8.6 gives an example of the data structures used in IMPACT to process requests. Regarding these example data structures a request "Find

$(k =)$ 2 nearest agents that provide a service (rent, car()) of renting cars"
will be processed as follows.

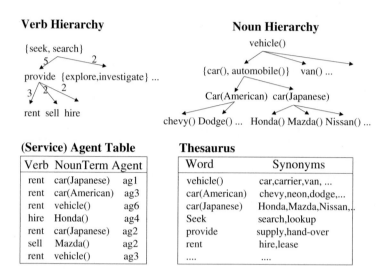

Fig. 8.6. Example of data structures used for service matchmaking in IMPACT

Firstly, an agent table is searched to find at most 2 agents that provide the
exact service (rent, car()). Since this search returns the empty set the service
related word pair (rent, car()) is now relaxed to (rent, vehicle()) by taking
an immediate neighbor of the verb 'rent' and the noun 'car' in the verb and
noun hierarchy, respectively. The type car() is now instantiated using values
specified in the data type hierarchy of the IMPACT type server which leads
in this example to noun terms car(Japanese) and car(American). As an intermediate result we get the following list of information on relevant services in
the form ((verb,noun),composite distance): ((rent, car(Japanese), 1), ((rent,
car(American)), 1), ((provide, car()), 3). Searching the agent table for exact
matching service names rent:vehicle() and rent:car(Japanese) is successful in
this example and returns agent6 and agent1 as relevant P-agents.

8.3.3 RETSINA/LARKS

The RETSINA (Reusable Task Structure-based Intelligent Network Agents)
[580, 512] multiagent infrastructure has been developed at the Carnegie Mellon University in Pittsburgh, USA. It consists of a system of three different
reusable agent types that can be adapted to address a variety of different
domain-specific problems.

Interface agents interact with the user, receive user input and display results. Task agents help users perform tasks by formulating problem solving plans and carrying out these plans through querying and exchanging information with other software agents. Information/resource agents provide intelligent access to a heterogeneous collection of information sources.

A collection of RETSINA agents forms an open society of reusable agents that self-organize and cooperate in response to task requirements. The RETSINA framework has been implemented in Java and is being used to develop distributed collections of intelligent software agents that cooperate asynchronously to perform goal-directed information retrieval information integration and planning tasks in support of a variety of decision making tasks.

Similar to the InfoSleuth system mediation in the RETSINA multiagent systems basically relies on service matchmaking. However, the specification of capability and service descriptions differ. The ACDL developed for matchmaking in RETSINA is called LARKS (Language for Advertisement and Request for Knowledge Sharing)[579]. Application domain knowledge in agent advertisements and requests can be currently specified as local ontologies written in a specific concept language ITL or by using WordNet. In the LARKS approach advertisements and requests are expressed using the same language. It is assumed that every LARKS specification is wrapped up in an appropriate KQML-like message by the sending agent indicating if the message content is to be treated as a request or an advertisement.

A service specification in LARKS is a frame comprised of the following slots:

1. *Context*: Keywords denoting the domain of the description,
2. *Types*: User-defined data types found in the signature definitions,
3. *Input* and *Output*: Input and output parameter declarations defining the signature of the operation,
4. *InConstraints* and *OutConstraints*: Logical constraints on input/output variables (pre-/post conditions),
5. *ConcDescriptions*: Descriptions of used potentially disambiguating words in terms of the concept language ITL, or keyword phrase, and
6. *TextDescription*: A free text description of the agent's capabilities.

Table 2 shows an example of both a request and matching capability description. In this example a P-agent advertises its capability to provide a list of deployed AWAC air combat missions which have been launched in a given time interval. This advertisement matches with the shown request for agents that are capable of providing information on any kind of air combat missions launched in a given time interval. The request is also formulated in LARKS by simply specifying a desired agent capability. Constraints on the input and output of a capability description or request are specified as conjunction of finite Horn clauses. Both the request and advertisement contain ontological annotations of disambiguating word 'Mission' by the concepts 'AirMission' and AWAC-AirMission', respectively, each of which is defined in the Con-cDescriptions slot in terms of a common KL-ONE [89] like concept language based on a shared minimal vocabulary.

LARKS is fairly expressive and capable of supporting automated infer-ences. The implemented matchmaking process for LARKS specifications em-ploys different techniques from information retrieval, AI, and software engi-neering to compute the syntactical and semantic similarity among advertised and requested agent capability descriptions. The matching engine contains five different filters for (1) keyword-based context matching, (2) TF-IDF based profile comparison, (3) concept-based similarity matching, (4) type-inference rule-based signature matching, and (5) theta-subsumption based constraint matching of finite Horn clauses. Any user may individually con-figure these filters to achieve the desired tradeoff between performance and matching quality. In the following we briefly summarize each of the filters of the proposed LARKS matchmaking process; it is described in more detail in [577].

The *context matching* consists of two consecutive steps:

1. For every pair of words u, v given in the `Context` slots compute the real-valued word distances $d_w(u, v) \in [0,1]$. Determine the most similar matches for any word u by selecting words v with the minimum distance value $d_w(u, v)$. These distances must not exceed a given threshold.
2. For every pair of most similar matching words, check that the semantic distance among the attached concepts does not exceed a given threshold.

The *comparison of the profiles* of LARKS specifications treated as doc-uments relies on a standard technique from the information retrieval area, called term-frequency-inverse document frequency weighting (TF-IDF). The similarity $dps(Req, Ad)$ of a request Req and an advertisement Ad under consideration is then calculated by :

$$dps(Req, Ad) = \frac{Req \bullet Ad}{|Req| \cdot |Ad|}$$

where $Req \bullet Ad$ denotes the inner product of the weighted keyword vectors. If the value $dps(Req, Ad)$ does exceed a given threshold $\beta \in \mathbf{R}$ both docu-ments pass the profile filter. For example, the profiles of both specifications in the example are similar with degree 0.65.

The matchmaker then checks if the declarations and constraints of both specifications for a request and advertisement are sufficiently similar. This is done by a pairwise comparison of declarations and constraints in two steps: Similarity and signature matching.

Similarity matching relies on a combination of distance values as calcu-lated for pairs of input and output declarations, and input and output con-straints. Each of these distance values is computed in terms of the distance

ReqAirMissions	
Context	Attack, Mission*AirMission
Types	Date = (mm: Int, dd: Int, yy: Int), DeployedMission = ListOf(mType: String, mID:String‖Int)
Input	sd: Date, ed: Date
Output	missions: Mission
InConstraints	sd <= ed.
OutConstraints	deployed(mID), launchedAfter(mID,sd), launchedBefore(mID,ed).
ConcDescriptions	AirMission = (and Mission (atleast 1 has-airplane) (all has-airplane Airplane) (all has-MissionType aset(AWAC,CAP,DCA,HVAA)))
TextDescription	capable of providing information on deployed air combat missions launched in a given time interval

AWAC-AirMissions	
Context	Combat, Mission*AWAC-AirMission
Types	Date = (mm: Int, dd: Int, yy: Int) DeployedMission = ListOf(mt: String, mid:String‖Int, mStart: Date, mEnd: Date)
Input	start: Date, end: Date
Output	missions: DeployedMission;
InConstraints	start <= end.
OutConstraints	deployed(mID), mt = AWAC, launchedAfter(mid,mStart), launchedBefore(mID,mEnd).
ConcDescriptions	AWAC-AirMission = (and AirMission (atleast 1 has-airplane) (atmost 1 has-airplane) (all has-airplane aset(E-2)))
TextDescription	capable of providing lists of deployed AWAC air combat missions launched in some given time interval

Fig. 8.7. Example of an advertised and requested agent capability description in LARKS

between concepts and words that occur in their respective specification section. These values are computed at the time of advertisement submittal and stored in the matchmaker database. The overall similarity value among two specifications in LARKS is computed as the average of the sum of similarity computations among all pairs of declarations and constraints.

The *signature filter* first considers the declaration parts of the request and the advertisement, and determines pairwise if their signatures of the (input or output) variable types match according to a given set of type inference rules. Both filters, the similarity and signature matching are used to determine if considered LARKS specifications syntactically match.

Finally, the matchmaker checks if both specifications *semantically match* in terms borrowed from the software engineering area. A software component description D_2 'semantically plug-in matches' another component description D_1 if (1) their signatures match, (2) the set of input constraints of D_1 logically implies that of D_2, and (3) set of output constraints of D_2 logically implies that of D_1. In our case the logical implication among constraints is computed using polynomial and sound θ-subsumption checking for Horn clauses [442].

8.3.4 Other approaches to service description and matching

Other approaches on (annotated) specification and matching of descriptions of capabilities and services via standardized markup languages, ontologies, and agent capability description languages include SHOE [385], OntoBroker [474], Osirix [504], GMD XML Broker [315], MIX [56], eCo system [277], and JAT/CDL [144], respectively.

JAT/CDL. The capability description language (CDL) [144] has been developed at the university of Edinburgh. Capabilities of and requests for services are described in CDL either in terms of achievable objectives or as performable actions. Figure 8.7 below shows an example of a request specified as a task description and a capability description in CDL. The latter describes the capability of a hospital to move patients to its location via ambulance and treat them as injured persons. The agent who is representing this hospital also advertises that its problem-solving behavior is complete with respect to this capability, i.e. that, if there is a solution to a problem it will find it. In the context of the particular capability in the example this implies that the hospital will get only injured people.

A request of service is specified in CDL as a task description; for example, the requested capability defined in the task description shown in figure 8.7 is subsumed by the capability of the hospital agent described above. For the purpose of automated logic-based reasoning on capability descriptions the statements are formally specified in a first-order predicate logic based format like KIF [354].

Logic-based reasoning over descriptions in CDL is based on the notion of capability subsumption or through instantiation. *Capability subsumption* in

Advertisement: **Query:**

(capability   **(task**

    :isa   move   **:isa**   move

    :properties   (complete)   **:properties**   (complete)

    :state-language fopl   **:state-language** fopl

    :input   **:input**

      ((To Hospital2)(Ambulance ?a))   ((Thing JohnSmith)

    :input-constraints   (From PowerPlant)

      ((elt ?thing Person)   (To Hospital2)

       (Is ?thing Injured))   **:input-constraints**

)   ((elt JohnSmith Person)

                           (Is JohnSmith Injured))

)

Fig. 8.8. Example of an advertised capability description and query in CDL

CDL refers to the question whether a capability description can be used to solve a problem described by a given task description in CDL: A capability C subsumes a task T if

1. in the result of performing C all output constraints of T are satisfied, means if the capability C achieves the desired state as specified in T, and
2. if in the situation that precedes the result of performing C, all input constraints of C are satisfied, means that capability C is applicable.

It is assumed that there is a model-theoretic semantics defined for every state language used to express constraints in CDL descriptions. This implies that reasoning relies on *model-based constraint satisfaction*. A constraint is satisfied in a situation if the model corresponding to the situation is a model of the expression representing the constraint. Regarding capability subsumption this means that the input constraints of a task description T define a set of models, one of which is corresponding to the actual situation before the capability is to be applied. Similarly, the output constraints of T define a set of models, all of which correspond to situations in which the objective has been achieved. Therefore a capability C subsumes a task T (a) if every model of T's input constraints is also a model of the C's input constraints (input match condition), and (b) if every model of C's output constraints is also a model of T's output constraints. This definition of capability subsumption resembles that of semantic plug-in matching of LARKS descriptions as described in section 8.3.3 above.

Both the CDL and the proposed matching of CDL descriptions have been implemented in Java and tested in selected application scenarios for brokering in multiagent systems developed in JAT (Java Agent Template)[327]. In summary, CDL is to some extent similar to LARKS but the matching methods proposed for each of the languages differ significantly in terms of the process and quality of reasoning.

eCo CBL. The eCo system's [277] common business library (CBL) consists of business descriptions and forms represented in an extensible, public set of XML building blocks that service providers in the domain of electronic commerce can customize and assemble. Semantics of the CBL are derived through analysis of industry standards, such as EDI X12850 for specification of purchase orders. This led to a base set of common terms, term mappings in the domain of e-commerce, and corresponding XML data elements, attributes, and generic XML document type definitions (DTD). Any request for a service is transformed to an appropriate standard DTD which then can either be used to find similar DTDs of available service descriptions or to produce a stream of information events routed to and processed by business applications.

SHADE and COINS. The SHADE and COINS [364] are matchmakers based on KQML. The content language of COINS allows for free text specification of services and its matching algorithm utilizes the tf-idf information retrieval method. The content language of the SHADE matchmaker consists of two parts, one is a subset of the knowledge interchange format (KIF), another is a structured logic representation called MAX. MAX uses logic frames to declaratively store the knowledge. SHADE uses a frame like representation and the matcher uses a prolog like unifier.

Other techniques and formalisms related to capability descriptions. The problem of capability and service descriptions can be tackled at least from the following different approaches.

1. *Software specification techniques.*
   Agents are computer programs that have some specific characteristics. There are numerous works for software specifications in formal methods, like model-oriented VDM and Z, or algebraic-oriented Larch. Although these languages are good at describing computer programs in a precise way, the specification usually contains too much detail to be of interests to other agents. Besides, those existing languages are so complex that the semantic comparison between the specifications appears to be impossible. The reading and writing of these specifications also require substantial training.
2. *Action representation formalisms.*
   Agent capability can be seen as the actions that the agents perform. There are a number of action representation formalisms in AI planning like the classical one STRIPS. The action representation formalisms are

inadequate in our task in that they are propositional and not involving data types.

3. *Concept languages for knowledge representation.*
   There are various terminological knowledge representation languages. However, ontology itself does not describe capabilities. On the other hand, ontological descriptions provide auxiliary concepts to assist the specification of the capabilities of agents.

4. *Database query capability description.*
   The database query capability description technique is developed as an attempt to describe the information sources on the Internet, such that an automated integration of information is possible. In this approach the information source is modeled as a database with restricted querying capabilities.

8.4 Conclusions

The Internet is an open system where heterogeneous agents can appear and disappear dynamically. As the number of agents on the Internet increases, there is a need to define middle-agents to help agents locate others that provide requested data and services. In this chapter we introduced several different classes of basic services any middle-agent needs to appropriately instantiate to perform a meaningful, effective, and reliable mediation between agents within and across multiple agent societies.

We have proposed a classification of middle-agents with respect to these service classes, presented a compact description of service matchmaking and brokering, and, finally, surveyed some prominent examples of multiagent systems and platforms which are coordinated by special kinds of middle-agents, namely broker and matchmaker agents. A comparative overview of selected matchmaker, broker, and mediator agents according to the service-oriented classification of middle-agents is given in figure 8.8.

Issues for future research in the domain of mediation via middle-agents include, for example, approaches to cope with the problems of trust establishment and management by middle-agents; scalability in terms of interoperation across heterogeneous agent societies; a thorough analysis and development of efficient methods supporting distributed real-time collaboration between different types of middle-agents [340]; investigations in system load balancing using middle-agents; standardized compositional design of middle-agents according to the proposed service-oriented classification enabling, e.g., component-based re-use and prototyping of such agents for different application scenarios.

Main application domains of assisted coordination of multiagent systems by middle-agents are intelligent cooperative information systems and agent-mediated electronic business in the Internet and Web. Farther in the future one could imagine middle-agents coordinating different agent societies which

Mediation Services	**IMPACT**	**InfoSleuth Broker**	**RETSINA Matchmaker**	**GMD Broker**	**MIX Mediator**
ACDL processing					
• ACDL descriptions	HTML-like	frame	LARKS frame	XML	XML
• matching	k-nearest neighbor	structural matching	TF-IDF, plug-in, type inference, constraint match, concept subsumption	DTD matching	DTD matching
Semantic interoperation					
• ontology services	verb/noun hierarchy, thesaurus	infosleuth ontology	WordNet, ITL concepts	XML namespaces	
• semantic reconciliation	synonym, word distance	synonym, value matching	synonym, word distance, subsumption		
• information model	global, collection	global, collection	part. integrated collection	global, collection	global, integrated
Data management	X	X	concept base, databases	XML data warehouse, XQL	XML schema, views, BBQ
Query processing					
• distributed query planning					X
• transaction_services				intermediate	intermediate
Agent interaction	register, matching	register, matching	register, matching	searchbots cooperation	wrapper cooperation
Mediation_protocol	matchmaking	matchmaking	matchmaking	brokerage	brokerage
Access sources				(search bots)	(wrapper)

Fig. 8.9. A service-oriented comparison of selected matchmaker, broker and mediator agents

are involved in, for example, inter-planetary information networks, UMTS cell phone videoconferences, traffic management, and negotiation of content provided by different information providers for embedded databases in mobile information appliances.

9. Agent Naming and Coordination: Actor Based Models and Infrastructures

Gul Agha, Nadeem Jamali, and Carlos Varela

Open Systems Lab, Department of Computer Science
University of Illinois at Urbana Champaign,
1304 W. Springfield Ave., IL 61801, USA
http://osl.cs.uiuc.edu/ {agha,jamali,cvarela}@cs.uiuc.edu

Abstract

Flexible and efficient naming, migration and coordination schemes are critical components of concurrent and distributed systems. This chapter describes actor naming and coordination models and infrastructures, which enable the development of mobile agent systems. A travel agent example is used to motivate the requirements and proposed solutions for naming, migration and coordination.

Universal Actor Names provide location and migration transparency, while ActorSpaces enable the unanticipated connection of users, agents and services in the open, dynamic nature of today's networks. An actor-based architecture, the World Wide Computer, is presented as a basis for implementing higher-level naming and coordination models for Internet-based agent systems. Finally, multiagent coordination is accomplished with *cyborgs*, an abstraction which provides a unit for group migration and resource consumption through the use of e-cash.

9.1 Introduction

The *World Wide Web* is an open distributed system where information and services are heterogeneous, distributed and dynamically evolving. The Web operates over the Internet which is characterized by the availability of enormous computational power and information resources but relatively small communication bandwidth. An efficient mechanism for resource discovery and service utilization on the Web is through use of *(software) agents*. We characterize agents as autonomous, persistent, mobile, and resource bound computational entities. The obvious advantage of agents is that they can act on behalf of users at remote locations, thus reducing the need for communication.

A large number of specialized agents navigating and computing over the Web allows considerable parallelism. Effectively using this parallelism requires dynamically dividing problems into sub-problems and integrating partial solutions as they are concurrently computed and communicated. Thus, scaling up the problem solving potential of agents requires effective solutions for coordinating their concurrent activities. We envision a *World Wide Computer* using the present Internet and Web infrastructures to provide seamless coordinated agent-based services to geographically distributed and mobile users.

9.1.1 A Motivating Scenario

Consider an agent that makes travel reservations on behalf of its owner. In the simplest case, reservations requests specify a starting point, a destination, and departure and arrival dates. A certain amount of "money" is allocated for searching for good rates as well as making the actual purchases. To perform its search, the *travel* agent creates additional agents to search for best airline ticket prices, hotel accommodations and car rental possibilities. These specialized agents themselves create other agents to perform additional searches in parallel, all bound by the shared goals and available resources.

Travel plans can be specified in the form of constraints. These constraints lay out specific requirements, but allow significant flexibility beyond those requirements. For example, a client interested in traveling from Paris to Champaign, specifies desired departure and arrival dates for all or parts of the journey, preferences for means of travel, financial constraints, etc. These constraints are absolute, relative, or a combination of the two. Airline ticketing agents look for airline fares, car rental agents look for rental deals, hotel reservation agents search for hotel rates, and so on.

Although different agents search independently, the constraints that guide them need not be static: this requires the agents to coordinate dynamically. For example, if hotel, car rental, and airline reservations need to be synchronized, they would need to be committed together. Not only does this require enabling synchronization protocols between agents and service providers, the agents must also coordinate their actions. For example, if the flight is to arrive in Chicago from Paris later than when the last flight leaves Chicago for Champaign, alternate plans would need to be considered: a train, bus, or a rental car is used, or alternatively, a hotel room is reserved for the night and further travel is postponed to the following day. Alternative flights from Paris to Chicago are also considered as an option that results in earlier arrival in Chicago. This entire activity may also be in interaction with the client.

From the perspective of the user, it is important to ensure that certain properties hold. For example, it is imperative to guarantee that the user's credit card will not be charged more than once to buy the same itinerary with different airline companies. More complex properties would enable the user to establish the probabilities of modifying the original travel plan, so as to minimize the total traveling cost, considering penalties incurred in changing departure or arrival dates.

9.1.2 What is Coordination?

Coordination is what fills the gap between autonomously acting agents and the problems they are collectively solving. In a multi-agent system, agent-to-agent messages offer the simplest form of coordination, using which complex coordination requirements can be satisfied. However, if implementation of coordination requirements is to be practical, where the language must support appropriate mechanisms for coordination, it must also provide abstractions that satisfy software engineering concerns such as modularity and reuse. For example, incentives engineering builds incentives into the system to drive interaction patterns of autonomous agents, but implemented without due attention to software engineering concerns, the code for functional behavior and that for coordination between agents will be mixed together.

Because coordination abstractions build on communication facilities provided by the underlying computation model, they are defined with respect to the model. Blackboard models (e.g., Linda) offer support for coordination through placement of content in a shared space. In the case of agents (actors), because communication is typically by asynchronous message passing, coordination can exploit the message ordering flexibility of the model, without disturbing the model's semantics. Specifically, separately specified synchronization constraints are enforced by ordering message deliveries, as shown in Frølund [250]. Because this is achieved without interfering with the functional behaviors of individual agents, modularity and reusability properties are achieved. Ren [511] extends this idea further to enable (soft) real-time constraint satisfaction.

9.1.3 Outline

This chapter introduces the Actor formalism as a natural model for agents, describes Universal Actor Names as an Internet-based naming scheme with location and migration transparency, and ActorSpaces as abstractions for decoupled publish-and-subscribe pattern-based communication. Following, we present the World Wide Computer infrastructure as a testbed for experimenting with high level agent naming and coordination mechanisms. One such mechanism, Cyborgs, is presented as a model for resource-bound multi-agent systems, with an example illustrating its use of local synchronization constraints and synchronizers. We conclude with some remarks and potential future research directions.

9.2 Actors and Agents

Agents are naturally modelled by the Actor formalism. In fact, implementations of agents are typically just implementations of actor systems. An actor is autonomous and persistent. The Actor model of computation has a built-in notion of local component and interface which provides a basis for reasoning about and building agent-based applications in open distributed systems. Actors are inherently concurrent and autonomous enabling efficiency in parallel execution [356] and facilitating mobility [10]. The actor model and languages provide a useful framework for understanding and developing open distributed systems. For example, actor systems have been used for enterprise integration [601], fault-tolerance [9], and distributed artificial intelligence [235].

Actors [8, 302] extend sequential objects by encapsulating a thread of control along with procedures and data in the same entity; thus actors provide a unit of abstraction and distribution in concurrency. Actors communicate by asynchronous message passing (see Figure 9.1). Moreover, message delivery is weakly fair – message delivery time is not bounded but messages are guaranteed to be eventually delivered. Unless specific synchronization constraints are enforced, messages are received in some arbitrary order which may differ from the sending order. An implementation normally provides for messages to be buffered in a local mailbox and there is no guarantee that the messages will be processed in the same order as the order in which they are received. Actor names (also called *mail addresses* in the actor literature) are bound to identifiers. Similar to cons cells in Scheme [567] or Java object references, and unlike pointers in C, the representation or binding of names is not visible. Thus, it is not possible to "guess" actor names (or corresponding locations); a name must be communicated before it can be used.

To define agents, the Actor model is extended with mobility and bounded resource use [10]. Mobility requires explicitly mapping actor names to locations. By bounded resource use, we model the fact that an agent is not able to consume an arbitrary amount of physical resources (e.g. processor time, memory, or network bandwidth) or logical resources (e.g. threads). We have used a uniform cybercurrency to express limitations on the use of resources. The term "energy" for a similar notion has been coined by Queinnec [438].

9.2.1 Programming Languages for Concurrent and Distributed Systems

Early programming languages for concurrent and distributed systems include Occam [303] and Ada [606]. A more recent and popular language for implementing concurrent systems is Java, which among other things, provides platform compatibility through the use of a virtual machine, support for multithreading, a clean object model and automatic garbage collection [281].

However, Java suffers from a number of deficiencies as a language for concurrent and distributed programming. We describe these below:

Java uses a passive object model in which threads and objects are separate entities. As a result, Java objects serve as surrogates for thread coordination and do not abstract over a unit of concurrency. We view this relationship

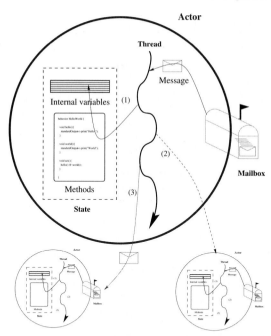

Fig. 9.1. In response to a message, an actor can: (1) modify its local state, or (2) create new actors, or (3) send messages to acquaintances.

between Java objects and threads to be a serious limiting factor in the utility of Java for building concurrent systems [611]. Specifically, while multiple threads may be active in a Java object, Java only provides the low-level *synchronized* keyword for protecting against multiple threads manipulating an object's state simultaneously, and lacks higher-level linguistic mechanisms for more carefully characterizing the conditions under which object methods may be invoked. Java programmers often overuse *synchronized* and resulting deadlocks are a common bug in multi-threaded Java programs.

Java's passive object model also limits mechanisms for thread interaction. In particular, threads exchange data through objects using either polling or wait/notify pairs to coordinate the exchange. In decoupled environments, where asynchronous or event-based communication yields better performance, Java programmers must build their own libraries which implement asynchronous message passing in terms of these primitive thread interaction mechanisms. Although actors can greatly simplify such coordination and are a natural atomic unit for system building, they're not directly supported in Java.

9.2.2 Supporting Actor Programming

It is possible to create a library in Java which enables actor programming. The Actor Foundry [476] is a framework developed in Java to provide concurrent object oriented programmers with a discipline for actor programming and a set of core services to facilitate this task. This is similar to earlier work on Actalk which supported actors in Smalltalk [99], and Act++ and Broadway which supported actors in C++ [344, 571]. However, there are several advantages to using a language over defining a library:

- Certain semantic properties can be guaranteed at the language level. For example, an important property is to provide complete encapsulation of data and processing within an actor. Ensuring there is no shared memory or multiple active threads, within an otherwise passive object, is very important to guarantee safety and efficient actor migration.
- By generating code from an actor language, we can ensure that proper interfaces are always used to create and communicate with actors. In other words, programmers can not incorrectly use the host language that has been used to build an actor framework.
- An actor language improves the readability of programs. Often writing actor programs using a framework involves using language level features (e.g. method invocation) to simulate common actor operations (e.g. actor creation, message sending, etc.). The need for a permanent semantic translation, unnatural for programmers, is a common source of errors.

A number of actor languages have been developed (e.g. [602, 311, 355]). More recently, we have developed SALSA (Simple Actor Language, System and Applications) [477] for enabling the development of Internet-based agent systems. The syntax of SALSA is a variant of Java. SALSA supports primitive actor operations, token-passing and join continuations, universal naming, remote asynchronous communication and migration. In the following sections, we will use SALSA pseudo-code to illustrate our travel agent sample application.

9.3 Naming in Open Systems

Software agents acting over the World Wide Computer require a scalable and global naming mechanism. Such naming mechanism must also enable transparent agent location and migration, i.e. the agent name should completely encapsulate the current location for such agent and migration should not break inverse acquaintance references.

Because of the heterogeneous nature of devices connected to the Internet, an agent naming mechanism should also be platform independent. Furthermore, because agents are different in nature and use different protocols for communication, the name should provide openness by including a protocol (or a set of protocols) to communicate with such agent.

Two additional critical characteristics of naming in Internet-based agent systems include safety and human readability. Safety includes the inability to "steal" messages by creating an agent with an existing name. Human readability of actor names implies that it is possible to "make" and "guess" actor names, very much like we make up and guess Web document URLs today. However, because names encapsulate addresses, unlike Actors, it is not possible to enforce at the language level that an agent name is valid (i.e. that it corresponds to a valid actor address or location.)

We describe two complementary proposed solutions for agent naming in open systems: Universal Actor Names (UAN), which abstract over particular Internet locations and ActorSpaces which address openness by detaching services from particular agents providing such a service.

9.3.1 Universal Actor Names

Universal Actor Names (UAN) are identifiers used in the World Wide Computer prototype infrastructure for naming universally accessible actors.

The Universal Actor naming strategy, based on Uniform Resource Identifiers (URI) [70], allows transparent migration and interconnection of distributed objects. Such transparency is accomplished by separating names from locations. Universal Actor Names (UAN) persist over the life-time of an actor, while Universal Actor Locators (UAL) uniformly represent the current location for a given actor.

A major motivation behind our work is the potential of the World Wide Web [69]. Much of the Web's fast growth is due to its strategy for uniformly identifying multiple resources. Berners-Lee envisioned location-independent Uniform Resource Names (URN), Uniform Resource Locators (URL) and Uniform Resource Citations (URC) for metadata. However, only URLs are currently widely deployed, hindering the transparent mobility of Web resources.

An important characteristic of the Web's addressing scheme from a practical perspective is the ability to "write the URL of a Web page in a business card." This characteristic not only enables, but also encourages the unanticipated connection of network resources worldwide. Therefore, we follow a scheme for actor naming and location in an open worldwide context, based on Uniform Resource Identifiers.

We define Universal Actor Names (UAN) as globally unique identifiers, which persist over the life-time of an actor and provide an authoritative answer regarding the actor's current locator. Universal Actor Locators (UAL) uniformly represent the *current* Internet location of an actor, as well as the communication protocol to use with such actor.

When an actor migrates from one host to another, its UAN remains the same, but its UAL is updated in its corresponding Naming Server to reflect

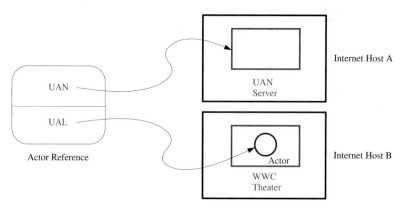

Fig. 9.2. By providing a persistent name to an actor (UAN), the actor can migrate from a host to another without breaking existing references.

the new locator. Notice that migration is transparent to client actors, which still hold a valid UAN reference.

A sample UAN for an actor handling air travel reservations is:

```
uan://wwc.travel.com/reservations/air/agent
```

A sample UAL for such actor is:

```
rmsp://wwc.aa.com/international/reservations/agent
```

The protocol specified in the UAL determines the communication protocol supported by such actor. In this case, the travel agent uses the Remote Message Sending Protocol (RMSP), which enables the delivery of messages among universal actors in the WWC.

SALSA provides support for binding actors to UANs and UALs. The pseudocode for a sample travel agent program in Salsa is presented in figure 9.3.

This program creates an agent and binds it to a particular UAN and UAL. After the program terminates, the Universal Actor Naming Server has been updated with the new (UAN, UAL) pair and the actor can be remotely accessible either by its name or by its locator.

9.3.2 ActorSpaces

ActorSpaces [120] is a communication model that compromises the efficiency of point-to-point communication in favor of an abstract pattern-based description of groups of message recipients. ActorSpaces are computationally passive containers of actors. Messages may be sent to one or all members of a group defined by a destination pattern. The model decouples actors in space and time, and introduces three new concepts:

```
behavior TravelAgent {

  void printItinerary(){...}

  public void act(String[] args){
    TravelAgent a = new TravelAgent();
    try {
      a<-bind("uan://wwc.travel.com/reservations/air/agent",
        "rmsp://wwc.aa.com/international/reservations/agent");
    } catch (Exception e){
      standardOutput<-println(e);
    }
  }
}
```

Fig. 9.3. A TravelAgent implementation in SALSA: Support for universal naming.

- **patterns** – which allow the specification of groups of message receivers according to their attributes
- **actorspaces** –which provide a scoping mechanism for pattern matching
- **capabilities** – which give control over certain operations of an actor or actorspace

ActorSpaces provide the opportunity for actors to communicate with other actors by using their attributes. The model subsumes the functionality of a Yellow Pages service, where actors may publish (in ActorSpace terminology, "make visible") their attributes to become accessible. Berners-Lee, in his original conception of Uniform Resource Citations, intended to use this metadata to facilitate semiautomated access to resources. Actorspaces bridge this gap between actors searching for a particular service and actors providing it.

Following our travel agent application, one could think of three actorspaces, one for air travel, one for car rental, and one for hotel reservations. Requests could be sent to these three actorspaces and different agents that match the proper request patterns could bid with the deals they find. An additional actorspace could be used for placing the bids and coordinating different schedules and combined travel constraints.

ActorSpaces enable unanticipated communication of actors. That is to say, an actor cannot only send messages to its acquaintances, but also to actors for which it does not have direct references. In actor semantics, an actor can only send messages to its acquaintances, an important property which allows local reasoning about the safety property of actor systems [11]. Furthermore, communication in actors is secure; in other words, it is not possible to "steal" messages by creating an actor with the same name as an existing actor. Both Universal Actor Names and ActorSpaces preserve this latter property.

Actorspaces' management of messages, which involves redirection rather than preprocessing, enables different strategies for load balancing (or replication) to be incorporated at the actorspace level, without affecting the semantics of particular applications. Such message management transparency anticipated the current use of name resolution algorithms for Web *portals* scalability.

9.4 World Wide Computer Prototype

The *World Wide Computer* (WWC) architecture provides a basis for developing Internet-based agent systems.

The WWC consists of a set of virtual machines for universal actors, which we name *Theaters*. Actors can freely move between theaters, in a transparent way, i.e. their names are preserved under migration. Naming servers provide the mapping from Universal Actor Names to Universal Actor Locators. The Remote Message Sending Protocol (RMSP) enables delivering messages to actors on remote theaters. A universal actor can be moved to a new theater by simply sending a *migrate(UAL)* message to such actor. The SALSA programming language enables high-level programming for actor creation, message sending, remote communication and migration. ActorSpaces can be implemented on top of the WWC architecture to enable resource discovery (through patterns) in large-scale systems.

Following, we will describe universal theaters, remote communication, and migration using the WWC architecture.

9.4.1 Universal Theaters

A WWC Theater is a virtual machine that provides runtime support to Universal Actors. A Theater (see figure 9.4) contains:

- an RMSP server with a hashtable mapping relative UALs to actual SALSA/Java actor references
- a runtime system for universal and environment actors.

Since references to Universal Actors can be created from their names (UAN) or even directly from their locators (UAL), universal actors cannot be garbage collected.

A Theater provides access to its host environment (for example, standard output, input, and error streams) through static, non-mobile system actors. In the prototype WWC implementation, all incoming actors get references to environment actors upon arrival. Future security policies may enable resource ownership rights to be used to control access to the Theater environment.

Theaters may run on applets and in such case, the RMSP server in charge of communication with actors in such applet theater must reside in the same

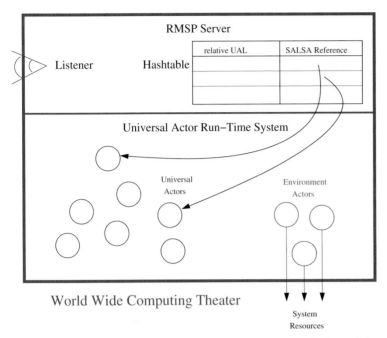

Fig. 9.4. A WWC Theater provides runtime support to Universal Actors. A Theater contains: (1) a RMSP server with a hashtable mapping relative UALs to actual Salsa actor references, and (2) a runtime system for universal and environment actors.

server as the HTTP server which hosts the applet. This is due to security restrictions prohibiting arbitrary Internet communications by untrusted Java applets. Applet theaters executing in a Web browser can safely host universal actors providing WWC applications with access to local computational resources.

9.4.2 Remote Communication

The Remote Message Sending Protocol (RMSP) is an object-based protocol on top of TCP/IP for remote actor communication and migration.

When the target of a message is found to be remote, the SALSA run-time system connects to the appropriate RMSP server listener and sends the message using a specialized version of Java object serialization. A message is a Java object containing the source and target actor references, the method to invoke at the target actor, the argument values, and an optional token-passing continuation [613] (which is represented as another message object). All actors in a serialized message are passed by reference. These actor references are updated in the serialization process to speed up local computation.

When an incoming message is received at a theater, all its actor references are updated in the following manner (see figures 9.5a, b). If the UAL for the

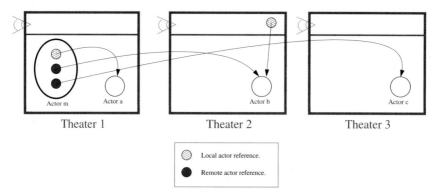

Fig. 9.5a. Before migration of actor m from Theater 1 to Theater 2, its references to actors b and c are remote, while its reference to actor a is local.

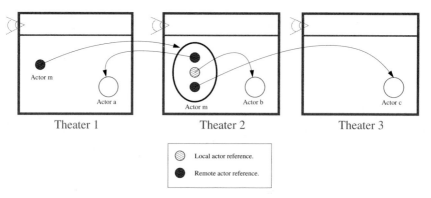

Fig. 9.5b. After migration of actor m, its reference to actor a becomes *remote* and its reference to actor b becomes *local*. Its reference to actor c remains unchanged. A temporary forwarder for actor m is left in Theater 1.

actor reference points to the current theater, we update it with the actual Java reference for that actor found in the internal RMSP server hashtable and we set its `local` bit to true. If the UAL for the actor reference points to another theater, we leave such reference unchanged (it remains remote).

After updating all actor references, the target actor reference in the message object has a valid internal Java reference pointing to the target actor in the current Theater. We can then proceed to put the message object in such local actor's mailbox. If the target actor has moved in the mean time, it leaves behind a *forwarder* actor (the same reference with the `local` bit set to false.) In such case, the RMSP server at the new location (the *forwarder*'s UAL) is contacted and the message sending process gets started again.

However, these *forwarder* actors are not guaranteed to remain in a theater forever. Thus, if the RMSP server hashtable doesn't contain an entry for the target actor's relative UAL, the UAN service for the target actor needs to be contacted again to get the actor's new location. Once a location has been received, the message sending process gets started again and a "hops" counter gets incremented in the message object. If such counter reaches a predetermined maximum (by default set at 20 hops) the message is returned to the sender actor as undeliverable.

RMSP in SALSA. SALSA provides support for sending remote messages to actors using the RMSP. For example, the code for sending a printItinerary() message to the travel agent created above, is given if figure 9.6.

```
//
//  Getting a remote actor reference by name
//  and sending a message:
//
TravelAgent a = new TravelAgent();
a<-getReferenceByName
   ("uan://wwc.travel.com/reservations/air/agent") @
   a<-printItinerary();
//
//  Getting the reference by location:
//
TravelAgent a = new TravelAgent();
a<-getReferenceByLocation
   ("rmsp://wwc.aa.com/international/reservations/agent") @
   a<-printItinerary();
```

Fig. 9.6. A TravelAgent implementation in SALSA: Support for remote messaging.

The SALSA syntax a<-m1() @ b<-m2(); is a simple case of a token-passing continuation, used to guarantee that message m2() is sent to actor b, only *after* actor a has finished processing message m1().

In the current prototype implementation, the behavior for a remote actor (e.g. the TravelAgent code) needs to be locally accessible in order to get a remote reference successfully. We intend to extend our prototype to allow remote code downloading, once a theater security policy is in place.

9.4.3 Migration

Migrating a passive object (such as a Java object with potentially several threads accessing it concurrently) requires a guarantee that the execution context and synchronization locks of all these threads will remain consistent after the passive object's migration. On the other hand, migration of an actor can be accomplished in a relatively easy and safe manner. This is because an actor encapsulates a thread of execution and is processing at most a single message. Migrating an actor involves waiting until the current message has been processed, serializing the actor's state (along with its mailbox), and restarting the thread of control in the new actor's location.

Universal actors migrate in response to an asynchronous message requesting migration to a specific UAL. This ensures that the actor is not busy processing any other messages: when migration takes place, the actor must be processing the `migrate` message. We describe in greater detail the algorithm we use for actor migration, from the perspective of the departure and arrival theaters.

Arrival Theater The RMSP server described in section 9.4.2 is also used for incoming actor migration. The server provides a generic input gate for SALSA-generated Java objects and the actions associated with receiving an incoming object depend upon the received object's run-time type.

When the incoming object is an instance of the `salsa.language.Message` class, the algorithm for message sending described in the previous section is used. If the object is an instance of the `salsa.language.UniversalActor` class, the internal RMSP dæmon hashtable gets updated with an entry mapping the new actor's relative UAL to its recently created internal Java reference. Then, all actor references in the incoming actor get validated in the same way as in messages. At this point, the actor is restarted locally. Lastly, if the object is an instance of the `salsa.language.Messenger` class, the Theater's run-time system automatically sends a `deliver()` message to such actor. The default implementation of a messenger contains a single message as an instance variable and upon receiving the `deliver()` message, the message instance is delivered with the same algorithm as a passive message.

Departure Theater When an actor is migrating away from a Theater, the actor state is serialized and moved to the new Theater. The current actor's internal reference is updated to reflect the new UAL and its `local` bit is set to false. Thus, this internal reference becomes a *forwarder* actor. The forwarder actor ensures that messages en-route will be delivered using the Remote Message Sending Protocol. Lastly, the UAN server containing the migrating actor's universal name gets updated to reflect the new actor location.

Actor Migration in SALSA. SALSA provides support for migrating an actor to a given WWC Theater. For example, the code for migrating the travel agent is given in figure 9.7.

9.5 Multiagent Coordination

The World Wide Computer infrastructure does not directly support coordination beyond asynchronous message passing, and simple delegation and value synchronization mechanisms such as token-passing continuations and

```
//
//  Migrating a travel agent to a remote WWC Theater:
//
TravelAgent a = new TravelAgent();
a<-getReferenceByName
   ("uan://wwc.travel.com/reservations/airline/agent") @
   a<-migrate("rmsp://wwc.nwa.com/usa/reservations/agent");
```

Fig. 9.7. A TravelAgent implementation in SALSA: Support for migration.

join continuations.[1] In this section, we discuss a model for supporting more complex types of coordination.

The travel agent we introduced earlier can be seen as a problem to be solved while incurring bounded costs, requiring coordination between activities. At the application level, two types of cost may apply. First, there is the financial cost of the airline ticket, the car rental, etc. The second type of cost is that of the inconvenience of a chosen solution. For example, there may be an inconvenience cost of late night travel. The application also has constraints that must be satisfied. For example, there are consistency constraints such as the requirement that a flight in the later part of journey depart after the earlier flight arrives, that a hotel is reserved for the day the flight arrives, etc. We will present a model of coordination that is useful in satisfying these constraints.

9.5.1 Multiagent Systems

Multiagent systems are systems of autonomous mobile agents pursuing shared goals. Goals of multiagent systems typically have spatial, temporal and functional requirements. Agents navigate their way through distributed systems, searching for environments suited for their execution.

Protection against a set of agents and/or hosts collectively causing undesirable behavior is a particularly challenging problem. Emergent behaviors may be controlled by using preventive mechanisms. These mechanisms may rely on linguistic support for precluding undesirable patterns of behavior, or they may be reactive, i.e., attempt to detect an imminent threat and take steps to prevent it. Either approach has its problems: while protection for all conceivable types of threats cannot be incorporated into a language, detecting threat or imminent threat in a dynamic complex system is also difficult. How group functionality emerges from behaviors of constituent entities is not well understood [265]. Even passive messages can flood a network [394]. However, certain group behaviors may be amenable to analysis at higher levels of abstraction, if one focuses on observable properties which can be measured for entities as well as systems of entities.

---

[1] Token-passing continuations and join continuations are described in [613]

Modeling. We treat a large multi-owned network of computers such as the Internet as a set of resources with rights of ownership assigned to them. Once we have introduced *ownership rights* and means for transferring these rights, it turns out that a distributed computation using mobile agents begins to resemble the activity of organisms in the "real world." The entities executing in this space can solve problems similar to those solved by mobile living organisms, and they face similar challenges. Specifically, while they may navigate in space in search of solutions, they are also constrained by the resources they have available to them.

A biological organism is typically a collection of co-located organs encapsulated inside a wrapper, collectively bound by the set of resources available to them. Each organ has the biological analog of a thread of control, and these organs interact under tighter constraints, as opposed to the type of looser constraints which determine how one organism interacts with another. For example, even though the legs of an ant can move simultaneously and independently of each other, the goal of self-preservation or preservation of the colony is hard-wired in the ant through evolution. The resources needed for this pursuit are also secured at the level of an ant. The way in which individual legs act is determined by how the resources available to the ant are distributed among its organs, including the legs, and the ways in which the legs are constrained to behave with respect to the rest of the organism. A significant implication of co-location is that the organs share, and are known to share, a common external environment in which they operate. This allows enforcement of interaction constraints that can be fine-tuned to very precise details.

In the following section, we introduce *Cyborgs* (cyber organisms) as an actor-based model for complex distributed computation inspired by organisms in the real world.

9.5.2 Cyborgs

Actors do not directly model multi-agent systems. Specifically, actors are single threaded, and the model does not represent locations and resources. We define cyborgs (cyber organisms) as a model for complex resource-bounded mobile agents. A cyborg encapsulates a set of tightly constrained *actors* bounded by shared resources, responsibility,[2] and goals (see figure 9.8)

Couplings between actors within a cyborg may be spatial, temporal or functional. For example, actors may require to be co-located, they may need to be synchronized to follow a protocol, and they may be attempting to solve parts of the same problem.

A cyborg defines the smallest granularity for assignment of goals, allocation of resources, and for migration from one ROD (*resource ownership*

---

[2] in terms of penalties for improper behavior

Requirements
Specification

Task Manager

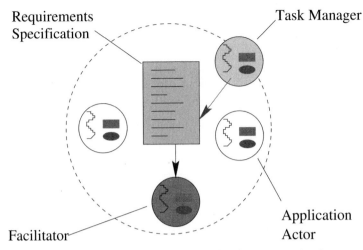

Facilitator

Application
Actor

Fig. 9.8. A cyborg encapsulates a set of tightly constrained actors

domain) to another (see figure 9.9). An ROD defines the boundaries of resource ownership. Each ROD has an ROD Manager with which a potential
client cyborg or an existing client may negotiate terms of arrival and subsequent execution. A contract reached between a cyborg and an ROD may
be static or it may be amendable. In either case, there can be penalties for
violation of the terms of a contract.

A cyborg is sustained by the *allowance* it receives. Allowance is in the form
of units of one of a set of accepted currencies, and is held in a *bank account*
for the cyborg. A cyborg may receive its allowance from its creator or from
another cyborg, typically as part of a message. Using its allowance, a cyborg
may purchase computational resources in its current ROD, and redistribute
them among its actors, as needed.

In the degenerate case, a cyborg may be viewed as an actor with mobility
and bounded resources as discussed in [10]. We now describe a typical cyborg
architecture.

Example Cyborg Let us consider a cyborg containing two special purpose
actors: *facilitator* and *task-manager*. A facilitator actor constantly monitors[3]
the execution environment(s) of the host ROD and explores the possibility of migrating to another ROD. Migration may be prompted by availability of a better execution environment (better suited hardware and software
or special services), more affordable resources, or application requirements.
Because RODs do not necessarily represent physical boundaries, migration
across them may be logical rather than physical. Cyborg migration may be
implemented by a synchronized migration of all the contained actors using
mechanisms provided for actor migration. The task-manager actor serves as

---

[3] Diagnostic information must be made available to facilitators by the system

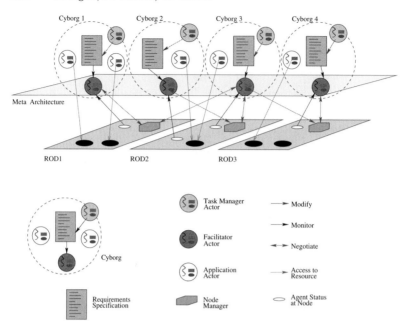

Fig. 9.9. Cyborg System Architecture: Cyborg carries dynamic specification of its requirements from one resource ownership domain to another.

a default receptionist for messages intended for the cyborg. When there are no other application actors, the task-manager acts as the default application actor and services received messages itself. More typically, the task-manager will organize application actors to solve problems. Furthermore, the task-manager redistributes available computational resources among the cyborg's actors according to a resource utilization strategy. It also updates environmental requirements specification of the cyborg as and when they change. □

The behavior of a cyborg is constituted by behaviors of the actors contained in it, and the way they are constrained with respect to each other. Hence, a cyborg's behavior may be modified by the individual actors changing their personal behaviors or by the task-manager modifying the constraints defined on them.

Communication in a system of cyborgs is multi-layered. Cyborg communication is resource oriented; cyborgs communicate with other cyborgs by exchanging asynchronous messages (similarly to actors), but messages may now contain some representation of remuneration for the requested service.

Actors inside cyborgs are encapsulated from directly receiving cyborg-level messages/requests, but they may still receive messages from other actors who know their addresses. The message syntax is identical to that of actor messages. An example of the usefulness of allowing such messages is motivated by considering the organism analogy described earlier. Many organs within an organism depend on external stimuli for survival. Even though these may be thought of as incoming messages, it will be incorrect to treat them as service requests; these stimuli are for the organism's own benefit, making them qualitatively different from explicit messages. Similarly, a cyborg may subscribe some of its actors to such stimulus messages from outside.

Example: Coordinating Travel Agents

In our example, we assume that a `TravelAgent` is created for a particular travel plan. As a result of searching for feasible travel possibilities, multiple air, hotel and car subagents are created. These agents search their own space of possibilities, sending messages back to the travel agent, who keeps track of all entries and consolidates ⟨AirReservation, CarReservation, HotelReservation⟩ entries to be sent back to the `Traveler`. When the traveler makes a decision regarding a travel plan, the original subagents get contacted to actually buy their particular reservations. The `TravelAgent` corresponds to a cyborg's task-manager, and all subagents are the cyborg's application actors. Even though functionally autonomous, all actors inside the cyborg share common bounded resources and goals, requiring coordination.

We consider examples of functional and temporal coordination in this travel agent application. Functional coordination includes data consistency in the selected travel plans, and temporal coordination involves atomic travel commitment by different agents involved in different subparts of a travel plan. Spatial coordination constraints could enable more efficient travel plan generation, by for example co-locating the air, hotel and car reservation agents after a fixed period of time, to locally coordinate valid travel plans, as an alternative to message passing. We leave the description of such spatial constraints in this example as an exercise to the reader.

We will use local synchronization constraints and synchronizers [250, 251] to specify functional and temporal coordination constraints respectively.

Local synchronization constraints allow to specify *when* certain messages can be received by a particular actor. Synchronizers are linguistic constructs that allow *declarative* control of coordination activity between multiple actors. Synchronizers allow two kinds of specifications: messages received by an actor may be disabled and, messages sent to different actors in a group may be atomically dispatched. These restrictions are specified using message patterns and may depend on the synchronizer's current state.

Local synchronization constraints in our `Traveler` example describe valid ⟨AirReservation, CarReservation, HotelReservation⟩ triplets. That is to say, triplets which do not go over the given budget and have consistent dates. The example is illustrated in figure 9.10 (the notation is taken from [250]):

Messages containing all possible combinations of travel are sent by the `TravelAgent` to the `Traveler` but only those satisfying the synchronization

```
class Traveller {

  disable
    plan(airReservation, carReservation, hotelReservation)
  if
    ((airReservation.price + carReservation.price +
      hotelReservation.price) > budget                              ||
     airReservation.arrivalDate != hotelReservation.arrivalDate ||
     ...
    )
}
```

Fig. 9.10. Local synchronization constraints disable invalid travel plans.

constraints are accepted by such agent and presented to the user. Once the user selects his/her preferred travel plan, the subagents in charge of specialized reservations get notified to purchase them.

A synchronizer ensures atomic commitment to a travel plan by an airline agent, a car agent and a hotel agent. The synchronizer is instantiated after the user decides the best travel itinerary. Such synchronizer makes sure that the combined state of the multiagent application is consistent. The example is illustrated in figure 9.11 (the notation is taken from [250]):

```
synchronizer TravelCommit(airAgent, carAgent, hotelAgent,
                          airReservation, carReservation,
                          hotelReservation) {

  bought := false;

  atomic
    ( airAgent.buy(airReservation),
      carAgent.buy(carReservation),
      hotelAgent.buy(hotelReservation) );

  disable
    airAgent.buy, carAgent.buy, hotelAgent.buy if bought;

  trigger
    airAgent.buy(airReservation)
      -> { bought := true; };
}
```

Fig. 9.11. A synchronizer enforces a single atomic travel purchase.

Atomicity constraints in synchronizers enforce the atomic dispatching of messages satisfying the given constraints. In other words, the "buy" message for one of the agents above will be dispatched atomically with the "buy" message for the other two agents. That is to say, no partial travel plans will be purchased. Furthermore, once a plan has been purchased, no additional purchases are allowed.

Synchronizer implementation

Two issues deserve further research regarding synchronizers as declarative constructs for specifying multiagent coordination. First, exception handling and failure considerations, and second, more active synchronizer implementation strategies.

While synchronizers provide a semantically clean and modular way to describe desired coordination properties in distributed systems, there is a need for enabling applications to take action in case failures happen. An exception-handling mechanism attached to synchronizers would for example, enable source actors to be notified when a message has been delayed for longer than an acceptable time limit.

Secondly, certain coordination requirements may be inconvenient to specify using synchronizers, given their passive nature: synchronizers can not receive or send messages, nor be "coordinated" by other synchronizers. A starting point for a more "active" implementation of synchronizers, is to use a hierarchy of *directors* to coordinate groups of actors [612].

9.6 Discussion

Building large complex systems is difficult without appropriate abstractions that impose some type of discipline on the software development process. The abstractions in wide use today, such as those offered by object oriented programming, result in significant benefits in terms of reusability of code, modularity and extensibility. Actors (agents) take object orientation one step forward into the realm of distributed systems, resulting in significantly simplifying a developer's task. Actors and the abstractions developed in the authors' research group have resulted in at least an order of magnitude reduction in the size and complexity of code over implementations using traditional object-oriented platforms.

The programming language abstractions we have developed provide universal naming, remote communication, migration and coordination. These abstractions not only streamline the distributed software development process, but also provide an opportunity for systematic code optimization (e.g. through compilation techniques [356].) Furthermore, the worldwide computing infrastructure we developed enables the execution of programs using these abstractions. In particular, this infrastructure offers support for building multiagent systems over the Internet. Cyborgs are an example of such a multiagent system.

Although these abstractions represent important steps in filling the gap between what is offered by the traditional agent paradigm and what is required of a platform to implement complex systems, there are still many open research questions.

Higher-level coordination abstractions and their efficient run-time support are needed. To eliminate redundant searches by agents working cooperatively, dynamic constraint propagation algorithms must be available. Economic models are required for studying resource consumption behaviors of cyborgs and groups of cyborgs. Reasoning mechanisms and logics must also be developed for constraint validation and resource redistribution, for example, algorithms for automatically deciding when and where to migrate agents or groups of agents. Different granularities for migration should therefore be supported by the underlying system.

Acknowledgments

We'd like to thank past and present members of the Open Systems Lab, specially Po-Hao Chang, for many discussions and readings of initial versions of this chapter. We're also grateful to Grégory Haïk for part of the design and implementation of universal naming and remote messaging in the World Wide Computer prototype. Jean-Pierre Briot at LIP6, provided insightful discussions and feedback. This research was made possible by support from the National Science Foundation (NSF CCR 96-19522) and the Air Force Office of Scientific Research (AFOSR contract number F49620-97-1-03821). The second author was also partially supported by a graduate fellowship from Eastman Kodak Corporation. Any opinions, findings, and conclusions are those of the authors and do not necessarily reflect the views of these agencies.

Part IV

Emerging Issues of Coordination

Emerging Issues of Coordination

Introduction

The increasing diffusion of the Internet, together with the fermenting research activities in the areas of both autonomous agents, coordination, and distributed systems, are rapidly paving the way for agent-based Internet applications. We can already envision a world where a multitude of interacting agents will populate the Internet, to perform task on our behalf and, by interacting with each other, to mimic and support our societal activities. However, as the researches on distributed systems, coordination, and autonomous agents advances and tend to converge as far as the Internet is involved, new fundamental research issues related to Internet-agent coordination emerge and have to be addressed before agent-based Internet applications can be effectively deployed and widely accepted.

This part of the book focuses on a specific set of issues that are emerging as being of primary importance in the development of Internet applications. In particular, the three chapters will focus on the issues of mobility, security, and scalability, respectively. Why these issues are of primary importance in the context of Internet agent coordination, and why they have to be considered as emerging issues is worth a brief introductory discussion.

Mobility of code is already widely exploited in the Internet, in the forms of both simple code fragments, such as JavaScript ones, and whole applications, as in the case of Applets. In the near future, we expect agent mobility to be widely exploited too, to enable autonomous entities to roam the Internet looking for data and resources – and interacting with remote environments – in an autonomous way [348, 614]. This can provide for a more dynamic and efficient execution model than the one of traditional distributed systems, and can also provide for a higher degree of autonomy in agent systems [467]. However, mobility in the Internet has not to be considered simply as a feature to be exploited in our software. Instead, since the Internet is becoming a necessary tool for our everyday life, the capability of effectively handling Internet connections and interactions for nomadic users, mobile devices [489], as well as of whole mobile networks [123] will be a compulsory necessity. In this context, once provided for low-level network protocols and mechanisms to enable interactions in the presence of mobility, coordination models and infrastructure must be provided to act as the middleware enabling and facilitating the developments of Internet applications based on mobile components [113], whether these are code fragments, agents, users, or devices.

Security has always been and will always be a critical issue in the Internet and in the Web [527]. In fact, while the Internet promotes the openness of application environments, it is also exploited in domains where safe, reliable, and secure execution models are required, as it may be the case of virtual enterprises and e-commerce. The secure execution of a networked software system requires, at the lower-level, the exploitation of appropriate mechanisms for authentication, verification, authorization, and data communication. Among the others, these mechanisms include cryptography, digital signatures, as well as access control models. At a higher-level, an appropriate security policy must be defined by exploiting the lower-level mechanisms. At this level, however, security issues and coordination issues are strictly related. In fact, while coordination technology for the Internet is typically concerned with ruling interactions so as to make them fruitful, security models and technologies are typically meant to build security policies aimed at bounding interactions so as to make them harmless [196]. In some sense, security and coordination policies represent different perspectives on the same problem and, as that, the definition and implementation of security policies in systems of interacting agents cannot abstract from the presence of specific coordination models and infrastructures.

Scalability issues naturally arise in the coordination of Internet agents, due to the world-wide scale of the Internet itself, as well as to the need of enabling and promoting interactions in systems in which agents are likely to be distributed (and possible able to move) across the whole Internet. However, in addition to its dimensions, there are other characteristics of the Internet and of its potential applications that introduce peculiar problems related to scalability. On the one hand, unlike a small network, the Internet is dynamic and unreliable, thus making it impossible to manage interactions and coordination activities relying on traditional models and infrastructures [123, 411]. On the other hand, the dynamic forming and dismissing of virtual enterprises – likely to exploit an agent-based Internet environment for collaboration – require the capability of dynamic structuring and scaling of applications or, more precisely, require the capability of the coordination infrastructure to enable and support a change-of-scale perspective in applications. In this context, the capability of the adopted coordination model and of the corresponding infrastructure of supporting application scaling in the presence of a wide-scale, unreliable, and dynamic execution scenario is a compulsory requirement for any proposal to gain acceptance.

Although the issues of mobility, security, and scalability are very important in Internet-agent coordination, only in the recent years they have become mainstream research issues for both the research communities of coordination models [123, 196, 411] and of multi-agent and autonomous-agent systems [616, 656].

A few earlier works exist focusing on mobility [520], scalability [353, 525], and security [424] in the context of coordination models and systems. However, most of past research has concentrated on applications and systems for which the above were simply non-issues. On the one hand, applications were typically running on systems closed to external access – therefore intrinsically secure – and locally distributed – thus having limited occasions to face the peculiar scalability issues raised by the Internet. On the other hand, either mobility was not present at all as a feature or it was merely exploited to re-distribute the execution load, transparently from applications and users [654, 655].

A similar restricted perspective also affected, since recently, most of the researches in the area of autonomous agents and multi-agent systems. On the one hand, most of the earlier researches in the area of multi-agent systems were focused on distribute collaborative problem solvers, i.e., closed agent systems with a limited number of agents explicitly designed to collaborate with each other, which do not introduce any problem related to scalability or security [626, 333, 112]. On the other hand, mobility issues were addressed mostly with regard to the capability of autonomous agents/robots of moving in an environment and plan their actions accordingly [389].

The convergence of the problems faced by different research communities, as induced by agent-based Internet computing, and the consequent emergence of new research issues, is well represented by the three chapters in this part of the book.

The contributions

Chapter 10, by Gruia-Catalin Roman, Amy Murphy, and Gian Pietro Picco, addresses the issues of mobility and coordination in a very general way. Starting from the fact that coordination problems intrinsically arise when two or more active components come in contact and are in need to interact with each other, the authors introduce a working definition of coordination and explore this concept in a way that makes it possible to transcend the distinctions between mobility of software and devices.

In the first part of the chapter, the authors analyze the various design dimensions that have to be taken into account in governing the interactions in a system of mobile components. These dimensions include: the modeling of the mobile components, of the space in which they move, and of the environment in which they execute and interact.

In the second part of the chapter, the authors presents three different coordination models, i.e., Mobile Unity, CodeWeave, and Lime, explicitly designed for systems of mobile components. The presentation of these three models is very useful to better illustrate the range of options that can be considered in the definition of a coordination model and, consequently, in the implementation of coordination architecture founded on that model.

Chapter 11, by Ciaran Bryce and Marco Cremonini, focuses on Linda-like coordination models, by analyzing the issues arising in the definition of a secure Linda-like coordination architecture for open and distributed agent systems, and by surveying the relevant work in the area.

The authors start by introducing a general secure coordination architecture, based on the concept of shared dataspace. The introduced architecture is exploited as a reference model towards an in-deep analysis of the problems related to the definition of mechanisms and policies for a secure coordination system.

Then, the authors survey the proposals of several coordination models and systems integrating some sort of security-oriented features. Again, the reference architecture introduced in the first part is exploited as a basis for discussions and comparison. The survey shows that very different models, technologies, and architectural solutions for security can be adopted in the context of Internet applications exploiting shared dataspaces as the main coordination media.

Chapter 12, by Ronaldo Menezes, Robert Tolksdorf, and Alan Wood, discusses the scalability issues that arise in the shift from LANs to WANs (e.g., the Internet) and, on this base, analyzes the architectural solution that can be adopted in a Linda-like coordination systems.

The shift from LANs – typically of small dimension and under the control of a centralized administration – to WANs – of geographical size and with decentralized management – makes it impossible to enforce location transparency, induce high-fluctuations in the available bandwidth, and it is also likely to notably increase the probability of network partitioning and faults. This considered, the authors analyze how Linda-like models and technologies can be extended so as to take into account these issues and still provide effective coordination.

By analyzing the possible extensions to Linda and the proposal of several models and systems, the authors argue that the challenge of implementing Linda-like coordination on the Internet can be faced without undermining the main advantages of the Linda model, that is, asynchronous and associative coordination.

10. Coordination and Mobility

Gruia-Catalin Roman[1], Amy L. Murphy[1], and Gian Pietro Picco[2]

[1] Department of Computer Science, Washington University
Campus Box 1045, One Brookings Drive, Saint Louis, MO 63130-4899, USA
{roman, alm}@cs.wustl.edu
[2] Dipartimento di Elettronica e Informazione, Politecnico di Milano
P.za Leonardo da Vinci 32, 20133 Milano, Italy
picco@elet.polimi.it

Summary.

Mobility entails the study of systems in which components change location, in a voluntary or involuntary manner, and move across a space that may be defined to be either logical or physical. Coordination is concerned with what happens when two or more components come in contact with each other. In this paper we put forth a working definition of coordination, we construct arguments that demonstrate that coordination is central to understanding mobility, we explore the intellectual richness of the notion of coordination, and we consider the practical implications of coordination-centered system design strategies. We develop these ideas in two steps. First, we analyze the different dimensions that govern the definition of a coordination strategy for mobility: the choice of an appropriate unit of mobility, the treatment of space and its implications on the way we think about mobility, and the manner in which contextual changes induced by component movement are perceived and managed. Then, we explore mechanisms that enable us to model and reason about coordination of mobile components, and to make it available to software developers in the form of middleware. Three very different models of mobility (Mobile UNITY, CODEWEAVE, and LIME) are used as principal sources for illustration purposes.

10.1 Introduction

The term mobility has grown to the point that it encompasses a very broad range of meanings and technological subcultures spanning from formal theoretical models to wireless transmission protocols and standards. In this paper we seek to explore the richness of this concept in a manner that transcends the distinctions between physical and logical mobility but to the exclusion of concerns having to do with the communication technology and low level protocols. As such, the kinds of issues we are about to consider are likely to be of interest primarily to researchers concerned with models, languages, and middleware.

While logical mobility involves the movement of code (in all its forms) among hosts, physical mobility entails the movement of hosts (of all sorts and sizes) in the real world. Future generations of mobile systems are likely to include both forms of mobility even though so far they have been treated as distinct and have been studied by different research communities. For now, logical mobility is viewed as offering designers a new set of conceptual and programming tools that seek to exploit the opportunities made available by the distributed computing infrastructure deployed over the last decade. Physical mobility, on the other hand, is assumed to be closely tied into the next evolutionary step in the development of the worldwide communication infrastructure, the extension of wireline networks to fluid clouds of wireless devices. This new environment presents designers with enormous challenges not the least among them being the seamless integration of programming models with both the wired and wireless platforms. It is for this reason that a unified treatment of physical and logical mobility is important at this time. Clearly, at the most basic level they share a view of the world in which components move through space (be it logical or physical) and interact with each other in accordance with the rules governing some particular model of mobility. Yet there is a wide range of variations among models and systems involving mobility. It is our contention that variability is essentially the result of differing decisions with respect to a narrow set of issues: unit of mobility, properties of space, context definition, and the coordination constructs that facilitate component interactions.

Our coordination perspective on the subject is fostered by the recognition that building open systems requires designers to adopt a new viewpoint. In defining a component, the designer must minimize any dependencies on the mechanics of data communication. Coordination [393] accomplishes this by separating the functionality of individual components from the manner in which interactions take place. Components may be logical or physical. Laptops and PDAs equipped with wireless connectivity may travel around a building or across the country alongside their owners. Code fragments may move from host to host across both wireline and wireless networks and even among various points in the structure of a single program. Mobile agents move of their own volition while class definitions are downloaded on demand. Components may be simple or complex structures. The types of components involved relate closely with the kind of spatial domain one must consider.

Logical level interactions among components are made possible by specialized constructs which specify the coordination services to be provided and define the interface to such services, when necessary. In the most extreme case, components are totally oblivious to the coordination process. As movement occurs and coordination takes place, components find themselves having access to a changing array of resources, making new acquaintances, losing contact with each other, etc. In other words, the dynamics of mobility place each component in a continuously changing contextual setting. The very definition of the context and the manner in which components handle change vary with the coordination constructs available to them.

Coordination is the thread that ties together the dominant themes in mobility today and the principal subject of this paper. Three specific models will be used as primary sources for illustrative examples. Mobile UNITY is a formal model of mobility that provides a notation and proof logic for describing a broad range of mobile systems, paradigms, and coordination constructs. CODEWEAVE is a model that assumes a very fine grained perspective on code mobility, at the level of single variables and statements. Finally, LIME is a middleware designed to provide transient and transitive sharing of tuplespaces among agents and hosts.

The remainder of the paper is organized as follows. Section 10.2 discusses issues that are central to understanding the relation between coordination concepts and mobility: Section 10.2.1 considers choices regarding the unit of mobility; Section 10.2.2 explores variations in the definition of space and discusses issues having to do with movement; Section 10.2.3 analyzes the definition of context and the manner in which it is perceived by the mobile components. Section 10.3 is concerned with the kinds of coordination constructs one may encounter. The emphasis is not so much on offering a survey of coordination languages and models as is on examining the range of options that may be considered and the mechanics of how context is constructed in three different models: Mobile UNITY, CODEWEAVE, and LIME. Conclusions appear in Section 10.4.

10.2 Mobility Issues

Basic to the notion of mobility is the requirement that there be some entities that perform the moves, some space within which movement takes place, and rules that govern motion. Equally important is the way in which mobile entities perceive the environment that surrounds them, the changes in such environment, or the way it is actively being explored by them. This section considers each of these issues in turn. We start by discussing possible choices regarding the unit of mobility. We follow with a discussion of physical and logical space and its relation to the units of mobility. Finally, we conclude the section by examining the notion of context, i.e., the worldview of the individual units.

10.2.1 Unit of Mobility

The entities that move through space can be physical or logical, simple or composite. Physical components are generally referred to as mobile hosts and they can vary in size from a laptop to a PDA or other wearable device. The trend towards miniaturization is likely to lead to the emergence of minuscule devices and smart sensors that can be attached to people's clothing, movable structures and everyday objects. Robots of all sizes also serve as hosts. They can move through space in a purposeful way under their own volition, can communicate with each other, and are able to orchestrate activities none of them could accomplish in isolation. It is generally expected that the number of mobile hosts connected to the Internet will rapidly reach into the millions. At the same time the size of ad hoc networks [190] (i.e., wireless networks having no wireline support) is also expected to reach into the hundreds. Some networks may be relatively stable, e.g., an assembly line or an office involving tens of devices that use wireless communication to interact with each other. Other situations are much more dynamic and unpredictable, e.g., cars on a highway exchanging information among themselves and with stationary data kiosks. Finally, there are situations in which the underlying application is a complex enterprise mobile in nature, e.g., an emergency response team consisting of many vehicles and individuals. What makes this kind of situation different is the heterogeneity of the computing platforms involved and the level of logistics interwoven into the behavior of the overall system. We rarely think of physically mobile units as coming together and breaking apart, yet such applications clearly point to a future in which the physical units of mobility will vary greatly in size and capabilities and will engage in interactions that go beyond just relative movement and wireless communication to include docking and complex physical reconfiguration.

In the realm of logical mobility, the unit of mobility naturally shifts from being a host to being a code fragment. It should be noted from the onset that the term "code fragment" implies some sort of syntactic element recognized by the programming language. This is because of the necessity to reference it in the code itself. Programs, agents, procedures, functions, classes, and objects are reasonable choices frequently encountered in mobile code languages and agent systems. Of course, language syntax recognizes also much finer grained elements such as statements, expressions, and variables. They can also be moved and such level of mobility it is referred to in this paper and others as fine-grained mobility. Later in the paper we will show examples of units of mobility associated with different syntactic elements and of various granularity. Another point of differentiation among mobile units is the state of execution at the time the movement takes place. If the code fragment is relocated by creating a fresh copy at the destination point or prior to the start of its execution, the movement involves pure code and it is often referred to as weak mobility. By contrast, strong mobility entails the movement of code being executed, i.e., the execution state is relocated along with the code thus allowing it to continue running even after the move. Of course, since the relocation may result in changes to some of the program bindings the actual state may have components that are no longer the same as before the move. Associated with strong mobility is usually the ability to exercise control over the movement both with respect to timing and destination although one can easily envision systems in which the fixed infrastructure has total control over who moves and when.

Is it possible to envision units of mobility that have no syntactic correspondence? While we can argue that the basic unit of mobility must have a syntactic correspondent, we can also see the possibility of creating, through a composition process, computational environments which no longer have any relation to program syntax. A simple example might be a swarm of agents that, once bound to each other, may become a new entity endowed with the ability to move and to restructure itself. Our own work on fine-grained mobility comes very close to this view of mobility, as it will become evident in a later section.

10.2.2 Space

Current work on mobility has made very little effort to investigate and formalize the concept of space and its properties. To date, physical components can vary greatly in size and capabilities but, most of them perceive location as a pair of coordinates on the earth surface provided by some GPS service. This is useful in terms of being able to exhibit location-dependent behaviors in PDAs and laptops. Robots can go one step further and actually control their position in space. Such capability, however, brings with it the added complexity of a space that is no longer continuous and homogeneous due to the presence of walls and other limitations to movement. Space acquires structure and maybe even semantics. Space can actually change over time as components move relative to each other. A robot moving out of a doorway may all of a sudden open new possibilities of movement for the others. Moreover, locations can be relative rather than absolute and knowledge of the space may be limited to those areas explored to date. This may become important when knowledge is shared among components since in the absence of a global reference system it may be difficult to reconcile the different views acquired by different components.

Can we think of physical space in a new light? We believe that we can and we must rethink our treatment of physical space. Space can have structure and the structure may be essential to making it possible to address important application needs. Consider, for instance, the problem of delivering messages among a group of mobile components that move through space and communicate only when in immediate proximity to each other. Can we guarantee message delivery? In general, this is impossible because one cannot be sure that two specific components ever meet. Yet, if we assume that the components move back and forth along a single line (a train track), the problem is easily solved. Many situations are amenable to similar treatment. Of course these kinds of issues can be handled in the application by superposing a suitable interpretation on top of what amounts to a primitive space. But, a more formal and higher level treatment may give us the tools to reason about such situations and to provide programmers with high level interfaces that reduce the complexity of the development effort.

Since much of the communication among mobile components entails the use of wireless transmission, space and distance metrics are playing growing roles in the way one thinks about the relation among components. Cellular networks provide a prime example of structure being imposed onto the physical space. The space is divided into regular patches with a base station supporting all the communication needs of the components in that specific area. Transitions among cells entail special handoff protocols, i.e., communication behavior is tied to space structure. In the case of ad hoc networks, the space lacks structure but the distance metric is important because communication can take place only when components are within range. If ad hoc routing is available, i.e., mobile components serve as mobile routers as well, the space acquires structure dynamically in response to the very presence of the mobile components. This structure is being used in new kinds of protocols that factor relative location information into their decision process, e.g., discovery protocols interested in determining what neighbors are within a certain distance of a given component. More sophisticated approaches are likely to take advantage of both distance and velocity by predicting future component locations. The density of components in a given region of space may also be exploited in the design of certain systems. In natural situations, distance may be affected by terrain topology. Even in the air, winds may be viewed as altering the properties of space, thus affecting the predictive equations. In artificial environments apparent distances may be altered by the presence of communication resources such as wireless bridges that offer extended connectivity through wireline networks.

To the best of our knowledge no systems to date provide what we would call a non-trivial view of physical space. The situation is quite different when it comes to considering logical space in programming languages and models. One can encounter a great deal of variability with respect to the choice of unit of mobility, the perception of logical space, and even the kind of movement that is permitted.

In Mobile UNITY [405], for instance, a program consists of a set of statements and the set of local variables being read and modified. A program becomes mobile through the addition of a distinguished location variable. Changes to the location variable represent movement and programs change location always as a whole. Since movement is reduced to value assignment, reasoning about mobility can be handled by employing the standard UNITY [147] logic. By contrast, CODEWEAVE [400] shares a common formal foundation with Mobile UNITY but adopts a fine-grained paradigm. Single variables and individual statements can be moved from one location to another and can be injected in, aggregated into and extracted from programs created on the fly. Large-grained aggregates can be manipulated in exactly the same manner. The mobility and restructuring of programs is not unique to CODEWEAVE. Algebraic models accomplish the same thing by allowing for the movement of processes, be they elementary or composite. In Mobile Ambients [123], for instance, rules are provided for moving processes from one context to another regardless of the complexity of the process involved in the move (the reader should think of context as being a location).

While our mental image of mobility is usually associated with some form of autonomy this cannot be assumed in all cases. In mobile agent systems the decision to move may indeed rest with the agent itself. Classes, however, are loaded on demand. One can also envision systems in which agents are pushed along (forced to move) when their services are no longer needed or when a need arises at some other site. When modeling physical systems, devices are carried around from one location to another without having any say. The motion is actually induced by outside forces, which may need to be modeled when reasoning about the resulting system.

In our discussion so far, we casually mentioned location without actually considering what it might be. In the context of logical mobility, location is often equated with a host in the network. Things are a little more complicated than this because the ability to execute code presupposes the existence of an appropriate computing environment. Nevertheless, treating space as a graph with vertices representing locations and edges constraining movement is a reasonable model. However, this is only one among many models one encounters in the literature and there are many more that are likely to be studied in the future. Consider, for instance, a program residing on a host and its structure which, for discussion purposes, we assume to be hierarchical in nature. Each node in its tree structure can be viewed as a location. The very structure of the programs provides a notion of space. Code fragments may move to locations in the program and may even extend the program. Thus, the notion of space induced by the program may be used to support mobility and as the basis for redefining the space itself. This is precisely the view adopted by CODEWEAVE, which recognizes both hosts and structured programs residing on hosts. In Mobile Ambients, the model is structured in terms of nested processes that define administrative domains. Mobility is constrained by the structure of the model while motion alters that very structure, i.e., the definition of space. MobiS [399] too is a model that offers a hierarchical structure with mobility restricted among parent child locations consisting of tuple spaces. Finally, in Mobile UNITY the space is left completely outside the model. Spatial properties may be used, however, in reasoning about the behavior of the system.

This latter strategy allows one to explore a broad range of spaces having different formal properties, purely abstract constructions or models of physical reality. In general, the ability to unify logical and physical views of mobility is useful in the analysis of mobile systems and also as the basis for developing new models. Moreover, if such efforts result in a practical integration of logical and physical mobility, a wide range of novel applications can be contemplated. LIME [493] is one such attempt to integration. Mobile agents reside on mobile hosts that can form ad hoc networks when in proximity of each other. When this happens, the agents appear to be sharing a common data environment (tuple space) and have the opportunity to jump from one host to another.

With the advent of mobility, space is fast becoming the new research frontier. Our treatment of space impacts our ability to analyze systems and shapes the models and languages we develop. The assumptions we make about the structure of space and the mobility profile of the components that inhabit it have profound effects on the kinds of protocols and algorithms we develop. Problems specific to mobility are often impossible to solve unless proper restrictions are imposed. A more precise and formal evaluation of space holds the promise for significant intellectual and practical advances in our treatment of mobility.

10.2.3 Context Management

As components move through space, their relation to other components and to fixed resources changes over time. Of course, even if a component is stationary, other components may move relative to it. The notion of context relates to the way in which a component perceives the presence of other components and available stationary resources at each point in time. While location plays an important role in determining the current context, it is not the sole controlling factor. Similar components at the same location are likely to see very distinct contexts. Two components, for instance, may not have the same access rights at that particular location because one is local while the other is a visitor. Their respective needs may also be distinct thus forcing the components to look for different things among the locally available resources. Even more interesting is the fact that components may obey different binding rules, i.e., ways to associate names to resources. Depending on the nature of the mobile system, when a component leaves a site existing bindings may be severed permanently, may be disabled temporarily and restored upon return, or may continue to be preserved in spite of the location change. The first option is most common in settings involving physical mobility while the third is readily implemented when logical mobility takes place across connected sites, as in the case of the Internet.

A purely local context (i.e., involving a single location) is often favored because it appears to be easier to maintain and implement. This is only partially true because even a local context may involve transparent coordination among multiple hosts. In the ad hoc mobility setting, for instance, the maintenance of a local context is very complex. Components need to discover each other and to negotiate the extent to which they are willing to collaborate among themselves. Keeping track of who else is in immediate proximity and which resources they are willing to provide or seek to use is not an easy task. The level of complexity is affected by the assumptions one can make about disconnection patterns, the relative speeds of components, and the reliability of both components and wireless links. The degree of consistency demanded by the application is another major factor. The trend is towards weak versions of consistency but they may not be acceptable in all situations. Even in the case of logical mobility, a component arriving at a site is required to establish new bindings. From the point of view of the component, this entails a resource discovery process and possible negotiations.

A distributed context (e.g., one that refers to distant hosts) entails all the complexities associated with a local one plus a lot more. At a minimum, the component navigating across the network must remember the identity of the resources it needs from different locations (e.g., IP addresses) and the network must provide the ability to support communication with the resources. However, this is adequate only if the resources are essentially passive, i.e., respond to requests but they do not initiate any. If the relation is such that resources can actually initiate communication, the complexity rises dramatically. The network must support delivery to components that move in space, be they agents or nomadic devices that rely on base station support. Mobile IP [488] is one protocol that provides this kind of service. Of course, the ultimate challenge is to allow mobile components to send messages to each other while offering delivery guarantees. Recently, we proposed several algorithms that support this kind of communication in a nomadic setting [444, 445]. Systems that provide notification services are another example in which resources need to contact mobile components. It should be noted, however, that providing messaging support is only the first step towards supporting the context management needs of a mobile computing system.

While context management can be left in the hands of the individual components, this is not a strategy likely to lead to rapid software development. It is more reasonable to provide middleware that enforces a certain clean conceptual view while offering the right tools for managing contextual changes. We draw a distinction here between maintaining the context and responding to contextual changes, a topic we will return to at the end of this section. Regarding context maintenance, two issues seem to be particularly important in differentiating among various software support strategies, whether they are implemented as part of middleware, agent systems, or mobile code language: the level of support provided by the underlying runtime system and the conceptual model enforced. Regarding the former, the two extremes seem to be making context maintenance explicitly the responsibility of the component or achieving full transparency. When an agent changes location on its own and arrives at a new site, it may be required to decide: how visible it is necessary to be to others by engaging in some registration process; which old acquaintances should be preserved; what services to register with the local site for availability to other agents; what resources it needs to discover and access at the new location; etc. All these activities, even if supported by some sort of mobility middleware, provide flexibility but also place significant demands on the component designer.

Much of our own work has centered on making context maintenance fully transparent. In such cases, the conceptual model that underlies the basis for the context maintenance is of paramount importance. The designer relies on its understanding to generate correct code. One of the models supported by Mobile UNITY is the notion of transparent transient sharing of program variables. Component code is simply written under the assumption that variables may undergo spontaneous value changes in response to the arrival and departure of other components in the vicinity or due to modifications made by them. What variables are shared and under what conditions is specified using a declarative notation—its operational semantics are ultimately reduced to coordination actions associated with statements in the basic Mobile UNITY notation. The condition for sharing variables can be arbitrary but it is usually related to relative positions among components, e.g., at the same location or within radio contact.

A more complex example of transparent context management involves the use of global virtual data structures. In a virtual memory system the application program perceives the memory space to be larger than the physical reality and the support system takes upon itself the responsibility of maintaining this illusion in a seamless manner. Similarly, a global virtual data structure creates the appearance that the individual mobile unit has access to shared data despite the presence of mobility. Consider, for instance, a graph and two very distinct settings, one involving agents and the other ad hoc networks. In one case, the graph is stored in a distributed fashion across the nodes of a fixed network. Agents move from node to node like crawling ants carrying data from vertex to vertex. Each agent is aware of the graph and of the presence of other agents co-located at the same vertex. In the second case, the graph is distributed among the mobile hosts but only that portion of the graph that is connected and stored among hosts within communication range is accessible to the application. Hosts can trade sections of the graph as long as such changes cannot have any effect on hosts that are out of contact. In both cases, behavior analysis is carried out by reasoning about the global structure but all actions are local. Furthermore, the actions involving the structure are specific to it. LIME is one system that follows this strategy by employing a tuple space partitioned among both hosts and agents.

Context changes can be induced not only by movement (through associated changes in data and resource availability) but also due to quality of service considerations, e.g., variations in bandwidth and delay. Regardless of their source, context changes are always important to the application and mechanisms for responding to such changes are needed. The most commonly used strategy is to provide an event notification mechanism. A predefined set of events is made available to the application, which can register in turn appropriate responses for specific events. A more general approach is to furnish the application with a general event notification mechanism and allow it to define both the set of events of interest and the choice of responses. A very different alternative involves the notion of reactive statements. As used in Mobile UNITY and LIME, the execution of reactions is not triggered by events, rather by specific state properties. Once activated, they continue to execute at high priority for as long as the condition persists. We will return to this topic in the next section that covers coordination constructs and the manner in which they contribute to context definition and maintenance.

10.3 Coordination Constructs

Coordination is a programming paradigm that seeks to separate the definition of components from the mechanics of interaction. In traditional models of concurrency, processes communicate with each other via messages or shared variables. The code of each component is explicit about the use of communication primitives and the components are very much aware of each other's presence. Actually, communication fails when one of the parties is missing. By contrast, coordination approaches promote a certain level of decoupling among processes and the code is usually less explicit about mechanics of the interactions. Ideally, the interactions are defined totally outside the component's code. Linda [267] is generally credited with bringing coordination to the attention of the programming community. By using a globally shared tuple space, Linda made temporal and spatial decoupling a reality in parallel programming and simplified the programming task by providing just three basic operations for accessing the tuple space. Interactions among processes were brought up to a new level of abstraction and the programming task was made simpler. Reasonable implementations of the tuple space made the approach effective.

Our concern, however, is not with coordination in general but with the role it can play in simplifying the task of developing mobile applications. Mobility can benefit from a coordination perspective because decoupling enhances one's ability to cope with open systems. At the same time, mobility adds a new and challenging element to coordination, the dynamic changes taking place as components move through space. Some properties that may be desirable in general become even more important in the mobile setting. Promoting a coordination style that is totally transparent to the participating components, for instance, may enhance decoupling and increase the ability to interact with components previously unknown. Other interesting properties are specific to mobility. The notion of transient interactions is a direct result of the fact that components move relative to each other going in and out of communication range. The concept of transitive interactions surfaces when one needs to consider establishing group-level interactions out of pairwise communications. At the other extreme, logical mobility in the presence of full server access across global networks leads to almost unreal modes of distant interaction where components move from location to location while preserving the ability to access resources as if they were local. In general, space becomes a major factor in formulating coordination issues. In physical mobility, the distance between components can become a barrier to wireless communication thus making interactions conditional on relative positions of components. Even in logical mobility, components may be limited to interacting only when present at a common location. Finally, spatial properties are commonly combined with quality of service and security considerations to define the nature of the coordination process.

In the remainder of this section we discuss three models corresponding to three distinct modes of coordination. While they involve both physical and logical mobility, separately and in a fully integrated fashion, the distinctions among the three models are most striking when we examine the way coordination is used to address similar problems in very different contexts. Mobile UNITY is illustrative of what one might call an *active* coordination strategy. Coordination is specified operationally and bridges (in a mostly transparent manner) the states of components when they are found in specific relations to each other. LIME is representative for a *passive* coordination style very similar to Linda but adjusted to the realities of ad hoc mobility. Transiently and transitively shared tuple spaces provide the coordination medium but programs need to make explicit use of tuple space operations to gain access the tuples located on hosts within proximity. Finally, CODEWEAVE illustrates one of the more exotic applications of coordination. Components (codes fragments and aggregates) are provided with primitives that facilitate code mobility. An operational specification defines the meaning of these operations in terms of simpler coordination primitives. One might call this style of coordination *constructivist*. The three examples exhibit a great degree of similitude at the conceptual level but also variability in the range of coordination constructs being employed. We view this to be indicative of two complementary facts. On one hand, one can build a common foundation and use it to examine the way coordination is used in mobility. Mobile UNITY seems to have many of the features required to accomplish this. On the other hand, mobility covers such a vast expanse of possibilities that many distinct models are likely to emerge. They will provide the conceptual foundation for software systems (mostly middleware) designed to support the development of mobile applications.

10.3.1 Mobile UNITY

Mobile UNITY [405] proposes a new notation and underlying formal model supporting specification of and reasoning about mobile systems. The approach is based on the UNITY [147] model of concurrent computation. Its notation is extended with constructs for expressing transient interactions among components in the presence of movement and reconfiguration.

UNITY was conceived as a vehicle for the study of distributing computing, and defined a minimalist model for specifying and reasoning about such systems. The key elements of the UNITY model are the concepts of variable and conditional multiple assignment statement. Programs are simply sets of assignment statements that execute atomically and are selected for execution in a weakly fair manner. Multiple programs can be composed through the *union* operator. The result is a new system that consists of the union of all the program variables and the union of all the assignment statements. Variables with the same name are assumed to be identical, i.e., they reference the same memory location. Our interest in mobility forced us to reexamine the UNITY model with the following goals in mind: to provide for a strong degree of program decoupling, to model movement and disconnection, and to offer high-level programming abstractions for expressing the transient nature of interactions in a mobile setting.

One key design decision in the development of Mobile UNITY was the choice of the program as the unit of mobility. This is a natural choice for UNITY because it allows for simple functional decomposition and composition (e.g., through program union and the use of similarly named variables). Therefore, the first major aspect of a Mobile UNITY system description is the specification of the individual mobile components, a standard UNITY program for each. However, unlike standard UNITY, Mobile UNITY seeks to foster a highly decoupled style of programming by requiring the namespaces of the programs to be disjoint. This allows each program to operate without interference from the other programs it is composed with. As shown later, coordination among components is allowed, but it is separated from normal processing. Additionally, each program is augmented with a distinguished location variable. This variable may correspond to latitude and longitude for a physically mobile component, or it may be a network or memory address for a mobile agent. The specific definition is left intentionally out of the model. However, by making location a part of the program specification, it can be manipulated from within the program to allow a program to control its own location. Furthermore, the location of the individual components can be used in reasoning about the system behavior. Actually, by reducing movement to value assignment, the standard UNITY proof logic may be used to verify program properties despite the presence of mobility.

The second major aspect of a Mobile UNITY specification is the **Interactions** section which defines all interactions among components. Because the namespaces of the programs are disjoint, no statement within a program can reference a variable in another program. The **Interactions** section is the only place where variables from multiple programs can be addressed. In this manner, the definition of coordination is separated from the definition of standard processing.

In our work we have shown that only a very small set of primitive constructs is needed to build a wide range of high-level coordination constructs and models. These primitives include asynchronous value transfer, statement inhibition, and reactive statements. Statement inhibition restricts the execution of a statement in one program based on the state of another program. Reactive statements are enabled by programmer specified global conditions and continue to execute at high priority until they no longer cause any state changes. The standard UNITY proof logic has been extended to incorporate the new Mobile UNITY primitives, but the underlying proof logic remains unchanged. Using these three primitives and a minor technical change to the basic UNITY notation, Mobile UNITY allowed us to define a number of interesting coordination constructs including: variables which are shared in a transient and transitive manner based on the relative positions of the mobile programs; statements that are synchronized in a transient and transitive manner according to a variety of synchronization rules; clock synchronization with and without drift; etc.

Reactive statements provide a mechanism for extending the effect of individual assignment statements with an arbitrary terminating computation. This construct allows us to simulate the effects of the interrupt processing mechanisms that are designed to react immediately to certain state changes. The construct is particularly useful when its guard involves the relative locations of components. The result is the execution of an additional state transition in response to a new connection or disconnection.

The standard UNITY model for shared variables is static. In Mobile UNITY transient variable sharing is implemented using the reactive statements. High level constructs are provided for symmetric and asymmetric update of variables throughout the period during which they are shared, for establishing a single common value when a new sharing relation is established (engagement), and for defining the values resulting from the disengagement of variables as components move away. Transient statement synchronization is defined using variable sharing as a building block.

The constructs provided by Mobile UNITY have been put to test in the specification and verification of Mobile IP [406] and of a variety of mobile code paradigms including code-on-demand, remote evaluation, and mobile agents [495]. In the next two subsections we will present two other uses of Mobile UNITY. One involves its application to fine-grained code mobility and the other relates to defining the formal foundation for mobility middleware involving transient sharing of tuple spaces.

10.3.2 CodeWeave

The core concepts of Mobile UNITY are geared towards the mobility of components. Programs may represent mobile hosts moving across space, or mobile agents roaming network hosts. Nevertheless, this coarse-grained view of mobility is indeed limited, as evidenced by state of the art technology. In the realm of logical mobility, mobile agent technology still awaits for massive exploitation in the design of distributed applications, while finer-grained forms of mobility, often collectively referred to as mobile code, already found their way into recent proposals for distributed middleware. For instance, Java

Remote Method Invocation (RMI) exploits the dynamic class loading capabilities of the Java language to allow, on both client and server, on-the-fly retrieval of stub and application classes that are needed to support a remote method invocation. The capability of relocating portion of the code and of the state of a mobile unit, rather than always moving all the constituents together, brings additional flexibility in the design of distributed applications.

CODEWEAVE [400] is a specialization of Mobile UNITY conceived for modeling fine-grained mobility. CODEWEAVE retains the operational model underlying Mobile UNITY, but allows the designer to specify migration of the constituents of a Mobile UNITY program. The unit of mobility in CODEWEAVE can be as small as a single UNITY statement or variable. The former is referred to as a *code unit*, while the latter is called a *data unit*. Units take part into the general system behavior only when they are part of a *process*. Processes can be organized in hierarchies, and the containment relation constrains the ambit of visibility of a unit. Thus, processes are the unit of scoping and execution. Processes and units exist at a given location, which may be a process or a site. Units that reside on a site do not belong to any process, they represent available resources that may be shared among the co-located processes.

CODEWEAVE provides primitives for moving (or cloning) units. Migration of units across hosts may represent the relocation of a class or an object in a distributed middleware. Migration of a unit from a host into a process may represent dynamic linking or deserialization mechanisms. Relocation of state and behavior is not the only dimension relevant to logical mobility. As discussed in [253], logical mobility is often exploited to gain access to a site's shared resources, hence the management of bindings to shared resources upon migration is a key issue. CODEWEAVE provides a notion of *reference* that enables processes to access a unit without explicitly (and exclusively) containing it.

The same primitives discussed thus far actually apply to processes. For instance, a **move** operation applied to a process causes its migration together with all its constituents. Hence, the fine-grained model put forth by CODEWEAVE subsumes, rather than replace, the coarse-grained perspective where the units of execution and of mobility coincide. For instance, mobile agents are still modeled naturally by using the process abstraction. Furthermore, the ability to represent nested processes enables the modeling of complex structures built by sites, places, and agents like those introduced in Telescript [631], similarly to what Mobile Ambients or MobiS provide.

CODEWEAVE represents fine-grained mobility by relying completely on the semantics of Mobile UNITY. The units of mobility of CODEWEAVE, i.e., statements and variables, are reinterpreted as Mobile UNITY programs, whose movement and sharing is ruled by statements in the **Interactions** section, according to the semantics specified in CODEWEAVE. For instance, the movement of a process along with all its constituents is actually reduced to the movement of a Mobile UNITY program representing the CODEWEAVE process, followed by a set of reactions that migrate the Mobile UNITY programs representing its constituents in the same atomic step.

Several reflections can be made about the model fostered by CODEWEAVE. The fact that the model's semantics is reduced completely in terms of Mobile UNITY is indicative of the fact that the constructs of Mobile UNITY effectively capture the essence of mobile interactions. However, the ability to model and reason about mobile systems at a level of abstraction that is closer to the domain opens up new possibilities.

On one hand, the availability of fine-grained constructs fosters a design style where mobile agents are represented at increasing levels of refinement. Existing systems typically do not allow a mobile agent to move along with all its code, due to performance reasons. Different systems employ different strategies, ranging from a completely static code relocation strategy that separates at configuration time the code that must be carried by the agent from the one that remains on the source host (like in Aglets [373]), to completely dynamic forms under the control of the programmer (like in μCODE [494]). Our approach allows modeling of a mobile agent application at different levels of detail. One can start with a high level description in terms of processes representing the mobile agents and continue to refine this view using the fine-grained constructs that specify precisely which constituents of an agent are allowed to move with it and which are not.

On the other hand, the perspective put forth by CODEWEAVE sheds a new light on coordination. Coordination no longer involves just communication about parties, which at most may be mobile and migrate to achieve local coordination. When fine-grained logical mobility is part of the picture, components are malleable and open to changes that may occur as part of the coordination protocol. The cooperative behavior of components is no longer determined only by the information exchanged during coordination, but also by new behaviors that can be exchanged as program fragments, and dynamically become part of a component. Examples include the ability to exploit new coordination primitives and coordination protocols downloaded on the fly while the computation is being executed.

This view may even lead to new models of computation. Insofar we always assumed that moving a statement or a variable in a CODEWEAVE system does not necessarily imply achieving this also in the implementation language. We thought of it allowing us to model the movement of a unit of mobility (e.g., a Java object or class) that is finer grained than the unit of execution (e.g., a Java thread). Nevertheless, the ability to move a single statement or variable in a real programming language is an intriguing possibility, one that may be realized by exploiting the new generation of scripting languages. Some researchers [224] proposed schemes where XML tags are migrated and dynamically "plugged in" an XML script already executing at the destination. This scheme may amplify the improvement in flexibility and customizability brought in by mobile code. An even wilder scenario is the one where it is possible not only to add or substitute programming language statements that conform to the semantics of the language, but also to extend such semantics dynamically by migrating statements along with a representation of the semantics of the constructs they use. As proposed at a recent conference [275], this could open up an economic model where the concept of software component includes not only application code or libraries, but even the very constituents of a programming language.

Another interesting opportunity is grounded in the binding mechanism that rules execution of units within a process. In our model, a statement can actually execute only if it is within a process, and if all of its variables are bound to corresponding data units. This represents the intuitive notion that a program executes within a process only if the code is there and memory has been allocated for its variables. In languages that provide remote dynamic linking, it is always a code fragment that gets dynamically downloaded into a running program. However, the symmetry between data and code units in our model suggests a complementary approach where not only the code gets dynamically downloaded, but also the data. Thus, for instance, much like a class loader is invoked to resolve the name of a class during execution of a program, similarly an "object loader" could be exploited to bring an object to be co-located with the program and thus enable resumption of the computation. Another, even wilder, follow-up on this idea is an alternative computation model where code and data are not necessarily brought together to enable a program to proceed execution, rather it is the program itself (or a whole swarm of them, to enhance probability of success) that migrates and proceeds to execute based on the set of components currently bound to it. This way, a program is like an empty "pallet" wandering on the net and occasionally performing some computation based on the pieces that fill its holes at a given point.

Verification may be considered under a new light as well. CODEWEAVE inherits the temporal logic of Mobile UNITY and thus, besides enabling reasoning about the location of mobile programs, it also allows reasoning about the location of their constituents. Hence, verification can be exploited not only to prove the overall correctness of the system, but also to optimize the placement of the constituents of its mobile components, placing them only on the nodes where they will be needed. For instance, a mobile agent could be written in such a way that it does not need to carry with it a given class, because a formal proof has been developed to guarantee that, for the given system in a given state, the class will be already present at destination. Clearly, this approach potentially enables bandwidth and storage savings, and is particularly amenable for use in environments where resources are scarce, e.g., wireless computing with PDAs.

10.3.3 LIME

LIME [493] takes a pragmatic step toward the development of applications for mobility by describing a model for coordination among mobile components which frees the application programmer from direct concern with many complexities of the environment while still providing a powerful programming paradigm. The model itself is formed by adapting the well-known Linda coordination model to accommodate the essential features of mobility, and the paradigm is presented to the application programmer in the form of middleware.

The fundamental properties of the Linda model are a globally accessible, static tuple space and a set of processes which interact by writing to and reading from the shared tuple space. None of the processes need to co-exist in either time or space to coordinate, and because access to the data is based on pattern matching, a process need not know the identity of the other processes in order to successfully interact. This decoupled style of interaction is of great utility in a mobile setting where the parties involved in communication change dynamically due to migration or shifts in connectivity patterns. On the other hand, the decoupled nature of Linda is made possible by the global accessibility and persistence of the tuple space.

When mobility is considered, especially the ad hoc model of physical mobility, no predefined, static, global context can exist for the computation. The current context is defined by transient communities of mobile components. The idea underlying LIME is to maintain a global *virtual* tuple space, physically distributing the contents of this structure among the mobile units. As connectivity among components changes, different projections of the global virtual tuple space are accessible to each component. From a more local perspective, each mobile unit is responsible for a portion of the global state (i.e., one partition of the global virtual tuple space). When two or more components are within communication range, the contents of their tuple spaces are shared transiently and transparently.

To the application programmer, all interactions with the shared data space occur via local accesses to a component known as the *interface tuple space*, or ITS. The ITS effectively provides a window into the global virtual tuple space which expands as mobile components come within range and contracts as connectivity among components is lost. Transient sharing of the contents of the tuple spaces within the ITS constitutes a very powerful coordination abstraction, as it provides a mobile unit with the illusion of a local tuple space that contains all the tuples belonging to the members of the currently connected community, without the need to explicitly know their identities. Additionally, because access to the ITS is entirely local, the application programmer can issue local operations, while reasoning about their effect in the global context.

The operations provided on the ITS are identical to the basic Linda operations, and by default operate over the currently accessible data. This permits a context dependent style of interaction by fulfilling queries based on the current connectivity state. Additionally, LIME extends the basic Linda operations to allow data to be placed with a specific mobile component as connectivity allows, and also to query a specific projection of the tuple space based on the mobile component responsible for storing that data. Such interactions enable a programming style in which the application programmer can access data based on a specific, known location. Thus, LIME provides both location-transparent and location-aware styles of data access, in order to support applications requiring different styles of programming.

Thus far, the description of the mobile components has been left intentionally abstract, however the LIME model provides a unique integration of physical and logical mobility. Basically, the logically mobile components, or mobile agents, form the active computational units of the LIME system, and it is their responsibility to hold individual partitions of the tuple space. As an agent migrates, it carries its portion of the tuple space with it as part of its state. The integration with physical mobility comes because these logically mobile components must reside on physical hosts that move through space and connect with one another based on the distance between them. We assume that when two agents reside on the same host, they are able to communicate, thus forming a *host level tuple space* containing the tuples of the agents located on that host. Similarly, when hosts are within communication range, the host level tuple spaces are shared to form a *federated tuple space*. To emphasize the power of the abstraction provided by the model, we note again that the basic Linda operations function over the federated tuple space. This makes coordination visible only as a changing set of tuples over which operations are evaluated, protecting the programmer from the changes inherent in the mobile environment.

As previously noted, the mobile environment is highly dynamic, and it is often desirable for applications to react to changes in the environment. In Mobile UNITY, this led to the development and integration of the reactive programming model. Linda already supports one model to react to the state of the system, namely a "pull" model in which a process blocks until a tuple matching a query appears in the tuple space. Because LIME provides the same primitive operations as Linda, this functionality is present in the mobile environment, however LIME also makes available Mobile UNITY's reactive model of programming, enabling a "push" style of coordination. In other words, instead of a process waiting to pull information from the tuple space when it is written, the tuple space itself is charged with pushing information about the state to a process or executing a piece of code which has been registered. Because the reactions are controlled from within the LIME system, a higher degree of atomicity between the discovery of a matching tuple and the execution of the user's registered reaction can be guaranteed. Pragmatic considerations about how to enforce atomicity guarantees in the distributed setting forced us to incorporate in LIME two kinds of reactions, weak and strong. They provide differing degrees of atomicity and are subject to different applicability constraints motivated by the need to provide an effective implementation. In our experience, the combination of this form of reactive programming with the transiently shared tuple space provides a programming abstraction that is extremely powerful and useful. Thus, for instance, programmers are able to specify once and for all that a reaction must be executed whenever a given condition takes place in any point of the federated tuple space, and possibly even within the context of a component that was unknown at registration time.

The reactive mechanism of LIME has proven useful not only for reacting to changes in the data state of applications, but also for reacting to changes in the system context, specifically the arrival and departure of agents and hosts. This hints at another feature of LIME, namely the exposure of the system context to the application programmer. Specifically the system context consists of the mobile hosts that are within communication range and the mobile agents contained on each of those hosts. It is also possible to augment this basic information with other system characteristics such as the available bandwidth between a pair of hosts or the resources available within a host. We approach the system context as the dual to the data context, making it available as a read only tuple space maintained wholly from within the LIME system and accessible with the same primitives as all other transiently shared LIME tuple spaces. In other words, the application programmer can query and react to this LIME system tuple space in the same manner it operates over the data tuple space, with the exception that the system tuple space cannot be written to.

LIME has been successful primarily on two fronts. First, a formal specification of the LIME model has been written in Mobile UNITY, providing both clear semantics for the operations, and serving as an example of the practical use of Mobile UNITY as the specification language for a mobile middleware system. With this semantic definition in hand, it is possible to prove properties about the overall LIME system. Examples include the completion of the engagement protocol when a new host joins the LIME system and properties of applications which have been specified in Mobile UNITY using the LIME constructs. Second, an implementation of LIME exists as a Java package available for distribution. It has been used to develop a variety of mobile applications ranging from collaborative work scenarios to spatial games. The simplicity of the Linda coordination model and its natural adaptation to transiently shared tuple spaces leads to a shallow learning curve for the LIME programmer and to ease of implementation.

10.4 Conclusions

Mobility is an area rich in research opportunities, both intellectually and pragmatically. It demands a new way of thinking and requires design strategies that are distinct from the traditional distributed computing. Our own research into mobility spans a broad range of issues, from formal models to middleware development. Regardless of the direction we explored, three issues emerged as central to our investigation in each case: the choice of the unit of mobility, the definition of space, and the manner in which context is maintained and perceived. In this paper we tried to develop these themes by exploring the range of options one can envision and by contrasting what is possible with what we actually employed in three specific models. Another important message of this paper is the notion that coordination played a key role both in our ability to provide a clean formal treatment of mobility and in our attempt to simplify the development of mobile applications. On one hand, a coordination perspective facilitated an abstract and modular treatment of mobility. On the other hand, a coordination-centered design of the middleware made it possible to offer the programmer a simpler conceptual model of interaction among mobile units and to delegate to the runtime support system much of the effort associated with maintaining and updating the context visible to the individual units. Because coordination promotes global thinking and local action, it is ideally suited for addressing the needs of mobility in all its forms.

Acknowledgements

This research was supported in part by the National Science Foundation under Grant No. CCR-9970939. Any opinions, findings, and conclusions or recommendations expressed in this paper are those of the authors and do not necessarily reflect the views of the National Science Foundation.

11. Coordination and Security on the Internet

Ciarán Bryce[1] and Marco Cremonini[2]

[1] Centre Universitaire d'Informatique
   Université de Genève , 24, rue Général-Dufour, CH-1211 Genève 4 , Switzerland
   `Ciaran.Bryce@cui.unige.ch`
[2] LIA, Dipartimento di Elettronica, Informatica e Sistemistica
   Università di Bologna, Viale Risorgimento 2, I-40136 Bologna, Italy
   `mcremonini@deis.unibo.it`

Summary.

This chapter examines the impact of security on the design of coordination models for agent-based systems deployed over the Internet. A reference architecture for secure coordination in shared space models is presented. In this context, we argue that the interaction of agents and system components throughout a shared space should be governed by policies that satisfy both coordination and security requirements. A distributed scenario, composed of multiple independent shared spaces, is then considered. The integration of cryptographic primitives into tuple-based communication is necessary, but this has subtleties that system designers must be aware of. Some examples of these subtleties are discussed. Finally, existing coordination models and systems are analyzed with respect to the general security framework presented.

11.1 Introduction

Coordination models deal with the interaction of independently developed active components. In the context of agent systems [626, 614], they address the issue of how agents interact, and permit developers to design systems without necessarily having to understand the internals of agents. Though a component-oriented approach to programming exists under many guises, coordination models are specifically concerned with formally expressing the interaction occurring among several concurrent entities in a uniform framework. In this chapter, we restrict our discussion to *data-driven coordination* models [482], like Linda [267], in which agents communicate by reading and writing messages or *tuples* to and from a *shared space.*

Tuple-based coordination is receiving renewed interest because it is increasing seen as a suitable model for managing the interaction among components of open, distributed and heterogeneous systems. In particular, the perceived scalability and uniformity of coordination models has also pushed many to consider them for agent-based systems in the Internet [597, 249, 472]. In this context, the shared space model is convenient since agents do not need to be synchronized to communicate; an agent can read any message from the space. The space model is also simple enough to use without the hindrance of site specific naming conventions; in an open system with several administrative domains, this is a significant advantage. However, aside the new opportunities that agent systems have brought to coordination models (and vice versa), new concerns, driven by the openness of the environment, affect the applicability of basic shared spaces.

Security is a major concern for open networks like the Internet, and this has important implications for the coordination models used. It basically means that interacting agents are mutually mistrusting. One reason for this is that the agents execute on or originate from mistrusting network sites. Another reason is that the agents are coded independently or act from unknown sources. Further, agents might simply contain bugs. In this reason, agents must be isolated from each another, and the information flows between agents and their access to application information must be controlled.

Security and coordination exhibit complementary facets in the Internet context. Security is the conceptual counterpart of coordination: While coordination deals with how system components interact, security deals with what they are allowed to do [196].

The aim of this chapter is to present a general security framework for agent systems based on the shared space coordination model. The underlying message is that security requirements cannot be effectively satisfied simply by adding on security functionality to existing agent systems. Rather, a system should be build with security as a key goal from the outset. To this end, we present a reference architecture for secure coordination. We overview aspects of agent authentication and authorization in this architecture.

To enforce security in an open environment, the architecture relies on cryptographic techniques and protocols. However, it is worth noting that the development of cryptographic communication protocols can present subtleties in the coordination environment, so they must be carefully analyzed before deployment. Some examples of this are presented and discussed.

Plan of the chapter: Section 2 presents the reference architecture. Section 3 looks at meaningful security policies in the coordination context, and at mechanisms for authentication and authorization. The case of a distributed scenario composed of multiple shared spaces is also described. Section 4 discusses principles of cryptographic communication protocol design. Section 5 then presents some of the existing coordination models and systems, and Section 6 concludes the chapter.

11.2 A Reference Architecture for Secure Coordination

This section presents a *reference architecture* for secure interaction in coordination systems. The role of this architecture is to define the components that should be included in a traditional shared space to define and implement security policies. We will refer to this architecture throughout the chapter, and use it when explaining security in existing coordination models and systems in Section 11.5.

11.2.1 The Shared Space Model

In *shared space* models, i.e., the ones based on Linda [267], all information and data to be exchanged between processes are stored in a shared data space. Entries in the space are *tuples* made up of sequences of typed values. In agent systems, a user can start several agents that use this space to communicate. An agent places a tuple in the space with the `out` operation, and reads and removes a tuple with the `in` operation. The `read` operation is like an `in` except that the tuple is not removed from the space.

A tuple is read by specifying a template tuple as a parameter to the `in` or `read` operation. For tuple t_2 and tuple variable t_1, $t_1 := in(t_2)$, searches the shared space for a tuple that *matches* with t_2. A template tuple matches a tuple if both have the same number of attributes, and if each attribute of the template tuple has the same type or value of the corresponding attributes of the matched tuple. The `in` operation blocks until a match is found; this may mean waiting for another agent to do an `out`. An important feature of matching is that a template tuple attribute may be a *wild card*, usually denoted by ? or by _. A wild card matches with any entry. Thus, the templates $\langle 1,a \rangle$, $\langle ?,a \rangle$, $\langle 1,? \rangle$ and $\langle ?,? \rangle$ all match with the tuple $\langle 1,a \rangle$.

This communication model is *associative* and *weakly connected*. Associative access means that information is accessed by its attributes, rather than by names or addresses. Communication is weakly connected since communicating agents do not need to know each other; a message sent by one agent can be read by any other agent.

The original aim of the shared space model was to facilitate the programming of scientific applications. These applications usually possess a large data set, and exploit parallelism in a closed system to improve performance. The shared space was seen as a convenient way of coordinating these processes. In this context though, security is not a real issue. However, interest has been renewed in the shared space model as a means of coordinating agents in open distributed systems [597, 472]. In this context, the fact that communicating agents need only be weakly connected is useful when running over unreliable networks. Associative data access is useful in a network where there are no agreed upon naming conventions and where data is created dynamically. On the other hand, open environments are by nature insecure, so the shared space model must be redesigned to handle security attacks.

Throughout this chapter we will adopt as a case study a conference review system [170] that automates the review process of a conference. Authors submit papers to the conference (by depositing them into a shared space). Reviewers read papers, write reviews (into the space), and exchange information with other committee members and the program chair. The program chair assigns papers to reviewers and collects the reviews. This scenario is often cited as a good coordination case study since interactions - the exchange of papers and reviews - can be efficiently carried out in an asynchronous manner and by means of weakly connected agents.

The conference system, when deployed on the Internet, highlights many security deficiencies of the basic shared space model. For instance, any agent can read any data entry in the space, i.e., by a *read*($\langle ?, ..., ? \rangle$). This means that all papers and all reviews are accessible to anyone's agent and this is not acceptable in many cases. The problem arises from the fact that in the shared space model there is no notion of agent identity when accessing data and therefore no inherent notion of authentication. There is thus no way to distinguish a reviewer agent that attempts to legally read a review from an author's agent. In addition, an agent can saturate the shared space by continuously outing tuples to it. This constitutes a *denial of service* attack, since memory saturation can cripple any system. Integrity is also easily violated because there is no way to prevent a malicious agent from fabricating a review, or from modifying an existing one. Unless all of these concerns are addressed, the basic shared space model can be used neither to implement the conference review system, nor many other Internet applications.

11.2.2 Towards a Security Architecture

In order for any system to be made secure, it must possess a *trusted computing base* (TCB) [145]. A TCB is the set of code and data needed for secure system operations. The TCB is used for instance to store access rights and encryption keys. It also houses the authentication procedures that are executed when a user logs onto the system and the authorization procedures that verify whether an agent attempting access to information possesses the needed access rights. Clearly, the TCB must be protected from tampering or intrusion for the system to operate securely. If the TCB fails (through error or malicious attack) then the overall system's security is compromised.

A system is only secure if no user agent is able to modify or gain access to information that is normally forbidden to him. This necessitates that each access to data made by an agent is checked, to ensure that the access is permitted by the system's security policy. For this reason, the primary component of a system's TCB is the *reference monitor* [145]. The role of a reference monitor in coordination models is to intercept each access by an agent to the tuple set and to verify that this access is allowed by the security policy.

An illustration of a reference monitor is given in Figure 11.1 for the shared space. A reference monitor is interposed between the agents and the shared space; the reference monitor intercepts calls to operations out, in and read on the space. The security policy, programmed into the reference monitor is consulted for each operation invoked by a user's agent. The TCB of this architecture includes the reference monitor, and all code and data of a system needed to implement the security policy. In existing systems, the implementation of the reference monitor ranges from the definition of a specific system component acting as a proxy for the shared space [422], to its implementation within the shared space itself [100, 472]. We give examples of such systems in Section 11.5.

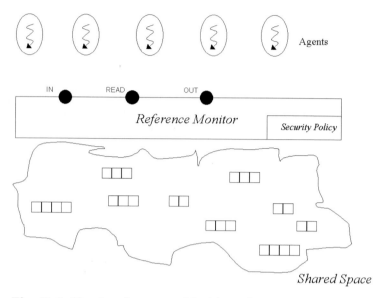

Fig. 11.1. The shared space model with a reference monitor

A reference monitor must possess two fundamental properties for it to work correctly: *total mediation* and *encapsulation* [145]. By total mediation is meant that the reference monitor intercepts *every* access to the data. By encapsulation is meant that the reference monitor is protected from tampering by malicious user agents. In this way an agent is unable to prevent the reference monitor from mediating each data access. Once these properties have been satisfied (a representation of) the security policy can be linked to the reference monitor.

One reason why security in a real system is difficult to achieve is that the properties of encapsulation and total mediation are hard to implement. To ensure total mediation, there must be no backdoor pointers to data placed in the shared space by user agents. This means that an agent may not read a data item in the space without using in or read. This has several implications for implementing a space. In an object-oriented environment for instance [43], *aliasing* is endemic [305]. Aliasing arises when an object is referenced (or named) by more than one other object. Aliasing provokes much undetected sharing and is the cause of many errors and security failures in object-oriented systems [304]. For this reason, an object placed into the shared space using in must have references to that object removed by the reference monitor (so that future accesses to that object pass through the system's in and out operations) [100].

A well-known attack on encapsulation happens when a user is able to insert malicious code into the reference monitor. This may also happen in object-oriented environments where inheritance is used to define the matching procedure of objects placed within the shared space. Recall that the template object of the in and read operations is matched with each object in the space. The meaning of the match comparison is specific to each data type. In object-oriented systems, the match procedure can be defined for each object type (or class) using inheritance. However, this also poses a security risk, since a class can be introduced with a malicious matching function. This function, for example, could contain an infinite loop and thus block the searching process, leading to a denial of service attack. The function could also attempt to steal or modify information in the object that it is being matched with, leading to a confidentiality or integrity attack. This issue is becoming more important since many of today's coordination systems are developed using object-oriented technology [169, 648, 249].

11.3 Security Policies

A *security policy* is a set of rules specifying how sensitive information has to be accessed in a computer system [145]. Meaningful security policies depend on the purpose of the system used and on the nature of the applications. Aside from their definition, policies must also be *enforced*, i.e., agents must be compelled to act according to the defined policies. In addition to a reference monitor, a TCB must also provide basic mechanisms for identifying agents (*authentication*) and for verifying the privileges of agents in the shared space (*authorization*).

There are several issues to consider for security in the Internet coordination context. On the Internet, the number of agents can be large, so verify identities may be hard if not impossible. Further, networks are made up of mistrusting sites, so a site might be unsure of the authenticity of a request from a remote site. With respect to coordination, the associative access mode is the main benefit brought by the model to agent systems; a security infrastructure must strive not to undo this benefit. This is possible if security policies can be defined in a flexible way. Flexibility requires that a wide range of security policies be supported, from a policy permitting unlimited associative access to the whole tuple set, as in original Linda, to a totally controlled scenario, in which an agent has access only to those tuples explicitly reserved for it, e.g., an author's agent in the conference example must only be allowed access to that author's papers.

The following subsections look at the implications of all of these aspects for coordination security policies. We consider authentication and authorization aspects first, and then look at the treatment of distributed infrastructures for shared spaces.

11.3.1 Authentication

Models. Agent authentication is a pre-condition for authorizing a request. It is needed to determine the access rights that can be granted to an agent [145]. Authentication in open systems is more general than identifying the individual that owns an agent. This is because an agent could depend on more individuals or no individual at all. Furthermore, in the Internet, often user identities are not meaningful for authorizing requests [77]. In fact, sometimes the identity of the user must not be revealed; this is the case for some electronic commerce applications where clients should not have to reveal their identity to the server. In this case, an agent must only prove to the server that it is running on behalf of a registered user for the server to authorize access. Other application-dependent attributes can be defined, such as, roles, affiliations, memberships or an available amount of electronic cash [439].

The set of data that an agent presents to be authenticated and then used for authorization is generally called *credentials*, while the entities (individuals or hosts) responsible for the agent credentials are called *principals*.

In the conference case study, for example, a reviewer's agent must be allowed to insert a review. Consequently, a reviewer is the agent principal and the credential to be verified for this authentication process is the fact that the agent acts on the behalf of a reviewer. This information derived from the authentication is then used to grant access permissions to this agent upon the shared space.

Agents use the shared space within the context of an application or protocol, and each protocol implements its own authentication policy. For this reason, each application performs its own authentication phase within a typical protocol that runs over the reference monitor. For this, each protocol can designate an agent, or a system process, to specifically handle authentication for that protocol. We term it the *protocol authentication process*, or PAP, as shown in Figure 11.2.

An agent that seeks to participate in an application protocol must first authenticate itself to the PAP by furnishing its set of credentials. If this authentication is successful, the PAP may return a data item called an *authentication token* to the agent. The agent then presents the authentication token to the reference monitor when writing to the space or when reading tuples written by other agents participating in the application (see Figure 11.2).

We term this the *reference* authentication protocol because of its generality. Many existing systems have effectively developed protocols exchanging tokens, which agents present for authentication, such as Kerberos [568] or cryptographic protocols that use secret or random values [1]. On presentation of these tokens, the space takes a supplementary authorization decision to determine the exact privileges that agents can be assigned. Sometimes the token corresponds to access keys or to access rights. For instance, many protocols providing for a cryptographic key exchange return a shared key to agents; this key is used to decrypt subsequent messages [1]. Other interesting

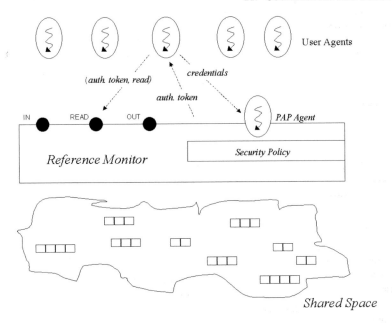

Fig. 11.2. The protocol authentication process

examples of authentication protocols include cryptographic keys used in the context of shared spaces [100], virtual money [585] and signed statements proofing that the possessor agent belongs to some registered principal of the system [568].

Another important aspect for authentication is that it should be *mutual*. Not only must an agent authenticate itself to a PAP; the PAP must authenticate itself to the client agent. This is necessary since the PAP is a service agent, and so one must ensure that a malicious agent does not launch a so-called *masquerade attack* against an application by impersonating the PAP agent. A final aspect of mutual authentication is that the data tuples must authenticate themselves to an agent that **read**s or **in**s them. In other words, a tuple placed in the space and read by an agent must be *believable*: An agent that later reads the tuple must be sure that it was not a fake one, but was written by an agent participating in that application. In the conference system for instance, one must be able to prove that a paper came from the specific author, and that a review is written by a certain reviewer.

Basic Concepts and Notation. Cryptography is the obvious security mechanism that can be used to implement authentication protocols over the reference architecture. Cryptography can be either *symmetric* or *asymmetric* [538].

In symmetric algorithms, a key $\widehat{K}$ used to encrypt a data item X is also used to decrypt the cipher-text; $\{X\}_{\widehat{K}}$ denotes an item X encrypted with key $\widehat{K}$, while $\{\{X\}_{\widehat{K}}\}_{\widehat{K}}$ returns X. Symmetric algorithms are mostly used to grant confidentiality of data exchanged between two parties, say A and B. In this case, the key is usually denoted with a subscript, e.g., $\widehat{K}_{ab}$, and must be shared by the parties. Another important usage of symmetric mechanisms is to record data in a ciphered format on a persistent storage.

Asymmetric algorithms deal with key pairs (K, K^{-1}), where K is called the *public key* and K^{-1} the *private key*. The two keys are unequivocally related to each other, and it is infeasible to derive one key from the other. The public key is publicly available, e.g., from Web sites, while the private key must be kept secret by its legal owner. We write $\{X\}_K$ for the encrypted representation of X under K. $\{\{X\}_K\}_{K^{-1}}$ yields X.

The value $\{X\}_K$ can be computed by any agent that possesses X (as K is assumed to be public), but can be decrypted only by the one holding K^{-1}. This operation is performed to preserve the confidentiality of X.

On the other hand, the value $\{X\}_{K^{-1}}$ can be computed only by the legal possessor of K^{-1} and represents the *digital signature* of X. Everyone knowing the value X can verifies that $\{\{X\}_{K^{-1}}\}_K$ effectively yields X. This is used for *authentication*: When a user signs a message X, he appends the digital signature $\{X\}_{K^{-1}}$ to the message and sends it. The recipient verifies the signature by decrypting the signature with the sender's public key K. If this decryption yields X, then the receiver knows that only an agent that holds K^{-1} could have signed it.

From the possession of a certain private key K^{-1}, one or more personal attributes of the owner could be inferred, such as its name, role or others. This association is stated by *certificates*. For our purposes, a certificate is a data structure that securely binds a public key K to one or more personal attributes of the owner of the key pair (K, K^{-1}). We denote a certificate by C_A, where A is the principal whose personal attributes are stated in the certificate.

Hence, the approach to authentication with public-key cryptosystems is: principal A signs X with K_A^{-1} and sends $\{X, \{X\}_{K_A^{-1}}\}$; another principal B verifies $\{X\}_{K_A^{-1}}$ using K_A. If the operation succeeds than it can be inferred that: While C_A binds A with K_A, K_A and K_A^{-1} are unequivocally related to each other, and K_A^{-1} is known only by its legal owner, then A has effectively signed X. For details about specific models and certificate management, we forward interested readers to the literature about current security frameworks, like PKIX [6, 312], SPKI [222, 223] or PGP [260].

Mechanisms. Authentication requires that each agent have the possibility of obtaining or generating asymmetric key pairs. An agent's key pair can be that of its owning user, or it could be generated by the agent itself. These keys are needed for establishing a secure communication channel between a client agent and the PAP, as well as for exchanging authentication tokens. A client agent that requests authentication with a PAP could present its credentials $Cred$ by outing the tuple

$$\langle C_{PAP}, C_{client}, \{Cred, \{Cred\}_{K^{-1}_{client}}\}_{K_{PAP}} \rangle$$

where the client has first signed its credentials using its private key K^{-1}_{client} and then has encrypted both credentials and signature with PAP's public key K_{PAP}. C_{PAP} and C_{client} are certificates for the PAP and client respectively.

The important aspect of this tuple is that even if the tuple is read by an agent other than the PAP, the credentials are not disclosed. The PAP ins authentication requests with

$$\langle C_{PAP}, ?, ? \rangle$$

and after verification of the credentials, the PAP may reply with

$$\langle C_{client}, C_{PAP}, \{AuthToken, \{AuthToken\}_{K^{-1}_{PAP}}\}_{K_{client}} \rangle$$

With respect to the conference example, suppose that the interacting agent is the program chair, PC, willing to in a review from the shared space and that $AuthToken$ is a symmetric key. The review should be kept in encrypted form in the space for confidentiality. As a result of the authentication protocol PC and PAP share a symmetric key, say $\widehat{K}_{PC-PAP}$.

PC ins a review by

$$\langle C_{PC}, ? \rangle$$

which matches tuples like

$$\langle C_{PC}, \{review\}_{\widehat{K}_{PC-PAP}} \rangle$$

that contains an encrypted review that only the program chair is able to decrypt.

Authentication associates an identity or a privilege level to agents. In the case where access constraints on information is statically defined, the authentication tokens can be sufficient for authorization also. However, access constraints to information are often dynamic in nature. First, constraints on information vary over time: In the conference system for instance, reviews are private during the review phase but are then made accessible to the author at a later date. Further, agents could be dynamically created and a means must exist to assign them privileges. These issues are treated under the authorization heading.

11.3.2 Authorization

Basic Concepts. Authorization is concerned with defining, enforcing and protecting access rights for agents. The fundamental problem in the shared space model is that a tuple and a space can in principle be accessed by *any* agent, which is clearly unacceptable for security reasons. One issue to consider is then the *granularity* of access control: Whether rights are granted to agents for tuple attributes, for tuples, or for spaces. In the conference case study, for example, an author agent should not read tuples containing reviews or, as in the previous example, if reads them it must be unable to interpret their content. In this case the access control is at tuple-level or attribute-level, though space-level control is also possible if all reviews are stored in the program chair's space.

Other issues that may be considered for authorization are: Whether rights are statically or dynamically allocated; and who grants and revokes rights. In the conference system, rights can be dynamically allocated. First, author agents transfer the rights to their papers to the program chair agent, which then transfers `read` rights to reviewer agents. Review agents grant rights for their reviews to the program chair agent, who then selectively grants access to each author agent for that author's review.

Finally, several other practical questions must be answered for authorization to work. For instance, care must be taken regarding access right storage so that agents do not steal, fabricate or tamper with rights. For this reason, a secure system must clearly specify how it protects access rights and the mechanisms used to prevent an uncontrolled transfer of rights.

Typing. A common way to protect access rights and authentication tokens is simply through typing [451, 100]. Several systems are now programmed in Java, e.g., SecOS, T Spaces or JavaSpaces. Java is a programming language with safe typing. This means that a data declared as type `AccessRight` cannot be interpreted as another data type, and that no data type may be used as an `AccessRight`. Typing thus safeguards against rights fabrication; it also makes rights propagation easier to detect and control [451].

However, protection through typing is only possible when processes are run and data is manipulated in type-safe environments. This is no longer the case when data is transferred over the network or stored on disk, or when tuples are stored in spaces of untrusted environments. Further, in an open network, a site might not trust another site's ability to guarantee type safety. In this case, encryption must be used to protect rights transferred outside of the environment [585, 100]; a site needs to sign access rights that it sends out, and then verify these signatures whenever an agent presents them.

Capabilities, ACLs and Roles. Several important models and mechanisms for access control have been developed in the security area. *Capabilities* and *Access Control Lists* (ACLs) are the most well-known mechanisms [372] that coordination models should implement [377, 100, 194].

A capability is a data structure binding a resource name to an access right. In the case study, the authentication token resulting from a PAP could act as a capability in the following way. For example, the program chair's authentication token $AuthToken_{PC}$ can be defined as $\{(Papers, \text{in}), (Reviews, \text{in})\}$. The reviewer authentication token $AuthToken_{Reviewer}$ can be defined as $\{(Papers, \text{read}), (Reviews, \text{out})\}$ while $AuthToken_{Author}$ can be $\{(Papers, \text{out})\}$. The reference monitor must tag each tuple as being *Papers* or *Reviews* in order to control access to tuples. The capabilities can then be presented to the reference monitor as part of the in, out or read operations. In order to control access to *Papers* or *Reviews* sets of tuples, the program chair ins:

$$\langle C_{PC}, \{AuthToken_{PC}, \{AuthToken_{PC}\}_{K_{PAP}^{-1}}\}_{K_{PC}}, ?\rangle$$

The reference monitor verifies the believability of the $AuthToken_{PC}$ capability and decides, accordingly to the rights granted, if the requested operation could be carried out.

In the access control list approach, access to data items is controlled by a list stored in the reference monitor. An entry in this list is a credentials and access rights pair. The meaning of this pair is that an agent that furnishes credentials C in its authentication token is granted the access rights associated with C in the access list. In the conference example, access control lists may look like: $Papers_{ACL} := \{[ProgramChair_{cred}, \text{in}], [Reviewer_{cred}, \text{read}], [Author_{cred}, \text{out}]\}$; and $Reviews_{ACL} := \{[ProgramChair_{cred}, \text{in}], [Reviewer_{cred}, \text{out}]\}$, where square brackets denote *lists*, and where $Program Chair_{cred}$ denote the credentials needed for an agent to be authenticated as a program chair agent. As an example, a PC agent would in

$$\langle C_{PC}, \{ProgramChair_{cred}, \{ProgramChair_{cred}\}_{K_{PAP}^{-1}}\}_{K_{PC}}, ?\rangle$$

The reference monitor first matches the PC credentials with those on the ACL to obtain its rights (e.g., $ProgramChair_{cred}$ has in for both papers and reviews). Then, accordingly to these rights, it decides whether to allow the requested operation.

This latter example leads also to introduce another convenient choice of authorization policy model for coordination applications called the *role-based* access control model (RBAC) [533]. In this framework, organizational *roles* are defined for a system and rights are assigned to roles, not to individuals. Then, each individual is assigned one or more roles. The underlying motivation for applying role-based access control systems is that they reduce the number of access control decisions, since they map principals to roles (one/few mappings for each principal), and then roles to access rights; the number of roles is typically much smaller than the number of different principal identities. Another advantage of this model is that it separates the assignment of access rights from the authentication phase; access rights are assigned based on *what* and not *who*.

In our case study, the application of roles might be outlined as follows:

- *Program Chair, Reviewer* and *Author* can be defined as roles and used in an ACL;
- agents first interact with the reference monitor carrying their principal credentials (e.g., the identity). A PAP is executed and the resulting authentication token carries the role assigned;

– for subsequent operations, the role is always added to the request to let the reference monitor match it against the access policy.

It is worth noting that the theory developed for the RBAC model is much more complex than the example here described, which simply highlights the basic idea of RBAC. In particular, roles can be defined in hierarchies so as to model the administrative relations within an organization, rights are usually inherited through a hierarchy of roles, and roles could be used for managing roles as well. Further information about RBAC can be found in [533].

11.3.3 Federation of Shared Spaces

In an open system, it is more likely that each site or enterprise will have its own space, as in [268, 195, 100], rather than there being a single global space, as in [597]. The former approach is more usual for several reasons. First, a global distributed space is hard to implement because it requires a centralized server which constitutes a performance bottleneck and single point of failure, or else replication mechanisms with data consistency being hard to implement in a system the size of the Internet. Second, multiple spaces correspond better to the organization and security requirements of information. Each organization has its own access policies on the information it stores, with restricted access for remote users. In the conference example, each reviewer could use his local TCB to store papers and reviews. This subsection looks at some of the issues involved in federated systems.

Topology. Topology is concerned with how shared spaces are distributed throughout a system (*network modelling*) and how agents learn about and get access rights for spaces (*network knowledge*). The problem of network modelling is particularly evident when dealing with intrinsically structured domains, as Internet-based organizations frequently are. In fact, Internet nodes are often grouped into clusters, subject to highly coordinated management policies and possibly protected by firewalls. Moreover, large clusters can be further characterized by the presence of sub-clusters, forming a web of protected organizational domains. Different enclosed clusters provide protected domains of shared spaces and are largely independent from the rest of the organization in the definition of policies for the usage of their resources.

As far as network knowledge is concerned, it is unrealistic to assume that agents have a complete knowledge of the whole network topology, as well as of resources availability. In fact, Internet-based domains are typically *dynamic* and *unpredictable*, due to their complex structure, the multitude of decentralized authorities and the absence of a central repository of information. As a consequence, knowledge about the environment should be dynamically and incrementally acquired by agents. This actually affects the coordination protocol, since part of the agent interaction concerns the acquisition of information about topology, and makes network knowledge a coordination-related issue in a highly distributed context.

A federated shared space system could then be modelled by means of a topology of connected secure shared spaces, each one providing for its own reference monitor, security policy and mechanisms. Two general models of topology can be considered: web-like or hierarchical. Figure 11.3 provides for an example of hierarchical topology of spaces.

Authentication and Authorization. One of the main problems in open and widely distributed systems arises from *partial knowledge* of the environment. A reference monitor may not contain all information needed to authenticate an agent, or judge whether it can be allowed access or not. Requests for tuple space operations can originate at remote sites, which are not fully trusted; this implies establishing a set of rules for remote users, and another set for local users. In this scenario, each reference monitor is responsible for storing the data and code needed for protecting tuples in its local space.

For instance, in Figure 11.3, author agents could out their papers in the program chair's shared space, which in turn could allocate them to reviewers' spaces. Then, reviewers could keep some papers for themselves and further allocate others to fellow reviewers. Reviews could be ined by reviewers from fellow reviewers, by the program chair from reviewers, and eventually by authors from the program chair. Policies held by local reference monitors should be designed and enforced for such management. Thus, author's agents should not be allowed to access reviewer's spaces but only the program chair's one. Reviewers cannot in reviews or out papers to other reviewer's spaces, and so forth.

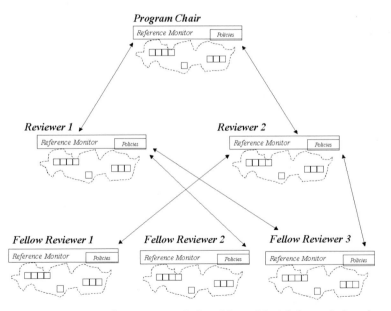

Fig. 11.3. The conference example in a hierarchical federated shared space

With regard to authentication, only the program chair's TCB should have the knowledge for authenticating author agents; reviewers simply have to verify the program chair identity (or reviewers identity in case of fellow reviewers). This observation leads to mention *delegation* as an additional issue that in coordination contexts composed of multiple spaces could be useful for distributed authentication, as discussed in [371, 380] among others. Delegation here is meant to be an action performed by a space, whose effect is to invest another space with the onus of doing something on its behalf. For instance, let us assume that each reviewer has to be allowed to read the papers allocated to the other reviewers. But, as we have said, a reviewer's space could be aware of only the program chair identity and ignore every others, thus it may be unable to authenticate the access of another reviewer. A possible solution could be to delegate reviewer's authentication to the program chair, since it is aware of all the identities. In this case, a reviewer agent could first interact with the program chair's space acquiring a signed authentication token. Then, it could access a reviewer's space by presenting that token, which can be authenticated because signed by the program chair.

The example done is extremely simple, but the benefits of delegating security operations are well-known and general. In many contexts and frameworks this approach has been adopted: Public key infrastructures (PKIs) are based on similar hierarchical relationships for authentication [6, 312]. Differently, SDSI/SPKI, an innovative security framework, explicitly defines delegation between entities for authorization reasons [222, 223]. Among coordination models, TuCSoN, discussed in Section 11.5, is an example of system adopting such an approach [194].

11.4 Cryptographic Protocols in Coordination Models

In this section we add some more details about the development of cryptographic protocols for tuple-based communication. In particular, the problem to tackle is the subtleties that the development of cryptographic protocols can have and that could make implementations prone to breaches. Today, few experiences exist about this topic in the area of coordination systems, and clear guidelines for the development lack. For these reasons, it is important that designers of tuple-based systems over the Internet be aware of the possible problems of cryptographic protocols.

Conversely, in the area of security, some principles and practices for cryptographic protocols have been defined to help system designers avoid some well-known errors derived from subtleties of such protocols. Dozen of distributed systems have been developed by relying on cryptographic protocols that a subsequent and more careful analysis has proven to be flawed. Systems based on tuple spaces may suffer from the same errors, even though the communication model differs from traditional message passing exploited by systems usually analyzed in the security area [1].

As we have already seen, the integration of cryptographic techniques with tuple-based communication provides considerable benefits, even though it may be harder than it looks. We present some examples applied to tuple-based communication.

Encryption, Signatures and Timeliness. One of the main concerns for the design of cryptographic protocols which is likely to affect also the development of secure tuple-based communication, is the possible ambiguity about who is responsible for a communication event (i.e., an operation upon a shared space) and who is the final destination. As a rule of thumb, it can be stated that: If some principal's credentials are essential to the meaning of a communication event, it is prudent to mention those credentials explicitly in the event itself [1]. In the conference management example, suppose that the PC agent, willing to assign a paper to the reviewer agent R, outs a tuple like

$$\langle\ C_{PC},\ C_R,\ \{paper,\ \{paper\}_{K_{PC}^{-1}}\}_{K_R}\ \rangle$$

where C_{PC} and C_R are certificates. This way, R should know that PC has outed the paper (by verifying the signature with K_{PC}^{-1}). R should also know that he is the legal recipient because of the encryption with K_R.

This solution is nevertheless flawed: any possible reviewer R willing to act maliciously could re-direct the paper to another reviewer R' and neither PC nor R' are able to detect it. When R ins that tuple, it simply retrieves the publicly available certificate $C_{R'}$, decrypt the signed paper, re-encrypt it using the public key $K_{R'}$ of R' and out the tuple:

$$\langle\ C_{PC},\ C_{R'},\ \{paper,\ \{paper\}_{K_{PC}^{-1}}\}_{K_{R'}}\ \rangle$$

As a result, R' believes that the tuple is from PC. The problem here is that the intended destination is inferred by the use of the encryption key K_R or $K_{R'}$, which is ambiguous in this case. A possible well-formed tuple from PC, instead, might be:

$$\langle\ C_{PC},\ C_R,\ \{PC_{cred},\ R_{cred},\ paper,\ \{PC_{cred},\ R_{cred},\ paper\}_{K_{PC}^{-1}}\}_{K_R}\ \rangle$$

This way, some credentials of both the source and the recipient are bound to the content of the communication event (i.e., the paper). The example presented can be easily generalised to many other application cases, this kind of protocol being widely used in open distributed systems. In particular, in its original formulation, it was proposed to let two parties exchanging a cryptographic key. The key exchanged was then used for subsequent encrypted communications [1]. As we have discussed in the previous section, in secure coordination models, cryptographic keys may be exchanged as authentication tokens. In this case the flaw may be particularly serious because R, the malicious reviewer, knows the key, and may thus read sensitive information exchanged between PC and R'.

Another simple example, concerning the use of signatures, can be made by assuming that the reviewer agent R needs to exchange a review with the program chair agent PC. The outed tuple might be:

$$\langle\ R_{cred},\ PC_{cred},\ \{review\}_{K_{PC}},\ \{R_{cred},\ PC_{cred},\ \{review\}_{K_{PC}}\}_{K_R^{-1}}\ \rangle$$

This way, the review is encrypted with K_{PC} for confidentiality, and together with the names of the parties is signed with K_R^{-1} for authenticity. Again, the protocol is flawed. Another malicious reviewer agent R' can intercept the tuple, remove the signature, copy the encrypted review, add its own signature using $K_{R'}^{-1}$ and out

$$\langle\ R'_{cred},\ PC_{cred},\ \{review\}_{K_{PC}},\ \{R'_{cred},\ PC_{cred},\ \{review\}_{K_{PC}}\}_{K_{R'}^{-1}}\ \rangle$$

Hence, R' appears to be the author of the review in place of R. While this situation could be harmless in the conference case, in other systems, such as those dealing with electronic commerce or allocation of resources, it could have dramatic consequences. An elementary solution might be that R first signs the review, then encrypts together the three attributes.

Usually in these cases, additional techniques are adopted, like *one-way hash functions* that permit recipients to verify the integrity of the data (i.e., namely that no one has illegally modified them). Data are first hashed and then the hash is signed [538]. This way, where $H(X)$ denotes the hash of X, reviewer agent R may out the tuple

$$\langle\ R_{cred},\ PC_{cred},\ \{review\}_{K_{PC}},\ \{H(R_{cred},\ PC_{cred},\ review)\}_{K_R^{-1}}\ \rangle$$

which is no longer prone to the previous flaw, because one-way hash functions cannot be inverted, nor re-computed with R'_{cred}, because the content of the review is encrypted.

As the last issue to highlight in this section, let us consider *temporal information* such as timestamps and sequence numbers. Temporal information states the freshness of a communication event or of a data, and the correct sequencing of events. The main concern about timeliness is the possibility for an attacker, to replay a message already sent and make the recipient believe that message is new. Hence, what is required to a protocol is that the proof of freshness and the message be encrypted together, to recognize the authenticity of their association. In case of tuple-based communication, this may imply that tuple's attributes, whose freshness must be ensured, or tuples that have to be consumed in a given order or have to be cryptographically bound, encrypted or signed, with timestamps or sequence numbers.

In practice, many cryptographic protocols can be developed in coordination models for which similar classes of flaws have been recognized. We forward interested readers to [1] for more details of the examples presented, which have been inspired by well-known cryptographic protocols for distributed systems and applied in this section to a tuple-based scenario.

11.5 Security in Existing Coordination Systems

This section reviews security in some relevant existing coordination models and systems. It uses the reference security architecture of Sections 11.2 and 11.3 to pinpoint strengths and weaknesses of these systems.

11.5.1 KLAIM

KLAIM (Kernel Language for Agent Interaction and Mobility) is a shared space coordination model, developed at the University of Florence (I), designed for use by mistrusting agents [451, 453]. The KLAIM model supports multiple tuple spaces distributed over several locations. The access control model of KLAIM enables tuple creators to grant rights for their tuples to other agents, and also allows a network coordinator agent to grant access rights for tuples.

An implementation of the KLAIM model does not contain a reference monitor because the access rights of agents are *statically* checked. This means that one verifies that an agent does not attempt to use a space without the appropriate access right *before* the agent runs. In KLAIM, the network administrator declares a security policy by specifying the spaces that each agent has access to, and the corresponding access rights. Security is verified by first determining the "intentions" of each agent, that is, the spaces that the agent is going to access and the kind of operations that it will effect in each. Analyzing the program text of an agent is sufficient to deduce this information. The second stage of security verification entails verifying that an agent's intentions do not exceed the security policy specified by the network administrator.

Access rights in KLAIM are first class values, meaning that they can be named and passed around by agents (using the space as a communication medium). As access rights are typed, security is equated with type correctness. This is a significant step since security is now seen as a primary property of an application. The fact that security in KLAIM is statically verified has the advantage that no supplementary security mechanisms need to be implemented in the model run-time, since a program that passes the verification phase is known to be secure before it runs. The absence of security mechanisms not only simplifies the architecture, but it also avoids performance overheads typically associated with security.

However, in the context of the Internet, static security checks are hardly enough. For instance, the system must ensure that an agent that has been verified is not tampered with between the time of verification and the time that it runs. This is not an easy assumption to make unless the application possesses a trusted storage subsystem for programs. Further, all sites of the application must trust each other; this is also an assumption that cannot be generalized in the Internet context. In the general case, information exchanged between sites needs to be encrypted for security. While there is nothing to prevent an implementation of KLAIM from doing this, the security of the system can then no longer be explained from the KLAIM security model. Thus, a dynamic security mechanism would have to be implemented - in other words, a security architecture in the style of that presented in 11.2.

KLAIM is designed to support a single application, so there is no authentication phase. The access control mechanism is present to cater for mistrusting application agents. The main feature of KLAIM is its static security verification. Though systems also require dynamic mechanisms, the systems should attempt to exploit the benefits of static security verification where possible.

11.5.2 JavaSpaces

JavaSpaces is a development by JavaSoft of the shared space model and is implemented in Java [43]. JavaSpaces forms part of the JINI framework [619], whose goal is to permit the interconnection of all sorts of hardware devices that run Java virtual machines. A JavaSpaces system consists of a set of interconnected machines, each running its own space.

Currently, JavaSpaces does not incorporate security access control mechanisms. Any agent that contains a reference to a space may read or write a tuple to or from that space. The only way to control access is to control the propagation of space references in the system, or to program an access control policy into the RMI (remote method invocation) mechanism that is used by an agent on one site to get access to information on another site. For this reason, JavaSpaces is not yet ready to support security critical applications.

One feature of the JavaSpaces model that is relevant to security is *leases*. This is a resource control measure. In the shared space model, a tuple placed in the space might never be read by another agent. In order to prevent the space from becoming saturated, the system must be able to remove garbage tuples. However in the shared space model there is no "garbage" since a tuple can be read then it is not garbage at any moment. In JavaSpaces, an application that places a tuple in a space can associate a lease with that tuple. A lease is a period of time; when this time has passed, the tuple is removed from the space. The only alternative to resource control is for each application to define its own garbage collector agent that removes tuples from the space using application specific rules.

At the same time, JavaSpaces can later have a security policy model integrated since it contains a carefully designed reference monitor. This is the JavaSpaces component that intercepts each access to the tuples, and implements the in and out operations. Recall that a reference monitor must be tamperproof and ensure total mediation. JavaSpaces is written in the Java object-oriented programming language and has to take extra measures to ensure these properties.

For total mediation: This means that no tuple in the space may be accessed without using the provided in and out operations. JavaSpaces handles this problem by making a copy of each object placed in a tuple of the space.

For encapsulation: This means that a possibly malicious user agent must not be able to tamper with the implementation of the in and out operations. This particularly means that the pattern matching mechanism must be furnished by the system. In JavaSpaces, the copy of an object placed in the space is transformed to a byte array (*serialized*). The matching operation used is that of the serialized object class.

Security is one of the reasons that JavaSpaces prohibits redefinition of its match operation; in contrast Jada [169] and T Spaces [377, 648] - also based on Java - permit the redefinition of the match function, and are therefore open to this form of attack.

Finally, the security of JavaSpaces is also dependent on the security and safety features of the Java language. For instance, language safety ensures that an integer can never be treated as an object pointer, and that a reference cannot be fabricated. For this reason, access to a space is impossible unless an agent creates that space or is transferred a reference for that space. The reference monitor could not function without these properties.

11.5.3 SecOS

In contrast to KLAIM, the *SecOS* model, developed at the University of Genève (CH), uses a dynamic security model [100]. This means that the reference monitor exists at run-time and is integrated into the system. SecOS (for Secure Object Spaces) is designed to allow for coordination between agents in mistrusting environments.

The basic idea of SecOS is that *keys* are associated with objects in tuples. An agent needs to furnish a matching key before it can access the corresponding tuple's object. Keys can be symmetric or asymmetric. For symmetric keys, the same key that locks an object is used to unlock that object. In the asymmetric case, key pairs are used; when one key of the pair is used to lock an object, the other key of the pair is used to unlock the object. Consider the tuple $\langle \widehat{K}:v_1, K:v_2 \rangle$ where $\widehat{K}$ is a symmetric lock and K is an asymmetric lock with K^{-1} being its pair; the object v_1 can only be read by an agent that possesses $\widehat{K}$, and v_1 can only be read by an agent that knows K^{-1}.

SecOS is implemented in Java [101]. Like JavaSpaces, its reference monitor relies on users not being able to redefine the matching process, and on object copies being stored in the space. With regards to locking, this is implemented through Java typing in a Java environment. However, whenever a key and object pair $K:v$ are exported outside of a Java environment, then an encryption key is associated with the key object K and this then encrypts the object v. In this way, an object need never be exposed in untrusted environments. The TCB includes the Java virtual machine since if this is compromised, then the typing that enforces locking is undone. The storage area allocated for encryption keys is also part of the TCB.

With respect to the outline architecture of Section 2, the reference monitor is implemented within the SecOS kernel. The reference monitor properties of encapsulation and total mediation are implemented using the same techniques employed by JavaSpaces (deep copy of objects and a system provided match function). Any agent can act as a PAP for an applications security policy; mutual authentication with the PAP can be done using asymmetric keys. Secure communication is done using either symmetric or asymmetric locking. Access control is implemented at the granularity of tuple entries, where keys are used as access rights. Keys are distributed in tuples, themselves protected with other keys.

11.5.4 Law-Governed Interaction

Law-Governed Interaction (LGI), developed at Rutgers University (USA), is a coordination mechanism that allows an open group of distributed active entities (agents, processes) to interact with each other, with confidence that an explicitly specified policy - called the *law* of the group - is strictly observed by each of its member [422, 421]. Policies could be both coordination and security ones. Groups are open because the membership may change dynamically and each agent may join any number of groups, operating under different laws. Laws in LGI are composed of reactive rules having the typical form: *on <event> do <action>*. The underlying assumption stated by LGI is that a law is global with respect to a group of agents, but it is locally defined at each member. This implies that a law regulates only local events at individual agents and depends only on the combination of the local event itself and a set of attributes - called control state - that characterize each agent.

With respect to the outlined architecture, the reference monitor facility is realised in LGI by defining, for each member of a group, a *controller*. A controller is a specific system component that holds the law governing an agent (i.e., the security and coordination policy) and the agent's control state, and totally mediates each event involving the associated agent. Thus, a controller has complete knowledge and authority over the associated agent. Hence, any interaction between two entities, say $Agent_X \leftrightarrow Agent_Y$, is carried out in LGI by means of three communication events: $Agent_X \leftrightarrow Controller_X$, $Controller_X \leftrightarrow Controller_Y$ and $Controller_Y \leftrightarrow Agent_Y$. The above design applied to agents also holds for shared spaces, which are mediated by a controller.

LGI inherits the suitability as a coordination model from its ancestor called Law-Governed Linda [424]. Differently from LGI, Law-Governed Linda was strictly focussed on improving the traditional Linda coordination model, making it applicable to a scenario composed by multiple open tuple spaces. In particular, the primary motivation for the introduction of Law-Governed Linda has been to improve Linda's safety in an open environment.

Hence, the real novelty of LGI is its application to the security area by exploiting, in particular, the possibility to model and to support various access control policies. It is interesting to note how a security policy is defined, managed and enforced exactly as a coordination one, in LGI, and this is truly compliant with what we stated for a reference secure coordination model. The set of rules composing a policy can be configured so as to model the main access control schemes, like traditional discretionary models based on capabilities or access control lists and mandatory lattice-based models. Some other application-specific access control models have been analysed, as well. Role-based models are not addressed, although their application to LGI seems feasible.

In summary, Law-Governed Interaction is an example of integrated management of coordination and security policies. As a final note, with respect to the issues discussed in this chapter, LGI does not consider the application of cryptographic techniques that, however, seem necessary for an effective deployment of LGI; and does not fully consider the issues of a trusted computing base (TCB), such as tamperproof and encapsulation.

11.5.5 T Spaces

T Spaces is a development by IBM Almaden Research Center that consists of the combination of database, tuple space, mobile computing and Java [377, 648]. The aim of T Spaces is to foster the interoperability between heterogeneous systems. Salient features of the T Spaces system concerning our discussion are:

- tuple spaces operators – the standard Linda-based set of operators has been implemented. In addition, some novel primitives have been introduced, namely Scan, ConsumingScan and Rhonda. The first two primitives have the same semantic of traditional in and read but apply to the set of all matching tuples in the space. The latter is used for atomic synchronization between two processes exchanging tuples.
- dynamically modifiable behaviour - in addition to the built-in set of primitives, T Spaces allows applications to dynamically define new operators that are immediately supported by a T Spaces server.
- access control - access control in T Spaces is based on Access Control Lists applied to tuple spaces. Principals that occurs in ACLs are defined as users or groups. Users are identified by means of the pair UserName and Password. Permissions occurring in ACLs are defined as Read, Write or Take.

Most of the security of T Spaces depends on the features of the Java language. Aside from Java native security features, T Spaces does not exhibit the characteristics of a secure coordination model. T Spaces does not implement the concept of reference monitor, thus it is prone to problems due to the lack of total mediation and encapsulation, if applied in open environments. Conversely, T Spaces provide for flexible and customizable interfaces, letting primitive operations to be dynamically re-defined. Clearly, while this facility could be fruitful in heterogeneous and dynamical distributed environments, it has strong security implications that seems still not fully addressed.

As far as security mechanisms are concerned, T Spaces does not fully applies cryptographic techniques, and both the authentication and the access control model supported by T Spaces supports only some very basic features. However, an interesting aspect of T Spaces concerns the hierarchical architecture for the access control. T Spaces has been designed with a hierarchical topology of shared spaces as the reference architecture. This way, a shared space holds the access control policy both for the creation and deletion of sub-shared spaces, and the access to their tuples. The purpose is to enable users to create and administer structured domains of shared spaces. The benefit is the improved scalability of the overall system.

11.5.6 TuCSoN

TuCSoN is an agent-oriented system developed at the University of Bologna (I) based on multiple shared spaces, whose goal is to face to the unpredictability and the dynamics of open distributed environments, dealing with their intrinsic heterogeneity and remoteness of resources, as well as with decentralized coordination and security policies [472, 196, 194]. Key elements of TuCSoN are:

- A coordination model based on multiple enhanced tuple spaces – called *tuple centres*;
- A hierarchical infrastructure, modelling the system organization, upon which tuple centres are deployed;
- The integration of advanced mechanisms for the access control within the tuple-based environment and their application to the hierarchical infrastructure.

TuCSoN tuple centres are shared spaces enhanced with the notion of *behaviour specification*: The behaviour in response to communication events of every tuple centre can be defined according to the system requirements. The definition of a new behaviour for a tuple centre basically amounts to specifying a new state transition in response to a standard communication event. This is achieved by allowing any admissible TuCSoN communication event to be associated to specific computations, called *reactions*. In particular, a *specification tuple* associates the event generated by an incoming communication operation Op to the reaction R and is denoted with reaction(Op, R). As a consequence, the result of the invocation of a communication primitive from the agent's viewpoint is the sum of the effects of the primitive itself and of all the reactions it triggered, perceived altogether as a single-step transition of the tuple centre state. This makes it possible to uncouple the agent's view of the tuple centre (which is perceived as a standard shared space) from the tuple centre actual state, and to connect them so as to embed the laws of coordination. Since each TuCSoN tuple centre stores both its data (*ordinary* tuples) and its behaviour specifications (*specification* tuples) locally, coherently with the distributed nature of component-based systems, coordination intelligence can be spread where needed all over the agent space The interaction space provided by a TuCSoN node relies on a multiplicity of tuple centres: So, TuCSoN shares the advantages of models based on multiple tuple spaces and goes beyond, since different coordination media can encapsulate different coordination laws, providing system designers with a finer granularity for the implementation of global coordination policies.

As far as security is concerned, TuCSoN shows several characteristics of a secure coordination model: The reference monitor concept is fully achieved by the reaction layer, which totally mediates and encapsulate each communication event.

Access control policies, in TuCSoN, are enforced both locally by each node holding resources by means of the programmability of tuple centres' behaviour, and by some decentralised components called *gateways* acting as proxies for protection domains composed by groups of nodes. Furthermore, gateways are supposed to be connected in a tree-like infrastructure, which permits to define nested protected domains each one controlled by a specific access control policy.

A peculiar design choice of TuCSoN concerns delegation. While node's administrators have to locally define policies governing the interaction with tuple centres, gateways can be delegated with the authority to enforce those policies. This way, policies could be conveniently shared along the hierarchy of gateways, so as to limit local interactions. To this extent, the role-based access control model has been introduced as a well-suited model for such a scenario.

Finally, cryptographic techniques have not yet fully integrated in the system, although cryptographic-based interactions have been modelled and analysed.

11.6 Conclusions

This chapter has looked at security issues for coordination. We have presented an outline architecture for implementing coordination security policies and examined the meaning of authentication and authorization in the coordination context. Some detail about cryptographic protocols have been examined. Finally we have looked at existing coordination systems and models, and discussed how they treat security.

It is clear that security is still an under-treated issue in the coordination domain. This should change as coordination models are adapted to open environments, such as the Internet, and as models continue to be used in embedded and safety critical systems [249, 80]. Nevertheless, security is particular in the coordination context, given for instance the associative access style of Linda-like models.

We expect that while the deployment of open agent systems based on shared spaces proceeds, coordination models will evolve to cope better with security requirements. In particular, the adoption of both cryptography technology and access control models are likely to strongly impact on tuple-based coordination, especially in case of distributed shared space systems.

Thus, in the long run, integrating security into coordination models can be as useful to the security domain as it is to the coordination domain.

12. Scalability in Linda-like Coordination Systems

Ronaldo Menezes[1], Robert Tolksdorf[2], and Alan M. Wood[3]

[1] University of Ulster at Magee College, Faculty of Informatics
   Northland Road, BT48 7JL, Derry, UK,
   r.menezes@ulst.ac.uk, http://www.infm.ulst.ac.uk/~ronaldo/
[2] Technische Universität Berlin, Fachbereich Informatik, FLP/KIT,
   Sekr. FR 6–10, Franklinstr. 28/29, D-10587 Berlin, Germany,
   tolk@cs.tu-berlin.de, http://www.cs.tu-berlin.de/~tolk/
[3] University of York, Department of Computer Science
   Heslington, York, YO10 5DD, UK
   wood@cs.york.ac.uk, http://www.cs.york.ac.uk/~wood

Summary.
  Coordination systems research has concentrated on developing and studying models with the principal aim of ensuring that they are meaningful, and useful. This is clearly the correct approach, and the focus has therefore been on getting the right *abstractions*. However, it is in the nature of coordination models that they are to be implemented and used *practically* over a large range of system sizes. Consequently it is important to assess questions of scalability (of implementations) of coordination languages and systems. In this chapter we address the ways in which Linda — the most common practical coordination language — scales, or fails to scale. This chapter uses some general characteristics which distinguish between LANs and WANs to structure the discussion of scalability. In most cases theses features suggest that current Linda-like models need some modifications in order to move from small systems to a WAN scale. These modifications are discussed in the chapter. However, it is encouraging to find that none appear to be *fundamental* in the sense that the underlying Linda model — asynchronous, non-deterministic, associative coordination — remains intact.

12.1 Introduction

Systems utilizing the Internet allow fewer assumptions on their structure and behaviour to be made than closed and homogeneous systems of former days. It has been argued [125] that the Web violates common assumptions in distributed computing by making virtual and physical locations, bandwidth fluctuations and failures visible, and that programming for the Web reduces to programming with these additional observables. Mobile computing is advocated as a notion that can deal with these additional phenomena being visible when changing from a LAN to a WAN environment.

Scaling programming from a LAN to a WAN context is the topic of this chapter. We use these observables to structure the chapter, but focus on the question of how current coordination technology can scale to cope with such a changed environment.

The coordination language Linda [269] introduced the view that the coordination of a concurrent system is an activity orthogonal to the calculation performed therein. Linda and the subsequent work on the family of Linda-like languages demonstrated that it is worthwhile to design languages and systems that focus exclusively on the aspects of coordination of components, agents, processes, objects etc. and to abstract from the calculations they perform.

Since Linda is the most prevalent coordination language, and it can be used to model most other coordination structures, it will be the prime focus of this chapter. However, the discussions and conclusions are applicable to all other coordination languages.

Linda was developed in the context of parallel computing, and both the coordination model and its implementations assumed, for example, reliability of processors, an upper bound on communication times, a static set of processes etc. Thus, while the separation of coordination from calculation seems to be beneficial, Linda as such seems not well suited for modern distributed computing environments.

The challenge that the Linda concept faces is the question of *scalability*. While the notion of scalability is often tied to a quantitative measure, e.g. how well a system can take advantage of additional processing resources, we consider it also a *qualitative* notion. That is, we look at how good a solution to some problem will work when the characteristics of the problem change. Size and available resources are certainly within that set of characteristics, but others are at least equally important.

Influenced by the discussion in [125], we consider the following set of characteristics as the challenges of computing in wide area networks:

- Static systems can assume a fixed set of components. In an open system, fluctuation is the norm. Coordination has to be aware of that and must be able to handle it.
- A conventional program has a defined point in time where it starts executing and some termination time. Modern agent-based or reactive systems tend to be long-living, perhaps even without the possibility of termination. Coordination has to be aware of this change in duration and persistence.
- While closed systems know only one fixed border, an open system introduces multiple and changing borders. The domains — security domains, naming domains, knowledge domains etc. — formed by those borders are visible to components and their coordination has to deal with them.
- Mobility can be used to minimize distance between collaborating components. Coordination systems must provide means for identifying distance of components and use this information on the coordination strategies.
- Whereas for stationary processes the location of execution is invariant, in mobile computing location becomes visible and components can be aware of it. Most certainly, coordination strategies have to take the location of those to be coordinated into account.

- Centralized systems can assume an upper bound for communication time. In a networked system, there is no such upper bound and delays are visible to components. Coordination has to deal with such delays.
- An open system is also open in terms of unpredicted behaviour. Failures are a common phenomenon and cannot be simply dealt with by restarting a computation. Coordination has to be failure aware and to provide means to cope with it.

Beyond the dimensions of execution speed, memory requirements, number of clients per server, we consider the above dimensions, and the increase of the problem sizes along their scales the real problems for modern systems and the methods used to engineer them. Linda was designed with assumptions made along those dimensions that can no longer be upheld. Existing Linda implementations face severe problems when exposed to such environments. Thus, the question we try to answer in the following is *how Linda-like languages can scale to such environments and still provide coordination*. To do so, we will explore and review existing approaches from the literature on Linda-like systems. These approaches add to the existing Linda concept in terms of language design and/or engineering principles. We will assess how they provide support for scalability along the named dimensions, what an integration of suitable concepts could look like, and sketch examples of scalable coordination technology.

The rest of the chapter covers the four main consequences of the observables mentioned earlier viz. awareness of domains (§ 12.2), location and distance (§ 12.3), bandwidth fluctuation (§ 12.4), and failures (§ 12.5). The final section summarises the conclusions to be derived from these discussions and suggests a way forward for Linda at the WAN level.

12.2 Domain Awareness

The distinctions between WANs and LANs described by Cardelli[1] [125] are to some extent subjective — although at the extremes it is possible to agree on whether a network is 'wide' or 'local' in extent based on the Cardelli observables, these metrics have no *absolute* values for differentiating, say, a local-area delay from a wide-area delay. However, distinguishing between the two kinds of network *is* useful in practice, especially when considering the ways in which a process can 'see' the system's resources. These resources can be viewed as forming collections whose *visibility* to a process can vary — in general *dynamically* over time. These collections will be termed 'domains', and hence processes will be more or less *aware* of their existence according to their visibility.

---

[1] These are that a process becomes 'aware' of *locations* (virtual and physical), *bandwidth fluctuations*, and *failures*.

Given this view of domains, the distinction between LAN and WAN will be taken to be that of *closed-* versus *open-*systems. In a *closed* system, there are known bounds on the number and lifetimes of domains and processes ... an *open* system is in principle unbounded.

In terms of Linda-like systems, a closed system would consist of a number of interacting processes, coordinating through a number of tuple-spaces, to achieve a particular computation. Both (bounds on the) numbers would be known before the computation started, and once this computation was complete, the closed system would cease to exist. An open system implies that there is at least one *universally visible* tuple-space with unbounded lifetime, and that the numbers of processes and tuple-spaces that might become part of the system are also unbounded.

12.2.1 Linda and Domains

The original Linda [267] had no notion of domain in the sense defined above — a single tuple-space was visible to all processes. Although this early version of Linda was most suited to closed systems — it was seen as principally applicable in scientific, and other, parallel computation — there was nothing which prevented the model being used for open systems, at least in principle. However, in practice the single tuple-space is far too restrictive as the basis of open systems both in terms of performance (it creates an intolerable bottleneck), and software engineering (the impossibility of isolating distinct process groups). Consequently, the original Linda model was limited to closed systems, primarily as a result of its lack of a domain concept.

The first major modification of the Linda model was the incorporation of *multiple* tuple-spaces. This idea was almost universally accepted and forms the best known variation of the original idea, to the extent that it is now reasonable to refer to it as *the* Linda model.

The introduction of multiple tuple-spaces was the necessary condition for the inclusion of domains into Linda-like systems: a (proto) domain is identified with a tuple-space. However, the ability to create and use multiple distinct tuple-spaces is not *sufficient* to provide a complete domain concept — for this it is necessary to be able to control the *visibility* of domains (and hence their accessibility) to collections of processes. At first sight, there seems little problem in achieving visibility management since the possession of references to tuple-spaces can be restricted ... if you don't know a tuple-space's name, you can't see it. This is *trivially* true of closed systems as the implementor can determine which references are available to which processes, and can code this explicitly. It is *partially* true of open systems — once an ensemble of processes is running, provided that no member of the group communicates a tuple-space reference to another process that should *not* know it, the constraints on visibility are maintained. The problem which arises in open systems is how this situation can be attained ... how can an ensemble with these properties be constructed dynamically?

To answer this question requires consideration of the means by which a process can be 'aware' of a tuple-space's existence. There are three principal mechanisms:

1. The tuple-space is universally visible — it has a constant, unique, predefined and universally known reference. The existence of such an object is a defining feature of an open system.
2. A process spawns a child process and passes the tuple-space reference as a parameter of the spawning mechanism.
3. A tuple-space reference is passed between processes in a tuple, via a tuple-space.

In the first case, since the tuple-space is universally visible, there can be no domain access control (at least at the tuple-space level) as the tuple-space must *remain* universally accessible.

For case 2, domain management is simple, since making a tuple-space visible to a child process is completely under the control of the parent — this is essentially the same situation as exists in a closed system. However, it should be noted that the parent gives *complete* control of visibility to the child, which could make the domain accessible to any of *its* children, or even to unrelated processes via mechanism 3 — the parent cannot place any restrictions on the transitivity of visibility.

The final mechanism is the most general, and is the most consonant with the spirit of an *open* tuple-space coordination system — it must be possible for new 'unknown' processes to join an existing process ensemble which means that they must gain knowledge of the ensemble's common domains, and this knowledge cannot be transferred by any spawning mechanism (otherwise we'd have a closed system). Unfortunately, in the classical Linda model there is a fundamental problem — since tuples are retrieved *associatively*, there is no way of preventing the 'wrong' process from getting a tuple containing a tuple-space reference. Worse still, this can happen accidentally, in a benign system, as well as maliciously.[2] Therefore, the question of domain management in open systems will be focussed on the effects of mechanism 3.

This section has argued for the *necessity* of a domain concept, and mechanisms for domain management, in open coordination systems and has shown that Linda-like systems do not have an adequate domain concept. The next section discusses ways in which this problem has been addressed. Since open systems are, in principle, unbounded, it is clear that the only acceptable solutions to the domain awareness problem must be *scalable*. In the context of open coordination systems this will be taken to mean that they must be able to be feasibly *distributed*.

---

[2] Attempting to make the tuple's contents too 'complex' for a process to accidentally match is no solution ... this is equivalent to attempting to achieve security by means of obscurity.

12.2.2 Solutions

The simplest form of domain is the tuple-space. As discussed above this is not sufficient, however, to give a full domain concept since there are no mechanisms for the management of these domains' visibilities. In addition, the flat structure of simple multiple tuple-space systems makes it difficult to *organise* domain structures, even if there were visibility management facilities.

One of the earliest, and still intriguing, developments of the Linda idea was Bauhaus [138], which introduced structure into the coordination spaces. The idea there was to merge the concepts of tuple and tuple-space by having multiple *nested* bags as the coordination media, with processes existing *within* the (sub-)bags. In this way a primitive form of domain management was available since a process could only directly access data in the bag in which it existed. If it needed to coordinate with processes outside that bag, it (or the other processes) had to 'move' to a common domain (bag). However, although the additional structure gives more flexibility in the *definition* of domains, the issues of visibility control are not addressed in the Bauhaus publications.

A recent proposal [411] has generalised the idea of nested tuple-spaces to allow, amongst other things, *overlapping* tuple-spaces. In this work, tuple-spaces are replaced by 'scopes' which are first-class values and which can be combined to produce other scopes using scope expressions. By generalising the tuple-space notion, the simple domain concept ('domain = tuple-space') is automatically extended.

These three extensions of the original Linda tuple-space idea — multiple tuple-spaces, nested hierarchy of bags, and scopes — all supply the basis of a domain concept with varying degrees of flexibility. They all require that tuple-spaces (or their analogues) be first-class in some sense.[3] Hence visibility of tuple-spaces can at most be obscured, not prevented (as argued above). Therefore, although all three have significant advantages over the original Linda, none can supply a full domain concept.

The proto-domains, whether multi-sets or scopes, all have reasonable scalability. Distributing tuple-spaces over multiple processors is not difficult, with the major performance degradation (relative to a non-distributed system) being due to network overheads, and these are no worse than in any other distributed system. In addition, the advantages of Linda over other distribution models lie in its asynchrony, which means that any Linda 'computation' must be made explicitly delay-insensitive, and so will automatically work in an arbitrarily distributed environment. Consequently, it can be expected that any domain *structure* based on a Linda-like system will scale adequately. This does not mean, however, that every domain *management* mechanism will scale in the same benign way.

From these consideration it can be seen that the basis for scalable domain *structure* exists in the extensions of the Linda model, but something extra

---

[3] At least that tuple-space *references* be storable in, and retrievable from tuples.

is needed for domain *management*. It is necessary to add mechanisms for visibility control to the model, but this must be done without destroying the fundamental properties of Linda-like open systems.

The simplest way of supplying visibility control mechanisms to the coordination spaces is to incorporate *access control* attributes, for instance read and write access, to tuple-spaces. In fact, as discussed in [641], the addition of such attributes can in general be applied to both tuple-spaces and tuples if a standard access control list (ACL) implementation is adopted. This gives a very fine degree of control over domains and enables a richer *concept* of domain to be developed since the visibility of an *element* (tuple) of a domain can be restricted independently of the domain (tuple-space) in which it is located. In addition, the associative, non-deterministic retrieval method fits well with a tuple being inaccessible due to its visibility attribute as opposed to its non-existence — the two cases are indistinguishable and consequently the model's semantics remain unchanged.

The major disadvantage for access control lists is that they scale very badly, since the sets of 'users'[4] need to be maintained by the distributed kernel which would be unacceptable in an unbounded, open system. A further disadvantage is that the number of sets of users is *static*, and defined before the system starts, making their utility in dynamic open systems questionable.

A solution to these problems is to use a distributed *capability*-based system. Capabilities can be though of as 'permits' which confer on the holder a set of rights over specific objects. In this way a process would only be able to 'see' a domain (e.g. a tuple-space or scope) if it holds a capability for operations on that domain. The standard implementation of capabilities [586] frees the kernel from having to maintain knowledge of all the rights of all the processes in the system — this is distributed since each process holds its own set of capabilities. In addition, process cliques can set up coordination ensembles by passing capabilities amongst themselves.

However, capabilities have disadvantages too, the main one being the difficulty in *altering* a process's set of rights once given. In an ACL-based system, the 'write' bit, say, for a tuple-space can be cleared by the kernel for a complete set of users, but there is no way of removing a capability from all processes that hold copies of it. Another disadvantage is that capabilities require objects to be *named*, whereas ACLs can be attached to *any* object. Thus, the former will work well with tuple-spaces and scopes, but not for individual tuples (since they are identified by *contents* not names).

It seems then, that using a combination of capabilities (wherever possible) and ACLs (whenever essential) gives just the right levels of domain definition and management for open Linda-like systems. As an example, the prime problem of how to pass information between processes in an open system without danger of interception, has been shown [641] to be solvable using a mixture

---

[4] These sets are usually called 'domains' in the operating system literature — a term not used here to avoid confusion.

of ACL visibility control on tuples, together with capability management of tuple-spaces.

12.2.3 Directions for Domain Awareness

It has been argued that domains, and mechanisms for visibility control, are an essential requirement for open distributed systems in general, and Linda-like systems in particular. Several solutions have been proposed, and any of these can be used to provide a complete domain concept by the addition of visibility management constructs such as capabilities. However, there are still some open issues which require investigation, two of which are:

Domain dynamics. The definition of domains will need to be modified over time. Although the techniques described above allow a degree of re-definition — for instance the scopes concept [411] allows the dynamic creation of new domains from existing ones — the question of how well these mechanisms scale *temporally* is not clear.

Domains and mobility. When explicit mobility of code and data is introduced as in Lime [493], the question of how domain *management* will be affected becomes important. It is expected that formal treatments of mobility semantics, such as the Ambient Calculus [123] will provide starting points for investigating these effects.

Work will also continue on investigating how to apply the scalability advantages of capability-based domains in an associative environment.

12.3 Location and Distance Awareness

Location is part of our everyday life, everything around us is based on location. At a given point in time, you may be in a room, in your house, in your neighborhood, in a city which is in a country which is on a planet and so on. One could easily consider two forms of location that are part of everyone's world:

– Everyone likes to associate things with places. Remove this concept from our lives and we would not be able to perform most of our everyday tasks, like parking a car (where?), going to the dentist (where?), or even going to the bathroom (where?). It easy to see that everything has a place — an absolute *location*.

– Another variation of the concept of location is the one of distance. In our lives sometime we want to go to *a place* which is close enough to where we are. For instance, one wants to go to *a petrol station* which is the closest to them. The particular location (address) of the petrol station, although important to allow one to get there, is secondary to the decision of which petrol station to visit.

In a computerized world, where information is distributed across the globe, users need to know where the resources they require are and how far they are from them, as this can be used when deciding where to place their own resources. Applications where the time taken to execute operations has to be kept within certain limits demand that the distance between two objects which are communicating be maintained within some acceptable range (distance awareness). In other situations the applications need to guarantee that some data is confined to given places; this may be necessary, for instance for security reasons (location awareness).

The original Linda [267] was proposed with a primary goal of hiding location. Users were not required to understand this concept and the model would create the notion of a location-free environment for them. It worth noticing though, that Linda was also primarily concerned with parallel computation where location is indeed irrelevant. Since then, Linda has been used as a model for distributed computing while maintaining most of its characteristics as proposed by Gelernter [267] more than a decade ago.

But what is location and distance in the computer world? One cannot measure distance in terms of miles or kilometers as the "roads" of the information super-highway are not measured in these terms. The best way to measure distance is use the concept of time: *how long does it take to get the needed information?* As for location, the notion of geography is sufficient for the computer world since computers are normally arranged in a network topology that somehow mimics the world geography.

It is easy to see that in systems that span the world the concepts of location and distance cannot be hidden any longer, implying that Linda has to evolve to cope with these concepts. Two simple scenarios would help to motivate this argument: how would Linda cope with these?

Scenario 1 (Distance awareness): If one is in Brazil the difference in time to retrieve information from the USA when compared to Argentina is at least ten-fold in favour of the USA. Therefore if one has to choose a location based on this, the USA would be the natural choice even though it is geographically more distant.

Scenario 2 (Location awareness): If one is in Brazil and they want to store some confidential information that should not be disclosed to countries outside the South America, the notion of location need to be present. In this case, although in terms of distance the USA seems the closest, Argentina should be the choice.

It might sound as if the concepts described above are the same, but although related to location, distance awareness does not depend on the awareness of location. One could be aware of the distance of an object and not know its location. This can be understood as *relative distance*: given two objects X and Y on different locations a process can only tell which is closer based on some measurements. Conversely one could talk about *absolute distance* which basically says how far is an X from a given source. Clearly pure absolute distance does not exists as the concepts of "far" and "close" are relative by definition. However in absolute distance one can consider that means of comparison (geographically for instance) are always available. For the purpose of this section it is important to elaborate on relative distance (distance for short) as absolute distance is achieved with the introduction of location awareness.

Mobility is the "buzz-word" in distributed computing. However mobility only exist given the concept of location. As locality becomes explicit, computations (processes) can react in their specific way to various network problems (e.g. failures, bandwidth fluctuations). In practice this seems more appropriate than delegating the job to a general purpose environment.

Linda is exactly this: a general purpose environment which hides location from processes. The idea of a shared dataspace [515] implemented in Linda-like systems, although suitable for parallel up to large LAN applications (closed systems) is inappropriate for WAN applications (open systems). Linda has had some success and has attracted interest from the research community as well as the industry because its communication metaphor, in which interprocess communication is independent of the life history of the processes involved, achieves decoupling of processes in both space and time characterising Linda as a model of communication different from others available (e.g. shared variables, message-passing).

12.3.1 Linda and Distance

The original Linda proposal [267] does provide some level of distance awareness. The retrieval primitives of Linda, namely in, rd, in and rdp, can be used to build an experiment to find about the distance of resources (tuple-spaces). In a perfect network if an in takes longer to retrieve a tuple from tuple-space A than it does from tuple-space B, A should be closer to the process than B. Even if geographically this is not true, from the point of view of a process, tuple-space A *is* closer (assuming that in and rd are always satisfied). The assumption of a perfect network although not satisfactory in the real world is used here for simplicity. In Section 12.4 the problem of bandwidth fluctuation in Linda is discussed.

Kielmann [353] has improved the notion of distance in Linda with his Objective Linda model. Basically Objective Linda assumes different semantics for the primitives accessing tuple-spaces. These semantics are different because there is the concept of timeout. Blocking primitives (in and rd) do not block indefinitely; an upper bound for the blocking time is one of the primitive's parameters. Although this does not directly tell how far apart two entities are (in this case a process and a tuple-space), it can be used to give a notion of relative distance. For instance, if an in from a tuple-space A succeeds with a timeout t but another in from a tuple-space, B, with the same timeout fails, this should indicate that B is (relatively) more distant than A. In addition to this simple example one could vary the value of the timeout within a loop statement until the primitive successfully returns a tuple. This improves the notion of distance since here it is not required for the primitive in to be satisfied.

Similar to Objective Linda, Bonita [525] primitives can also improve the idea of distance. Bonita is a variant of Linda which enhances performance by parallelising the blocking time of primitives. This is achieved by separating the process of finding a tuple from checking whether the tuple has been delivered (locally). For instance, the primitive in is implemented by a dispatch plus an arrived followed by an obtain. The primitive arrived is the primitive that checks locally whether the tuple requested has arrived. Of course, arrived was not proposed for this purpose but one could imagine its use improving the notion of distance inside the system. Again, if one assumes that tuples stored in nearer tuple-spaces should arrive sooner, arrived can be used to test for a relative distance of two tuple-spaces.

Neither Objective Linda nor Bonita were proposed with the intent of providing relative distance, however their primitives allow one to build an experiment and gain some notion of distance. The problem with this is that the notion gained represents the situation at that point in time which is not necessarily a realistic view of the situation. In a dynamic system where the configuration of the system changes one would perhaps like Linda itself to be able to provide an idea of distance.

12.3.2 Linda and Location

It is true to say that Linda systems seem to be promising for WANs. Probably the main reason for this common belief is the decoupling of space and time achieved by the model. Linda is also similar to other models that already include the notion of location such as the Messenger Environment [604]. In Messengers, as in Linda, computations can start new processes in remote hosts and they communicate via shared memory. The difference lies in the fact that in Messengers the processes have the choice of which remote host to use when spawning new processes whereas in Linda this decision is hidden (provided by the underlying system). All communication is local; processes "hop" between hosts and if they are located in the same host they can communicate via a shared memory locally.

Messengers are a good example of a coordination paradigm based on shared memory communication which is particularly suited to mobile systems. This happens because its functionality is based on the operation hop which controls how messengers should move in the system. Messengers are autonomous messages: they carry a process and not just data. The hop operation governs the movement of messengers; each node visited resumes the execution of the messenger until a hop which causes the process to leave the current node is encountered.

Although Messengers are interesting for proving that models including location are successful in open environments, they do not provide the concept of time decoupling which differentiates Linda from other models, therefore it is reasonable to explore the topic in Linda environments.

Some work has been done to bring the concept of location to Linda. As expected the work on location in Linda is very much attached to mobility of processes and tuple-spaces within the kernel.

Tolksdorf [593] proposed a Linda-like system called Mobile Object Spaces (MOS) in which each entity has a locality attribute. In fact, both logical and physical locality can be identified uniquely. After an agent is spawned in MOS it can be moved between agentbags (collections of active agents). Agentbags have a locality attribute which represents the host where the agentbag is currently located. The model also allows for an agentbag to be moved between physical hosts — by changing its locality attribute.

The Kernel Language for Agents Interaction and Mobility (KLAIM) [453] is a language which consists of multiple tuple-space Linda primitives with a set of CCS process operators. Location is a first class attribute which is used in the distribution of the tuple-spaces and processes. The Linda-like operations are adapted to work with explicit locations — locations are used as indexes which identify the set of tuple-spaces the given operation should consider. The question of what level of location should be included appears here. KLAIM uses the concept of logical location of tuple-spaces which do not necessarily match the physical location. Still the level is sufficient to give the user more control over the coordination components. Decisions can be made based on the information available.

Jada [169] is a coordination system for mobile agents which combines Java and Linda. It implements mobility of code; code that satisfies a request can be sent over the network to execute remotely (as an agent). Java makes it easier for sending code across a network while Linda provides the basic coordination infrastructure. Jada is location aware and clients (`TupleClient`) are created and told what is the location of the server (IP number and port).

Ligia [409] is similar to Jada in two ways. Ligia is also a combination of Linda and Java, which makes mobility of code more easily implemented, and Ligia also requires that IP number and a port of a server. However, in Ligia, the work of finding a server is hidden from the users. Ligia may not give control to users to choose the server explicitly but in its full description [410] an operation to deal with I/O is proposed (`link`) which increases the notion of location in the system. The operation `link` allows programmers to attach a tuple space to a file. Although proposed to solve problems related to garbage collection of tuple spaces it implicitly improves the notion of location of tuple spaces since location is an important attribute of the file descriptor. Additionally, `link` could in principle be used to associate a tuple space with a URL, therefore defining its location.

Lime [493] is a proposal for mobility of processes in Linda. The central idea that governs the operations in Lime is that agents are mobile but have locations attached to them (as an attribute). The primitives are then adapted to work based on this idea of location.

Lime introduced the notion of a *transient shared tuple-space* (TSTS) which behaves like a globally accessible tuple-space (GTS) but which is dynamically reconfigured based on the processes at a given location. It is as if the contents of GTS were divided amongst the agents — each agent "owns" a piece of GTS called an *interface tuple-space* (ITS). When an agent migrates from one location to another it takes its ITS along. The TSTS in a given location is formed by the collection of all ITSs belonging to the processes at this location.

By default, a process dealing with TSTS stores tuples in its own ITS. This means that if a process stores a tuple t and migrates, it takes t along with it. This generates a problem because other processes may be waiting for t at the original location (before migration). To cope with this situation the agent can use a modifier in the out operation. For instance A.out[x](t) takes the location of process x into consideration; t would be stored in the ITS of x.

Retrieval operations (namely in and rd) take this concept of the modifier one step further. Consider the operation A.in[x,y](t). This would try to get a tuple matching t from the subset of tuples of A which are in x's ITS but are destined for y's ITS. This situation only happens when y is not connected to the system, which can occur frequently in mobile systems. If y was present the tuple would be automatically moved to y's ITS and the operation would equivalent of A.in[y,y](t). In the case of in and rd, mobile hosts could be used instead of an agent as the first modifier. Therefore the operation A.in[B,-](t) would perform an in on the subset of tuples of A which are in the host B.

Lime is successful in including location in Linda to the extent that the semantics of the primitives are as much as possible unchanged. Yet, Lime is based on the assumption that a process knows about others which is not generally true in open systems and in particular Linda open systems. Lime is very fine-grained — location is attached to tuples and not to tuple-spaces. This may cause the reactive nature of the system (which makes tuple migrate to the proper locations) to slowdown the system considerably.

In a mobile system where location is explicit, user should be able to say that a given component is attached (fixed) to a location. In Lime this would correspond to having primitives to limit the migration of processes. This would allow the implementation of systems where security (where the data is physically stored) is a concern.

One has to be able to express mobility in Linda systems, or generally speaking generative communication systems in which location explicit. Ciancarini and colleagues [160] have proposed an algebra for generative communication which can be adapted to represent mobility in Linda. Their original proposal consists of only one tuple-space which is known to all processes. If one uses a variation where multiple tuple-spaces can be considered, mobility can be represented implicitly: a process moves by creating a copy of itself at a new tuple-space and ends its execution in the current tuple-space. Still this algebra would only cope with locations abstracted as tuple-spaces, or in other words, would not cope with "real" locations.

LLINDA [452] is another language/calculus for Linda systems which is based on the existence of multiple tuple-spaces extended to cope with the concept of location being explicit. LLINDA assumes the existence of a set of sites (physical locations) which are where processes and tuple-spaces are located, and symbolic localities (domains) which allow for the distribution while not paying attention to the physical location.

12.3.3 Directions for Distance and Location Awareness

From the description above one can see that the inclusion of the notion of distance and location in Linda is not only desirable but required if Linda is to become a model adopted for the implementation of large scale (open) applications. There are several approaches to tackle the idea, some more complete than others but no solution can be said to be a "killer" proposal. One of the reasons for the differences on how they tackle the problem comes from the fact that there is a tradeoff between expressiveness and simplicity.

The solution for including the notion of distance in Linda may not lie in modifications of the standard primitives but in a component which maintains global system information. Distance may be a Quality of Service (QoS) issue. A global component could for instance tell a process at any given point in time which one of a set of tuple-spaces is the closest based on average response time. Implementation of QoS has been envisioned in Lime [493].

Location is at the centre of the idea of mobility. Strictly speaking mobility is only achieved in full when the system gives the users some level of control of the location of their resources. Although some level of mobility can be achieved without requiring the users to understand the concept of location, it would not be expressive enough to implement WAN based applications in general. The problem previously mentioned, where security is an issue exemplifies very well the situation. Users need to have some control over where resources are allocated. The core of the problem when introducing location is that the simplicity of the model is affected. An introduction of an API for Linda could provide some sort of standardization of the primitives and at the same time introducing different levels of control.

12.4 Fluctuation Awareness

Wide area networks do not provide constant transfer rates. Instead, the bandwidth provided to applications fluctuates in an unpredictable manner. It is affected by various parameters, such as capacities along a certain route, the choice of a route, current usage of that route etc. For any two transfers from a node A to a node B, the time necessary can vary. In an asynchronous system, this fluctuation even makes it impossible to distinguish long network delays from failures at the destination node.

12.4.1 Linda and Fluctuation Awareness

The original Linda design did not look at network delays and their fluctuation at all. This was justified by the assumptions of relative stable upper bounds on communication delays in parallel computers as in [130]. In wide-area computing, fluctuation of available network bandwidth affects Linda systems in two dimensions:

- At the *application level*, algorithms may depend on upper bounds of communication or not. For example, a voting application has to decide whether to wait for further votes that might still be underway in the network or not. In order to deal with timing variations at the application level, a coordination language has to offer some notion of time and a way to make timing statements with respect to coordination operations.
- At the *implementation level*, the management of the tuple-space itself may rely on upper communication bounds or not. For example, distributed kernels in which parts of the tuple-space are replicated usually rely on similar communication delay amongst the nodes holding replicas. Timing variations affect strongly the chosen distribution schema for a shared coordination space.

There are some proposals from the Linda literature that try to deal with such fluctuations. The language Sonia [51] considers the notion of time and delays as vital for coordination in open distributed systems. It is argued that any application coordinating activities in the real world needs a notion of time, as the world is inherently real-time. Thus, timing of activities caused by messages is explicitly seen as an issue for the application which knows the application semantics with respect to time. Sonia allows an expiry to be placed on messages posted to a shared space and a timeout on requests for message extracted from it.

Objective Linda [353] introduces timeouts as additional parameters to in, rd, out, and eval operations. A timeout of 0 leads to immediate failure in the case of out 1and eval and is equivalent to the predicates inp and rdp in the case of in and rd. Combinations with other parameters stating the minimum and maximum number of tuples to match for in and rd gives further variants of the operations up to the extreme case that causes a process to block for a certain time without retrieving any tuples.

Both approaches leave the problem of defining upper bounds for semantically correct execution of Linda's operations to the application. At the implementation level, bandwidth fluctuations can be of severe impact on the overall system, if the distribution structure depends on it.

For the case of a centralised implementation with only one tuple-space server, a slow connection affects only one client's interactions and delays the work of other clients waiting for tuples generated there. The same holds for distributed implementations that use partitioning of a tuple-space by hashing schemas.

However, in a full replication of the tuple-space delays can affect more clients than would be expected. It is common to apply some locking schema across all replicas, because one specific replicated tuple cannot serve as a successful match to two different templates and has to be locked in all replicas until it is decided whether it is removed or not. Thus, any bandwidth fluctuations between the replica servers and the requesting clients affect the complete system.

Xu and Liskov [650] use methods from distributed computing to deal with fluctuations up to network partitioning. The approach introduces dynamic sets of replica servers and involves votes within those on whether a tuple is to be delivered.

Chiba, Kato, Masuda [156] relax the consistency requirements on the contents of replicated tuple-spaces. The approach defines and compares strict, non-exclusive, and weak protocols to establish some consistency amongst replicas. All three are included in a multi-protocol tuple-space in which the programmer can select the kernel behavior for in operations amongst these protocols.

12.4.2 Directions for Fluctuation Awareness in Linda

The implementation level mechanisms try to make bandwidth fluctuation transparent to the user of a tuple-space. While this approach is suitable for distributed systems, we do not consider it appropriate for wide-area computation where delays can have a meaning at the application level. Thus, delays should be visible to applications in order to react in a semantically correct manner to them.

This means that delays might have to be expressed at the language level as timeouts for communication or upper bounds for processing. The primitives might be expanded to take this into account and some mechanism is necessary to communicate the violation of such a bound to the applications. On the other hand, the language extensions aiming at the application level leave the burden of the interpretation of delays completely to the programmer. There is no hint at all on how long the delay might persist, whether the system can try to handle it etc.

At the system level, a WAN-ready Linda-kernel has to employ flexible distribution schemas that do not rely on fixed upper communication bounds. Also the system should provide support for the application level visibility of delays by making them visible in a suitable manner and offering some assessment of the importance of a delay for the applications' semantics.

12.5 Failure Awareness

A WAN is inherently unreliable, thus WAN computing has to be able to deal with failures. In this section, we describe means that have been proposed to establish some form of fault-tolerance into Linda-like systems. We use several categories to talk about aspects of fault tolerance. These are:

- *The locus of faults.* Although tuple-space based systems provide an uncoupled peer-to-peer communication and coordination model, the implementation of the Linda operations distinguishes at least two locations: the *server* is a component that keeps the tuple-space and provides operations on it, whereas the *client* is the agent performing computation and using the server for coordination operations. Thus, faults can occur on the *server side* and on the *client side.*
- *The transparency of fault recovery.* If faults are made visible to clients, then some language construct has to be introduced in order to express how to deal with an error. We speak of *language-level mechanisms* if new primitives etc. are introduced, whereas mechanisms expressed and executed in the environment of a client provide *transparent fault tolerance.*
- *Openness of a system.* As a general characteristic, tuple-space based systems and languages can be *closed,* that is they require the complete set of agents be known before the system starts. *Open* systems, instead, allow clients to join and leave the system at any time. Some mechanisms for fault tolerance below make assumptions on whether they will be used in closed or open systems.

In the following, we focus on the *design aspects* of providing fault tolerance for tuple-space based languages and systems. For a comprehensive discussion of fault-models, a formal view on fault tolerance, and fundamental mechanisms to achieve properties of systems in the case of faults see [264].

12.5.1 Linda and Fault Tolerance

One approach to fault tolerance in tuple-space based systems is to provide *no guarantees* at all, i.e. neither to foresee any fault tolerance masking at the server side, nor to change anything about the coordination language.

This is basically how the original kernels from Yale, such as the S/Net Kernel [130], deal with the issue. Ignoring fault tolerance problems can well be a reasonable choice in the field of parallel processing. Here, applications have rather short lifetimes and therefore are relatively simple to restart in the case of failures. As parallel applications tend to be closed systems, failures cannot affect an environment.

The major benefit of ignoring faults is the avoidance of any performance loss and rather simple communication protocols. The obvious disadvantage is the absence of fault tolerance. Thus, while ignoring faults is a plausible solution in a LAN environment, particularly for closed programs, it cannot be suited for a WAN environment.

Originating in DBMS, *transactions* are a mechanism for fault tolerance that has been incorporated into various tuple-space based languages. It usually extends the language with primitives to start, commit, or abort a transaction.

Languages like PLinda [26], Paradise [542], JavaSpaces [249], or TSpaces [648] consider a transaction to be a sequence of local processing and accesses to the tuple-space. The effects of changes to the tuple-space content become visible to other agents only after the transaction is committed, thus preventing failing agents from introducing inconsistencies into the shared space.

Transactions are usually introduced because long term parallel processing makes restarts expensive, as all intermediate results would be lost. For example, DNA processing — one application cited often in the Linda literature — can have a lifetime of several weeks.

The advantage of the transaction mechanism is that it is an understood approach that is cheap to implement. Its disadvantages are that it alters the semantics and that it cannot provide fault tolerance for presence notification when intermediate tuples have to be seen by other agents but the transaction prevents this. Also, transactions are a rather heavy weight mechanisms.

Transactions seem a good approach to provide fault tolerance for both WAN and LAN environments, if rather traditional "closed" programs and open non-interactive programs are considered.

Checkpointing is another mechanism to tolerate failures. In general, it means to store a copy of some state of interest and the ability to reestablish it in the case of a failure. There are some variations on this concept in the Linda literature. FT-Linda [49, 48] uses checkpointing at the server level by retaining a copy of tuples handed out to clients via an in primitive. MOM [122] takes the same approach and introduces an additional "busy" tuple-space to store those copies. PLinda 2.0 [339, 338] also uses checkpointing of the tuple-space at the server side, but also provides a language level extension for clients to request checkpointing of their local state.

Similar to transactions, checkpointing is intended for long term parallel processing. Advantages include the option for a transparent implementation of checkpointing at the server side, and that restarts are even cheaper as the last checkpointing might be done later than some transaction commit.

A disadvantage is the need for a reliable backing store for the checkpointed data. If checkpointing is implemented transparently at the language level, this calls either for complex analysis to determine when to checkpoint or brute force checkpointing after every state change, which is inefficient. If the backing store is available only via a network, serious problems may arise from network congestion.

Thus checkpointing seems a good option at the server side, but is suited to a LAN environment only if offered at a language level for the client.

Replication is a means to increase both fault tolerance, and as availability. It is usually applied at the server side by replicating the contents of a tuple-space. Various distributed Linda-like systems, such as the S/Net kernel or Laura [597], replicate for performance in a distributed setting.

Xu and Liskov [650] use replication to address fault tolerance. Tuples outed are stored on a set of servers. An in then queries this set of servers. Even if a server fails, a majority of answers leads to the delivery of a matched tuple to the client. Kambhatla [346, 345, 347] studies the effects of replica size and number on performance.

Amongst the advantages of replication are increased availability and the potential to cope with non-transient failures of communication. The main disadvantages are that total replication does not scale, that reconciliation is in general unsolvable, and that replication of all tuples can be inefficient as the application specific usage of tuples is not accounted for.

Replication seems to be well suited for a LAN environment, especially if physically mobile devices are involved. In a WAN environment, replication might be suitable if a limited number of replicas is maintained. Application aware kernels and dynamic replication might be necessary in this setting. The effect of reduced latency by higher availability might be even more valuable in a WAN than in a LAN.

Mobility of code is a yet another mechanism that can contribute to fault tolerance, as described in [520]. It aims at providing an alternative to transactions in a WAN setting. Here, a sequence of code using coordination primitives is packaged as a coordination operation into an object and passed to the tuple-space server. Upon its complete arrival, the server executes the operation, thus providing all-or-nothing fault tolerance for the operation. If the client agent fails, consistency of the tuple-space can be established by executing a "will" that is passed with the operation object and that contains code that can compensate changes to the tuple-space state.

The mechanism incorporates changes to the coordination language and requires additional functionality at the server. The server side processing is transparent to the programmer and does not alter the semantics of the coordination primitives. If allows for presence notification and has been proved to exhibit a good performance.

As disadvantages, the mobility approach potentially increases the server load. Also, it increases the complexity of the server's functionality, and — most of all — requires the provision of an execution environment by the server as part of an infrastructure for mobile code.

Mobility for fault tolerance seems most attractive in a WAN setting, where it provides an alternative to transactions.

While the mechanisms reviewed show a variety of ways to deal with failures, the *detection of failures* is a a crucial issue. Chandy and Misra [146] show that in asynchronous systems, failures cannot be distinguished from network delays.

For tuple-space based systems, there are two approaches that attempt to detect failures. MOM [122] allows a client to place an upper bound on how long another client can process that tuple. When the upper bound is exceeded then the client consuming the tuple is assumed to have failed, and the tuple is recreated. Kambhatla [347] uses "I am alive tuples" that are issued periodically by all clients. A recovery manager tries to read them and deduces failure of the client from their absence.

12.5.2 Directions for Fault Tolerance in Linda

This review shows that there is a variety of possible fault-tolerance mechanisms available for integration into Linda-like systems. However, each of them shows different benefits and disadvantages. The solutions differ along the dimension of the transparency they provide to applications and by the performance overhead introduced.

Thus, there is no single best solution to offer the required fault-tolerance in a WAN-ready Linda-like language. However, it seems necessary to alter the original high-level view of Linda that neglected the possibility of faults at all. While the language definition itself only defines a functional interface to a tuple-space with some operations, features beyond the primitives are important.

A first step towards an integration of the various mechanisms described can be taken by talking about a system of types of tuple-spaces that capture both non-functional issues like replication characteristics and functional extensions like primitives for transactions.

Whereas the Linda language can be seen as an interface to server- or runtime-objects in an object-oriented sense, non-functional issues have to be made explicit by differentiating classes implementing that interface. Extensions of the language have to be understood as subtypes of the Linda interface.

12.6 Conclusions

In this chapter, we discussed how and whether Linda-like languages can scale to WAN environments and still provide coordination. We understood scalability as a qualitative notion along several dimensions that have been identified as important differences from LAN characteristics.

We reviewed the concepts of the original Linda and possible solutions for the issues concerning domains, locations, fluctuation, and faults. We have seen that the Linda literature provides a variety of potential adjustments of the original Linda. However, these ideas have been developed for particular problems, and it is unclear how they can be integrated to a WAN-ready Linda which covers all the mentioned aspects of WAN environments.

From the conclusions drawn for each aspect, it seems that there are two levels on which a WAN-ready Linda has to differ from the original Linda: at the *language level* introducing functional changes and at the *system level*, introducing non-functional changes (such as quality of service).

We have seen that at the language level, a notion of *location* is necessary both logically and physically. Logically, domain structures such as multiple, nested, and overlapping tuple-spaces are necessary to reflect the application requirements for structuring the computational world to be coordinated. Physically, network locations have to reflect the concrete structure of that computational world. Both kinds of locations call for a new data type in Linda, a polymorphic extension of the primitives, and an adjusted semantics.

Operations on locations include some definition of *distance*. This is simple to see for distance in space or networks, but it is also important in time, as network fluctuations affect the temporal distance between executed operations. One can also understand faults as being states of the system being 'at a distance' from correct states. Thus, distance might be yet another data type necessary to formulate WAN-ready coordination. Distance might be even more important than location, as it is a relative and non-global measure.

At the system level, a WAN-ready Linda has to provide additional services for *management*. Domains have to be managed, by providing resolution of domain identifiers and to deal with dynamic domains. Distance has to be managed by providing mobility of agents. Fluctuation has to be channelled into services that estimate the temporal distance of events or that enforce some quality of service. And finally, the system has to provide enabling services for the detection and management of failures.

In order to bring a WAN-ready Linda into existence, the definition of a standard Linda API could be a first step. This API would have to provide a framework in which the functional issues at the language level are captured as types of language-objects that are implemented by concrete Linda-like systems. The non-functional issues would have to be attributed as interfaces to certain implementations that provide certain system level services.

Part V

Applications of Coordination Technology

Applications of Coordination Technology

Introduction

Just as *coordination* is nearly invisible when conducted successfully, the supporting coordination technology works behind the stages in distributed applications on the Internet. Good coordination technologies make "things run smoothly" so that the management of dependencies amongst users and processes in applications is hidden. Thus, it is not an easy task to point at a specific application and make the benefits of advanced coordination technologies clearly visible. While being almost invisible, coordination is also pervasive in all aspects of interaction, such as in a discussion where only one participant speaks at a time, in the design of organizations by prescribing workflows, or in computing systems by mechanisms in parallel and distributed computations such as scheduling, locking etc. Thus, one could even claim, that every information technology application in which interaction occurs or is supported is an application of coordination mechanisms.

With the introduction of the Web as a platform for information distribution that is easy to deploy and easy to use both for information providers and users, the Internet has increased the need for coordination support for distributed applications. While being a static hypermedia system in its beginnings, the Web has evolved into a collection of services provided at different levels. The immediate popularity of the Web made it attractive to offer local services at a worldwide scale. And commercially driven innovation has brought across new services that take advantage of the Web's scale and availability ([171]). The more services are available, the more difficult becomes the task of gluing them together into applications and coordinating their interactions. The core Web technology offers only very limited support for such distributed coordinated applications and makes this lack very visible. It is coordination mechanisms as enabling technologies that provide means for processes, components, or agents to work smoothly together. But still, is it not easy to select specific flavors of coordination technology for an application. A variety of application scenarios demands for different coordination technologies ranging from agent-based to tuplespace-based models ([600, 599, 598]).

Figure 12.1 illustrates the set of application given forces that guide the choice of a concrete coordination technology. These tradeoffs all affect the design of a coordination manager differently. For example, a centralized server is easier to maintain and changes to the documents and deadlines implies

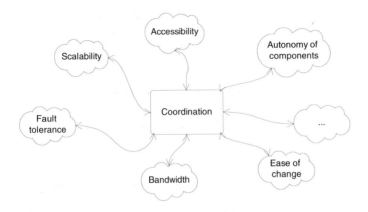

Fig. 12.1. Tradeoffs on coordination technologies

fever risks of inconsistencies than in a replicated architecture. Or: A centralized coordination manager also is easier to adapt to changes in different organizational structures which have their particular demands.

The following four chapters report on applications of coordination technologies. They represent specific situations in which sets of tradeoffs are given by applications and have been matched by specific choices of what technology to apply where. Although they look at application domains that are not related per se, they share the fact that their implementation in a distributed Internet context *requires* some sort of coordination technology. They provide insights on how to design coordinated applications, and show how to provide coordination behind the stages in cooperative and more computational applications.

The contributions

Chapter 13 by *Franco Zambonelli, Nicholas R. Jennings, Andrea Omicini,* and *Michael Wooldridge* deals with the development of complex Internet based applications. The authors focus on the field agent-based computing as an approach to develop applications in terms of autonomous software agents whose specifics are proactive behavior and and high-level interaction protocols. While models and technologies of agents become more and more mature, the question on *how* the analysis and design applications in terms of agents can be supported has not yet been examined in sufficient depth. However, having such suited methodologies available is crucial to the deployment of agent technologies at an industrial scale.

An existing methodology – Gaia – is evaluated against the requirements of the Internet context. It turns out, that it lacks support for openness of a system, does not deal with non-cooperative agents as usually found on the Internet, and does have a concept to group agents as societies and to establish social rules in them. The authors propose to apply a coordination model within the methodology to cover the mentioned shortcomings and to extend it towards a coordination-oriented methodology.

With a different emphasis, but equally devoted to the development of co-ordinated applications, *Dwight Deugo, Michael Weiss*, and *Elizabeth Kendall* present in chapter 14 a set of reusable patterns for agent coordination. There is a variety of options to design agents interactions and their coordination. While patterns like master-slave coordination dominate, the designer of an application should be aware of other known patterns and be able to make an educated choice amongst them. Similar to an object-oriented programming, agent-oriented development is influenced by a set of forces that determine the actual choice of a specific design. The authors identify mobility and communication, standardization, coupling, problem partitioning and failures as the ones most important in agent-oriented designs. Based on that, the chapter presents a catalog of five patterns for agent coordination and describes their context and problem, forces involved, and known solutions.

Workflow systems are yet another application domain in which coordination models and technologies are of major importance. In chapter 15, *Monica Divitini, Chihab Hanachi*, and *Christophe Sibertin-Blanc* discuss how such systems help to coordinate actors involved in business processes. They show, that the use of the Internet open new ways to work together. Organizational cooperation is enabled by masking spatial distances by communication and further enhanced by the possible dynamics of forming teams of people from different organizations. Current Workflow Management Systems, however, do not support such inter-organizational workflows as required. The authors define a framework which is enabling to analyse such workflows and to understand the characteristics involved. They go on to study two approaches to inter-organizational workflows within their framework.

The final chapter 16 of this applications part, written by *Eric Monfroy* and *Farhad Arbab*, shows an example of applying coordination models by embedding them in yet another technology. They study constraint programming, where a solution to a problem is characterized by a set of constraints. Constraint solvers then try to find a solution that satisfies the conjunction of constraints. With distribution and communication provided by a network, the setup of multiple constraint solvers becomes an option and the way of their cooperation a challenge. The authors look at the relation of coordination languages and existing solver cooperation solutions. They advocate the use of coordination models for cooperation of solvers and demonstrate two possible approaches to do so.

13. Agent-Oriented Software Engineering for Internet Applications

Franco Zambonelli[1], Nicholas R. Jennings[2], Andrea Omicini[3], and Michael J. Wooldridge[4]

[1] Dipartimento di Scienze dell'Ingegneria
Università di Modena e Reggio Emilia, Via Campi 213b,I-41100 Modena, Italy
mailto:franco.zambonelli@unimo.it
[2] Department of Electronics and Computer Science
University of Southampton, Highfield, Southampton SO17 1BJ, United Kingdom
mailto:nrj@ecs.soton.ac.uk
[3] LIA, Dipartimento di Elettronica, Informatica e Sistemistica
Università di Bologna, Viale Risorgimento 2, I-40136 Bologna, Italy
mailto:aomicini@deis.unibo.it
[4] Department of Computer Science
University of Liverpool, Liverpool L69 7ZF, United Kingdom
mailto:M.J.Wooldridge@csc.liv.ac.uk

Summary.

The metaphors of *autonomous agents* and *agent societies* have the potential to make a significant impact on the processes of analysis, design, and development of complex software systems on the Internet. In this chapter, we concentrate predominantly on agent societies, and show how work on coordination models and technologies provides a powerful framework for the engineering of Internet-based, multi-agent systems. First, we introduce the concepts of agent, multi-agent system, and agent-oriented software engineering, and highlight the specific issues that arise when we take the Internet as the environment that agents inhabit. We then provide a brief survey of the state of the art in the area of agent-oriented methodologies, paying particular attention to the Gaia methodology for agent-oriented analysis and design. Gaia was originally conceived for benevolent agents inhabiting closed systems. However, to broaden its scope, we show how insights from the area of coordination models can be incorporated in order to make it more suitable for developing Internet-based applications.

13.1 Introduction

Agent-based computing [552, 332, 643] is rapidly emerging as a powerful technology for the development of complex software systems, synthesising contributions from many different research areas, including artificial intelligence, software engineering, robotics, and distributed computing. Developing applications in terms of *autonomous software agents* that exhibit proactive and intelligent behaviour, and that interact with one another in terms of high-level protocols and languages, leads to a new programming paradigm. This paradigm, which we term *agent-oriented software engineering*, is well suited to tackling the complexity of today's software systems. Firstly, today's software systems are required to deal with complex and unpredictable execution environments which object-oriented languages and applications seem unable to model and tackle in a natural and clean way [82]. The Internet is probably the most complex and unpredictable environment that application designers have to face today, and Internet applications are arguably the most important area in which the agent paradigm can fulfill its potential. Secondly, the abstraction level defined by the agent-based approach is higher than that of the object-oriented paradigm, as the behaviour of agents more closely reflects that of the human beings whose work they are delegated to perform and/or support.

By dint of being a new programming paradigm, the development of agent-based applications implies new programming abstractions and techniques. This necessity is born out by the significant body of research that has been undertaken in defining and developing new models and systems for building agent-based, and multi-agent, systems. These efforts include problems related to the definition of suitable architectures for agents [358], agent communication languages [240, 239], coordination model for agents [472, 116], as well as models for the specification and verification of multi-agent systems [93]. However, the development of complex multi-agent systems requires not only new models and technologies, but also new *methodologies* to support developers in an engineered approach to the *analysis* and *design* of such systems. This need is especially pressing if multi-agent systems are to break out of being a niche technology used by the few, to something that is part of the armoury of a mainstream software engineer.

In the last few years, several attempts have been made to develop *agent-oriented modelling techniques and methodologies* [321, 330]. However, none of these techniques can yet be regarded as a comprehensive methodology for the analysis and design of multi-agent systems. The *Gaia* methodology [642] is one of the few attempts that is specifically tailored to the analysis and design of multi-agent systems and that deals with both the micro (intra-agent) level and the macro (inter-agent) level of analysis and design. However, Gaia, as it presently stands, is not a general methodology for all kinds of multi-agent system. Rather, it is intended to support the development of distributed problems solvers in which the system's constituent components are known at design time (i.e., a closed system) and in which all agents are expected to cooperate towards the achievement of a global goal. For these reasons, Gaia is not suitable for the analysis and design of Internet applications, where openness and self-interest are key factors.

One of the main reasons why most extant agent-oriented methodologies (including Gaia) are ill suited to open systems are that they conceive all interactions as occurring directly between agents. This makes it difficult to enforce any form of control on interactions as required, for example, to handle the arrival of new agents into the system or to constrain the actions of possibly self-interested agents. From a more general perspective, these methodologies fail to adequately address the concept of "agent societies". Agents need to be conceived as populating a society, whose global activities are expected to proceed according to specific social laws and conventions. In other words, the proper functioning of a multi-agent system usually relies on some form of global laws that the agents living in it have to obey when interacting with other agents. For example, the correct functioning of agent-mediated auctions require participating agents to comply to the conventions that rule each specific auction type [460].

In this chapter, we propose the adoption of *coordination models* [269, 163] as the conceptual abstraction that can be exploited in the analysis and design of multi-agent systems for the Internet. Furthermore, we sketch how a coordination model can be exploited to make a methodology, such as Gaia, suitable for Internet applications. The key idea stems from the fact that a coordination model abstracts the concept of coordination media, intended as the place where interactions occur, and of coordination laws, intended as the rules that the coordination media enforces in interactions. Therefore, in general, a coordination model could be exploited so as to act as the repository of the social laws of an application, which all agents, having to interact with each other through the mediation of the coordination media, are forced to respect. More specifically, a coordination model could be exploited as a mediator (so as to enable interactions between entities that do not know one another), as well as a global controller for all interactions (so as to control and – if necessary – constrain, the behaviour of possibly self-interested agents).

The remainder of this chapter is organised as follows. Section 13.2 discusses the basic characteristics of the agent paradigm and of multi-agent systems, and motivates the need for software engineering methodologies for multi-agent systems. Section 13.3 analyses a number of methodologies for agent-oriented software engineering (paying particular attention to Gaia) and shows the limitation of these methodologies when dealing with Internet applications. Section 13.4 shows how a coordination model can be used as a powerful framework for the analysis and design of multi-agent systems on the Internet. On this base, section 13.5 sketches a new methodology for the analysis and design of multi-agent systems on the Internet. Section 13.6 concludes the chapter and outlines open issues and research directions in the area.

13.2 Engineering Multi-Agent Systems on the Internet

13.2.1 What is a Multi-agent System?

The very notion of *agent* is one of the most debated and controversial in the fields of Computer Science and Artificial Intelligence. According to [643], an agent is characterised by *autonomy, social ability, reactivity*, and *pro-activeness*. Since we are mainly interested in Internet agents, here, we may think of an agent as an autonomous software entity which interacts with its environment (the Internet) and with other agents pro-actively (that is, by its own initiative) in order to achieve its own goals (typically accomplishing some information gathering or dissemination task).

These agents typically represent different users and thus there are many of them in a given environment. Thus, *multi-agent systems* can be considered as ensembles of autonomous agents, acting and working independently from each other, each representing an independent *locus* of control of the whole system. Each agent tries to accomplish its own task(s) and, in so doing, will typically need to interact with other agents and its surrounding environment in order to obtain access to information/services that it does not possess or to coordinate its activities to ensure its goals can be met. In many cases, however, a multi-agent system, as a whole, achieves more complex or wider goals than the mere sum of its component agent's goals. As an example, in a system composed of autonomous agents, each looking for computational resources to exploit, a global load balancing of the activities can be achieved, despite the fact that no single agent explicitly worries about load balancing. As another example, in systems for agent-mediated auctions, the opposing forces of buyers and sellers (the former attempting to sell a good at a high-price, the latter attempting to buy it at a low-price) can naturally lead to a reasonable pricing of goods.

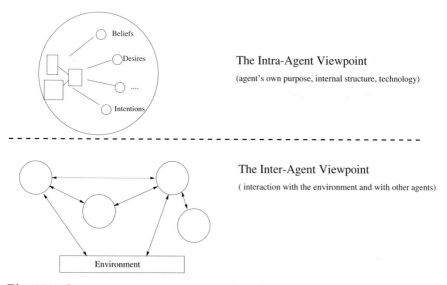

Fig. 13.1. Intra-agent versus inter-agent viewpoints

The above perspective typically leads to the conception of a multi-agent system as a *society* of agents, where the mutual interactions between agents and with their environment leads to a useful global behaviour. Correspondingly, each agent of a multi-agent system may be observed according to two different perspectives (see Figure 13.1): from the inside, as an individual (software) system, with its own purpose/structure/technology (the *intra-agent* viewpoint), and from the outside, as part of a society, interacting with other individuals, accessing resources, and exploiting the social infrastructure (the *inter-agent* viewpoint). The latter aspect is what makes a multi-agent system something of radical departure from more traditional (software) systems, and is therefore the main topic of interest in this chapter.

More precisely, we may describe a multi-agent system by abstracting three fundamental concepts: *(i)* the agents, taken as individuals, *(ii)* the interactions among agents, like communication acts [239, 240], and *(iii)* the mutual dependencies between agents and social relationships, or *organisational relationships* [642, 236]. Clearly, the aspects related to the inter-agent viewpoint are represented by the last two concepts and characterise a multi-agent system as a society of interacting individuals. In particular, we may think of *(ii)* and *(iii)* as two different levels of social interaction. Speech acts and agent communication languages [558, 239, 240] constitute the basic elements of interaction, while organisational relationships provide the conceptual framework upon which each agent finds a well-specified position (or *role*) in the society, which motivates and structures the interactions among the agents.

It is the organisation of agents that gives a multi-agent system more than the knowledge, competence, and abilities provided by all its individual agents, and represents the value-added of the multi-agent approach. In fact, it is possible to change the behaviour of a multi-agent system without changing the constituent agents merely by altering the organisational relationships between them. Generally speaking, this means that the very essence of a multi-agent system implies that the organisational structures, that is, the societies of agents, have to be taken into account as *first-class entities*, and analysed, designed and implemented as such.

13.2.2 Engineering a Multi-agent System

In seeking to develop an agent-oriented methodology, the most obvious point of departure is to consider object-oriented methodologies [82]. These methodologies have gained widespread acceptance and use. In particular, the emphasis of such techniques on both encapsulation and interaction among entities suggests that a multi-agent system could actually be built by exploiting an object-oriented methodology [465, 103, 485].

However, object-oriented approaches fall short in supporting the full notions of agents , and organisations as first-class entities [247, 330]. This is hardly surprising since these represent the two main distinguishing features of multi-agent systems with respect to object-based systems. Object-oriented methodologies have objects as their basic conceptual model and therefore have no support for capturing reactive and proactive behaviour, nor for maintaining a balance between the two. Additionally, there is no first class notion of an *organisational structure* in the object-oriented world. Organisation structure in object-oriented systems is implicit within `public` and `private` qualifiers, and the "handles" that agents have on one-another. Where entities in systems represent real-world entities that do have organisational relationships to one-another, this level of representation is inadequate.

Consequently, we believe what is needed is the definition of suitable engineering methodologies that are specific for multi-agent systems. These need to go beyond traditional object-oriented approaches by providing explicit support for the notions of agenthood and agent society.

13.2.3 Agent-oriented Analysis and Design

As with traditional methodologies, agent-oriented analysis starts from the definition of a system's requirements and goals. The application domain is studied and modelled, the computational resources available and the technological constraints are listed, the fundamental application goals and targets are devised, and so on. Then, the application's global goals are typically decomposed into smaller sub-goals, until they become manageable at the abstraction level provided by the approach adopted – which is when the design phase comes in.

In particular, when dealing with the analysis of an agent, we are no longer limited to defining computable functionalities, as in procedure-oriented methodologies, or sets of related services, to be encapsulated into an object or a component. Instead, since, by definition, agents have goals which they pursue pro-actively and in an autonomous way, agent-oriented analysis must identify the *responsibilities* of an agent. That is, the activities it has to carry out to perform one or more *tasks*, which may include specific *permissions* to access and influence the surrounding environment, as well as *interactions* with the other agents in the application. Design is concerned with the representation of the abstract models resulting from the analysis phase in terms of the design abstractions provided by the methodology. In agent-oriented software engineering, this means responsibilities, tasks, and interaction protocols, should be mapped onto agents, high-level interactions and organisations.

When assigned to an agent, a task defines both its inner structure, in terms of its environment representation and capabilities (from the competence required by the task), and its interaction protocol (roughly, from the information required and provided and the actions to be performed to accomplish the task). More precisely, an agent will be designed so as to be able to represent that portion of the environment with which it is concerned (its *sphere of influence*), to infer new information from this knowledge, and to act somehow on the environment. Moreover, its interaction protocols will be defined so as to enable the agent to contact other agents, get from them the information it needs, transmit newly inferred information to them, and coordinate its activities with the other agents.

One may think that "grown-up" objects may be charged with responsibilities, tasks and complex interaction protocols towards a useful representation of agents. However, this perspective misses what is peculiar to multi-agent systems engineering, that is, the concept of an *agent society*, structured according to organisational relationships. When agents have to live in an organised society, the analysis phase should identify not only the responsibilities of the agents as individuals, (i.e., their *individual tasks*), but also their global responsibilities to the multi-agent system as a whole, (i.e., its *social tasks*).

Individual tasks are associated with one specific competence in the system, related to the need to access and effect a specific portion of the environment and carry out some simple task. Each agent in the system is assigned one or more individual tasks, and the agent assumes full responsibility for carrying out assigned tasks. From an organisational perspective, this corresponds to assigning each agent a specific role in the organisation/society. Of course, multiple agents in a system can be assigned the same task/role.

In contrast, social tasks represent the global responsibilities of the agent system. In order to carry out such tasks, several, possibly heterogeneous competences, will usually need to be combined. The achievement of social tasks leads to the identification of global *social laws* that have to be respected and/or enforced by the society of agents, to enable the society itself to function properly and accordingly to the global expected behaviour.

To clarify the above concepts, let us consider the problem of engineering a multi-agent software system to manage the review process for an international conference. An individual task that easily comes out from the analysis phase is picking up a given number of papers, and taking the responsibility for reviewing them. The task can be defined as an individual one in that it can be easily and naturally charged to a single agent, representing a referee. A social task, instead, could be to ensure that each submitted paper has at least three reviews, by three different referees of different institutions. This task requires that a given number of entities have the competence for reviewing papers, and that they can assume the responsibility for such a task (an individual one). However, the task also requires that the reviewing competence and tasks are coordinated and organised so as to ensure the required number and variety of reviews. Therefore, the task cannot naturally be committed to a single agent, but its achievement involves several of the agents in the system.

According to the above considerations, any methodology for agent-oriented software engineering must provide suitable abstractions and tools to model not only the individual tasks of agents, but also the social ones.

13.2.4 Engineering Systems for the Internet

The choice of the Internet as the target environment for the multi-agent system has a number of implications for the engineering of the system.

The first consequence of such a choice arises from the nature of the Internet as a global, distributed, and heterogeneous *information system*. Many of the activities of the agents are concerned with accessing, understanding, relating, modifying, and producing information. Apart from the abilities required of the individual agents, this makes it easy and natural to design multi-agent systems as information-based systems, where *all* the activities are interpreted and modelled in terms of the information required or made available. In particular, this also applies to the interactions of the agents. As a result, methodologies supporting this view of multi-agent systems naturally fit their engineering on the Internet.

Another feature which is intrinsic to the Internet is *openness*. One may easily envision a (not so far) future where the Internet will host thousands of multi-agent systems, some of which interact directly or indirectly, with agents moving from one multi-agent system to another. This makes it difficult to use methodologies that assume the multi-agent system is *closed* – that is, that the number and the nature of the agents are known once and and for all a priori. Rather, the ability to support *openness* – as a feature, rather than as a problem – seems to be a mandatory requirement for any methodology for Internet-based multi-agent systems. This obviously holds for other typical Internet features, too: unpredictability, dynamicity, and unreliability. In particular, this is relevant for large-scale multi-agent systems, where the absence of centralised control makes it impossible to have a complete and reliable static picture of the agent's environment, on which analysis and design might be grounded on.

Furthermore, the properties of openness and unpredictability mean it is simply not feasible to make the cooperativeness of agents a basic assumption in the analysis and design phases. Some agents may indeed be cooperative, accepting goals on behalf of other agents, for instance, or agreeing on some protocol for cooperative interaction. However, many other agents will be purely *self-interested* and will pursue their own goals.

A methodology for agent-based Internet applications should therefore be able to support the engineering of MAS that incorporates not only well-known agents with a cooperative attitude, but also previously unknown agents that dynamically join the system (i.e., the agent society) and that are likely to exhibit self-interested behaviour.

13.3 Software Engineering Methodologies for MAS

This section provides a brief overview of the state of the art in the area of software engineering methodologies for MAS. In particular, we detail the main characteristics of the Gaia methodology and outline its limitations with respect to dealing with Internet-based applications.

13.3.1 State of the Art

A number of different methodologies have been proposed in recent years for modelling and engineering agents and multi-agent systems (see [321] for a survey).

As already observed, traditional methodologies for analysis and design are poorly suited for multi-agent systems because of the fundamental mismatch between the respective levels of abstraction. Despite this mismatch, however, several proposals do take object-oriented modelling techniques or methodologies as their basis. On the one hand, some proposals directly extend the applicability of object-oriented methodologies and techniques to the design of agent systems. For example, some proposals attempts to directly apply the UML notation to represent agent systems and their patterns of interaction [350, 583]. However, these proposals fail to capture the autonomous and proactive behaviour of agents, as well as the richness of their interactions. On the other hand, some proposals seek to extend and adapt object-oriented models and techniques to define a methodology for use in multi-agent systems. This can lead, for example, to extended models for representing agent behaviour and their interactions [103, 358, 485], as well as to agent-tuned extensions of UML [465, 485]. However, although these proposals can sometimes achieve a good modelling of the autonomous behaviour of agents and of their interactions, they lack the conceptual mechanisms for adequately dealing with organisations and agent societies.

A different set of proposals build upon and extend methodologies and modelling techniques from knowledge engineering [93, 94, 274]. These techniques provide formal and compositional modelling languages for the verification of system structure and function. These approaches are well-suited to modelling knowledge- and information- oriented agents (as are found in several Internet applications). However, since these approaches usually assume a centralised view of knowledge-based systems, they fail to provide adequate models and support for the societal view of multi-agent systems. The CommonKads approach [320] attempts to overcome these limitations by explicitly introducing into the methodology the abstraction of agent society. However, this simply reduces to modelling a society as a collection of interacting entities, with no identification of concepts such as social tasks or social laws.

Other models and approaches attempt to model and implement multi-agent systems from an "organisation-oriented" point of view [247]. These help pave the way towards agent-oriented methodologies by explicitly conceiving multi-agent systems as organisations [236] or as societies. However, these proposals define an organisation merely as a collection of interacting roles, thus failing, again, to deal with the key point of social tasks.

13.3.2 The Gaia Methodology

Gaia is a methodology for agent-oriented analysis and design that makes explicit use of an organisational point of view. In Gaia, analysis and design are well-separated phases (see Figure 13.2). Analysis aims to develop an understanding of the system and its structure, in terms of the roles that have to be played in the agent organisation and of their interactions, without any reference to implementation details. The design phase aims to define the actual structure of the agent system, in terms of the agent classes and instances composing the system, of the services to be provided by each agent, and of the acquaintances' structure.

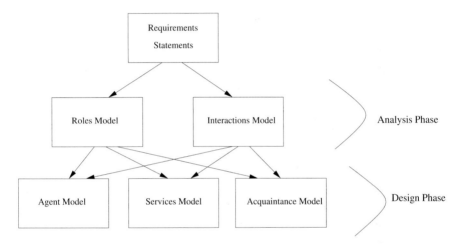

Fig. 13.2. The basic concepts of the Gaia methodology

In more detail, the analysis phase aims to identify what the actual organisation of the multiple agents should look like. It does this by decomposing the system into abstract "loci of control"; i.e., the *roles* to be played in the organisation, and the way in which they interact accordingly to specific *protocols* (this, respectively, defines the *roles model* and *interactions model*). In particular, Gaia suggests the following steps:

1. Identify the roles in the system (these typically correspond to individuals within an organisation, departments, or organisations themselves) and define a list of the key roles in an informal description language.
2. For each role, identify the associated protocols, i.e., the patterns of interaction that are likely to occur between roles.
3. Elaborate the complete roles model and interactions model and, if required, iterate the previous stages.

The expected outputs of the analysis phase are a fully elaborated roles model – describing each role in terms of responsibilities, permissions, interaction protocols, and activities – and an interactions model – describing each protocol in terms of data exchanged and partners involved.

The design phase starts from the models defined during the analysis phase and aims to define the actual agent system in such a way that it can easily be implemented. To this end, the design phase has to decide which classes of agents (and how many) have to play the roles identified during the analysis phase, which services agents must provide to fulfill their role, and what is the actual topology of the interactions that flows from the interaction and the agent models. In more detail, the design phase involves the following stages:

1. Identify the agent model, that is, aggregate roles into agent types and refine, to form an agent type hierarchy, and evaluate the number of required instances for each class;
2. Identify the services that agents have to provide in order to fulfill their assigned roles, by analysing the activities and responsibilities, as well as the protocols defined by each of the roles;
3. Develop the acquaintance model, to identify inefficiencies in the design and, if required, iterate the previous stages.

The expected output of the design phase is the actual architecture (i.e., organisation) of the agent system, which can then be implemented using more traditional techniques (such as object-orientation and component-ware).

13.3.3 Applying Gaia

To illustrate the principles of the Gaia methodology, we will consider how it can be applied to the task of developing a software system to support the task of managing the review process of an international conference [161]. Once the submission deadline has passed, the program committee (PC) has to handle the review of the papers; contacting potential referees and asking them to review some of the papers by a given deadline. After a while, reviews come in and they are then used to decide about the acceptance/rejection of the submissions. The process is essentially a workflow: the activities of a number of different individuals have to be synchronised, data has to be exchanged, and each person involved may be required to perform different activities depending on the global status of the process. The whole process can be effectively supported by means of a multi-agent system (as in ADEPT [333]), which assists with workflow management.

Depending on the size of the conference (i.e., the number of submissions it receives), different ways of handling the review process can be adopted. Let us consider the case of a large conference, in which the PC Chair does not handle the assignment of individual papers to referees and in which the PC Members need to recruit external referees in order to assist them with their reviewing task. In this organisation, the PC Chair can simply partition the submitted papers and then send one of the partitions to each of the PC members. The duty of each PC Member is then to find three different referees for each of the papers in their assigned partition, collect the corresponding reviews, and send them back to the PC Chair. The PC Chair eventually collects and ranks the reviews.

In Gaia, the first step of the analysis phase is to identify the roles involved. In this case, the following roles are easy to identify:

- *paper partitioner*: in charge of partitioning the papers and assigning the partitions to PC members according to some criterion (for example, based on load balancing or competences of PC Members);
- *review allocator*: in charge of finding three reviews for each of the papers in a given partition, and collating the reviews that are returned;
- *reviewer*: in charge of receiving a paper and reviewing it by the stated deadline;
- *review collector*: in charge of collecting all the reviews, ranking them and deciding upon acceptance and rejection.

For each of these roles, the associated permissions, activities, and responsibilities need to be identified. The role reviewer, for example, requires the permission to read the paper it is assigned for review and the permission to write the corresponding review form. Its activities involve receiving a paper to review, reviewing it in due time, and sending the completed review form back. Its main responsibility is to ensure that the completed review form is sent back on time.

The interaction model follows very naturally from the definition of the roles. It basically amounts to specifying which protocols involve which role pairings and what information is exchanged during the execution of the protocol. By means of illustration, consider the exemplar protocol that involves the reviewer (as initiator of the protocol) and the review allocator in which the reviewer checks the correctness of the completed review form and sends it back to the review allocator.

Having completed the analysis phase, the first step of the design phase is to assign roles to agents (definition of the agent model). In this application, this is a trivial mapping for most of the roles since the agent model naturally derives from the real-world organisation: one PC Chair agent will assume both the roles of paper partitioner and review collector. One agent for each of the PC Members will assume the role of review allocator. Also, PC Member agents are likely to assume the role of reviewer, for those papers they review by themselves. Each external referee will be associated to an agent that will play the role of reviewer (for each paper that he is assigned).

From the agent model, the service model specifies which services the agent must implement to enable all the roles it has to play to be fulfilled. This amounts to transforming the abstract activities that the roles have to perform (as identified in the analysis phase) into more coherent blocks of computational activity. In the case of the reviewer role, for example, the only required service is the one that starts when the paper is received from the review allocator and then executes in order for the paper to be actually reviewed, and eventually sends back the completed review form.

Finally, the acquaintance model is constructed. This model, which simply identifies the communications pathways that exist between agents, provides a check of whether the structure of the interactions in the system are poorly organised. In this case, there are no obvious bottlenecks since the structure of the agent organisation closely resembles that of its real-world counterpart.

13.3.4 Limitations of the Gaia Methodology

Gaia was intended for use in *closed systems* of *distributed problem solvers*, in which:

- the organisational structure of the system is static; i.e., neither the number of agents, nor their inter-agent relationships change at run-time;
- agents exhibit globally collaborative behaviour: they have a global goal in mind and do not exhibit competitive or self-interested behaviour.

However, these characteristics make Gaia, as it currently stands, unsuitable for Internet applications for the three main reasons that are dealt with in the remainder of this sub-section. Each limitation is illustrated in the context of our conference management scenario.

No Open Systems. Gaia requires that all agents in a system, as well as all interaction protocols between them, are known a priori. However, there are cases, especially on the Internet, in which two agents need to interact with one another, although they do not know each other at design time and they do not have a preset interaction protocol for so doing.

In our application example, an external referee may want to rely on his own agent – well trusted and with a behaviour tuned to his own personal needs – for all its activities. Therefore, he may refuse to use an externally provided agent and, instead, insist that the PC member agent interacts directly with his personal agent (in order to receive the papers to review and to send them back to the PC Member agent). This type of situation is likely to become increasingly common as personal agents become more widespread.

In a system designed with Gaia, either the personal agent explicitly advertises itself and completely complies with the interaction protocols of the PC member agent or no interaction could take place. For example, Gaia would be unable to model a situation in which a PC Member agent has to contact an external referee agent to dynamically discover its area of competence.

No Self-interested Agents. Gaia does not explicitly deal with situations in which interactions are non-cooperative in nature. However, the Internet is populated predominantly by self-interested entities that compete to achieve their own objectives. It should be noted that Gaia does not preclude the development of such systems. Rather, it provides no explicit mechanisms for controlling or monitoring for such situations.

In the conference management example, if the system design does not account for self-interested behaviour then: *(i)* an author could make its own agent assume the role of reviewer for his own paper or *(ii)* a reviewer could obtain a significant number of papers to review and thus may exert a strong influence over the nature of the conference.

No Social Laws. More generally, perhaps the main drawback of Gaia is that it does not identify an organisation of agents as a *society* in which there are global laws that have to be respected by the society of agents.

As already stated, the definition of a multi-agent system has to rely not only on the individual task of each agents, but on the social task too and on the enforcement of the related social laws.

In the conference management example, a situation in which a reviewer receives too many (or too few) papers to review should be avoided. However, such situations can be difficult to monitor. On the one hand, an agent may be likely to exhibit self-interested behaviour and it may also lie in order to review either a lot of papers (to increase their influence in setting the scientific program) or a very few (to do less work). On the other hand, when PC Members autonomously allocate referees, one has to enforce the control of how many papers a single referee has received, possibly from different PC Members. The enforcement of this control requires specific interaction protocols that may impact in the definition of both PC Chair, PC Members, and Reviewer agents.

Gaia, by lacking the abstraction of a social task, does not explicitly model social laws and, as a consequence, either completely misses them or leaves them implicit in the definition of each agent.

13.4 Exploiting a Coordination Model

This section introduces the concept of a *coordination model* [269] and shows how it can be exploited in the context of designing multi-agent systems for use on the Internet. In particular, a coordination model makes it possible to enact social laws in the system and to control the execution of foreign and self-interested agents.

13.4.1 Coordination Models

In general terms, coordination is the art of managing interactions and dependencies among activities, and a coordination model provides a formal framework in which the interaction of a set of concurrent activities can be expressed [269, 393].

In computer science, in its broadest conception, a coordination model deals with the creation and destruction, the communications, the distribution and mobility in space, as well as synchronisation over time [163], of a set of active software entities, whether processes, objects, or agents [482]. However, in most cases, a more restricted (and more manageable) view of a coordination model is adopted, as the framework dealing with the communication and synchronisation of a system of autonomous software agents.

From this latter perspective, a coordination model can be thought as consisting of three elements:

- the *coordinables*: the entities whose mutual interaction is ruled by the model, e.g., the agents in a multiagent system;
- the *coordination media*: the abstractions enabling agent interactions, as well as the core around which the components of a coordinated system are organised. Examples are semaphores, monitors, channels, or more complex media like tuple spaces, blackboards, etc.
- the *coordination laws*: define the behaviour of the coordination media in response to interaction events. The laws can be defined in terms of a *communication language* (a syntax used to express and exchange data structures) and a *coordination language* (a set of interaction primitives and their semantics)

According to [482], coordination models can be divided in two classes: *data-driven* and *control-driven*.

In *control-driven* coordination models, (e.g., Manifold [39]), coordinables (agents) interact with one another and with the external world via well-defined input/output ports, connecting the agents, and actually representing the coordination media. The observable behaviour of the coordinables, from the point of view of the coordination media, is in terms of state changes and events occurring on these ports. The coordination laws establish how events and state changes can occur and how they propagate though the coordination media. Therefore, the coordination media basically handle the interaction space by controlling how the flux of events connects the coordinables and how it propagates in the system, with no concern for the data exchanged between coordinables.

In *data-driven* coordination models, (e.g., Linda [267]), coordinables interact with the external world by exchanging data structures through the coordination media, which basically acts as a shared data space. The observable behaviour of the coordinables, from the point of view of the coordination media, is one of entities requesting data (either reading or extracting it from the dataspace). The coordination laws determine how data structures are represented and how they are stored, accessed, and consumed. Therefore, the coordination media basically handles the interaction space in terms of entities interacting via data exchange and synchronisation over data occurrences.

Although not all coordination models provide for a way of programming the coordination laws, which are then built into the coordination media, several recent proposals define flexible coordination media in which the default coordination laws can be changed and adapted to the specific coordination needs of a system [472, 116].

We refer the interested reader to Chapters 2 and 3, respectively, for a more detailed and formal characterisation of coordination models and for a survey on several control-driven and data-driven models. What is of interest here is that a coordination model, (whether data- or control- driven), models a system in terms of inter-agent interactions occurring occurring via coordination media embedding coordination laws, possibly programmable, to which all the interactions have consequently to conform. Adopting the above modelling in the analysis and design of multi-agent system provides a means of dealing with some of the shortcomings of the Gaia methodology.

Although both control-driven and data-driven models can be adopted to handle multi-agent system interactions, data-oriented models have an additional, important, advantage. In the Internet, in the majority of cases, agents exhibit an "information-oriented" view of their world (as argued in Subsection 13.2.4). Therefore, adopting a data-driven coordination model, which ensures all interactions occur via shared dataspaces, is a natural choice for such an information-oriented view of interaction.

The remainder of this section highlights how a coordination model perspective helps alleviate some of Gaia's aforementioned shortcomings.

13.4.2 Open Systems

When a coordination model is adopted, the coordination media mediates all interactions occurring between agents, and influences the effect of the interaction events according to its embedded coordination laws. As a consequence of this mediation, inter-agent interactions are intrinsically less coupled: for instance, a message sent by an agent crosses the coordination media before being delivered to another agent. If the coordination laws in the coordination media can programmed so as to embed any kind of behaviour or intelligence, the coordination media themselves can provide for a very loosely-coupled model of interactions. On the one hand, two agents can interact even if they do not know each other: the coordination media can take care of virtually connecting agents by appropriately delivering messages. On the other hand, two agents can interact even if they are heterogeneous in terms of their communication language or their interaction protocols: the coordination media can handle any necessary translation of messages and adaptation of protocols.

From the analysis and design point of view, the presence of the coordination media implies that it is no longer necessary to determine all the interaction links between all the possible agents that the application will meet – which a priori rules out the possibility of unforeseen agent arrivals – and to define all the possible interaction protocols. Instead, provided there is an appropriate design of the behaviour of the coordination media: *(i)* some of the interaction links between agents can be left unbound, by making the coordination media dynamically connect the interaction links to agents, according to its coordination law; *(ii)* agents do not need to be a priori aware of all possible interactions protocols, because the coordination can embed the functionality necessary to act as a "translator" in the interaction between heterogeneous agents.

In the conference management example, and with reference to the protocol involving the PC Member agent and the Reviewer agent in assigning a paper to review, the design should no longer consider that the PC Member agent will necessarily have an interaction link with a priori known reviewer agents. Instead, the design can leave the interaction link unbound, and the coordination media can be programmed so as to dynamically connect the link to the agent that will assume the role of reviewer. Then, the PC Member agent does not have to worry about whether the reviewer agents is a known reviewer agent or an unknown personal agent of the referee.

13.4.3 Self-interested Agents

The coordination media, by mediating all interactions between agents, is intrinsically able to monitor and influence all interactions. Therefore, it can also be programmed in such a way as to constrain the behaviour of the agents during their interactions, for example by forbidding agents to send a specific kind of message to another agent. This can occur either by simply denying the access of the agents to the coordination media, or by modifying the semantics of the agents' interactions, for example by forwarding a forbidden message to a controller agent instead of delivering it to the original recipient.

This characteristic of the coordination media makes it comparatively easy to monitor and identify the presence of self-interested or opportunistic behaviours in the multi-agent system. Therefore, whenever these kinds of behaviour are likely to be damaging to the multi-agent system, the coordination media can be programmed so as to *(i)* recognise the appearance of such damaging behaviours and, thereafter, *(ii)* either forbid the access to the coordination media by the offending agent or simply constrain/modify the semantics of their accesses in order to make it harmless.

In the conference management example, a self-interested Reviewer agent that tries to collect too many papers to review, can be simply detected by the coordination media and can be excluded from further executing the interaction protocol needed to obtain papers.

13.4.4 Social Laws

Since societies of any kind are grounded on the interaction among the individual components, it seems natural to identify the space of agent interactions as the place where social laws have to be represented and embodied. The interaction space has to be recognised as an independent design space for multi-agent system design, and abstractions and tools are needed to enable agent interaction to be shaped according to the social laws. If the interaction space is not recognised as a primary abstraction, (as is the case in Gaia), social laws have to be left implicit within the definition of roles and agents. However when the interaction space is recognised as the place where social tasks have to be modelled and social laws enforced, a coordination model is the appropriate conceptual abstraction around which to build a society of agents.

The adoption of a coordination model naturally leads to conceptualising a multi-agent system as a society, in which the individual tasks of agents have to be modelled separately from the social tasks. The definition of social tasks, in particular, instead of being mixed in the definition of roles and agents, find an appropriate model in the definition of the behaviour of the coordination media. In particular, by having the capability of monitoring and controlling all interactions between agents, the coordination media can take care of enforcing whatever social laws have to be respected by the agent system, in its entirety, in order for the social tasks to be met.

By considering the conference management example, we can make the concept of social laws clearer. The review process, to be effective and polite, has to be subject to several laws. For example: an author cannot act as a referee for their own paper; a referee should not be assigned to review two different papers of the same author; and the workload should be evenly distributed between the organising committee. All the above constraints cannot simply be reflected in the definition of a few roles and protocols. Instead, they are likely to impact the whole organisation of the conference. Therefore, once the social tasks are identified, the coordination media can become the place where the interactions between agents are appropriately monitored and controlled, so as to make agent interaction respect global goals.

13.5 Toward a Coordination-oriented Methodology

The adoption of a coordination model introduces a further abstraction into the Gaia methodology that necessarily influences the way a multiagent system is analysed and designed (see Figure 13.3).

In the analysis phase, and with reference to the terminology adopted in Gaia, the characteristics of the multi-agent system have to be analysed and understood so as to identify not only the roles to be played in the system and their required interactions, but also the social laws to be respected by the multi-agent system. In other words, the analysis should clearly identify those aspects of the system that are spread across multiple roles and protocols, and therefore properly belong to the multi-agent systems as a whole, i.e., as a coherent organisation of agents with an expected global behaviour.

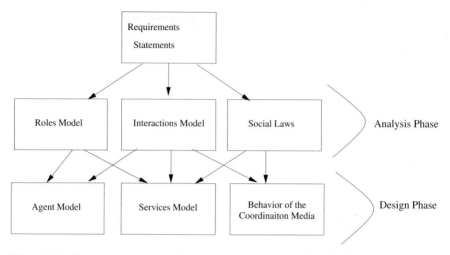

Fig. 13.3. The basic concepts of a coordination-oriented methodology

The expected output of the analysis phase are well-defined role and inter-action models, in addition to a well-defined model of social laws. The latter specifies the social laws that must be respected and enforced by the system if it is to work properly.

In the design phase, the role model and the interactions model drive the design of individual agents and of their internal structure (i.e., with reference to the Gaia methodology, of the agent and service models). In addition, social laws, together with the identified interactions model, drive the definition of the actual expected behaviour of the coordination media in response to the interaction events of the agents. Note that, because a methodology centered around a coordination model leads to an agent system intrinsically open and with dynamically bounded interaction links, the acquaintance model (defined by Gaia) is almost meaningless.

The expected output of the design phase should produce an agent and a service model detailed enough for the agents to be implemented (or designed making use of traditional object-oriented techniques). In addition, the be-haviour of the coordination media should make it possible to implement the coordination media, whatever media it is actually exploited.

A coordination-oriented methodology obviously leads to a design specifi-cation of the coordination media that can very easily implemented by making use of a programmable coordination system, such as MARS [116], TuCSoN [472], and Law Governed Interactions [425], in which the concepts of me-diated interactions via a programmable media have already found a clean and efficient implementation. Otherwise, should the multi-agent system rely on a traditional communication infrastructure (e.g., TCP/IP based message-passing), the actual implementation of the system should also include the implementation of the infrastructure needed to make all interactions compliant with the expected behaviour of the coordination media. For instance, this can be done by associating (even dynamically) specific communication stubs to the agents in the system, as was done, for example, in the FishMarket project [460].

13.6 Conclusions and Future Work

This paper has analysed the main issues that arise in engineering multi-agent systems for the Internet. Specifically it has shown how a coordination model can act as a powerful abstraction for both the analysis, design, and actual development of multi-agent systems.

An analysis of the state of the art in the area has shown that only a few complete and well-grounded methodologies for the analysis and design of multi-agent systems have been proposed so far. In particular, we focused on the Gaia methodology. However, as it currently stands, Gaia falls short when dealing with open agent systems. It does so because it lacks the necessary abstractions to deal with the dynamic arrival and departure of agents, and with self-interest agents. More generally, we have identified how Gaia does not support the concept of a multi-agent system as a society, in which agents have to act accordingly to specific social laws.

The adoption of a coordination model as the conceptual abstraction to be exploited in the analysis and design of multi-agent systems for the Internet, enables open systems, self-interested agents, and social laws, to find a suitable accommodation. On this basis, we have shown how the methodological concepts introduced by Gaia can be effectively complemented by the concepts of social laws and coordination media, leading to the definition of a coordination-oriented methodology suitable for multi-agent Internet systems.

In the latter part of this chapter, we identified the basic concepts and guidelines to be integrated in a methodology for the analysis and design of multi-agent systems on the Internet. Naturally, the sketched coordination-oriented methodology is far from being well-defined; it requires a more detailed specification, supported by appropriate formalism. In addition, there are several other issues – not specifically addressed by this chapter – that a software engineering methodology for multi-agent system on the Internet has to take into account. In particular:

– Object-oriented technologies have already recognised the need for re-use in object-oriented software architectures, and exploited them via design-patterns [258]. In the area of agent-oriented programming and multi-agent systems, we expect the same could apply with regard to the most widely used patterns of interactions between agents (see Chapter 14) and, even more generally, to the most widely used patterns after which a society of agent can be shaped. In other words, we expect agent-patterns to catalogue

widely used social laws, to be exploited to re-use well-known behaviours of
the coordination media.

– Interacting in open environments, such as the Internet, requires authentication mechanisms that allow agents to recognise each other, and control
policies for enabling safe interactions (see Chapter 11). Therefore, analysis and design methodologies should provide appropriate abstractions to
analyse security issues and define security policies. In this context, it is
important to investigate whether a coordination model could be a suitable
abstraction to define and handle security issues, by assuming the coordination media embed, in addition to embed the social laws, also the "security
laws".

14. Reusable Patterns for Agent Coordination

Dwight Deugo[1], Michael Weiss[2], and Elizabeth Kendall[3]

[1] School of Computer Science
   Carleton University, 1125 Colonel By Drive, Ottawa, Ontario, Canada, K1S 5B6
   `deugo@scs.carleton.ca`
[2] School of Computer Science
   Carleton University, Ottawa, Canada
   `weiss@scs.carleton.ca`
[3] Sun Microsystems Chair of Network Computing, School of Network Computing
   Monash University Peninsula Campus McMahons Rd. Frankston, VIC 3199 Australia
   `kendall@infotech.monash.edu.au`

Summary.

Much of agent system development to date has been done ad hoc. These problems limit the extent to which "industrial applications" can be built using agent technology, as the building blocks, reusable techniques, approaches and architectures have either not been exposed or have not yet been fully elaborated. In the mid 80's, supporters of object-oriented technology had similar problems. However, with the aid of software patterns, objects have provided an important shift in the way developers successfully build applications today. In this paper, after describing an agent pattern's generic format, we identify a set of software patterns for agent coordination.

Much of agent system development has been done on an ad hoc basis [92], resulting in many problems [349, 210]:

1. lack of agreed definition of an agent
2. duplicated effort
3. inability to satisfy industrial strength requirements
4. difficulty identifying and specifying common abstractions above the level of single agents
5. lack of common vocabulary
6. complexity
7. research presents only problems and solutions

These problems limit the extent to which "industrial applications" can be built using agent technology, as the building blocks, reusable techniques, approaches and architectures have either not been exposed or have not yet been fully elaborated. In contrast, agent and agent-based system researchers are starting to understand many of the principles, facts, fundamental concepts, and general components [626]. Take for example, the call for papers of the workshop on Mobile Agents in the Context of Competition and Cooperation [420] at Autonomous Agents '99. We found comments such as, "we are uninterested in papers that describe yet another mobile agent system." The question we had after reading this was, if we know so much about agents and agent-based systems, why do we have the above problems?

In the mid 80's, supporters of object-oriented technology had similar problems. However, with the aid of software patterns, objects have provided an important shift in the way developers successfully build applications today. Since we believe that agents are the next major software abstraction, we find it essential to begin the effort of documenting that abstraction so that others can share in the vision. Patterns provide a means of documenting the building blocks in a format already accepted by the software engineering community. Patterns also have the added benefit that no unusual skills, language features, or other tricks are needed to benefit from them. As with objects, software patterns can be an enabling technology for agents.

In this chapter, after describing a pattern's generic format, we identify a set of software patterns for agent coordination. Agent patterns generally fall into architectural, communication, travelling and coordination patterns. Typically, agent coordination mechanisms are based on a master-slave or a contract-net like architecture, but the reasons for either choice are rarely made explicit. What's missing are the forces influencing the choices.

Therefore, before our discussion of particular patterns, we identify in section 14.2 an initial set of global forces surrounding the task of coordination. These forces identify the trade-offs that push and pull solutions proposed by coordination patterns. They help you, the developer, make a more informed decision about when and when *not* to use a particular coordination mechanism. These forces may not be applicable to all coordination patterns. However, they are ones that are important for anyone developing coordination patterns to consider. In sections 14.3 through 14.7, we select different combinations of forces; place them in coordination contexts that give rise to specific problems; and solve the problems, generating our initial set of coordination patterns.

14.1 Software Patterns

Software patterns have their roots in Christopher Alexander's work [22] in the field of building architecture. He proposed that a pattern is a three-part rule that expresses a relation between a certain context, problem and solution. Although there are different formats for patterns today, it is generally agreed that the mandatory parts include the following [413]:

- **Name:** As the saying goes, a good name is worth a thousand words and a good pattern name, although just a short phrase, should contain more information than the number of words would initially suggest. Would the word agent be a good pattern name? The answer is no. Although it means much more than the single word suggests, it has too many meanings! One should strive for a short phrase that still says it all.

- **Context:** A description of a situation when the pattern would apply. However, in itself the context does not provide the only determining factor as to the situations in which the pattern should be applied. Every pattern will have a number of forces that need to be balanced before applying the pattern. The context helps one determine the impact of the forces.
- **Problem:** A precise statement of the problem to be solved. Think from the perspective of a software engineer asking him/herself, How do I ....? A good problem for a pattern is one that software engineers will ask themselves often.
- **Forces:** Description of items that influence the decision as to when to apply the pattern in a context. Forces can be thought of as items that push or pull the problem towards different solutions or that indicate trade-offs that might be made [185].
- **Solution:** A description of the solution in the context that balances the forces.

Optional parts include resulting context, rationale, related patterns, examples, code examples, indications, aliases, known uses and acknowledgements.

A good pattern provides more than just the details of these sections; it should also be generative. Patterns are not solutions; rather patterns generate solutions. You take a "design problem" and look for a pattern to apply in order to create the solution. The greater the potential for application of a pattern, the more generative it is. Although very specific patterns are of use, a great pattern has the potential for many applications. For this to happen, pattern writers spend considerable time and effort attempting to understand all aspects of their patterns and the relationships between those aspects. This generative quality is difficult to describe, but you will know a pattern that has it once you read it. It is often a matter of simplicity in the face of complexity.

Although patterns are useful at solving specific design problems, we can enhance the generative quality of patterns by assembling related ones, positioning them among one another to form a pattern language. Pattern languages can help a developer to build entire systems. For example, an individual pattern can help you design a specific aspect of your agent, such as how it models its beliefs, but a pattern language can help you to use those beliefs to build agents that plan and learn.

The development of agent pattern languages is important for agent patterns to be successful. Forcing each pattern to identify its position within the space of existing patterns is not only good practice, it is also good research. This activity is not only helpful to you as a pattern author, but to all those other software engineers who will use your patterns to develop their systems.

14.2 Global Forces of Coordination

Forces identify the different types of criteria engineers use to justify their designs and implementations. For example, computer scientists usually consider the force of efficiency, along the dimensions of time and space, when developing algorithms. Forces will both positively and negatively interact with one another, even within the same criterion. Time and space is a good example. Database access would be very fast if the database was maintained in memory. However, this solution is usually inappropriate due to the amount of data. Is it better for the database to provide fast access for limited data or slower access for a large amount of data? The answer is, it depends. The conflict between the forces and between the forces and the goals surrounding the problem reveal the intricacies of the problem and indicate the trade-offs that must be considered by the pattern's solution.

In this section, we discuss a number of forces that we believe impact many coordination patterns. Coordination "refers to the state of a community of agents in which actions of some agents fit in well with each other, as well as to the process of achieving this state... Two manifestations of coordination that play particularly important roles in Distributed Artificial Intelligence (DAI) are competition and cooperation." [626], pp 598. Our goal here is to propose an initial list of forces for agent coordination patterns authors to consider when writing their patterns. We expect this list to be continually enhanced with new forces as the issues, factors and conflicts involved in agent coordination are better understood.

14.2.1 Mobility and Communication

Agents that are mobile and must coordinate their activities will need to communicate with other mobile agents, statically located agents, resources and hosting environments.

For two agents to communicate, at least one of them needs to know where the other one is located. Although the initial sender must know where to send the message, it can include its location in the message so that the receiving agent can respond. There are potentially three solutions to this problem. One solution is for an agent to carry either the itineraries of the other agents or a directory of where they are located. The second solution is for it to use a lookup service to find the locations of the other agents. Another solution is to have an agent broadcast its message to all environments, so that eventually the desired agent will receive the message. All solutions have their own problems.

The first one requires that mobile agents carry extra data with them on their trips to other environments. The extra size of an agent implies that it will take longer to transport and that it will consume more memory within the environments. This situation may not be a problem for agent systems that have very few agents (mobile or static). However, this solution may not even be possible due to memory limitations in an agent system containing thousands of agents that need to communicate and coordinate with one another.

The second solution involves agents informing a lookup service of where they are currently located. It also requires that other agents using the lookup service are able to find those locations. The problems with this solution are the latency of the network and the possible failure of the service. In highly mobile agent systems, agents may move so often that the lookup service is never in sync with where the agents have gone. Therefore, when an agent asks where another one is located, it gets an old address rather than the new one. Even worse, if the lookup service fails, an agent will not be able to find the location of any agent.

The final solution is not without its performance and security problems either. Sending a message everywhere takes time and effort by the sending environment and consumes time, effort and space in the receiving environment. Most of this is wasted since the message is actually only for one agent. When the ratio of agents to environments becomes very large, this solution is impractical. This becomes even more true when the overhead of managing the security of the messages – making sure a message reaches the correct agent – is considered.

Even if agents know where others are located, any coordination solution must deal with latency and failure of messages over the network. Messages can get lost or take a long time to reach their destinations.

On one hand, you want to have fast, reliable messaging between coordinating mobile agents. However, you also need a solution that does not increase the memory requirements of agents and their execution environments. You also need one that does not involve complex failure and security mechanisms to handle lost or slow messages, failures in lookup services and message broadcasts.

14.2.2 Standardization

The computer industry has seen the benefits of standardization. Java and XML are two good examples of it in action. Although much of agent framework development done today is in Java [427], there are still many differences in the implementations of the following: environments, execution and management of agent types, management of identifiers, persistence, navigation, communication, the interaction with external resources and security. [514]. The OMG's Mobile Agent System Interoperability Facility (MASIF) [419] and the Foundation for Intelligent Physical Agents (FIPA) [155] are two attempts at standardizing agent technology. Agent communication is outside MASIF's scope, leaving it extensively addressed by CORBA. Coordination is also not standardized. The implication is that agents of different types and implemented using different languages will potentially need to coordinate with one another, each using their own control mechanisms.

Assuming for the moment that agents can send messages between one another, there is also the question of the content of a message.

On one hand, it would be good to have a standardized coordination and communication protocol. However, this takes a great deal of time and money to put into place and dedicated individuals to drive the process. The Mobile Agent List [427] indicates that there are at least sixty-four different mobile agent frameworks, as of September 29, 1999. Therefore, it would be difficult to get all of the associated designers to agree to an expensive update of their systems, even if they could agree on a reference model.

14.2.3 Temporal and Spatial Coupling

Assuming that agents have the ability to communicate with one another, developers must also consider the spatial and temporal coupling between the agents in their systems. Spatially coupled models require that agents share a common name space [114]. Therefore, agents can communicate by explicitly naming the receiving agents. In order to support this ability, a naming or locating service is often used to prevent the need for explicit references to receiving agents' locations by the sending agents.

Spatially coupled agent systems allow agents to communicate in a peer-to-peer manner. However, the ease of communication comes at a cost of using agreed communication protocols, locations and times. It also requires the assumption that network connections and intermediate network nodes will be stable and reliable. In the case of mobile agent systems, this approach is not adequate. Since mobile agents move frequently, locating and direct messaging are expensive operations, and rely heavily on the stability of the network. Statically located agents, especially those located in the same environment, can benefit from spatially coupled models, since the protocols, locations and coordination times can be agreed upon a priori and network involvement is minimized.

Spatially uncoupled models allow agents to interact without having to name one another. With these models, the information an agent has to share and its type are more important than its name. Therefore, several different agents can serve the same purpose, making the system more redundant and less likely to fail. In addition, naming services are not required, resulting in fewer system components to manage.

Temporally coupled models imply that there is some form of synchronization between the agents. Temporal coupling is very important for spatially uncoupled models. Agents still need to agree on what to share, when to share it, and how to share it. Spatially uncoupled models put less emphasis on direct agent-to-agent communication, as the environment is used more often as the medium for information exchange. This architectural decision increases the complexity of the environment and increases its computational requirements. Moreover, the model requires that the agents share a common knowledge representation and are aware of schedules and positions for information exchange.

Temporally uncoupled models relax the synchronization requirement. Therefore, agents are no longer dependent on meeting and exchanging information with others at specific times, and they do not have to worry as much about other agents' schedules. However, this model increases the importance of knowledge representation and on how the environment is used to transfer knowledge. It is easy for two agents to communicate directly, but effective multi-agent communication (one agent with many other agents) increases the complexity of the agent.

You want it to be easy for agents to exchange information. Direct agent-to-agent messaging seems to be the best approach. There are fewer synchronization problems, as an agent can just send messages to another when it needs to. However, in the dynamic case, such as mobile agents, the implementation and execution costs of locating and getting a message to another are high and message reliability is a problem when network problems occur. Even the static solution is not without its problems. For example, it would be impossible for a large number of agents to inhabit one environment and send messages to one another. The environment would not have the computational capacity.

So you try the spatially uncoupled approach. Even with this, agents have to agree where and when to meet, and doing so at the same place causes the same overhead problem as when static agents try to send messages to one another from the same place. In addition, the environment must now handle the information exchange. Therefore, you allow agents to come and go as they please and let them leave whatever information they want to in the environment for others agents to read. However, now your environment is more complex and getting the agents' knowledge representation correct can be difficult.

14.2.4 Problem Partitioning

An agent can partition a task between others in order to increase reliability, performance and accuracy. For example, rather than have one agent look for the best airfare, why not have three, or four, or one hundred. If part of the network fails, killing a few agents, you will still get answers from the others. A benefit is that one answer may be better than the rest. In the situation where you also need to book a hotel, you could have other agents doing that task while the rest are finding the best airfare. This solution involves coordinating and collating the agents' results, which increases the overall computational effort of the global task, not only in the home environment, but also in those environments that agents visit.

The trade-off one makes between reliability, performance, accuracy, complexity and computation depends on the problem. For simple problems the overhead of partitioning is usually too large. However, more complicated problems can benefit from task partitioning.

14.2.5 Failures

You can make two assumptions with respect to failures when developing coordination models: nothing ever fails, or entities like messages, connections and even agents will fail sometimes.

The first assumption will often make the problem much easier to solve, resulting in protocols and solutions that are easy to understand. The down side is that these solutions will never work in practice.

The second assumption makes problems harder to solve, requiring more time to get them right and requiring complex solutions. The benefit is that you can use the solutions on a live network.

We all want simple solutions to problems. We also want simple solutions that work with "real" systems. Time constraints put on developers often make these two forces conflict.

14.2.6 Summary

Now that we have summarized the major forces acting on agent coordination, the remainder of this chapter covers particular patterns of agent coordination. The patterns we will cover are: Blackboard, Meeting, Market Maker, Master-Slave, and Negotiating Agents.

14.3 Blackboard Pattern

Context You already have a set of agents that are specialized to perform a particular subtask of an overall task. You need to provide a medium that allows them to monitor each other and build on their mutual progress.

Problem How to ensure the cohesion of a group of specialized agents.

Forces Agents need to collaborate to perform complex tasks that extend beyond their individual capabilities. One way to enable collaboration is to hard wire the relationships between agents, for example, through a list of acquaintances in each agent. However, this is difficult to achieve if the locations of the collaborating agents are not fixed; some agents haven't been created at the time an agent wants to interact with them; or if agents are mobile.

Agents may have been independently designed. In this case, it could be difficult to enforce a common way of representing relationships between agents that each agent has to implement. It would more suitable if the agents did not make assumptions about which specific agents will be available to collaborate with, and were built with the notion that there will be *some* agents available, unknown to the agent at design time.

The coordination protocol needed for agent collaboration can be expressed using the data access mechanisms of the coordination medium. That means that the coordination logic is embedded into the agents. Although a logical separation between algorithmic and coordination issues would provide more flexibility, the cost of a more complex coordination medium is considered too high. Keeping the interface to the coordination medium small allows agents to be easily ported to use another coordination medium.

Solution The solution to the problem involves a blackboard to which agents can add data and which allows them to subscribe for data changes in their area of interest. Agents can also update data and erase it from the blackboard. The agents continually monitor the blackboard for changes and signal when they want to add, erase or update data.

When multiple agents want to respond to a change, a supervisor agent decides which specialist agent may make a modification to the blackboard. The supervisor agent also decides when the state of the blackboard has sufficiently progressed and a solution to the complex task has been found. The supervisor only acts as a scheduler for the specialists, deciding when and whether to let a specialist modify the blackboard. It does not facilitate their interaction with each other. Note that because the blackboard is a passive coordination medium, we chose not to represent it by an agent. The structure and main interactions of this pattern are shown in figures 14.1 and 14.2.

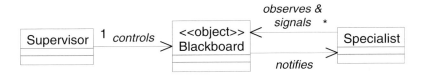

Fig. 14.1. Role diagram of the Blackboard pattern

Rationale The Blackboard pattern decouples interacting agents from each other. Instead of communicating directly, agents interact through an intermediary. This intermediary provides both time and location transparency to the interacting agents. Transparency of time is achieved because agents who want to exchange data don't have to receive it when it is sent but can pick it up later. The locations of the receiving agents are transparent in that the sending agent does not need to address any other agent specifically by its name; the mediator forwards the data accordingly.

Time transparency can not always be guaranteed when using this pattern. Shared state data may persist on the blackboard for as long as it is needed. However, events (data of a transient type) will typically not persist, unless they are converted to persistent data. In particular this implies that agents

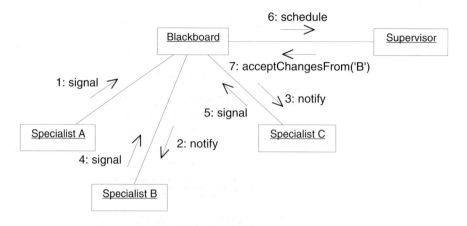

Fig. 14.2. Interactions between the participants of the Blackboard pattern

only get notified about events after they subscribe. We thus cannot uphold time transparency for event-style data when using the Blackboard pattern.

Mobility is also supported well by this pattern once a small extension is made to the protocol between specialists and the blackboard. Since exchange of non-event data is asynchronous, agents can leave data for other agents on a blackboard. Agents that arrive after the originator of the data has left the place can still read the data from the blackboard. A small change is required to the protocol between specialists and the blackboard. Upon arrival at a place that hosts a blackboard, an agent subscribes to all areas of interest. In addition, the blackboard should notify the agent about any data that was posted to the blackboard before the agent subscribed.

The blackboard is an example of a passive coordination medium. While it allows agents to share data, it does not specify how the agents are expected to react to the data they receive. In other words, all the real coordination knowledge remains hidden in the agents. The reason for this is that coordination protocols need to be expressed using the data access interface to a blackboard. If it is not possible to express a coordination protocol in this way, the agents are forced to implement the coordination protocol in their own code. Extensions of the Blackboard paradigm such as [627] and [473] avoid this, but we would therefore really consider them instances of the Market Maker pattern.

Known Uses This pattern has been documented in many forms. We can only reproduce some of the pointers to the literature here. The blackboard concept, as described here, that includes a control component, goes back to Hayes-Roth's BB1 system [298]. Various agent-based systems have employed the blackboard pattern in their design (for example, [584] and [627]). The tuple space concept originally introduced by Gelernter is another type of blackboard, although it lacks its control features [266]. Recent extensions of tuple spaces to reactive tuple spaces make them much more powerful. For the reasons expressed above, we consider this type of blackboard a broker as discussed in the Market Maker pattern (section 14.5).

14.4 Meeting Pattern

Context Agents in a system you are developing need to interact in order to coordinate their activities without the need for explicitly naming those involved in the overall task. These agents may be statically located or mobile. Direct messaging between agents and between environments and agents is possible. However, the precise time and location for agents to coordinate their activities are not known a priori.

Problem How do agents agree to coordinate their task and mediate their activities?

Forces Messaging between agents located within the same environment is fast, secure and simple. By not involving the network and its connections, agents can communicate using the built-in facilities of the environment's infrastructure. Since these infrastructures are often constructed using languages that support message passing, such as Java, communication is reliable.

Building applications that force agents to reside permanently on the same machine fails to make use of potential gains in efficiency by not allowing agents to execute partial tasks in other environments. Moreover, it is unlikely that the information sources agents require can be located on the same machine. However, remote agents will require several messages and interactions with other agents across the network to perform a task. For example, buyer and seller agents negotiating on the terms of a transaction from different locations incur a significant messaging overhead. If the amount of information is large, this can impose severe loads on remote environments providing the information and on the current environment handling the responses.

Direct interaction is a technique that people understand well. Although we may live in distant places, the phone and mail have helped us to use this form of interaction. Direct interaction between remote agents is possible, but it requires a dedicated connection between both agents' environments. This approach is not feasible when the number of agents involved in the coordination task is large since an environment can only support a small number of connections. The reliability of direct interaction is also dependent on the reliability of the network. Agents could send mail to one another, but this is slow and requires a more complex synchronization strategy to coordinate a task because of unpredictable delays.

It is easier to build applications that have agents interact (remotely or directly) with knowledge of one another's names. To send a message, all an agent has to do is use the messaging services provided by the application.

Name servers help with the mobility issue. However, application developers must now consider failures and network delays.

If agents are not required to have names, messaging to the appropriate one seems difficult. However, it does allow an application to use many different agents for the same purpose, provided they support the coordination requirements. However, using different agents for the same task raises security concerns. Is the agent helping with the task the right one for the job and will it act in a rational manner?

On the one hand, you want only the required agents, named or unnamed, to coordinate with one another. You want to minimize the number of messages passed between agents. You don't want to force them to be statically located and you want your application to be secure. On the other hand, you don't want to suffer problems due to network reliability and unpredictability. You don't want coordination to be slow or complex and you don't want to add to the load on the network.

Solution Create a place in an environment for agents to meet. Let an agent call for a meeting at that meeting place. Permit interactions to occur in the context of the meeting that enable agents to communicate and synchronize with one another in order to coordinate their activities.

The first part of the solution involves the construction of a named meeting place in the context of an existing environment. Permit agents to move to this meeting place and allow them to message to a statically located, named agent at the meeting place, called the Meeting Manager.

Consider a meeting as an event, and make the Meeting Manager responsible for notifying agents interested in a meeting when one is proposed. Therefore, the Meeting Manager and agents interested in the meeting are an instantiation of the Observer pattern [257]. The Meeting Manager accepts messages from remote or local agents wanting to register for notification of specific meetings. In their registration messages, agents must identify who they are and where they can be located. The Meeting Manager also accepts messages from remote or local agents interested in calling a meeting and informs registered agents of when the meeting will occur. Since the Meeting Manager is located at one physical location, it can make meeting announcements and registered agent information persistent, permitting it to recover its current state should the underlying node crash. The Meeting Manager has the additional responsibilities of controlling the meeting, registering agents as they arrive and deregistering them as they departure. The structure and main interactions of this pattern are shown in figures 14.3 and 14.4.

Use the solution many times if several different meetings are required. The structure of the MeetingManager handles more than one meeting and since a MeetingManager exists on each environment, meetings can occur at different places.

Rationale The solution does not completely remove the use of named agents, but it does minimize the number of names that other agents must

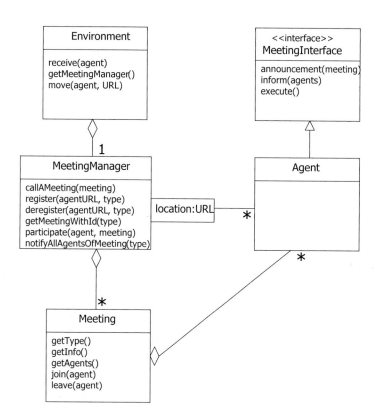

Fig. 14.3. The Meeting Role Diagram

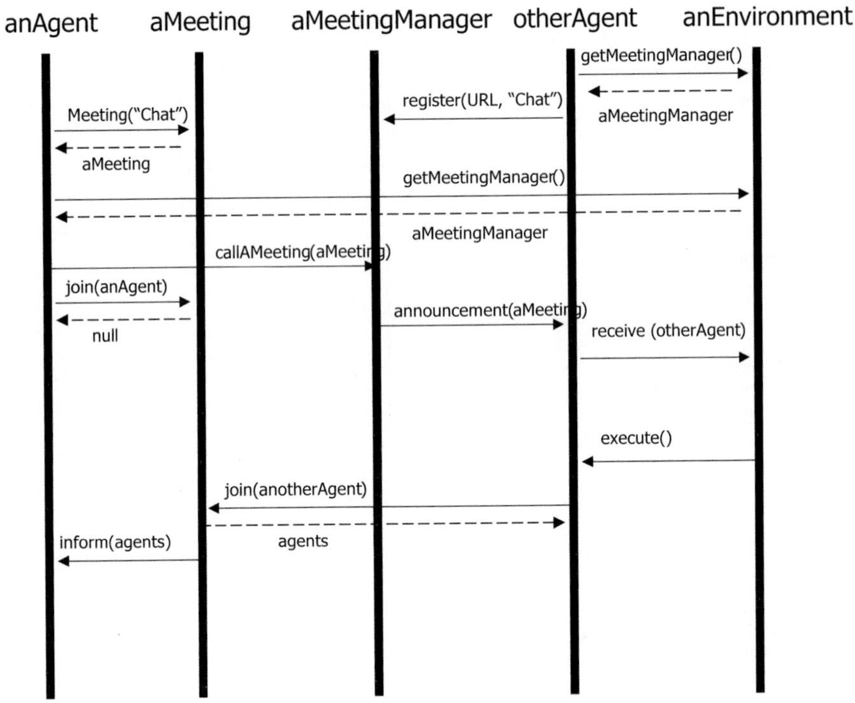

Fig. 14.4. Meeting Lifecycle Sequence Diagram

remember to one: the name of the MeetingManager – or the environment where the MeetingManager is located. The act of calling or registering for a meeting requires that all agents know about the MeetingManager. And, while it is true that the MeetingManager must know the names of the other agents in order to notify them of meetings, it is only loosely coupled to their names since agents inform the MeetingManager of their names (locations) when registering for a meeting. The MeetingManager does not have to know the names a priori.

This solution does not restrict agents from telling others about a meeting, provided they know the names of the other agents, but it does not require it. Having agents go to one place for a meeting cuts down on the overhead of messaging between agents since the network is not involved. Security is still an issue, but it can be localized to the responsibility of the environment the meeting is held at. In addition, coordination between agents is no longer susceptible to network failures or delays since all agents meet at one location. If an environment fails, the environment can use its persistent services to reinitialize the agents and the meeting to the state preceding the crash.

The solution does not restrict how agents collaborate. Once a meeting begins, it is up to the agents to decide how to proceed, athough, they must still use messages to communicate with one another.

Known uses IBM's Aglet's framework makes use of a meeting structure similar to the one shown here [41]. Concordia [638] uses the pattern's MeetingManager for its EventManager, which manages group-oriented events enabling collaborating agents to communicate. Place-oriented communication [360] is another example of where a community of agents can coordinate and cooperate with one another by moving to a single place to exchange information.

14.5 Market Maker Pattern

Context Your agent system evolves constantly. Instead of setting up relationships between agents up-front you let the agents locate appropriate transaction partners on-the-fly.

Problem How to match up buyers and sellers of goods (services or resources).

Forces Agents need to collaborate to perform complex tasks that extend beyond their individual capabilities. As discussed for the Blackboard pattern, one could hard wire the relationships between the agents, but this isn't always practical.

Again, the agents may have been independently designed. In this case, it would more suitable, if the agents did not make assumptions about which specific other agents will be available for collaboration.

Embedding the coordination logic into the agents would notably increase the agents' complexity. It would also affect the global application design, because now coordination rules are distributed between the coordination medium and the agent. Although a logical separation between algorithmic and coordination issues increases the cost of the coordination mechanism, you need the flexibility to implement and modify coordination protocols, while keeping any changes hidden from the collaborating agents.

Solution The solution involves a broker or market maker that accepts requests from buyers for bids for goods (resources or services) and matches them up with sellers. The broker handles the coordination logic needed to advertise requests to sellers, collect their bids, and introduce the selected seller to the buyer. To emphasize that agents may play the roles of buyers and sellers at the same time, we have introduced the role of a trader that contains the buyer and seller roles. The structure of this pattern is shown in figure 14.5.

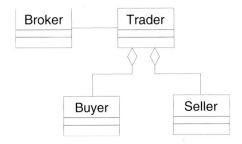

Fig. 14.5. Role diagram of the Market Maker pattern

Like a real-estate broker, the broker does not simply select a matching seller on behalf of a buyer, but leaves the ultimate choice between multiple bids to the buyer. The rationale for this is that the individual definitions of what buyers consider a "good" fit may be different from one buyer to another, depending on what attributes of the requested good they care most about (such as cost or quality of service).

The broker, acting on behalf of the buyer, sends requests for bids to all sellers. The seller agents decide if they want to provide the good requested and submit bids, which may also spell out any attached conditions that constrain their ability or willingness to provide the good. For example, sellers may ask for a minimum price to be paid for the good. The broker, now acting on behalf of the sellers, presents the list of bids to the buyer requiring it to select the "appropriate" bid. It then sets up a direct relationship between the chosen seller and the buyer, which lasts until the good has been delivered (for a service that is the whole duration of providing the service). Figure 14.6 shows the main interactions of this pattern.

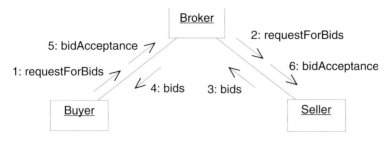

Fig. 14.6. Interactions between the participants of the Market Maker pattern

Rationale The broker at the core of this pattern is an example of a coordination medium that takes an active role in the coordination process. The broker essentially enforces the house rules of agent interaction. These other agents are therefore delegating their coordination duties to the broker. Agent designers only need to define the application logic, not the coordination protocol.

Once buyers have located appropriate sellers, they may still need to negotiate the terms of the transaction (such as the delivery conditions). This leads to the Negotiating Agents pattern.

Known Uses There are many accounts of the Market Maker pattern in the literature. One of the first examples is the Contract Net protocol pioneered by Smith [561]. Wellman's market-oriented programming framework supports a variety of auction types each imposing a set of market rules on the agent interactions [647]. Freeman [249] describes a marketplace framework based on the JavaSpaces technology that allows producers and consumers to interact to find the best deal. The MAGNET market infrastructure [569] provides support for a variety of transactions, from simple buying and selling to multi-contract negotiations. Our formulation of the pattern has also been influenced by the role-based agent modelling approach practiced at BT [181].

14.6 Master-Slave Pattern

Context You decide to partition a task into subtasks to increase the reliability, performance, or accuracy of its execution.

Problem How to delegate subtasks and coordinate their execution.

Forces An agent can partition a task, and delegate subtasks to other agents in order to improve the reliability, performance, or accuracy with which the task is performed. For example, while an agent has other agents working on subtasks, the agent could continue with its own work in parallel. In particular, an agent can move to a remote host to execute a subtask there and offload work from the client host. However, this solution also increases the overall computation effort of the global task. Simple problems may not benefit from partitioning for this reason.

Whether a task is partitioned or not, this should remain transparent to clients. When the task is partitioned the agent could return a set of partial results back to the client. However, the client may not be capable of processing the separate results and synthesizing them into one solution. It doesn't want to be concerned with the internals of the computation. As an aside, this is a principle that PC and operating system makers mostly seem to violate.

Solution The solution to these forces involves a master who divides the task into subtasks, delegating the subtasks to slaves and computing a final result from the partial results returned. In the process the master creates a slave for each subtask and dispatches it to a remote host. While the slave computes the partial result to the task it has been assigned, the master can continue its work. When the slaves have all finished their work, the master compiles the final result and returns it to the client. The structure of the pattern is shown in figure 14.7.

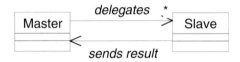

Fig. 14.7. Role diagram of the Master-Slave pattern

In the basic pattern the slaves are created by the master and then move to a remote host to perform their tasks. Upon completion they send their results back to the master. The slaves then dispose of themselves. In a variation of the pattern, the slaves exist permanently in remote locations and can be assigned new tasks once they have completed their current task. Figure 14.8 shows the main interactions of this pattern.

A typical application of the Master-Slave pattern is parallel computation. A number of slaves can be assigned to a work pool which is controlled by a master. Each of the slaves offers the same services. Clients send their requests to the master that handles these requests by dividing each one into subtasks and dispatching them to idle slaves in the work pool.

Rationale The Master-Slave pattern is an example where vertical coordination is used to coordinate the activity of two or more agents. Vertical coordination is an interaction where one agent carries out a subtask for another agent, but this subtask is still logically part of the former agent's task. The term was introduced by Collins [180] in the context of a new theory of action.

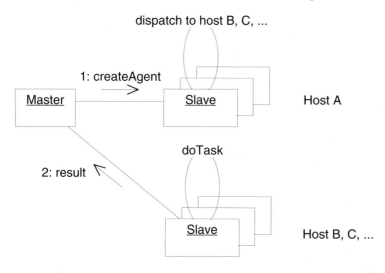

Fig. 14.8. Interactions between the participants of the Master-Slave pattern

Known Uses The Master-Slave pattern has its roots in parallel computation. Consult [131] for a much more detailed account of various applications of this pattern. Descriptions in patterns format first appeared in [104] (using objects) and [41] (using agents). The primary distinction between the object and the agent formulations of the pattern is that the agent pattern specifically accounts for mobility, where the object pattern does not.

14.7 Negotiating Agents Pattern

Context In your application agents interact as peers. That may cause them to give conflicting instructions to the environment.

Problem How to detect and resolve conflicting intentions between agents.

Forces Agents need to align their actions, because this can be useful, desirable, or even essential to the achievement of their individual goals. One possible solution is for each of the agents to implement the "ostrich's algorithm", that is, to ignore the possibility of conflicts and respond to them only after they have occurred. The disadvantage of this algorithm is that it may not always be possible to rollback the agents' and the environment's states to where they were before the conflict happened. For example, an instruction to the environment may be to forward a call to a blocked number. By the time the conflict is detected, the phone might already have been picked up at the receiving end.

Solution These forces drive a solution where the agents make their intentions explicit. For example, they exchange constraints on what the other agents are allowed to do. In response to the intentions disclosed by other agents, the agents may replan their actions to avoid detected interactions with their own intentions. Replanning involves choosing among alternative courses of action.

In selecting alternative courses of action, agents are guided by policies such as giving preference to one kind of action over another or maximizing the utility associated with their actions. The agents subsequently exchange their revised intentions with each other. The exchange of intentions and subsequent replanning proceeds until the agents manage to align their actions, or if they reach an impasse which makes further negotiation futile.

The solution involves an initiator who starts a negotiation round by declaring its intention to its peers, which are all the other agents who must be consulted before the initiator can go ahead with its action as intended. The peers take on the role of critics in the negotiation. They test if there is a conflict between the declared intention and their own intended course of action. If there is none, a critic accepts the proposed action, otherwise it makes a counter-proposal or rejects the action outright. Counter-proposals contain alternative actions that are acceptable to the critic. Rejections indicate that there is an impasse that can only be handled outside the negotiation framework. Figure 14.9 shows the structure of this pattern.

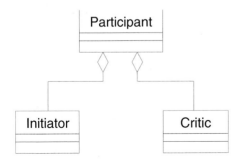

Fig. 14.9. Role diagram of the Negotiating Agents pattern

An agent can be an initiator and a critic in different negotiations at the same time. Therefore we create another role, that of a participant, which contains the initiator and critic roles. Participants often act on behalf of other agents for whom they are negotiating. For instance, an initiator may negotiate on behalf of a buyer agent about the terms of a transaction. Once the terms have been determined the buyer pays the negotiated amount to the seller and receives the good. The main interactions of this pattern are shown in figure 14.10.

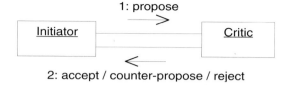

Fig. 14.10. Interactions between the participants of the Negotiating Agents pattern

For purpose of illustration, consider that agents represent their alternative courses of actions as an AND/OR tree as in figure 14.11. AND nodes
designate a set (possibly a sequence) of actions that needs to be performed
together, or not at all. OR nodes indicate choices between alternative action
trees. This model of actions is fairly generic as the literature suggests (for example, [53] or the recent work on the theory of actions by Collins [180]). But
it is by no means all-inclusive. This should be kept in mind when applying
this solution.

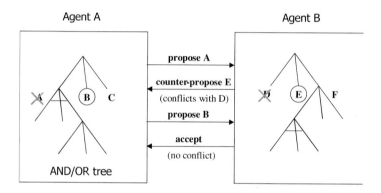

Fig. 14.11. Example of using the pattern

In the example, agent A decides to perform action A. Before it goes ahead
with its execution, however, it publishes its intention to do so to its peer, agent
B (propose A). Assume that B detects a conflict between the proposed action
and its own action D that it was about to perform. B therefore searches
for an alternative, and, via backtracking, arrives at action E. B makes a
corresponding counter-proposal to A. Agent A can now rule out action A
and search itself for an alternative course of action, which it finds in B. Upon
receiving the updated proposal, B agrees by accepting the action proposed
by A. A and B now proceed by executing their actions B and E.

Rationale The Negotiating Agents pattern deals with the situation where
the interacting agents appear as peers to each other, but need to align their

actions for some reason. Unlike the Master-Slave pattern, the tasks of the interacting agents are not instances of one agent's carrying out another agent's subtask. We refer to this type of coordination as horizontal.

Once you adopt the key idea in this pattern that agents declare their intentions to each other, there is a multitude of protocols that the agents can follow in their negotiation. The example given serves only as an illustration; many other protocols are possible. This suggests that there is a whole pattern language for agent negotiation waiting to be written, with this pattern only providing the root from which the other, more specific patterns descend.

Known Uses This pattern is popular in the telecommunications [288] and the supply-chain domains [53]. In the first domain an example may involve two agents controlling different parties in a phone call. The agents interact with the underlying switch by listening for events and independently proposing a next action in response to these events. The actions proposed by the agents may, however, conflict with each other. For example, the callee's agent proposes to forward the call to another destination, but the caller does not want to be connected to this destination. If instead, the callee's agent identifies its intention to forward the call, the caller's agent is now able to reject that action. As a result the call is not forwarded.

The concept of market sessions in MAGNET [569] also exemplifies this pattern. Sessions encapsulate a transaction on the market. Agents can play two roles with regard to a session. The agent that initiates a session is known as the session initiator, while the other participating agents are known as session clients. The supply chain role model in the ZEUS agent building toolkit introduces similar roles: negotiation initiator and partner [181].

14.8 Summary

We have provided only a small sampling of the possible coordination patterns. Since assembling related patterns and positioning them relative to others will form a pattern language that ultimately increases the generative quality of the patterns, we encourage others to develop coordination patterns. We believe that agent pattern languages are essential for the future success of agent systems. They are not only helpful to you, but also to all the software engineers who will use the patterns to develop their systems in the future.

15. Inter–Organizational Workflows for Enterprise Coordination

Monica Divitini[1], Chihab Hanachi[2], and Christophe Sibertin–Blanc[3]

[1] Norwegian University of Science and Technology
email: Monica.Divitini@idi.ntnu.no
[2] University Toulouse I
Place Anatole France, 31042 Toulouse, France
email: hanachi@univ-tlse1.fr
[3] IRIT/University Toulouse I
Place Anatole France, 31042 Toulouse, France
email: sibertin@univ-tlse1.fr

Summary.

Workflow systems are widely adopted by organizations for supporting business processes. In particular, workflow systems help organizations to coordinate the different actors involved in the business process by automating repetitive tasks and facilitating the distribution of documents, information, and control. Today's workflow systems however do not adequately support processes that cross the boundaries of multiple organizations. The enhancement of workflow systems in this direction, *Inter-Organizational Workflows* (IOWs), is essential given the growing need for organizations to cooperate and coordinate their activities in order to meet the new demands of highly dynamic markets. This paper starts by describing some of the issues related to the collaboration among organizations, pointing out a number of factors that can impact on the required support. After having introduced the basic terminology of traditional workflow and workflow systems, the chapter outlines some requirements for IOW, distinguishing between loose and tight IOW. *Loose IOWs* refer to occasional cooperation, free of structural constraints, where neither the involved partners nor their relationships are defined a priori. *Tight IOWs* refer to a structural cooperation among organizations, i.e., a cooperation based on a well-established infrastructure among pre-defined partners. Based on this distinction and the related requirements, the chapter presents two approaches to the design and the implementation of IOWs. The first approach adopts the notion of software agents for enhancing workflow systems and allowing their use in loose IOWs. The second approach, which can be supported by an agent based implementation, combines Petri Nets and Federated Databases for providing the more structured support needed by tight IOWs. Both approaches are compliant with the Workflow Management Coalition reference architecture. This guarantees the possibility to tailor the support provided by the IOW to the needs of the collaborating organizations, remaining within a coherent framework of reference.

15.1 Inter-Organizational Coordination

The last decade has witnessed the emerging of new and numerous forms of cooperation among organizations. Various factors, like the emerging of a global economy and more dynamic markets, require combining different competencies in a flexible and ad-hoc manner in order to meet the changing requirements of the market. The realization of these needs is made possible by the widespread of Internet and of network and infrastructural facilities. Thanks to technology, communication is eased and geographical distances are reduced. People, within or without organizations can dynamically join to work on a project, organizations can restructure themselves into teams, possibly outsourcing a relevant part of their activities. In this way varied types of cooperation are recognizable, going from electronically linked organizations with no conventional boundaries, up to distributed "traditional" organizations with multiple modes of communication [625]. Cooperation can take place within a long-term project, e.g. a strategic alliance among organizations covering complementary business niches, as well as within the context of shorter business processes like those set up in Electronic Commerce for satisfying a specific customer's request.

It is clear that these forms of organizational cooperation are characterized by varying degrees of physicality, as well as varying degrees of heterogeneity or coherence among the participants, being them individuals or smaller organizations. What is in common to all of them is the need to have work flowing through several enterprises to achieve a common goal. Therefore, it dramatically emerges the need to *coordinate* the distributed effort of such a polyedric reality.

In this chapter the term coordination indicates the work needed for "... putting together tasks, task sequences, task clusters, and even the work done in aligning larger units such as subprojects, in order to accomplish the work" [570]. It is all the overhead work that is required in order to make cooperation possible, the price to pay whenever the work to be done requires the orchestrated contributions of more than one individual.

In general, the more distributed the activities to perform are (in terms of time, space, knowledge, organizational backgrounds and the like), the more complex it becomes to coordinate them [535]. In order to support coordination, organizations have developed in the years different mechanisms for specifying the "expected" flow of work, mainly in the form of work procedures and business processes. These mechanisms are intended to support the cooperating actors by describing their expected behavior while working with recurrent coordination activities. For example, a work procedure "Insurance claim" can describe the steps that each actor involved in an insurance claim has to take (e.g., for the customer: fill in form, submit form to secretary; for the secretary: forward form to the appropriate employee, register claim, and the likes). The procedure is an experimented means to reach a business goal and its observance reduces the need to renegotiate the patterns of interaction among co-workers under standard condition.

The capabilities of organizations and individuals of handling the complexity of coordination can be augmented thanks to computer-based technology.

Many systems have been developed lately with this purpose, e.g., scheduler and group calendars. Among these tools, workflows are of foremost importance for organizations. They developed as an evolution of the office information systems of the 1970s [220]. A *workflow* is "an automation of a business process, in a whole or a part, during which documents, information or tasks are passed from one participant to another for action, according to a set of procedural rules" [646]. This definition is provided by the Workflow Management Coalition, a non-profit international organization for the development and promotion of workflow standards.

Given the definition of a workflow, a *Workflow Management System* (WfMS), or workflow system for short, is the software that helps organizations to specify, analyze, execute and monitor workflows.

Different types of workflow systems have been developed both as research prototypes and commercial products. Among the research prototypes are, e.g., Regatta [576], MILANO [13], APM [127], and WIDE [287]. Among the products are, e.g., ATI ActionWorkflow^{TM}, Xsoft InConcert^{TM}, and TeamWARE Flow^{TM}. (See [566] for an evaluation of different workflow products.). An agreed-upon taxonomy of workflow systems is still missing, though they are often characterized in terms of the type of process that they support: administrative, production, ad-hoc, and collaborative [396].

Workflow systems have been in use for many years and successes and failures on their adoption have been reported in the literature, see for example [502, 88]. These experiences have allowed improving the existing tools, resulting in a growing number of installations. However, supporting the flow of work across different organizations arises challenges that are only partially supported by the existing tools. Considering the complexity of coordinating work across organizations, the extension of WfMS to support these situations is of paramount importance. In the following, we will refer to these workflows as *Inter-Organizational Workflows* (IOW).

The availability of low-level tools which ease distributed objects interoperability (OMG technology and especially Corba) and of Internet provides a basic "communication" infrastructure. However, many of the problems emerging in the new working contexts cannot be solved at this level. In fact, semantic interoperability at the workflow and business level is still a challenge [483] and current WfMS are too rigid.

Overcoming rigidity is already a key issue in traditional workflow systems. Flexibility is required in order to adapt to business process evolution, often in connection to Business Process Reengineering [575], and for handling exceptions [219]. Moreover, in workflow systems, flexibility opens the problem of assuring correct and reliable workflow executions independently by changes in the process. Different solutions have been proposed. Some of these solutions focus on the model of the business process, e.g., [221]. Others have proposed to extend the notion of database transactions to workflow, in order to support the consistent and reliable execution of business processes in a multi-user environment, e.g., [216].

However, in IOW systems flexibility takes also new meanings because they have to answer to extremely varied needs and they have to take into account the different dimensions that characterize the different forms of cooperation. Among these, we recall:

- Time spanning of the cooperation, i.e. short time vs. long time interactions. For example, the organizations are joining for a transaction, a single project or are combined into an alliance.
- Typology of actors involved. In general, when we talk about actors in IOW, we can have individuals, software agents, departments, and organizations.
- Coupling of the actors, e.g. to what extent the actors involved in the IOW can be identified or identify themselves as a single supra-organization, with specified policies, strategies, and the likes.
- Motive for cooperation: sharing skills, sharing resources.
- The properties of the data and information that are exchanged and shared by the organization: amount, complexity, confidentiality, volatility, etc.

All these dimensions imply that IOW must support not only organizationally defined procedures, but also coordination as an emerging phenomenon in the cooperation among organizations [213]. In fact, given the heterogeneity of the possible contexts of use, in terms of policies, objectives, authorities, local and global commitments, security, it is not always conceivable the definition of a global business process, not is possible to provide a unique organizational view of how work is arranged.

In relation to the different forms of cooperation outlined by the dimensions mentioned above, it is necessary to distinguish two main cases with respect to the definition of the flow of work in terms of business process:

- No definition of a process, but only of a common goal with self-organization of the parties that are involved. Coordination is realized through awareness and explicit communication. Information sharing is key to this types of IOWs.
- Detailed definition of a process, with different degree of tailorability of the tasks by the actors.

In both cases, policies and constraints can be defined locally to the actors or globally for all of them, and they determine the degree of freedom for organizations to organize the part of work under their responsibility, as they prefer.

These two main cases deeply impact on the type of support that the IOW system can provide. Common to all the IOW is however the need to find a balance between, on one hand, the need to explicitly define processes for reducing the complexity of coordinating the work to be done, and on the other hand the dynamic nature of work contexts that makes these processes "unstable". In fact, the speed of changes in modern work environments is increasing

[175] and people working in these dynamic conditions need to adapt both to local contingencies and to completely new demands from their environment. Moreover, the dynamicity of the environment impacts the cooperative ensemble itself, e.g., new organizations can join the IOW for integrating new competencies, or the responsibilities of the single organizations can change according to the changes in the market. This dynamicity calls for continuous changes in the way the work is performed and thereby coordinated, requiring changes to the defined process. For example, the "insurance claim" procedure can be changed for taking into account the outsourcing of the claim verification to a new organization.

The rest of the chapter is organized as follows. Section 15.2 introduces some of the main concepts related to Workflow systems. This is essential for providing a shared background and a common terminology for Inter-Organizational Workflow. Section 15.3 describes the requirements for IOWs and introduces a framework for their study. Two opposite scenarios are identified and their requirements developed. Section 15.4 presents two comprehensive approaches to design and implement IOW: an agent-enhanced approach and another one combining Petri Nets and Federated Databases. Each approach fits the needs of one scenario.

15.2 Overview of Main Concepts of Workflow

This section recalls the necessary workflow concepts for clarifying the vocabulary and underlining the most relevant criteria which should be investigated later on, in the context of Inter-Organizational Workflows. We shall present the main issues that cover a workflow lifecycle:

- Workflow conceptual models, which provide an answer to the question: What to define, i.e. what are the entities involved in a workflow?
- Workflow definition languages, i.e.: How must workflows be expressed? Or, What is the expressive power required for their definition?
- Execution models, i.e.: How should workflow models be executed?
- Architecture and implementation issues, i.e.: How to design and implement software supporting the three previous issues?

Furthermore, there are two different stages in a workflow life-cycle which must be well-identified and distinguished since they structure the workflow domain and determine possible architectures for the WfMS:

- *Build time* during which a designer builds, analyzes and simulates the workflow model;
- *Run time* during which occurrences of the workflow model (called cases) are initiated and executed under the control of a WfMS which schedules and assigns tasks to the appropriate performers (person, machine, or software).

15.2.1 Workflow Conceptual Models

A workflow model consists of three models: the organizational model, the information model, and the process model. They are described below.

The *organizational model* (OM) has two roles. First, it structures resources in classes of objects sharing the same characteristics. A class is called a *role* when it comprises agents having the same capabilities, and an *organizational unit* for agents belonging to a same organization structure. Second, the organizational model attributes to each resource authorization to perform tasks. Roles and Organizational Units are abstraction that can be used to define business processes without referring explicitly to the individual participants in a workflow, but rather to the quality they must have. In real time, the WfMS assigns the tasks to individual performers. Therefore, change of individuals has no consequence for the workflow definition. Moreover, we distinguish two assignment modes: the *pull* and the *push* modes. In the push mode, the WfMS dispatches a given work to a performer even if he has not asked for it. In the pull mode, tasks are recorded in the worklist of each authorized performer who can decide when to perform it. As soon as a performer pulls a task, it is removed from all the worklists where it was recorded. It is important to stress that an OM also defines authorizations to perform meta-level tasks as defining new processes, enacting cases, and, particularly important, modifying process definitions or occurrences. For example, a unit manager can be allowed to change the procedure for travel reimbursement; an executive secretary can be allowed to change the procedure in a specific case (the reimbursement of travel A for employee X), but not globally.

The *information model* (IM) describes the structure of the forms, documents, and data that are used and produced by a workflow. Even if the structure of this information is not necessarily defined in the context of a workflow, since it often pre-exists to workflow creation, the model of this information must be known in order to be exploited. In particular, the existence and the values of this information determines whether a task is likely to be executed or not (pre-condition of a task). Three types of data in connection with a WfMS are usually distinguished:

- *Workflow relevant data* created and used during workflow enactment.
- *System and environmental data* internal to the WfMS and describing the progress of each workflow instance through time. They provide a view on the current state of each instance and facilitate recovery.
- *Application data* manipulated by external tools.

The *(business) process model* (PM) defines the component tasks, their coordination, and the information and performers involved in each task. This model refers to both the organizational model, which defines and organizes the set of potential performers, and the information model, which allows access to the objects to be processed. A process model is described with a language, formal or not, able to express different forms of task coordination (e.g., parallel and sequential routing, split, join, iteration). Generally, a task includes the following items: an identity, a pre-condition describing a situation (resources or data availability, event occurences) that must be satisfied to start the task, an action which corresponds to the activity to perform, and a post-condition establishing the configuration to reach in order to consider the task as completed.

15.2.2 Workflow Description Language

To define a workflow we need languages to express the three models described in the previous section. There are a great number of languages, nearly as many as the number of existing systems (e.g., DartFlow [119], Panta Rhei [217], WebWork [417], WIDE [140]). The information model is usually described with a data description language (Entity-Relationship, Relational or object). Most of the time, the organizational model is mapped onto a data model in order to be easily accessed by the WfMS, so that the information and the organizational models are both described with the same data description language. Sometimes, actor assignment policies are expressed with rules to add more flexibility and dynamicity. On the other hand, processes are specified with formalisms able to express behavior like Petri Nets, State Charts, or Active Rules. The ideal language would be one with a very large expressive power to describe the three models in a uniform way, or at least languages allowing interactions between these models. For example, the WIDE system [140] has its own Workflow Description Language with a specific graphic interface; it relies on Active Databases which provide on the one hand a data description language to define the information and the organizational models, and on the other hand active rules to express processes.

Given the focus of this chapter on coordination, we will now concentrate on the process description since, in this perspective, it constitutes the core concept of workflows.

As an example, consider the process that allows an employee to obtain the required authorization to travel. First he (or she) initiates the process by creating a new `TravelRequest` form. Then, information about the location, the expenses and the subject have to be feed in any order. Using the location and expenses information, the Financial Manager gives his agreement or not, while using expenses and subject information, the Team Manager gives his agreement or not. If both agree, the Big Chief gives or not the final agreement while in the other cases the authorization is denied. Figure 15.1 shows the Petri Net model of this process:

- The *transitions* represent the tasks that can be performed during the process.
- The *places* stand for the state of the process, and they may contain data referred to as *tokens*; the input places of a transition correspond to the

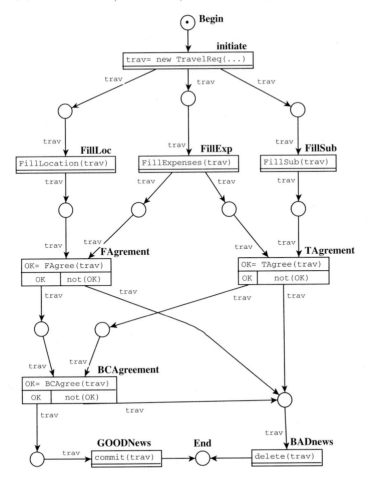

Fig. 15.1. The travel authorization workflow process

enabling conditions of the transition's task, while the output places correspond to the state resulting from the task achievement.
- The *variables* along the arcs correspond to the data that flow from a place
to a transition (the task needs data in this state and will use them) or from
a transition to a place (the task achievement sets a data in this state). In
this example, the variable trav is a reference toward the informational
entity of type TravelRequest that has been created by the initiate task
and is stored in the Information Model Database.

At the very beginning of the process, only the initial Begin condition
is fulfilled so that only the initiate task may occur. Then, the tasks are
concurrently or sequentially enabled according to the flow of tokens, until the
GoodNews or the BadNews task allows the reach the End final state. The task

allocation specification (stating which (kind of) actor may perform each task) is not shown in this definition. This can be done in various ways, namely in introducing places concerning the state of the actors registered in the Organizational Model Database.

The general features usually expected from a Process Definition Language are the following:

- *A graphical interface* which eases the process definition.
- *Different levels of granularity* in the definition of tasks to allow reuse and progressive definition of processes. This is made possible thanks to abstraction mechanisms. For example, the Panta Rhei Workflow Description Language [217] supports the nesting of activities (tasks). Thus, an activity within a WF can be expanded itself as a workflow process. The WIDE system [140] supports subprocess, supertask and multitask. The first two constructors are modularization units, while the multi-task makes possible the simultaneous execution of several copies of the same task.
- *An appropriate expressive power* to allow the description of:
  1. *Tasks' structure*, and particularly their pre-conditions, actions, and post-conditions. Pre-conditions correspond to several types of events (e.g., temporal, predicate, database queries). Actions may be manual and therefore linked to the organizational model, or automated and linked to applications.
  2. *Control flow* especially conventional constructors like parallel and sequential routing, split, join, or iteration.
  3. *Data flow* that defines the path that must be followed by the data. Often, the expression of control flow and data flow are mixed.
  4. *Transactions* to guarantee consistent and reliable executions. Database transactions structure the actions performed on a database to guarantee its transition from a coherent state to another. When a transaction fails, all its already executed actions are undone and the database previous state is restored. In workflow systems, processes are long-living, cooperative and complex (comparatively to conventional transactions consisting of a few read and write actions) and consequently conventional transaction mechanisms do not apply. Indeed, it is not reasonable to systematically undo all the tasks made in the context of a process but we need more flexible attitudes relaxing the classical ACID properties (Atomicity, Consistency, Isolation, Durability). Extended transaction mechanisms (like saga, contracts, nested transactions), fitting workflow requirements, must be used and made available at build time [632].
  5. *Failure and exception handling* ranging from technical failures (system and software) to unexpected semantics exceptions which manifest themselves by inconsistencies between a running case and its corresponding workflow description [139].
- *An operational semantics* enabling an easy mapping from specification to implementation;

- *Theoretical foundations* allowing analysis and validations of behavioral properties;
- *Simulation facilities.*

[378] provides an interesting and extensive comparison of different workflow formalisms (Wide, Flow Mark, Action, StateCharts, Triggers) with regard to some of these requirements.

15.2.3 Workflow Execution Model

The workflow execution model defines how the workflow interpreter (engine) behaves once a workflow has been defined. There is no single algorithm for the execution since there are many alternatives depending on:

- How transactions are treated;
- How tasks are selected (conflict resolution);
- How tasks are assigned (push or pull mode);
- How exceptions are handled.

Thus, the workflow interpreter must be provided with knowledge to decide, according to the context, what task to perform (in the case of alternatives among several enabled tasks); when to perform (in the case of several possible schedules); where to perform an operation that may be executed on more than one site and/or by different engines; and possibly by whom in push mode. There are several possible execution models depending on these choices. A general algorithm of a workflow engine that executes a process looks like the following one:

Algorithm ProcessExecution
       ActiveTask = 0 //number of tasks in progress
       Repeat
          While some tasks are Enabled and NotAssigned **do**
              Select a task T
              Assign T
              ActiveTask=ActiveTask +1
          EndWhile
          If (ActiveTask > 0) and (no task is completed) **Then**
              Wait(task completion)
          Endif
          For each completed Task
              ActiveTask=ActiveTask -1
          End For
       Until Process is completed
          // may coincide with (No task is enabled) and (ActiveTask=0)
End

15.2.4 WfMS Architecture and Implementation

A WfMS supports three main functions:

– The definition of workflows;
– The execution of workflows;
– The administration of workflows and the monitoring of their executions.

The WfMC has proposed an architecture including these three functions (see Figure 15.2). This abstract architecture, which is followed by most systems, is organized around six components:

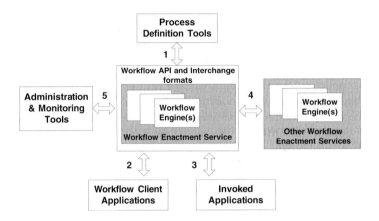

Fig. 15.2. The Workflow reference architecture [645]

– The *Workflow Enactment Service* supports the execution of workflow processes. For that purpose, it may use one or several workflow engines and invoke the other components through interfaces (numbered 1 to 5) based on set of API calls. The Workflow enactment service drives the execution of each case by interpreting its definition.
– The *Workflow Definition Tools* help the workflow designer in specifying and analyzing workflow models.
– The *Workflow-Client Applications* invoke the Workflow Enactment Service and enable the end user to interact with the WfMS. For example, client applications may ask the worklist handler to retrieve the list of works corresponding to a given performer.
– *Invoked Applications* are called by the Workflow Engine to perform a task. For example, a DBMS may be called to retrieve information needed by the workflow or to store information produced by it.
– *Administration and Monitoring tools* enable the workflow administrator to set parameters, follow workflow executions through time and react to possible problems.

– *Other WfMSs* may be connected to the current one via interface 4.

The interfaces supporting the communication between the different components are being unified and standardized by the WfMC under the term Workflow Application Programming Interface (WAPI). WAPI is made of a set of API, interchange formats and protocols. However, as observed by [607], this proposition remains at a technical level since it only specifies syntax features while semantic features, and consequently conceptual consensus, are required.

Besides, the WfMC architecture remains general since the components are not decomposed and specified precisely. For example, concerning the Workflow Enactment Service, there are still many choices to make:

– Its decomposition into modules (scheduler, transaction-manager, etc);
– The modular definition of these modules with a high-level formalism (Object, Agent, etc);
– The way these modules share data (message passing, repository, client-server model, mediator);
– Their control (e.g., centralized, distributed, event-driven).

Once refined, this architecture must be implemented. Regarding design and implementation, one desirable requirement is an easy mapping between the conceptual formalisms and the implementation language.

Workflow systems can exploit various existing technologies. In [2], for example, the authors distinguish between e-mail and database driven workflows. The first use electronic mail for the routing and the presentation of work to users. An example of this class of systems is given by MILANO [13]. The second class is based on database technology, generally for storing routing and status information. Examples of workflows of this type are WIDE [139] and Pantha Rei [217]. Workflows of this type are generally more robust, but also more complex to use and configure. Lately, a number of workflow systems have started adopting the Web as technical infrastructure, focusing on distribution and accessibility. Examples of such systems are WebFlow [285], WebWork [417], and DartFlow [119]. WebWork has the particularity to be completely implemented with web-technology (Web browsers, Web servers, HTML, java script and CGI). DartFlow combines Web technology and Agent Tcl. A Process is initiated by filling a form which in its turn dynamically creates an Agent to fulfill the process. Each agent transports with itself the description of the process it must perform.

15.3 Inter-Organizational Workflow Requirements: A Framework for Studying IOW

Now that we have defined the concepts and the vocabulary of workflows, let us make clear the requirements for Inter-Organizational Workflows. First, we outline the computing context in which IOW may be deployed and identify two main IOW scenarios to illustrate the presentation. Then, we examine general and key issues of IOWs. Finally, we provide a structuring and systematic framework in which requirements can be investigated. Within this framework, we examine the requirements of the two proposed scenarios.

15.3.1 Context and Possible Scenarios for IOWs

The *computing context* in which IOW takes place has several characteristics:

- *Heterogeneity*, which apart from interconnectivity issues, concerns the differences in structure, syntax, and semantics of the workflow models in each organization.
- *Distribution*, which manifests itself by the geographical dispersion of information, resources, processes and control, and which consequently implies defining infrastructure to make them interact.
- *Autonomy*, which requires that each organization participating in an IOW should be able to decide by itself the conditions of the cooperation, i.e. when, how, and with whom. Besides, the organization should be able to preserve the control over local tasks of the IOW, and maintain the privacy of other tasks.
- *The technological environment*, made up also of legacy systems, which must be preserved and exploited rather than ignored. On the other hand, the emergence of Web-based technology must be integrated since it provides many facilities to ease communication and interoperability between different organizations.

Without an application in mind, IOW requirements cannot be precisely examined. Consequently, we have identified two main scenarios, representative of a large class of applications, and leading to quite different requirements:

- *Loose IOW* refers to occasional cooperation, free of structural constraints, where the partners involved and their number are not pre-defined. For example, the cooperation of organizations in the context of Electronic Commerce generally falls into this scenario.
- *Tight IOW* refers to a structural cooperation among organizations. A structural cooperation means a cooperation based on a well-established infrastructure among pre-defined partners. This kind of IOW is necessary when the organizations involved are engaged in a long-term cooperation and when a strong interdependence between their workflows (business processes) exists. This interdependency manifests itself by frequent interactions between workflow cases of the different enterprises, and consequently by the need to synchronize several cases running simultaneously.

Obviously, there is a continuum of scenarios between these two extremes depending on the level of structural constraints between the partners, the presence or otherwise of interaction between cases, and the nature of this interaction.

In the *loose scenario*, the computing context has two additional features:

– *Openness*, meaning that the composition of an IOW could evolve through time and that it is not necessarily fixed a priori but should be decided dynamically at runtime.
– *Scalability*, inherent to Internet, that increases the complexity of the system to be modeled.

15.3.2 General and Key Requirements

In the environment described in the previous sub-section, IOW raises a lot of specific problems which concern at the same time component WfMS in a group of WfMSs (*local issues*), and the group of WfMSs viewed as an entity (*global issues*).

The first class of problems is related to the social abilities of a WfMS, e.g.:

– Cooperating with other WfMSs, which assumes sharing workflow description (information, organization and process models), workflow relevant data and workflow activity (execution).
– Reasoning, which assumes modeling knowledge and capabilities concerning the other WfMSs.

The problems that are specific to the WfMS group concern:

– The organization and architecture of the group, their coordination and the common protocols and commitments that enable them to cooperate.
– The common information needed for the cooperation, and which must be set up and maintained.

In addition, IOW must generically guarantee properties such as:

– *Adaptability.* Inter-Organizational Workflows must be "adaptable" to a wide variety of conditions, from the ones that require only a macro definition of the process to the ones that require a strict definition of all the steps in order, for example, to guarantee process quality. Moreover, since situations that involve IOW are highly dynamic it is necessary for the IOW to provide a smooth transition from one situation to the other.
– *Lightweight deployment.* Since IOWs have to be used in situations that are "less-stable" than the ones where traditional WfMSs are used, IOW needs: minimal technical requirements, especially in terms of common platform for the client; reduced "set-up" time; openness with respect to continuous changes in the group of people that are involved in it.

– *Visibility.* information and activities sharing in a highly dynamic environment such as IOW requires a flexible mechanism that assures the sharing of entities, as well as the preservation of privacy.

15.3.3 A Systematic Framework to Study IOW

In the light of the previous considerations, IOW requirements can be considered in the framework depicted in Table 15.1. Inasmuch as our final objective is to design and implement IOW, we consider the four dimensions that are specific to workflows (see Section 15.2), namely:

– Workflow Description models;
– Workflow Description languages;
– Architecture;
– Execution models.

   For each dimension, we consider both local and global issues. In accordance with the above discussion, we emphasize on social abilities and especially on information and activity sharing issues, which constitute the central problematic of IOW. All the requirements are examined in the computing context previously established: heterogeneity, distribution, autonomy, technological environment, and possibly openness and scalability.

   Now let us examine each scenario within this framework.

Loose IOW. In this open and dynamic context, – where potential partners (workflow service requesters, workflow service providers) are numerous, leaving and joining the global system freely, ignoring one another a priori –, it is highly desirable to have *middle resources* that help to select and locate partners, and ease interoperation with them. For this scenario to work, the following features are required:

– At the global level, the availability of matchmakers and ontology servers. *Matchmakers* can structure, record and advertise partners capabilities and connect requesters to providers. In our context, the use of Matchmakers requires the definition of a *Workflow Capability Description Language* allowing providers to publish their capabilities and requesters to express their needs. Such a language must be able to structure the format and the protocol of the interactions between requesters, providers and matchmakers. On the other hand, *Ontology servers* can assist semantic interoperability [550] by allowing nodes to adopt or propose a domain specific ontology, and by offering translating services.
– At the local level, each node needs to be provided with specific models for negotiating and sharing information and activity with middle resources and partners. Negotiations require protocols, and rules to use protocols appropriately in real time. To share activities, each node must explicitly define its offered and requested processes within its workflow models. It

	Loose IOW	Tight IOW
Workflow Description models	**Global level:** – Middle resources (Matchmaker, Ontology Servers) **Local Level:** – Negotiation Protocols (selection of partners, services, …) – Models of the mediating resources – Sub-contracted task definitions – Requested and offered task definitions – Dynamic shared inf. space – Flexible behavior: exceptions, adaptability, …	**Global level:** – Rules to join or leave the Federation, global integrity constraints – (possibly a) Global Workflow Model. **Local Level:** – Imported, Exported, and Integrated workflow models (information, organization and process models) – Interaction models: WF Coordination patterns – Commitments (information and services offering)
Workflow Description Language	– Contract based language – Workflow capacity description language – Shared Information Space definition language	– Abstract and transparent WDL – Meta-protocol definition – Global validation – Import, export and integration mechanisms. – WF Coord. constructors
Architecture	Workflow agentification compliant with the WfMC architecture **Global:** – Mediator, Matchmaker, … **Local:** – Social interface (publishing skills, managing contracts, selecting partners) **Enabling Technology:** – Agent and the Web	Federated WfMS compliant with the WfMC architecture **Global:** – a Federation manager (distributed or centralized) – a Global Model (not necessary) **Local:** – Component(s) for Model Exportation, Importation, and Integration – Coordinator (if not global) **Enabling Technology:** – Agent, Federated-DB
Execution model	Distributed execution based on contracts and dynamic information shared space	Distributed and concurrent execution according to well-established coordination patterns

Table 15.1. IOW requirements

must also be provided with a local database storing information about external middle resources. To share information with partners, the workflow models must integrate specific tasks to create dynamically shared information space to exchange tasks, cases and workflow relevant data needed by the cooperating nodes.

The previous requirements impact the Workflow Description Language that must provide additional features like:

- Contract-based protocol to support negotiation. This idea is currently being investigated in the CrossFlow European Project which examines inter-organizational workflows around the notion of contracts [384].
- Workflow Capability Description Language as previously mentioned. Works on Agent Capability Description Languages [578] could be followed and adapted to the workflow context.
- Mechanisms to create and manage "Shared information space". The use of associative blackboards, like the Linda tuple-space model [269], could be investigated in this context. [140] organizes information exchange in IOW around an event publish/subscribe model. Each WfMS is provided with a specific software component called the Event Manager responsible for publishing its capabilities as a producer or consumer of events, and for managing IOW interactions caused by event occurrences. Workflow interactions are explicitly described with "send nodes" and "request nodes" respectively capable of notifying and handling events.
- Flexible definitions of process models where parts of the activities can be specified at execution time in different ways. Let us consider a simple example. The process "business travel" can have an activity "reimbursement request". Even if the business travel involves actors from different organizations, a single process can be defined. Still for the "reimbursement request" it could be necessary to adopt a local procedure specified within the organization each actor belongs to. In the definition of the process "business travel" it must therefore be specified that a certain step, "reimbursement request", can be expanded, in specific ways.

From an architecture point of view, all these features require to provide conventional WfMS architecture with specific components devoted to social interface. Agent technology is a good candidate to deal with these features and the challenge could be to enhance WfMS with Agent features. The Workflow Enactment Service must be thought in terms of agents, and specific components must be added to support high-level communications with middle resources. Web technology is also very valuable since it provides both a simple and widely available interface (web browsers, HTML forms, . . .) and a communication infrastructure (CGI scripts, Java applets, . . .), on top of which agents could be deployed [119].

From an execution point of view, the Workflow Enactment Service must be able to control contract-based distributed execution and make shared information space available to partners.

Tight IOW. First, let us draw a useful analogy between this scenario and Federated Databases [102]. Indeed, both aim at enabling cooperation between heterogeneous, distributed, autonomous and pre-defined components belonging to different organizations. However, they differ by the nature of the components involved, which are structured information sources in the context of Federated Databases, while they are workflows in the context of IOW. This analogy originated the definition of Tight IOW requirements. However, the analogy should not be pushed too far, since IOWs gives rise to specific and more difficult issues due to coordination problems raised by processes.

Let us now precise tight IOW requirements. In this context, the partners know one another and they agree on global behavioral rules establishing, for example, how they can leave or join the group, and on some integrity constraints to respect. They could possibly agree, when it is feasible, on a global workflow model. The definition of a global model, which corresponds to a centralized approach, could be interesting to provide a uniform view to each partner, but requires a lot of efforts to be created and maintained and could limit the autonomy of each node. A preferable solution is that each node constructs its own view made of local models and imported models from the other participating systems. Each local node must specify:

– *Local models*, as usual (see Section 15.2).
– *Exported workflow models*, which are views on its local models and made available to the cooperating systems. Providing these views commits the local node to provide the related information and/or to perform the tasks published in those views.
– *Imported workflow models*, which are views on external workflow models belonging to other cooperating systems.
– *Integrated workflow models*, which correspond to a view combining local and imported models. These models should be combined thanks to interaction models.
– *Workflow interaction models*, which are coordination patterns synchronizing imported and local models. [607] has identified several possible workflow coordination patterns (called "forms of workflow interoperability"): *capacity sharing*, based on central control and distributed execution; *chained execution*, corresponding to a distributed but sequential execution; *subcontracting*, corresponding to a distributed and hierarchical control between a manager and several contractors; *case transfer*, where a process description is duplicated in several nodes and the most appropriate node is selected at each time; *loosely coupled* workflow processes, corresponding to a distributed and parallel execution of processes synchronized at certain pre-defined points.

From a Workflow Description Language (WDL) point of view, we need abstractions enabling the manipulation of external models with different levels of granularity, considering for example external models as atomic or expanding them to examine details. We also need mechanisms to import, export, translate, integrate, and coordinate models. To limit translation effort, a common WDL is required for expressing exported models. The Workflow Description Language should also provide constructors to express "coordination patterns" and enable their manipulation as first-class objects. Finally, the WDL must ease the validation of integrated workflow models even if we do not have all the details about the imported models but only some external properties.

From an architecture point of view, we need a *Federation manager* corresponding to a Federated WfMS (by analogy with federated Databases) which may be centralized or distributed. The federated manager is responsible for first, administrating the component nodes (arrival and departure according to protocols, global integrity constraints checking, ...) and the possible global model, and second, coordinating global workflows (versus local workflows). Each node should be provided with specific software components guaranteeing interoperability (Model Integration, Model importation, Model exportation). Coordination patterns, which are specific to IOW, need to be thought as first-class objects since they are useful at different steps (during design by providing "coordination patterns", and during execution for synchronizing processes and for monitoring remote executions). Consequently, a *Coordinator* is needed. In a centralized approach, it could be part of the federated manager while in a distributed approach each node needs its own coordinator within or interacting with the corresponding Workflow Enactment Service.

From an execution point of view, each Workflow Enactment Service in cooperation with the coordinator should support consistent, concurrent and distributed execution models implementing the different coordination patterns.

15.4 Two Comprehensive Approaches for IOW

The previous section has outlined two main IOW scenarios: loose and tight IOW. For each of them, we present a general approach for their design and implementation. The first approach adopts the notion of software agent for enhancing workflow systems and allowing their use in loose IOWs. The second approach combines Petri Nets and Federated Databases for providing the more structured support needed by tight IOWs. Both approaches are compliant with the Workflow Management Coalition reference architecture. This guarantees the possibility to tailor the support provided by the IOW to the needs of the collaborating organizations, remaining within a coherent framework of reference.

15.4.1 Agent-Based Approach to Support Loose IOW

Software agents have lately been adopted for the development of workflow systems due to their compositionality and flexibility [559]. There are two broad approaches for exploiting the agent technology in the context of workflow:

– Agent-enhanced Workflow aims at adding value to WfMS by providing an agent layer in charge of social facilities. Nowadays, many research prototypes as well as commercial systems integrate software agents to perform specific services (e.g. filtering messages or signaling pending commitments). For example, in the workflow system MILANO [13] agents are used for the elaboration of messages and for keeping the overall status of the on-going processes, by combining information provided by the system and by the users.
– Agent-based Workflow takes a more radical approach, fully rethinking the system in terms of agents. An example of work in this direction can be found in [84], where the focus is on reflective agents. Along the same vein, in ABACO [557] the architecture of the workflow is rethought in terms of agents. Another example is provided by ADEPT, an agent-based system for process management [509]. However, ADEPT focuses on the business perspective, rather than on the coordination among people actually involved in the process.

The use of agents becomes even more relevant in the case of IOW, given the heterogeneity and dynamicity of the contexts where they are used. As pointed out in Section 15.3, IOW requires a high degree of compositionality and openness. Being (semi-) autonomous entities, software agents provide a computational paradigm for the development of systems characterized by a high degree of distribution, compositionality, and openness [329, 591, 270]. In addition, the distributed nature of agent systems enables a decentralized control [440], making it easier to change the specification as well as the execution of workflow processes. Finally, due to their social ability agents can handle sophisticated interactions [643]. This feature of agents, combined with their intelligent behavior, makes it possible to provide a high level support to the users, with respect to both the heterogeneity and to the dynamicity of the environment.

Figure 15.3 presents the architecture of an agent-enhanced workflow approach. It complies with the WfMC's architecture shown in Figure 15.2 since it keeps the same components and the same interfaces between these components. More precisely, it details the workflow Enactment Service and indicates which software entities implement the Workflow process instances.

According to this architecture, the Workflow Enactment Service includes as many agents as the number of workflow process instances being currently in progress, an *Agent Manager* (AM) in charge of these agents, and a *Connection Server* (CS) that helps the agents to extend their acquaintances according to their needs.

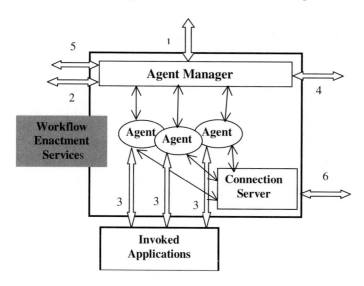

Fig. 15.3. An agent-based architecture for Workflow Enactment Service

Workflow concepts	Agent concepts
A definition of a workflow process	An agent type
A process instance and its engine	An agent
A process execution	The run of an agent

Table 15.2. Mapping from workflow concepts to agent concepts

The key idea is to implement each workflow process instance as a software process, and to encapsulate this process within an active agent (see Table 15.2). This agent continuously executes its *main procedure* and this run is actually the execution of the workflow process instance. Thus, the definition of the work to be done by a workflow process instance and the engine that carries out this work are gathered into a single unit that is an agent. Such an agent is an instance of an *agent type* generated from the definition of the workflow process, and it is provided with the means necessary to interact properly with the environment and to carry out the execution of a process instance. Therefore, each type of workflow process generates an agent type, each workflow process instance gives rise to the creation of a new instance of the corresponding agent type, and the execution of a workflow process instance is performed by the run of its agent. This agent supports Interface 3 with the applications that are used to perform the piece of work associated to a step (or a *task* according to the WfMC's terminology) of the process.

The *Agent Manager* controls and monitors the activation of the agent instances, which consists in the four following tasks.

1. *To generate agent types*: For each workflow process, the AM generates an agent type, whose instances will implement the process instances. Notice that this creation may be done only once, when the model of the Workflow process is defined.

2. *To make agents running*: Upon a request for the creation of a new instance of a workflow process, the AM creates a new instance of the corresponding agent type and, according to the context, initializes its parameters with the appropriate values. Then, it launches the running of the agent's main procedure.

3. *To support agent persistency*: Some workflow processes support long-term business processes that extend for a long time. In such processes, task performances are interleaved with periods of inactivity. During these periods, the process does not go on and it is not desirable that the corresponding agent stays active and unnecessarily consumes computing resources. Instead, it may be unloaded for storage in a long-term memory (disk) as long as it has nothing to do, and loaded again to become active as soon as it has some task to perform. In this way, the agent is persistent and can be alive for a long time while being active just when it has something to do. This feature is supported by the AM that makes agents go from the active to the inactive state and vice-versa.

4. *To assume Interfaces 1, 2, 4 and 5*: The AM uses Interface 1 to get the definition of workflow processes. It also supports Interfaces 2, 4 and 5 that, roughly speaking are concerned with receiving the definition of a workflow process, creating new workflow process instances, receiving events that enable instances to go one step ahead and supplying information about the state of instances.

A key principle of the agent paradigm is that the efficiency of agents to a large extent relies upon their ability to get in touch with one another and to collaborate. The role of the *Connection Server* is to help each agent to find partners (e. g., organization, workflow instance agent, provider agent) that stay outside the organization and can contribute to the achievement of its own goal. To do this, the CS interacts with Mediator and MatchMaker agents which are specialized in finding agents able to fulfil a particular need (search engines are an example of such agents in the Web). Assuming that this architecture becomes widespread, the definition of a new interface, *Interface 6*, could allow the CS of different Workflow Enactment Services to interact with one another too. In addition, the CS stores the collected information in an *inter-organizational model* database which is an extension of the organizational model of the WfMS in that it stores the same kind of information but about the environment of the organization. In some way, the CS strips, or relieves the instance agents of a part of their social abilities, but it is necessary to warrant the quality of the information maintained in the inter-organizational model.

The classical structure of a Workflow Enactment Service consists of a Workflow Engine that, as and when a Workflow process instance progresses, reads its definition in a database and triggers the appropriate action(s). Within the agent-enhanced approach, the structure of the Workflow Enactment Service mirrors the real world phenomenon it supports: there is a one-to-one correspondence between the agents and the Workflow process instances and both are processes. Thus, the computer-based entities (the agents) and the real world entities (the business processes) have the same constituent properties, so that the former ones can quite easily adapt to the requirements of the latter ones. Flexibility, inheritance and mobility may be used to illustrate this fact.

Flexibility is known as being one of the most challenging issues in WfMSS [219]. Indeed, each instance of a business process is a specific case featuring distinctive characteristics with regard to its objectives, constraints and environment. These differences arise both in a diachronic perspective – considering successive instances of a business process that evolves according to business requirements –, and in a synchronic perspective – considering the exceptions encountered by contemporaneous instances of a business process. Agents are commonly provided with generic facilities for supporting flexibility. Each of the agents supporting Workflow process instances is provided with two additional capabilities to deal with flexibility. First, each agent includes its own definition of the process – what is to be performed is specific to the agent – and second, it includes its own engine for interpreting this definition – how to perform it is also specific[1]. Tailoring an agent to the distinctive features of its Workflow process has an effect both on its structure and on the value of its attributes and acquaintances. This tailoring mainly takes place at the time the agent is instantiated but it may also occur dynamically as the agent is running.

Inheritance among processes means that the behavioral properties of a process are supported by another one. Although this relationship raises open theoretical issues [382], some practical approaches have been proposed [608, 297]. The facilities of the agent technology to support inheritance may be applied to the process definitions embodied into instance agents.

Another very valuable capability is to consider agents that are mobile and thus can move from the Workflow Enactment Service of an Organization to the one of another Organization. However, supporting this functionality would require a significant enhancement of the services supported by Interface 4 of the WfMC's architecture.

15.4.2 Federated Databases and Petri Nets to Support Tight IOW

As shown in Section 15.3, tight IOW needs to set up an infrastructure allowing the organizations to share a part of their Information Models and Process

---

[1] This property agrees with efficiency concerns, namely the fact that agents must be sparing of memory size [554]

Models. The aim of this section is to show how the combined use of Federated Databases and Petri Nets can support this requirement.

Database technology is one of the core technologies commonly used to support Workflow Management Systems [287, 217], and while moving from intra- to inter-Organizational Workflow it is quite natural to go from local Databases to Federated Databases. In WfMS, Databases are usually used to structure, record and provide information and views about the workflow models (organization, information and process) and the workflow relevant data for which they constitute a shared information space. Databases are also known for guaranteeing good properties like data integrity and consistent execution of transactions. Federated Databases [102] extend databases by providing an architecture and mechanisms to support interoperability between several heterogeneous, distributed and autonomous databases. Roughly speaking, they provide mechanisms allowing to:

– Export views from a local database schema to the other cooperating nodes;
– Import views of database schemas from other cooperating nodes to a local database;
– Integrate a local schema with imported ones to produce a global view on the federated databases;
– Control global transactions;
– Administrate the federation (global integrity constraints, membership management, etc);
– Process global queries, i.e. to decompose them in sub-queries to be executed on local databases, to synthesize the sub-queries results, and to compose the final result.

In the context of IOW, the use of Federated Databases, hiding distribution and heterogeneity, eases information sharing at different levels:

– Each organization can import and export fragments of the information and organizational models and therefore can build a global and integrated view on these models.
– Workflow relevant data can be made available to each partner involved in a given process.
– The global Information Model of the inter-organizational cooperation can be made explicit so that one may study characteristics such as its consistency.
– In addition, this Federated Database can be the support to import and export the definition of the processes of the participating Organizations.

With regard to Process interaction, we propose to use Petri nets as a reference framework and to introduce a new model called coordination model to define how the Organizations Workflow processes interact. In tight IOW, the role played by each of the participating Organizations is not negotiated for each cooperation case but it is the matter of a lasting agreement. To put this role allocation into practice and determine how they will cooperate, the partners also agree upon a *coordination model* which is a process specifying the task(s) to be performed by each Organization and when these tasks can or must be executed. This coordination model is the gathering of the process model exported by each Organization and states the mutual commitment between participating Organizations. As a simple example, Figure 15.4 shows a coordination model concerning only two Organizations A and B. Starting

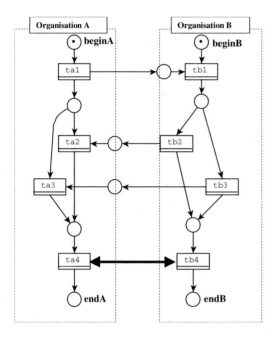

Fig. 15.4. A coordination model between two organizations

the cooperation is done by A as performing task **ta1**. Then, B must perform **tb1** followed by either **tb2** or **tb3**. Afterwards, A has to perform **ta2** in the former case, and **ta3** in the latter. Finally, **ta4** and **tb4** are the respective contributions of A and B to the ending task that they achieve together. Each task that appears in such a coordination model, referred to as a *coordination task*, is also a part of a local Workflow process of one of the Organizations. Thus, tight IOW makes arise a global Workflow process resulting from the combination of a number of local Workflow processes through a coordination model. The coordination model is the glue that gathers into a *global workflow process* all the local Workflow processes including one of its coordination task. Continuing the current example, Figure 15.5 shows a possible local Workflow process that allows Organization B to collaborate according to the coordination model of Figure 15.4. As for Organization A, we assume that its local process is just its part (the left side of Figure 15.4) of the coordination model. Then, replacing the A (resp. B) part of the coordination model by the local process of A (resp. B) results in the global Workflow process (Figure 15.6) that they execute in cooperation.

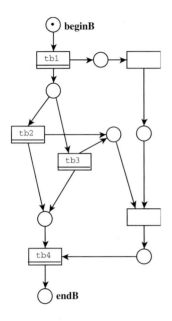

Fig. 15.5. The local workflow process of Organization B

As a consequence, the possibility to execute a coordination task is determined by enabling conditions set by both the coordination model and the local workflow process of the task. This fact raises issues about the consistency of these constraints: if they are not compatible, some cooperation tasks (and probably some internal tasks too) will never be able to occur. Thus, there is a drastic need to validate and verify a global workflow process in order to warrant each participating organization that this process behaves properly and effectively allows to reach the goal of the cooperation. In any case, no organization may accept to enter into a cooperation that could lead its own activity to fail. Let us notice that this guarantee is difficult to establish because none of the organizations has a full knowledge of the global process: each one only knows its local Workflow processes and the collectively agreed coordination model. Indeed, each organization exports and makes visible to the others only the part of its processes that is related to the cooperation. This is a matter of privacy and corresponds to the meaning of the commitment expressed by the coordination model. In fact, this is primarily a matter of viability since some of the participating organizations are likely to modify their local Workflow processes. It is essential that the cooperation should not

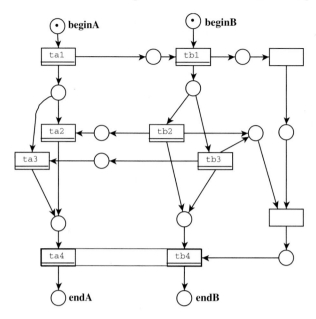

Fig. 15.6. Global workflow process jointly performed by Organization A and B

systematically be called into question by such changes. Another difficulty is that a global Workflow process is a concurrent process, since each organization executes its Workflow processes on its own disregarding the activity of other organizations (except for the constraints entailed by the coordination model). It tends to be a complex process since it results from the coordination of several processes, so that its modeling and analysis requires a powerful Description Language featuring the properties mentioned in Section 15.3.3.

Petri net formalisms, and more specifically High-Level Petri nets (see, e.g. [335, 510, 553]), satisfy these requirements. Their suitability for modeling and analyzing business or workflow processes has been advocated by many authors for a long time. Indeed, they enjoy formal semantics (process definitions are unambiguous and precise), a graphical nature (process models are intuitive and easy to understand), a wide expressive power (all the synchronization constructs are supported, the interaction between the data structure and the control structure is accounted for by high-level tokens referring to entities stored in a Database), the availability of analysis techniques supported by tools allowing to check many properties, the possibility to easily make simulations and, last but not least, well-established implementation techniques. Among these topics, we will just illustrate validation and implementation issues.

Validation concerns a huge number of properties, and the ones of interest depend to a large extent on the process under consideration. As an example, the *effective ending* property will be considered, because it is relevant for any process. A process effectively ends if, starting from the initial state (where only the begin place contains one token), whatever state is reached there exists a sequence of task occurrences that leads to the final state (where the end place contains one token). The reader can easily verify that the processes of Figures 15.1 and 15.5 effectively end, as does the coordination model of Figure 15.4 where at the initial (resp. final) state, all the begin (resp. end) places contain one token. Up to a simple condition, this property may be checked automatically [443]. Now, we are faced with the following question: How to prove a property such as the effective ending of a global workflow process while its structure is not defined? Indeed, we cannot refer to the structure of the local workflow processes since they can be changing, and we can only use the fact that they fulfil the constraints imposed by the coordination model. Thus we have to express these constraints formally. Let us consider a coordination model cm and a state Scm of cm (that is a distribution of tokens in the places of cm), O an organization involved in cm, wpo the local workflow process of O and So a state of wpo, and finally Tcoordo the set of coordination tasks of O that appear in cm (by definition, they are the very same appearing in wpo). We say that So *is similar to* Scm if [499]:

1. if there exists a sequence of tasks of cm that is enabled, contains exactly one task tc of Tcoordo and whose performance leads to the state Scm', then there exists a sequence of tasks of wpo that is enabled, contains exactly the task tc of Tcoordo and whose performance leads to a state So';
2. So' is also similar to Scm' (namely So' and Scm' satisfy condition 1)[2].

A local Workflow process wpo fulfils the constraints imposed on O by a coordination model cm if the initial state of wpo is similar to the initial state of cm, since, informally speaking, in each situation where the coordination model requests O to perform a coordination task, O is actually able to carry out this task. Notice that the similarity property may be checked automatically. Thanks to this formal definition of the constraints imposed by a coordination model, many properties of a global workflow process can be checked without dealing with the precise definition of the local workflow processes. Namely, we have the following result. Let cm be a coordination model and $wpo_1, \ldots wpo_n$ be the local Workflow processes of the organizations involved in cm. If

1. cm and each of the wpo_i effectively end,
2. each of the wpo_i fulfils the constraints imposed by cm,

then the resulting global workflow process effectively ends.

Regarding implementation issues, the use of high-level Petri nets as Process Description Language supplies several standard techniques for support-

---

[2] Similarity being a very technical property, we only intend to give an intuition of its meaning.

ing the enactment of process instances. Within the IOW context, the agent-based and Active Database-based ones deserve to be mentioned. The agent-enhanced architecture outlined in the previous sub-section accommodates very well Petri net-defined processes. Each agent includes a compact definition of the Petri net it has to execute, and its main procedure is a generic Petri net interpreter that maintains the current state of the process instance and, according to this state, makes the tasks associated to the enabled transitions active . The implementation of the CoOperative Objects formalism, a fully concurrent Object-Oriented language based upon Petri nets, works in this way [554]. Another way to implement Petri nets is to map each net into a set of rules of the *event-condition-action* form and execute these rules by an inference engine that implements the Petri net semantics [47]. In the tight IOW context, Active Databases [632] are a very appropriate technology to store and execute such rules. Besides, these rules can associate reactive behaviors to events occurring to the objects stored in the (Federated) database or occurring in the environment (temporal event, signals from other software, . . .). All these functions are guaranteed without user intervention. This mechanism is interesting when one bears in mind that with conventional DBMSs, the user has to query the database periodically to know if an interesting event has occurred. Consequently, active rules enable the coordination of the different tasks. For example, each time the state of a task evolves, a database-update event is generated and an appropriate action can be performed (agent notification, task chaining, task allocation, history recording). [139] has shown how to implement a WfMS on top of an active Database. In our context, combining federated and active databases features turns the shared information space into a distributed blackboard: each node has a local blackboard available to it.

15.5 Conclusions

This chapter has presented some of the issues that needs to be addressed in order to make workflow systems able to support business processes that span across multiple organizations, i.e. Inter-Organizational Workflows. In particular, the chapter has focused on the support to coordination of cooperating organizations and, consequently, on the modeling and enactment of business processes. Though the focus is on the process, the importance of information and organization models in the context of IOW has been stressed.

After having introduced the basic terminology of traditional workflow and workflow systems, the chapter has outlined some requirements for IOW. In particular, a framework for organizing these requirements has been presented. The framework is structured along 4 dimensions: the WF description model, the WF description language, the Architecture, and the Execution model. In addition, a distinction is made between local and global issues. The first are related to the individual WF systems that can possibly be involved in a IOW, while the latter are connected to the group of these systems as a whole.

Given the different ways in which organizations can cooperate, the requirements have been identified in relation to two scenarios that represents the two extreme of the range of variability: loose and tight IOW. Loose IOWs refer to occasional cooperation, free of structural constraints, where neither the involved partners nor their relationships are defined a priori. Tight IOWs refer to a structural cooperation among organizations, i.e., a cooperation based on a well-established infrastructure among pre-defined partners. Based on this distinction and the related requirements, the chapter presents two approaches to the design and the implementation of IOWs. The first approach adopts the notion of software agents for enhancing workflow systems and allowing their use in loose IOWs. The second approach combines Petri Nets and Federated Databases for providing the more structured support needed by tight IOWs.

Both the approaches are compliant with the Workflow Management Coalition reference architecture. This guarantees the possibility to tailor the support provided by the IOW to the needs of the collaborating organizations, remaining within a coherent framework of reference.

This chapter does not aim at providing a final answer to the problem of IOWs, rather it fully acknowledges the complexity of the problem, and suggests a framework where different contributions can be compared and integrated.

Clearly, the distinction between loose and tight workflows is mainly analytical, necessary for organizing requirements and solutions. In the real world there is a continuum between these two extremes. Our future research will aim at developing a continuum also in the support that a IOW system can provide. The goal is to build a bridge between the two proposed approaches, so to assure a smooth transition from the less structured to the more structured support (and vice versa), and, on the overall, a support that can be adapted to the evolution of the organizations and the way they cooperate.

16. Constraints Solving as the Coordination of Inference Engines

Eric Monfroy[1] and Farhad Arbab[1]

CWI, Kruislaan 413, 1098 SJ Amsterdam, the Netherlands
mailto:Eric.Monfroy@cwi.nl, mailto:Farhad.Arbab@cwi.nl

Summary.

In this chapter we consider the application of coordination to (cooperative) constraint solving. This topic raises several issues and questions, such as: Why use coordination models for (cooperative) constraint solving? What are the possible approaches and what categories of coordination models are best suited for this task? Are coordination languages just a new way of implementing solver (cooperation), or do they also improve solving techniques/methodologies and open new directions? What can constraint solving expect from coordination languages and models?

In the following we attempt to address these issues and at least hint at some possible directions. In the first section, we discuss the general problems and highlight two approaches: using coordination for cooperation of solvers (Section 16.2), and designing solvers with a coordination language (Section 16.3). Finally, we conclude by advocating the use of coordination models for realizing both constraint solvers and cooperation of constraint solvers.

16.1 A Generic Approach to Coordination-based Constraint Solving

In this section we present a number of very generic problems that must be considered to use coordination for (cooperative) constraint solving. After a brief review of constraint programming and more specifically of constraint solving, we present a basis for evaluating the appropriateness of coordination models for constraint solving.

16.1.1 Constraint Programming

In the last 15 years, constraint programming has emerged as a new programming paradigm. In this alternative approach the programming process is merely a specification of a set of requirements, a solution for which will be found using some general or domain specific constraint solvers.

These requirements are called constraints, and they can be seen as statements of relationships that must exist among the set of variables in a problem. Thus, constraint programs are highly declarative: you just state what is required, not how to find the solutions. This approach to modeling of problems can be introduced in many traditional programming environments.

Solvers aim at computing/finding solutions for constraint problems, i.e., values for variables such that all constraints are satisfied. Solvers for domain specific constraints are usually provided in the form of specific algorithms (such as programs for solving systems of linear equations), packages, or libraries (such as linear programming packages/libraries), whereas general methods are usually presented as techniques for reducing the search space combined with specific search algorithms. Most of these general methods are based on constraint propagation which extracts information from constraints in order to reduce the set of possible values that can be assigned to a variable.

Constraint programming has been successfully used for solving many difficult real-life problems in numerous domains including operations research problems, physics and chemical applications, computer graphics, database systems, molecular biology, financial applications, electronic circuit design and validation, art, etc.

Although constraint programming is a multidisciplinary research area, we can split it into two main directions: programming languages and constraint solving. In the following we focus on the second direction and show that constraint solving is intrinsically linked to coordination models and languages.

16.1.2 Constraint Solving

The Need for Solver Cooperation. Constraint programming utilizes a collection of largely independent techniques, notably various specialized constraint solving techniques. These specialized techniques have been successfully used in practical constraint programming tools for solving real-life problems in specific domains. However, combining these existing techniques and tools generally requires their reprogramming or re-engineering. Given that the development of solvers is, generally, an expensive and tedious task, the interest for re-using existing constraint solvers and for connecting to solvers dispatched on the Internet is obvious [562]. More importantly, integrating several solvers, each working in a different domain or based on a different technique, is an appealing and realistic approach when dealing with problems that cannot be tackled or efficiently solved with a single solver.

Thus, combining various existing methods and techniques within a single framework is both a powerful tool and a major challenge in constraint programming. Such a framework must provide tools to easily configure and integrate existing components, and a language to control and coordinate their actions in a distributed environment. Particularly, one of the continuing challenges in this area is the integration of symbolic and numerical computing [65, 436]. So far, such frameworks consider either a specific constraint domain (such as linear constraints [67], non-linear constraints over real numbers [436]), a fixed solving strategy, or a fixed scheme of collaboration (either sequential or concurrent). More recently, BALI [429, 433], an environment for domain-independent solver collaboration, was proposed. Its high-level language is based on primitives that allow one to combine solvers using collaboration primitives (such as sequentiality, concurrency, and parallelism) and control primitives (such as conditional, guarded, iterative, and fixed-point collaborations).

Solver vs. Solver Cooperation. Recall that we have identified two different schemes for solving constraints: constraint solvers and solver cooperation. A constraint solver can be seen as a single technique, or a "low-level" combination of several solving techniques. On the other hand, solver cooperation techniques consider constraint solvers as black boxes and compose them in "high-level" combinations to produce new solvers.

The difference between the two schemes is not always structurally obvious. For example, consider constraint propagation with chaotic iteration (CI) [30, 31] (this topic is detailed in Section 16.3). The reduction functions can be considered as components of the algorithm, or they can be seen as black-box functions, i.e., solvers. Then, is the chaotic iteration algorithm a solver or a cooperation of solver? The distinction is generally made by considering where the components come from. If their code is included in the code of the CI algorithm, then, we can say that we deal with a solver. If one re-uses external functions in the form of executable files, libraries, or connects to Internet agents, then one should think in terms of solver cooperation.

Some approaches (such as BALI) create instances of solver cooperation among constraint solvers. But then, these cooperation instances can recursively be considered as constraint solvers in their own right, that can in turn be used in other cooperation instances. Sometimes (such as [143]), a special language is used to design both constraint solvers and solvers cooperation schemes, at the same level. Thus, each primitive of the language can be used to create a solver or a cooperation of other solvers.

Although the distinction between constraint solvers and solver cooperation is not clear cut, it is still helpful for us to consider them as motivation for two separate approaches: (1) designing constraint solvers using coordination languages, and (2) using a coordination language to realize cooperation of solvers.

Agents. In solver cooperation schemes the notion of an agent is natural and straightforward: individual solvers are computing agents that can be threads on a single machine, processes located on different machines on a network of computers, or processes dispatched all over the world and communicating through the Internet. There is a one to one mapping from solvers to agents. These computational components are then controlled by coordination agents.

Within an individual solver, the concept and the role of agents are less clear. Generally, the underlying hardware architecture and the development framework may define what agents are. One may say that in a solver that is the combination of different solving techniques, each technique constitutes an agent. But generally, there is no clear rule for deciding what agents are and what role they play within an individual solver. For instance, an agent can be a function, a variable, a program module, etc.

Inter-operability Issues. A solver is generally programmed from scratch, and thus all of its agents (however they may be defined) are normally written in the same language. As such, inter-operability is not an issue for developing individual solvers.

The situation is very different for solver cooperation schemes because generally, solvers are heterogeneous: they may be written in different languages, execute on different operating systems, and may be adapted to take advantage of specific hardware platforms. In this case, the choice of the coordination language is crucial. It must be able to support many computational languages and must be ported to many different platforms so that it does not restrict the solvers that may be integrated in such a framework.

It is a safe bet to assume that every solver has its own representation of data. This makes integration one of the main issues in solver cooperation. We can illustrate this problem with a simple, but usual example. What does it mean (semantically) when a real number is exchanged between two solvers? They both knows what it is (a real number), but they are likely to have two different representation for floating point numbers (8 bits, 16 bits, infinite precision,...). This creates many problems at the level of constraint solving that are not especially related to coordination. This way, converter agents do not become the bottleneck in the system, and adding a new solver requires at most the minimum effort of providing converter agents to support its specific representation format.

If we know how to translate data from one representation to another, then coordination models provide an easy way for two black-box solvers to communicate with one another. We need to provide new computational agents that convert data from one representation to the other. However, two other issues must now be considered. First, what exactly should a data converter agent know? Should we have a data converter agent for every possible pair of different representation format, or should a data converter have global knowledge of all representation formats used in an application? Second, should a converter agent convert directly from one representation to another, or should converter agents translate individual solver representation formats to and from a unique global representation format? The proper answer to these questions depends on the number of solvers involved in cooperation schemes, the potential for the evolution of the framework (which may involve connection and integration of new solvers), and the volume of the data that flows between various heterogeneous solvers. However, it is safe to say that an open architecture for a system to allow connection to solvers and inference engines dispatched on the Internet, it is reasonable to use a global external representation format and provide converter agents to translate back and forth between this representation format and that of the individual solvers.

Although, coordination does not solve the problem of integration (of heterogeneous solver agents), it significantly facilitates its realization. For example, the Openmath consortium [587] is working on the design of a standard language for mathematical objects (i.e., the most commonly used objects in constraints). Such a standard should thus be integrated as a low level layer in constraint systems so that mathematical tools can exchange data with each other. Coordination languages allow us to realize this layer as just a converter agent. This way, the code of the converter can be separated from the code of the solvers, and used with tools that do not adhere to this standard.

16.1.3 Coordination Models

Coordination languages [269, 482] offer language support for composing and controlling software architectures made of parallel or distributed components. As such, they can be thought of as the linguistic counterpart of software libraries and platforms, like MPI of Dongarra et al. or PVM of Geist et al, which offer extra-linguistic support for parallel and distributed programming ([36]). By providing explicit linguistic support for otherwise ad-hoc constructs offered by such standards and libraries, coordination languages advocate a programming paradigm that can be described by the slogan *Programming = Computation + Coordination*, as proposed by Gelernter and Carriero in their seminal 92 paper [269].

The conceptual significance of such a programming paradigm is a clear separation between the *components of the computation* and their *interaction* in the overall application or system. On the one hand, this separation facilitates the reuse of components; on the other hand, the same patterns of interaction occur in many different problems – so it might be possible to reuse the coordination components as well.

Coordination languages have been applied to the parallelization of computation intensive sequential programs in the fields of: simulation of Fluid Dynamics systems, matching of DNA strings, molecular synthesis, parallel and distributed simulation, monitoring of medical data, computer graphics, analysis of financial data integrated into decision support systems, and game playing (chess).

Coordination models and languages can be classified [482] as control-driven vs. data-driven. Orthogonally, they can also be classified [36] as endogenous vs. exogenous.

Data-driven Coordination Models. The main characteristic of data-driven coordination models is that they tend to organize the communication of all components through a substantial shared body of data.

Mixing coordination and computation. Most data-driven coordination models are endogenous. Endogenous coordination models provide primitives that must be incorporated *within* a computational agent for its coordination. In applications that use such models, primitives that affect the coordination of each agent are inside the agent itself. Thus, an agent is responsible for both examining and manipulating data as well as coordinating its own activity with other agents.

To devise solver cooperation schemes, solvers are usually considered as black-boxes that cannot be modified. In fact, they are often provided in binary form and their source code is not available. Solvers can also be agents to which queries can be sent through an interface. In both cases, only their front-ends may be adaptable for special purposes, but their source code cannot be modified to accommodate the coordination primitives of endogenous models.

In contrast, the realization of a constraint solver is usually programmed from scratch. Thus, agents can be defined with the appropriate coordination and computation primitives.

Shared data-space. Almost all data-driven coordination models have evolved around the notion of a shared data-space [515]. All agents involved in an application communicate indirectly through this medium: each agent serves itself (i.e., puts or gets data) in the shared data-space without any global organization.

Shared data-spaces can be convenient for designing individual solvers. However, they are generally completely inadequate for solver cooperation schemes. Indeed, this way of communication would lead to a framework close to pure concurrent cooperation. This component interaction mechanism is generally proven to be inefficient for solver cooperation [283]. The techniques used in individual constraint solvers are by now well-understood, to the extent that it is possible to define "identity cards" for most solvers. Furthermore, experimental results have shown that certain cooperation schemes lead to significant improvements, whereas others are catastrophic. It is, thus, not reasonable to think that a "random" exchange of data between solvers can lead to more efficient cooperation than what can be built based on ten years of knowledge and experiments.

Data-driven coordination models built around shared-data-spaces can also raise security problems when agents connect through the Internet. However, there is some recent work that addresses some of these privacy and security issues.

Flat structures. Data-driven models generally organize agents in a flat structure. This is opposed to the notion of solver cooperation that considers incremental construction of solving processes [433, 143]. With such coordination models, a solver cooperation instance cannot be considered as a solver that may itself be integrated into yet another cooperation.

Control-driven Coordination Models. Control-driven coordination models emphasize processing or the flow of control. They induce a view on an application as a collection of autonomous agents that consume their input data and subsequently produce new data for other agents. Furthermore, in exogenous control-driven models, such as **MANIFOLD**, there is a complete separation of computation and coordination concerns. The state of an application is defined in terms of the agents and the coordination patterns that they are involved in. The actual values of the data the agents manipulate or exchange are almost never involved.

Control. Data is of only secondary importance in defining solver cooperation schemes, and in some systems, of no importance at all. The key is to know certain generic properties of the results produced by various solvers. A cooperation scheme can be seen as a design to exploit such invariant properties and other relevant information about its participating solvers. This may seem counter-intuitive when one considers a construct like the conditional primitive of BALI. It appears that this primitive must examine some actual data value to decide which solver to send a request to. However, this appearance is misleading because in fact the examination of the data value is *not* done at the same level as the primitive itself; it is done inside a specialized agent. Thus, the coordination pattern that corresponds to this primitive is generic and independent of the actual data values. The specialized agent that examines the actual data value, simply signals the coordination pattern to react and create one of the two alternative data-flow pipelines.

Complete separation of computation and coordination. An exogenous control-driven coordination model completely separates computational and coordination concerns into separate components. It is, thus, possible to define a full language purely concerned with coordination. **MANIFOLD** is such a language where computational components are considered as black-boxes with clearly defined input/output interfaces.

Such models are good candidates for defining solver cooperation schemes, and even more so, for defining solver cooperation languages. The main motivation is to re-use and integrate already existing and already programmed solvers, and to connect to solvers through the Internet. Hence, solvers are generally provided as black-boxes the insides of which cannot be modified, or as Internet agents which are known only through their interfaces. These components then naturally make up the purely computational part of the system, i.e., its computing agents. The necessary coordination components can then be written in a pure exogenous coordination-oriented language, such as **MANIFOLD**.

Adequacy. To summarize, data-driven coordination models aim at coordinating the production and consumption of data within a shared data-space, whereas control-driven models directly coordinate active entities, or agents. Analogously, constraint solvers manipulate constraints that are stored in a special data-space (i.e., the constraint store), whereas solver cooperation schemes mainly deal with the control of the application of individual solvers.

Thus, the two main categories of coordination models can be associated with the two main approaches for constraint programming: data-driven models to solvers, and control-driven models to solver cooperation. However, just as there is no clear cut dichotomy of data-driven and control-driven coordination models, the boundary between constraint solvers and solver cooperations schemes is not clear either. Consequently, the association of data-driven and control-driven coordination models with the design of solvers and solver cooperation schemes cannot be considered as a strong and universal dichotomy.

For example, it is clear that concurrent constraint programming [534] defines a data-driven coordination framework for constraint programming and constraint solving. On the other hand, the solver collaboration language of BALI defines a set of cooperation primitives that matches coordination patterns of a control-driven coordination model. When dealing with chaotic iteration, the association becomes more hazardous because several alternative realizations are possible. Using a data-driven coordination model, we can consider a shared data-space (representing the variables and their values) used by agents (the reduction functions) to asynchronously post and retrieve values until they reach a fixed-point. Alternatively, a control-driven framework can be used to implement chaotic iteration techniques. Here, variables become coordinators that request computing agents to perform reductions. Nevertheless, consistent with our classification, the first scheme is more appropriate when chaotic iteration is used to design solvers, whereas the second scheme better suits the design of solver cooperation schemes.

16.2 A Solver Cooperation Language

In this section, we consider a language for solver cooperation. Such a language is built out of predefined cooperation primitives (or patterns) that enable one to design composite solvers made of cooperative solvers. The approach that we propose in this section consists of transcribing each collaboration pattern into a coordination pattern, i.e., a topology of agents, some streams for their communication, and some control for their coordination. This approach captures the notion of *solver cooperation languages* in the field of constraint programming. As an example, we study one such system: BALI [429, 433, 430].

16.2.1 BALI

BALI is an alternative way of designing cooperative constraint solver systems using a generic and domain-independent control-oriented language. In order to deal with the integration of constraint solvers, re-usability, and cooperation, BALI provides a glass-box mechanism which enables one to link and control black-box tools, i.e., the solvers. This system allows one to design and implement solver collaboration schemes [1] with a high-level language to compose solvers using collaboration primitives (such as sequentiality, concurrency and parallelism) and control primitives (such as iterators, fixed-points and conditionals).

---

[1] Solver collaboration means either solver cooperation or solver combination. Solver combination consists of creating a solver for a union of theories from its component solvers, while solver cooperation deals with communication among component solvers each defined for a single domain but based on different techniques, or working on different constraints. For a more formal definition of both of these concepts see [430].

Heterogeneous solvers can be involved in the solver collaboration language of BALI, and we want to be able to use every software we need, i.e., not only the software we can locally access on our own network of machines, but also software located on other networks to which we can connect through the Internet.

In BALI, a solver collaboration is itself considered as a solver. This means, that it can be re-used in another (higher level) collaboration scheme.

The Coordination Model and Language. Due to the dynamic aspect of the formal model of BALI, the use of heterogeneous solvers, and the incremental composition of cooperation, only a coordination language able to deal with dynamic processes and channels (creation, duplication, dis-/re-/connection), able to handle external heterogeneous solvers (routines for automatic data conversions), and able to manage non-flat structures can fulfill the requirements of the formal model of BALI. This guided us through the different coordination models and lead us to the IWIM (Ideal Worker Ideal Manager) model [33, 34], i.e., a control-driven model, and the **MANIFOLD** [81, 35] language, which is an implementation of the IWIM model ported to several platforms, supporting many different programming languages.

The Solver Collaboration Language. A detailed description of the solver collaboration language of BALI can be found in [433, 429]. In this section, we give a brief overview of some of its collaboration primitives, and the complete syntax of the language is given in Table 16.1.

$Id \in \mathcal{I}$ (identifiers)
$S \in \mathcal{S}$ (solvers)
$\psi \in \Psi$ (concurrency functions)
$n \in \mathbb{N}$ (positive integers)
$OA \in \mathcal{OA}$ (arithmetic observation functions)
$OB \in \mathcal{OB}$ (boolean observation functions)
$Col ::= Id = E$
$E ::= \Diamond \mid Id \mid S \mid seq(SE) \mid dc(\psi, SE) \mid split(SE) \mid f\_p(E) \mid rep(Ar, E) \mid if(B, E, E)$
$SE ::= E \mid E, SE$
$Ar ::= n \mid Ar + Ar \mid Ar - Ar \mid Ar * Ar \mid OA$
$B ::= true \mid false \mid Ar < Ar \mid Ar \leq Ar \mid Ar = Ar \mid B \wedge B \mid B \vee B \mid \neg B \mid OB$

Table 16.1. Syntax of the solver collaboration language

Sequentiality (denoted seq) means that the solver E_2 will execute on the constraint store C', which is the result of the application of the solver E_1 on the constraint store C.

When several solvers are working in *parallel* (denoted split), the store C is sent to each and every one of them. The results of all solvers are gathered together to constitute a new constraint store analogous to C. This primitive represents a cooperative concurrency.

Concurrency (denoted dc) is interesting when several solvers based on different methods can be applied to non-disjoint parts of the constraint store. The result of such a collaboration is the result of a single solver S composed with the constraints that S did not manipulate. The result of S must also satisfy a given property ψ which is a *concurrency function* (set Ψ in Table 16.1). For example, *basic* is a standard function of Ψ that returns the result of the first solver that finishes executing. Some more complex ψ functions can be considered, such as *solved_form* which selects the result of the first solver whose solution is in solved form on the computation domain. The results of the other solvers (which may even be stopped as soon as S is chosen) are not taken into account. The concurrency primitive is similar to a "don't care" commitment but also provides control for choosing the new store (using ψ functions). This primitive represents a competive concurrency.

These primitives (that comprise the computation part of the collaboration language) can be connected with combinators (which make up the control part of the language, using primitives such as iterators, conditionals, and fixed-points) in order to design more complex solver collaborations schemes.

The *fixed-point* combinator (denoted f_p) repeatedly applies a solver collaboration until no more information can be extracted from the constraint store.

The primitives and combinators presented above are statically defined. Using a set of *observation functions* on the constraint store allows one to get more dynamic primitives. These functions are evaluated at run-time (when entering a primitive) using the current store. They may be either arithmetic (set $\mathcal{OA}$ in Table 16.1, such as *card_var* which computes the number of distinct variables in the store),) or Boolean (set $\mathcal{OB}$ in Table 16.1, such as *linear* that tests whether all the constraints in the store are linear).

The *repeat* combinator (denoted rep) is similar to the *fixed-point* combinator, but applies a solver n times (n being the result of a composition of a number of *observation functions*). Since this primitive takes into account the constraint and its form at run-time, it improves the dynamic aspect of the collaboration language.

Finally, the *conditional* combinator (denoted if) applies one solver or another depending on the evaluation of a condition (also expressed as a composition of a number of observation functions on the constraint store).

The following example illustrates the solver collaboration language:

$$\text{seq}(A,\text{dc}(\text{basic},B,C,D),\text{split}(E,F),\text{f\_p}(G))$$

Consider applying this collaboration scheme to the constraint store c[2]. First A is applied to c and returns c_1. Then, B, C, and D are applied to c_1. The first one that finishes gives the new constraint store c_2. Then E, and F execute

---

[2] In order to simplify the explanation, we consider here solvers that return only one solution (one disjunct).

on c_2. The solution c_3 is a composition of c_3' (the solution of E) and c_3'' (the solution of F). Finally, G is repeatedly applied to c_3 until a fix-point, c_4, is reached, which is the final solution of the collaboration.

Agents. Solvers in BALI are black-boxes and heterogeneous. This is readily supported by **MANIFOLD** which integrates or connects the solvers as external workers. Then, communication and coordination can be defined among solvers in the same way as with common agents, regardless of whether they are located on a local network, or dispatched on several networks.

Individual solvers are encapsulated to create *component solvers*. As shown in [429], a solver collaboration is itself a solver. Applying this concept to the architecture, encapsulation becomes a hierarchical operation. Hence, several component solvers can be encapsulated in order to build a *composite solver agent*. However, viewed from the outside of a capsule, component and composite solvers become identical.

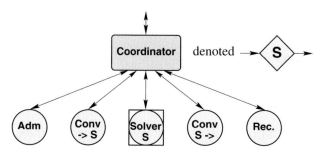

Fig. 16.1. Simple solver

A component solver (see Figure 16.1) consists of several agents:

- a coordinator for managing the messages and agents inside the encapsulation. This coordinator is also the in/out gate of the capsule (when communicating with superior agents).
- a solver, that can be a "local" solver, or a de-located solver,
- four *filters* (**MANIFOLD** workers):
  - to filter the constraints the solver can handle. In fact, when re-using (or connecting to) solvers, not all of them are able to treat every type of constraint in the store. Thus, only those constraints *admissible* by a solver must picked.
  - to convert the data from the global representation format to the format of the solver,
  - to convert the solutions of the solver into the global format,
  - to re-compose equivalent solutions based on the solutions of the solver and the constraints it cannot handle.

A composite solver (see Figure 16.2) is the encapsulation of several component/composite solvers together with some filters. The filters and the coordinator are specialized for the collaboration primitive the agent represents. See [37] for more details.

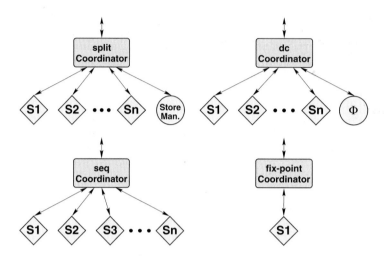

Fig. 16.2. Composite solver

The dynamic facilities of **MANIFOLD**, provide several advantages here, such as sharing of agents (filters, and solvers) among composite solvers (see Figure 16.3). The creation of another instance of an agent (solver or filter) will depend on the activity of the already running instances.

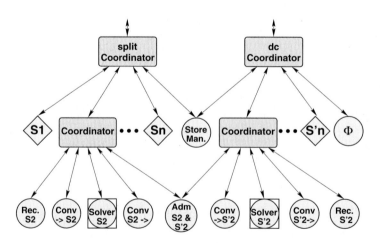

Fig. 16.3. Shared solvers and filters

BALI requires dynamic facilities in a coordination language for several reasons.

Dynamic handling of solvers. The set up of the distributed architecture and its use are not disjoint phases in BALI. This means that when a solving request is issued, the collaboration will be built incrementally (agent after agent) and only the necessary agents will be created. For example, in a conditional or guarded collaboration, only the "then" or the "else" sub-collaboration will be launched. If another request is sent to the same collaboration, the launched components will be re-used, possibly augmented by some newly created agents.

Dynamic handling of disjunctions. Disjunctions of constraints (i.e., created when a solver computes several solutions) are treated dynamically in BALI. We demonstrate this for the case of sequential collaboration $\mathsf{seq}(S_1,S_2,\ldots,S_n)$. All disjuncts produced by S_1 must be sent to S_2. MANIFOLD allows us to use pipelines to solve c_2 as soon as it is produced by S_1. If S_2 is still working on c_1, and all the other instances of S_2 are busy, then a new instance of S_2 is created for solving c_2. The treatment of c_2 is thus not postponed. This mechanism applies to all sub-agents of the sequential agent.

Coordination. We now informally describe the coordination (performed by the coordinator agent) related to some of the primitives of the solver collaboration language of BALI. More details, including some formal definitions can be found in [37, 430].

Recall that each solver can produce several solutions (i.e., constraints, or stores of constraints). When a solver has enumerated all its solutions, it sends the solution termination message (end). Thus, to manage all these solutions we consider a backtrack-like mechanism among solvers.

We also consider that several instances of an agent can be created, and that there is no concern about using one instance or the other. This is just a matter of efficiency that enables the treatment in parallel (or in a pipelined way) of several solutions given by a solver. Thus, in the following, we just consider a solver (not its instances). Instance management is described in [37].

Sequential primitive. $\mathsf{seq}(S_1,S_2,\ldots,S_n)$ solves a constraint by sequentially applying several solvers. As soon as the coordinator receives a solution (i.e., a constraint or a store of constraints) from an agent S_i, the constraint is forwarded to S_{i+1}. The process is initialized by sending a constraint to S_1. Solutions from S_n are forwarded to the superior agent of this collaboration. In a sequential collaboration, several agents are "pipelined" and work in "parallel", but the solutions are passed "sequentially" from one agent to the next.

Another interesting feature is that the order of solution is not preserved. Assume that S_i produces several solutions $c_1,\ldots,c_n$ one after the other. They are then forwarded to S_{i+1} in the same order. But it can happen that the instance of S_{i+1} that treats c_{m+1} (produced after c_m) is faster than the one treating c_m. Then, the solution created from c_{m+1} will be sent before the one of c_m. This is in fact an important feature, since a treatment will never be delayed by another one. Thus, we obtain a kind of parallel and quick-first search.

The split primitive. $\mathsf{split}(S_1,S_2,\ldots,S_n)$ applies several solvers in parallel on the same constraints. The solution of split is a Cartesian-product-like re-composition of all solutions returned by $S_1,S_2,\ldots,S_n$. When a split agent receives a solve request from its superior, it forwards the request to all its S_i's. Then, it waits and stores all partial solutions of individual S_i's. The split agent creates the elements of the Cartesian-product of the solutions as soon as possible (i.e., as soon as at least one solution from each S_i is received) and forwards them to its superior agent.

The ψ_don't care primitive. $\mathsf{dc}(\psi_1,S_1,S_2,\ldots,S_n)$ introduces concurrency among solvers. Upon receiving a constraint c from its superior, the don't care agent forwards c to all its sub-agents, S_i's. Then it waits for a solution c' from any of its sub-agents. If c' does not satisfy ψ_1 [3] then c' is forgotten and the don't care agent waits for a solution from another sub-agent (other than the one that produced c'). As soon as the don't care agent receives a solution c' from some S_i that satisfies ψ_1, all other sub-agents are stopped and c', as well as all other solutions produced after by S_i, are forwarded to the superior agent.

The fix-point primitive. $\mathsf{f\_p}(S)$ repeatedly applies S on a constraint, until no more information can be extracted from the constraint. The solving process starts when the fix-point agent receives a constraint c from its superior. This is an iterative process in which each solution is sent again to an instance of S untill a fixed point is reached, i.e., the constraint sent to an instance of S and the solution the fix-point coordinator gets from the same instance of S are the same. Then, this solution is sent to the superior agent.

An application of S can create a disjunction of solutions, i.e., enumerate several solutions. But we do not force all these solutions to be treated by the same instance of S. Thus, we do not know how many applications of S may be required, but we favour efficiency [4].

For a description of the coordinators for the repeat and the conditional primitives, as well as a detailed description of the sequential coordinator, see [37].

The Contribution of Coordination. We see that coordination languages, and **MANIFOLD** in particular, are helpful for implementing cooperative constraint solving. However, the advantages of using coordination languages are

---

[3] ψ_1 is an element of the set ψ of boolean functions. They test whether or not a constraint satisfies some properties.

[4] We could consider well defined iteration steps, i.e., waiting for all answers of S before entering the next iteration. But then, already enumerated solutions would always be delayed by the still coming solutions.

not only at the implementation level. MANIFOLD allows an implementation of the formal model of BALI (as opposed to an implementation of a "simplification" of BALI when coordination is not used) and this implies some significant benefits for constraint solving.

We illustrate this point with the treatment of disjunctions which is a key point in constraint solving. The most commonly required search is depth-first: each time several candidates appear, take one, and continue with it until a solution is reached, then backtrack to try the other candidates. One of the reasons for this choice is that, generally, only one solution is required and producing all solutions would be too slow. The coordination we described with MANIFOLD leads to what we call a "parallel depth-first and quick-first" search. The parallel depth-first search is obvious. The quick-first search arises from the fact that each constraint flows through the agents independently from the others. Hence (ignoring the boundary condition of reaching certain resource limits) a constraint is never delayed by another constraint, nor stops at the input of a solver or in a queue. The outcome is that the solution which is the fastest to compute (even if it is not originated from the first disjunct of a solver) has a better chance to become the first solution given by the solver collaboration. We thus obtain a solution faster, and when all solutions are required, we also get all results quicker using parallel computation.

16.2.2 Other Realizations

BALI is not the only realization of a system for solver cooperations, but it is certainly the most demanding one from the point of view of coordination.

Other realizations of solver cooperation systems are of two types: (1) based on a single fixed cooperation scheme, or (2) based on a solver cooperation language somewhat like BALI. In systems that are built out one coordination pattern the topology of agents, the communication streams, and the control are fixed. In languages that define several parameterized coordination patterns the control is fixed, but for each pattern, the topology of its agents is dynamic depending on the solvers involved, and the communication streams must be created according to this topology. There are numerous examples of systems in the first category in the literature, including the system of Marti-Rueher [397] which uses a monitor to coordinate several solvers communicating asynchronously through the monitor. This system basically contains only one coordination pattern. The same can be said about the system of [65] and the solver cooperation of [283] where the coordination pattern is a fixed sequential primitive of BALI. CoSAc [436] is a distributed cooperative system for solving non-linear polynomial constraints. CoSAc fits somewhere in between the two categories above, because it uses several fixed coordination patterns. In CoSAc five heterogeneous solvers cooperate through a client/server architecture, and they can be involved in three different collaborations.

A solver cooperation language is defined in [85] in terms of a set of strategies over a rule-based programming language. Some of these rules are able to call external processes. This cooperation language defines several parametrized coordination patterns, similar to the ones in BALI.

In [143] a control language for designing solvers and solver cooperation is proposed. Such a language can also be translated into several coordination patterns.

16.3 Design of a Constraint Solver

In this section we discuss the design of a constraint solver using a coordination model. Contrary to the case of BALI (see Section 16.2), the transcription leads to a single coordination pattern:

- the structure of the topology is fixed. This means that the number of agents can vary, but they will be of previously defined types in the coordination pattern,
- patterns of communication are fixed, i.e., each agent is linked by a net of streams depending on its type,
- the control is fixed.

However, the coordination pattern can still be parameterized with some strategies. Several agents of a type can be proposed, each of them implementing a strategy. For example, consider agents of type "scheduler" that aim to schedule the actions of a set S of agents. Then, each scheduler agent represents a different strategy, and each of them can be used in the same coordination pattern.

We consider the highlights of one main example in this section: a coordination-based chaotic iteration (CI) algorithm for constraint propagation. Interested readers can also see [432] for more details and technical considerations about this example.

16.3.1 A Coordination-based CI Algorithm

Constraint propagation is one of the most important techniques for solving constraint satisfaction problems [5] (CSP's). It aims at reducing a CSP into an equivalent but simpler one, i.e., the solution space is preserved while the search space is reduced.

Constraint propagation algorithms usually aim at computing some form of "local consistency" described as a common fixed point of some *domain reduction functions*. These algorithms are instances of a more general mathematical framework, the framework of *chaotic iterations* [30] (CI). CI is a basic technique used for computing limits of iterations of finite sets of functions.

---

[5] A constraint satisfaction problem is given by a set of constraints, and for each variable occuring in these constraints, a domain representing the values the variable can assume.

By "feeding" domain reduction functions into a chaotic iteration algorithm, we generate an algorithm that enforces local consistency.

We present a generic framework for constraint propagation using coordination languages. More precisely, we consider the realization of a coordination-based version of the Generic Iteration Algorithm for Compound Domains (CD) of K.R. Apt. Our main motivation is to explain constraint propagation as coordination of cooperative agents, and to provide a flexible, scalable, and generic framework for constraint propagation that overcomes the problems that are inherent in the parallel and distributed algorithms of [434, 435]. Another benefit of our coordination-based framework is that it does not require special modeling of CSP's.

Overview. The basic idea is to exploit the intrinsic relation between constraint propagation and cooperative agents. The main components of the CD algorithm are mapped to basic components of **MANIFOLD**: variables associated with their domains are transformed into extended variables, and domain reduction functions (drf's) are converted into workers. Some channels related to the domains and co-domains of functions are established among variables and workers. In order to compute the limit of the application of the drf's, the execution progresses in the following way: when a variable is modified, it sends a request to its related drf's; when a drf receives a request, it computes a new value and sends it to its output variables. The process terminates when no drf is able to change the value of a variable. Using the features of **MANIFOLD**, we can detect that no worker is busy and no message in pending in a stream.

Constraint Propagation. Many algorithms for constraint solving can be described using a simple component-based framework based on two main interleaving processes: constraint propagation and splitting (i.e., a kind of enumeration mechanism).

Constraint propagation consists of reducing a constraint satisfaction problem (CSP) by computing a common fixed point of domain reduction functions. Each variable of a CSP is associated with a domain, i.e., the set of values the variable can assume. Reducing the CSP generally means reducing these domains, which means removing values for which the constraints do not hold.

Domain reduction functions are related to domains of constraints, and they have been widely studied for standard domains (e.g., Boolean constraints [179], integers, interval arithmetic [66, 431]). For less common domains, either these functions must be designed by hand, or, if the domain is finite, techniques such as in [32] can automate generations of its reduction functions.

We first informally describe our constraint propagation framework. Given a CSP, a set F of domain reduction functions is deduced according to the domain of computation. Then, by feeding these functions and a sequence of domains of variables to the CDA algorithm [6] (see Table 16.2) a fixed-point for the functions in F is computed, i.e., the reduced domains.

Assume that the domains of the variables are finite. Then, every execution of the CDA algorithm terminates and computes in d the largest common fixed point of the function h defined by:

$$h(x) = \bigcap_{f \in F} (x \cap f^+(x))$$

where f^+ denotes the extension of f to D.

CDA ALGORITHM

Input: $d = d_1, \ldots, d_n \in D$: a sequence of domains
            % *associated to variables* $x_1, \ldots, x_n$ *respectively*
            F: a set of domain reduction functions
            % *each from a subset of* $x_1, \ldots, x_n$ *to a subset of* $x_1, \ldots, x_n$
Output: $d' = d'_1, \ldots, d'_n \in D$: a sequence of domains

% *Initialization*
$d' \leftarrow d$
$G \leftarrow F$

% *Loop until no function can modify anymore the domains*
while $G \neq \emptyset$ **do**
     % *Select a domain reduction function*
     choose $g \in G$; suppose g is from $x_{i_1}, \ldots, x_{i_m}$ to $x_{i_1}, \ldots, x_{i_l}$
     $G \leftarrow G \setminus \{g\}$
     % *Application of g to narrow domains*
     $d'_{i_j} \leftarrow d_{i_j} \cap g(d_{i_1}, \ldots, d_{i_m})_{i_j}$ for each $j \in [1..l]$
     % *Update of the list of functions still to be applied*
     $G \leftarrow G \cup \{f \in F - G \mid f$ depends on some $i \in [1..l]$ such that $d \neq d'\}$
     % *Update of the current domains with the newly computed values*
     $d_{i_j} = d'_{i_j}$ for each $j \in [1..l]$
od

Table 16.2. The CDA Algorithm

The Network of Agents and its Behavior. We now consider the realization of a coordination-based version of the CDA algorithm to explain constraint propagation as coordination of cooperative agents. To this end, we map the main components of constraint propagation to certain IWIM processes, and we describe the global behavior of the network of processes.

---

[6] The CDA algorithm is a restriction of the Generic Iteration Algorithm for Compound Domains of [31] and of the CI algorithm of [434] to constraint propagation by domain reduction.

The network. We map the components of the CDA algorithm to two types of agents and introduce an additional special agent (see Figure 16.4): variables (each variable is represented by one coordination variable), drf's (each drf is represented by one worker agent), and an initialization/termination agent. The initialization agent (IP for short) builds the network of variables and drf's, collects solutions, and also detects termination using a standard coordination pattern in **MANIFOLD**.

In the following, we denote by upper-case letters the representation of components of the CDA algorithm: a coordination variable X will represent a domain variable x, and a worker F will represent the implementation of a domain reduction function f.

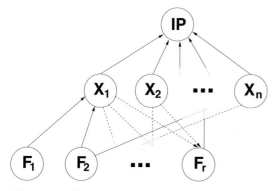

Fig. 16.4. General Network

We proceed in three steps: first, initialization of the network of processes, then computation and reduction of the CSP, and finally, collection of the solutions.

The first phase is carried out by the initialization agent (IP). Given a CSP, and a set of "meta" domain reduction functions, the IP deduces the domain reduction functions required for reducing the given CSP. From these drf's, the IP generates the network of processes together with the channels connecting variables and drf's. Consider a drf f. An input variable of f is a variable whose value is required by f, and an output variable of f is a variable that f potentially modifies. Hence, the drf agent F will have one input channel for each of the input variables of f, and one output channel for each output variable of f. In the second phase, which corresponds to the core of the CD algorithm, only variables and drf's are active. The last phase is just an exchange of messages between IP and the variables for collecting their values.

Behavior of the network. The computation proceeds as follows: variables send requests containing their domain values to domain reduction functions; drf's compute new values and send them to the corresponding variables. The process terminates when no drf is able to change the value of a variable.

A variable X is modified when it receives a new value whose intersection with its current domain value is smaller than its current domain value. Each time a variable X is modified, it requests the drf's F_1, ..., F_n (all drf's that use x in their input) to work with its new domain value. F_1, ..., F_n thus have new tasks to perform. Then, they send their results to each of their output variables $X_1, \ldots, X_m$. $X_1, \ldots, X_m$ may eventually be modified by these values, and this will iterate the process.

The termination is detected when no variable and no function is busy anymore, and no message is pending in a stream between a coordination variable and a domain reduction function. Using the results of [435], it is possible to prove the correctness of the framework, i.e., that the result computed by the coordination-based CDA algorithm is indeed the limit defined by chaotic iteration.

Contribution of Coordination. Managing termination requires mechanisms that generally must be mixed with the computation. Using certain coordination features, and a standard termination pattern, we can neglect this task when designing our agents and control.

In systems such as [434], algorithms are designed considering an implicit termination. However, this "implicit" termination becomes a big issue when real implementations are considered. Using coordination, the termination is easily implemented by introducing some new independent agents, and by adding standard guarded actions to the agents involved in computation.

Due to the coordination and dynamic facilities of the IWIM model, we obtain clear, simpler and more elegant algorithms than in [434, 435] with enhance scalability and distributability. The granularity of the reduction agents can be adapted: simple reduction functions, complex functions, compositions of functions, or even complex solvers. The underlying levels of the coordination language then manage either threads, processes, or connection through the Internet. The designer does not have to care about mapping agents to threads or processes, and connecting them with either pipes, sockets, or through the Internet. Calls to external processes also enable quick implementations of complex drf's and solvers. Scalability allows both solvers and solver cooperations to be designed in this framework.

Certain strategies can be integrated in the framework, simply by adding a scheduling mechanism or replacing agents. This results in more efficient cooperation than pure concurrency can offer. Aside from these "implementation" concerns, solver design can also benefit from coordination. For example, we can transform the CDA algorithm into the Simple Iteration algorithm of [31] by simply ordering the application of functions. This requires a scheduler agent that sequentially raises specific events, each of which is captured by only one DRF.

16.4 Conclusion

The purpose of this chapter was to clarify the issues and concepts involved in solving constraints using a coordination model/language. The way we consider the problem and the point of view we adopt lead to several conclusions on various aspects of this symbiosis.

From a constraint programming point of view, we identified two main areas or directions for processing constraints:

- designing solvers using a single technique or combining tools at a low level,
- solver cooperation that deals with high-level combination and control of black-box solvers.

These two concepts can be associated with data-driven and control driven coordination models, respectively. The first focus on constraint manipulation and emphasizes the data, whereas the second describe control of solvers independently of the data that are exchanged.

Coordination can be used to realize

- families of solver processes that can be transcribed into a single (but parameterized) coordination pattern for specific computation domains; and
- families of constraint solver processes that require several (parameterized) coordination patterns.

The first category consists of constraint solvers and fixed solver cooperation systems, while the second contains solver cooperation languages.

Solver cooperation languages are usually the most demanding of the coordination models and languages. They require intensive use of control constructs to coordinate agents, some event-like mechanism, constructs for dynamic re-configuration of the topology of agent interconnections, and support for heterogeneous programming languages and platforms.

We are convinced that constraint solving can greatly benefit from coordination-based programming. This is because:

- the separation of concerns in coordination (i.e., computation vs. control) matches well the separation of solving techniques and solver cooperations strategies;
- scalability, flexibility, and manageability issues for constraint solving have natural solutions in a coordination framework. Heterogeneous solvers and solving techniques can be combined or connected as black-boxes to build more efficient composite solvers;
- coordination languages transparently takes care of details such as to integrate solvers, one does not have to consider whether the implementation of solvers that are being integrated are threads, processes on a local machine, on a local network of machines, or spread across the Internet;
- unlike parallel computing techniques that focus on performance efficiency, coordination languages provide flexible modeling and design paradigms and can transparently parallelized and/or distribute an application.

Part VI

Visions

Visions

Introduction

Since its birth, the Internet has passed through a so dramatic and fast evolution to make it very hazardous to foresee its evolution in, say, the next twenty years.

Conceived in the late 60's as a tool to support remote access to time-sharing mainframes [407], the Internet has rapidly assumed the role of a communication tool (the very first E-mail has been sent in 1971), of a tool for information sharing (e.g., NFS), of a tool for remote access to information and resources (e.g., ftp, telnet), and, more generally, of a distributed repository for any kind of digital information (e.g., gopher).

The definition of the Web architecture in 1989 [68], integrating effective interoperability solutions and suitable user-friendly metaphors, followed by the deployment of easy-to-use and easy-to-install browsers (e.g., Mosaic, in 1993), provided for another, significant, change of role. Within a few years, the Internet was no longer a tool for the use of researchers and academics only but, instead, a very popular tool that could be made easily available to any kind of people.

Since then, the continuous appearance of new application software and the co-evolution of network and hardware technologies have been changing once again the role of the Internet. From a very general perspective, one can say that the today's Internet is a general-purpose global distributed computing system, in which complex forms of computation, communication, and data manipulation can take place to support, facilitate, and expedite our activities related to information management, telecommunication, and collaboration.

The next step can be agent-based computing. Despite the great deal of talking about intelligent agents, they do not still populate the Internet. Some simple software tools already exist that attempt (or pretend) to exploit agent-based concepts to assist users in accessing and navigating the Internet (e.g., E-mail filters). In the next few years, however, we expect that intelligent agent technology will be able to fulfill its premises and to deploy effective agent-based solutions for personal support to Web access – such as intelligent agents for information retrieval and for data filtering [390] – management – such as mobile agents for the maintenance and the coordination of distributed services [72] – as well as for support to cooperation and coordination activities – such as meetings schedulers and agenda organizers.

The likely-probable success of agent-based computing, together with the trend toward pervasive Internet connectivity and embedded computing, let us envision a world in which a multitude of agents will populate our physical environment and will be in charge of supporting and making more comfortable our everyday lives. For example, we can easily imagine that, in each and every room, a population of embedded agents will be in charge of monitoring or activities and our personal physiological status, and will be able to modify the environment accordingly, e.g., by properly regulating heating and air conditioning. As another example, an agent associated to the fridge will be able to tell us which food items are expired and which ones need refurbishing. And it will be an Internet agent, too. In fact, it will be able to connect itself to the Internet and will be able to automatically re-order the needed items. This agent, by cooperating with the other agents in the kitchen and possibly by consulting a book of recipes in a remote site, will also be able to suggest us the available alternatives for our dinner.

For the above scenario to become reality, suitable and practical development tools will be needed to make the building of such agent systems easier and practical [90]. Also, since communication and coordination between agents will play a primary role, much more than it is currently available from todays coordination models and infrastructures will be needed. In particular, one has to consider that agents will form some sorts of virtual organizations mimicking (when not actively participating in) our real-world organizations. Thus, the engineering of the interactions in such systems will have to necessarily rely on interaction and coordination models inspired by the ones that already play a fundamental role in real-world organizations. On the one hand, since agents will live in an environment with limited resources available, market-based models have to regulate their interactions so as to avoid a global degradation of the organizational efficiency [292, 95]. On the other hand, models and methodologies must be available to support the development of agent-based systems based on appropriate organizational and societal abstractions [656, 142, 314].

The two chapters that conclude this book focus on the above two topics, respectively, and show that, although we still have to wait several years before agent societies will populate the Internet, the research is already headed in that direction and is already confirming the feasibility of the approach.

The contributions

Chapter 17, by Jonathan Bredin, David Kotz, Daniela Rus, Rajiv T. Maheswaran, Çagri Imer and Tamer Başar, focuses on market-based models for mobile-agent systems, with the goal of presenting both an architecture for agent marketplaces and planning algorithms to allow agents an effective expenditure of their budgets.

The described marketplace architecture is a very general one. It involves agents having to purchase the computational resources they consume from hosts, as well as agents able to sell their services to users and other agents. It provides support for commercial transactions between agents (and between agents and hosts), based on the exchange of electronic currency, no matter whether it is redeemable for legal tender currency or not. Finally, the marketplace architecture supports secure transactions via cryptographic protocols and trusted third-party arbiter agents.

Given that agents have a limited endowment, and have to purchase the resources they need to complete their execution, the authors describe an algorithm to allow a mobile agent to plan its execution in a network so as to minimize its global execution time. For the agent to effectively plan its optimal execution, the presented algorithm requires the agent to have the availability of perfect information about the network, the hosts' resources, and their prices. Of course, these assumptions cannot easily apply when Internet agents are involved. However, the authors show, via simulation, that even in the presence of non-accurate information about the status of the network, and despite the presence of dynamically varying prices, the algorithm still enables agents the achievement of good execution times. These results are strongly promising and encourages the development of agent systems in which all coordination activities can be effectively planned in respect of the available budget and accordingly to the marketplace rules.

Chapter 18, by Rune Gustavsson and Martin Fredriksson, puts the focus on the next generation of agent-based Internet applications, e.g., distributed health-care and smart homes, and analyzes the issues that arise in the coordination and in the control of such systems.

The authors identify "computational ecosystems" as a promising direction for advanced Internet applications. Currently, the Internet is shifting from rigid vertical e-business systems connecting buyers and sellers towards worlds – ecosystems – of smart e-services built around a common area of interest. In such ecosystems, value-chains of smart e-services can be seen as being realized and maintained by societies of cooperating agents.

After having introduced the concept of computational ecosystems, together with several application examples, like the COMFY comfort management systems, the authors focuses on the engineering of such systems, and show how societal concepts – such as ownership, responsibility, accessibility – can and have to play a fundamental role in their design.

17. A Market-Based Model for Resource Allocation in Agent Systems

Jonathan Bredin[1], David Kotz[1], Daniela Rus[1], Rajiv T. Maheswaran[2], Çagri Imer[2], and Tamer Başar[2]

[1] Department of Computer Science, Dartmouth College, 6211 Sudikoff Laboratory, Hanover, NH 03755-3510, USA
  {jonathan,dfk,rus}@cs.dartmouth.edu
[2] Coordinated Science Laboratory, University of Illinois
  1308 West Main Street Urbana, Illinois 61801, USA
  maheswar@uiuc.edu,{imer, tbasar}@control.csl.uiuc.edu

Summary.

In traditional computational systems, resource owners have no incentive to subject themselves to additional risk and congestion associated with providing service to arbitrary agents, but there are applications that benefit from open environments. We argue for the use of markets to regulate agent systems. With market mechanisms, agents have the abilities to assess the cost of their actions, behave responsibly, and coordinate their resource usage both temporally and spatially.

We discuss our market structure and mechanisms we have developed to foster secure exchange between agents and hosts. Additionally, we believe that certain agent applications encourage repeated interactions that benefit both agents and hosts, giving further reason for hosts to fairly accommodate agents. We apply our ideas to create a resource-allocation policy for mobile-agent systems, from which we derive an algorithm for a mobile agent to plan its expenditure and travel. With perfect information, the algorithm guarantees the agent's optimal completion time.

We relax the assumptions underlying our algorithm design and simulate our planning algorithm and allocation policy to show that the policy prioritizes agents by endowment, handles bursty workloads, adapts to situations where network resources are overextended, and that delaying agents' actions does not catastrophically affect agents' performance.

17.1 Introduction

Agents are clean abstractions for constructing multiple-user applications. In particular, the abstraction is useful for networked applications where agents represent competing or cooperating principals. We believe that using the agent model, it is possible to quickly construct openly networked architectures where computational resources are distributed around the network for remote and visiting agents to use. There is, however, little incentive for service providers (hosts) to accommodate arbitrary agents. Hosts expose themselves to additional resource contention and risk inherent in offering any additional network service. Conversely, agents have no incentive for responsible resource usage nor mechanisms to assess the costs of their actions.

We solve these problems by having agents use electronic currency to purchase the computational resources that they use. The currency's value gives hosts incentive to entertain arbitrary agents, finite budgets bound agents' impact on the network, prices convey the cost of an agent's actions, and market competition serves as a primitive coordination mechanism.

We argue in Section 17.2 that markets solve problems at many levels faced by agent systems. In Section 17.3, we summarize work we have done to provide a secure marketplace for mobile agents. We provide a resource-allocation policy in Section 17.4 on which we derive an algorithm to minimize a mobile agent's execution time of a sequence of tasks given a budget. Section 17.5 presents simulation results of agents visiting hosts using our resource-allocation policy. We show that it effectively prioritizes agents according to endowment and that our planning algorithm's performance degrades gracefully as network delay increases. We summarize relevant related work in Section 17.6 and conclude by fleshing out our future research direction and describing the applicability of our results to more general agent systems in Section 17.7.

17.2 Markets

We promote agent architectures where agents' potentials are represented through a common parameter– their endowments. Agents may spend their endowments how they see fit to optimize their performance. Rather than specify absolute rules, hosts specify policies to guide agents. While agents may deviate from these policies to tune their performance, they do so at the expense of depleting their endowments, and possibly their lifetimes. The architecture type we propose is that of a market, though the extent of market implementation may vary. In this section, we give a high-level description of market structures applied to agent systems.

Our computational markets involve agents purchasing the computational resources that they consume from hosts. Agents can sell their services to users and other agents. Hosts accumulate revenues that they redistribute to their users, who use the currency to launch their own agents. Figure 17.1 sketches the exchange of money in our market.

Currency exchange can happen at many levels to provide a cleaner design, fault tolerance, and incentive mechanisms. At the most basic form, an agent's currency represents its potential to act in the network. Currency exchange can be modeled at the design level to provide a useful architectural tool by quantifying the limits of agents' actions.

More involved markets have agents and hosts exchange cryptographically verifiable electronic cash. Electronic cash serves as a security mechanism and verifies the spender. This type of budget constraint bounds the havoc that a malicious agent can wreak and provides a limited form of fault tolerance.

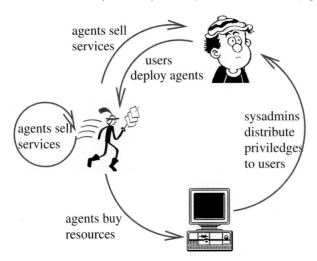

Fig. 17.1. The flow of money in our computational market.

In a still stronger market, participants exchange virtual currency that is redeemable for legal tender currency (e.g, U.S. dollars). Here, the currency verification process is more important and requires more scrutiny. The benefit, however, is that administrative domains become flexible. Resource owners may lease their equipment to agents outside their domain, recouping the cost of capital. Conversely, system administrators may temporarily expand their domains when the need for extra computation arises by buying outside resources.

In each of these examples, we rely on a pricing system. Prices signal the costs of agents' actions and allow agents to plan accordingly. When agents crowd resources, resource prices rise and deter further congestion. Thus, prices serve to balance computational load over time and through the network [620, 149].

17.3 Secure Transactions

The first step towards establishing any market is to promote methods of secure exchange. The most obvious part of secure transactions is a verifiable currency. Sometimes, exchange requires more than just valuable currency and we have implemented a protocol for a trusted third party to mediate transactions between agents who may not trust one another. Agents must be able to find and negotiate with vendors of computational resources, and we have implemented an architecture for agents to locate machine resources through a network of resource management agents. Finally, agents are ultimately subject to the wishes of their hosts, but we argue that interaction between hosts and agents is beneficial to both and that repeated interaction is likely. Repeated interaction and exchange foster cooperation between hosts and agents.

17.3.1 Currency

There are many existing electronic currency systems [276, 363, 449, 500]. As a proof of concept, we have implemented electronic currency and a hierarchy of banks in Agent Tcl, a mobile-agent system [95]. Our currency is verified using PGP and incurs a lot of overhead in comparison to other electronic currency systems, but clearly any of the existing more efficient mechanism could also be used. Most mobile-agent systems cryptographically verify the identity of agents, so verifying currency on agents' arrival does not pose significant additional overhead. After agents verify their currency at a host, they can convert a global currency to local "script" similar to what is done in the Millicent electronic currency system [276]. This local verification reduces transaction costs enough to allow small efficient transactions.

17.3.2 Repeated Interaction

It is frequently the case that repeated interaction among agents creates incentive for cooperation. In this subsection we focus on the effects of frequent interaction between *mobile* agents and their hosts. In this context, a mobile agent is a computational process that may autonomously relocate its execution from one host to another.

Currency validation protects sellers, specifically mobile-agent hosts. Protecting agents from agents and hosts from agents appear to be tractable problems and there has been much progress in the area. Protecting mobile agents from their hosts is difficult, however. A host provides an agent with an execution environment and hence, the mobile agent is at the mercy of its host. There is little to prevent the possibility of the host robbing visiting mobile agents.

While it may always be possible for hosts to molest mobile agents, we believe that it is in hosts' best interests to provide safe and reliable execution environments. In establishing a market for computation, it must be the case that transactions benefit both hosts as well as agents. If this were not the case, then either agents or hosts would not participate in the exchange.

Additionally, we believe that mobile-agent applications will likely rely on frequently sending small agents to remote sites. Thus, a mobile-agent market for computational resources will see repeated interaction between hosts and agents. Since molesting an agent risks upsetting a host's income stream, there is incentive for the host and agents to cooperate. Axelrod sees many examples of cooperation development in scenarios where there is repeated interaction among human agents and that often little communication is necessary between agents to foster cooperation [46].

17.3.3 Arbiter

While we believe that in many circumstances an agent will deal with known agents and facilities, it is likely that at some point it will be necessary to conduct transactions between untrusting parties. There may be little reason to believe that there will be future transactions, or agents may prefer to conceal their identities. To support such transactions, we have implemented an arbiter protocol for use within Agent Tcl [95].

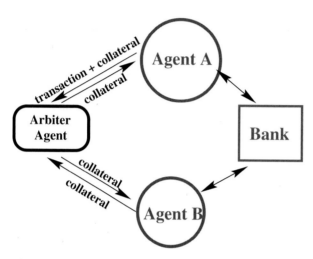

Fig. 17.2. The arbiter protocol for secure transaction between agents. Agents A and B send collateral and the transaction to a trusted third party, the arbiter agent. Once the arbiter agent receives payments from the agents, it delivers the product and payment to the agents. After an agreed upon time, if neither agent complains, the arbiter returns the collateral to agents.

In our arbiter protocol, agents arrange for a trusted third party, an arbiter, to conduct the transaction. The arbiter asks each agent for the information to be exchanged between the agents, and an amount of collateral equal to the value of the transaction from each agent. If, by an agreed upon time, neither agent is unhappy with the resulting transaction, the arbiter returns the collateral to the agents. If, however, one agent does not receive the goods or payment that it expected, the arbiter retains both agents' collateral until the transaction can be policed.

17.3.4 Resource Managers

To facilitate resource location and access negotiation in the D'Agents mobile-agent system, every host machine has a set of well-known resource-management agents [286]. These agents are responsible for allocating their respective resources and all resource consumption requests are directed to them.

Resource managers are agents and use the same communication protocols as every other agent, so transactions between an agent and a resource manager do not require any additional protocol. Any agent request to use a resource is automatically forwarded to the relevant resource manager, however, and resource consumption can be transparent to consumer agents.

Resource managers allow system administrators to tune resource access to fit individual resource consumption habits. Certain resources may require specialized policies or coordination with other resources. Several resource managers may work together to prevent deadlock or to track suspicious resource usage.

17.4 Allocation Mechanism

We now provide a specific market model that for use in allocating computation to mobile agents. For a more rigorous system formulation, we refer the reader to [97, 96]. In our model, a mobile agent attempts to minimize the time taken to execute a series of tasks each requiring consumption of a particular service.

For example, an agent may wish to retrieve an image at one site, process the image using a computationally intensive algorithm at another, and then deliver the image to be displayed at a display located near its user. Figure 17.3 depicts the agent's example itinerary. Each of the three sites that the agent visits may allow the agent to pay more to complete its task faster.

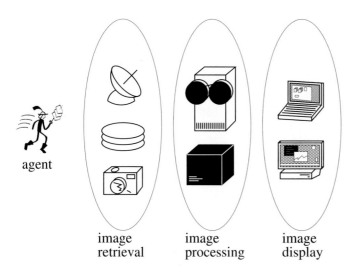

Fig. 17.3. An example of a mobile agent's itinerary. The agent must visit one host in each group and choose at what priority to execute at each host visited.

After an agent finishes all execution, its remaining endowment vanishes. Each host offers one of K computational services to the set of agents at the site. To extract agent demand, hosts solicit bid functions from the agents. The bids represent rates at which the bidder will pay for access to the service. The i-th agent receives service at a rate equal to the capability, c_k^i, of the k-th host times the agent's bid, u_k^i, relative to the sum of all bids the host receives, $\theta_k = \sum_i u_k^i$. So the i-th agent computes its task at site k at a rate of:

$$v_k^i = c_k^i \left(\frac{u_k^i}{u_k^i + \theta_k^{-i}} \right) \tag{17.1}$$

where $\theta_k^{-i} = \theta_k - u_k^i$ represents the sum of competing agents' bids. The amount of time an agent spends to complete its task is the size of the job, q_k^i, divided by the computational rate, v_k^i, which is:

$$t_k^i = \frac{q_k^i(u_k^i + \theta_k^{-i})}{c_k^i u_k^i} \tag{17.2}$$

The amount of currency an agent spends is its bid, u_k^i, multiplied by the time taken, t_k^i, is:

$$e_k^i = \frac{q_k^i(u_k^i + \theta_k^{-i})}{c_k^i}. \tag{17.3}$$

We derive a bidding strategy that minimizes the time to complete an agent's itinerary given knowledge of the itinerary's task sizes, the amounts competing agents bid, the capacities of all hosts to be visited, a fixed budget constraint, and the assumption that the agent has no need for currency other than to complete its set of tasks at hand.

We begin by assuming that the agent's bid is small enough that competing agents will not change their bids significantly in response to the agent's bid. From this assumption, we derive $f^i(\theta_1^{-i})$, the i-th agent's optimal bid at the first host as a function of competing agents' bids, θ_1^{-i}. The agent's naive bidding strategy for the i-th is:

$$u^i = f^i(\theta_1^{-i}) = \max \left(\frac{\alpha^i - \beta^i \theta_1^{-i}}{\beta^i + \frac{\gamma^i}{\sqrt{\theta_1^{-i}}}}, 0 \right). \tag{17.4}$$

The parameters α^i, β^i, and γ^i describe the i-th agent's itinerary and the state of the hosts it will visit:

$$\alpha^i = I - \sum_{k \neq 1} \frac{q_k^i}{c_k^i} \theta_k^{-i} \tag{17.5}$$

$$\beta^i = \frac{q_1^i}{c_1^i} \tag{17.6}$$

$$\gamma^i = \sum_{k \neq 1} \frac{q_k^i}{c_k^i} \sqrt{\theta_k^{-i}} \tag{17.7}$$

where I is the agent's remaining endowment.

In reality, however, other agents will change their bids in response to the agent's bid. We must augment our bidding strategy to accommodate other agents' responses by finding an equilibrium bidding level at which all agents' bidding functions are satisfied. We can find the equilibrium by transforming each agent's bidding function domain to a domain common to each agent. The original domain operates over the over the space of the sum of all other agents' bids, θ_1^{-i}, while the transformed domain, θ_1, includes the bid of the i-th agent. The result is:

$$u^i = g(\theta_1) = \frac{(\alpha^i - \beta^i \theta_1)^2}{2\gamma^{i2}} \left(-1 + \sqrt{1 + \frac{4\gamma^{i2}\theta_1}{(\alpha^i - \beta^i \theta_1)^2}} \right) \tag{17.8}$$

when $\theta \in (0, \alpha^i/\beta^i)$ and $u^i = g(\theta_1) = 0$ otherwise. The fraction α^i/β^i represents the rate at which the agent can pay to compute at the first host. If α^i/β^i is less than θ_1, the agent does not have enough money to be serviced given the current level of site congestion. If the quotient is negative, then the agent must wait until congestion at future hops subsides. To ensure that $g(\theta)$ is continuous, we require γ^i to be strictly positive. Normally, γ^i would only be zero when the agent bids for its last task. We approximate the situation by assigning γ^i an arbitrarily small positive value to keep $g(\theta)$ continuous.

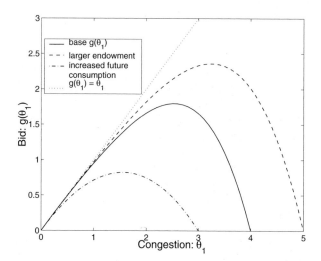

Fig. 17.4. The form of an agent's bid as a function of all bids submitted to the server. As the agent's endowment increases, the function scales outward. Increasing the size of future tasks results in a smaller gentler curve.

Figure 17.4 sketches three examples of agents' bidding functions for the next task. The function, $g(\theta)$, has a few important properties. First, a positive bid computed with $g(\theta)$ guarantees that the agent can complete the task at the current level of congestion. After completing the task with the bid computed from $g(\theta)$, the agent will have enough cash remaining to finish its itinerary given current network conditions. The function is continuous and concave in the upper right quadrant. Finally, $du/d\theta$ equals one at the origin.

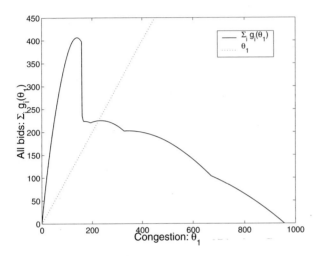

Fig. 17.5. Sample plot of the sum of 16 agents' bids a function of the sum of all bids at the server. Equilibrium occurs at the intersection of the dotted line and the plotted curve, where no agent wishes to change its bid.

We complete the description of our resource-allocation policy by allowing each agent to submit the parameters α^i, β^i, and γ^i that describe its itineraries, wealth, and perceived state of the network. If there are multiple agents visiting, the host constructs all the bidding functions, sums them, and finds a value of θ at which $\theta = \sum_i g(\theta)$ and allocates a fraction of the computational resources to the i-th agent equal to $g^i(\theta_1)/\theta_1$. This determines a Nash equilibrium for the underlying non-cooperative game. If there is only one agent, then there is no contention for the resource and the host assigns the agent the full share of resources. Figure 17.5 demonstrates an example of 16 agents' bidding function and the resulting equilibrium, which we show as the intersection of the sum of the individual bidding curves and the 45° line. In [97], we prove that when there are two or more agents at a server, there is exactly one bidding level at which agents will be satisfied with their bids given their bidding functions. This means that the underlying game has a unique Nash equilibrium.

Note that to utilize Equation 17.8, an agent must already have formulated a route. If we fix the costs and times required for an agent to complete its tasks at every host, the problem of choosing the hosts to visit to minimize execution time under its budget constraint is NP-complete. The problem is the constrained shortest path problem to which the knapsack problem can be reduced [15, 96]. We are currently working on algorithms that use dynamic programming to approximate optimal routing with performance guarantees.

As a reasonable heuristic, the i-th agent can use Equation 17.8, by setting the values of θ_k^i and c_k^i parameters for tasks after the present task, to represent the mean values of hosts that may complete the agent's k-th job. We demonstrate the effectiveness of the heuristic in the next section.

17.5 Simulation

We generate a network topology with the GT-ITM stochastic network topology generator [121] to implement a simulation of a network of mobile-agent hosts in the Swarm simulation system [374]. In GT-ITM, a network consists of a hierarchal system of transit domains connecting stub domains. The networks in our simulation have 100 host nodes in three levels of transit domains. Because we focus on expenditure planning, we choose network delays that do not dominate job execution times.

Host capacity is determined by a positively truncated Gaussian random variable with a positive mean. Hosts offer one of eight services to mobile agents that are created at a Poisson rate uniformly across the network.

At creation, we give each agent an itinerary of tasks and an endowment of currency with which to buy computation from hosts. The number of tasks comprising itineraries is exponentially distributed. We choose tasks uniformly from the eight services that hosts offer. In our simulations, job sizes are either exponentially or Pareto distributed. We choose the endowment to be a positively truncated random variable multiplied by the sum of the agent's task sizes. This random variable represents the agent's owner's preference that the agent completes its itinerary quickly.

1:	$t_{min} := \infty; \quad nextHost := \emptyset$
2:	**for all** hosts k offering service next in itinerary **do**
3:	$t_k :=$[`transferLatency` `to:` k `from:` $currentHost$]
	$\quad + q_k g(\theta_k^{-i}) / (c_k(\theta_k^{-i} + g(\theta_k^{-i})))$
4:	**if** $t_{min} > t_k$ **then**
5:	$t_{min} := t_k; \quad nextHost := k$
6:	**end if**
7:	**end for**
8:	return $nextHost$

Fig. 17.6. Algorithm: Choose Next Site for Agent i

The algorithm in Figure 17.6 demonstrates how agents choose which sites to visit. For all but the next set of hosts to be visited, the agent plans to visit sites with average capacity, c_k, and congestion, θ_k, for hosts offering the k-th service. The agent assumes that there will be no change in bidding level, θ_k^{-i}, and chooses the next site to be the one that minimizes the sum of execution times and network transfer times for the next hop. Thus, our routing algorithm is greedy and naive.

When an agent arrives at the site, it commits itself to finishing its next task at the site. The agent submits parameters α_i, β_i, and γ_i, from Equations 17.5-17.7, to describe its current task and ability to pay for service. The host uses the algorithm in Figure 17.7 to redistribute priority whenever an agent arrives or departs. The algorithm forms a bid-response function, $\sum_i g_i(\theta)$, and conducts a bisection search to find a positive value of θ at which no agent wishes to change its bid.

```
1:    while true do
2:        t := time since last arrival/departure
3:        for all agents i do
4:            deduct tg_i(θ) from agent i's endowment
5:        end for
6:        add new agent or remove departing agent
7:        for all agents i do
8:            query agent i for α, β, and γ
9:            use Equations 17.5-17.7 to build g_i(θ)
10:       end for
11:       search for θ = Σ_{i=1}^{N} g_i(θ) in (0, max_i(α_i/β_i))
12:       for all agents i do
13:           v_k^i := c_k g_i(θ)/θ
14:       end for
15:   end while
```

Fig. 17.7. Algorithm: Allocate Resources for Host k

17.5.1 Effectiveness

We would like to first verify that our resource-allocation method stratifies agents' performance in a reasonable fashion. After the network has reached a steady state, we designate seven percent of all new agents to be test agents. These test agents all share a common start host and task-type sequences, but their endowments uniformly span two standard deviations, σ, around the mean endowment, μ. We measure the performance of each test agent against what it could achieve in a network with zero resource contention. This idealized measure is the shortest path from the start host to visit hosts that offer services to complete the agent's itineraries. The edge lengths of the path are the sum of the network transfer latencies from the previous host and the time required to process the job given that no other agent requests service, q_k/c_k.

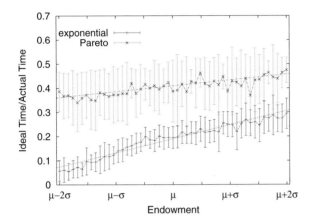

Fig. 17.8. Endowment versus ideal time relative to actual time. We plot the observed mean and standard deviations for each endowment level for two experiments for agents two standard deviations, σ, around the mean endowment, μ. One experiment has exponentially distributed job sizes and the other uses a Pareto distribution.

We run four experiments to show how agents are prioritized. There are two variables describing the experiments: workload and utilization. The two workloads are differentiated by agents' job size distribution. One workload uses an exponential distribution and the other uses a Pareto distribution.

There are two levels of utilization in the experiment. One level is approximately 70 percent of capacity while the other has agents arriving with jobs of about 140 percent of capacity. In the latter situation, it must be the case that some agents will not be able to complete their tasks.

Figures 17.8 and 17.9 show the performance of agents with different endowments at 70 and 140 percent utilization, respectively. We plot the means as well as the standard deviations for each endowment level. The Pareto distribution has a much lower median than an exponential distribution with the same expected value. Hence there are more small jobs that are easier to schedule and agents with Pareto distributed jobs generally perform their itineraries more quickly than those with exponentially distributed job sizes.

In the experiments run at 70 percent utilization, there is a weak linear relationship between agents' expenditure and their performance. Since the system can accommodate all agents, there is little need to discriminate against agents with low endowments to improve the performance of agents with larger endowments.

When agent demand exceeds system capacity, however, hosts must ignore poorer agents to allow richer agents to complete their tasks. In this scenario,

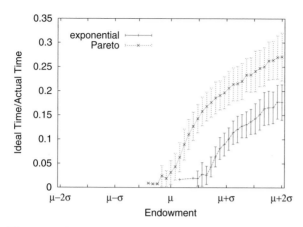

Fig. 17.9. Endowment versus ideal time relative to actual time when agent requests exceed capacity. We plot observations two standard deviations, σ, around the mean endowment μ.

there is a strong relationship between agents' endowment and performance and agents with endowments below the mean do not complete their jobs.

17.5.2 Network Delay

One criticism of market systems is the belief that they are sensitive to the accuracy of knowledge concerning the state of the world. We test this belief by varying the latency incurred by agents jumping from one host to another. Agents have accurate information concerning the current state of the network, but increasing the transfer latency delays agents' actions and simulates agents using aged information.

Figure 17.10 demonstrates that agents' performance decays gradually as the quality of their network information decreases. The figure plots network delay compared to a reference network with the performance that agents receive in the reference network. We observe that increasing network delays does not cripple our resource-allocation or planning algorithms.

17.5.3 Price Structure

Figure 17.11 shows a histogram of the logarithm of price of computation at a server in our simulation. We observe that price is log-normally distributed over time. With a log-normal distribution, agents can expect that price will be stable for the most part, punctuated with intense, but brief, periods of high prices.

These periods of contention aggravate agents' ability to complete their tasks. When the price of computing is high, it is frequently the case that

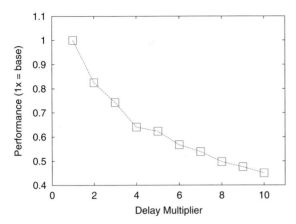

Fig. 17.10. The mean performance of agents over all endowment levels versus network delays relative to the mean performance of agents operating in a network with a delay multiplier of one.

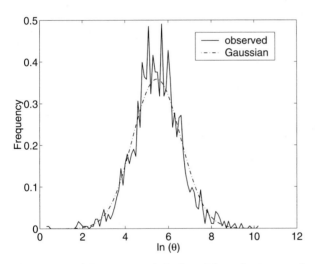

Fig. 17.11. A histogram of the logarithm of price at a host over time. We observe that price is roughly log-normally distributed, resulting in intense but brief periods of high prices.

one agent is consuming the majority of the host's computational resources to complete a small task. While the price is high, other agents' tasks are put on hold, but the flow of agents into the system continues. So it is imaginable that the host's load will not fall back to its initial level for an extended period. These periods add to the variability of agents' performance and in Section 17.7 we will discuss methods for agents to trade risk to decrease their performance volatility.

17.6 Related Work

Economic ideas for controlling computational resources are not new; in the sixties, Sutherland established auctions to schedule computer time among users [574]. Spawn is perhaps the most cited work dealing with computational economic systems [620]. In Spawn, agents participate in auctions to buy processor time to run computationally intensive jobs. The pricing system pairs idle processors with jobs and improves utilization in distributed systems. Clearwater *et al.* use double auctions to allow agents to trade climate-control resources within an office building [178]. The result is that climate control resources are more effectively allocated with energy saving of up to ten percent.

Forms of market-based control have been a part of mobile-agent systems from the field's beginnings. One of the first mobile-agent systems, Telescript [631], supports a fault-tolerance and security measure where agents carry "permits" to access specific resources. A permit's power diminishes over an agent's lifetime, thus limiting the agent's lifetime. A permit for one resource is not easily converted to another resource permit. A more general policy would be for hosts to issue a common permit in the form of a verifiable electronic currency.

The Geneva Messengers project [605] applies market ideas to allocate CPU usage and memory to visiting "messengers," lightweight mobile programs implemented in a Postscript-like language. Host sites heuristically set prices by examining the amount of resources requested by the present messengers.

POPCORN [508] is a system for distributing "computelets" to hosts on the network. POPCORN assigns computelets to anonymous entrepreneurial hosts through a double auction. Because agents do not choose their sites and no mobility after initial placement is allowed, there is no reason for agents to plan their expenditures. Additionally, the framework does not permit inter-computelet communication. POPCORN is ideal for parallel computation intensive programs where interaction among threads is limited. Our system is more general, but mobile agents must weigh many factors in choosing their hosts and agents are accountable for planning their routes and expenditures.

Boutilier *et al.* solve sequential resource-allocation problems [87]. It is difficult to construct mechanisms where it is rational for buyers to truthfully reveal their preferences, but Boutilier *et al.* resolve the problem by ensuring that all users vying for resources interact with identical agents. They prove that it is rational for users to express their preferences to their agents, who then compete in iterated sequential auctions until a stable resource allotment is found. The method can handle many traditionally difficult assignment problems where goods may be complements or substitutes to one another. The technique is centralized and more general than what we model in that it makes no assumptions on resource values and relations, but it is also computationally more expensive.

Tatonnement is another centralized resource-allocation method where buyers iteratively adjust purchase amounts in response to sellers' changing prices. The WALRAS algorithm [152] is a system for finding equilibrium where participants have convex utility functions and there is gross substitutability among goods (goods are not complementarities for one another), but often converges to a solution even when gross substitutability is violated.

Market-based resource control appears in non-research applications. In 1997, *distributed.net* [376] entered a contest held by RSA Labs to break a 56-bit secret-key encrypted message. The project wrote a client that users downloaded to search portions of the key space on users' computers. The winning user, or team of users, received a prize from *distributed.net*. The prize is a probabilistic payment for users' computing resources by *distributed.net*.

Another use of market-based control is Enron Communications' [341] establishment of bandwidth trade among its customers. Enron Communications' customers can resell their unused bandwidth to other customers in an automated fashion. Currently, trade is restricted to bandwidth of a single link connecting New York and Los Angeles.

17.7 Conclusions

We provide the framework upon which to build market-based resources in the D'Agent mobile-agent system. This framework includes a secure currency, well-known resource manager agents, arbiter agents for larger transactions, and an environment with repeated interaction to foster cooperation among agents and their hosts. We provide a resource-allocation method for computational priority and derive an algorithm that allows a mobile agent to plan execution of a sequence of tasks to minimize execution time given a budget constraint.

It is possible to supplement our serial bidding algorithms with other algorithms to minimize parallel task execution time. An extension would likely accompany more complex task planning as well. Our model applies to general agent uses, not just mobile ones, as our policy and algorithms minimize execution time for sequential tasks. Using our policy, it is possible to allocate any divisible resources. For example, we can apply our algorithm as a decentralized method of flow control for network bandwidth by auctioning off bandwidth.

We simulate our allocation mechanism and agents using our planning algorithms to show that our system handles different workloads and adapts to handle situations where resources are over-constrained by ignoring lower-priority agents' requests. Additionally, our system degrades gracefully as network latency increases and suggests that agents can reason effectively without complete network state information.

We observe that prices in our computational markets can be volatile, however. This volatility adds uncertainty to agents' performance and it is desirable for users to have the knowledge of how their agents will perform when agents are launched. For this reason, we are currently researching reservation systems where hosts issue call options to agents. A call option gives an agent the right, but not the obligation, to buy computation at a specified time and price in the future. There will still be volatility in agents' performance, but the uncertainty associated with an agent's performance will be eliminated once the agent holds options for its computation.

Another limitation with our work is that we assume that we can parameterize every application through controlling access to a single good. In reality, the good that we control is a bundle of resources that we label "computational priority." If agent applications have similar resource usage habits, controlling the bundled resources will suffice to regulate the system. If the application space is more diverse, then it may be more efficient to separately allocate multiple resources among agents. For example, some agents may wish to purchase high-quality network connections, but not consume very much processor time, while there may be other agents with opposite needs.

Traditionally, multiple resource allotment has been a computationally difficult problem. The problem becomes intractable when an agent may substitute one good for another. Recently, however, there has been much effort spent towards allocating many resources to agents [87, 254, 484, 532]. So far, there are no bounds on the amount of time necessary to compute an allotment, but these recent projects investigate allocating numbers of goods ranging from ten to hundreds. We imagine that allocating half a dozen resources to agents will provide an efficient allocation and it may be reasonable to allocate multiple resources to agents.

Acknowledgements

This work is supported in part by Department of Defense contract MURI F49620-97-1-0382, DARPA contract F30602-98-2-0107, and an ARO/EPRI contract. We would like to thank Robert Gray for implementing the core D'Agents system and Joe Edelman for implementing the banking, arbiter, and currency systems inside Agent Tcl.

18. Coordination and Control in Computational Ecosystems: A Vision of the Future

Rune Gustavsson and Martin Fredriksson

Department of Software Engineering and Computer Science,
University of Karlskrona/Ronneby,
S-37225 Ronneby, Sweden.
rgu@ipd.hk-r.se, mfe@ipd.hk-r.se

Summary.

In computational ecosystems the focus is on creating and maintaining value-adding chains of e-services. The e-services are created, maintained and used by actors with a common interest in an ecosystem. Ecosystems can be seen as hubs supporting, for instance, financial services, distributed health-care or smart homes. We argue that coordination and control in an ecosystem have to support trust among participating parties. This means, among other things, that the architecture and infrastructure of the ecosystem have to incorporate societal support to meet requirements such as trust creation and maintenance. More precisely, we advocate that basic societal concepts to support are Ownership, Responsibility, and Accessibility (ORA). The paper gives an introduction to the concept of ecosystems. We also provide an example of a potential e-service in the form of a comfort management system (COMFY) in a smart home. The paper also includes an layered ORA architecture built on top of SUNs Jini platform.

18.1 Introduction

In earlier chapters of the book the focus has been on existing and emerging models and technologies of agent coordination as such. In this chapter, we will put the focus on a next generation of Internet applications with a visionary touch. These visions will be articulated in the next section, 18.2 Towards Computational Ecosystems. The bottom line is that the driving force in this type of Internet applications is the ability to create value-adding chains, composed by more or less smart e-services available in a system built around a common area of interest. A basic revenue model in the computational ecosystem is built around e-services on a pay-per-use basis (see [314] for a general outline of computational ecologies and ecosystems). Finally, acceptance and hence use of the offered services is based on the concept of trust.

We will see that coordination and control in ecosystems has more complementary purposes and patterns than those found in the usual setting of distributed problem solving. This is the main theme of this chapter and will be treated in more details in sections 18.4 Coordination and Control in Ecosystems and 18.5 Methodological Issues and the Engineering of Ecosystems.

In section 18.3.3 The Comfort Management System, we give an example of a computational ecosystem, the COMFY physical comfort control. The purpose of the COMFY example is threefold. Firstly it exemplifies a multi-agent solution for a quite sophisticated comfort control service. The solution is interesting in itself and we can show that the solution also has a clear business potential. Secondly, it supports the following argument; in order to create accepted business opportunities around the COMFY service it should be part of an ecosystem around smart homes or buildings. The COMFY solution can thus be seen as an e-service built as a well-defined value-chain of reusable e-services. From this example we can also exemplify how we can create a trust relationship between the COMFY service and its users based on the fundamental concepts of ownership, responsibility, and accessability (ORA) connected to e-services. The concepts of Ownership, Responsibility, and Accessability as well as their grounding in the real world is the focus of section 18.6 ORA: Merging of the Real and Virtual. Thirdly, the COMFY generated ecosystem also gives us a concrete motivation for our methodological approach towards engineering of ecosystems, specifically on coordination and control in ecosystems. Section 18.4 addresses these topics. Also, our implementation of COMFY on a Jini (see chapter 4 for more information) based platform, called SOLACE, illustrates our methodological approach.

The chapter ends with section 18.7 SOLACE: A Layered ORA Architecture and the section 18.8 Conclusions.

18.2 Towards Computational Ecosystems

We have rapidly entered the era of e-business and e-commerce. Whole industries have been turned upside down in the efforts of giving the customer direct access to parts of the company's business model. New startups have become billion dollar companies. Well-known examples are Amazon.com, eToys.com, and eBay.com. Thousands of businesses got wired with e-business. Millions, soon billions, of customers came or will come online, e-commerce was born. Not only products are for sale but also competencies. Keen.com connects people to a rich variety of experts, you can even apply to become a new expert and your success depends on how many customers you got. At epinions.com you get paid for expressing your opinion on services and offers on the Internet. Collab.net allows you for instance to join software development teams or to share software.

A recent trend on the Internet is a transition from more rigid vertical e-business systems connecting buyers and a seller towards ecosystems with buyers, sellers, service providers, and content providers exploring opportunities in areas of common interests.

At the core of an e-services world is an ecosystem, the total trading community in which a company exists. If you are a utility company, for example, you sell kWh or water. But, the ecosystem that you live in is the total exchange of goods and services related to what people do with kWh and water. Buying home appliances is part of the utility ecosystem, as is the building and building maintenance where electric grids and plumbing are important infrastructures for kWh usage and water supply. The concept of smart homes can most naturally be regarded as a new type of ecosystem overlapping the earlier mentioned utility ecosystem. We will return to this example in the next chapter on e-comfort services. That ecosystem is much larger than just one company's single ecosystem. There is a fundamental difference between a dot com company of today and e-services. Dot com companies are mainly about making money by selling products. E-services make money by developing value in an ecosystem. Through the use of hubs ecosystems of e-services can be allied on the fly. Rather than determining all entities in a transaction in advance, e-services will permit the spontaneous composition of services to meet a specific need.

Swedish banks are already quite advanced utilizers of the web. More and more of financial services are already done electronically by letting customers, via the Internet, have access to a broad range of bank services. As an obvious next step, at least one major Swedish bank will create an electronic hub connecting customers of the bank and supporting creation of new customer-to-customer business patterns. Of course, the bank will support this by providing services such as a secure cash flow in the hub and also broker and matching services. In essence, the former centralized banking model of treating each customer individually has been replaced by an ecosystem consisting of the bank, its customers and their customers forming a system built on trusted and value-adding services, or e-services.

Concrete examples of ecosystems are emerging as companies are building their net-based business models around providing services rather than products. We, the authors of this chapter, are involved in several projects aiming at identifying new ecosystems out of the possibilities of connecting people and smart equipment in networks. The idea is to break vertical applications into chains of services that can be reused and to focus on selling functions and information (i.e. services) rather than products. Some examples are:

- From selling a commodity such as kWh to services such as COMFY comfort (see section 18.3.3).
- From selling heat-exchange hardware to selling heating services.
- From selling washing machines to selling washing services.
- The banking example above, i.e., opening a hub connecting customers to the bank and thus creating an ecosystem.
- Home based health care as an ecosystem around the patient.

Needless to say, the necessary transformation of business models can be very dramatic for companies and organisations. Many issues have to be properly addressed and solved before the expectations will become fulfilled. As a matter of fact the European Commission has made an initiative, Universal Information Ecosystems, as a part of the Fifth Framework IST programme. We are participating in that programme with a project called Alfebiite - A logical Framework for Ethical Behaviour between Infohabitants of the Universal Information Ecosystem [23]. A key area of investigation in that particular project is how we can understand, create and support the concept of trust in future information ecosystems.

Where do agents fit in and play a natural role in ecosystems and the value-chains of e-services? Again a shift from products toward services allow us to shift from agents as such to the smart e-services they offer. Value-chains of smart e-services can thus be seen as being realized and maintained by cooperating agents. However, there is a change of focus concerning the purpose of the agent coordination. Most multi-agent systems of today are geared towards collaborative problem solving, e.g., resource management realized as a computational market [651]. In the ecosystem world the focus is value-creation as a result of the cooperation, i.e., (re-) combining services in a purposeful way. A methodology for agent based ecosystems thus has a specific flavor. We will return to this topic in section 18.5 Methodological Issues and the Engineering of Ecosystems.

The concepts of e-services and ecosystems are supported by companies such as Hewlett-Packard, Ariba, Computer Science Corporation, and Nortel as a basis for their new system solutions [481].

18.3 Smart E-Services to Achieve Customer Satisfaction

The purpose of agent based services (smart e-services) in software applications is to increase customer satisfaction for the users they represent. However, in today's personal interface agents, for example for information search and filtering on the web, it is the end user who is made fully responsible for specifying what customer satisfaction precisely means.

In foundational theories for agents, such as game, decision, and microeconomic market theory, utility functions as a numerical measure for customer satisfaction are simply supposed to preexist as known input. In practical applications this assumption is usually false. In many services, customer satisfaction and customer preferences are qualitative concepts, often rather tacit to both producers and users of these services, hard to quantify and measure, and difficult to understand in terms of the causal factors and control parameters that produce customer satisfaction. In summary, such electronic service agents simultaneously need an integrated range of rather advanced capabilities. Nevertheless, our COMFY system shows how this is possible in practice.

The rest of this section is organized as follows. section 18.3.2 describes how to formalize the concept of comfort. Here, scale methods from social science research [211] are a good starting point to express customer satisfaction.

This scale is then linked to an underlying causal factor model, originally developed by Fanger, and available as an international ISO standard [478]. This model provides the baseline of an e-service for comfort delivery. The service is outlined in the form of an agent-based application for automatic comfort management system (COMFY). For a full description of the system, please refer to [78]. In that particular paper a certain procedure is described that has been used in order to convert the comfort scale into cardinal utility functions that underlie economically rational behavior of the COMFY agents. The paper also describes how to optimize comfort at runtime over a selected period of time (e.g. a day), such that the agents achieve customer-desired comfort at the lowest possible cost in a real-time dynamic price setting. The agents' dynamics and the role of utility, observation and control variables, and resource market prices in the optimization process are also discussed. Simulations of several scenarios have been carried out and quantitative results are presented in section 18.3.3 The Comfort Management System.

18.3.1 Energy Saving

The COMFY system is an extension of our previous research on so-called HomeBot agents, see for example [651][21][294]. The HomeBot agents act as, communicating and economically rational, individual representatives of building offices, rooms, and energy-consuming smart equipment or appliances. The economic context is one of a deregulating energy and telecom industry sector. This is underway now in many countries, including the US, UK, Scandinavia, The Netherlands, and other European countries. The liberalization of the energy market induces strong price competition as well as the need for better customer service [19]. Rather than sticking to the usual fixed tariffs, there is an economic incentive to exploit dynamic, real-time prices for energy as they may lower costs and improve the required real-time match between production, distribution, and consumption. Several countries already have a spot market for energy.

The present work is set in the context of a business scenario where users have the possibility to optimize their energy consumption based on real-time dynamic pricing. Such a scenario is already a reality for distributors, retailers and big users in deregulated markets, and is a marketable service for the small end users in the very near future.

18.3.2 Comfort

Another good example of a customer service issue is the concept of "comfort". For a full treatment of the involved issues, we refer to the full paper in the references [78]. Comfort, in the sense of the quality of the climate as perceived by people living and working in buildings and homes, poses an interesting challenge for electronic agent-based services for several reasons:

- Comfort is clearly a qualitative concept for the end user: people will typically be able to say whether or not they "like" the climate in a building, but they will find it extremely hard to make this more explicit beyond qualitative statements.
- Comfort is a personal concept: users will generally differ concerning to what extent a given building climate is perceived as comfortable, and what climate they personally prefer.
- Comfort is a sophisticated multi-dimensional concept, as it causally depends on many interacting factors such as temperature, humidity, clothing, sunshine and other environmental conditions.
- Delivering comfort in buildings is a large-scale and real-time problem, as it depends on the many living and working functions that different parts of a home or building are intended for, and on the ever-changing external and internal factors (weather, presence of people, what they are actually doing, etc.).
- Delivering comfort in buildings is an economic issue: from marketing studies [375] it is known that the financial costs of energy and equipment needed for heating, cooling, air quality, and climate control are key issues for customers and building managers.
- Comfort can be implemented as a service, accessible in a smart home ecosystem containing business partners and end users.

Comfort is the sensation experienced by a person caused by the combination of atmospheric factors like temperature, humidity and air velocity. Although aspects as illumination and noise are sometimes considered to be part of the comfort in a building as well, we focus on thermal comfort only. Comfort is subjective; some persons like it hot and humid, while others prefer a more fresh and dry environment. The atmospheric factors sometimes strengthen and sometimes weaken each other's effect on a certain sensation.

These aspects of comfort are combined in Fanger's comfort model [478]. This model identifies a quantification of the notion of comfort and is based on extensive empirical research on how people experience comfort. The model gives six aspects that together constitute the comfort a person experiences in a room. These underlying causal factors are:

- air temperature
- radiant temperature (sunshine)
- humidity
- air velocity (wind, draught)
- the person's clothing
- the person's metabolism (a measure of the person's activity)

The equations in Fanger's model map the combined values of these aspects onto a linear scale giving a comfort level (Predicted Mean Vote) ranging from -3 (very cold) to +3 (very hot). The mapping is constructed in such a way that only 5% of the people in Fanger's experiments (Predicted Percentage

Dissatisfied) claim to be dissatisfied with a comfort level 0, while 75% of the people are expected to be dissatisfied with comfort level -2 or 2. A situation with average humidity, clothing, metabolism and air velocity corresponds to a Fanger comfort level equal to zero if the air and radiant temperatures are equal to 23 degrees Centigrade. The same average causal factor conditions with a temperature equal to 20 degrees maps onto a comfort level of -1, while the +1 level is achieved when the temperature reaches 27 degrees Centigrade.

18.3.3 The Comfort Management System

We have above clarified the notion of comfort and explained how comfort can be measured and controlled. The COMFY system's functionality is illustrated by two different customer scenarios, describing the system's possible behavior in a real-life setting. The section ends with a summary of results from simulations and some lessons learned concerning the need for an ecosystem approach to the COMFY service.

Two Customer Scenarios: Erik & Erika. Erik is a poor student, and manages to pay the rent of his condo in central Amsterdam by economizing on anything but the rent. His comfort agent should keep comfort levels acceptable, but should economize as much as possible. So when he's gone, Erik accepts the comfort in his house to fluctuate very much, as long as little energy is used by the system.

When Erik comes home at 6 p.m., the comfort in the kitchen is -0.5, which is slightly under Erik's preferred comfort level. This is due to the fact that energy prices were relatively high that afternoon. Erik's comfort agent knew that Erik was willing to accept a certain deviation in order to keep the cost down. During cooking, the kitchen becomes a bit damp, so the system opens some ventilation grids to let the humid air out. The system knows that a person's metabolism decreases during the evening. It therefore increases temperature gradually by a few degrees. At 11.30 p.m., Erik goes to sleep. The radiators have been turned off half an hour before by the comfort management system.

Coming from a wealthy family, Erika is not particularly concerned about the costs of living. Although the activities of Erik and Erika differ, their times of leaving and entering their houses are much the same. The big difference is that Erika wants to make no concessions to her comfort level whatsoever, especially when it concerns having it "nice and warm". Her comfort agent should therefore keep comfort levels as closely as possible to the ones preferred by Erika, irrespective of cost. That is why it is perfectly comfortable when she comes home, despite the high energy prices during that afternoon.

At present Erik and Erika do not know of each other. However, we can foresee a scenario where they will meet each other and decide to live together in Eriks little flat. This new situation will bring into focus issues such as combining and adapting preferences, challenging issues to consider in the next version of COMFY (i.e. COMFY II).

Results of Simulation Scenarios. We have implemented a prototype of the COMFY comfort management system to illustrate and simulate the ideas discussed above. In the COMFY system, clothing and metabolism are treated as exogenous, and are described in user configuration files. The same holds for external temperature, external humidity and electricity prices. For the measurements of current air temperature, radiant temperature, humidity and air velocity we take the values that the system calculates from the settings of the devices. During the simulation of the two scenarios described above, Erik and Erika are assumed to prefer the same comfort level. Their cost preferences differ however. Erika wants a comfort level equal to the preferred one at those times that she is present, at any cost. Erik, however, is more concerned with saving energy, and accepts a deviation if that reduces costs significantly.

We compare these situations with one in which no comfort management system is present. Consider a situation in which a thermostat regulates the heating. This is a reactive system, with no planning done in advance. If the air temperature is below the preferred one the heaters are turned on. If the air temperature is above the preferred one, the heaters are switched off. Cost preferences and energy prices are not taken into account. We assume that the user turns the thermostat down when s/he leaves or goes to sleep, and turns the thermostat up when the user is present in a room. Furthermore, we assume that each room has its own thermostat.

Each of the three scenario situations is simulated for the kitchen and the living room in a flat. The environmental setting corresponds to a sunny winter day with outside air temperatures fluctuating between 15 degrees Centigrade at night and 21 in the afternoon, and on a winter day with outside temperatures between -5 and +5 degrees Centigrade. Dynamic energy prices have been taken from a published UK example. The prices fluctuate considerably in present day energy market, being very low at night, very high in the morning, relatively low during the day, and quite high again in the evening. There are even quite frequent situations when we have negative prices for short times, that is, energy buyers are paid for taking care of surplus energy!

Discussion of Results. Figure 18.2 shows some of the simulation results by the COMFY system for a winter day during 25 periods of 1 hour each, starting at midnight. Outside temperatures fluctuate between -5 Centigrade at night and +5 Centigrade in the afternoon. As can be derived from the graphs, comfort management by the COMFY system in the luxurious setting saves about 15% compared to the conventional situation without any comfort management.

Differences between the economy setting (Erik) and luxurious setting (Erika) are as expected: in the economy setting less energy is used than in the luxurious setting, the difference being about 40 percent. The cost savings in the "economical" comfort management scenario compared to the conventional non-management scenario are 45%.

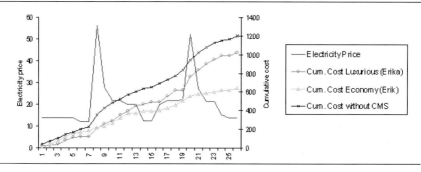

Fig. 18.1. Cumulative costs for three different scenarios on a winter day: the "luxurious" way of comfort management saves about 15%, and the "economical" way of cost management saves about 45%, compared to the scenario without comfort management. CMS in the figure stands for Comfort Management System.

A key difference between the COMFY system and the conventional thermostat is that the thermostat only controls heaters, while the COMFY system also controls other devices. Figure 18.2 illustrates the consequences of this difference. It shows the comfort levels on a winter day in the kitchen, the kitchen's windows facing south. On the one hand, the COMFY system saves energy and energy costs by controlling devices other than the heaters only. It can heat a room by opening ventilator grids when outside temperatures are higher than inside (periods 9-11), or by raising the sunblinds to let heat from the sun enter a room. On the other hand, the COMFY system is able to keep comfort closer to the preferred level than a thermostat. By lowering the sunblinds, it prevents the kitchen from heating up too much (periods 10-18).

Summary of Results. We have shown how software agents can be designed to model and deliver customer satisfaction in electronic service applications. Our agents are rather sophisticated. Agents for comfort management need a wide range of capabilities, including sensing and acting (related to observation and control of critical variables such as humidity and temperature). Furthermore we need forecasting (by model-based prediction of the energy need for the upcoming day), communication (monitoring going price vectors, possibly market-based negotiation with other agents) and reasoning (by optimizing actual resource use over time and thereby balancing service needs with cost considerations). The presented agent-based COMFY system delivers and manages comfort in buildings, and does so at the lowest possible cost in a real-time pricing scenario for needed energy resources.

The main reason to include the COMFY system in this chapter is to illustrate a general problem that we have encountered in many projects with industry partners, especially when we have been developing Internet-based demonstrators. The problem can be summarized in two sentences. "The application is interesting, but we can not afford the investments". "The application is interesting but, it is not in our core business of selling products such as

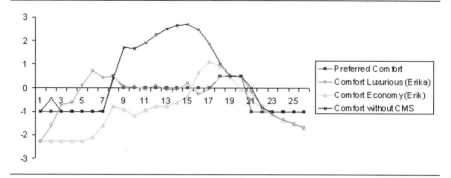

Fig. 18.2. Comfort levels for three different scenarios on a sunny winter day. Without comfort management it gets way too hot. The comfort management system uses mostly the natural no-cost ways (sun heat, natural ventilation) to achieve the desired comfort levels. The "economical" setting does this more strongly than the "luxurious" setting: the latter uses some additional heating early in the morning. CMS in the figure stands for Comfort Management System.

kWh or thermostats". Having said that, the same companies also acknowledge that they have to change their business models in order to survive in a highly competitive world. They even acknowledge the need to go from low profit commodities such as kWh to more profitable user demanded services.

Lessons Learned. We have demonstrated, for instance by the COMFY system, that it is possible to design and implement powerful new applications based on connecting smart equipment and people in networks. However, these new applications might be difficult to realize because the old business model between supplier and consumer either does not easily support the new service or entirely new business opportunities might be possible if some investments can be shared. In order to exploit the full potential of the COMFY system we need to recast the old supplier and consumer model into an appropriate ecosystem.

18.3.4 Ecosystems Supporting Smart Buildings

In order to tackle the cited statements above up-front we regard, as said above, the COMFY system as a component in an ecosystem around smart buildings. In that ecosystem the COMFY system as such is represented by the e-service of comfort management. In the ecosystem setting the COMFY application is unbundled into a set of e-services corresponding to the different measurements or controls (Figure 18.3). At this point in time it is however an open question who the active service providers will be in that ecosystem. Service providers might include utilities, providers of smart equipment, house owners, financial institutions, insurance companies, residents and so on.

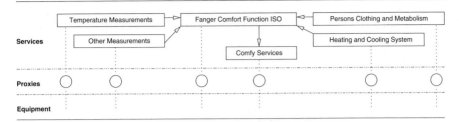

Fig. 18.3. The COMFY system as a value-chain of e-Services.

We will come back to the contents of Figure 18.3 in sections 18.7 and 18.8 below. At this point we make the following observations: The COMFY service is realized by the following e-services:

- The Fanger comfort function.
- The heating and cooling services.
- Temperature measurements.
- Other measurements grouped as one service.
- The information on clothing and metabolism.

As depicted in Figure 18.3 (smart) equipment and users as well as the high-level services are connected to the system using proxies. Obviously, the components of the COMFY service can be reused in other value-chains.

The purpose of the ecosystem is, as we stated in section 18.2 Towards Computational Ecosystems, to enable creation of useful and profitable value-chains of e-services. A crucial issue is therefore to create and maintain value-chains for all participants as well as mechanisms for making profit by a pay-per-use of e-services.

Among services provided by agents in the ecosystem we can thus at this point identify two types. The first type of service is the societal support to either find out new value-chains of existing services or to find out if an expressed need could be realized by existing e-services. We can call this service value-chain creation. Obviously, in creating the value-chain we need information about the different potential services in the chain. We have identified three important concepts, mentioned above, associated with each service and supporting the formation of a potential new service. The concepts are ownership, responsibility, and accessibility. The second type of service that can be identified at this point is related to the formation of trust in the service or trust creation.

Referring to Figure 18.3 we would like to evaluate the quality of the end service, responsibilities and the costs involved as well as the overall trust in the end service before we sign a contract. Also, service providers would like to estimate revenues as well as potential markets for maintaining services in the ecosystem.

The issues of value-chains and trust creation will be in the focus of section 18.6. In order to investigate these issues further, we are at present implementing the COMFY system on an extended Jini platform called SOLACE. We will return to the SOLACE system in section 18.7.

18.4 Coordination and Control in Ecosystems

The purpose and methodologies of coordination and control in a traditional goal-oriented multi-agent application are discussed in other chapters of this book. However, as we have motivated above, in an ecosystem an additional purpose is to identify and create profitable and trusted value-chains. A principled approach to the coordination and control of that process is a key issue for the success of the ecosystem as a conceptual and engineering idea.

An ecosystem is per definition implemented as a distributed system and is hence a set of distributed applications. This means that fundamental aspects of distributed systems have to be part of a methodology supporting the engineering of computational ecosystems. Functionality such as advertising services and look-up services supporting value-chains and trust creation have to be an integral part of the ecosystem's infrastructure. The same holds for support of an ecosystem economy based on a pay-per-use of services and for survivability against failure, as well as tampering or malicious outside attacks on the ecosystem. Business creation in an ecosystem presupposes a common understanding of concepts and rules, e.g., ontology services. Last, but not least, the ecosystem has to be trustworthy and must also support a clear ownership-responsibility model. For example, who is responsible if an application (service) fails due to, e.g., an upgrading of a component resident in a subservice? The latter questions are addressed in the earlier mentioned EC project Alfebiite.

In summary, coordination and control in ecosystems are intrinsically more complex than in more traditional agent based applications. Part of the coordination and control is done by, or is supported by, the underlying infrastructure of the ecosystem. Norms, social laws and ethos as well as survivability are underpinnings of a rational behavior in an ecosystem. A precision of these statements is the topic of the next section.

18.5 Methodological Issues and the Engineering of Ecosystems

A comprehensive methodology for development of multi-agent systems is still lacking although there is an increasing interest in a multi-agent approach to development of complex systems [261]. There are several attempts in methodological approaches, e.g., within a Special Interest Group of the EC AgentLink

Process Support   **Components of a (use–specific) Methodology**

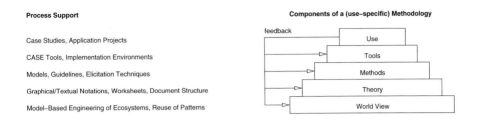

Case Studies, Application Projects

CASE Tools, Implementation Environments

Models, Guidelines, Elicitation Techniques

Graphical/Textual Notations, Worksheets, Document Structure

Model–Based Engineering of Ecosystems, Reuse of Patterns

Fig. 18.4. The Methodological Pyramid.

NoE. We also refer to Chapter 13, on software engineering, in this book. Most often agents per se are the focus of these efforts. We advocate a more evolutionary approach where agent modeling and technologies are selected parts of a system development life cycle; requirement engineering, design, implementation, and maintenance. In an ecosystem the main requirements concern adaptivity, sustainability and survivability of the system. We also believe that there is no single unifying agent based methodology for agent-based applications in general, but that we can find some basic underlying principles, i.e., as expressed in the Methodological Pyramid, Figure 18.4.

A basic principle is that we take the characteristics of the goal system into account even at requirement analysis and in high level design. Of course, this insight is not new. A classical example is logic programming. In theory we can have a declarative (high-level) approach to logic programming, but in practice every Prolog programmer has to have basic knowledge of implementation specifics, e.g., the top-down and depth first execution model of the Warren Abstract Machine, in order to write useful and efficient code.

18.5.1 The Methodological Pyramid

Our application domain is distributed systems (ecosystems), with characteristics such as [618]:

– Latency
– Memory access
– Partial failure
– Concurrency

These characteristics are naturally also valid in distributed multi-agent systems. We can not have a high-level design of agent systems ignoring these facts or postpone the issues to the implementation stage and still hope that everything will work out fine. On the contrary, acknowledging these fundamental characteristics can support us in early phases of the requirement analysis and design of ecosystems.

As an example, let us suppose that we have a specific distributed task that is time critical. A first coordination task between the agents involved would be to re-allocate data and computations in the system in order to minimize the latency. A next step would be to minimize deliberation time during the task execution by compiling efficient interaction protocols. A third step can be to minimize interaction time by minimizing message exchange overhead, i.e., avoiding high-level ACL messages in favor of short messages or reading from a blackboard. However, in order to do this context dependent articulation work, the agents have to be aware of the latency problem as such and have the capabilities to reason about how to solve it and how to utilize the support from the underlying system to set up an arrangement as above.

The Methodological Pyramid (see Figure 18.4) captures the main components and their interdependencies of a comprehensive methodology. The given pyramid is an adaptation of ideas from decades of practice in knowledge engineering and can be found for example in a new book on knowledge management and knowledge engineering [539].

The Methodological Pyramid can be seen as a pyramid with a fixed base but where the content of intermediate layers depends on what kind of applications are in focus at the top of the pyramid. The Methodological pyramid thus captures the fact that the contents of the components of a methodology vary and is engineered to suit a class of applications. However we have a common base, the World View, unifying the methodologies. In our case the application area is ecosystems as described above with an underlying distributed infrastructure. As a goal system for implementation we have an extension of Sun Microsystems' Jini platform called SOLACE (see 18.7 SOLACE: A Layered ORA Architecture).

18.5.2 A World View of Computations

We propose in our Methodological Pyramid a high level societal world view of complex system such as ecosystems [293]. Similar approaches have been proposed by for instance Jennings [332]. The components of the world view are:

- Context
- Coordination
- Agents

The computation is driven by rational behavior of the agents with respect to their mental attitudes. The meanings of rationality and mental attitudes have been extensively studied and discussed, not the least in connection with agents, during the last decades. A well-known set of attitudes, the Belief-Desire-Intention (BDI) model, has been proposed and investigated mainly by Georgeff and his colleagues [506]. The ideas behind the BDI models come from Bratman in an attempt to give a formal model for reasoning about

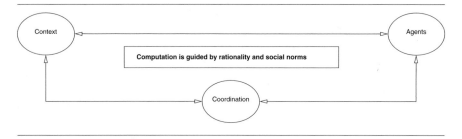

Fig. 18.5. Computation model at the society level.

individuals. Later, researchers have extended the model into a multi-agent setting incorporating team formation and coordination. The BDI external view of agents has also been translated into agent architectures such as PRS, dMARS and COSY [296].

Shoham and Cousins classification of mental attitudes according to their relevance to computational applications is as follows [551]:

- Informational: Belief, knowledge, awareness.
- Motivational: Intention, choice, plan, goal, desire, commitment, preference, wish, want.
- Social: Obligation, permission, norms

We have added norms to take care of a multi-agent situation and following Castelfranchi and his colleagues [184]. A social agent, according to Shoham, knows and is aware of society norms and acts rationally with respect to this awareness and according to its informational and social intentions when invoking its motivational attitudes in selecting an action to perform.

In an ecosystem, the agents also have to take into account the obligations, reputations, criminal acts, law enforcement, societal support and so on in order to act rationally in the given context [23].

An often used example of societal support in our real society is traffic laws and their enforcement. Traffic regulations are a solution to the society problem of coordination of access to a scarce resource, traffic lanes. The society implements a support infrastructure in the form of traffic lights in road crossings and the norms of access as green-yellow-red traffic signals. Simultaneously, the society demands that all drivers have learned about these norms and, not the least, about the consequences of breaking the norms (e.g., loss of driver's license). The agents (drivers) believe that all other drivers know and accept the coordination mechanism. Coordination between the drivers (agents) can thus be done without any explicit communication between the agents by means of just only interpreting the signs and acting accordingly. Of course, accidents still happen due to failure in the infrastructures or failure on the driver's part to follow the norms.

The important observation here is that we explicitly state that the agent exists in a society that supports certain coordinations by norms and implemented coordination mechanisms. This means for instance that we do not need to model the reasoning of an agent and the communication plan with other agents in order to drive across an intersection. The interaction is captured by the simple protocol: red = stop, yellow = wait/prepare to stop, green = drive, executed by drivers. This example illustrates the fact that coordination in complex situations can be simplified by implementing societal (contextual) support in infrastructures, and also that the agents of the society have to be aware of the norms and their enforcement, see section 1.7.

We make the following two observations of our choice to have Coordination as a component of the World View. The first observation is that this approach allows us to have a common framework for, e.g., stationary and mobile agents. On the one side, the coordination between agents can be entirely modeled as a dialogue of message exchanges between stationary agents as in approaches such as FIPA ACL [497]. On the other extreme the coordination is entirely due to mobile agents going to places as in systems such as Voyager. In a real situation, however, the natural coordination can be a mixture of the two models, or as in the traffic signal example, by observation of signals. In an EC ACTS project on load balancing in telecommunication networks we have indeed a hybrid model between stationary and mobile agents for coordination [328]. In effect, the contextual knowledge of properties of the actual network components is used as an input to the decision of which model of coordination is the most appropriate in a given dynamic situation.

The other observation is that do have a high level core Agent Communication Language (ACL) as a part of the Coordination component. The core ACL is used in the articulation work of the agents not as a default language of type one size fits all. We prefer to derive an appropriate communication exchange model from the Context, the Coordination model, and the Agent capabilities [20]. Again, this methodological choice is a consequence of our experiences and also reflects well-known difficulties with an general ACL such as KQML or FIPA ACL [497].

As a final remark, we have developed a methodology for modeling value-chains, E3-Value [279].

The efforts in the Theory and Methods parts of the Methodological pyramid connects the World View components with a focus on the application domain at hand. In our case it is computational ecosystems that are grounded both in a real and a virtual environment.

18.6 ORA: Merging of the Real and Virtual

As previously stated, we consider the driving force of the next generation of Internet applications to be the creation of value-adding chains composed by pay-per-use based e-services. The reason for us to consider this type of applications can be found in not only agent-based application development, but also in the recent development trend concerning software components and physical devices; to enable interconnectivity between diverse software components and hardware devices. This trend is a consequence of the possibility that the resulting environment of interconnected software and hardware components offers added customer value, at least from the perspective of the industry. Considering the exponential growth of the Internet and its success in terms of added customer value, the emergence of such an environment has an enormous potential. Further analysis of this topic implies that it is important to grasp the profound implications that the emergence of such a complex environment might have.

It is not very difficult to see that the resulting environment in question will be constituted by an extremely large amount of hardware devices (e.g. workstations, cellphones, appliances, etc.) and that each device will have to continuously execute a computer program of a more or less complex nature, if a specific device is supposed to communicate with other devices. Due to the fact that each device of this type will be able to communicate with the surrounding environment, a very important feature will emerge: information and functionality previously only associated with the physical environment a certain device resides in is suddenly accessible by all parties that are allowed to communicate with the device in question. The statement does not only apply to the physical devices, but consequently also to the software running on them. In other words, if we enable hardware devices and the software running on them to communicate with each other we have suddenly made all information and functionality associated with them accessible by potentially all other actors in the environment. From an industrial perspective this situation would probably be considered as a dream come true, just think of all the new business opportunities that could emerge. However, there is another side to the story that is worthwhile to consider. As soon as someone (e.g. individual or organization) buys one of these devices (including the software that is supposed to execute on them), all information or functionality that potentially could be accessed by anyone is actually owned by someone. Furthermore, if a device is owned by someone and also possible to communicate with, it is implied that a device and its owner has certain obligations and responsibilities towards the accessing party.

As a consequence of this reasoning, it should be quite obvious that we cannot treat the next generation of Internet applications the same way as we treat them today. We believe that the next generation of Internet applications should be considered as a (large) set of services in need of coordination (see 18.4 Coordination and Control in Ecosystems). In effect, we need an infrastructure that not only accommodates the notion of services and the coordination of them, but also fundamental concepts such as ownership, responsibility, and accessibility (ORA).

Primarily, the Internet can be conceptualized as a large number of computational entities that are interconnected with each other using some kind of communication protocol. However, at this point it is important to note the difference between the notion of a conceptualization and the notion of an embodiment of that particular concept. An embodiment of a concept is a physical entity (something that has a separate and distinct existence), and a concept is a descriptive construction of our minds that we make use of when we reason about a specific entity or class of entities. But why is this somewhat philosophical perspective on the nature of things so important in the discussion of Internet applications?

Due to the fact that an entity can exhibit a number of properties concerning its physical existence, an entity can be conceptualized in different ways depending on what subset of its properties we currently refer to. In other words, concepts are context dependent. If we now relate this line of reasoning to the notion of the Internet, we see that traditionally we make use of a one-to-one relationship between the concept of the Internet and the embodiment of that particular concept, i.e. we do not make room for different interpretations of the same entity. In that context, the Internet is solely considered to be the communication platform for whatever application we choose to contemplate. However, due to its physical existence this particular entity actually exhibits yet another property that has quite profound consequences if appropriately considered - spatial scope.

The Internet can possibly be viewed as not only a communication platform, but also as a physical entity with a global spatial scope. Considering this aspect of the Internet it should be treated as a very real part of our society as such. However, as soon as we treat the Internet as a natural part of our societies, and not merely a communication platform, activities related to conceptual notions such as e-commerce and e-services must be treated the same way as we would treat their counterparts in human societies. The treatment we refer to involves the concepts of ownership and responsibility. Both of these concepts are strongly related to what we refer to as trust, i.e. the confidence a human attaches to the certainty that an act of communication between him- or herself and another entity will generate a positive outcome from the perspective of the individual itself. Furthermore, if computational ecosystems as we envisage them on the Internet are to achieve acceptance and customer-added value, they have to address the fundamental notion of trust as we refer to it in human societies (see section 18.6.1).

We believe that a possible way to achieve this goal is to assert that services in computational ecosystems in one way or the other is owned by a physical person or an organization, but also to make sure that the services are obliged to exhibit certain responsibilities towards the persons or organizations that interact with them. In the following subsections we will delve further into these topics.

18.6.1 Trust

The concept of trust is a crucial concept in ecosystems, e.g., in electronic commerce. A recent book on the concept of trust in line with our point of view is [142]. An origin of trust emanates from institutional power, e.g., from institutions such as the Swedish national bank. Through proper delegation of authority we can trust a civil servant to perform a certain task for us, e.g., we accept bank-notes from a clerk in a bank office as a payment of a check. We can trust an agents ability and willingness to perform a task or we can have trust in the reliability of the information transmitted. We model the concept of trust as a 4-place relation:

$$trust :< person, person, task, context >$$ (18.1)

There are several attempts in giving a formal treatment of and providing semantics for such types of trust relations [342]. In the context of an ecosystem a task is typically a service (i.e. entity) which has an owner (see 18.6.2 Ownership). We thus have the following implicit trust relation:

$$trust :< person, entity, task, value - chain >$$ (18.2)

This corresponds to our everyday trust of an ATM in the wall of a bank building when we insert our ATM card and provide our pin code and accept the paper money eventually delivered from the machine. We trust that the money are valid and that the transactions are reliable. The trust relation has to be earned and can not be engineered in a system. However, by clarifying concepts such as ownership, responsibility, and accessibility of an entity we can support different models of trust creation. We will show how the latter concepts, e.g., the ORA concepts, can be architecturally supported on our platform SOLACE (see section 18.7 SOLACE: A Layered ORA Architecture).

18.6.2 Ownership

One important aspect of trust concerning the use of services in computational ecosystems is that it implies a relation between a person and the services (entities with responsibilities) that he or she accesses, see the trust relation above (18.2). However, there are many different ways of enforcing this relation. We suggest that one way of handling this enforcement of the relation is to focus on who actually owns an entity. The reason for this is that if an entity fails to fulfill its responsibilities towards a certain user, it must be possible to propagate this failure into a complaint directed towards an entity that is in charge of the entity. However, since a computational entity will not care whether or not an accessing user is happy with its ability to fulfill its responsibilities, this has to be dealt with by someone that does care. This someone is of course the person or organization that is the owner of the entity. The concept of ownership in a computational ecosystem manifests itself as a certain relation:

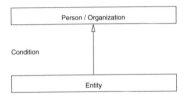

Fig. 18.6. The Ownership relation.

$$ownership :< person, entity, condition > \qquad (18.3)$$

Perhaps the term person could be substituted with the term organization, but the key point is that the term person refers to someone per definition legally responsible in a real environment (society). The entity referred to in the relation is an embodiment of a concept (e.g. a service) that exists in a virtual environment. Furthermore, between person and entity there must also exist a condition that proves the validity of the ownership. The concept of ownership in the ORA model is obviously of great importance, since without it the notion of trust a user puts in a computational ecosystem and its constituents will be difficult to enforce. Proper implementation of the concept of ownership is therefore one of the fundamental tools at hand to enable a merging of the real world and computational ecosystems. However, by incorporating ownership as a key concept in the ORA model it is also very important that we incorporate another concept that is tightly coupled with ownership, namely responsibility.

18.6.3 Responsibility

A fundamental property of an entity that is to be accessed by another entity is that it must be owned by someone that is situated in a physical environment. The reason for this is that if an entity is not owned by anybody its responsibilities towards an accessing party in a societal setting cannot be enforced in a legal fashion. But exactly what does it mean to have certain responsibilities towards an accessing party? The issue can be perceived from two different perspectives:

– Owner. The owner of an entity offers a set of information or functionality to an accessing party for a certain price for using the entity in question. Therefore, the owner of the entity has the right to require a mutual understanding in the form of a contract (i.e. a legally binding agreement) before allowing a specific party to access the entity. The contract outlines the responsibilities of the entity (and consequently also the responsibilities of the entity owner). If the entity in question does not fulfill its responsibilities

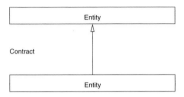

Fig. 18.7. The Responsibility relation.

in accordance with the contract the negatively affected party has the right to take legal actions.

- User. The user of an entity is willing to pay a certain price for the access to a set of information or functionality offered by a second entity that is owned by someone. However, due to the fact that there is a possibility that the actually accessed set of information or functionality does not match the offered set of information or functionality and that the user is asked to pay a certain price for the access, a contract is required between the user and the owner of the accessed entity.

As a consequence of these two perspectives the concept of responsibility can be viewed as a relation between two entities (that are owned by two different persons) in the form of a legally binding agreement:

$$responsibility :< entity, entity, contract > \qquad (18.4)$$

18.6.4 Accessibility

The two concepts of ownership and responsibility can be viewed as the cornerstones in the ORA model concerning the support for trust in computational ecosystems. However, yet another fundamental concept needs to be considered in order to enable ownership and responsibility, namely accessibility. If an entity is supposed to access another entity there are two important issues involved that have to be properly handled:

- Manifestation. In order for one entity to access another entity, there has to be some way for the first entity to address the other entity. When it comes to Internet applications this is often achieved using some kind of addressing scheme (e.g. a Uniform Resource Locator). For example, an entity makes use of a URL in order to access another entity that is located on a webserver. However, such an addressing scheme presupposes that the context that the addressed entity adheres to is already known. In computational ecosystems an entity can offer a set of information or functionality that could possibly adhere to many different contexts. Therefore, since we

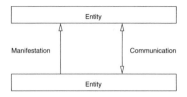

Fig. 18.8. The Accessibility relation.

do not know what addressing scheme to use in order to access an entity in a computational ecosystem, all entities make use of the manifestation concept in order to address other entities. The concept of manifestation is twofold, it refers to the fact that an entity actually exists, but also to the fact that an entity in some way must be possible to perceive by other entities inhabiting its environment. In the ORA model, an entity is perceived by other entities as a description of the various concepts it supports (i.e. its manifestation). Therefore, if an entity wishes to address another entity in the environment it can do so by matching a sought-for manifestation with the manifestations of other entities in the environment.

– Communication. Once an entity has found another entity it must know the nature of its interface in order to be able to communicate with it. Traditionally, if we would have presupposed the addressing scheme to use in order to find an entity, we would by now probably also know what communication interface to use. However, since an entity in a computational ecosystem must make use of manifestation as a way of finding other entities it is not clear what interface a newly found entity makes use of. The only way to solve this issue is that all entities agree to make use of the same primitive communication interface, no matter what manifestation they have chosen to make use of, cf., Core ACL in section 18.5.2.

Therefore, in order to support the concept of accessibility in a computational ecosystem it is important to realize that manifestation and communication are fundamental parts of the relation between two entities:

$$accessibility :< entity, entity, manifestation, communication > \quad (18.5)$$

In summary, we state that an entity choses its own manifestation as soon as it enters the computational ecosystem, and this (possibly dynamic) manifestation can be perceived and therefore used by other entities in order to locate the entity in question. However, the approach also implies that one entity would not know how to actually communicate with an entity once it has found one. Therefore, a common communication interface must be used by all entities, thus making it possible for an entity to at least know one way of communicating with the others.

18.6.5 Architecture and Infrastructure

As described in section 18.6.1, we believe that a possible way to achieve acceptance and customer-added values in the setting of computational ecosystems is to enforce the notion of trust. In order to focus on the notion of trust we introduced three fundamental concepts: ownership, responsibility, and accessibility. Each one of these concepts involves a certain relation between a person (or organization) and an entity or between an entity and some other entity. The various relations identify the necessity of certain issues to be appropriately handled. In the case of ownership, a person can only be the owner of an entity if he or she fulfills a certain condition required by the computational ecosystem. When it comes to the responsibilities a certain entity (and consequently its owner) has towards another entity this can be expressed in terms of a contract. And finally, the accessibility relation deals with the manifestation of an entity (i.e. in what way an entity is perceived by other entities in its environment) and its capability to communicate with other entities. The ownership, responsibility, and accessibility relations deal with the notion of trust as we previously outlined in the beginning of this chapter. However, there is one fundamental issue that we have not discussed yet, namely architectures and infrastructures.

In order to enforce the notion of trust in computational ecosystems, it is not enough to just model the entities and the coordination of them according to the three concepts of ownership, responsibility, and accessibility. It is fundamentally important that we also address the concepts in terms of a supporting architecture and a supporting infrastructure. The architecture aspect of the ORA model is important because it must exist in order to offer a basic structure and methodology for the modeling and implementation of entities in a computational ecosystem. The infrastructure consists of a number of primitive entities and system functions that need to exist in order to enforce the purpose and goal of the ORA model and consequently also the implied architecture. In summary, we need both an architecture and an infrastructure in order to handle methodological issues.

In the next section we will delve further into an ORA related architecture, and also outline a number of the primitive entities (i.e. an infrastructure) that offer the actual support for trust in that they enforce ownership conditions, responsibility contracts, and accessibility manifestation and communication.

18.7 SOLACE: A Layered ORA Architecture

The concept of trust in computational ecosystems can be modeled in many different ways, and one approach is to address it in terms of ownership, responsibility, and accessibility (ORA). Previously in this chapter we have discussed the difference between a concept and the embodiment of that par-

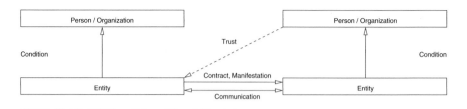

Fig. 18.9. A combined view over the three relations of ownership, responsibility, and accessibility.

ticular concept. Therefore, we will treat the implementation of services and trust in a similar manner, i.e. separating the concept and the embodiment.

In terms of implementation, an embodiment of a concept must rely on a defined architecture, since the intent of an architecture is to support the modeling and deployment of entities that address the concept. However, an architecture does not by itself enforce the concept in question. This task must be achieved by the entities themselves. Therefore, we must introduce the notion of an infrastructure, i.e. a set of primitive entities that always exist in the infrastructure of a computational ecosystem. Thus, in our case (considering the ORA model) these primitive entities must support the concepts of ownership, responsibility, and accessibility. To conclude this line of reasoning, we must define both an architecture and an infrastructure in order to enforce the notion of trust in computational ecosystems. In this section we will delve further into an attempt to define such an architecture and infrastructure. Our approach is called SOLACE (Service-Oriented Layered Architecture for Communicating Entities).

18.7.1 Architecture

The SOLACE architecture is divided into three logical layers on a functional basis (see Figure 18.10): Entity Layer, Proxy Layer, and Access Layer. At the entity layer we find the actual implementation of the various services and other important functions that address the ORA concept as a whole. In other words, the entity layer enables us to consider the concept of trust on a level separated from the technical perspective on how to implement the concept of accessibility. At the proxy layer, the concepts of manifestation (i.e. in what way other entities are supposed to perceive the entity) and communication (i.e. message passing) are handled. Thus, a proxy is used in order to take care of issues related to accessibility that are of a somewhat technical nature, rather than assigning this task to the entity itself. Finally, below the proxy layer we have defined the access layer. At the access layer a number of different communication channels can be supported, thus giving

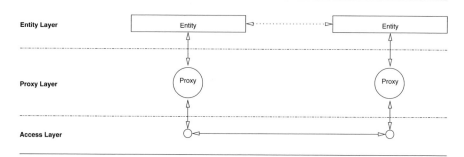

Fig. 18.10. At the entity level of an ORA architecture the concepts of ownership and responsibility are taken care of, and at the proxy level as well as the access level, the concept of accessibility is addressed.

an entity the indirect opportunity to communicate with other entities as well as advertising its manifestation.

Entity Layer. At the entity layer the two concepts of ownership and re-sponsibilities are handled through entity behavior, such as providing certain services and handling current conditions and contracts. Furthermore, it is at this level that an entity is actually considered to exist, not on the layers below the entity layer. However, each of the entities represented at the entity layer must in some way handle the requirement of accessibility and therefore each entity has a counterpart in the proxy layer.

Proxy Layer. The next layer of an ORA architecture is the proxy layer. A proxy is responsible for the successful handling of the manifestation of an entity and its communication capabilities. These capabilities are not related to the bahavior of an entity, but rather to the necessary mechanisms that are needed in order for an entity to exhibit support the concept of accessibility. The proxy layer contains an equally large amount of proxies as there are entities at the entity layer. The reason for this is that each entity at the entity layer will have a counterpart in the proxy layer that is responsible for handling the technical details of creating a successful mapping between a real environment and its corresponding virtual environment. All entities at the entity layer of an ORA architecture are associated with a proxy that handles the technical details of the accessibility concept (i.e. manifestation and communication).

Access Layer. This layer of an ORA architecture very much corresponds to the three lowest layers of the ISO OSI model: link layer, network layer, and transport layer. In other words, the access layer of an ORA architecture can be viewed as the communication medium of a computational ecosystem. Using this layer entities can get access to a wide range of different communi-cation channels, as long as they are supported by the access layer.

Fig. 18.11. The internals of an entity proxy, supporting the two concepts of manifestation and communication.

In order for a proxy to be successful when it comes to communication, it is important that it does not consider only the existence of one type of access channel, but rather to offer the ability for its associated entity to make use of as many different access channels as possible. The reason for this is that the architecture would then address the issue of entity interaction and integration in a more effective manner than if only one channel type was used.

18.7.2 Infrastructure

When we consider the next generation of Internet applications in the context of computational ecosystems it is very important that we address the notions of trust and coordination of services in a societal setting, as opposed to solely considering services and their users from an application perspective. As previously described, we can not handle the notion of trust in an effective manner if we do not include functions into an ecosystem that are normally only to be found in human societies (institutionalized power). Therefore, the entity layer of an ORA architecture must at least be inhabited by entities that correspond to the following fundamental societal functions and institutions:

- Entity Registry. As soon as an entity wishes to be part of an computational ecosystem it must register its existence if it desires to take part in any kind of mediation in the system. This is handled by the Entity Registry. Furthermore, at registration of its presence in the ecosystem the entity must also supply the Entity Registry with a number of descriptive properties that can be used to distinguish it from other registered entities (i.e. in order to ensure the uniqueness of an entity).
- Condition Registry. As previously described, an entity must be owned by someone. The fact that an entity (registered at the Entity Registry) actually is owned by someone is handled by a Condition Registry. If there is no explicit ownership of an entity it is impossible to sign a contract between an entity and the user of an entity.
- Contract Registry. When someone wishes to make use of an entity there has to exist a contractual agreement between the two parties. However, if a contract for some reason is broken and one party wishes to take legal action, the validity of the contract has to be confirmed by a trusted third

party. In SOLACE this is taken care of by the Contract Registry. Every time a contract is signed between two entities, it must be registered at the Contract Registry for future reference.

A computational ecosystem will of course consist of an extremely large amount of entities, but the three registry types outlined above is the absolute minimum requirement of initial entities inhabiting the environment. The reason for this is that they constitute the actual support for the concept of trust in the form of a number of societal institutions that by default must be possible to perceive as trusted.

18.8 Conclusions

We argue in this chapter that computational ecosystems represent a very promising direction for advanced Internet applications. Conceptually, a computational ecosystem can be seen as a hub where service providers can create profitable value-chains of services meeting demands of customers. We also argue that in order to accept a service, a user must have trust in the service its functioning and also how to handle failures of different kinds. Trust creation and maintenance are thus challenging issues in a computational ecosystem. The trust relation as such can basically not be engineered but we claim that it can be grounded on a set of system properties. We argue that the ownership, responsibility, and accessibility relations (ORA) enable trust creation and maintenance and hence are important architectural components of an computational ecosystem. The ownership relation, for instance, makes a necessary link between the real world and the ecosystem.

The chapter also includes a framework for computational ecosystems. We illustrate some ideas and concepts with the Comfort Management System COMFY and also in our architecture of the Jini based platform SOLACE. Finally, computational ecosystems can also be seen as a new challenge for coordination of Internet agents. The work reported is under development but is supported by several industrial applications of multi agent systems in the areas of Smart homes and energy management.

Acknowledgements

We happily acknowledge the importance of the sharing of ideas and experiences within our R&D group Societies of Computation (SoC) as well as with colleagues in national and international projects. Some explicit names can be found in our list of references.

References

1. Martin Abadi and Roger Needham. Prudent Engineering Practice for Cryptographic Protocols. *IEEE Transactions on Software Engineering*, 22(1):6–15, January 1996.
2. Kenneth R. Abbott and Sunil K. Sarin. Experiences with Workflow Management: Issues for the Next Generation. In Richard Furuta and Christine Neuwirth, editors, *Proceedings of the Conference on Computer–Supported Cooperative Work, CSCW'94, Chapel Hill, North Carolina, U.S.A.*, pages 113–120. ACM Press, October 1994.
3. Franz Achermann, Stefan Kneubühl, and Oscar Nierstrasz. Scripting Coordination Styles. Submitted for publication, April 2000.
4. Franz Achermann, Markus Lumpe, Jean-Guy Schneider, and Oscar Nierstrasz. Piccola – a Small Composition Language. In Howard Bowman and John Derrick, editors, *Formal Methods for Distributed Processing: An Object-Oriented Approach*, chapter 18. Cambridge University Press, 2000.
5. Franz Achermann and Oscar Nierstrasz. Application = Components + Scripts – A tour of Piccola. In Mehment Aksit, editor, *Software Architectures and Component Technology*. Kluwer Academic Press, 2000.
6. C. Adams and S. Farrell. Internet X.509 Public Key Infrastructure Certificate Management Protocols. In *RFC 2510, The Internet Society*. IETF, 1999.
7. Tilak Agerwala. Putting Petri Nets to Work. *Computer*, pages 85–94, December 1979.
8. G. Agha. *Actors: A Model of Concurrent Computation in Distributed Systems*. MIT Press, 1986.
9. G. Agha, S. Frølund, R. Panwar, and D. Sturman. A Linguistic Framework for Dynamic Composition of Dependability Protocols. In *Dependable Computing for Critical Applications III*, pages 345–363. International Federation of Information Processing Societies (IFIP), Elsevier Science Publisher, 1993.
10. G. Agha and N. Jamali. Concurrent Programming for Distributed Artificial Intelligence. In G. Weiss, editor, *Multiagent Systems: A Modern Approach to DAI.*, chapter 12. MIT Press, 1999.
11. G. Agha, I. A. Mason, S. F. Smith, and C. L. Talcott. A Foundation for Actor Computation. *Journal of Functional Programming*, 7:1–72, 1997.
12. Aglets. http://www.trl.ibm.co.jp/aglets/aglets.
13. Alessandra Agostini, Giorgio De Michelis, and Maria Antonietta Grasso. Rethinking CSCW systems: the architecture of Milano. In John A. Hughes, Wolfgang Prinz, Tom Rodden, and Kjeld Schmidt, editors, *Proceedings of the Fifth European Conference on Computer Supported Cooperative Work, ECSCW'97, Lancaster, U.K.*, pages 33–48, Dordrecht, August 1997. Kluwer Academic Publishers.

14. S. Ahmed, N. Carriero, and David Gelernter. A program building tool for parallel applications. In *DIMACS Workshop on Specifications of Parallel Algorithms*, 1994.

15. Ravinda K. Ahuja, Thomas L. Magnanti, and James B. Orlin. *Network Flows: Theory, Algorithms, and Applications*. Prentice Hall, Upper Saddle River, NJ, 1993.

16. S. Ahuja, N. Carriero, D. Gelernter, and V. Krishnaswamy. Matching language and hardware for parallel computation in the Linda machine. *IEEE Transactions on Computers*, 37(8):921–929, 1988.

17. B. Aiken and et al. A Report of a Workshop on Middleware (RFC2768). http://www.ietf.org/rfc/rfc2768.txt.

18. Ajanta Mobile Agents Research Project. http://www.cs.umn.edu/Ajanta.

19. J.M. Akkermans and H. Ottosson (Eds.). *The KEES Project En-ergy Efficiency in a Deregulated Market*. EnerSearch AB, Malm, Sweden, http://www.enersearch.se, 1999.

20. J.M. Akkermans, R. Gustavsson, and F. Ygge. Structured Engineering Process for Agent Communication Modelling. In *Knowledge Engineering and Agent Technology*. IOS Press, 2000.

21. J.M. Akkermans, F. Ygge, and R. Gustavsson. HOMEBOTS: Intelligent Decentralized Services for Energy Management. In J.F. Schreinemakers, editor, *Knowledge Management: Organization, Competence and Methodology*. Ergon Verlag, Wuerzburg, D, 1996.

22. C. Alexander. *The Timeless Way of Building*. Oxford University Press, New York, 1979.

23. Alfebiite. A Logical Framework for Ethical Behaviour Between Infohabitants in the Information Trading Economy of the Universal Information Ecosystem. Technical Report EC IST-1999-10298, www.iis.ee.ic.ac.uk/alfebiite, 1999.

24. D. Amselem. A window on shared virtual environments. *Presence-teleoperators and virtual environments*, 4(2):140–145, 1995.

25. Paul C. Anagnostopoulos. *Writing Real Programs in DCL*. Digital Press, 1989.

26. Brian G. Anderson and Dennis Shasha. Persistent Linda: Linda + Transactions + Query Processing. In J.P. Banâtre and D. Le Métayer, editors, *Research Directions in High-Level Parallel Programming Languages*, number 574 in LNCS, pages 93–109. Springer-Verlag, 1991.

27. Jean-Marc Andreoli, Paolo Ciancarini, and Remo Pareschi. Interaction Abstract Machines. In Gul Agha, Peter Wegner, and Akinori Yonezawa, editors, *Trends in Object-Based Concurrent Computing*, pages 257–280. MIT Press, Cambridge (MA), 1993.

28. Jean-Marc Andreoli and Remo Pareschi. Linear Objects: Logical Processes with Built-in Inheritance. *New Generation Computing*, 9(3-4):445–473, 1991.

29. Apple Computer. *AppleScript Language Guide*. Apple Technical Library. Addison-Wesley, 1993.

30. K. R. Apt. The Essence of Constraint Propagation. *Theoretical Computer Science*, 221(1–2):179–210, 1999.

31. K. R. Apt. The Rough Guide to Constraint Propagation. In J. Jaffar, editor, *Proc. of the 5th International Conference on Principles and Practice of Constraint Programming (CP'99)*, volume 1713 of *LNCS*, pages 1–23. Springer-Verlag, 1999. Invited lecture.

32. K. R. Apt and E. Monfroy. Automatic Generation of Constraint Propagation Algorithms for Small Finite Domains. In J. Jaffar, editor, *Proc. of the 5th International Conference on Principles and Practice of Constraint Programming (CP'99)*, volume 1713 of *LNCS*, pages 58–72. Springer-Verlag, 1999.

33. F. Arbab. Coordination of Massively Concurrent Activities. Technical Report CS–R9565, CWI, Amsterdam, The Netherlands, November 1995. Available on-line http://www.cwi.nl/ftp/CWIreports/IS/CS-R9565.ps.Z.

34. F. Arbab. The IWIM Model for Coordination of Concurrent Activities. In Paolo Ciancarini and Chris Hankin, editors, *Coordination Languages and Models*, volume 1061 of *LNCS*, pages 34–56. Springer-Verlag, April 1996.

35. F. Arbab. *Manifold2.0 reference manual*. CWI, Amsterdam, The Netherlands, May 1997.

36. F. Arbab. What Do You Mean, Coordination? *Bulletin of the Dutch Association for Theoretical Computer Science, NVTI*, pages 11–22, 1998. Available on-line http://www.cwi.nl/NVTI/Nieuwsbrief/nieuwsbrief.html.

37. F. Arbab and E. Monfroy. Coordination of Heterogeneous Distributed Cooperative Constraint Solving. *Applied Computing Review*, 6(2):4–17, 1998.

38. Farhad Arbab. *Manifold Reference Manual*. Department of Software Engineering, CWI, Amsterdam, NL, June 1998.

39. Farhad Arbab, Ivan Herman, and Per Spilling. An Overview of MANIFOLD and its Implementation. *Concurrency: Practice and Experience*, 5(1):23–70, February 1993.

40. Y. Arens, C. A. Knoblock, and C. Hsu. Query Processing in the SIMS Information Mediator. In Austin Tate, editor, *Advanced Planning Technology*. AAI Press, 1996.

41. Y. Aridor and D. Lange. Agent Design Patterns: Elements of Agent Application Design. In *The Second International Conference of Autonomous Agents*. IEEE, 1998.

42. K. Arisha, T. Eiter, S. Kraus, F. Ozcan, R. Ross, and V.S.Subrahmanian. IMPACT: Interactive Maryland Platform for Agents Collaborating Together. *IEEE Intelligent Systems*, 14(2), 2000.

43. Ken Arnold and James Gosling. *The Java Programming Language*. The Java Series. Addison-Wesley, Reading (MA), second edition, 1998.

44. Ken Arnold, Bryan O'Sullivan, and et al. *The Jini Specification*. Addison Wesley, 1999.

45. *Proceedings of the First International Symposium on Agent Systems and Applications and Third International Symposium on Mobile Agents (ASA/MA'99)*, California (USA), October 1999.

46. Robert M. Axelrod. *The Evolution of Cooperation*. Basic Books, New York, NY, 1984.

47. P. Azema, F. Vernadat, and P. Gradit. A Workflow Specification Environment. In *Proceedings of the Workshop on Workflow Management: Net-based Concepts, Models, Techniques and Tools, June 1998, Lisboa (Portugal)*, 1998.

48. David E. Bakken and Richard D. Schlichting. Tolerating Failures in the Bag-of-Tasks Programming Paradigm. In *Proceedings of the 21st International Symposium on Fault-Tolerant Computing*, pages 248–255, 1991.

49. David E. Bakken and Richard D. Schlichting. Supporting Fault-Tolerant Parallel Programming in Linda. *IEEE Transactions on Parallel and Distributed Systems*, 6(3):287–302, March 1995.

50. Jean-Pierre Banâtre and Daniel Le Métayer. Programming by Multiset Transformation. *Communications of the ACM*, 36(1):98–111, January 1993.

51. M. Banville. Sonia: an Adaptation of Linda for Coordination of Activities in Organizations. In P. Ciancarini and C. Hankin, editors, *Proc. 1st Int. Conf. on Coordination Models and Languages*, volume 1061 of *LNCS*, pages 57–74. Springer, 1996.

52. Fernanda Barbosa and Jose C. Cunha. A Coordination Language for Collective Agents Based Systems: GroupLog. In *Proceedings of the 2000 ACM Symposium on Applied Computing (SAC 2000)*, pages 189–195, Como (I), March 19 - March 21 2000. ACM. Track on Coordination Models, Languages and Applications.

53. M. Barbuceanu. Coordination with Obligations. In *Second International Conference on Autonomous Agents*, pages 62–69. IEEE, 1999.

54. M. Barbuceanu and M.S. Fox. Capturing and Modeling Coordination Knowledge for Multi Agent Systems. *International Journal on Cooperative Information Systems*, 5(2–3):275–314, 1996.

55. Mihai Barbuceanu and Mark S. Fox. COOL: A Language for Describing Coordination in Multiagent Systems. In Victor Lesser, editor, *Proceedings of the First International Conference on Multi–Agent Systems*, pages 17–25, San Francisco, CA, 1995. MIT Press.

56. C. Baru, A. Gupta, B. Ludascher, R. Marciano, Y. Papakonstantinou, P. Velikhov, and V. Chu. XML-Based Information Mediation with MIX. In *ACM Conf. on Management of Data (SIGMOD'99)*, Philadelphia, USA, 1999.

57. A. Barua, A.B. Whinston, and F. Yin. Value and productivity in the Internet economy. *IEEE Computer*, May 2000.

58. Len Bass, Paul Clements, and Rick Kazman. *Software Architecture in Practice*. Addison-Wesley, 1998.

59. J. Baumann, F. Hohl, K. Rothermel, and M. Straßer. Mole - Concepts of a Mobile Agent System. *World Wide Web*, 1(3):123–137, 1998.

60. J. Baumann and N. Radouniklis. Agent Groups in Mobile Agent Systems. In *IFIP WG 6.1 International Working Conference on Distributed Applications and Interoperable Systems*, Cottbus , Germany, September, 30 – October, 2 1997. Chapman & Hall.

61. Paolo Bellavista, Antonio Corradi, and Cesare Stefanelli. An Open Secure Mobile Agent Framework for Systems Management. *Journal of Network and Systems Management*, 7(3):323–339, September 1999.

62. Paolo Bellavista, Antonio Corradi, and Cesare Stefanelli. An Integrated Management Environment for Network Resources and Services. *IEEE Journal on Selected Areas in Communication*, 8(5), May 2000.

63. Paolo Bellavista, Antonio Corradi, and Cesare Stefanelli. A Mobile Agent Infrastructure for Terminal, User and Resource Mobility. In James Hong and Robert Weihmayer, editors, *NOMS 2000 – Proceedings of the 2000 IEEE/IFIP Network Operations and Management Symposium: The Networked Planet: Management Beyond 2000 (NOMS 2000)*, pages 877–890, Honolulu (USA), April 11 - April 13 2000. IEEE Press.

64. Paolo Bellavista, Antonio Corradi, and Cesare Stefanelli. Protection and Interoperability for Mobile Agents: A Secure and Open Programming Environment. *IEICE Transactions on Communications*, E83B(5), May 2000.

65. F. Benhamou and L. Granvilliers. Combining Local Consistency, Symbolic Rewriting, and Interval Methods. In *Proc. of AISMC3*, Steyr (Austria), 1996.

66. F. Benhamou and W. Older. Applying Interval Arithmetic to Real, Integer and Boolean Constraints. *Journal of Logic Programming*, 32(1):1–24, March 1997.

67. Henri Beringer and Bruno DeBacker. Combinatorial Problem Solving in Constraint Logic Programming with Cooperative Solvers. In Christoph Beierle and Lutz Plümer, editors, *Logic Programming: Formal Methods and Practical Applications*, Studies in Computer Science and Artificial Intelligence. North Holland, 1995.

68. T. Berners-Lee.   WWW: Past, Present, and Future.   *IEEE Computer*, 29(10):69–78, October 1996.

69. T. Berners-Lee, R. Cailliau, A. Luotenen, H. F. Nielsen, and A. Secret. The World-Wide Web. *Communications of the ACM.*, 37(8), Aug 1994.

70. T. Berners-Lee, R. Fielding, and L. Masinter. Uniform Resource Identifiers (URI): Generic Syntax. IETF Internet Draft Standard RFC 2396, August 1998. http://www.ietf.org/rfc/rfc2396.txt.

71. Gérard. Berry and Gérard Boudol. The Chemical Abstract Machine. *Theoretical Computer Science*, 96:217–248, 1992.

72. A. Bieszczad, B. Pagurek, and T. White. Mobile Agents for Network Management. *IEEE Communications Surveys*, 1(1), 1998.

73. J. Billington, M. Farrington, and B. B. Du. Modelling and Analysis of Multi-agent Communication Protocols using CP-nets. In *Proceedings of the third Biennial Engineering Mathematics and Applications Conference (EMAC'98)*, pages 119–122, Adelaide, Australia, July 1998.

74. A. D. Birrell and B. J. Nelson. Implementing Remote Procedure Calls. *ACM Transactions on Programming Languages and Systems*, 2(1), February 1984.

75. R. Bjornson. *Linda on distributed memory multiprocessors*. PhD thesis, Yale University, 1992. YALEU/DCS/RR-931.

76. R. Bjornson, N. Carriero, and D. Gelernter. The implementation and performance of Hypercube Linda. Technical Report YALEU/DCS/RR-690, Yale University, 1989.

77. Matt Blaze, Joan Feigenbaum, and Jack Lacy. Decentralized Trust Management. In *Symposium on Secure Programming*, Oakland (CA), May 1996. IEEE Computer Society.

78. E. Boertjes, H. Akkermans, R. Gustavsson, and R. Kamphuis. Agents to Achieve Customer Satisfaction: The COMFY Comfort Management System. In *The Fifth International Conference on The Practical Application of Intelligent Agents and Multi-Agents (PAMM 2000)*. The Practical Application Company, April 2000.

79. J. Bolliger and T. Gross. A framework-based approach to the development of network-aware applications. *IEEE Transactions on Software Engineering*, 24(5):376–390, May 1998.

80. M. Bonsangue, J. Kok, M. Boasson, and E. DeJong. A software architecture for distributed control systems and its transition system semantics. In J. Carroll and et al, editors, *Proc. ACM/SIGAPP Symp. on Applied Computing (SAC '98)*. ACM Press, 1998.

81. M.M. Bonsangue, F. Arbab, J.W. de Bakker, J.J.M.M. Rutten, A. Scutellá, and G. Zavattaro. A Transition System Semantics for the Control-driven Coordination Language Manifold. Technical Report SEN–R9829, Centrum voor Wiskunde en Informatica, Kruislaan 413, 1098 SJ Amsterdam, The Netherlands, 1998.

82. G. Booch. *Object-oriented Analysis and Design (second edition)*. Addison Wesley, Reading (MA), 1994.

83. N.S. Borenstein. E-Mail with a Mind of its Own: The Safe-Tcl Language for Enabled Mail. *IFIP Transactions C (Communication Systems)*, C-25:389–402, 1994.

84. U. Borghoff et al. Reflective Agents for Adaptive Workflows. In *Proceedings of Second International Conference on the Practical Application of Intelligent Agents and Multi-Agent Technology, London, UK*, 1997.

85. P. Borovansky and C. Castro. Cooperation of Constraint Solvers: Using the New Process Control Facilities of ELAN. *Electronic Notes in Theoretical Computer Science*, 15:379–398, September 1998.

86. S.R. Bourne. An Introduction to the UNIX Shell. *Bell System Technical Journal*, 57(6):1971–1990, July 1978.

87. Craig Boutilier, Moises Goldszmidt, and Bikash Sabata. Sequential Auctions for the Allocation of Resources with Complementarities. In *Proceedings of the International Joint Conference on Artificial Intelligence*, Stockholm, Sweden, 1999.

88. John Bowers, Graham Button, and Wes Sharrock. Workflow from Within and Without: Technology and Cooperative Work on the Print Industry Shopfloor. In Hans Marmolin, Yngve Sundblad, and Kjeld Schmidt, editors, *Proceedings of the Fourth European Conference on Computer–Supported Cooperative Work, ECSCW'95, Stockholm, Sweden*, pages 51–66. Kluwer Academic Publisher, September 1995.

89. R.J. Brachman and J.G. Schmolze. An Overview of the KL-ONE Knowledge Representation System. *Cognitive Science*, 9(2), 1985.

90. J. M. Bradshaw, M. Greaves, H. Holmback, T. Karygiannis, W. Jansen, B. G. Silverman, N. Suri, and A. Wong. Agents for the Masses? *IEEE Intelligent Systems*, 6(2):53–63, March-April 1999.

91. Jeffrey M. Bradshaw. KAoS: An open agent architecture supporting reuse, interoperability, and extensibility. In *Tenth Knowledge Acquisition for Knowledge-Based Systems Workshop*, 1996.

92. J.M. Bradshaw, Dutfield. S., P. Benoita, , and J.D. Woolley. KaoS: Towards and Industrial-Strength Open Distributed Agent Architecture. In J.M. Bradshaw, editor, *Software Agents*, pages 375–418. AAAI/MIT Press, 1997.

93. F. Brazier, B. Dunin-Keplicz, N.R. Jennings, and J. Treur. Formal Specifications of Multi-agent Systems: a Real-World Case. In *First International Conference on Multi-agent Systems (ICMAS95)*, pages 25–32, June 1995.

94. F.M.T. Brazier, B.M. Dunin-Keplicz, N.R. Jennings, and J. Treur. DESIRE: Modelling Multi-Agent Systems in a Compositional Formal Framework. *Journal of Cooperative Information Systems*, 6(1):67–94, 1997.

95. Jonathan Bredin, David Kotz, and Daniela Rus. Market-based Resource Control for Mobile Agents. In *Proceedings of the Second International Conference on Autonomous Agents*, pages 197–204, Minneapolis, MN, May 1998. ACM Press.

96. Jonathan Bredin, David Kotz, Daniela Rus, Rajiv T. Maheswaran, Cagri Imer, and Tamer Başar. Computational Markets to Regulate Mobile-Agent Systems. December 1999.

97. Jonathan Bredin, Rajiv T. Maheswaran, Cagri Imer, Tamer Başar, David Kotz, and Daniela Rus. A Game-Theoretic Formulation of Multi-Agent Resource Allocation. In *Proceedings of the Fourth International Conference on Autonomous Agents*, June 2000.

98. M. Breugst and T. Magedanz. On the Usage of Standard Mobile Agent Platforms in Telecommunication Environments. In S. Trigila and et al, editors, *Intelligence in Services and Networks: Technologies for Ubiquitous Telecom Services Multi-Agent Systems Engineering*, volume 1430 of *LNCS*. Springer-Verlag, 1998.

99. J.-P. Briot. Actalk: a testbed for classifying and designing actor languages in the Smalltalk-80 environment. In *Proceedings of the European Conference on Object Oriented Programming (ECOOP'89)*, pages 109–129. Cambridge University Press, 1989.

100. C. Bryce, M. Oriol, and J. Vitek. A Coordination Model for Agents Based on Secure Spaces. In P. Ciancarini and A. Wolf, editors, *Proc. 3rd Int. Conf. on Coordination Models and Languages*, volume 1594 of *LNCS*, pages 4–200, Amsterdam (NL), April 1999. Springer-Verlag, Heidelberg (D).

101. Ciaran Bryce and Jan Vitek. The JavaSeal Mobile Agent Kernel. In *Proceedings of the 1st International Symposium on Agent Systems and Applications, 3rd International Symposium on Mobile Agents (ASAMA '99)*, pages 176–189, Palm Springs (CA), 1999. ACM Press.

102. O. Bukhres and A. Elmagarmid, editors. *Object-Oriented Multidatabases Systems : A Solution for Advanced Applications*. Prentice Hall, Englewood Cliffs, New Jersey, USA, 1996.

103. B. Burmeister. Models and Methodologies for Agent-oriented Analysis and Design. In *Working Notes of the KI96 Workshop on Agent-oriented Programming and Distributed Systems*. DFKI, 1996.

104. F. Buschmann. The Master-Slave Pattern. In J. Coplien and D. Schmidt, editors, *Pattern Languages of Program Design 1*, pages 133–142. Addison-Wesley, 1995.

105. Nadia Busi, Roberto Gorrieri, and Gianluigi Zavattaro. Three Semantics of the Output Operation for Generative Communication. In David Garlan and Daniel Le Métayer, editors, *Coordination Languages and Models – Proceedings of the 2nd International Conference (COORDINATION'97)*, volume 1282 of *LNCS*, pages 205–219, Berlin (D), September 1–3 1997. Springer-Verlag.

106. Nadia Busi, Roberto Gorrieri, and Gianluigi Zavattaro. A Process Algebraic View of Linda Coordination Primitives. *Theoretical Computer Science*, 192(2):167–199, 1998.

107. Nadia Busi, Roberto Gorrieri, and Gianluigi Zavattaro. Comparing Three Semantics for Linda-like Languages. *Theoretical Computer Science*, 240(1):49–90, 2000.

108. Nadia Busi, Roberto Gorrieri, and Gianluigi Zavattaro. On the Expressiveness of Linda Coordination Primitives. *Information and Computation*, 156:90–121, 2000.

109. Nadia Busi, Roberto Gorrieri, and Gianluigi Zavattaro. Process Calculi for Coordination: from Linda to JavaSpaces. In Teodor Rus, editor, *Algebraic Methodology and Software Technology – Proceedings of the 8th International Conference, AMAST 2000*, volume 1816 of *LNCS*. Springer-Verlag, 2000.

110. Nadia Busi and Gianluigi Zavattaro. Event Notification in Data-driven Coordination: Comparing the Ordered and Unordered Approaches. In *Proceedings of the 2000 ACM Symposium on Applied Computing (SAC 2000)*, pages 233–239, Como (I), March 19–21 2000. ACM. Track on Coordination Models, Languages and Applications.

111. Nadia Busi and Gianluigi Zavattaro. On the Expressivenes of Event Notification in Data-Driven Coordination Languages. In *Proceedings of ESOP 2000*, volume 1782 of *LNCS*, pages 41–55. Springer-Verlag, 2000.

112. S. Bussmann. Agent-Oriented Programming of Manifacturing Control Tasks. In *Proceeding of the 3rd International Conference on Multi-Agent Systems (IC-MAS 98)*, pages 57–63. IEEE CS Press, June 1998.

113. G. Cabri, L. Leonardi, and F. Zambonelli. Mobile-Agent Coordination Models for Internet Applications. *IEEE Computer*, 33(2):82–89, 2000.

114. Giacomo Cabri, Letizia Leonardi, and Franco Zambonelli. Reactive Tuple Spaces for Mobile Agent Coordination. In K. Rothermel and F. Hohl, editors, *Mobile Agents – Proceedings of the 2nd International Workshop (MA'98)*, volume 1477 of *LNCS*, pages 237–248, Stuttgart (D), September 1998. Springer-Verlag.

115. Giacomo Cabri, Letizia Leonardi, and Franco Zambonelli. Design and Implementation of a Programable Coordination Architecture for Mobile Agents. *Proceedings of the TOOLS EUROPE '99 Conference*, June 1999.

116. Giacomo Cabri, Letizia Leonardi, and Franco Zambonelli. MARS: a Programmable Coordination Architecture for Mobile Agents. *IEEE Internet Computing*, 2000.

117. Giacomo Cabri, Letizia Leonardi, and Franco Zambonelli. Mobile-agent Coordination Models for Internet Applications. *IEEE Computer Magazine*, 33(2), February 2000.

118. Giacomo Cabri, Letizia Leonardi, and Franco Zambonelli. XML Dataspaces for Mobile Agent Coordination. In *Proceedings of the 2000 ACM Symposium on Applied Computing (SAC 2000)*, pages 181–188, Como (I), March 19 - March 21 2000. ACM. Track on Coordination Models, Languages and Applications.

119. T. Cai, P. Gloor, and S. Nog. DartFlow: a workflow management system on the web using transportable agents. Technical report, Dartmouth College, 1997.

120. C. Callsen and G. Agha. Open Heterogeneous Computing in ActorSpace. *Journal of Parallel and Distributed Computing*, pages 289–300, 1994.

121. Ken Calvert and Ellen Zegura. GT-ITM: Georgia Tech Internetwork Topology Models, 1996. http://www.cc.gatech.edu/fac/Ellen.Zegura/gt-itm/gt-itm.tar.gz.

122. Scott R. Cannon and David Dunn. Adding Fault-tolerant Transaction Processing to LINDA. *Software: Practice and Experience*, 24(5):449–466, May 1994.

123. L. Cardelli and A. Gordon. Mobile Ambients. *Theoretical Computer Science*, 240(1), 2000.

124. Luca Cardelli. A Language with Distributed Scope. *Computing Systems*, 8(1):27–59, 1995.

125. Luca Cardelli. Wide Area Computation. In Jiri Wiedermann, Peter van Emde Boas, and Mogens Nielsen, editors, *Proceedings of the 26th International Colloquium on Automata, Languagese and Programming, ICALP'99*, volume 1644 of *LNCS*, pages 10–24. Springer-Verlag, 1999.

126. Luca Cardelli and Andrew D. Gordon. Mobile Ambients. In Maurice Nivat, editor, *Proceedings of Foundations of Software Science and Computation Structures (FoSSaCS), European Joint Conferences on Theory and Practice of Software (ETAPS'98)*, volume 1378 of *LNCS*, pages 140–155, Lisbon, Portugal, 1998. Springer-Verlag.

127. Steinar Carlsen. Action Port Model: A Mixed Paradigm Conceptual Workflow Modeling Language. In Michael Halper, editor, *Proceedings of the 3rd IFCIS International Conference on Cooperative Information Systems, New York City, USA*, pages 300–309, Los Alamitos, California, August 1998. IEEE Computer Society.

128. J. Carreria, L. Silva, and J. Silva. On the design of Eilean: A Linda-like library for MPI. Technical report, Universidade de Coimbra, 1994.

129. N. Carriero. *Implementation of Tuple Space Machines*. PhD thesis, Yale University, 1987. YALEU/DCS/RR-567.

130. N. Carriero and D. Gelernter. The S/Net's Linda Kernel. *ACM Transactions on Computer Systems*, 4(2):110–129, 1986.

131. N. Carriero and D. Gelernter. *How to Write Parallel Programs: A First Course*. The MIT Press, 1990.

132. N. Carriero and D. Gelernter. Tuple Analysis and Partial Evaluation Strategies in the Linda precompiler. In D. Gelernter, A. Nicolau, and D. Padua, editors, *Languages and Compilers for Parallel Computing*, Research Monographs in Parallel and Distributed Computing, pages 114–125. MIT Press, 1990.

133. N. Carriero and D. Gelernter. A foundation for advanced compile-time analysis of Linda programs. In *Languages and Compilers for Parallel Computing*, volume 589 of *LNCS*, pages 389–404. Springer-Verlang, 1991.

134. N. Carriero and D. Gelernter. New optimization strategies for the Linda precompiler. In G. Wilson, editor, *Linda-like systems and their implementation*, Edinburgh Parallel Computing Centre, pages 74–82. Technical Report 91-13, 1991.

135. Nicholas Carriero and David Gelernter. How to Write Parallel Programs: A Guide to the Perplexed. *ACM Computing Surveys*, 21(3):323–357, September 1989.

136. Nicholas Carriero and David Gelernter. Linda in Context. *Communications of the ACM*, 32(4):444–458, April 1989.

137. Nicholas Carriero and David Gelernter. Case Studies in Asynchronous Data Parallelism. *International Journal of Parallel Programming*, 22(2):129–149, 1994.

138. Nicholas Carriero, David Gelernter, and Lenore Zuck. Bauhaus Linda. In Paolo Ciancarini, Oscar Nierstrasz, and Akinori Yonezawa, editors, *Object-Based Models and Languages for Concurrent Systems*, volume 924 of *LNCS*, pages 66–76. Springer-Verlag, 1995.

139. F. Casati. *Models, Semantics and Formal Methods for the design of Workflows and their Exceptions.* PhD thesis, Politechnico di Milano, 1998.

140. F. Casati. Semantic Interoperability in interorganizational workflows. In *WACC workshop on cross-organizational workflows, San Francisco, CA*, February 1999.

141. A. Cassandra, D. Cassandra, and M. Nodine. Capability-based matchmaking. In *Agents-2000 Conference on Autonomous Agents, Barcelona*. ACM Press, 2000.

142. C. Castelfranchi and Y.-M. Tan (Eds.). *Trust and deception in virtual societies.* Kluwer Academic Publishers, Dordrecht-Holland, 2000.

143. C. Castro and E. Monfroy. A Control Language for Designing Constraint Solvers. In *Proceedings of Andrei Ershov Third International Conference Perspective of System Informatics, PSI'99*, volume 1755 of *LNCS*, Novosibirsk, Akademgorodok, Russia, 1999.

144. CDL. Capability Description Language. http://www.aiai.ed.ac.uk/~oplan/cdl.

145. Computer Security Center. Trusted Computer Systems Evaluation Criteria. Technical Report CSC-STD-001-83, DoD Computer Security Center, Fort MEade, MD, 1983.

146. K. M. Chandy and Jayadev Misra. How Processes Learn. *Distributed Computing*, 1:40–52, 1986.

147. K.M. Chandy and J. Misra. *Parallel Program Design: A Foundation.* Addison-Wesley, 1988.

148. Deepika Chauhan. JAFMAS: A Java-Based Agent Framework for Multiagent Systems Development and Implementation. Master's thesis, ECECS Department, University of Cincinnati, 1997.

149. Anthony Chavez, Alexandros Moukas, and Pattie Maes. Challenger: A Multi-agent System for Distributed Resource Allocation. In *Proceedings of the First International Conference on Autonomous Agents, Marina Del Ray, CA*, 1997. ACM Press.

150. Q. Chen, P. Chundi, U. Dayal, and M. Hsu. Dynamic Agents. *International Journal on Cooperative Information Systems*, 8(2–3):195–223, 1999.

151. Ye Chen, Yun Peng, Tim Finin, Yannis Labrou, and Scott Cost. A Negotiation-Based Multi-Agent System for Supply Chain Management. In

Working Notes of the Agents '99 Workshop on Agents for Electronic Commerce and Managing the Internet-Enabled Supply Chain., Seattle, WA, April 1999.

152. John Q. Cheng and Michael P. Wellman. The WALRAS Algorithm: A Convergent Distributed Implementation of General Equilibrium Outcomes. *Journal of Computational Economics*, 12:1–23, 1998.

153. D. Chess and et al. Itinerant Agents for Mobile Computing. *IEEE Personal Communications Magazine*, 2(5):34–59, May 1995.

154. D. Chess, C.G. Harrison, and A. Kershenbaum. Mobile Agents: Are They a Good Idea? In *Mobile Object Systems - Towards the Programmable Internet*, volume 1222 of *LNCS*, pages 25–47. Springer-Verlag, 1997.

155. L. Chiariglione. Foundation for Intelligent Physical Agents, 1997.

156. S. Chiba, K. Kato, and T. Masuda. Exploiting a Weak Consistency to Implement Distributed Tuple Space. In *12th International Conference on Distributed Computing Systems*, pages 416–425, Washington, D.C., USA, June 1992. IEEE Computer Society Press.

157. Martin Chilvers. *Fnorb User Guide*. CRC for Distributed Systems Technology, University of Queensland, AU, April 1999.

158. Søren Christensen and Niels Damgaard Hansen. Coloured Petri Nets Extended with Place Capacities, Test Arcs and Inhibitor Arcs. Technical Report DAIMI PB-398, Computer Science Department, Aarhus University, Aarhus C, Denmark, May 1992.

159. P.E. Chung and et al. DCOM and CORBA Side by Side, Step by Step, and Layer by Layer. *C++-Report*, 10(1), January 1998.

160. P. Ciancarini, R. Gorrieri, and G. Zavattaro. Towards a Calculus for Generative Communication. In E. Najm and J. Stefani, editors, *Proc. First IFIP Workshop on Formal Methods for Open Object-Based Distributed Systems (FMOODS)*, pages 289–306, Paris, France, 1996. Chapman and Hall, London.

161. P. Ciancarini, O. Nierstrasz, and R. Tolksdorf. A Case Study in Coordination: Conference Management on the Internet. http://www.cs.unibo.it/~cianca/wwwpages/case.ps.gz.

162. P. Ciancarini and D. Rossi. Coordinating Java Agents over the WWW. *World Wide Web Journal*, 1(2):87–99, 1998.

163. Paolo Ciancarini. Coordination Models and Languages as Software Integrators. *ACM Computing Surveys*, 28(2):300–302, June 1996.

164. Paolo Ciancarini, F. Franzé, and Cecilia Mascolo. Using a Coordination Language to Specify and Analyze Systems Containing Mobile Components. *ACM Transactions on Software Engineering and Methodology*, 2000.

165. Paolo Ciancarini and Chris Hankin, editors. *Coordination Languages and Models – Proceedings of the 1st International Conference (COORDINATION'96)*, volume 1061 of *LNCS*, Cesena (I), April 15–17 1996. Springer-Verlag.

166. Paolo Ciancarini, Keld K. Jensen, and Daniel Yankelewich. On the Operational Semantics of a Coordination Language. In Paolo Ciancarini, Oscar Nierstrasz, and Akinori Yonezawa, editors, *Object-Based Models and Languages for Concurrent Systems*, volume 924 of *LNCS*, pages 77–106. Springer-Verlag, 1995.

167. Paolo Ciancarini, Andrea Omicini, and Franco Zambonelli. Coordination Technologies for Internet Agents. *Nordic Journal of Computing*, 6(3):215–240, Fall 1999.

168. Paolo Ciancarini, Andrea Omicini, and Franco Zambonelli. Multiagent System Engineering: the Coordination Viewpoint. In Nicholas R. Jennings and

Yves Lespérance, editors, *Intelligent Agents VI — Agent Theories, Architectures, and Languages*, volume 1767 of *LNAI*, pages 250–259. Springer-Verlag, February 2000.

169. Paolo Ciancarini and Davide Rossi. Jada - Coordination and Communication for Java Agents. In Jan Vitek and Christian Tschudin, editors, *Mobile Object Systems: Towards the Programmable Internet*, volume 1222 of *LNCS*, pages 213–228. Springer-Verlag, Heidelberg (D), April 1997.

170. Paolo Ciancarini, Davide Rossi, and Fabio Vitali. A Case Study in Designing a Document-Centric Coordination Application over the Internet. In D. Clarke, A. Dix, and F. Dix, editors, *Proc. Workshop on the Active Web*, pages 41–56, Staffordshire (UK), January 1999.

171. Paolo Ciancarini and Robert Tolksdorf. Coordination Mechanisms for Web Agents. *Autonomous Agents and Multi-Agent Systems*, 2(3):215–216, September 1999. Guest editorial.

172. Paolo Ciancarini, Robert Tolksdorf, and Fabio Vitali. The World Wide Web as a Place for Agents. In Manuela Wooldridge, Michael J. AD Veloso, editor, *Artificial Intelligence Today. Recent Trends and Developments*, volume 1600 of *LNAI*, pages 175–194. Springer-Verlag, 1999.

173. Paolo Ciancarini, Robert Tolksdorf, Fabio Vitali, Davide Rossi, and Andreas Knoche. Coordinating Multiagent Applications on the WWW: A Reference Architecture. *IEEE Transactions on Software Engineering*, 24(5):362–375, May 1998.

174. Paolo Ciancarini and Alexander L. Wolf, editors. *Coordination Languages and Models – Proceedings of the 3rd International Conference (COORDINATION'99)*, volume 1594 of *LNCS*, Amsterdam (NL), April 26–28 1999. Springer-Verlag.

175. Claudio U. Ciborra. *Teams, markets and systems. Bussiness innovation and information technology*. Cambridge University Press, Cambridge, 1993.

176. P. Clayton, F. de Heer-Menlah, and E. Wentworth. Placing Processes in a Transputer-based Linda programming Environment. Technical report, Rhodes Uiversity, 1992.

177. P. Clayton and E. Wentworth. Placing processes in a transputer-based Linda programming environment. Technical report, Rhodes Uiversity, 1992.

178. Scott H. Clearwater, Rick Costanza, Mike Dixon, and Brain Schroeder. Saving Energy Using Market-Based Control. In Scott H. Clearwater, editor, *Market-Based Control*, pages 253–273. World Scientific, Singapore, 1996.

179. P. Codognet and D. Diaz. A simple and efficient Boolean constraint solver for constraint logic programming. *Journal of Automated Reasoning*, 17(1):97–128, 1996.

180. H. Collins and M. Kusch. *The Shape of Actions. What Humans and Machines Can Do*. The MIT Press, 1998.

181. J. Collis and D. Ndumu. The Role Modelling Guide. In *ZEUS Methodology Documentation*. British Telecom Laboratories, 1999.

182. Nora Comstock and Clarence Ellis, editors. *Proceedings of the Conference on Organizational Computing Systems, COOCS'95, Milpitas, California, USA*. ACM Press, August 1995.

183. Concordia. http://www.meitca.com/HSL/Projects/Concordia.

184. R. Conte and C. Castelfranchi. Norms as mental objects: From normative beliefs to normative goals. In *Spring Symposium on Reasoning about Mental States: Formal Theories and Applications*. AAAI Press, 1993.

185. J.O. Coplien. *Software Patterns*. SIGS Management Briefings Series. SIGS Books & Multimedia, 1996.

186. CORBA/IIOP Rev 2.2, OMG Document formal/98-07-01. `http://www.omg.org/library/c2indx.html`, February 1998.
187. Proposal for a Migration Service. `http://www.omg.org/docs/ec/99-01-07.pdf`, 1999.
188. CORBA Services – OMG Document formal/98-12-09. `http://www.omg.org/library/`, December 1998.
189. Antonio Corradi, Marco Cremonini, Rebecca Montanari, and Cesare Stefanelli. Mobile Agents Integrity for Electronic Commerce Applications. *Information Systems*, IS24(6), November 1999.
190. M. Corson, J. Macker, and G. Cinciarone. Internet-Based Mobile Ad Hoc Networking. *IEEE Internet Computing*, 3(4), July 1999.
191. R. Scott Cost, Ye Chen, Tim Finin, Yannis Labrou, and Yun Peng. Modeling Agent Conversations with Colored Petri Nets. In *Working Notes of the Workshop on Specifying and Implementing Conversation Policies*, pages 59–66, Seattle, Washington, May 1999.
192. R. Scott Cost, Tim Finin, Yannis Labrou, Xiaocheng Luan, Yun Peng, Ian Soboroff, James Mayfield, and Akram Boughannam. Jackal: A Java-based tool for agent development. In Jeremy Baxter and Chairs Brian Logan, editors, *Working Notes of the Workshop on Tools for Developing Agents, AAAI '98*, number WS-98-10 in AAAI Technical Reports, pages 73–82, Minneapolis, Minnesota, July 1998. AAAI, AAAI Press.
193. Michail F. Cowlishaw. *The REXX Language: A practical Approach to Programming*. Prentice Hall, 2nd edition, 1990.
194. Marco Cremonini. *Security and Mobility Issues in Software Agent Systems*. Ph.D Thesis, D.E.I.S., University of Bologna, Bologna (I), 2000.
195. Marco Cremonini, Andrea Omicini, and Franco Zambonelli. Modelling Network Topology and Mobile Agent Interaction: an Integrated Framework. In *Proc. 1999 ACM Symposium on Applied Computing (SAC '99)*, S. Antonio (TX), 1999. ACM Press.
196. Marco Cremonini, Andrea Omicini, and Franco Zambonelli. Multi-Agent Systems on the Internet: Extending the Scope of Coordination towards Security and Topology. In Francisco J. Garijo and Magnus Boman, editors, *Multi-Agent Systems Engineering – Proceedings of the 9th European Workshop on Modelling Autonoumous Agents in a Multi-Agent World (MAMAAW '99)*, volume 1647 of *LNAI*, pages 77–88, Valencia (E), June 30 - July 2 1999. Springer-Verlag, Heidelberg (D).
197. Marco Cremonini, Andrea Omicini, and Franco Zambonelli. Ruling Agent Motion in Structured Environments. In Marian R. Bubak, Hamideh Afsarmanesh, Roy Williams, and Bob Hertzberger, editors, *High Performance Computing and Networking — Proceedings of the 8th International Conference (HPCN Europe 2000)*, volume 1823 of *LNCS*, pages 187–196, Amsterdam (NL), May, 8–10 2000. Springer-Verlag.
198. L.R. Crow and N.R. Shadbolt. IMPS - Internet Agents for Knowledge Engineering. In *11th Workshop on Knowledge Acquisition, Modeling and Management (KAW'98)*, Calgary, April, 18–23 1998. SRDG Publications.
199. W.H.E. Davies and P. Edwards. Agent K: An Integration of APO and KQML. Technical Report AUCS/TR9406, Department of Computer Science, University of Aberdeen, 1994.
200. F. de Heer-Menlah. Analyzing communication flow and process placement in Linda programs on transputers. Technical report, Rhodes Uiversity, 1991.
201. K. Decker, K. Sycara, and M. Williamson. Middle-agents for the Internet. In *IJCAI-97 International Joint Conference on Artificial Intelligence, Nagoya, Japan*, 1997.

202. Serge Demeyer, Sander Tichelaar, and Patrick Steyaert. FAMIX 2.0 - The FAMOOS Information Exchange Model. Technical report, University of Berne, Institute of Computer Science and Applied Mathematics, August 1999.

203. Enrico Denti, Antonio Natali, and Andrea Omicini. Programmable Coordination Media. In David Garlan and Daniel Le Métayer, editors, *Coordination Languages and Models – Proceedings of the 2nd International Conference (COORDINATION'97)*, volume 1282 of *LNCS*, pages 274–288, Berlin (D), September 1–3 1997. Springer-Verlag.

204. Enrico Denti, Antonio Natali, and Andrea Omicini. On the Expressive Power of a Language for Programming Coordination Media. In *Proceedings of the 1998 ACM Symposium on Applied Computing (SAC'98)*, pages 169–177. ACM, February 27 - March 1 1998. Track on Coordination Models, Languages and Applications.

205. Enrico Denti and Andrea Omicini. An Architecture for Tuple-based Coordination of Multi-Agent Systems. *Software — Practice & Experience*, 29(12):1103–1121, October 1999.

206. Enrico Denti and Andrea Omicini. Engineering Multi-Agent Systems in LuCe. In Stephen Rochefort, Fariba Sadri, and Francesca Toni, editors, *Proceedings of the ICLP'99 International Workshop on Multi-Agent Systems in Logic Programming (MAS'99)*, Las Cruces (NM), November 30 1999.

207. Enrico Denti, Andrea Omicini, and Vladimiro Toschi. Coordination Technology for the Development of Multi-Agent Systems on the Web. In Evelina Lamma and Paola Mello, editors, *Proceedings of the 6th AI*IA Congress of the Italian Association for Artificial Intelligence (AI*IA'99)*, pages 29–38, Bologna (I), September 14–17 1999. Pitagora Editrice.

208. Department of Computer Science, University of Aarhus, Denmark. *Design/CPN Occurrence Graph Manual*, version 3.0 edition, 1996.

209. L. Deri. *A Component-based Architecture for Open, Independently Extensible Distributed System*. PhD thesis, University of Bern, June 1997.

210. D. Deugo and M. Weiss. A Case for Mobile Agent Patterns. In *Workshop on Mobile Agents in the Context of Competition and Cooperation (MAC3), Autonomous Agents 99*, pages 19–23, 1999.

211. R.F. DeVellis. Scale Development: Theory and Application. *Applied Social Research Methods Series*, 26, 1991.

212. Ian Dickenson. Agent Standards. Technical report, Foundation for Intelligent Physical Agents, October 1997.

213. Monica Divitini. *Coordinating Cooperative Work: A framework for the design of flexible computer–based support*. PhD thesis, Aalborg University, Aalborg, Denmark, 1999.

214. A. Douglas, A. Rowstron, and A. Wood. ISETL-LINDA: Parallel Programming with Bags. Technical Report YCS 257, University of York, 1995.

215. A. Douglas, A. Wood, and A. Rowstron. Linda implementation revisited. In *Transputer and occam developments*, pages 125–138. IOS Press, 1995.

216. J. Eder and W. Liebhart. The workflow activity model wamo. In *Proceedings of 3rd Int. Conference on Cooperative Information Systems*, Vienna, Austria, 1995.

217. Johann Eder, Herbert Groiss, and Walter Liebhart. The Workflow Management System Panta Rhei. In Asuman Doğaç, Leonid Kalinichenko, M. Tamer Özsu, and Amit Sheth, editors, *Workflow Management Systems and Interoperability*, NATO ASI Series. Springer, Berlin, 1998.

218. Renée Elio and Afsaneh Haddadi. On Abstract Task Models and Conversation Policies. In *Working Notes of the Workshop on Specifying and Implementing Conversation Policies*, pages 89–98, Seattle, Washington, May 1999.

219. C. A. Ellis. Workflow Technology. In Michel Beaudouin-Lafon, editor, *Computer Supported Co–operative Work*, Trends in Software, pages 29–54. John Wiley & Sons, New York, 1999.
220. C. A. Ellis and G. J. Nutt. Office Information Systems and Computer Science. *Computing Surveys*, 12(1):27–60, 1980.
221. Clarence A. Ellis and Grzegorz Rozenberg. Dynamic Change Within Workflow Systems. In Comstock and Ellis [182], pages 10–21.
222. C. Ellison. SPKI Requirements. In *RFC 2692*. The Internet Society, IETF, 1999.
223. C. Ellison, B. Frantz, B. Lampson, R. Rivest, B. Thomas, and T. Ylonen. SPKI Certificate Theory. In *RFC 2693*. The Internet Society, IETF, 1999.
224. W. Emmerich, C. Mascolo, and A. Finkelstein. Incremental Code Mobility with XML. Technical Report 99-95, University College London, October 1999.
225. Robert S. Englemore and Antony J. Morgan, editors. *Blackboard Systems*. Addison-Wesley, Reading (MA), 1988.
226. Entrust Home Site. http://www.entrust.com.
227. J. Eriksson, N. Finne, and S. Janson. SICS MarketSpace An Agent based Market Infrastructure. In *First International Workshop on Agent-Mediated Electronic Trading (AMET-98)*, volume 1571 of *LNAI*, Minneapolis, MN, May 10 1998. Springer-Verlag.
228. C. Faasen. Intermediate uniformly distributed tuple space on transputer meshes. In J.P. Banâtre and D. Le Métayer, editors, *Research Directions in High-Level Parallel Programming Languages*, volume 574 of *LNCS*. Springer Verlag, 1991.
229. A. El Fallah-Seghrouchni, S. Haddad, and H. Mazouzi. A Formal Study of Interactions in Multi-Agent Systems. In *Proceedins of ISCA International Conference in Computer and their Applications (CATA '99)*, April 1999.
230. A. El Fallah-Seghrouchni and S. Haddad H. Mazouzi. Etude des interactions basée sur l'observation réepartie dans un systéme multi-agents. In Hermés, editor, *Proceedings of JFIADSMA '98*, Nancy, France, November 1998.
231. Amal El Fallah-Seghrouchni and Hamza Mazouzi. A Hierarchial Model for Interactions in Multi-agent Systems. In *Working Notes of the Workshop on Agent Communication Languages, IJCAI '99*, August 1999.
232. Jalal Feghhi, Jalil Feghhi, and Peter Williams. *Digital Certificates: Applied Internet Security*. Addison Wesley, October 1998.
233. Jesse Feiler and Anthony Meadow. *Essential OpenDoc*. Addison-Wesley, 1996.
234. M. Feng, Y. Gao, and C. Yuen. Implementing Linda tuple space on a distributed system. *International Journal of High Speed Computing*, 7(1):125–144, 1995.
235. J. Ferber and J. Briot. Design of a Concurrent Language for Distributed Artificial Intelligence. In *Proceedings of the International Conference on Fifth Generation Computer Systems*, volume 2, pages 755–762. Institute for New Generation Computer Technology, 1988.
236. J. Ferber and O. Gutknecht. A Meta-Model for the Analysis and Design of Organizations in Multi-Agent Systems. In *Proceeding of the 3rd International Conference on Multi-Agent Systems (ICMAS 98)*. IEEE CS Press, June 1998.
237. Jaques Ferber. *Les Système Multi-Agents*. InterEditions, 1996.
238. P. Ferreira, M. Shapiro, X. Blondel, O. Fambon, J. Garcia, S. Kloosterman, N. Richer, M. Robert, F. Sandakly, G. Colouris, J. Dollimore, P. Guedes, D. Hagimont, and S. Krakowiak. PerDiS: Design, Implementation, and Use of a PERsistent DIstributed Store. In S. Krakowiak and S. Shrivastava, editors, *Advances in Distributed Systems*, volume 1752 of *LNCS*, pages 427–452. Springer-Verlag, 2000.

239. Timothy W. Finin, Richard Fritzson, Donald McKay, and Robin McEntire. KQML as an Agent Communication Language. In *Proceedings of the 3rd International Conference on Information and Knowledge Management (CIKM'94)*, pages 456–463, Gaithersburg (Maryland), November 1994. ACM Press.

240. FIPA Home Site. `http://www.fipa.org/`.

241. FIPA. FIPA 97 Specification Part 2: Agent Communication Language. Technical report, FIPA - Foundation for Intelligent Physical Agents, October 1997.

242. David Flanagan. *JavaScript: The Definitive Guide*. O'Reilly & Associates, 2nd edition, January 1997.

243. R.A. Flores-Mendez. Towards the Standardization of Multi Agent Systems Architectures: An Overview. *ACM Crossroads - Special Issue on Intelligence Agents*, 5(4), Summer 1999.

244. Jean-Luc Fontaine. Simple Tcl Only Object Oriented Programming. Available at http://www.multimania.com/jfontain/stooop.htm, 1998.

245. MPI Forum. MPI Specification. `http://www.mpi-forum.org/`.

246. I. Foster, J. Geisler, B. Nickless, W. Smith, and Tuecke S. Software infrastructure for the I-WAY high-performance distributed computing experiment. In *Proceedings of the 5th IEEE International Symposium on High Performance Distributed Computing*, pages 562–571. IEEE Computer Society Press, 1996.

247. M. S. Fox. An Organizational View of Distributed Systems. *IEEE Transactions on Systems, Man, and Cybernetics*, 11(1):70–80, January 1981.

248. S. Franklin and A. Graesser. Is it an Agent or just a Program? A Taxonomy for Auotnomous Agents. In J. P. Müller, Michael J. Wooldridge, and Nicholas R. Jennings, editors, *Intelligent Agents III — Agent Theories, Architectures, and Languages*, volume 1193 of *LNAI*, pages 21–35. Springer-Verlag, 1997.

249. Eric Freeman, Susanne Hupfer, and Ken Arnold. *JavaSpaces: Principles, Patterns, and Practice*. The Jini Technology Series. Addison-Wesley, 1999.

250. S. Frølund. *Coordinating Distributed Objects: An Actor-Based Approach to Synchronization*. MIT Press, 1996.

251. S. Frølund and G. Agha. A Language Framework for Multi-Object Coordination. In *Proceedings of ECOOP 1993*. Springer Verlag, 1993. LNCS 707.

252. M. Fuchs. Domain Specific Languages for ad hoc Distributed Applications. In *USENIX Conference on Domain Specific Languages*, Santa Barbara (CA), October 15–17 1997.

253. Alfonso Fuggetta, Gian Pietro Picco, and Giovanni Vigna. Understanding Code Mobility. *IEEE Transactions on Software Engineering*, 24(5):342–361, May 1998.

254. Yuzo Fujishima, Kevin Leyton-Brown, and Yoav Shoham. Taming the Computational Complexity of Combinatorial Auctions: Optimal and Approximate Approaches. In *Proceedings of the International Joint Conference on Artificial Intelligence*, Stockholm, Sweden, 1999.

255. Alan Galan and Albert Baker. Multi-Agent Communications in JAFMAS. In *Working Notes of the Workshop on Specifying and Implementing Conversation Policies*, pages 67–70, Seattle, Washington, May 1999.

256. Doreen Galli. *Distributed Operating Systems – Concepts & Practice*. Prentice Hall, August 1999.

257. E. Gamma, R. Helm, R. Johnson, and J. Vlissides. *Design Patterns: Elements of Reusable Object-Oriented Software*, chapter Observer, pages 293–303. Addison Wesley, 1995.

258. Erich Gamma, Richard Helm, Ralph Johnson, and John Vlissides. *Design Patterns*. Addison-Wesley, 1995.

259. H. Garcia-Molina and et al. The TSIMMIS Approach to Mediation: Data Models and Languages. In *Workshop NGITS-95*, 1995. ftp://db.stanford.edu/pub/garcia/1995/tsimmis-models-languages.ps.

260. Simson Garfinkel. *PGP: Pretty Good Privacy*. O'Reilly & Associates, Inc., Sebastopol (CA), 1995.

261. F.J. Garijo and M. Boman (Eds.). *Multi-Agent System Engineering. Proceedings of the 9th European Workshop on Modelling Autonomous Agents in a Multi-Agent World (MAAMAW99)*, volume 1647 of *LNCS*. Springer Verlag, Berlin, D, 1999.

262. David Garlan, Robert Allen, and John Ockerbloom. Architectural Mismatch: Why Reuse Is So Hard. *IEEE Software*, 12(6):17–26, November 1995.

263. David Garlan and Daniel Le Métayer, editors. *Coordination Languages and Models – Proceedings of the 2nd International Conference (COORDINATION'97)*, volume 1282 of *LNCS*, Berlin (D), September 1–3 1997. Springer-Verlag.

264. Felix C. Gärtner. Fundamentals of fault-tolerant distributed computing in asynchronous environments. *ACM Computing Surveys*, 31(1):1–26, March 1999.

265. Les Gasser and Jean-Pierre Briot. Object-Based Concurrent Programming and Distributed Artificial Intelligence. In Nicholas M. Avouris and Les Gasser, editors, *Distributed Artificial Intelligence: Theory and Praxis*, pages 81–107. Kluwer Academic, 1992.

266. D. Gelernter, N. Carrierio, S. Chandran, and S. Chang. Parallel Processing in Linda. In *International Conference on Parallel Processing*, 1985.

267. David Gelernter. Generative Communication in Linda. *ACM Transactions on Programming Languages and Systems*, 7(1):80–112, 1985.

268. David Gelernter. Multiple Tuple Spaces in Linda. In E. Odijk, M. Rem, and J. C. Syre, editors, *Proceedings of the Conference on Parallel Architectures and Languages Europe : Vol. 2*, volume 366 of *LNCS*, pages 20–27. Springer-Verlag, Heidelberg (D), June 1989.

269. David Gelernter and Nicholas Carriero. Coordination Languages and their Significance. *Communications of the ACM*, 35(2):97–107, February 1992.

270. M. R. Genesereth and S. P. Ketchpel. Software Agents. *Communication of the ACM*, 37(7):48–54, 1994.

271. M.R. Genesereth, A.M. Keller, and O. Duschka. Infomaster: An Information Integration System. In *ACM SIGMOD Conference*, May 1997.

272. J.A. Giampapa, M. Paolucci, and K. Sycara. Agent Interoperation Across Multi-agent System Boundaries. In *4th International Conference on Autonomous Agents (Agents 2000)*, Barcelona (Spain), June 3–7 2000. ACM Press.

273. Simon Gibbs and Dionysios Tsichritzis. *Multimedia Programming*. Addison Wesley, March 1995.

274. N. Glase. *Contributions to Knowledge Modelling in a Multi-agent Framework (The CoMoMAS Approach)*. Ph.D Thesis, Université Henry Poincaré, Nancy (F), 1996.

275. G. Glass. Agents and Internet Component Technology. Invited talk at 3rd *Int. Conf. on Autonomous Agents (Agents'99)*, May 1999.

276. Steve Glassman, Mark Manasse, Martín Abadi, Paul Gauthier, and Patrick Sobalvarro. The Millicent Protocol for Inexpensive Electronic Commerce. *World Wide Web Journal*, 1(1), Winter 1996.

277. R.J. Glushko, J.M. Tenenbaum, and B. Meltzer. An XML framework for agent-based e-commerce. *Communications of the ACM*, 42(3), March 1999.

278. H. Gomaa. Inter-Agent Communication in Cooperative Information Agent based Systems. In *Third International Workshop on Cooperative Information Agents (CIA99)*, volume 1652 of *LNAI*, pages 137–148, Uppsala (Sweden), July 31–August 2 1999. Springer-Verlag.

279. J. Gordijn, H. Akkermans, and H. Van Vliet. Value Based Requirements Creation for Electronic Commerce Applications. In *The 33rd Hawaii International Conference on System Sciences (HICSS-33)*. IEEE Computer Society Press, January 2000.

280. Rob Gordon. *Essential Java Native Interface*. Prentice Hall, 1998.

281. J. Gosling, B. Joy, and G. Steele. *The Java Language Specification*. Addison Wesley, 1996.

282. James Gosling and Ken Arnold. *The Java Programming Language*. Addison Wesley, December 1997.

283. Laurent Granvilliers. Cooperative Interval Narrowing. In *Proceedings of International Workshop on Frontiers of Combining Systems*, LNAI, Nancy, France, 2000. Springer-Verlag.

284. Grasshopper Home Site. `http://www.ikv.de/products/grasshopper`.

285. Antonietta Grasso, Lean-Luc Meunier, Daniele Pagani, and Remo Pareschi. Distributed Coordination and Workflow on the World Wide Web. *Computer Supported Cooperative Work: The Journal of Collaborative Computing*, 6(2–3):175–200, 1997.

286. Robert Gray. *Agent Tcl: A flexible and secure mobile-agent system*. PhD thesis, Dartmouth College, June 1997. Available as Dartmouth Computer Science Technical Report TR98-327.

287. P. B. Grefen, B. Pernici, and G. Sanchez, editors. *Database support for Workflow Management – The WIDE Project*. Kluwer Academic Publishers, Dordrecht, The Netherlands, 1999.

288. N. Griffeth and H. Velthuijsen. Reasoning about goals to resolve conflicts. In *International Conference on Intelligent Cooperating Information Systems*, pages 197–204. IEEE, 1993.

289. Ralph E. Griswold and Madge T. Griswold. *The Icon Programming Language*. Peer-to-Peer Communications, December 1996.

290. Thomas R. Gruber. A Translation Approach to Portable Ontology Specifications. *Knowledge Acquisition*, 2:199–220, 1993.

291. T. Gschwind, M. Feridun, and S. Pleisch. ADK Building Mobile Agents for Network and Systems Management from Reusable Components. In *First International Symposium on Agent Systems and Applications and Third International Symposium on Mobile Agents (ASA/MA99)*, pages 13–21, Palm Springs, October, 3–6 1999. IEEE Press.

292. A. Gupta, B. Jukic, M. Parameswaran, D. O. Stahl, and A. B. Whinston. Streamlining the Digital Economy: How to Avert a Tragedy of the Commons. *IEEE Internet Computing*, 1(6), Nov.-Dec. 1997.

293. R. Gustavsson. Multi Agent Systems as Open Societies - A design framework. In *Intelligent Agents IV, Agent Theories, Architectures, and Languages*, volume 1365 of *LNAI*, pages 329–337. Springer Verlag, Berlin, D, 1998.

294. Rune Gustavsson. Agents with Power. *Communications of the ACM*, 42(3):41–47, March 1999.

295. R. Guttman, A. Moukas, and Patty Maes. Agent-Mediated Electronic Commerce: A Survey. *Knowledge Engineering Review*, 13(3):147–160, 1998.

296. A. Haddadi. *Communication and Cooperation in Agent Systems. A Pragmatic Theory*, volume 1056 of *LNAI*. Springer Verlag, Berlin, D, 1995.

297. N. Hameurlain and C. Sibertin-Blanc. Behavioural Types in CoOperative Objects. In *Proceedings of the Second Workshop on Semantics of Objects as Processes, SOAP99–ECOOP99*, 1999.

298. B. Hayes-Roth. A Blackboard Architecture for Control. *Artificial Intelligence*, pages 251–321, 1985.

299. Mathias Hein and David Griffiths. *SNMP: Simple Network Management Protocol – Theory and Practice, Versions 1 and 2*. Van Nostrand Reinhold, September 1995.

300. Michael Held. Scripting für CORBA. Master's thesis, University of Bern, Institute of Computer Science and Applied Mathematics, April 1999.

301. A. Herzberg, Y. Mass, J. Mihaeli, D. Naor, and Y. Ravid. Access control meets public key infrastructure, or: Assigning roles to strangers. In *IEEE Symposium on Security and Privacy*, May 2000.

302. C. Hewitt. Viewing Control Structures as Patterns of Passing Messages. *Journal of Artificial Intelligence*, 8-3:323–364, June 1977.

303. M. G. Hinchey and S. A. Jarvis. *Concurrent Systems: Formal Development in CSP*. McGraw-Hill, 1995.

304. John Hogg. Islands: Aliasing Protection in Object-Oriented Languages. In *Proceedings of the OOPSLA '91 Conference on Object-oriented Programming Systems, Languages and Applications*, pages 271–285, November 1991.

305. John Hogg, Doug Lea, Alan Wills, Dennis deChampeaux, and Richard Holt. The Geneva Convention on the Treatment of Object Aliasing. *OOPS Messenger*, 3(2):11–16, April 1992.

306. T. Holvoet. Agents and Petri Nets. *The Petri Net Newsletter*, (49):3–8, 1995.

307. T. Holvoet and P. Verbaeten. Synchronization Specifications for Agents with Net-based Behavior Descriptions. In *Proceedings of CESA '96 IMACS Conference, Symposium on Discrete Events and Manufacturing Systems*, pages 613–618, Lille, France, July 1996.

308. Tom Holvoet and Thilo Keilmann. Behavior Specification of Active Objects in Open Generative Communication Environments. In Hesham El-Rewini and Yale N. Patt, editors, *Proceedings of the HICSS-30 Conference, Track on Coordination Models, Languages and Systems*, pages 349–358. IEEE Computer Society Press, January, 7–10 1997.

309. Tom Holvoet and Pierre Verbaeten. Using Petri Nets for Specifying Active Objects and Generative Communication. In G. Agha and F. DeCindio, editors, *Advances in Petri Nets on Object-Orientation*, Lecture Notes in Computer Science. Springer-Verlag, 1998.

310. Kohei Honda and Mario Tokoro. An Object Calculus for Asynchronous Communication. In Pierre America, editor, *Proceedings of the European Conference on Object Oriented Programming (ECOOP'91)*, volume 512 of *LNCS*, pages 141–162. Springer-Verlag, 1991.

311. C. Houck and G. Agha. HAL: A High-level Actor Language and Its Distributed Implementation. In *Proceedings of the 21st International Conference on Parallel Processing (ICPP '92)*, volume II, pages 158–165, St. Charles, IL, August 1992.

312. R. Housley, W. Ford, W. Polk, and D. Solo. Internet X.509 Public Key Infrastructure, Certificate and CRL Profile. In *RFC 2459*. The Internet Society, IETF, 1999.

313. Timothy Howes, Mark Smith, and Gordon Good. *Understanding and Deploying LDAP Directory Services*. MacMillan Technical Publishing, 1999.

314. B.A. Huberman and T. Hogg. The Emergence of Computational Ecologies. In L. Nadel and D. Stein, editors, *SFI Studies in the Sciences of Complexity, Vol. V*. Addison-Wesley, 1993.

315. G. Huck, P. Fankhauser, K. Aberer, and E.J. Neuhold. Jedi: Extracting and Synthesizing Information from the Web. In *Conference on Cooperative Information Systems CoopIS'98*. IEEE Computer Society Press, 1998.

316. S. Hupfer, D. Kaminsky, N. Carriero, and D. Gelernter. Coordination Applications of Linda. In J.P. Banâtre and D. Le Métayer, editors, *Research Directions in High-Level Parallel Programming Languages*, volume 574 of *LNCS*, pages 187–194. Springer-Verlang, 1995.

317. Susanne Hupfer. Melinda: Linda with Multiple Tuple Spaces. Technical Report RR YALEU/DCS/R-766, Dept. of Computer Science, Yale University, New Haven, CT, 1990.

318. IAIK JCE Home Site. http://jcewww.iaik.at/jce/jce.htm.

319. Roberto Ierusalimschy, Luiz Henrique de Figueiredo, and Waldemar Celes Filho. Lua – an Extensible Extension Language. *Software: Practice and Experience*, 26(6):635–652, 1996.

320. C. Iglesias, M. Garijo, J.C. Gonzales, and J.R. Velasco. Analysis and Design of Multi-agent Systems Using MAS-CommonKADS. In *Intelligent Agents IV (ATAL97), LNAI 1365*, pages 313–326. Springer-Verlag, 1998.

321. Carlos Iglesias, Mercedes Garijo, and Juan Gonzales. A Survey of Agent-Oriented Methodologies. In A. S. Rao J.P. Muller, M. P. Singh, editor, *Intelligents Agents IV (ATAL98)*, LNAI. Springer-Verlag, 1999.

322. IMPACT. Interactive Maryland Platform for Agents Collaborating Together. http://www.cs.umd.edu/projects/impact/.

323. ARPA Knowledge Sharing Initiative. *Specification of the KQML agent-communication language*. ARPA Knowledge Sharing Initiative, External Interfaces Working Group, July 1993.

324. Internet2 Home Site. http://www.internet2.edu/middleware.

325. Wilfred C. Jamison and Douglas Lea. TRUCE: Agent Coordination Through Concurrent Interpretation of Role-based Protocols. In Paolo Ciancarini and Alexander L. Wolf, editors, *Coordination Languages and Models – Proceedings of the 3rd International Conference (COORDINATION'99)*, volume 1594 of *LNCS*, pages 384–398, Amsterdam (NL), April 26–28 1999. Springer-Verlag.

326. M. Jarke, M.A. Jeusfeld, C. Quix, T. Sellis, and P. Vassiliadis. Metadata and data warehouse quality. In M. Jarke, M. Lenzerini, Y. Vassiliou, and P. Vassiliadis, editors, *Fundamentals of data warehouses*. Springer, 2000.

327. JAT. Java Agent Template. http://cdr.stanford.edu/ABE/JavaAgent.html.

328. B. Jennings, R. Brennan, R. Gustavsson, R. Feldt, J. Pitt, K. Prouskas, and J. Quantz. A FIPA-Compliant Multi-Agent System for Real-time Control of Intelligent Network Traffic Load. *Computer Networks and ISDN Systems*, 31, 1999.

329. N. R. Jennings and M. Wooldridge. Applications of Intelligent Agents. In N. R. Jennings and M. Wooldridge, editors, *Agent Technology Foundations, Applications and Market*, pages 3–29. Springer, Berlin, Germany, 1998.

330. N. R. Jennings and M. Wooldridge. Agent-Oriented Software Engineering. In *Handbook of Agent Technology*. ACM, 2000.

331. Nicholas R. Jennings and Michael J. Wooldridge, editors. *Agent Technology: Foundations, Applications and Markets*. Springer-Verlag, 1998.

332. N.R. Jennings. Agent-Based Computing: Promises and Perils. In *The Sixteenth International Joint Conference on Artificial Intelligence (IJCAI99)*, pages 1429–1436, 1999.

333. N.R. Jennings, T.J. Norman, and P. Faratin. ADEPT: An Agent-based Approach to Business Process Management. *ACM SIGMOD Record*, 27(4):32–39, 1998.

334. D. Jensen, Y. Dong, B.S. Lerner, E.K. McCall, L.J. Osterweil, S.M. Sutton, and A. Wise. Coordinating Agent Activities in Knowledge Discovery Processes. In *International Joint Conference on Work Activities Coordination and Collaboration (WACC99)*, pages 137–146, San Francisco (CA), February 22–25 1999.

335. K. Jensen. Coloured Petri Nets. In W. Brauer, W. Reisig, and G. Rozenberg, editors, *Petri Nets: Central Models and Their Properties, Advances in Petri Nets 1986 Part I*, volume 254 of *LNCS*, pages 248–299, Berlin, Germany, 1987. Springer-Verlag.

336. K. Jensen. *Coloured Petri Nets. Basic Concepts, Analysis Methods and Practical Use*, volume Volume 3, Practical Use of *Monographs in Theoretical Computer Science*. Springer-Verlag, 1997.

337. K. Jeong. *Fault-tolerant parallel processing combining Linda, checkpointing and transactions*. PhD thesis, New York University, 1996.

338. K. Jeong and D. Shasha. PLinda 2.0 : A Transactional/Checkpointing Approach to Fault Tolerant Linda. In *Symposium on Reliable Distributed Systems (SRDS '94)*, pages 96–105, Los Alamitos, Ca., USA, October 1994. IEEE Computer Society Press.

339. K. Jeong, D. Shasha, S. Talla, and P. Wyckoff. An Approach to Fault-Tolerant Parallel Processing on Intermittently Idle, Heterogeneous Workstations. In *Proceedings of The Twenty-Seventh Annual International Symposium on Fault-Tolerant Computing (FTCS'97)*, pages 11–20. IEEE, June 1997.

340. S. Jha, P. Chalasani, O. Shehory, and K. Sycara. A Formal Treatment of Distributed Matchmaking. In *2nd Conference on Autonomous Agents (Agents 98),Minneapolis, MN*, May 1998.

341. Claudia Johnson. Enron Communications announces first commodity bandwidth trade, December 1999.

342. A.J. Jones and B.S. Firozabadi. On the characterisation of a trusting agent Aspects of a formal approach. In C. Castelfranchi and Y-H. Tan, editors, *Trust and deception in virtual societies*. Kluwer Academic Publishers, Dordrecht-Holland, 2000.

343. Java Virtual Machine Profiler Interface (JVMPI). `http://java.sun.com/jdk/1.3/docs/guide/jvmpi/jvmpi.html`.

344. D. Kafura, M. Mukherji, and G. Lavender. ACT++: A Class Library for Concurrent Programming in C++ Using Actors. *Journal of Object Oriented Programming*, pages 47–55, 1993.

345. S. Kambhatla and J. Walpole. The Interplay between Granularity, Performance, and Availability in a Replicated Linda Tuple Space. In Viktor K. Prasanna and Larry H. Canter, editors, *Proceedings of the 6th International Parallel Processing Symposium*, pages 508–511, Beverly Hills, CA, March 1992. IEEE Computer Society Press.

346. Srikanth Kambhatla. Replication Issues for a Distributed and Highly Available Linda Tuple Space. Master's Thesis, Oregon Graduate Institute, 1991.

347. Srikanth Kambhatla and Jonathan Walpole. Recovery With Limited Replay: Fault-Tolerant Processes In Linda. Technical Report CS/E 90-019, Oregon Graduate Institute, 1990.

348. N.M. Karnik and A.R. Tripathi. Design Issues in Mobile-Agent Programming Systems. *IEEE Concurrency*, 6(3):52–61, 1998.

349. E. A. Kendall, P.V. Murali, Chirag Krishna, V. Pathak, and C.B. Suresh. Patterns of Intelligent and Mobile Agents. In *Autonomous Agents '98*, 1998.

350. E.A. Kendall. Role Modeling for Agent System Analysis, Design and Implementation. In *First International Symposium on Agent Systems and Appli-*

cations and Third International Symposium on Mobile Agents (ASA/MA99), pages 204–218, Palm Springs (CA), October 3–6 1999. IEEE Press.

351. L. Kerschberg and S. Banerjee. An Agency-based Framework for Electronic Business. In *Third International Workshop on Cooperative Information Agents (CIA99)*, volume 1652 of *LNAI*, pages 265–290, Uppsala (Sweden), July 31–August 2 1999. Springer-Verlag.

352. Grégor Kiczales, John Lamping, Anurag Mendhekar, Chris Maeda, Cristina Lopes, Jean-Marc Loingtier, and John Irwin. Aspect-Oriented Programming. In Mehmet Aksit and Satoshi Matsuoka, editors, *Proceedings ECOOP '97*, number 1241 in LNCS, pages 220–242. Springer, June 1997.

353. Thilo Kielmann. Designing a Coordination Model for Open Systems. In P. Ciancarini and C. Hankin, editors, *Coordination Languages and Models: Proceedings of COORDINATION '96*, number 1061 in Lecture Notes in Computer Science, pages 267–284. Springer, Cesena, Italy, 1996.

354. KIF. Knowledge Interchange Format. http://logic.stanford.edu/kif/.

355. W. Kim. *THAL: An Actor System for Efficient and Scalable Concurrent Computing*. PhD thesis, University of Illinois at Urbana-Champaign, May 1997.

356. W. Kim and G. Agha. Efficient Support of Location Transparency in Concurrent Object-Oriented Programming Languages. In *Proceedings of Supercomputing'95*, 1995.

357. W. Kim and et al. On resolving schematic heterogeneity in multidatabase systems. *Distributed and Parallel Databases*, 1:251–279, 1993.

358. D. Kinny and M. Georgeff. A Methodology and Modelling Technique for Systems of BDI Agents. In *Workshop on Modelling Autonomous Agents in a Multi-Agent World, LNAI 1038*, pages 56–71. Springer-Verlag, 1996.

359. V. Kisielius. Applying Intelligence Makes E-commerce Pay Off. *Electronic Commerce World*, 7(12), December 1997.

360. Y. Kitamura, Y. Mawarimichi, and T. Tatsumi. Mobile-Agent Mediated Place Oriented Communication. In *Proceedings of the Third International Workshop on Cooperative Information Agents*, volume 1652 of *LNAI*, pages 232–242. Springer-Verlag, 1999.

361. V. Krishnaswamy, S. Ahuja, N. Carriero, and D. Gelernter. The Linda machine. In *Proceedings 1987 Princeton Workshop on Algorithm Architecture and Technology Issues for Models of Concurrent Computations*, pages 697–717, 1987.

362. V. Krishnaswamy, S. Ahuja, N. Carriero, and D. Gelernter. Architecture of a Linda coprocessor. In *Proceedings 15th Annual International Symposium on Computer Archiatecture*, pages 240–249, 1988.

363. David M. Kristol, Steven H. Low, and Nicholas F. Maxemchuk. Anonymous Internet Mercantile Protocol. Technical report, AT&T Bell Laboratories, Murray Hill, NJ, 1994.

364. D. Kuokka and L. Harrada. On using KQML for matchmaking. In *CIKM-95 3rd Conf. on Information and Knowledge Management*. AAAI/MIT Press, 1995.

365. Kazuhiro Kuwabara, Toru Ishida, and Nobuyasu Osato. AgenTalk: Describing Multiagent Coordination Protocols with Inheritance. In *Proceedings of the 7th IEEE International Conference on Tools with Artificial Intelligence (ICTAI '95)*, pages 460–465, 1995.

366. Y. Labrou, T. Finin, and Y. Peng. Agent communication languages: The current landscape. *IEEE Intelligent Systems*, March/April 1999.

367. Yannis Labrou. *Semantics for an Agent Communication Language*. PhD thesis, University of Maryland Baltimore County, 1996.

368. Yannis Labrou and Tim Finin. A proposal for a new KQML Specification. Technical Report Technical Report TR-CS-97-03, University of Maryland Baltimore County, 1997.

369. Yannis Labrou and Timothy Finin. Semantics and Conversations for an Agent Communication Language. In *Proceedings of the Fifteenth International Joint Conference on Artificial Intelligence (IJCAI-97)*, Nagoya, Japan, August 1997.

370. C. Lakos and Søren Christensen. A General Systematic Approach to Arc Extensions for Coloured Petri Nets. Technical Report R93-7, Department of Computer Science, University of Tasmania, Hobart, Tasmania, August 1993.

371. B. Lampson, M. Abadi, M. Burrows, , and E. Wobber. Authentication in distributed systems: Theory and Practice. *ACM Transactions on Computer Systems*, 10(4):265–310, 1992.

372. Butler Lampson. Protection. *ACM Operating Systems Review*, 8(1), January 1974.

373. D. B. Lange and M. Oshima, editors. *Programming and Deploying Java Mobile Agents with Aglets*. Addison-Wesley, 1998.

374. Chris Langton, Roger Burkhart, Marcus Daniels, and Alex Lancaster. The Swarm Simulation System, 1999.

375. R. Larsson, J. Schnknecht, P. Sweet, and M. Driver. The Customer Side of Energy-Saving Activities Exploring Attitudes and Interests on the Karlshamn Energy Market. In J.M. Akkermans and H. Ottosson, editors, *The KEES Project Energy Efficiency in a Deregulated Market*, pages 39–60. EnerSearch AB, Malm, Sweden, 1999.

376. Jeff Lawson, Adam L. Beberg, Peter Gildea, David McNett, Chris Chiapusio, Peter DeNitto, and Tim Charron. distributed.net. http://www.distributed.net, visited March 2000.

377. T. Lehman, W. McLaughry, and P. Wyckoff. TSpaces: The Next Wave. In *Hawaii International Conference on System Sciences (HICSS-32)*, January 1999.

378. Yu Lei and Munindar P. Singh. A Comparison of Workflow Metamodels. In *Proceedings of the ER-97 Workshop on Behavioral Modeling and Design Transformations: Issues and Opportunities in Conceptual Modeling, Los Angeles, CA*, 1997.

379. J. Leichter. *Shared tuple memories, shared memories, buses and LAN's – Linda implementations across the spectrum of connectivity*. PhD thesis, Yale University, 1989. YALEU/DCS/TR-714.

380. N. Li, J. Feigenbaum, and B. Grosof. A Logic-based Knowledge Representation for Authorization with Delegation (Extended Abstract). In *Proceedings of the 12th Computer Security Foundations Workshop*, pages 162–174, Los Alamitos (CA), 1999. IEEE Computer Society Press.

381. Fuhua Lin, Douglas H. Norrie, Weiming Shen, and Rob Kremer. Schema-based Approach to Specifying Conversation Policies. In *Working Notes of the Workshop on Specifying and Implementing Conversation Policies, Third International Conference on Autonomous Agents*, pages 71–78, Seattle, Washington, May 1999.

382. B.H. Liskov and J.M. Wing. A Behavioral Notion of Subtyping. *ACM Transactions on Programming Languages and Systems*, 16(6), November 1994.

383. David C. Luckham, John L. Kenney, Larry M. Augustin, James Vera, Doug Bryan, and Walter Mann. Specification and Analysis of System Architecture Using Rapide. *IEEE Transactions on Software Engineering*, 21(4):336–355, April 1995.

384. H. Ludwig and Y. Hoffner. Contract-based Cross-Organisational Workflows - The CrossFlow Project. In *Workshop on Cross-Organisational Workflow Management and Co-ordination, February 22nd 1999, San Francisco*, 1999.

385. Sean Luke, Lee Spector, David Rager, and James Hendler. Ontology-based Web Agents. In *1st International Conference on Autonomous Agents*, 1997.

386. Markus Lumpe. *A π-Calculus Based Approach to Software Composition.* PhD thesis, University of Bern, Institute of Computer Science and Applied Mathematics, January 1999.

387. Markus Lumpe, Jean-Guy Schneider, Oscar Nierstrasz, and Franz Achermann. Towards a formal composition language. In Gary T. Leavens and Murali Sitaraman, editors, *Proceedings of ESEC '97 Workshop on Foundations of Component-Based Systems*, pages 178–187, Zurich, September 1997.

388. N. Lynch. *Distributed algorithms.* Morgan Kaufman, 1996.

389. D.M. Lyons and A.J. Hendriks. Planning for Reactive Robot Behavior. In *Proc. of the IEEE Int. Conf. on Robotics and Automation*, Nice, France, May 1992.

390. P. Maes. Agents that Reduce Work and Information Overload. *Communications of the ACM*, 37(7):31–40, July 1994.

391. Thomas Magedanz and Radu Popescu-Zeletin. *Intelligent Networks - Basic Technology, Standards and Evolution.* International Thomson Computer Press, July 1996.

392. Thomas Magedanz (ed.). Special Issue on Mobile Agents in Intelligent Networks and Mobile Communication Systems. *Computer Networks Journal*, 31(10), July 1999.

393. T.M. Malone and K. Crowston. The Interdisciplinary Study of Coordination. *ACM Computing Surveys*, 26(1):87–119, March 1994.

394. U. Manber. Chain Reactions in Networks. *IEEE Computer*, October 1990.

395. D.W. Manchala. E-commerce trust metrics and models. *IEEE Internet Computing*, 4(2), March/April 2000.

396. Ronni T. Marshak. Workflow: Applying Automation to Group Processes. In David Coleman, editor, *Groupware – Collaborative Strategies for Corporate LANs and Intranets*, chapter 6, pages 143–181. Prentice Hall PTR, 1997.

397. P. Marti and M. Rueher. A Distributed Cooperating Constraints Solving System. *International Journal on AI Tools*, 4(1&2):93–113, 1995.

398. Francisco Martin, Enric Plaza, and Juan Rodríguez-Aguilar. Conversation Protocols: Modeling and Implementing Conversations in Agent-Based Systems. In *Working Notes of the Workshop on Specifying and Implementing Conversation Policies*, pages 49–58, Seattle, Washington, May 1999.

399. C. Mascolo. MobiS: A Specification Language for Mobile Systems. In P. Ciancarini and A. Wolf, editors, *Proceedings of the 3rd Int. Conf. on Coordination Languages and Models (COORDINATION)*, volume 1594 of *LNCS*, pages 37–52. Springer-Verlag, April 1999.

400. C. Mascolo, G.P. Picco, and G.-C. Roman. A Fine-Grained Model for Code Mobility. In *Proc. of the 7th European Software Engineering Conf. held jointly with the 7th ACM SIGSOFT Symp. on the Foundations of Software Engineering (ESEC/FSE '99)*, LNCS, Toulouse (France), September 1999. Springer-Verlag.

401. Mobile Agent System Interoperability Facility (MASIF) specification. `ftp://ftp.omg.org/pub/docs/orbos/97-10-05.pdf`.

402. Y. Mass and O. Shehory. Distributed trust in open multi-agent systems. In *Autonomous Agents 2000 Workshop on Deception, Fraud and Trust in Agent Societies, June*, 2000.

403. G. Matos and J. Purtilo. Reconfiguration of Hierarchical tuple-spaces: Experiments with Linda-Polylith. Technical Report CSD TR 3153, University of Maryland, 1993.

404. F.G. McCabe and K. Clark. April Agent PRocess Interaction Language. In *Intelligent Agents — Agent Theories, Architectures, and Languages*, volume 890 of *LNAI*, pages 324–340. Springer-Verlag, 1995.

405. P.J. McCann and G.-C. Roman. Compositional Programming Abstractions for Mobile Computing. *IEEE Trans. on Software Engineering*, 24(2), 1998.

406. P.J. McCann and G-.C. Roman. Modeling Mobile IP in Mobile UNITY. *ACM Transactions on Software Engineering and Methodology*, 8(2), April 1999.

407. H. Meleis. Toward the Information Network. *IEEE Computer*, 29(10):59–67, October 1996.

408. R. Menezes and A. Wood. Garbage Collection in Open Distributed Tuple Space Systems. In *Proceedings of 15th Brazilian Computer Networks Symposium - SBRC'97*, 1997.

409. Ronaldo Menezes. Ligia: Incorporating Garbage Collection in a Java based Linda-like Run-Time System. In Raimundo J. Macedo, Alcides Calsavara, and Robert C. Burnett, editors, *Proc. of the 2nd Workshop on Distributed Systems (WOSID'98)*, pages 81–88, Curitiba, Paraná, Brazil, June 1998.

410. Ronaldo Menezes. *Resource Management in Open Linda Systems*. PhD Thesis, Department of Computer Science. University of York, 1999.

411. Iain Merrick and Alan Wood. Coordination with Scopes. In *Proc. ACM Symposium on Applied Computing*, pages 210–217. ACM Press, 2000.

412. M. Merz and W. Lamersdorf. Agents, Services, and Electronic Markets: How do they Integrate? In *Proceedings of the IFIP/IEEE International Conference on Distributed Platforms*, Dresden, Germany, 1996.

413. G. Meszaros and J. Doble. A Pattern Language for Pattern Writing. In *Pattern Languages of Program Design 3*, pages 529–574. Addision Wesley, 1998.

414. Microsoft. DCOM Specification. http://www.microsoft.com/.

415. Microsoft Corporation. *Visual Basic Programmierhandbuch*, 1997.

416. Sun Microsystems. Java Specification. http://java.sun.com/.

417. John A. Miller, Devanand Palaniswami, Amit P. Sheth, Krys Kochut, and Harvinder Singh. WebWork: $METEOR_2$'s Web-Based Workflow Management System. In *Journal of Intelligent Information Systems – Special Issue: Workflow Management Systems* [528], pages 185–215.

418. Robin Milner. *Communication and Concurrency*. Prentice-Hall International, 1989.

419. D. Milojicic, M. Breugst, I. Busse, J. Campbell, S. Covaci, B. Friedman, K. Kosaka, D. Lange, K. Ono, M. Oshima, C. Tham, S. Virdhagriswaran, and J. White. MASIF, The OMG Mobile Agent System Interoperability Facility. In *Proceedings of Mobile Agents '98*, 1998.

420. N. Minar and T. Papaioannou. Workshop on Mobile Agents in the Context of Competition and Cooperation (MAC3), Autonomous Agents 99, 1999.

421. N. Minsky and V. Ungureanu. A Mechanism for Establishing Policies for Electronic Commerce. In *Proc. of the 18th International Conference on Distributed Computing Systems (ICDCS '98)*, pages 322–331, 1998.

422. N. Minsky and V. Ungureanu. Unified Support for Heterogeneous Security Policies in Distributed Systems. In *7th USENIX Security Symposium*, San Antonio (TX), 1998.

423. Naftaly H. Minsky. The Imposition of Protocols over Open Distributed Systems. *IEEE Transactions on Software Engineering*, 17(2):183–195, February 1991.

424. Naftaly H. Minsky and Jerrold Leichter. Law-Governed Linda as a Coordination Model. In Paolo Ciancarini and Oscar Nierstrasz, editors, *Object-Based Models and Languages for Concurrent Systems – Proceedings of the ECOOP'94 Workshop on Models and Languages for Coordination of Parallelism and Distribution*, volume 924 of *LNCS*, pages 125–146. Springer-Verlag, 1994.

425. Naftaly H. Minsky, Yaron M. Minsky, and Victoria Ungureanu. Making Tuple Spaces Safer for Heterogeneous Distributed Systems. In *Proceedings of the 2000 ACM Symposium on Applied Computing (SAC 2000)*, pages 218–226, Como (I), March 19 - March 21 2000. ACM. Track on Coordination Models, Languages and Applications.

426. http://www.npaci.edu/DICE/mix-system.html.

427. Mobile Agent List, 1999.

428. Daniel Moldt and Frank Wienberg. Multi-Agent-Systems based on Coloured Petri Nets. In *Proceedings of the 18th International Conference on Application and Theory of Petri Nets (ICATPN '97)*, number 1248 in Lecture Notes in Computer Science, pages 82–101, Toulouse, France, June 1997.

429. E. Monfroy. *Collaboration de Solveurs pour la Programmation Logique à Contraintes*. PhD Thesis, Université Henri Poincaré - Nancy 1, France, November 1996. Also available in English as *Solver Collaboration for Constraint Logic Programming*.

430. E. Monfroy. An Environment for Designing/Executing Constraint Solver Collaborations. *ENTCS (Electronic Notes in Theoretical Computer Science), Elsevier Science Publishers*, 16(1), 1998.

431. E. Monfroy. Using "Weaker" Functions for Constraint Propagation over Real Numbers. In *Proc. of The 14th ACM Symposium on Applied Computing, SAC'99, Scientific Computing Track*, San Antonio, Texas, USA, March 1999. ACM Press.

432. E. Monfroy. A Coordination-based Chaotic Iteration Algorithm for Constraint Propagation. In J. Carroll, E. Damiani, H. Haddad, and D. Oppenheim, editors, *Proceedings of the 2000 ACM Symposium on Applied Computing (SAC'2000)*, pages 262–269, Villa Olmo, Como, Italy, 2000. ACM Press.

433. E. Monfroy. The Constraint Solver Collaboration Language of BALI. In D.M. Gabbay and M. de Rijke, editors, *Frontiers of Combining Systems 2*, volume 7 of *Studies in Logic and Computation*, pages 211–230. Research Studies Press/Wiley, 2000.

434. E. Monfroy and J.-H. Réty. Chaotic Iteration for Distributed Constraint Propagation. In *Proceedings of The 14th ACM Symposium on Applied Computing, SAC'99, Artificial Intelligence and Computational Logic Track*, San Antonio, Texas, USA, March 1999. ACM Press.

435. E. Monfroy and J.-H. Réty. Itérations Asynchrones: un Cadre Uniforme pour la Propagation de Contraintes Parallèle et Répartie. In *Proceedings of Journées Francophones de Programmation Logique et Contrainte (JFPLC'99)*, Lyon, France, 1999. Hermès. (in French).

436. E. Monfroy, M. Rusinowitch, and R. Schott. Implementing Non-Linear Constraints with Cooperative Solvers. In K. M. George, J. H. Carroll, D. Oppenheim, , and J. Hightower, editors, *Proceedings of The 11th ACM Anual Symposium on Applied Computing, SAC'96*, pages 63–72, Philadelphia, PA, USA, February 1996. ACM Press.

437. Scott Moore. On Conversation Policies and the Need for Exceptions. In *Working Notes of the Workshop on Specifying and Implementing Conversation Policies*, pages 19–28, Seattle, Washington, May 1999.

438. Luc Moreau and Christian Queinnec. Design and semantics of quantum: a language to control resource consumption in distributed computing. In *Usenix*

Conference on Domain Specific Language, DSL'97, pages 183–197, Santa-Barbara (California, USA), October 1997.

439. Jean-Henry Morin and Dimitri Konstantas. HyperNews: A MEDIA Application for the Commercialization of an Electronic Newspaper. In *Proceedings of ACM Symposium on Applied Computing (SAC '98)*, Atlanta (GE), 1998. ACM Press.

440. B. Moulin and B. Chaib-draa. An Overview of Distributed Artificial Intelligence. In G. M. O'Hare and N. R. Jennings, editors, *Foundations of Distributed Artificial Intelligence*, pages 3–57. John Wiley & Sons, New York, NY, 1996.

441. Thomas J. Mowbray and Raphael C. Malveau. *CORBA Design Patterns*. Wiley, 1997.

442. S. Muggleton and L. De Raedt. Inductive logic programming: Theory and methods. *Logic Programming*, 9(20), 1994.

443. T. Murata. Peti Nets:Properties, Analysis, and Applications. *Proc. of the IEEE*, 77(8), April 1989.

444. A.L. Murphy and G.P. Picco. Reliable Communication for Highly Mobile Agents. In *Proc. of the 1st Int. Symp. on Agent Systems and Applications and 3rd Int. Symp. on Mobile Agents (ASA/MA '99)*, pages 141–150, Palm Springs, CA, USA, October 1999. IEEE Computer Society.

445. A.L. Murphy, G.-C. Roman, and G. Varghese. Tracking Mobile Units for Dependable Message Delivery. Technical Report WUCS-99-30, Washington University, Dept. of Computer Science, St. Louis, MO, USA, December 1999.

446. David R. Musser and Atul Saini. *STL Tutorial and Reference Guide*. Addison-Wesley, 1996.

447. R. Neches, R. Fikes, T. Finin, T. Gruber, R. Patil, T. Senator, and W. Swartout. Enabling Technology for Knowledge Sharing. *AI Magazine*, 12(3):36 – 56, Fall 1991.

448. Bruce J. Nelson. *Remote Procedure Call*. PhD thesis, Carnegie-Mellon University, May 1981.

449. B. Clifford Neuman and Gennady Medvinsky. Internet Payment Services. In Lee W. McKnight and Joseph P. Bailey, editors, *Internet Economics*, pages 401–415. MIT Press, Cambridge, MA, 1997.

450. Next Generation Internet Home Site. `http://www.ngi.org`.

451. R. De Nicola, G. Ferrari, and R. Pugliese. Coordinating Mobile Agents via Blackboards and Access Rights. In *Proc. 2nd Int. Conf. on Coordination Models and Languages*, volume 1282 of *LNCS*, September 1997.

452. Rocco De Nicola, Gian Luigi Ferrari, and Rosario Pugliese. Locality Based Linda: Programming with Explicit Localities. In Michel Bidoit and Max Dauchet, editors, *TAPSOFT '97: Theory and Practice of Software Development*, volume 1214 of *LNCS*, pages 712–726. Springer-Verlag, 1997.

453. Rocco De Nicola, Gian Luigi Ferrari, and Rosario Pugliese. KLAIM: A Kernel Language for Agents Interaction and Mobility. *IEEE Transactions on Software Engineering*, 24(5):315–330, May 1998.

454. B. Nielsen and T. Sorensen. Distributed programming with multiple tuple space Linda. Technical report, Aalbrog University, Department of Mathematics and Computer Science, 1994.

455. Oscar Nierstrasz and Laurent Dami. Component-Oriented Software Technology. In Oscar Nierstrasz and Dennis Tsichritzis, editors, *Object-Oriented Software Composition*, pages 3–28. Prentice Hall, 1995.

456. Oscar Nierstrasz, Jean-Guy Schneider, and Franz Achermann. Agents Everywhere, All the Time. Submitted for publication, March 2000.

457. Oscar Nierstrasz, Dennis Tsichritzis, Vicki de Mey, and Marc Stadelman. Objects + Scripts = Applications. In *Proceedings Esprit 1991 Conference*, pages 534–552, Dordrecht, NL, 1991. Kluwer Academic Publisher.

458. M. Nodine, J. Fowler, T. Ksiezyk, B. Perry, M. Taylor, and A. Unruh. Active information gathering in InfoSleuth. *Cooperative Information Systems*, 9(1/2), 2000.

459. M. H. Nodine and A. Unruh. Facilitating Open Communication in Agent Systems: the InfoSleuth Infrastructure. In Michael Wooldridge, Munindar Singh, and Anand Rao, editors, *Intelligent Agents Volume IV – Proceedings of the 1997 Workshop on Agent Theories, Architectures and Languages*, volume 1365 of *Lecture Notes in Artificial Intelligence*, pages 281–295. Springer-Verlag, Berlin, 1997.

460. P. Noriega. *Agent-mediated Auctions: The Fishmarket Metaphor*. Ph.D Thesis, Universitat Autonoma de Barcelona, Barcelona (E), 1997.

461. H.S. Nwana, L. Lee, and Nicholas R. Jennings. Coordination in Multi Agent Systems. In *Software Agents and Soft Computing: Towards Enhancing Machine Intelligence*, volume 1198 of *LNAI*, pages 42–58. Springer-Verlag, 1997.

462. H.S. Nwana and Michael J. Wooldridge. Software Agent Technologies. In *Software Agents and Soft Computing: Towards Enhancing Machine Intelligence*, volume 1198 of *LNAI*, pages 59–78. Springer-Verlag, 1997.

463. Object Management Group. CORBA Specification. http://www.omg.org/ .

464. Object Management Group. *The Common Object Request Broker: Architecture and Specification*, July 1996.

465. J. Odell, H. Van Dyke Parunak, and C. Bock. Representing Agent Interaction Protocols in UML. In *OMG Document ad/99-12-01*. Intellicorp Inc., December 1999.

466. Odyssey. http://www.genmagic.com.

467. A. Ohsuga, Y. Nagai, Y. Irie, M. Hattori, and S. Honiden. PLANGENT: an Approach to Making Mobile Agents Intelligents. *IEEE Internet Computing*, 1(3):50–57, 1997.

468. OIL. Ontology Interchange Language. http://www.ontoknowledge.org/oil/.

469. OKBC. Open Knowledge Base Connectivity. http://www.ai.sri.com/ okbc/.

470. Andrea Omicini. On the Semantics of Tuple-based Coordination Models. In *Proceedings of the 1999 ACM Symposium on Applied Computing (SAC'99)*, pages 175–182. ACM, February 28 - March 2 1999. Track on Coordination Models, Languages and Applications.

471. Andrea Omicini. SODA: Societies and Infrastructures in the Analysis and Design of Agent-based Systems. In Paolo Ciancarini and Michael J. Wooldridge, editors, *Agent-Oriented Software Engineering – Proceedings of the 1st International Workshop (AOSE 2000)*, LNCS. Springer-Verlag, Limerick (Ireland), 2000.

472. Andrea Omicini and Franco Zambonelli. Coordination for Internet Application Development. *Journal of Autonomous Agents and Multi-Agent Systems*, 2(3), September 1999. Special Issue on Coordination Mechanisms and Patterns for Web Agents.

473. Andrea Omicini and Franco Zambonelli. Tuple Centres for the Coordination of Internet Agents. In *Proceedings of the 1999 ACM Symposium on Applied Computing (SAC'99)*, pages 183–190, San Antonio (TX), February 28 - March 2 1999. ACM. Track on Coordination Models, Languages and Applications.

474. OntoBroker project. http://ontobroker.aifb.uni-karlsruhe.de/.

475. Open Software Foundation. *DCE - The OSF Distributed Computing Environment*. Springer-Verlag, October 1993.

476. Open Systems Lab. The Actor Foundry: A Java-based Actor Programming Environment, 1998. Work in Progress. http://osl.cs.uiuc.edu/foundry/.

477. Open Systems Lab. SALSA: Simple Actor Language, System and Applications, 2000. Work in Progress. http://osl.cs.uiuc.edu/salsa/.

478. International Standard Organization. Moderate Thermal Environments: Determination of the PMV and PPD Indices and Specification of the Conditions for Thermal Comfort. European Standard Report EN-ISO-7730-1995, CEN, Brussels, 1995.

479. John K. Ousterhout. *Tcl and the Tk Toolkit*. Addison-Wesley, 1994.

480. John K. Ousterhout. Scripting: Higher Level Programming for the 21st Century. *IEEE Computer*, 31(3):23–30, March 1998.

481. Hewlett Packard. Home Page of Information About E-Services, 2000.

482. George A. Papadopoulos and Farhad Arbab. Coordination Models and Languages. In Marvin V. Zelkowitz, editor, *The Engineering of Large Systems*, volume 46 of *Advances in Computers*, pages 329–400. Academic Press, August 1998.

483. M. P. Papazoglou and W. Van Den Heuvel. From Business Processes to Cooperative Information Systems: An information Agents Perspective. In M. Klusch, editor, *Intelligent Information Agents*. Springer, Berlin, Germany, 1999.

484. David Parkes. iBundle: An Efficient Ascending Price Bundle Auction. In *Proceedings of the ACM Conference on Electronic Commerce*, Denver, CO, November 1999.

485. H.V.D. Parunak. Visualizing Agent Conversations: Using Enhanced Dooley Graphs for Agent Design and Analysis. In *Second International Conference on Multi-agent Systems (ICMAS96)*, pages 275–282, June 1996.

486. Y. Peng, T. Finin, Y. Labrou, R. S. Cost, B. Chu, J. Long, W. J. Tolone, and A. Boughannam. An Agent-Based Approach for Manufacturing Integration - the CIIMPLEX Experience. *International Journal of Applied Artificial Intelligence*, 13(1–2):39–64, 1999.

487. M.K. Perdikeas, F.G. Chatzipapadopoulos, I.S. Venieris, and G. Marino. Mobile Agent Standards and Available Platforms. *Computer Networks Journal*, 31(10), October 1999.

488. C. Perkins. IP Mobility Support. RFC 2002, IETF Network Working Group, 1996.

489. C. E. Perkins. Mobile Networking in the Internet. *Mobile Networks and Applications*, 3:315–334, 1998.

490. Dewayne E. Perry and Alexander L. Wolf. Foundations for the Study of Software Architecture. *ACM SIGSOFT Software Engineering Notes*, 17(4):40–52, October 1992.

491. Charles J. Petrie. Agent based Engineering, the Web, and Intelligence. *IEEE Expert*, 11(6):24–29, December 1996.

492. Simon Peyton Jones, Erik Meijer, and Daan Leijen. Scripting COM Components in Haskell. In *Proceedings of the Fifth International Conference on Software Reuse*, Victoria, British Columbia, June 1998.

493. Gian Pietro Picco, Amy L. Murphy, and Gruia-Catalin Roman. LIME: Linda meets Mobility. In David Garlan and Jeff Kramer, editors, *Proceedings of the 21th International Conference on Software Engineering (ICSE'99)*, pages 368–377. ACM, May 16–22 1999.

494. G.P. Picco. μCODE: A Lightweight and Flexible Mobile Code Toolkit. In *Proc. of the 2nd Int. Workshop on Mobile Agents*, volume 1477 of *LNCS*. Springer-Verlag, 1998.

495. G.P. Picco, G.-C. Roman, and P.J. McCann. Expressing Code Mobility in Mobile UNITY. In M. Jazayeri and H. Schauer, editors, *Proc. of the 6th European Software Engineering Conf. held jointly with the 5th ACM SIGSOFT Symp. on the Foundations of Software Engineering (ESEC/FSE '97)*, volume 1301 of *LNCS*, pages 500–518, Zurich, Switzerland, September 1997. Springer-Verlag.

496. J. Pinakis. A distributed typeserver and protocol for a Linda tuple space. Technical report, University of Western Australia, 1991.

497. J. Pitt and M. Mamdani. Designing Agent Communication Languages for Multi-Agent Systems. In *9th European Workshop on Modelling Autonomous Agents in a Multi-Agent World (MAAMAW99)*, volume 1647 of *LNAI*. Springer Verlag, Berlin, D, June 1999.

498. Jeremy Pitt and Abe Mamdani. Communication Protocols in Multi-Agent Systems. In *Working Notes of the Workshop on Specifying and Implementing Conversation Policies*, pages 39–48, Seattle, Washington, May 1999.

499. L. Pomello, G. Rozenberg, and C. Simone. A Survey of Equivalence Notions for Net Based System. In G. Rozenberg, editor, *Advances in Petri Nets 1992*, volume 609 of *LNCS*, pages 410–472. Springer-Verlag, 1992.

500. Tomi Poutanene, Heather Hinton, and Michael Stumm. NetCents: A Lightweight Protocol for Secure Micropayments. In *USENIX Workshop on Electronic Commerce*, pages 25–36. USENIX Association, September 1998.

501. Wolfgang Pree. *Design Patterns for Object-Oriented Software Development*. Addison-Wesley, 1995.

502. Wolfgang Prinz and S. Kolvenback. Support for Workflows in a Ministerial Environment. In Mark S. Ackerman, editor, *Proceedings of the ACM 1996 Conference on Computer Supported Cooperative Work, CSCW'96, Cambridge, Mass., U.S.A.*, pages 199–208, New York, November 1996. ACM Press.

503. M. Purvis and S. Cranefield. Agent Modelling with Petri Nets. In *Proceedings of the CESA '96 (Computational Engineering in Systems Applications) Symposium on Discrete Events and Manufacturing Systems*, pages 602–607, Lille, France, July 1996. IMACS, IEEE-SMC.

504. Rabarijaona and et al. Building and searching an XML-based corporate memory. *IEEE Internet Computing*, May/June 2000.

505. M. Ranganathan, V. Schaal, V. Galtier, and D. Montgomery. Mobile Streams: A Middleware for Reconfigurable Distributed Scripting. In *First International Symposium on Agent Systems and Applications and Third International Symposium on Mobile Agents (ASA/MA99)*, pages 162–175, Palm Springs (CA), October 3–6 1999. IEEE Press.

506. A.S. Rao and M.P. Georgeff. Modeling Rational Agents within a BDI Architecture. In *The International Conference on Principles of Knowledge Representation and Reasoning (KR-91)*, pages 473–484. Morgan Kaufmann, 1991.

507. RDF(S): XML-based Resource Description Framework Schema Specification. http://www.w3.org/TR/WD-rdf-schema/.

508. Ori Regev and Noam Nisan. The POPCORN Market— an Online Market for Computational Resources. In *Proceedings of the First International Conference on Information and Computation Economies*, pages 148–157, Charleston, SC, October 1998. ACM Press.

509. Manfred Reichert and Peter Dadam. *ADEPT_{flex}*-Supporting Dynamic Changes of Workflows Without Losing Control. In *Journal of Intelligent Information Systems – Special Issue: Workflow Management Systems* [528], pages 93–129.

510. W. Reisig. Petri nets with individual tokens. *Theoretical Computer Science*, 41(2-3):185–213, 1985.

511. S. Ren, G. A. Agha, and M. Saito. A Modular Approach for Programming Distributed Real-Time Systems. *Journal of Parallel and Distributed Computing*, 36:4–12, 1996.

512. RETSINA. http://www.cs.cmu.edu/ softagents/retsina.html.

513. P. Robinson and J. Arthur. Distributed process creation within a shared data space framework. *Software: Practice and Experience*, 25(2):175–191, 1995.

514. A. Rodrigues Da Silva O, A. Romo, D. Deugo, and M. Mira Da Silva. Towards a Reference Model for Surveying Mobile Agent Systems. *Autonomous Agents and Multiagents Systems Journal*, 2000.

515. G. C. Roman and H. C. Cunnigham. Mixed Programming Metaphors in a Shared Dataspace Model of Concurrency. *IEEE Transactions on Software Engineering*, 16(12):1361–1373, 1990.

516. Davide Rossi. *Coordination: an Enabling Technology for the Internet*. PhD thesis, Department of Computer Science, University of Bologna, Italy, February 2000.

517. Davide Rossi and Fabio Vitali. Internet-Based Coordination Environments and Document-Based Applications: A Case Study. In Paolo Ciancarini and Alexander L. Wolf, editors, *Coordination Languages and Models*, number 1594 in LNCS, pages 259–274. Springer, April 1999. Proceedings of Coordination '99.

518. K. Rothermel and F. Hohl, editors. *Mobile Agents – Proceedings of the Second International Workshop (MA'98)*, volume 1477 of *LNCS*, Stuttgart (D), September 1998. Springer-Verlag.

519. A. Rowstron. *Bulk primitives in Linda run-time systems*. PhD thesis, Department of Computer Science, University of York, UK, 1997.

520. A. Rowstron. Mobile Co-ordination: Providing Fault Tolerance in Tuple Space Based Co-ordination Languages. In P. Ciancarini and A. Wolf, editors, *Proceedings of the 3rd Int. Conf. on Coordination Languages and Models (COORDINATION)*, volume 1594 of *LNCS*, pages 196–210. Springer, 1999.

521. A. Rowstron, A. Douglas, and A. Wood. A distributed Linda-like kernel for PVM. In J. Dongarra, M. Gengler, B. Tourancheau, and X. Vigouroux, editors, *EuroPVM'95*, pages 107–112. Hermes, 1995.

522. A. Rowstron, S. Li, and S. Radina. C^2AS: A System Supporting Distributed Web Applications Composed of Collaborating Agents. In *WETICE*, pages 87–92, 1997.

523. A. Rowstron and S. Wray. A run-time system for WCL. In H. E. Bal, B. Belkhouche, and L. Cardelli, editors, *IEEE Workshop on Internet Programming Languages*, volume 1686 of *LNCS*. Springer-Verlag, 1998. Chicago, USA.

524. Antony Rowstron. WCL: A Web Co-ordination Language. *World Wide Web Journal*, 1(3):167–179, 1998.

525. Antony Rowstron and Alan Wood. BONITA: A Set of Tuple Space Primitives for Distributed Coordination. In Hesham El-Rewini and Yale N. Patt, editors, *Proc. of the 30th Hawaii International Conference on System Sciences*, volume 1, pages 379–388. IEEE Computer Society Press, January 1997.

526. Antony Rowstron and Alan Wood. Solving the Linda multiple rd problem using the copy-collect primitive. *Science of Computer Programming*, 31(2-3):335–358, 1998.

527. A. D. Rubin and D. E. Geer Jr. A Survey of Web Security. *IEEE Computer*, 31(9):39–41, September 1998.

528. Marek Rusinkiewicz and Abdelsalam Sumi Helal (eds.). Special Issue: Workflow Management Systems. *Journal of Intelligent Information Systems*, 10(2), March–April 1998.

529. *Proceedings of the 2000 ACM Symposium on Applied Computing (SAC 2000)*, Como (I), March 19–21 2000. ACM. Track on Coordination Models, Languages and Applications.

530. *Proceedings of the 1998 ACM Symposium on Applied Computing (SAC'98)*, Atlanta (GA), February 27 - March 1 1998. ACM. Track on Coordination Models, Languages and Applications.

531. *Proceedings of the 1999 ACM Symposium on Applied Computing (SAC'99)*, San Antonio (TX), February 28 - March 2 1999. ACM. Track on Coordination Models, Languages and Applications.

532. Tuomas Sandholm. An Algorithm for Optimal Determination in Combinatorial Auctions. In *Proceedings of the International Joint Conference on Artificial Intelligence*, Stockholm, Sweden, 1999.

533. Ravi S. Sandhu, Edward J. Coyne, Hal L. Feinstein, and Charles E. Youman. Role-Based Access Control Models. *IEEE Computer*, 29(2):38–47, February 1996.

534. V. Saraswat. *Concurrent Constraint Programming*. MIT Press, Cambridge, London, 1993.

535. Kjeld Schmidt and Liam J. Bannon. Taking CSCW Seriously – Supporting Articulation Work. *Computer Supported Cooperative Work – An International Journal*, 1(1–2):7–40, 1992.

536. Jean-Guy Schneider. *Components, Scripts, and Glue: A conceptual framework for software composition*. PhD thesis, University of Bern, Institute of Computer Science and Applied Mathematics, October 1999.

537. Jean-Guy Schneider and Oscar Nierstrasz. Components, Scripts and Glue. In Leonor Barroca, Jon Hall, and Patrick Hall, editors, *Software Architectures – Advances and Applications*, chapter 2, pages 13–25. Springer, 1999.

538. Bruce Schneier. *Applied Cryptography*. Wiley, New York, second edition, 1996.

539. A.Th. Schreiber, J.M. Akkermans, A.A. Anjewierden, R. de Hoog, N.R. Shadbolt, W. Van de Velde, and B.J Wielinga. *Knowledge Engineering and Management: The CommonKADS Methodology*. MIT Press, 2000.

540. Michael Schumacher, Fabrice Chantemargue, and Béat Hirsbrunner. The STL++ Coordination Language: A Base for Implementing Distributed Multi Agent Systems. In Paolo Ciancarini and Alexander L. Wolf, editors, *Coordination Languages and Models – Proceedings of the 3rd International Conference (COORDINATION'99)*, volume 1594 of *LNCS*, pages 399–414, Amsterdam (NL), April 26–28 1999. Springer-Verlag.

541. Scientific Computing Associates. *Paradise: User's guide and reference manual*. Scientific Computing Associates, 1996.

542. Scientific Computing Associates, Inc., New Haven, CT. *Paradise 4. Reference Manual*, 1996.

543. Adriano Scutellà. Simulation of Conference Management Using an Event-Driven Coordination Language. In Paolo Ciancarini and Alexander L. Wolf, editors, *Coordination Languages and Models*, number 1594 in LNCS, pages 243–258. Springer, April 1999. Proceedings of Coordination '99.

544. Roger Sessions. *COM and DCOM: Microsoft's Vision for Distributed Objects*. John Wiley & Sons, December 1997.

545. Ravi Sethi. *Programming Languages: Concepts and Constructs*. Addison-Wesley, 1989.

546. R. Seyfarth, S. Arumugham, and J. Bickham. Glenda Users Guide. Technical report, University of Southern Mississippi, 1994.

547. Mary Shaw and David Garlan. *Software Architecture: Perspectives on an Emerging Discipline*. Prentice Hall, April 1996.

548. A. Sheth and J.A. Larson. Federated Database Systems. *ACM Computing Surveys*, 22(3), 1990.

549. A. Sheth, E. Mena, A. Illaramendi, and V. Kashyap. OBSERVER: An approach for query processing in global information systems based on interoperation across pre-existing ontologies. In *Cooperative Information Systems CoopIS-96*. IEEE Computer Society Press, 1996.

550. Amith Sheth, Vipul Kashyap, and Tarcisio Lima. Semantic Information Brokering How Can a Multi-agent Approach Help? In M. Klusch, O. Shehory, and G. Weiss, editors, *Proceeding of the third International Workshop CIA, Uppsala, Sweden, July/August 1999, LNAI 1652*, pages 303–322. Springer, 1999.

551. Y. Shoham and S.B. Cousins. Logics of Mental Attitudes in AI. In *The International Conference on Principles of Knowledge Representation and Reasoning (KR-92)*. Morgan Kaufmann, 1992.

552. Yoav Shoham. Agent–Oriented Programming. *Artificial Intelligence*, 60:51–92, 1993.

553. C. Sibertin-Blanc. High Level Petri Nets with Data Structure. In K. Jensen, editor, *Proceedings of the 6th European Workshop On Application and Theory of Petri Nets, Finland*, 1985.

554. C. Sibertin-Blanc. CoOperative Objects: Principles, Use and Implementation. In G. Agha and F. De Cindio, editors, *Petri Nets and Object Orientation*, LNCS. Springer-Verlag, Berlin, 1999.

555. J. Silva, J. Carreria, and F. Moreria. ParLin: from a centralized tuple space to adaptive hashing. Technical report, Universidade de Coimbra, 1993.

556. L. Silva, B. Veer, and J. Silva. The Helios tuple space library. In *Proceedings 2nd Euromicro workshop on Parallel and Distributed Processing*, pages 325–333, 1994.

557. C. Simone and M. Divitini. Ariadne: Supporting Coordination through a Flexible Use of the Knowledge on Work Process. In *Information Technology for Knowledge Management* [84], pages 121–148.

558. M. Singh. Agent Communication Languages: Rethinking the Principles. *IEEE Computer*, 31(12):55–61, December 1998.

559. Munindar P. Singh and Michael N. Huhns. Multiagent Systems for Workflow. In *IJCAI Workshop on Business Applications of Artificial Intelligence*, Nagoya, Japan, 1998.

560. N. Skarmeas and Keith L. Clark. Component Based Agent Construction. Autonomous Agents and Multi Agent Systems, submitted, 1999.

561. R. Smith. The Contract Net Protocol: High-Level Communication and Control in a Distributed Problem Solver. *IEEE Transactions on Computers*, pages 1104–1113, December 1980.

562. Gert Smolka. Problem Solving with Constraints and Programming. *ACM Computing Surveys*, 28(4), December 1996. Electronic Section.

563. Secure and Open Mobile Agents (SOMA). `http://lia.deis.unibo.it/Research/SOMA`.

564. SPKI Simple PublicKey Infrastructure. `ftp://ftp.ietf.org/internet-drafts/draft-ietf-spki-cert-theory-02.txt`.

565. J.W. Stamos and D.K. Grifford. Implementing Remote Evaluation. *IEEE Transactions on Software Engineering*, 16(7):710–722, July 1990.

566. H. Stark and L. Lachal. Ovum evaluates: Workflow. Ovum report, Ovum Ltd., London, UK, 1995.

567. G. L. Steele and G. J. Sussman. Scheme, an Interpreter for Extended Lambda Calculus. Technical Report Technical Report 349, Massachusetts Institute of Technology, Artificial Intelligence Laboratory, 1975.

568. Jennifer Steiner, Clifford Neuman, and Jeffrey Schiller. Kerberos: An Authentication Service for Open Network Systems. In *USENIX Conference Proceedings (Dallas TX)*, pages 191–202, Berkeley, (CA), Winter 1988. USENIX Association.

569. E. Steinmetz, J. Collins, S. Jamison, and et al. Bid Evaluation and Selection in the MAGNET Automated Contracting System. In P. Noriega and C. Sierra, editors, *Agent-Mediated Electronic Commerce*, volume 1571 of *LNAI*, pages 105–125. Springer-Verlag, 1999.

570. Anselm Strauss. The articulation of project work: An organizational process. *The Sociological Quarterly*, 29(2):163–178, 1988.

571. D. Sturman. Fault-Adaptation for Systems in Unpredictable Environments. M.S. Thesis, May 1994.

572. R. Sukthankar, A. Brusseau, R. Pelletier, and R. Stockton. JGram: Rapid Development of Multi Agent Pipelines for Real-World Tasks. In *First International Symposium on Agent Systems and Applications and Third International Symposium on Mobile Agents (ASA/MA99)*, pages 30–40, Palm Springs (CA), October 3–6 1999. IEEE Press.

573. V. Sunderam, J. Dongarra, A. Geist, and R Manchek. The PVM Concurrent Computing System: Evolution, Experiences, and Trends. *Parallel Computing*, 20(4):531–547, 1994.

574. Ivan E. Sutherland. A Futures Market in Computer Time. *Communications of the ACM*, 11(6):449–451, June 1968.

575. Keith D. Swenson and Kent Irwin. Workflow Technology: Trade-Offs for Business Process Re-Engineering. In Comstock and Ellis [182], pages 22–29.

576. Keith D. Swenson, Robin J. Maxwell, Toshikazu Matsumoto, Bahram Saghari, and Kent Irwin. A Business Process Environment Supporting Collaborative Planning. *Collaborative Computing*, 1(1):15–34, 1994.

577. K. Sycara, M. Klusch, S. Widoff, and J. Lu. LARKS: Dynamic matchmaking among heterogeneous software agents in cyberspace. *Autonomous Agents and Multiagent Systems*, March 2001.

578. K. Sycara, J. Lu, and M. Klusch. Interoperability Among Heterogeneous Software Agents on the Internet. Technical report, Technical Report CMU-RI-TR-98-22, 1998.

579. K. Sycara, J. Lu, M. Klusch, and S. Widoff. Dynamic service matchmaking among agents in open information environments. *ACM SIGMOD Record*, 1999.

580. K. Sycara and D. Zeng. Coordination of multiple intelligent software agents. *Cooperative Information Systems*, 5(2/3), 1996.

581. Clemens Szyperski. *Component Software: Beyond Object-Oriented Programming*. Addison-Wesley, 1998.

582. Tromso And COrnell Moving Agents (TACOMA). http://www.tacoma.cs.uit.no.

583. Y. Tahara, A. Ohsuga, and S. Honiden. Agent System Development based on Agent Patterns. In *International Conference on Software Engineering*, pages 356–367. ACM, 1999.

584. S. Talukdar, E. Cordozo, and L. Leao. Toast: The Power System Operator's Assistant. *IEEE Expert*, pages 53–60, July 1986.

585. Andrew Tanenbaum and et al. Experience with the Amoeba Distributed Operating System. *Communications of the ACM*, 33(12):46–63, December 1990.

586. A.S. Tanenbaum. *Distributed Operating Systems*. Prentice Hall, 1995.

587. The OpenMath Society. (web page). http://www.nag.co.uk/projects/openmath/omsoc.

588. S.R. Thomas. The PLACA Agent Programming Language. In *Intelligent Agents — Agent Theories, Architectures, and Languages*, volume 890 of *LNAI*, pages 355–370. Springer-Verlag, 1995.

589. Stephen Thomas. *SSL and TLS Essentials: Securing the Web*. John Wiley & Sons, March 2000.

590. Sander Tichelaar. A Coordination Component Framework for Open Distributed Systems. Master's thesis, University of Bern, Institute of Computer Science and Applied Mathematics, May 1997.

591. M. Tokoro. The Society of Objects. In M. N. Huhns and M. P. Singh, editors, *Readings in Agents*, pages 421–429. Morgan Kaufmann Publishers, San Mateo, CA, 1998.

592. R. Tolksdorf. A machine for uncoupled coordination and its concurrent behaviour. In *Object-Based Models and Languages for Concurrent Systems*, volume 924 of *LNCS*, pages 176–193. Springer-Velag, 1995.

593. R. Tolksdorf. Coordination Patterns in Mobile Object Spaces. In *Proc. 7th IEEE Workshops on Enablings Technologies: Infrastructure for Collaborative Enterprises (WETICE)*, pages 126–131, Stanford, CA, June 1998. IEEE Computer Society Press.

594. Robert Tolksdorf. *Coordination in Open Distributed Systems*. Number Reihe 10, 362 in VDI Fortschrittsberichte. VDI Verlag, 1995.

595. Robert Tolksdorf. Coordinating Services in open distributed systems with LAURA. In Paolo Ciancarini and Chris Hankin, editors, *Coordination Languages and Models – Proceedings of the 1st International Conference (COORDINATION'96)*, volume 1061 of *LNCS*, pages 386–402, Cesena (I), April 15–17 1996. Springer-Verlag.

596. Robert Tolksdorf. Berlinda: An Object-Oriented Platform for Implementing Coordination Languages in Java. In David Garlan and Daniel Le Métayer, editors, *Coordination Languages and Models – Proceedings of the 2nd International Conference (COORDINATION'97)*, volume 1282 of *LNCS*, pages 430–433, Berlin (D), September 1–3 1997. Springer-Verlag.

597. Robert Tolksdorf. Laura — A Service-Based Coordination Language. *Science of Computer Programming*, 31(2–3):359–381, July 1998.

598. Robert Tolksdorf, Paolo Ciancarini, Mark Ginsburg, Jakob Hummes, and Wilfred Jamison. Working Group Report on Coordination Architectures for Distributed Web Applications. In *Proceedings of the 7th Workshops on Enabling Technologies: Infrastructure for Collaborative Enterprises (WET ICE '98)*, pages 133–137. IEEE Computer Society Press, 1998.

599. Robert Tolksdorf, Ted Goddard, Muralidharan Srinivasan, Stefan Fnfrocken, and Michael Schroeder. Working Group Report on Collaborative Agents in Distributed Web Applications. In *Proceedings of the 6th Workshops on Enabling Technologies: Infrastructure for Collaborative Enterprises (WET ICE '97)*, pages 133–137. IEEE Computer Society Press, 1997.

600. Robert Tolksdorf, Gustaf Neumann, Wolfram Conen, Peter Bertok, and Matthew Fuchs. Working Group Report on Web Infrastructure for Collaborative Applications. In *Proceedings of the 5th Workshops on Enabling Technologies: Infrastructure for Collaborative Enterprises (WET ICE '96)*, pages 340–345. IEEE Computer Society Press, 1996.

601. C. Tomlinson, P. Cannata, G. Meredith, and D. Woelk. The extensible services switch in Carnot. *IEEE Parallel and Distributed Technology*, 1(2):16–20, May 1993.

602. C. Tomlinson, W. Kim, M. Schevel, V. Singh, B. Will, and G. Agha. Rosette: An Object Oriented Concurrent System Architecture. *Sigplan Notices*, 24(4):91–93, 1989.

603. C.B.S. Traw and J.M. Smith. Striping within the Network Subsystem. *IEEE Network Magazine*, 9(4), July 1995.

604. Christian Tschudin. The Messenger Environment M0 — A Condensed Description. In *Mobile Object Systems: Towards the Programmable Internet*, volume 1222 of *LNCS*, pages 149–156. Springer, 1997.

605. Christian F. Tschudin. Open Resource Allocation for Mobile Code. In *Proceedings of The First Workshop on Mobile Agents*, pages 186–197, Berlin, April 1997.

606. United States Department of Defense. *Reference Manual for the Ada Language*, draft, revised mil-std 1815 edition, july 1982.

607. W. M. P. van der Aalst. Interorganizational Workflows: An Approach based on Message Sequence Charts and Petri Nets. *Systems Analysis – Modelling – Simulation*, 34(3):335–367, 1999.

608. W. M. P van der Aalst and T. Basten. Life-cycle Inheritance: A Petri Net-Based Approach. In P. Azema and G. Balbo, editors, *Application and Theory of Petri Nets 97*, volume 1248 of *LNCS*. Springer-Verlag, 1997.

609. Richard van der Stadt. CyberChair: An Online Submission and Reviewing System for Conference Papers. `http://trese.cs.utwente.nl/CyberChair/` , 1997.

610. Guido van Rossum. Python Reference Manual. Technical report, Corporation for National Research Initiatives (CNRI), October 1996.

611. C. Varela and G. Agha. What after Java? From Objects to Actors. *Computer Networks and ISDN Systems: The International J. of Computer Telecommunications and Networking*, 30:573–577, April 1998. http://osl.cs.uiuc.edu/Papers/www7/.

612. C. Varela and G. Agha. A Hierarchical Model for Coordination of Concurrent Activities. In P. Ciancarini and A. Wolf, editors, *Third International Conference on Coordination Languages and Models (COORDINATION '99)*, LNCS 1594, pages 166–182, Berlin, April 1999. Springer-Verlag. http://osl.cs.uiuc.edu/Papers/Coordination99.ps.

613. C. Varela and G. Agha. Linguistic Support for Actors, First-Class Token-Passing Continuations and Join Continuations. Proceedings of the Midwest Society for Programming Languages and Systems Workshop, October 1999. http://osl.cs.uiuc.edu/~cvarela/mspls99/.

614. Jan Vitek and Christian Tschudin. *Mobile Objects Systems*. Springer-Verlag, Heidelberg (D), 1997.

615. Voyager. `http://www.objectspace.com/voyager/prodVoyager.asp`.

616. T. Wagner and O. Rana. *Proceedings of the 1st Workshop on Instrastructure for Scalable Multi-agent Systems*. Springer-Verlage, Berlin (D), 2000.

617. Thomas Wagner, Brett Benyo, Victor Lesser, and Ping Xuan. Investigating Interactions Between Agent Conversations and Agent Control Components. In *Working Notes of the Workshop on Specifying and Implementing Conversation Policies*, pages 79–88, Seattle, Washington, May 1999.

618. J. Waldo, G. Wyant, A. Wollrath, and S. Kendall. A Note on Distributed Computing. In K. Arnold, J. OSullivan, A. Scheiffer, J. Waldo, and J. Wollrath, editors, *The Jini Specification*. Addison-Wesley, 1999.

619. Jim Waldo. The Jini Architecture for Network-centric Computing. *Communications of the ACM*, 42(7):76–82, July 1999.

620. Carl A. Waldspurger, Tad Hogg, Bernardo A. Huberman, Jeffrey O. Kephart, and W. Scott Stornetta. Spawn: A Distributed Computational Economy. *IEEE Transactions on Software Engineering*, 18(2):103–117, February 1992.

621. Larry Wall, Tom Christiansen, and Randal L. Schwartz. *Programming Perl*. O'Reilly & Associates, 2nd edition, September 1996.

622. U. Warrier, L. Besaw, L. LaBarre, and B. Handspicker. The Common Management Information Services and Protocols for the Internet (RFC 1189), October 1990.

623. Peter Wegner. Coordination as Constrained Interaction. In Paolo Ciancarini and Chris Hankin, editors, *Coordination Languages and Models – Proceedings of the 1st International Conference (COORDINATION'96)*, volume 1061 of *LNCS*, pages 28–33, Cesena (I), April 15–17 1996. Springer-Verlag.

624. Peter Wegner. Why Interaction is more Powerful than Computing. *Communications of the ACM*, 40(5):80–91, May 1997.

625. B. M. Weisenfeld, S. Raghuram, and R. Garud. Communication Patterns as Determinants of Organizational Identification in a Virtual Organization. *Journal of Computer Mediated Communication*, 3(4):1–21, 1998.

626. Gerhard Weiss, editor. *Multiagent Systems – A Modern Approach to Distributed Artificial Intelligence*. The MIT Press, Cambridge (MA), 1999.

627. M. Weiss and F. Stetter. A Hierarchical Blackboard Architecture for Distributed AI Systems. In *Fourth International Conference on Software Engineering and Knowledge Engineering*, pages 349–355. IEEE, 1992.

628. G. Wells and A. Chalmers. An Extended Linda System using PVM. In *PVM Users' Group Meeting, Pittsburgh*, 1995.

629. *Proceedings of the IEEE 8th International Workshops on Enabling Technologies: Infrastructure for Collaborative Enterprises (WET ICE 99)*, Palo Alto, California, 16 - 18 June, 1999 1999. IEEE Press.

630. J.E. White. General Magic White Paper – Telescript Technology: The Foundation for the Electronic Marketplace. http://www.genmagic.com, 1994.

631. J.E. White. Telescript Technology: Mobile Agents. In J. Bradshaw, editor, *Software Agents*. AAAI Press/MIT Press, 1996.

632. J. Widom and S. Ceri. *Active Database Systems*. Morgan Kaufmann Publishers, 1996.

633. G. Wiederhold. Mediators in the architecture of future information systems. *IEEE Computer Systems*, 25(3), March 1992.

634. Frank Wienberg. *Multiagentensysteme auf def Basis gefärbter Petri-Netze*. PhD thesis, Universität Hamburg Fachbereich Informatik, 1996.

635. G. Wilson. Improving the performance of generative communication systems by using application-specific mapping functions. In *Linda-like systems and their implementation*, volume Technical report 91-13, pages 129–142. EEPC, 1991.

636. Terry Winograd and Fernando Flores. *Understanding Computers and Cognition*. Addison-Wesley, 1986.

637. W. Wobcke, editor. *Agents and Multi-Agent Systems: Formalisms, Methodologies and Applications*. Springer-Verlag, July 1998.

638. D. Wong, N. Paciorek, T. Walsh, J. DiCelie, M. Young, and B. Peet. Concordia: An Infrastructure for Collaborating Mobile Agents. In *Proceedings of the First International Workshop on Mobile Agents*, 1997.

639. H.C. Wong and K. Sycara. A taxonomy of middle-agents for the Internet. In *Agents-1999 Conference on Autonomous Agents*, 1999.

640. H.C. Wong and K. Sycara. Adding security and trust to multi-agent systems. In *Autonomous Agents 1999 Workshop on Deception, Fraud, and Trust in Agent Societies*, May 1999.

641. A.M. Wood. Coordination with Attributes. In P. Ciancarini and A.L. Wolf, editors, *Coordination Langauges and Models*, volume 1594 of *LNCS*, pages 21–36. Springer-Verlag, 1999.

642. M. Wooldridge, N. R. Jennings, and D. Kinny. The Gaia Methodology for Agent-Oriented Analysis and Design. *Journal of Autonomous Agents and Multi-Agent Systems*, 2000.

643. Michael J. Wooldridge and Nicholas R. Jennings. Intelligent Agents: Theory and Practice. *The Knowledge Engineering Review*, 10(2):115–152, 1995.

644. Michael J. Wooldridge and Nicholas R. Jennings. Agent-based Software Engineering. *IEE Proceedings on Software Engineering*, 144(1):26–37, February 1997.

645. Workflow Management Coalition. Reference Model – The Workflow Reference Model. Technical Report WFMC-TC-1003, Workflow Management Coalition, November 1994.

646. Workflow Management Coalition. Workflow Management Coalition Terminology and Glossary. Technical Report WFMC-TC-1011, Workflow Management Coalition, February 1999.

647. P. Wurman, M. Wellman, and W. Walsh. The Michigan Internet AuctionBot: A Configurable Auction Server for Human and Software Agents. In *Second International Conference on Autonomous Agents*, pages 301–308. IEEE, 1998.

648. P. Wyckoff, S. McLaughry, T. Lehman, and D. Ford. T Spaces. *IBM Systems Journal*, 37(3):454–474, 1998.

649. XOL. Ontology Exchange Language. http://www.ai.sri.com/pkarp/xol/.

650. A. Xu and B. Liskov. A Design for a Fault-Tolerant, Distributed Implementation of Linda. In *International Symposium on Fault-Tolerant Computing (FTCS '89*, pages 199–207, Washington, D.C., USA, June 1989. IEEE Computer Society Press.

651. F. Ygge and H. Akkermans. Resource-Oriented Multi-Commodity Market Algorithms. *Autonomous Agents and Multi-Agent Systems*, 3(1):53–72, 2000.

652. Min-Jung Yoo, Walter Merlat, and Jean-Pierre Briot. Modeling and Validation of Mobile Agents on the Web. In *Proceedings of the International Conference on Web-Based Modeling & Simulation (SCS Western MultiConference on Computer Simulation)*, San Diego, California, January 1998.

653. B. Yu and M.P. Singh. A social mechanism of reputation management in electronic communities. In M. Klusch and L. Kerschberg, editors, *CIA-2000 Workshop on Cooperative Information Agents*, volume 1860 of *LNAI*. Springer, 2000.

654. F. Zambonelli. How to Achieve Modularity in Distributed Object Allocation. *ACM Sigplan Notices*, 32(6):75–82, June 1997.

655. F. Zambonelli. Exploiting Biased Load Information in Direct-Neighbour Load Balancing Policies. *Parallel Computing*, 25(6):745–766, June 1999.

656. F. Zambonelli, N. R. Jennings, and M. Wooldridge. Organisational Abstractions in the Analysis and Design of Multiagent Systems. *International Journal of Software Engineering and Knowledge Engineering*, 2001.

657. Gianluigi Zavattaro. Towards a Hierarchy of Negative Test Operators for Generative Communication. In *Proceedings of Express'98*, volume 16(2) of *Electronic Notes in Theoretical Computer Science*. Elsevier Science, 1998.

658. Gianluigi Zavattaro. *Coordination Models and Languages: Semantics and Expressiveness*. PhD thesis, Department of Computer Science, University of Bologna, Italy, February 2000.

659. S. Zenith. Linda coordination language; subsystem kernel architecture (on transputers). Technical Report YALEU/DCS/RR-794, Yale University, 1990.

660. T. Zhang, T. Magedanz, and S. Covaci. Mobile Agents vs. Intelligent Agents - Interoperability and Integration Issues. In *Proceedings of the 4th International Symposium on Interworking*, Ottawa (Canada), 1998.

About the Authors

Gul Agha is Director of the Open Systems Laboratory at the University of Illinois at Urbana-Champaign and Professor in the Department of Computer Science. He is Editor-in-Chief of ACM Computing Surveys, and is past Editor-in-Chief of IEEE Concurrency. Dr. Agha is an ACM International Lecturer. His research interests include models, languages and tools for parallel computing and open distributed systems. His other interests include studying mysticism, in particular the Sufis of Sindh, and campaigning for animal rights and environmental protection. He received an MS and PhD in computer and communication science, and an MA in psychology, all from the University of Michigan, Ann Arbor, and a BS from the California Institute of Technology.

Farhad Arbab received his PhD in Computer Science from University of California, Los Angeles in 1982. In 1983 he was a visiting faculty at UCLA, and joined the faculty of the Computer Science Department at University of Sothern California in January 1984. He became a senior researcher at the Dutch national research center for mathematics and computer science, CWI (Centre for Mathematics and Computer Science) in Amsterdam, the Netherlands, in January 1990. His current fields of interest include Coordination Models and Languages, Parallel and Distributed Computing, Visual Programming Environments, and Constraints Programming. He leads a group working on design, implementation, and applications of Manifold: a coordination language for managing the interactions among cooperating autonomous concurrent processes in heterogeneous distributed computing environments.

Paolo Bellavista received his Laurea in Electronic Engineering from the University of Bologna, Italy, in 1997. He is currently pursuing a Ph.D. in Computer Science and Engineering at the the Department of Electronics, Computer Science and Systems (DEIS) of the same university. His research interests include distributed computing, distributed objects, mobile agents, network and systems management, adaptive multimedia systems, and distance learning. He is a student member of the IEEE, ACM and AICA (Italian Association for Computing).

Nadia Busi is a researcher working at the Department of Computer Science at Bologna University. Her interests include concurrency theory, theory and application of Petri nets, semantics and expressiveness of concurrent languages.

Giacomo Cabri received his Laurea degree in Electronic Engineering from the University of Bologna and his Ph.D. in Computer Science at the University of Modena and Reggio Emilia. His current research interests include tools and environments for parallel and distributed programming, wide-scale network applications, and object-oriented programming. Currently, he has a research contract at the University of Modena and Reggio Emilia. He is a member of TABOO, the Italian Association for Object-Oriented Programming.

Paolo Ciancarini is Associate Professor of Computer Science at the Univ. of Bologna. His research interests include: coordination languages for agent-basedsystems, programming systems based on distributed objects, advnaced Web technologies, and formal methods in software engineering. He has been one of the main proponents of ESPRIT BRA Project COORDINATION on Coordination models and languages and a co-proponent of the PageSpace Open LTR project on extending the WWW infrastructure with provisions for coordinated agent-oriented programming. He is author of more than 100 scientific papers published in international journals and conference proceedings.

Enrico Denti received his Laurea degree in Electronic Engineering in 1991 and his Ph.D. in Computer Science and Engineering in 1998, both from the University of Bologna, Italy. His current research interests include coordination models, languages, technologies and infrastructure for agent-based and Internet-based applications, as well as programming languages and software engineering. Currently, he is a Research Associate at the Department of Electronics, Computer Science and Systems (DEIS) of the University of Bologna.

Dwight Deugo is an Assistant Professor in the School of Computer Science at Carleton University. He is also the Editor-In-Chief of Java Report. He holds a Ph.D. degree from Carleton University. Before joining Carleton, he was the Director of Java Services at The Object People. He has been involved with all forms of object technology for more than 16 years as a consultant, project mentor and educator. His research interests include using large numbers of mobile agents to solve distributed computing problems and developing agent patterns.

Monica Divitini holds a M.s. in Information Science from the University of Milano, Italy and a Ph.D. in Computer Science from the University of Aalborg, Denmark. She is currently employed as an Associate Professor at the department of Computer Science of the Norwegian University of Science and Technology (NTNU), in Trondheim, Norway. She has previously been senior researcher at the University of Milano, Italy and at the Risoe National Laboratory, Denmark. Her main area of expertise is in CSCW, with a focus on coordination. Her other domains of interest include user modeling, knowledge management, software agents, education.

Timothy Finin is a Professor of Computer Science and Electrical Engineering at the University of Maryland Baltimore County. He has had over 25 years of experience in the applications of Artificial Intelligence to problems in database and knowledge base systems, natural language processing, intelligent interfaces and robotics and is currently working on the theory and applications of intelligent software agents. He holds an SB degree in EE from MIT and a PhD in Computer Science from the University of Illinois. Prior to joining the UMBC, he held positions at Unisys, the University of Pennsylvania, and the MIT Artificial Intelligence Laboratory.

Roberto Gorrieri (Ms'86, PhD'91 both from Pisa University) is Professor of Computer Science at the Faculty of Science of the Universty of Bologna. His research interests include: theory of concurrency and coordination, formal methods, security and electronic commerce. Gorrieri is author of more than 80 papers published in international journals or proceedings of international conferences, and editor of three volumes. He is member of the executive board of EATCS, secretary of IFIP Technical Committee 1, chair of IFIP WG 1.7 on foundations of security analysis and design, member of IFIP WG 6.1 on architectures and protocols for computer networks, member of the steering committee of the European Educational Forum, member of the editorial board of a few journals (TCS-Elsevier, IJIS-Springer) and member of the steering committe for some international conferences (ICALP, IEEE CSFW, Coordination, PAPM, FMOODS). Gorrieri has taken part to many research projects funded by the European Community or by the Italian MURST and CNR.

Chihab Hanachi is currently an Associated-Professor at the University of Toulouse 1 (France). He received his Ph.D. thesis in Computer Science from the University Paul Sabatier (Toulouse III) in 1991. His research interests are software agents and their application to information gathering, workflow and manufacturing systems.

Nadeem Jamali is a doctoral candidate in the Open Systems Laboratory at the University of Illinois at Urbana-Champaign. His research interests include distributed artificial intelligence and the theory and design of multiagent systems. He received his BS from the University of Karachi and MS from Dalhousie University, both in computer science. He was named a Kodak Fellow in 1998.

Nick Jennings is a professor in the Department of Electronics and Computer Science at Southampton University where he carries out basic and applied research in agent-based computing. He has helped pioneer the use of agent-based techniques for real-world applications. He has also made a number of contributions to the area of agent-based interaction – including: social rationality, cooperation, coordination, negotiation and argumentation. Professor Jennings has been an invited lecturer at numerous national and international conferences related to agent systems, he has initiated and co-chaired two major international conferences (The Practical Application of Agents and Multi-Agent Systems (PAAM) and Autonomous Agents), and has initiated and co-chaired the Agent Theories, Architectures and Languages Workshop series. He was the recipient of the Computers and Thought award (the premier award for a young AI scientist) in 1999 for his contribution to practical agent architectures and applications of multi-agent systems (this is the first time in the award's 30 year history that it has been awarded to a European). He has published over 110 articles on various facets of agent-based computing, written one monograph and co-edited four books. He is the founding editor-in-chief of the International Journal of Autonomous Agents and Multi-Agent Systems.

Elizabeth A. Kendall is the Sun Microsystems Chair of Network Computing at Monash University. Prof. Kendall has over 20 years of experience in industry-based and academic research and development in information technology, with emphasis on object technology and distributed/ networked applications. For 11 years, she was a Senior Research Engineer at major research laboratories in the USA, including Xerox and Lockheed. Prof. Kendall holds B.S., M. S., and PhD degrees from the Massachusetts Institute of Technology and the California Institute of Technology. She has carried out significant research in agent systems, patterns, and role models. She spent 1998 as a Senior Research Fellow in Intelligent Business Systems at BT (British Telecom) Laboratories in England.

Matthias Klusch is a Senior Researcher in the Multi-Agent Systems Group at the German Research Center for Artificial Intelligence and an Assistant Professor in the Artificial Intelligence Department at Free University of Amsterdam. He is coordinating the Special Interest Group on Intelligent Information Agents as part of the European Network of Excellence for Agent-Based Computing (AgentLink), and the founder and general chair of the international workshop series on Cooperative Information Agents (CIA). He holds a PhD in Computer Science from University of Kiel, Germany, and spent 1998 as a visiting research scientist at Carnegie Mellon University in Pittsburgh, USA. Dr. Klusch is a co/editor of seven books, co/author of numerous papers and several tutorials, program committee member of major conferences in the field, and is on the editorial board of the Semantic Web journal. His past and current research focuses on the application of Artificial Intelligence and agent technology to advanced database and information systems in the Internet and Web.

Yannis Labrou is Director of Technology at Powermarket, Inc., a Silicon Valley Business-to-Business startup and a Visiting Assistant Professor at the Computer Science and Electrical Engineering Department, University of Maryland, Baltimore County (UMBC). He holds a PhD in Computer Science from UMBC (1996) and a Diploma in Physics from the University of Athens, Greece. Dr. Labrou's research focuses on intelligent agents, an area in which he has been actively involved for the past 8 years. Dr. Labrou is a founding member of the FIPA Academy and has been an active participant in the development of the FIPA specifications for software agents standards. Prior to joining UMBC, Dr. Labrou worked as an intern at the Intelligent Network Technology group of the I.B.M. T.J. Watson Research Center.

Markus Lumpe works as a research and teaching assistant in the Software Composition Group at the Institute for Computer Science and Applied Mathematics of the University of Berne, Switzerland. He is interested in the design and implementation of object-oriented and component-oriented languages using fully object-oriented compiler construction techniques. He completed his M.Sc. in 1990 at the University of Dresden and his Ph.D. in 1999 at the University of Berne. He worked in industry in the area of object-oriented system design and implementation. He joined the Software Composition Group in fall 1994.

Thomas Magedanz acts as an assistant professor at the Department for Open Communication Systems (OKS) of the Technical University Berlin since 1989, with focus on distributed information technologies and advanced telecommunication systems. In addition, he works since 1998 as technical director of the IKV++ GmbH, a start up company originating from GMD FOKUS, where he is leading the development of advanced telecommunications middleware products and applications. One famous product is the Grasshopper Agent Platform. He is working on IN evolution and advanced telecommunications middleware since more than ten years and thus he is an internationally recognised expert in this area. He is a member of the IEEE, editorial board member of several journals, and the author of more than 100 technical papers/articles related to IN standards and IN evolution. He also produced several special issues related to telecommunications middleware within various journals. He is the author of the first international book on IN standards, published in 1996, and he recently published in the IEEE communications magazine in June 2000 an IN evolution feature topic. Furthermore, he is an regularly invited tutorial speaker at major international IN events and conferences as he is famous for his comprehensive investigations and "easy to diggest" style of presentations. He also provides on demand onsite seminars as well as consultancy on IN related topics for different operators and vendors.

Eric Monfroy received his Ph.D. in Computer Science from the University Henry Poincaré-Nancy 1 in 1996. His research interests include constraint programming, languages and systems for constraint solver collaboration, design of constraint solvers and languages, combination of constraint solvers and symbolic transformations, and coordination languages.

Oscar Nierstrasz is Professor of Computer Science at the Institute of Computer Science and Applied Mathematics of the University of Berne where he leads the Software Composition Group. He is interested in all aspects of component-oriented software technology, and particularly in the design and implementation of high-level specification languages and tools to support reusability and evolution of open applications. He completed his M.Sc. in 1981 and his Ph.D. in 1984 in the area of Office Information Systems at the University of Toronto. He worked at the Institute of Computer Science in Crete (1985), and in the Object Systems Group at the Centre Universitaire d'Informatique of the University of Geneva, Switzerland (1985-1994).

Andrea Omicini is a Research Associate and a Professor of Computer Science at the University of Bologna, Italy. He received his Laurea degree in Electronic Engineering in February 1991 and his PhD in Computer Science in November 1995, both from the University of Bologna. His research interests include logic, constraint, and object-oriented programming, multiagent systems, coordination models and languages, as well as intelligent system engineering. He has published over fifty articles on those subjects, and has held several tutorials on coordination models and languages at international conferences. He has organised and chaired international conferences and workshops, and is currently serving as the Program Chair of the Special Track on Coordination Models, Languages and Applications of the ACM Symposium on Applied Computing. He is a member of ACM, IEEE CS, GULP - ALP, and AI*IA - ECCAI.

George A. Papadopoulos (Ph.D.) holds the (tenured) rank of Associate Professor in the Department of Computer Science. He has participated in a number of international and national projects (namely ESPRIT, MED-CAMPUS, INCO, LEONARDO DA VINCI, etc.), both as a researcher or partner, and as a (co-)coordinator. His research interests include modelling and design of multimedia systems, development of web-based distance learning and training environments, parallel programming and high performance computing, electronic commerce, cooperative information systems, software engineering and mobile computing. He has published over 50 papers as book chapters or in internationally refereed journals and conferences. He has been involved in the organisation of about 30 international conferences and has served in the Editorial Board of 5 international journals. Professor Papadopoulos is a recipient of an 1995 ERCIM-HCM scholarship award.

Davide Rossi received his Laurea degree in Computer Science from the University of Bologna and his Ph.D. in Computer Science from a consortium between the University of Bologna, University of Padua and the University of Venice. His research interest include coordination models and languages, software architectures for distributed collaborative application, programmable, document-based, collaborative platforms. Currently, he has a research contract at the University of Bologna.

Antony Rowstron is currently a researcher at Microsoft Research Ltd., Cambridge, UK. After completing a Ph.D. in Computer Science at the University of York, UK, in 1996 he moved to the Computer Laboratory at Cambridge University as a Research Associate in the Open Media Research Group. Subsequently, he moved to the Engineering Department at Cambridge University as a Senior Research Associate, where he was one of the founding members of the Laboratory for Communication Engineering and was principal investigator for the UK RoboCup 1998 robot football team. In 1999 he moved to Microsoft Research. His research interests over the last seven years have focused on coordination languages: developing tuple space based coordination languages (WCL and Bonita) and extensions to Linda, novel run-times to support them, and investigating mobile code for fault tolerance in Linda-like languages. Currently, his research interests are focused on using adaptation in middleware systems based on the information or data managed within the middleware.

Jean-Guy Schneider works as a research and teaching assistant in the Software Composition Group at the Institute for Computer Science and Applied Mathematics of the University of Berne, Switzerland. His main interests are in object-oriented and parallel programming, scripting languages, and the definition of formal methods for component-based software engineering. He completed both his M.Sc. in Computer Science in 1992 and his Ph.D. in 1999 at the University of Berne. He has been working for the Software Composition Group since 1994.

R. Scott Cost is a Visiting Research Assistant Professor in the Computer Science and Electrical Engineering Department of the University of Maryland Baltimore County, where he received his Ph.D. in 1999. His research interests include conversation modeling and agent communication, and the application of agent-based approaches to information retrieval and electronic commerce. Dr. Cost also holds and M.S.E. from Johns Hopkins University and an A.B. from Colgate University.

Christophe Sibertin-Blanc is member of the IRIT (Institut de Recherche en Informatique de Toulouse) research Laboratory and Professor at the Toulouse 1 University. He received is Ph.D. thesis in Computer Science from the Engineering School ENSEEIHT, Toulouse, in 1984. His main domain of research is in the integration of concepts from both the Petri net theory and the Object-Oriented approach: definition of appropriate formalisms, system modelling, system validation and implementation of tools. His other domains of interest include Software Engineering, modelling methodologies, Data bases.

Katia P. Sycara is a Professor in the School of Computer Science at Carnegie Mellon University. She has more than 20 years experinec in research and application of advnaced information systems technology, in particular multiagent systems. She holds a B.S, MS and PhD from Brown University, University of Wisconsin and the Georgia Institute of Technology respectively. She has authored or co-authored over 150 technical papers, has given many keynote talks and tutorials, and has been organizer and program committee member for many conferences. She has served as the General Chair of the Second International Conference on Autonomous Agents (Agents 98). She is a founding member and on the Board of Directors of the International Foundation of Multiagent Systems and Chair of the Steering Committee of the Autonomous Agents Conference. She is a Founding Editor-in-Chief of the Journal "Autonomous Agents and Multi Agent Systems"; an Editor-in-Chief of the Springer Series on Agents; on the Editorial Board of the Kluwer series on Multi Agent Systems; the Area Editor for AI and Management Science for the journal "Group Decision and Negotiation" and on the Editorial Board of the Semantic Web journal. She has served as member of the AAAI Executive Council, and is the Scholarship Chair of the American Association for Artificial Intelligence.

Robert Tolksdorf is Assistant Professor at the study group Formal models, Logic and Programming at the Technical University of Berlin, Department for Computer Science. He received his Dr.-Ing. in Computer Science from the TU Berlin in 1995. His research interests include coordination languages, open distributed systems, and Web-technology. He is author of several papers published in international journals, conferences proceedings, or as book chapters. He authored several german books on Web-technologies and is editor of an book series on XML technologies. He serves as program committee member for various conferences and workshops. He is member of the steering committee for the conferences on Coordination Models, Languages and Systems and general Chair of the IEEE WET ICE 2001 conference. He is member and co-proposer of various EU funded activities, including the networks Agentlink II and Coordina.

Carlos Varela is a doctoral candidate in the Open Systems Laboratory at the University of Illinois at Urbana-Champaign. His research interests include web-based computing, concurrent and distributed systems, and active object oriented programming languages. He expects to receive his Ph.D. in computer science in 2000. He received a BS in computer science with honors from the University of Illinois at Urbana-Champaign in 1992.

Michael Weiss is an assistant professor at Carleton University. He joined the School of Computer Science after a five year stint in industry following his PhD. His research interests are electronic commerce, agent patterns, and Internet applications. Most recently, he lead the Advanced Applications group within the Strategic Technology group of Mitel Corporation. At Mitel he was responsible for demonstrating the use of agent technology for managing the complexity of call control software, and for promoting Java and XML within the company. He obtained his PhD on agent-mediated collaborative design from the University of Mannheim, Germany in 1993.

Michael Wooldridge is Professor of Computer Science in the Department of Computer Science at the University of Liverpool, UK. He has been active in the research and development of multi-agent systems for ten years, gaining his PhD for work in the theoretical foundations of multi-agent systems from the University of Manchester, UK in 1992. Prof Wooldridge has published many articles in the theory and practice of agent-based systems, and has edited eight books in the area. He has served on many program committees for conferences and workshops in the area, and is a director of the International Foundation for Multi-Agent Systems (IFMAS). He also serves as an associate editor of the International Journal of Autonomous Agents and Multi-Agent Systems (Kluwer), and an editorial board member for the Journal of Applied AI (Taylor & Francis). He is coordinator of AgentLink, the ESPRIT-funded European Network of Excellence in the area of agent-based computing (see http://www.AgentLink.org/).

Franco Zambonelli is Research Associate and Professor of Computer Science at the University of Modena and Reggio Emilia, Italy. His current research interests include: parallel and distributed programming, coordination models and architectures for the Internet. He received his Laurea degree in Electronic Engineering in 1992 and his PhD in Computer Science in 1997, both from the University of Bologna. He is the secretary of the Italian Association for Object-Oriented Programming and a member of ACM, IEEE CS and EUROMICRO.

Gianluigi Zavattaro got Ms'94 and PhD'2000 in Computer Science from the Department of Computer Science of Bologna University. His research interests include concurrency theory, semantics and expressiveness of coordination languages, formal methods, and models for object-oriented distributed programming. He is author of several papers published in international journals, proceedings of conferences, or as chapters in books.

List of Contributors

Gul Agha
Open Systems Lab
Department of Computer Science
University of Illinois
at Urbana Champaign
1304 W. Springfield Ave.
IL 61801, USA
agha@cs.uiuc.edu

Farhad Arbab
CWI
Kruislaan 413, 1098 SJ Amsterdam
The Netherlands
Farhad.Arbab@cwi.nl

Tamer Başar
Department of Computer Science
Dartmouth College
6211 Sudikoff Laboratory
Hanover, NH 03755-3510, USA

Paolo Bellavista
Dipartimento di Elettronica
Informatica e Sistemistica
Università di Bologna
Viale Risorgimento 2
I-40136 Bologna, Italy
pbellavista@deis.unibo.it

Jonathan Bredin
Department of Computer Science
Dartmouth College
6211 Sudikoff Laboratory
Hanover, NH 03755-3510, USA
jonathan@cs.dartmouth.edu

Nadia Busi
Dept. di Scienze dell'Informazione
Università di Bologna
Mura Anteo Zamboni 7
I-40127 Bologna, Italy
busi@cs.unibo.it

Ciarán Bryce
Centre Universitaire d'Informatique
Université de Genève
24, rue Général-Dufour
CH-1211 Genève 4 , Switzerland
Ciaran.Bryce@cui.unige.ch

Giacomo Cabri
Dept. di Scienze dell'Ingegneria
Univ. di Modena e Reggio Emilia
Via Campi 213b
I-41100 Modena, Italy
giacomo.cabri@unimo.it

Paolo Ciancarini
Dept. di Scienze dell'Informazione
Universit'a di Bologna
Mura Anteo Zamboni 7
I-40127 Bologna, Italy
cianca@cs.unibo.it

R. Scott Cost
Dept. of Computer Science and
Electrical Engineering
University of Maryland
Baltimore County
Baltimore, Maryland 21250
cost@csee.umbc.edu

Marco Cremonini
Dipartimento di Elettronica
Informatica e Sistemistica
Università di Bologna
Viale Risorgimento 2
I-40136 Bologna, Italy
mcremonini@deis.unibo.it

Enrico Denti
Dipartimento di Elettronica
Informatica e Sistemistica
Università di Bologna
Viale Risorgimento 2
I-40136 Bologna, Italy
edenti@deis.unibo.it

Dwight Deugo
School of Computer Science
Carleton University
1125 Colonel By Drive
Ottawa, Ontario, Canada, K1S 5B6
deugo@scs.carleton.ca

Monica Divitini
Norwegian University of Science and
Technology
Monica.Divitini@idi.ntnu.no

Tim Finin
Department of Computer Science and
Electrical Engineering
University of Maryland
Baltimore County
Baltimore, Maryland 21250
finin@csee.umbc.edu

Martin Fredriksson
Dept. of Software Engineering
and Computer Science
University of Karlskrona/Ronneby
S-37225 Ronneby, Sweden
mfe@ipd.hk-r.se

Roberto Gorrieri
Dept. di Scienze dell'Informazione
Università di Bologna
Mura Anteo Zamboni 7
I-40127 Bologna, Italy
gorrieri@cs.unibo.it

Rune Gustavsson
Dept. of Software Engineering
and Computer Science
University of Karlskrona/Ronneby
S-37225 Ronneby, Sweden
rgu@ipd.hk-r.se

Chihab Hanachi
University Toulouse I
Place Anatole France
31042 Toulouse, France
hanachi@univ-tlse1.fr

Çagri Imer
Department of Computer Science
Dartmouth College
6211 Sudikoff Laboratory
Hanover, NH 03755-3510, USA

Nadeem Jamali
Open Systems Lab
Department of Computer Science
University of Illinois
at Urbana Champaign
1304 W. Springfield Ave.
IL 61801, USA
jamali@cs.uiuc.edu

Nicholas R. Jennings
Department of Electronics and
Computer Science
University of Southampton
Highfield, Southampton
SO17 1BJ, UK
nrj@ecs.soton.ac.uk

Elizabeth Kendall
Sun Microsystems
Chair of Network Computing
School of Network Computing
Monash University
Peninsula Campus, McMahons Rd.
Frankston, VIC 3199 Australia
kendall@infotech.monash.edu.au

Matthias Klusch
DFKI GmbH
German Research Center for AI
Multi-Agent Systems Group
Stuhlsatzenhausweg 3
D-66123 Saarbrücken, Germany
klusch@dfki.de

David Kotz
Department of Computer Science
Dartmouth College
6211 Sudikoff Laboratory
Hanover, NH 03755-3510, USA
dfk@cs.dartmouth.edu

Yannis Labrou
Department of Computer Science and
Electrical Engineering
University of Maryland
Baltimore County
Baltimore, Maryland 21250
jklabrou@csee.umbc.edu

Markus Lumpe
Institute of Computer Science
and Applied Mathematics (IAM)
University of Berne
Neubrückstrasse 10
CH-3012 Bern, Switzerland

Thomas Magedanz
IKV++ GmbH
Bernburger Strasse 24-25
D-10963 Berlin, Germany
magedanz@ikv.de

Rajiv T. Maheswaran
Department of Computer Science
Dartmouth College
6211 Sudikoff Laboratory
Hanover, NH 03755-3510, USA

Ronaldo Menezes
Univ. of Ulster at Magee College
Faculty of Informatics
Northland Road
BT48 7JL Derry, UK
r.menezes@ulst.ac.uk

Eric Monfroy
IRIN
Facult des Sciences
2, rue de la Houssinire
B.P. 92208
F-44322 Nantes Cedex 3
France
Eric.Monfroy@irin.univ-nantes.fr

Amy L. Murphy
Department of Computer Science
Washington University
Campus Box 1045
One Brookings Drive
Saint Louis, MO 63130-4899, USA
alm@cs.wustl.edu

Oscar Nierstrasz
Institute of Computer Science
and Applied Mathematics (IAM)
University of Berne
Neubrückstrasse 10
CH-3012 Bern, Switzerland

Andrea Omicini
Dipartimento di Elettronica
Informatica e Sistemistica
Università di Bologna
Viale Risorgimento 2
I-40136 Bologna, Italy
aomicini@deis.unibo.it

George A. Papadopoulos
Department of Computer Science
University of Cyprus
75 Kallipoleos Street
P.O. Box 20537
CY-1678 Nicosia, Cyprus
george@cs.ucy.ac.cy

Gian Pietro Picco
Dipt. di Elettronica e Informazione
Politecnico di Milano
P.za Leonardo da Vinci 32
20133 Milano, Italy
picco@elet.polimi.it

Gruia-Catalin Roman
Department of Computer Science
Washington University
Campus Box 1045
One Brookings Drive
Saint Louis, MO 63130-4899, USA
roman@cs.wustl.edu

Davide Rossi
Dipt. di Scienze dell'Informazione
Università di Bologna
Mura Anteo Zamboni 7
I-40127 Bologna, Italy
rossi@cs.unibo.it

Antony Rowstron
Microsoft Research
1 Guildhall Street
Cambridge, CB2 3HN, UK
antr@microsoft.com

Daniela Rus
Department of Computer Science
Dartmouth College
6211 Sudikoff Laboratory
Hanover, NH 03755-3510, USA
rus@cs.dartmouth.edu

Jean-Guy Schneider
Institute of Computer Science
and Applied Mathematics (IAM)
University of Berne
Neubrückstrasse 10
CH-3012 Bern, Switzerland

Christophe Sibertin–Blanc
IRIT/University Toulouse I
Place Anatole France
31042 Toulouse, France
sibertin@univ-tlse1.fr

Katia P. Sycara
Carnegie Mellon University
The Robotics Institute
5000 Forbes Ave
Pittsburgh PA 15213, USA
katia@cs.cmu.edu

Robert Tolksdorf
Technische Universität Berlin
Fachbereich Informatik, FLP/KIT
Sekr. FR 6–10, Franklinstr. 28/29
D-10587 Berlin, Germany
tolk@cs.tu-berlin.de

Carlos Varela
Open Systems Lab
Department of Computer Science
University of Illinois
at Urbana Champaign
1304 W. Springfield Ave.
IL 61801, USA
cvarela@cs.uiuc.edu

Michael Weiss
School of Computer Science
Carleton University
Ottawa, Canada
weiss@scs.carleton.ca

Alan M. Wood
University of York
Department of Computer Science
Heslington, York, YO10 5DD, UK
wood@cs.york.ac.uk

Michael J. Wooldridge
Department of Computer Science
University of Liverpool
Liverpool L69 7ZF, UK
M.J.Wooldridge@csc.liv.ac.uk

Franco Zambonelli
Dipartimento di Scienze dell'Ingegneria
Università di Modena e Reggio Emilia
Via Campi 213b
I-41100 Modena, Italy
franco.zambonelli@unimo.it

Gianluigi Zavattaro
Dipartimento di Scienze dell'Informazione
Università di Bologna
Mura Anteo Zamboni 7
I-40127 Bologna, Italy
zavattar@cs.unibo.it

Printing and Binding: Stürtz AG, Würzburg